Economics of Marketing

Edna Douglas
Washington State University

HARPER & ROW, PUBLISHERS
New York   Evanston   San Francisco   London

Sponsoring Editor: John Greenman
Project Editor: Pamela Landau
Designer: T. R. Funderburk
Production Supervisor: Will C. Jomarrón

ECONOMICS OF MARKETING

Library of Congress Cataloging in Publication Data

Douglas, Edna.
  Economics of Marketing.

  Includes index.
  1. Marketing.   I. Title.
HF5415.D73   380.1   75-3527
ISBN 0-06-041695-5

To the memory of
Henry Thomas Douglas
1874-1969

Contents

98617

Preface

In a letter to Carl Van Vechten, who had inquired about the last words of Gertrude Stein, Alice B. Toklas wrote:

> She said upon waking from a sleep—What is the question. And I didn't answer thinking she was not completely awakened. Then she said again—What is the question and before I could speak she went on—If there is no question then there is no answer. And she turned and went to sleep again.*

In all fields of inquiry we are seeking answers to questions. But the quantity and quality of our knowledge depend quite as much upon the questions we ask as upon our answers. Not only do the questions posed determine the direction of inquiry, but they also reveal the intellectual framework into which the answers must ultimately fit if they are to be meaningful and, hence, a basic part of our knowledge.

This is a volume about marketing in which the questions asked are derived within the framework of economics. Marketing is concerned with one of the most important areas of human behavior and one of the most fascinating of all social systems. While as a field of study it is not itself a discipline, marketing can be examined within the framework of any discipline that deals with aspects of social organization and behavior. Each of the social or behavioral sciences provides a basis for perceiving and analyzing various facets of marketing phenomena.

In recent years one of the most pervasive developments in business administration in general, and in marketing in particular, has been a movement away from economics as an orientation toward other disciplines in the social and behavioral sciences, particularly social psychology. This diffusion has arisen from the search for new insights into human behavior that would be helpful in understanding marketing organization and processes and in formulating policy in the business firm. Through these extensions marketing has broadened the bases upon which its tenets are structured.

It is my conviction that the movement of marketing into these new directions is both necessary and desirable if we are to understand fully how the market mechanism functions, how decision-making units behave within (and without) markets, and how the resulting structural and behavioral patterns affect human welfare. Nor should the study of marketing be restricted to the social and behavioral sciences, for the perceptions of the humanist may shed quite as much light upon the meaning and implications of the art of marketing as those of the social or behavioral scientist.

It is also my conviction that economics and marketing have, and will continue to have, a great deal to offer each other. Human behavior in the market place cannot be understood if its economic dimensions are ignored. Nor can its economic dimensions be fully understood unless the technological and sociopsychological milieu within which market behavior occurs is accurately perceived and related to economic vectors. I believe that neither the economist nor the marketing specialist has adequately appreciated what the other has to offer and that the potentials inherent in an exploration of their mutual concerns have not yet been fully exploited.

---

*Alice B. Toklas, *Staying on Alone: Letters of Alice B. Toklas,* Edward Burns, ed. (New York: Liveright, 1973), p. 276.

The study of the structure and functioning of markets has long occupied a central position in micro economics, industrial organization, and international trade. Although a market is not essential to the implementation of all economic decisions, markets are a significant part of the environment within which most economic choice-making entities operate and comprise a principal medium through which competition and complementarity both affect and effect allocation choices and procedures. For these reasons, the theory of economic value has evolved in micro economics primarily through the analysis of market behavior. The study of the structural and behavioral interrelations of the system of commodity markets has been centered in that curiously labeled area of economics known as industrial organization. It has been in the study of international economic relations, however, where an economic theory of trade has been developed that comes as close to being a systematic, cohesive theory of marketing as can be found in any of the social or behavioral sciences at this time.

It is not surprising, therefore, that marketing as an area of study in business administration originated in economics. Economists were among the first to examine marketing institutions as economic entities. Out of these early studies—essentially descriptions and classifications of marketing institutions, functions, and policies—marketing evolved as a specialized field of study.

Since those early days, both economics and business administration have moved through many stages of development. One significant parallel development in the two areas of study has been the structuring of formal decision-making and behavioral models and the search for realistic estimates of their parameters. Business administration has been primarily interested in micro decision models, while economics has concerned itself with both micro and macro models. In both areas mathematics and statistics have come to play increasingly important roles as analytical frames, tools, and language.

The proximity of business administration to problems of the firm has resulted in a rich reservoir of cases, data, and models appropriate to micro economic analysis. Too rarely have economists known about, appreciated, or utilized these. The refinement and testing of such models, drawing upon the theoretical foundations of economics, as well as other social and behavioral sciences, and upon the wealth of empirical data in marketing, should lead to better and more useful models. The economic theory of markets must be an integral part of any broader social theory of market behavior.

But economics is, above all, a social science, dealing not only with the positive aspects of economic organization and behavior, but also with both positive and normative issues concerning human welfare. During the last few decades we have seen the crossing of new frontiers in macro economics, with its focus on system structure and performance and social welfare. Recently we have seen the reexamination of still nagging unanswered questions in both micro and macro economics. The impact of market structure and performance on the level and distribution of income, the effects of specific marketing practices on consumer welfare, the role of markets in resource utilization and economic development, the interrelations of monetary and commodity markets, the social efficiency of the marketing system, and the impact of public policy on market performance are among those areas of inquiry where the subject matter of economics and marketing is contiguous if not overlapping. The social implications of market phenomena must be scrutinized if private and public policy are to be assessed and the social effects of the marketing system are to be measured.

The purpose of this volume is to attempt to bridge some of the gaps that have developed between economics and marketing by viewing a spectrum of market phenomena and problems within the framework of economics. This does not presume that the economic dimensions of marketing are its only dimensions nor that the treatment presented here is exhaustive. It merely proposes that economics can provide a systematic and meaningful way of asking some important questions about this important area of human activity. I would like to hope that this approach will help to preserve in marketing a measure of pride in its heritage as well as to strengthen the analytical framework within which markets and marketing are viewed, so that others who follow can more expeditiously find solutions to the many problems we cannot yet resolve.

In pursuit of these goals, I have become indebted to far more individuals than can be cited here. I owe an immeasurable amount to the many scholars in economics and marketing who have provided the intellectual foundations for this volume as well as the scaffolding and materials with which it has been structured. I have borrowed widely and heavily and hope that I have been reasonably successful in preserving and projecting accurately the core of those ideas.

In addition, many have helped me directly in the course of the book's development. I am particularly indebted to Lee E. Preston of the State University of New York at Buffalo, whose thorough and insightful review of the entire volume yielded a number of constructive suggestions for improvement of its organization and content. He is not, of course, responsible for its remaining shortcomings.

Shaikh M. Ghazanfar, former research assistant and now professional peer, contributed substantially to the empirical work undertaken during the first stages of writing. His range of technical skills added considerably to the data, graphs, and content of several chapters.

Other graduate assistants who contributed to various parts of the volume were Jagjit K. Dhesi, Leonard Roberts, Kenneth Anderson, and Michael Meek. Many of my other sutdents, both graduate and undergraduate, in economics and marketing at Iowa State University, Norges Handelshøyskole, and Washington State University have left their imprint on these pages through the often perceptive insights of precocious tyros.

I also express my appreciation to the Baker Library at Harvard University, which made its resources available to me during a sabbatical when some of these chapters were first drafted.

Kathleen Warfield was a loyal and expert typist of the entire manuscript. Others who typed at various stages were Glenda Boone, Joyce Niemi, Bonnie Gibbs, Devoughn Anderson, and Joyce Thompson. All of these deserve more out of life than the opportunity to demonstrate their competence at the keyboard, and my thanks.

The editorial staff of Harper & Row has been splendid to work with, and I appreciate their patience and competence.

I am especially grateful to Eugene Clark, Dean of the College of Economics and Business, and to the departments of Economics and Business Administration at Washington State University for providing the environment and the opportunity for bringing this volume to completion.

Edna Douglas

i Introduction

1

The Nature
of Marketing

An old-fashioned Moslem goes through the ablution before he opens
the [Koran]. He never puts it beneath another book, never reads it
except in a reverential tone and posture. If he is a book dealer, he won't
sell the book. He bestows a copy on the would-be purchaser, who in
turn bestows a specified sum of money—an act of mutual bestowal, but
not a business transaction.

—Philip K. Hitti

Among the inventions of man that have had the most far-reaching effects on human
behavior and welfare are some that have evolved over long periods and whose influence
has been felt, not through spectacular changes, but through a gradual transition to a
different mode of human activity. Many forms of social organization—the corporation,
the monetary and banking system, the marketing system, the political organization—are
of this type and rank among the most ingenious of human creations.

This volume is a study of one of these forms of social organization—the marketing
system: its structure, its behavior, and its effects on human welfare. Because it is an
integral part of the total economy, we shall examine it in terms of its role in the total
economic system. There are many kinds of markets—factor markets for natural, capital,
and human resources and commodity markets for consumer goods—and within each
category, a multitude of markets for particular types of goods and services. We shall be
concerned primarily with the marketing of goods, both industrial and consumer, although
many characteristics of the organization and behavior of commodity markets are also
relevant to the marketing of services, including labor.

THE CONCEPT OF MARKETING

Marketing

Marketing consists of those activities of business firms and consumers that are directly
related to achieving exchange relationships. These activities are primarily buying and
selling, although some other kinds of functions are so closely related to an exchange
transaction that we shall include them as a part of marketing. The evidence of a
marketing transaction is an exchange of assets by two parties: In a monetary economy
this transfer usually alters the liquidity pattern of buyer and seller: The buyer exchanges
a liquid asset (money or credit) for a less liquid asset (a good), while the seller increases
his liquidity. Once the exchange has taken place, the potential market roles of buyer and
seller become reversed. (See Figure 1.1.)

Marketing is a result of and necessary to specialization in our economy. It binds
specialized production and consumption units together into a unified economy. The
market structure is the adhesive tape, the coordinating and integrating mechanism, the

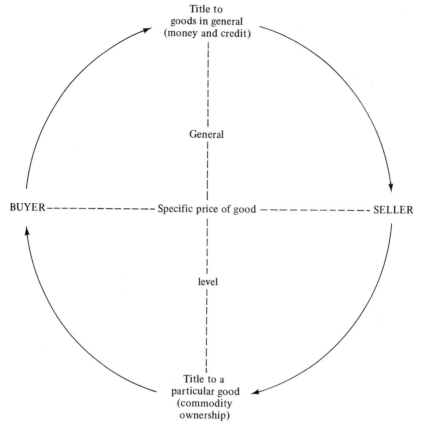

Figure 1.1. Market relationships.

aperture through which economic communication and control are effected in a highly specialized economy, and the more mature that economy, the more important marketing becomes.

One interesting consequence of trade is that both participants in the transaction are made better off. As Kenneth Boulding points out, trade involves the exchange of two inequalities.[1] A buyer will not exchange $5.95 for a pair of green overshoes unless he values the green overshoes more than the $5.95. Nor will the seller accept $5.95 unless he, in turn, values that more than the ownership of green overshoes. It does not follow that all marketing activities necessarily increase social welfare, although this is probably more often true than not. But in a free market it can be assumed that each transaction is beneficial to each participant.

The Market

While we define *marketing* as the particular cluster of activities necessary to achieve an exchange relationship between buyer and seller, we shall define a *market* as the exchange relationship itself.[2] When a buyer and seller meet, negotiate, and reach an agreement, a

---

[1] Kenneth E. Boulding, *Economic Analysis*, vol. I, *Microeconomics*, 4th ed. (New York: Harper & Row, 1966), p. 22.

market exists. Seldom, however, is a transaction completed in an economic vacuum. Usually, many buyers participate in purchasing a particular kind of good, and many sellers try to sell to a particular group of customers. When this occurs, there are aggregations of buyers and sellers whose negotiations and agreements impinge upon each other so that patterns of exchange relationships emerge. Thus, we speak of the automobile market or the textile market or, more specifically, the low-price automobile market or the cotton market, in which many specific transactions take place, but in which the tendency toward a single price unifies the forces of demand and supply.[3]

We do not, however, often find markets so nearly pure and perfect that there is, in fact, a single price. There is more likely to be a central core where price equality prevails and, surrounding that, fringes where one transaction merges into another and differences in terms of exchange exist. Not all buyers of Volkswagens pay the same price, and not all sellers of General Electric toasters receive the same price. Nor is the price of apples completely independent of the price of oranges. Much of our study of markets is directed toward what we call imperfect markets where variations in product, selling method, services, or numbers of buyers and sellers and their information and degree of market power create a far more complex pattern of exchange relationships and interactions than the classical concepts envisioned. But even in imperfect markets it is the buyer-seller relationship that comprises the market. Let us examine some of the attributes of this exchange relationship.

Dimensions of the Exchange Relationship

The concept of marketing as a cluster of activities directly related to achieving exchange relationships is not without ambiguity, for we have not yet defined what is "directly

[2] Were we to interpret an "exchange relationship" both literally and broadly, we would include not only exchanges that occur between buyers and sellers in markets but also exchanges of anything between two parties whether a market is involved or not. There are many "things" that have utility for an individual that might be transferred to him from another—a kind remark, an automobile, a safety pin, an affectionate St. Bernard, blue jeans, a love letter, a well-cooked meal. Transfer of one of these to another might well involve an exchange—a bag of peanuts for a dime, a love letter for happiness, a well-cooked meal for gratitude. All exchange relationships, whether they involve the market or not, have certain characteristics in common. However, we shall make no attempt to analyze anything except those exchanges that involve a buyer-seller relationship in the market. For an interesting and valuable treatment of both market and nonmarket exchange relationships, see Alfred Kuhn, *The Logic of Social Systems* (San Francisco, Calif.: Jossey-Bass, 1974). See especially pp. 172-231, where transactions are discussed, and pp. 381-395, where the market economy is described as a special-purpose informal organization.

[3] One of the most commonly quoted definitions of the term *market* is that of Augustin Cournot, which has been translated by Alfred Marshall as follows: "Economists understand by the term *market*, not any particular market place in which things are bought and sold, but the whole of any region in which buyers and sellers are in such free intercourse with one another that the prices of the same goods tend to equality easily and quickly." Augustin Cournot, *Récherches sur les Principes Mathématiques de la Théorie des Richesses*, new ed. (Paris: Marcel Riviére, 1838), p. 55, quoted in Alfred Marshall, *Principles of Economics*, 8th ed. (London: Macmillan, 1920), p. 324. A translation by Nathaniel T. Bacon is slightly different from that of Marshall: "It is well known that by *market* economists mean, not a certain place where purchases and sales are carried on, but the entire territory of which the parts are so united by the relations of unrestricted commerce that prices there take the same level throughout, with ease and rapidity." Augustin Cournot, *Researches into the Mathematical Principles of the Theory of Wealth*, trans. Nathaniel T. Bacon (New York: Augustus M. Kelly, 1960), pp. 51-52.

related" to the achievement of an exchange relationship. We shall do so by first delineating the dimensions of an exchange transaction and then showing that where we draw the boundaries depends on the purpose and framework of our investigation. A market transaction has four major dimensions: social, physical, economic, and political.

SOCIAL

The social aspect of a market concerns the interpersonal and intergroup relationships that characterize marketing activities. For marketing to take place there must be a meeting of minds. The most elementary facet of this social relationship is communication, and for this reason there is a similarity between communication models and market structure. The transmission of information necessary for primary decisions, the adaptation of buyers and sellers to information distortion (noise), the interpretation of information received, and the acquisition and use of control data are aspects of the social relationships that are basic to market transactions. These are among the more elusive aspects of marketing. Although necessary and important, they are difficult to measure and evaluate. A buyer must not only know what is available and on what terms, but he must also make an interpretation—that is, estimate the relative adaptabilities of available goods to meet a specific need and relate those to relevant costs. Sellers are equally concerned with the problem of ascertaining consumer demands, sales potentials, and costs.

There is, however, a second facet of the social relationship involved in a market transaction. Underlying consumer choices and, indirectly, production decisions, are basic determinants of individual and group behavior. Consumers' preference patterns, buyers' perceptions of alternatives, the expansion and contraction of demand through the product life cycle, and variation in demand through the family life cycle are examples of marketing phenomena deeply rooted in the cultural and social environment within which consumer needs and behavior are shaped. While the economist accepts the structure of wants and demand as given, the psychologist and sociologist who study marketing look behind market behavior for the sociopsychological roots of specific kinds of consumer activity. A similar sociopsychological approach is also appropriate to a study of the production of goods.

PHYSICAL

Physical aspects of marketing are particularly important where time and space "gaps" must be filled in order for goods, otherwise physically produced, to be made available to consumers. Transportation and storage, long objects of study by the marketing specialist, are the marketing activities most difficult to distinguish from those that we normally identify as nonmarketing. Abba P. Lerner comments on the importance of movement in all forms of economic production:

> Workers cannot create material things; they can only manipulate materials that already exist.... The farmer moves small pieces of earth with spade or plow; he moves fertilizer to where it is needed; he moves seeds from his bins to his fields; and, finally, he moves the ripe crops from the field to the barn. The automobile worker moves one piece of metal to join it on to another piece and moves the screws so that they hold tight. The textile worker draws cotton or wool into threads, or arranges the threads so that they are entangled with each other to form cloth or joined with other pieces of thread to form suits and dresses and shirts.[4]

---

[4] Abba P. Lerner, "The Myth of the Parasitic Middleman," *Commentary*, 8 (July 1949): 46.

If we were to limit our attention to the exchange relationship in marketing, we would exclude all physical activities from consideration. But if we wish to understand why trade takes place, we must understand the conditions under which specialization occurs, and a limiting factor is the cost of maintaining physical contacts between production and consumption units. Transportation is in a physical sense what communication is in a social sense. We shall therefore include in our concept of marketing the maintenance of physical contact between buyer and seller separated in space and in time, since such contacts are interunit in nature and germane to the exchange process.

ECONOMIC

The essential economic characteristic of marketing is price determination. The core of classical economics is the theory of price determination in purely and perfectly competitive or monopolistic markets. More recent work in pricing theory concerns price determination in markets of oligopoly and imperfect or monopolistic competition. Agreement on the terms of exchange is an essential element in the marketing transaction. No trade can take place without a mutually acceptable price, and the process of price determination and the effects of price on resource allocation and consumer welfare are among the most critical problems in economics. It is at this point that the identity of interest between economics and marketing is clearest.

POLITICAL

The political character of a market transaction lies in the legal nature of the exchange. It is within the framework of law that the mechanism for transferring ownership and the rights of ownership are defined. These are the most highly formalized social relationships in market transactions. The legal character of marketing is also reflected in the regulation of market transactions through policies such as price control, rationing, restrictions on output, limitations on price discrimination, labeling requirements, regulations of advertising, restrictions on market power, and control of competitive methods, as well as through broader policies concerning fiscal and monetary affairs. These aspects of marketing are determined politically and establish restrictions or boundaries within which market transactions are completed.

MULTIDISCIPLINARY APPROACH TO MARKETING

Figure 1.2 is a highly simplified classification scheme of some important fields of knowledge. Although it is neither complete nor unambiguous, it may serve to suggest certain significant relationships that will be helpful in clarifying the nature of marketing and its relationship to other fields.

Arts and Sciences

Philosophy, or the science of knowledge, is the parent field from which the arts and sciences spring. The main divisions of philosophy are *psychology*, the science of mental processes or events, *epistomology*, the theory of knowledge, and *ontology*, the theory of being. Philosophy also includes what have sometimes been identified as philosophical

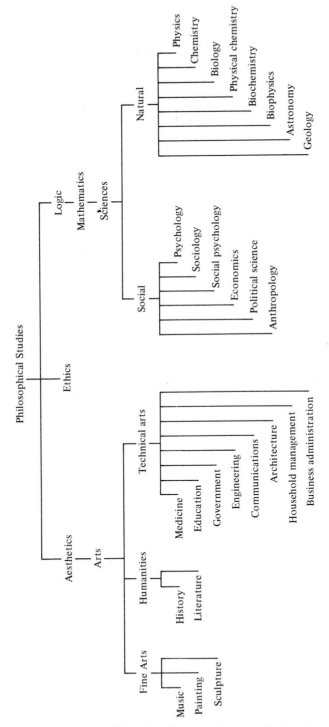

Figure 1.2. A simplified classification of certain fields of knowledge.

studies, and these we have included in Figure 1.2. They include *aesthetics*, a department of psychology that concerns itself with the nature of beauty, *ethics*, also a department of psychology concerned with the nature of good and of duty, and *logic*, which is the normative ("what-ought-to-be") science of thought. *Arts* and *Sciences* are derivations from aesthetics and logic.

Sciences are concerned with the understanding of natural and human phenomena and seek, through concepts, propositions, and theorems, to create an intellectually orderly structure through which the natural and social world may be viewed and comprehended.[5] The arts, on the other hand, are concerned with accomplishment of something that makes possible an experience, and do this through an intuitive, subjective, trial-and-error method that stands in contrast to the objective scientific method of observation, classification, deduction, and experimentation. The object of science is understanding of the fact; the object of art is understanding of the fact and the feeling about the fact.[6] The method of science is intellectual and objective; the method of art is intuitive and subjective.

It is important to note that many of the important breakthroughs in science have come in hybrid areas that represent the integration of two fields, such as physical chemistry and biochemistry. Hybridization in the social sciences has begun to emerge in social psychology and, to a limited degree, in the field of political economy. It is possible that important breakthroughs in the social sciences may some day come through the development of metaconcepts or metatheories embracing more than one of the social sciences as they now exist.

Social Sciences and Technical Arts

Between "pure" art and "pure" science lie those areas of knowledge that embrace most of the things that people "do" in the process of daily living. In this middle area are a group of "middle sciences" and "middle arts." These middle sciences are social sciences that use objective, logical procedures to structure a framework of propositions about humans and their organization and behavior. These are the sciences most intimately concerned with what people do and how they do it. They are not concerned with purely biological beings but rather with socialized biological beings whose values, needs, activities, and achievements arise out of the culture of which they are a part.

The social scientist is confronted with problems unique in the sciences. The subject that he studies has feelings, a mind, and a will, and it reacts to unseen forces that may be more powerful than the objective variables that the scientist measures. Often it reacts to the mere fact of being studied.[7] But although these facts make his task difficult, they should not obscure the role of objectivity and logical analysis in the approach of the social scientist to his data.

---

[5] ". . . the goal of science is to augment and order our experience." Niels Bohr, *Atomic Physics and Human Knowledge* (New York: Wiley, 1958), p. 88. See also his essay, "Unity of Knowledge," in ibid., 67-82, especially his discussion of the arts on pp. 79-81.

[6] See Joyce Cary, *Art and Reality—Ways of the Creative Process* (Garden City, N.Y.: Doubleday, 1961), p. 22.

[7] See Kenneth E. Boulding, *The Skills of the Economist* (Cleveland, O: H. Allen, 1958), chap. 5, "Trade—Not Aid for the Sciences." pp. 131-159, and Norbert Wiener, *Cybernetics* (New York: Wiley, 1948), p. 190.

The technical arts in Figure 1.2 are those whose object is to make possible an experience and whose method is eclectic, involving the use of artistic and/or scientific methods or principles. A technical artist is an opportunist, drawing on any useful field.[8] A business administrator or manager, for example, may employ the techniques and principles of economics or social psychology in his work, but the skillful blending of many kinds of relevant knowledge is itself an art that justifies our differentiation between economics and business management. The engineer who designs a bridge draws heavily upon principles and methods of physics but must, in the final analysis, exercise artistic judgment in choosing among and balancing the many facts and forces that bear upon the utility of his final design.

MARKETING AS A TECHNICAL ART

Marketing is clearly a social activity that falls within the province of business management, household management, and government. It is not a science but rather a cluster of activities that may or may not be based on science. Marketing management in either the business firm or the household may involve the use of economic and psychological principles, but final decisions and their execution involve the blending of both objective and subjective knowledge of many varieties. The best economic decision is not necessarily the best business decision, given the psychological and sociological characteristics of the environment within which marketing management must function. Nor is the best business decision necessarily the most economic decision. Until the day comes when there is a comprehensive theory of social behavior that embraces all relevant physical and social facts and relationships, an understanding of marketing management must be based on a multidisciplinary approach.

There is a second aspect of marketing that justifies a multidisciplinary approach. Marketing activities in the aggregate pervade the economy and provide a highly impersonal, integrating mechanism for fitting its components together. This function of marketing is not one that can be studied purely as an art; only the social sciences provide the necessary framework for identifying, organizing, and comprehending the relationships that are the essence of marketing. There is a sociology of marketing, which concerns itself not only with the internal structure of marketing groups but also with patterns of group interaction. There is a political science of marketing, which focuses on formal legislative, regulatory, and judicial determination of market structure and behavior. There is also a psychology of marketing, which examines market activities as manifestations of personalized behavior. There is a social psychology of marketing, within which marketing activities are viewed as the behavior of socialized individuals. There is an anthropology of marketing, dealing, for example, with the physical, social, and cultural origins of humans' market relationships. There is even an ecology of marketing, concerned with the relations of human market participants and their environment. And, of course, there is an economics of marketing, which analyzes market organization and the behavior and interaction of production and consumption units in terms of their effects on resource utilization and allocation.

It is not correct to say that only the marketing practitioner understands marketing. He may be the most competent in the art of marketing, but understanding comes not merely

---

[8] The field of operations research is an excellent example of such an approach. The objective is to get a job done by using any relevant analytical techniques.

from doing a job but also from comprehending its nature and its relationship to other natural and social things. Each of the social sciences provides a logical framework for studying human activities, and through each framework new insight can be gained, not only into why people organize themselves as they do and behave as they do, but also into how that organization and behavior might be modified in order that human objectives can be more nearly realized.[9]

We shall now indicate how economics is related to the subject matter of marketing.

ECONOMICS AS A SOCIAL SCIENCE

Economics is the social science that analyzes decisions concerning the allocation of scarce resources among alternative uses. It is concerned with decisions about what to produce, how to produce it, and how to distribute society's output. To this end the economist studies such things as the kinds and amounts of natural and human resources available; the creation and use of capital goods; technological production possibilities; the organization of business firms and the processes of making production decisions; the structure of consumer demand; the purposes, organization, and functioning of markets; the processes of price determination and trade; the effects of trade on the size and distribution of income; the pricing of productive factors; the determinants of national income and its cyclical and secular variations; and the welfare implications of private and public policies that affect the production, consumption, and distribution of goods and services.

While he can answer many questions that have economic implications, the economist cannot answer all such questions. He can, for example, measure and analyze the effects of an increase in the demand for refrigerators on the price and quantity sold, but he does not necessarily have in his toolkit the means for determining *why* demand has changed. He can describe, and perhaps explain, why a redistribution of personal income has occurred, but he cannot, within his discipline, say whether that redistribution is "good" or "bad" for society as a whole. Nor does he appear yet to have a complete explanation of the bases for long-run economic growth, although he is able to identify and measure certain variables known to be important determinants of a secular change in income. Even in spite of considerable competence in *ex post* description and analysis, he cannot yet accurately forecast many economic variables. If, however, he knows the structure of human wants, the structure of resources, and the technological possibilities for production, he is equipped with the data necessary for delineating rational behavior and for arriving at intelligent production decisions. His tools also enable him to analyze economic aggregates and to reach some conclusions concerning the effectiveness with which the total economic system meets certain criteria of economic welfare.

In the development of his field, the economist seeks relevant data—economic facts and significant relationships among those data. These are compounded by the accounting processes of economic units and become totaled, or added up, in the market place. For this reason, most of economics is concerned with the study of what goes on in markets—how they are organized, who participates, how participants behave, and the effects of these patterns of behavior on the welfare of society. It is at this point that

---

[9] We shall not at this point consider the extent to which the social sciences are positive or normative. For an opinion see F. S. C. Northrop, *An Introduction to the Logic of the Sciences and the Humanities* (New York: Macmillan, 1948), pp. 328-347. Two other enlightening discussions are Lionel Robbins, *Essay on the Nature and Significance of Economic Science*, 2d ed. (London: Macmillan, 1935), and A. G. Papandreou, *Economics as Science* (Philadelphia: Lippincott, 1958).

marketing and economics as fields of study share common interests. Marketing concerns itself with interunit relations that are primarily economic in nature, and economics, with decisions concerning resource utilization whose determining forces manifest themselves in market relations between economic units. We can sharpen these points of identity, contiguity, and difference by delineating some of the principal characteristics of economic organization and the role of markets in that organization.

ECONOMIC ORGANIZATION

Specialization and Production Organization

Production is the creation of utility, and most production in our economy is carried on by business firms.[10] A firm is characterized by two facts: (1) It is primarily a *production unit* (i.e., a utility-creating unit) rather than a consumption unit, and this objective determines its resource and organizational structure, and (2) somewhere within its structure it has a *managerial center* whose function is to decide what the organization's objectives are to be, what its resources shall be, and how they will be directed toward the organization's goals. The production system contains a large number and variety of firms, each engaging in some form of production and each directed by its management, which makes and administers decisions.

A major characteristic of our production system that is relevant to our study of marketing is the existence of specialization—geographic, personal, and institutional. Specialization on the basis of absolute or comparative advantage is one means of achieving increased efficiency in production.[11] Specialization cannot, however, exist without exchange, and the existence of an efficient exchange mechanism makes possible increased specialization, just as inefficiency in exchange reduces the amount of specialization. There are three conditions that make specialization economical: differences in productive resources, differences in consumer tastes, and economies of scale.[12]

---

[10] This should not obscure the fact that production can and often does take place within households or other consuming units. This alternative is one that gives many families additional economic choices, and omission of estimates of the value of household and other nonmarket production is a shortcoming of national income data. Ismail A. Sirageldin has estimated that in 1964 the average value of unpaid output for the American family was $3,939, which was nearly 50 percent of the average family disposable income (including imputed rent for home owners) of $8,115. About 90 percent of this unpaid production was in the form of housework and other types of home production. The balance was the value of volunteer work, educational tasks undertaken by family members, the family's car services, and any additional free help received by families. See Ismail A. Sirageldin, *Non-Market Components of National Income*, Institute for Social Research, Survey Research Center (Ann Arbor: University of Michigan, 1969), pp. 53-55.

According to the survey of food consumption by the U.S. Department of Agriculture in 1965, the value of food consumed by reporting families accounted for by home-produced food or gifts for which there was no direct money expense accounted for 5.6 percent of the total value of their food consumption. This varied from 2.6 percent for urban, 8.6 percent for rural nonfarm, and 29.5 percent for rural farm families. Computed from U.S. Department of Agriculture, Agricultural Research Service, *Food Consumption of Households in the United States, Spring 1965*, Household Food Consumption Survey 1965-66, Report No. 1 (Washington, D.C.: GPO, 1968), pp. 7, 56, 98, 145.

[11] An elementary theoretical analysis of this is presented in Chapter 2.

[12] For an excellent treatment of these, see Bertil Ohlin, *Interregional and International Trade*, rev. ed. (Cambridge: Harvard University Press, 1961), particularly pt. I, pp. 5-46.

DIFFERENCES IN PRODUCTIVE RESOURCES

These are most easily seen where the natural endowments of two areas are not the same, as, for example, Washington timber and California oranges. Another basis is differences in human capacities or the natural endowments of humans. Those talents that make a good army general do not necessarily make a good college president. Of great importance in the trade between areas that differ in levels of economic maturity are differences in the amount of captial in the two areas. This would include capital in the broadest sense, involving not only capital goods but also technology and "social capital" in the form of various kinds of social organization. Finally, we also find that factor proportions may differ between areas or firms, thereby providing a basis for specialization and trade.

DIFFERENCES IN CONSUMER TASTES

These may be the product of a vast range of conditions, many of which are cultural in origin. Assume that 75 percent of the people in one state are coffee drinkers, while 75 percent of those in the adjoining state are tea drinkers. If the two states have equal production advantages for both products, it may pay the tea-drinking state to export coffee and import tea and the coffee-drinking state to do the opposite. If, however, marketing costs are so high that each industry is consumer oriented, minority consumers in either state may find their sources of supply concentrated where consumption is also concentrated. How these patterns of taste arise is a problem in social psychology rather than ecomonics, but their impact on the production and marketing systems is considerable, and they are an important part of the data of the environment within which economic decisions are made. Moreover, positive action by marketing firms is sometimes undertaken to modify these patterns of taste, thereby altering the geographic structure of industry.

ECONOMIES OF SCALE

Also an important cause of specialization and trade, economies of scale refer to lower costs associated with an increase in the size of the firm where, because of indivisibilities, size is increased through a change in the quantity of all the productive factors, although not necessarily a proportionate change in each.[13] If such economies are possible, and if two economic "regions" become one in order to achieve them, both size of firms and market areas will be increased.

Given any or all of these three conditions, specialization of production will occur so long as the economies so achieved are not obliterated by increased costs of marketing that become necessary in order to exchange the specialized outputs. External coordinating costs are substituted for higher internal coordinating costs.[14]

The Organization of Consumption

Just as the production process is performed by units whose size, resource structure, and activities represent attempts to achieve efficient clusters, consumption also takes place in

---

[13]Note that this is not the same as increasing returns associated with a change in the quantity of a single productive factor. Such returns occur within a firm that has certain fixed resources and one or more variable resources and precede what are commonly known as diminishing returns.

[14]H. S. Houthakker, "Economics and Biology: Specialization and Speciation," *Kyklos* 9, fasc. 2 (1956): 181-189.

economic units that generally include more than one person, thereby making possible economies of scale.[15] The structure of consumption units is, however, less likely to be dominated by purely economic considerations than is the structure of production units. Nevertheless, economic considerations play an important role in consumer behavior. The direct influence of disposable personal income on consumer demand and its indirect effect, through the rate of household formation and the birthrate, show the impact of economic factors on both the structure and behavior of consumption units.

Consumption is the absorption of utilities, and generally this involves the destruction of utilities. By its nature, consumption is a very personal, individual act; that is, only an individual can experience satisfaction. Nevertheless, many of the goods from which these satisfactions are derived are shared by families, households, or groups of people who live together in institutional or communal arrangements, and certainly many of the decisions that determine what goods will be consumed are made collectively within some type of social organization. The most important consumption unit in our economy is the household, and its preferences and decisions constitute some of the most important data in marketing analysis.

HETEROGENEOUS CONSUMPTION

One of the dominant characteristics of household consumption is its heterogeneity. While production units specialize in order to achieve efficiencies associated with internal homogeneity, consumption units do just the opposite, for decreasing marginal utility places a premium on diversity in a family's consumption pattern. In fact, as the household's level of consumption rises, variety is likely to increase. This discrepancy between the structure of production and consumption units adds to the complexity and cost of marketing, for one of the functions of marketing is to coordinate these divergent patterns.

SUBJECTIVE VALUATIONS

Heterogeneity of consumption within the household bears some relationship to another characteristic of consumer demand that has considerable impact on the marketing system. Just as the business firm must undertake a calculus of the effects of alternative policies on its revenues and costs and on its asset-liability structure, so the household must make similar calculations in determining its economic course of action. It must decide whether to raise its own vegetables or to buy them, whether to purchase one make of car or another, whether to buy on credit or pay cash, whether to patronize a specialty store or a department store, whether to replace its refrigerator this year or next, whether to own one TV set or two. Some of the calculations can be made with considerable confidence in their precision, for the alternatives are known and their values measurable. But others involve the comparative evaluation of utilities whose measurement is elusive. For this reason, there are particular problems in arriving at rational consumer decisions that are less likely to arise in arriving at rational business decisions, where the calculus is generally one involving the use of measurable prices of inputs and outputs. The problem is partly that a wide range of consumption choices and the desire for a wide variety of goods make it extremely difficult for the average consumer to become competent in his choice

---

[15] See, for example, S. J. Prais and H. S. Houthakker, *The Analysis of Family Budgets*, University of Cambridge, Department of Applied Economics, Monograph 4, 2d impression abridged (Cambridge: Cambridge University Press, 1971), pp. 146-152, where the theory and estimates of economies of scale are discussed.

making even where objective criteria exist, and partly it is a problem of comparing goods whose utility can be measured only subjectively. Both of these facts help explain why expenditures for consumer goods advertising are far greater than for producer goods advertising.

Psychologists, and to a far lesser extent economists, have developed ingenious techniques for analyzing choice where subjective variables are involved. By using ordinal rather than cardinal relations, they have structured models of consumer choice that have greatly facilitated analysis in this area, although important analytical problems remain, as well as problems of empirical measurement.[16] Subjective valuation is particularly difficult to deal with when questions involving interpersonal comparisons arise. If a change in pricing policy, for example, affects different groups of society in different ways, what is the overall effect on society as a whole? The problem is particularly difficult when we are considering a case in which one group is benefited while another is hurt. Problems of this type should not, however, obscure the fact that many effective techniques of decision making for consumers do exist that have a bearing on important characteristics of the marketing system.

Economic Functions of Marketing

We have indicated that most production is carried on within business firms that are generally highly specialized if differences in resources, in tastes, or in costs of production according to scale of enterprise make specialization economical. Where specialization between firms is vertical in nature—that is, where it involves the breaking up of a sequence of processes, with each performed by a separate firm—some mechanism is needed for coordinating these separate functions into an organized and balanced process. This is one of the functions of the marketing system—to effect coordination between vertically related business firms. This coordination is achieved in *capital goods markets*, which we shall define broadly to include markets in which goods are purchased for processing or resale.

We have also indicated some of the characteristics of consumption in our economy—its heterogeneity and the subjective elements of its calculus. If the structure of consumption is laid alongside of the structure of production, it is apparent that some organization is necessary to effect integration between the two. This is accomplished in *consumer goods markets*. The sheer physical task of mixing the outputs of large numbers of specialized production centers into bundles of diversified goods desired by large numbers of consumer units is tremendous. Equally important is the intellectual task of programming such an allocation. Just as capital goods markets effect integration between firms that are vertically related, so consumer goods markets achieve integration between firms and consuming units (usually households), which are also vertically related.

Let us now examine these broad, coordinating functions of marketing in greater detail, indicating more specifically the ways in which marketing complements other economic activities and how, as it matures, it often assumes a more positive role in the economy. To simplify our discussion, we shall assume that marketing is performed by specialized

---

[16] A brief survey of the nature of scaling and techniques of measurement can be found in Donald S. Tull and Gerald S. Albaum, *Survey Research: A Decisional Approach* (New York: Intext Education, 1973), pp. 81-132. A review of utility measurement as developed in economics is in Tapas Majumdar, *The Measurement of Utility* (London: Macmillan, 1958).

marketing firms. This will help isolate and clarify the various facets of marketing. The nature of marketing is the same, however, whether it is performed by a specialized marketing firm or whether a single firm performs both marketing and nonmarketing functions.

The marketing system fits together into complementary relationships the separate decision-making units of the economy. In so doing, it is not only filling gaps of intelligence, time, and space, but it is also coordinating the termini of those gaps. Consumers must know what sellers have to offer; producers must know what buyers are willing to buy. Producers must anticipate consumer demand; consumers must anticipate the availability of goods. Finally, goods must be moved physically from where they are produced to consumers who can use them. It is the function of marketing to do these things. Can we describe these activities in terms of economic functions that indicate not only the kind of gap being filled but also the situation in which the function is performed and the general effect of its performance on the structure and behavior of the economic system as a whole? Figure 1.3 outlines the four economic functions of marketing that we shall consider.

FUNCTION I: SIMPLE COORDINATION

Suppose that we have a situation in which there is complete certainty. Consumers know what they want now and will want in the future; producers know their present output and costs and future output and costs. Because the relevant data are known, adaptations necessary by either producers or consumers can be made. The function of the marketing system under circumstances like these is simple coordination, and its identification as a specialized function to be performed by a specialized marketing firm is based on economies of specialization. Information must be exchanged between buyers and sellers, mixed outputs and demands must be matched, and time and space gaps must be filled. To perform these coordinating functions efficiently, specialized firms may be established.

Where the demand or supply occur irregularly, a specialized middleman has unusual value as an aperture for information. A buyer, for example, purchases a job lot of woodworking machinery from a bankrupt firm for $42,000 and resells it to a furniture firm 400 miles away for $78,000. This is commonly known as *arbitrage*, and its effect is to reduce price differences.[17] In a sense, all enterprise is arbitrage, but marketing is arbitrage without changes in the physical attributes of the product itself.

There is, however, a particular aspect of this marketing function that has some of the attributes of insurance and is an additional reason for the development of specialized marketing firms. The occurrence of a particular market transaction may be highly uncertain, while the probability of the occurrence of many may be known. A manufacturer of pencil sharpeners may, for example, be highly uncertain as to whether he will sell one to a particular filling station, but an office supply wholesaler may know with some degree of confidence the probability of selling pencil sharpeners to a large number of filling stations. An aggregate of many uncertainties may be a measurable risk. In this case, an economy is effected by specialization in the performance of the marketing functions.

The role of the marketing firm described here is passive in the sense that it responds to

---

[17] Boulding defines *arbitrage* as "the process of increasing the value of one's possessions by buying a commodity at one time or place and selling it at another time or place *at a higher price*." Arbitrage through time he defines as *speculation*. See his *Economic Analysis*, vol. I, pp. 134-139.

Nature of the Marketing Function	Prerequisite Conditions	Market Relationships		Schematic Diagram	General Effect on the Economy
		Vertical	Horizontal		
I. Simple coordination	certainty	complementary	competitive	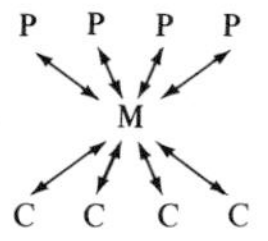	passive
II. Competitive speculation	uncertainty	complementary	competitive	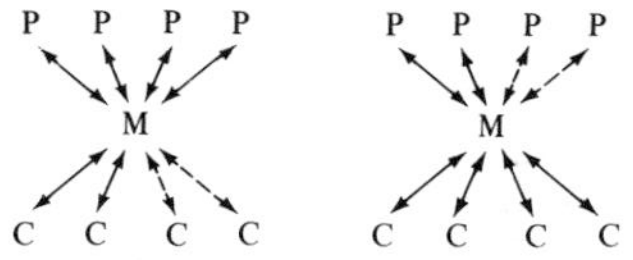	neutralizing
III. Monopolistic speculation	imperfection	competitive	monopolistic	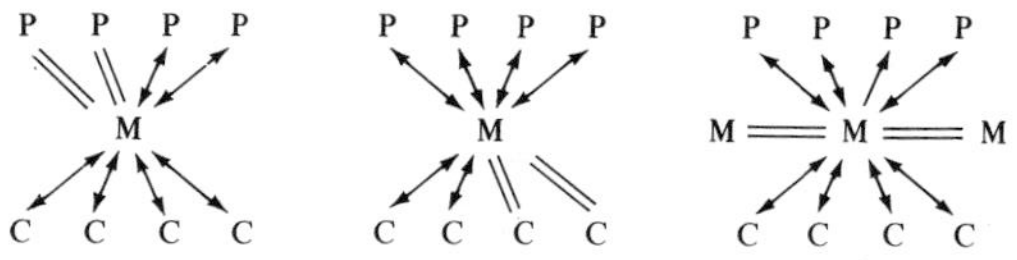	restrictive
IV. Creative speculation	imperfection	complementary	monopolistically competitive	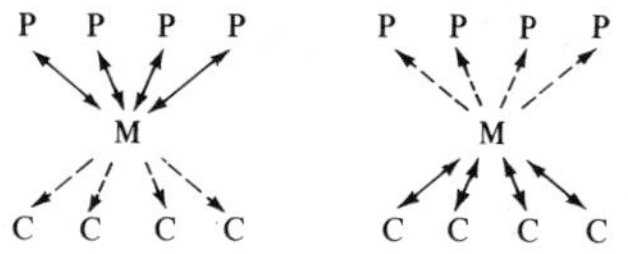	constructive

P = form producer

M = marketing firm

C = consumer

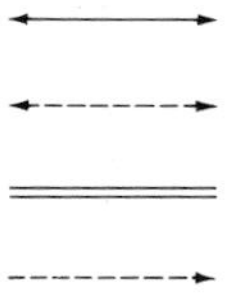

⟷ = perfect communication between independent units

⟷ (dashed) = imperfect communication between independent units

= = perfect communication between integrated units

→ (dashed) = imperfect communication between directing and directed units

Figure 1.3. The basic functions of marketing firms in the economy.

the aggregate economy, facilitating economic processes. It increases efficiency but is not an interfering type of activity. It enables vertically related units to complement each other better and enhances effective competition horizontally between producers and between consumers.

FUNCTION II: COMPETITIVE SPECULATION

Competitive speculation occurs in marketing under conditions of uncertainty.[18] Buyers may be uncertain of the present or future availability of goods; producers may be uncertain of present or future demand. The more dynamic the economy and the greater the distance in time and space between producer and consumer, the more likely it is that uncertainty will exist. The marketing specialist performs a very important role in this situation, for he assumes the uncertainty. If he makes an accurate projection, he does a service both to himself (through profit) and to society (by effecting an economically desirable allocation of resources).[19] A speculator, let us say, believes that soybeans will go up in price. He buys, stores, and resells at a profit. Both he and society are benefited. If, however, he buys, stores, and resells at a loss, the effect is not quite so clear. Either he or his creditors suffer a loss. If the loss were inevitable regardless of speculation, the speculator (or creditor) is bearing that loss for society. But if, on the other hand, there are many speculators who make independent decisions and collectively dominate the market, the effect is to exaggerate price fluctuations through time, and this is not economically desirable. The social utility of competitive speculation rests, therefore, on its effect's being genuinely neutralizing, bringing resource allocation nearer the optimum. It if is inefficient—for example, based on wrong information—its economic effects are restrictive and not desirable.

There is another special form of marketing activity that has attributes of monopoly horizontally but of competition vertically. If the effect of a marketing activity is basically an enhancement of vertical competition, it would be classified as competitive speculation. Assume, for example, that a marketing firm is faced with monopolistic practices on the part of producers. If it acquires market power equal to or greater than that of the producing firms and thereby breaks the monopolistic control of the producers, the effect is an enhancement of vertical competition, and the activity would be classified as competitive speculation. Because this creates a form of duopoly, the effect on consumer welfare depends on the extent to which profits are merely transferred from producer to middleman or passed on to consumers in the form of lower prices.

It is important to recognize that where gaps of space, time, or intelligence involve *calculable* risks, the bearing of these by the marketing firm is not competitive speculation but simple coordination. In these cases, there may be economies of scale arising out of the specialization possible by bunching large numbers of particular risks in the marketing firm. If there is a cost of risk calculation, there may also be possible economies from having a marketing firm specialize in such calculations. These are functions that do not involve uncertainty and should not be classified as speculative.

Schematic diagram II in Figure 1.3 illustrates the competitively speculative function of the marketing firm by indicating, first, a firm that buys outputs from production firms

---

[18] The terms *competitive speculation* and *monopolistic speculation* as used here are those of Abba P. Lerner. See his *Economics of Control* (New York: Macmillan, 1944), pp. 69-71, 88-95.

[19] This assumes no collusion among speculators, which would constitute monopolistic speculation.

with uncertain knowledge of total consumer demand. A second possibility is the firm that contracts to deliver an output for which a source of total supply is not certain. The marketing firm bears a complementary relationship to production and consumption units and a competitive relationship to other marketing firms. The effect on the economy is neutralizing, for the marketing firm helps effect equilibrium at a higher level of total satisfaction by setting in motion counterforces to those prevalent in the market.

FUNCTION III: MONOPOLISTIC SPECULATION

This function involves the use of market power to restrict the availability of goods in order that profits may be increased. Such power can be achieved by horizontal control or by vertical integration that has the effect of horizontal control and causes the market to become less than purely and perfectly competitive. A firm achieves monopolistic power in the market and uses it against other firms and against consumers.

Two conditions may give rise to this type of market control: (1) limitations on the amount of resources or their ownership—for example, natural resources, such as minerals; funds for capital investment; technology and managerial skill; patents, copyrights, franchises—and (2) economies of scale that give cost advantages to large firms and enable them to become dominant. A special situation that encourages this type of marketing function may develop in an expanding economy. During a period of economic growth, each specialized marketing firm is evolved to meet a particular need. Once established, however, these firms may become too powerful to be displaced, even though other kinds of firms or other kinds of functional arrangements might be more efficient. This occurs if the existing firms have a certain power inherent in their inside knowledge and good will, or if there is a sizable cost involved in converting a group of resources into a going firm. This is comparable to the difference between the amount of energy required to run an electric motor and the much greater amount required to start it. When this situation arises, "old" marketing firms can sometimes keep out "new" firms for quite a while. If the desire to keep out "new" types of firms or marketing practices is supported by legislation (e.g., through resale price maintenance and unfair practices laws), the power of existing firms may be greatly enhanced.

Monopolistic speculation, arising out of the exercise of market power, reduces output, lessens the amount of change in the economy, modifies resource allocation, and works against consumer interests.

FUNCTION IV: CREATIVE SPECULATION

This type of marketing function is more difficult to handle within the framework of economics, but its economic effects are considerable. It is at this point that the integration of marketing, production, and consumption becomes so marked that differentiation is extremely difficult. In this case, the marketing firm assumes some of the functions inherent in either production or consumption. It may, for example, decide what ought to be produced and place orders to specification or otherwise direct production. Decision making and control over production are thus centered, not in the processing unit, but in the marketing firm. This has the effect of vertical integration without outright ownership. This form of behavior is not uncommon among department stores, chain stores, and mail order firms that buy by specification and exercise control over the output of goods. If we adhere to our definition of marketing as the activities directly related to the achievement of interunit relations, we can identify product development (sometimes called *merchandising*) as marketing to the extent that it is an interpretation of consumer demand in terms of quantity and quality of product. When it becomes a question of technological alternatives in production, it ceases, of course, to be a marketing problem.

The ability of the marketing firm to exercise control over consuming units is far more limited, for a firm cannot control consumer choices or behavior. But the firm is not without power in this area, for it may attempt to persuade through advertising and sales promotion. Whether or not such persuasion is effective is a moot question, but there is no question that many producers believe that it is effective. This is one of the most interesting and difficult areas of marketing to analyze. It is not enough for us to say that it would not occur in markets that are purely and perfectly competitive. Nor is it enough to dismiss it as a waste of resources. It is a pervasive element in our marketing system, and we must cope with it analytically to the extent that our tools will permit.

AN ADDITIONAL NOTE ON MONOPOLISTIC AND CREATIVE SPECULATION

In the schematic diagram in Figure 1.3, we have simplified trade channels to show only a three-level channel consisting of processor-marketer-consumer. Were we to expand these to include a longer trade channel, it would be possible to show other ways in which market power is utilized to increase profits either through the restriction of output (function III) or through the shaping of demand or supply (function IV) at other levels in the trade channel. For example, wholesale firms may affiliate by contract with retail firms (e.g., a voluntary chain) and introduce merchandising and promotional policies that exploit or enhance the wholesalers' and retailers' market power. Consumer cooperatives may integrate back toward processing, or manufacturers may integrate forward, through sales branches and factory-owned retail outlets, to achieve advantages of cost or strategy not otherwise open to them. In later chapters we shall explore many of these alternative means of utilizing market power.

Production and Marketing

Many students of marketing refer to *production* and *marketing* as separate, complementary activities. Since we have defined production as the creation of utility, we shall have to classify marketing, as well as other service industries, as economically productive, as are also manufacturing, construction, mining, forestry, agriculture, and fishing. Marketing is utility creating and is therefore a phase of the total production process, concerning itself with ownership-time-space relations between separate economic units. Only Function III—monopolistic speculation—can be regarded as containing some clearly nonproductive elements.

Is there therefore any justification for separating out the marketing phase of production for special study? Many marketing functions are performed by firms whose primary activities are form production; that is, their principal function is to effect chemical, physical, and biological changes in the resources they use rather than to effect the social changes that characterize marketing. Why not study production and let the marketing aspects, as we define them here, emerge as a part of the overall activities of the firm?

One reason for isolating this particular cluster of production activities is their overall importance in the total production system. Another is that the development of specialized marketing firms has facilitated the identification, measurement, and evaluation of this particular area of activity. By studying marketing separately, we can (1) evaluate different organizational methods for getting this group of production functions performed, (2) show what happens when resource ownership and productive activities shift from one firm to another through integration or disintegration, and (3) distinguish between marketing activities that are truly utility creating and those that cannot be so identified. Just as the study of international trade, which takes place under artificial restrictions, has thrown light on domestic trade, so the study of marketing, which concerns interfirm relations, throws light on intrafirm activity. The behavior of the child away from his family often reveals more about that family than does his behavior at home.

RECAPITULATION

The purpose of an economic organization is to provide an orderly and efficient grouping of resources and activities so that society obtains the maximum satisfactions possible from its limited means. To achieve this, we have structured an economy of specialized production units to produce goods and services for nonspecialized consuming units or households. At the interface of these two broad segments of the economy, binding its separate parts together, is the marketing system, whose function is to provide a coordinating mechanism in the economy that transmits data, makes gap-bridging decisions, and assumes creative functions if they are lacking elsewhere in the economy. (See Figure 1.4.) In this sense, marketing is a control mechanism that facilitates the fitting together of the various parts of the economy and provides a feedback that will set into operation corrective measures where errors have occurred.[20]

Administrative and Marketing Control

Economic control may also be achieved by administration, which the economist identifies as management. The function of management within a firm or within a household is to make decisions concerning the organization's objectives and the use of available resources, to organize these resources into an effective organization, to communicate directions, and to control activities within the organization. This is precisely what the marketing system accomplishes between economic units, but by impersonal, nonauthoritarian means. A simple one-buyer-one-seller relationship sets up a control mechanism, for both buyer and seller are restricted by each other. When many buyers and sellers of the same or related products are involved, there is not only a vertical relationship but also a horizontal relationship, which arises because each buyer now has a wider range of alternatives and each seller a wider range of possible customers. This control is exercised horizontally as well as vertically, for a seller is limited not merely by customer reaction but equally by his competitors' behavior. A market provides an impersonal means of administration.

The marketing system must, in the aggregate, be judged not only by its contribution to efficiency, through its relationship to specialization, but also by its effectiveness as a

---

[20] ". . . the feedback principle means that behavior is scanned for its results, and that the success or failure of this result modifies future behavior." Norbert Wiener, *The Human Use of Human Beings* (Boston: Houghton Mifflin, 1950), p. 69.

Figure 1.4. A simple model of economic relationships.

control mechanism for the total economy. "Good" administration and an equally "good" market should produce identical results.

Even totalitarian economies must utilize the market mechanism, as the following statement by Trotsky indicates:

> The innumerable living participants of the economy, state as well as private, collective as well as individual, must give notice of their needs and of their relative strength not only through the statistical determination of plan commissions but by the direct pressure of supply and demand. The plan is checked and, to a considerable measure, realized through the market. The regulation of the market itself must depend upon the tendencies that are brought out through its medium. The blueprints produced by the offices must demonstrate their economic expediency through commercial calculation. . . . Economic accounting is unthinkable without market relations.[21]

We shall have occasion to examine some of the bases for and implications of vertical and horizontal integration. These are cases where administrative control is substituted for

---

[21] L. D. Trotsky, *Soviet Economy in Danger* (New York: Pioneer, 1933), pp. 30, 33.

market control. It is important to bear in mind, however, that what is economically desirable without integration is economically desirable with integration. Where the effects of integration are the modification of behavior, it is important that we determine why the change occurs and evaluate it in terms of whether the modified behavior is closer to or further from what would be economically optimum.

Before we conclude our consideration of the market system, we shall also consider the alternative means by which interunit coordination might be achieved in an economy and shall compare a market system with authoritarian or command systems of economic coordination and control.

Economics of Marketing

Economics is the science of decision making where those decisions concern limited resources and alternative uses. The forces that shape the patterns of decision manifest themselves most clearly in the market, and it is in the market that competition between forces is resolved and complementarity established. For this reason, economists have devoted more attention to the study of market structure and behavior than to any other single subject.

Marketing is a cluster of activities directed mainly toward the integration of economic units. It is therefore an economic activity, involving the use of scarce resources to achieve a desired end, and may be studied within the framework of economics and evaluated by economic criteria. But because economic tools can be used to accomplish other objectives than purely economic ones, and because the effective use of economic resources may require far more than merely economic knowlege, it will be appropriate for us to keep in mind throughout this study the broader social nature of marketing.

The purpose of this volume is to look at marketing activities through the eyes of an economist, hence, within the framework of economics. This is not to claim that only economics is useful in understanding marketing behavior, but rather that economics is one of the important social sciences that can throw light on marketing activities. We shall from time to time encounter problems of analysis that lie within other social and behavioral sciences, particularly areas such as psychology, social psychology, sociology, and political science. Our purpose, however, is to use economics as fully and effectively as possible and thereby to show its possibilities and limitations in helping us understand the complex structure and behavior of the marketing system. In time, we may hope that a theory of social behavior will be evolved that will provide an integrated framework within which this complicated and dynamic aspect of our society can be examined. In the meantime, we shall push as far as we can within the confines of a single, important discipline.

2

The Elementary Theory of Trade

Be abstract
And you'll wish you'd been specific; it's a fact.

—Marianne Moore

The economic importance of specialization, one of the most pervasive characteristics of our production system, lies in the fact that it makes possible a larger real income than would otherwise occur. The marketing system is a corollary of specialized production, and its extent and character are determined by the ways in which specialization manifests itself throughout the production system. If we explain the principles underlying specialization, we shall have also explained why marketing occurs. In Chapter 1 we discussed the three situations in which specialization is economical. In the discussion that follows, each of these will be examined in detail to show with greater precision why trade occurs and its effects on the total economy.[1]

THE BASES OF TRADE

We have identified three principal conditions that give rise to specialization and marketing: differences in resources, differences in demand, and economies of scale.

Differences in Resources or Resource Combination

DIFFERENCES IN COST RATIOS

Let us assume that we have two states, each capable of producing each of two products, and each with a cost advantage in a different product. (See Table 2.1.) Let us further assume that there are no marketing costs. In this case, it would be better for Washington to specialize in the production of apples and Idaho in the production of potatoes. Each has an *absolute advantage* in the production of one product, meaning that its costs of production are absolutely lower than those in the competing area.

---

[1] The presentation in this chapter is by no means a complete statement of trade principles and certainly not an exhaustive one. It is an attempt to bring together into a simple statement some of the propositions about trade developed in international and interregional trade theory that are useful in understanding certain aspects of trade within a domestic economy. Those studies that we have found particularly helpful for perceiving trade theory in terms of its relevance to domestic marketing are Charles P. Kindleberger, *International Economics*, 4th ed. (Homewood, Ill.: Irwin, 1968), especially pp. 19-54 and 86-101; Richard E. Caves, *Trade and Economic Structure: Models and Methods*, Harvard Economic Studies, vol. CXV (Cambridge: Harvard University Press, 1960); Bertil Ohlin, *Interregional and International Trade*, Harvard Economic Studies, vol. XXIX, rev. ed. (Cambridge: Harvard University Press, 1967); and Raymond G. Bressler and Richard A. King, *Markets, Prices, and Interregional Trade* (New York: Wiley, 1970). We have drawn upon these in developing this presentation.

24

Table 2.1 Constant Costs of Production per Bushel for Potatoes and Apples in Washington and Idaho: Case I

Commodity	Washington	Idaho
Potatoes	$4	$3
Apples	3	4

Let us, however, consider the cost ratios rather than the absolute costs. A bushel of apples can be produced in Washington at three-fourths the cost of a bushel of potatoes. A bushel of potatoes can be produced in Idaho at three-fourths the cost of a bushel of apples. So long as imported potatoes sell in Washington for anything less than one and one-third bushels of apples, residents of Washington gain; so long as imported apples sell in Idaho for anything less than one and one-third bushels of potatoes, Idaho residents benefit. The nearer the import price to the domestic price, the more the exporting area gains, of course.

Let us now assume a different cost relationship, as in Table 2.2. This is a case where Washington has an *absolute advantage* in the production of each product; its costs of production for each are absolutely lower than in Idaho. Idaho has an *absolute disadvantage* in the production of both products, for its costs are absolutely higher than those in Washington. Under these circumstances, one possible result is that potato and apple growers in Idaho will move to Washington, where production costs are lower. We shall not at the moment trace through the effects of this adjustment. Let us, on the other hand, assume that people in Idaho are reluctant or unable to move away, and that labor and management prefer to produce there even though their costs are higher than if they moved to a more productive area. It will obviously pay Idaho to buy something from Washington, since Washington's costs are lower than Idaho's. But will Washington gain by such an exchange? By examining costs ratios, we can show that it will.

If Washington grows its own potatoes, each bushel requires (costs) the resources that could have been used to produce one bushel of apples. Therefore, the price of potatoes and that of apples will be the same. But if Idaho produces both potatoes and apples, each bushel of apples costs two bushels of potatoes. Suppose, therefore, that Washington producers say to Idaho: You concentrate on the production of potatoes, and we will sell apples to you for $6 per bushel. There is an obvious gain of $2 per bushel to each Idaho consumer. Washington consumers, now equipped with $6 for each bushel of apples sold to Idaho consumers, can, in turn, enter the Idaho potato market and purchase one and one-half bushels of potatoes. Had they sold their apples at home, they would have received only one bushel of potatoes in exchange. Now they receive one and one-half bushels. It is obviously to their advantage to specialize, assuming that the gains so realized are not completely obliterated by increased marketing costs, which we have thus far assumed to be zero.

Because we are dealing with domestic trade, we have assumed that the money used by the two states is the same. Had their monetary systems been different, the principle

Table 2.2 Constant Costs of Production per Bushel for Potatoes and Apples in Washington and Idaho: Case II

Commodity	Washington	Idaho
Potatoes	$3	$4
Apples	3	8

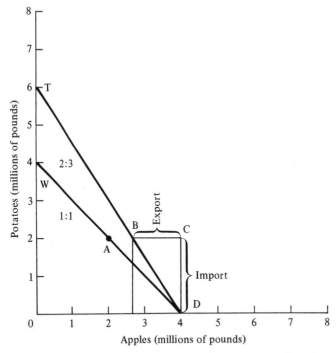

Figure 2.1. Transformation curve under conditions of constant costs: Washington.

would have been the same. An area (or person) should specialize in that in which it (he) has the greatest comparative advantage or the least comparative disadvantage. This is the principle of comparative advantage. Its marketing implications are apparent in the corollary principle: If resources differ in two areas and are immobile between the two, specialization and exchange between them will be economical if the costs ratios within one area differ from those in the other and if trade is costless. We shall examine later the limitations imposed by the cost of marketing, which we now assume is zero. In our last example of comparative advantage, Case II, the cost ratio in Washington was 1:1. In Idaho it was 1:2. The potential gain from trade lies in the difference between these two ratios.

PRODUCTION ALTERNATIVES: CONSTANT COSTS

We shall now examine the same proposition under the same circumstances—constant costs and no marketing costs—but in terms of alternative production possibilities. Line *W* in Figure 2.1 represents Washington's production possibilities: If it uses all of its resources to produce potatoes, it can produce 4 million pounds; if it produces 3 million pounds of potatoes, it can also produce 1 million pounds of apples; and if it produces only apples, it can grow 4 million pounds.

Line *I* in Figure 2.2 represents Idaho's position without trade. If Idaho produces only apples, it can produce 4 million pounds; if it produces only potatoes, it can produce 8 million pounds. Production of 4 million pounds of potatoes would also allow for the production of 2 million pounds of apples.

Let us see what happens if trade takes place between these two states. We shall first examine the position of Washington. Without trade, Washington has been producing 2 million pounds of potatoes and 2 million bushels of apples, represented by point *A* on

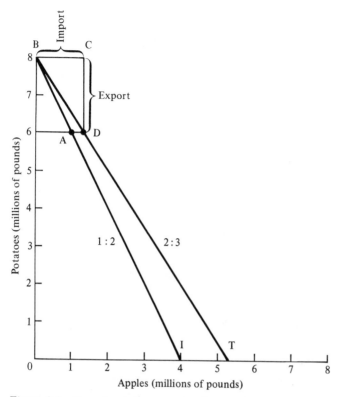

Figure 2.2. Transformation curve under conditions of increasing costs: Idaho.

Washington's constant-cost transformation curve in Figure 2.1. The exchange ratio between potatoes and apples will be 1:1. That is, if potatoes sell for $3, apples will also sell for $3. If trade relations are established with Idaho, Washington will concentrate its production on apples, in which it has a greater comparative advantage, producing 4 million pounds. If the prices established on the basis of trade are on a curve higher than Washington's original production possibility curve, as, for example, curve T in Figure 2.1, Washington will gain from the transaction, for now each pound of apples exchanges for one and one-half pounds of potatoes. If demand and supply conditions place the new consumption level of Washington at point B, Washington will export one and one-third million pounds of apples, BC, in exchange for 2 million pounds of Idaho potatoes, CD. Previously Washington consumers consumed only 2 million pounds of each. They continue to consume 2 million pounds of potatoes but increase their apple consumption to two and two-thirds million bushels, which represents a gain in total consumption or real income.

Figure 2.2 shows Idaho's transformation curve for potatoes and apples under constant costs. The exchange ratio without trade is 2:1; that is, two pounds of potatoes have the same value as one pound of apples. Let us say that Idaho has been operating at point A, producing and consuming 6 million pounds of potatoes each year and 1 million pounds of apples. Under trade, an exchange ratio of 2:3 is established. Each pound of potatoes is now worth two-thirds of a pound of apples instead of one-half pound, as it was previously. If Idaho now concentrates on the production of potatoes and uses all its resources, it can produce 8 million pounds. If it exchanges 2 million pounds of potatoes, CD, for one and one-third million pounds of apples from Washington, BC, it will be able

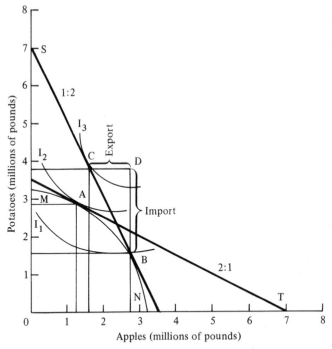

Figure 2.3. Transformation curve under conditions of increasing costs: Washington.

to sustain its usual consumption of potatoes at 6 million pounds and increase its apple consumption to one and one-third million pounds, which is one-third of a million pounds more than it was previously consuming. Both Idaho and Washington have gained.

PRODUCTION ALTERNATIVES: INCREASING COSTS

It is not likely that an area or producer will experience constant unit costs at all levels of output. It is far more likely that production possibilities will reflect increasing costs as output increases. This means, therefore, that the transformation curve will be convex to the origin, as is *MN* in Figure 2.3. With no trade, price ratios within Washington, let us assume, are 2:1, indicated by line *T*. If a pound of potatoes is priced at 40 cents, a pound of apples will be priced at 20 cents. At point *A*, the transformation ratio is 2:1, the price ratio is 2:1, and the marginal rate of substitution by consumers, as evidenced by the slope of the tangent to the indifference curve I_2, is 2:1. This would therefore determine Washington's optimal production if Washington is self-sufficient in the production of these two products. Washington consumers will have a little more than 1 million pounds of apples and not quite 3 million pounds of potatoes.

But suppose that Washington and Idaho engage in trade, and Idaho's advantage in producing potatoes is coordinated with Washington's advantage in growing apples so that the exchange ratio shifts to 1:2, indicated by line *S*. One pound of potatoes in the common market now costs as much as one-half pound of apples. It would now pay Washington to shift its production to point *B*, for at this point its transformation ratio is 1:2. Washington's potato production declines from nearly 3 million pounds to 1.6 million pounds. Resources released from the potato industry make it possible to increase apple production from a little more than 1 million pounds to about 2.7 million pounds. This would represent the optimum output for Washington under the new exchange ratios.

Now let's see what happens to Washington consumers. If Washington consumers do not trade with Idaho, production at point B is clearly inferior to that at point A. This is shown by the fact that B is on a lower indifference curve, I_1. The reason Washington would produce at point B and trade with Idaho is that this will enable Washington consumers to move to a higher indifference curve. Let us assume that with the demand and supply conditions in the two states, Washington's consumption under the new trading situation settles at point C. At this point, Washington consumers will have 1.6 million pounds of apples and about 3.8 million pounds of potatoes. Washington will export about 1.1 million pounds of apples to Idaho and import 2.2 million pounds of potatoes from Idaho. Point C represents a higher level of satisfaction than point A because it is on a higher indifference curve. We do not show the transformation and indifference curves for Idaho, but the same basic relationships would prevail there except that its advantage would lie in potato production. Consumers in Idaho would also be better off so long as the cost ratio established by trade permits them to move to a higher indifference curve. If both states are not better off, there is no reason for them to engage in trade.

Even under increasing costs, a difference in prevailing cost ratios in two areas will make trade economical and will benefit both areas so long as the price ratio established by trade lies between the price ratios in the two areas. However, under increasing costs, each area will probably produce *some* of each traded product. Specialization will not be complete, for as increasing costs are incurred with increased output, it will usually be more advantageous for a basically importing area to produce a small amount at low costs than to force added production onto the producers of the other area, where increasing costs are being experienced.

Differences in Tastes

Just as differences in costs of production may make trade economical, so also may differences in tastes or consumer demand. This is particularly likely under conditions of increasing costs. If Nebraska and Iowa are equally efficient in the production of beef and pork but differ in their consumption habits, it may be more economical for each state to produce both and for trade to fit the outputs to consumption patterns than for each to specialize.

One other minor condition that might give rise to trade is the case of goods whose marginal utility increases with increased consumption. Two pairs of red socks may be worth more to the wearer (or his launderer) than a combination of one red pair and one blue pair. This would be a case of increasing rather than decreasing marginal utility. A second place setting identical to a first one is of more added value to a homemaker than the first one, and two identical place settings are worth more than two different ones. Under such circumstances, it may pay for trade to take place if two producers have cost advantages in the production of diversified outputs. Such cost advantages are most likely to occur where there are joint costs. The marketing mechanism makes it possible for one to assemble a collection of red socks produced by several hosiery manufacturers, each of whom has a cost advantage in producing a range of colors of their particular brands and styles. Similarly, a devotee of socks can collect a variety of brands and colors through the services of a single retail firm that assembles the outputs of many manufacturers, each producing a range of types of selected brands and colors. This is a case of unspecialized production and specialized consumption, which necessitates trade to achieve the desired product mix in production and distribution.

Economies of Scale: Decreasing Costs

Decreasing-cost industries lead to complete specialization. If costs of production decline continuously as size of enterprise increases, it will be most economical to concentrate production in one firm. It is more likely, however, that the long-run cost curve for increasing scale will not show a continuous decline but will show a decreasing and then increasing average cost. Such a curve shows, not decreasing and increasing costs associated with the variation in output of a single enterprise with certain fixed costs of production, but rather, variation in costs associated with increasing size of the enterprise made possible through an increase in *all* productive resources of the firm. Under these circumstances, concentration of production up to the point where the lowest long-run average cost of production is achieved would be economical.

Another possibility for economies associated with scale of enterprise is particularly important to marketing under conditions of economic growth. This is based on economies that are external to the firm. As enterprises grow, it is possible for peripheral industries, particularly service and marketing industries, to develop around those basic enterprises which they service. These tertiary enterprises are themselves subject to cost variations according to scale, but because of the greater importance of social captial than physical capital to them, such firms are less likely to show internal efficiencies as volume increases but are more likely to show external efficiencies associated with market organization, internal administrative structure, and good will. Thus the automobile industry, once established in Detroit, gave rise to subsidiary industries and market organizations around it, which, once established, tended to perpetuate the automobile industry's continued existence in the area. By breeding the subsidiaries essential to its life, an industry may become, in turn, dependent on the subsidiaries. Parents sometimes find it hard to live without their children.

AGGREGATE DEMAND AND SUPPLY

Thus far we have sketched the basic conditions under which specialization and trade occur. By taking these singly, however, we have failed to show the interaction of supply and demand conditions to determine volume of trade or terms of trade. If we combine our separate markets into a single market, we can show the aggregate effects of demand and supply on the volume of trade and the price of traded goods. In the discussion that follows we shall use the traditional supply and demand curves from price analysis to show price determination where two markets become one.

Trade with No Marketing Costs

CONSTANT COSTS

Suppose that Washington, which we shall call area A, and Idaho, area B, have constant costs of production for apples, with Washington's costs markedly lower than those of Idaho. We illustrate this in Figure 2.4, where we show two positive quadrants of a graph placed back-to-back. Area B's output is shown on the right side of the X axis, increasing from 0 to Q_b'. Area A's output is shown in the reverse direction on the left side as it increases from 0 to Q_a'. The price for both areas is shown on the Y axis. The demand in

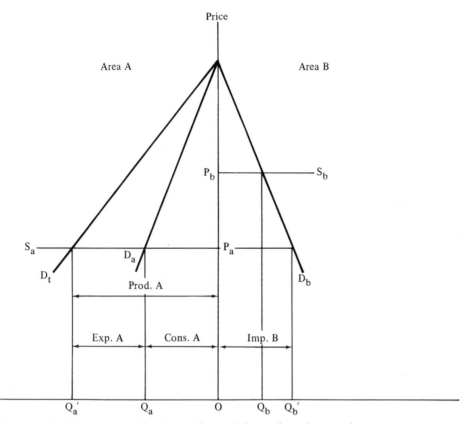

Figure 2.4. One-area specialization with equal demands and unequal constant costs.

each state is identical: $D_a = D_b$. The supply in both areas is perfectly elastic and is represented by S_a and S_b in areas A and B, respectively. The equilibrium price in Washington is shown in Figure 2.4 as OP_a; in Idaho it is OP_b. Without trade, area A would produce OQ_a output and area B, OQ_b output.

It would appear desirable for Idaho to buy its apples from Washington. If Idaho's demand, D_b, is added to Washington's demand, D_a, the total demand is doubled and becomes D_t. Washington's output would be increased to OQ_a', of which OQ_a would be consumed by Washington consumers and Q_aQ_a' would be exported to Idaho consumers. Thus, Idaho's consumption would be equal to OQ_b'. If all the advantage accrues to Idaho consumers, the new price will now be OP_a, the same as it was in Washington before specialization. It is not likely that the price will remain at OP_a, however, for Idaho must now shift its productive resources into some other industry by which it acquires the purchasing power necessary to purchase Washington apples, and this readjustment of related markets may cause the price of apples to rise to a point higher than OP_a.

Cost differentials between two areas under conditions of constant cost will tend to result in complete specialization by the low-cost area and an equilibrium price at the level of that in the low-cost area without specialization. This will not occur, however, if there are no other more attractive production alternatives in the high-cost area or if the resulting realignment of production modifies the income of productive resources, the demands for goods, and, hence, the price relationships among various commodities. We shall not develop the conditions underlying these qualifications to Figure 2.4 but mention them here as a reminder of their existence.

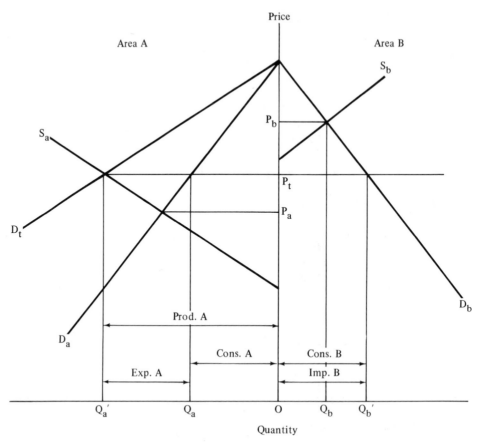

Figure 2.5. One-area specialization with equal demands and unequal increasing costs.

INCREASING COSTS

Figure 2.5 illustrates another case of complete specialization, but this time under conditions of increasing costs. Let us assume that the demand in area A is exactly the same as that in area B, but costs of production in A are substantially below costs of production in B except when A's output becomes quite large. If each area produces its own product, the price in area B is OP_b, while in area A it is OP_a. Area A obviously has a cost advantage. If it produces for the two markets combined, the demand becomes D_t, and the new equilibrium price becomes OP_t, which is higher than it was in A but lower than it was in B. We continue, of course, to ignore marketing costs.

This situation, however, raises an interesting question. If the price of apples rises in area A from OP_a to OP_t because of trade with area B, aren't Washington consumers worse off than they were before? The answer is yes if apples were the only product consumed by Washington consumers. But we must remember that trade is an exchange of goods and services, and the monetary transaction merely obscures the underlying real transaction. Idaho can buy apples from Washington only if it sells something in exchange, either to Washington or to other areas that trade with Washington. Therefore, the important question is not how much Washington consumers have to pay for apples but how much their total real consumption is because of the trading transaction. If I pay $4 for apples plus $50 for my weekly groceries, I am worse off than if I pay $5 for apples plus $45 for my weekly groceries. Under these new circumstances, I may even choose to eat slightly fewer apples and diversify my diet somewhat with more vegetables from Idaho sources.

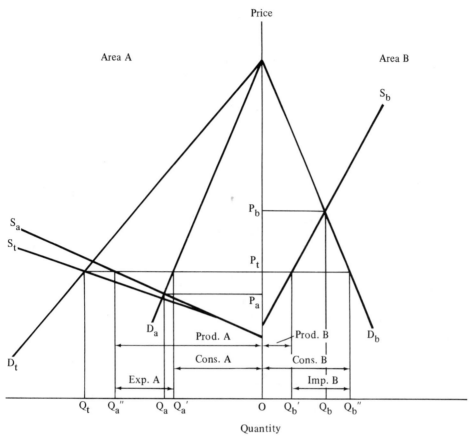

Figure 2.6. Partial interarea specialization with equal demands and unequal increasing costs.

Let us take a second example of identical demands and increasing costs in two areas. This is illustrated in Figure 2.6 and probably represents a more common situation, for in this case cost differences exist but are not great enough to justify complete specialization. As in the previous examples, area A has a cost advantage with a domestic price of OP_a, which is considerably lower than the price of OP_b in area B. Again, joint demand and supply warrant an output OQ_t, which consists of OQ_a'' produced in area A and OQ_b' produced in area B. The equilibrium price under trading conditions is OP_t, which is higher than the domestic price in area A but lower than the domestic price in area B without trade. But at this price consumers in area A curtail their consumption to OQ_a', and $Q_a'Q_a''$ of area A's output is exported to area B. In area B, on the other hand, the price of OP_t causes an increase in the quantity demanded, and consumers are willing to purchase OQ_b'', although only OQ_b' is produced there at that price. The balance is imported, and the amount imported by area B exactly equals the amount exported by area A, since the output and price were determined by the total demand and supply in the two markets. An increase in demand in the two areas would raise the new market price and cause an increase in the total production in the two markets combined and an increase in the volume of trade.[2]

---

[2] If there were no trade between the two areas, output in area A would be OQ_a, and output in area B would be OQ_b. The total of these is less than OQ_t.

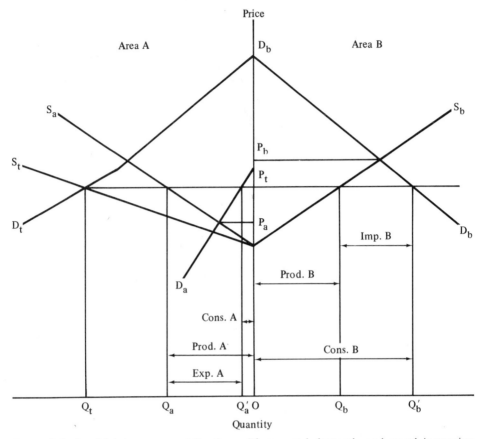

Figure 2.7. Partial interarea specialization with unequal demands and equal increasing costs.

A third example is illustrated in Figure 2.7. In this case, we assume that there are increasing costs of production and that the two areas have identical cost structures. The difference between the two is in demand. In area A the demand is quite limited, while in area B it is much greater. The price in area A is low, OP_a, but much higher in area B because of the larger demand. If the two markets become one, the combined demands are D_t and the combined supplies S_t, yielding a new trading price of OP_t, which is between the previous prices in A and B. Area A now increases its production greatly, to OQ_a.

But at a price of OP_t, area A's consumption is very small—only OQ_a'. This means that Q_aQ_a' will be exported by A to the consumers in area B, where the quantity demanded has increased to OQ_b'. Area B's production is exactly the same as area A's, but its consumption of OQ_b' is made possible by imports of Q_bQ_b' from area A.

DECREASING COSTS

If an industry has continuous decreasing costs, its supply curve will be negatively sloping. If there are two areas of demand, it will be most economical to combine them into a single market and to concentrate production in one firm in order to achieve the lowest possible cost of production. Figure 2.8 illustrates a case in which the demands in two areas are identical, and costs of production decline gradually as output increases. Under these circumstances, with no trade, the price will be the same in each area, since

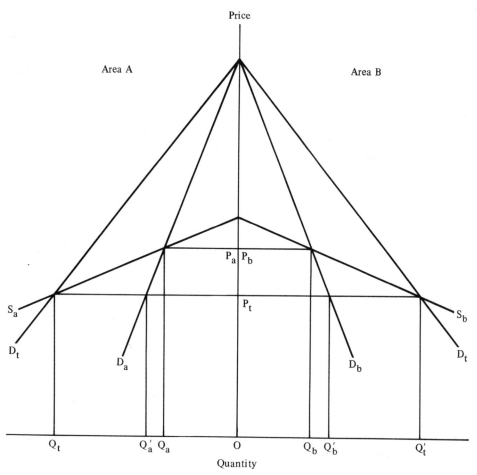

Figure 2.8. Partial interarea specialization with equal demands and equal decreasing costs.

$OP_a = OP_b$. If production is concentrated in *either* area A or area B, the new price will be at OP_t, reflecting the lower costs of production associated with larger output. If production is concentrated in area A, OQ_t will be produced, and half of this will be consumed by consumers in A, OQ_a', and half exported to consumers in B, $Q_a'Q_t$, which equals OQ_b', the amount that buyers in B are willing to purchase at price OP_t. If, on the other hand, production is completely concentrated in area B, then OQ_t' will be produced, and this equals OQ_t. Producers in B will export $Q_b'Q_t'$ to A, and consumers in B will absorb OQ_b' ($= OQ_a'$) at price OP_t. If, however, either area had experienced a greater cost reduction as volume increased than did the other area, it would have been more economical to concentrate production there.

As we have indicated, it is not likely that decreasing costs will continue indefinitely as volume of production increases. It is possible, however, for certain external economies— such as efficient commodity market organization, the development of significant service industries, and the maturation of factor markets—to develop that bring lower costs up to a point. Concentration of production at least up to that point will be economically justified.

Although we are here considering static market situations, it is appropriate to mention the possibility of decreasing costs that arise out of a dynamic situation. Technological

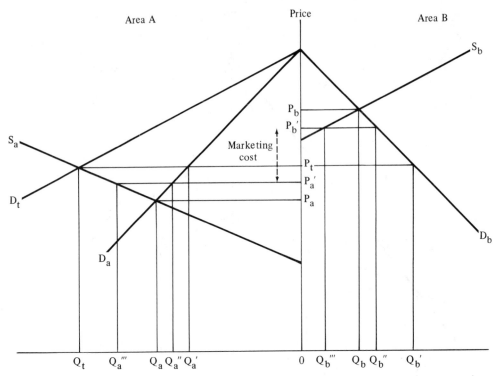

Figure 2.9. Partial interarea specialization where marketing cost is less than interarea price difference.

developments that breed new cost functions with lower minimums are stimulated by a growing level of output. These developments may be largely physical, or they may be social and cultural in nature. For example, the development of an efficient marketing system for automobiles and the maturation of credit institutions in automobile markets have interacted with scale of output, growth of consumer demand, and engineering technology as both cause and effect. The decreasing cost curve for some industries may therefore reflect a secular cost function that is as much a product of the evolution of the economic climate as it is a function of size of firms and industry.

Trade with Marketing Costs

We shall now lift our limiting and unrealistic assumption about no marketing costs and see how such costs modify the amount and terms of trade. We have already shown that an importing area obtains a good through trade at lower prices than would be possible through domestic production. A part of this "saving" must, however, be used to pay the marketing costs made necessary by trade. If the marketing cost is less than the differential, trade will take place in spite of this "tariff." Figure 2.9 shows the effect of marketing costs on output, volume of trade, and prices.[3]

Without trade area A will produce and consume quantity OQ_a at price OP_a. Area B will

---

[3] For a slightly different method of graphic presentation and an extension into a simple linear programming model, see Bressler and King, op. cit., pp. 86-107.

produce OQ_b at price OP_b. The difference between the prices in the two areas is P_aP_b. If there were no marketing costs, area A could produce OQ_t for both areas at a price of OP_t. A's exports to area B would be $Q_a'Q_t$, and its own consumption would be OQ_a' ($OQ_b' = Q_a'Q_t$). Suppose, however, that there are marketing costs involved in shipping goods from area A and selling them in area B. We shall assume that the marketing cost per unit is constant and equals $P_a'P_b'$. This cost will have to be added onto the price of the product in area B but not in area A. This marketing cost becomes a wedge driven between the price of the product in A and its price in B.[4] How much will area A now produce, and will area B now find it advantageous to produce any of this product? The amount that will be produced in area A will equal the amount that buyers in A are willing to buy at the price indicated by cost of production plus the amount that buyers in B are willing to buy at the price indicated by cost of production plus marketing cost.

We show this in Figure 2.9 as output OQ_a'''. Of this total amount, buyers in A will purchase OQ_a'' at price OP_a', and $Q_a''Q_a'''$ will be sold to buyers in area B. But the price in B will be OP_a' plus the marketing cost of $P_a'P_b'$, or OP_b'. At price OP_b' consumers in B will find that domestic producers will provide them with OQ_b''' output, and the balance of the quantity that it demands at that price, $Q_b'''Q_b''$, will come from A's exports. $Q_b'''Q_b''$ exactly equals $Q_a''Q_a'''$. Thus total output will equal total consumption, imports into B will equal exports from A, output in A will equal consumption in A plus exports to B, consumption in B will equal output in B plus imports from A, the price in B will exceed the price in A by the amount of the marketing cost, and all sellers will be able to cover their costs of production, including marketing costs. Note that while area B is paying the marketing cost on its imported goods, these costs have a bearing on the level of output of area A and, hence, on the cost of production and the price of the product in area A.

Figure 2.10 illustrates a situation in which unit marketing costs exceed the price differential between the two areas. Given the cost and demand structures described, we can see that without trade, area A would produce quantity OQ_a at a price of OP_a, and area B would produce OQ_b at price OP_b. The unit marketing cost is P_aP_b'. If A were to increase its output in order to export to B, unit cost would rise. But even without a rise in production cost, addition of the marketing cost to the equilibrium price in A would raise the price of B's import to OP_b'. At this price, output of B's own firms would increase to OQ_b', while the quantity demanded would be less than without trade. Therefore, if marketing costs between two areas are greater than the price differential between them, no trade will take place.

An interesting aspect of marketing costs is evident from the two situations we have just examined. Marketing costs tend to reduce the amount of specialization and trade, and their incidence is on both buyer and seller by causing higher prices in the import area and lower prices in the export area. Which of the two areas feels the greater burden will depend on the elasticities of demand and supply in the two areas. The area that has the more inelastic demand and supply will experience the greater price change; the area with the more elastic demand and/or supply will experience the greater quantitative change.

---

[4] "In a price system, transaction costs drive a wedge between buyer's and seller's prices and thereby give rise to welfare losses as in the usual analysis." Kenneth J. Arrow, "The Organization of Economic Activity: Issues Pertinent to the Choice of Market Versus Nonmarket Allocation," in *The Analysis and Evaluation of Public Expenditures: The PPB System*, vol. I, compendium of papers submitted to the Joint Economic Committee, Subcommittee on Economy in Government, 91st Congress, 1st sess. (Washington, D.C.: GPO, 1969), p. 60.

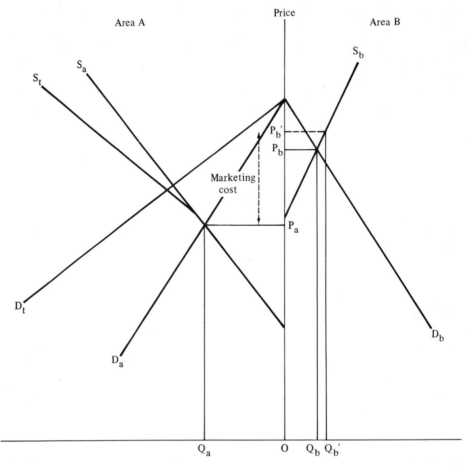

Figure 2.10. No interarea specialization where marketing cost exceeds interarea price difference.

Recapitulation

Trade takes place between two areas, two firms, or two people who have differences in resources, in demands, or in costs associated with scale of enterprise. The amount of trade will be such that it brings the aggregate demand and supply of the two areas into equilibrium at a single market price. The price of a traded good will differ between export and import areas by the amount of marketing costs, and trade will not take place unless this marketing cost is less than the difference in price without trade. Constant costs and decreasing costs will cause complete specialization, while increasing costs are more likely to cause partial specialization, with importing areas producing some for their own consumption. The incidence of marketing costs is on both buyers and sellers.

THE EFFECTS OF TRADE

We have examined certain specific cost and demand conditions that cause trade to take place. We have greatly oversimplified our presentation, taking one variable at a time and no more than two commodities and two areas at a time. Trade is in fact far more complex than this, reflecting varying degrees of specialization among a wide range of products and among a large number of producers and consumers. It is not two- or three-dimensional but multidimensional in scope. Laborers are, in effect, trading productive services for a wide variety of consumer goods; manufacturers of technical equipment exchange their output for textiles; textile producers, in turn, exchange their goods for automobiles and automobile producers theirs for clothing, and so on. Money obscures the basic barter aspects of trade and consequently many of its ramifications and implications. But directly or indirectly, every producer and every consumer is participating in a network of relationships that are designed to yield very real and significant gains to him. Let us examine briefly some of the significant effects of trade relationships.

Economic Effects of Trade

We shall consider the effects of trade on real income, resource utilization, demand, and the structure of the economy.

REAL INCOME

The justification for trade lies in its ability to increase real income. The purpose of specialization is to effect a more economical utilization of resources, which is reflected in a higher real income than would occur without specialization. Trade makes specialization possible and in so doing also makes a higher real income possible. In a narrow sense, this is the gain from trade. This gain manifests itself in the *aggregate* prices of traded commodities. It is not true that each product traded carries a lower price for each buyer than it did before trade but rather that the exchange ratios among all goods are such that both participants in each trading transaction realize a larger real income.

Increased trade is also likely to result in greater price equalization, with price differences reflecting the cost of marketing the traded goods. Bertil Ohlin has pointed out, however, that price equalization is achieved between exporting and importing areas but not necessarily between two importing areas that maintain no trading relations with one another either directly or via a common source of commodities.[5] We have demonstrated this effect in the preceding section, where we showed how independent markets become a single market through the establishment of exchange relationships.

While the gains of trade may conceivably accrue to only one participant—either buyer or seller—it is more likely that both parties will have some gains. Otherwise the reasons for both to participate in the transaction will not exist. But one very interesting fact emerges from our simplified analysis up to this point: When trade takes place between a large producing area and a small producing area, the small area is likely to gain more than the large one. The reason for this lies in the fact that the exchange ratio between the two areas is a result of reciprocal demand and supply. We have illustrated this by showing an aggregate demand and supply for two trading areas. If the larger producing area also has the larger demand, its output and demand will dominate the aggregate demand and supply. Therefore, the exchange ratio that finally emerges from the aggregate market is likely to be nearer that of the large area than that of the small one, whose demand and

---

[5] Ohlin, op. cit., pp. 107-109.

supply situation has little influence on the total.[6] In addition, the larger the exporting area, the more likely it is that it will not be able to specialize to the same degree as a smaller area with more limited resources. Therefore, the large area has more influence on a larger number of exchange ratios in interregional trade. To benefit from trade, a buyer or seller must enjoy through trade a more favorable exchange ratio than he had without trade. His gain is greatest the nearer the actual trading ratio is to this other more favorable ratio. Small producers often gain most through participation in markets dominated by big producers.

RESOURCE UTILIZATION

We have already indicated that trade makes possible greater specialization in production and, hence, greater efficiency in resource utilization. There are, however, some interesting secondary effects beyond this initial change in the pattern of resource use. As trade shifts the pattern of use, those resources that are used more intensively will tend to rise in price as the demand for them rises, and those used less intensively than previously will tend to fall in price. If Massachusetts exports large quantities of precision machinery to South Carolina, the wages of machinery workers will tend to rise as the demand for their services increases. But as Massachusetts increases its imports of textiles from South Carolina, the wages of textile workers in South Carolina will tend to rise and the wages of Massachusetts textile workers to fall, or at least not to rise as they would have without trade. These changes in factor prices tend to offset some of the short-run changes that occur as trade increases. Their overall effect is greater equalization of factor prices between trading areas. It is unlikely, however, that there will be perfect equalization of factor prices through trade, for there are always rigidities and imperfections that prevent the free movement of resources, and this is particularly true of human resources. Trade in commodities tends to decrease wage differences between Georgia and California, but because of the immobility of labor, some residents of Georgia will not be attracted to California in spite of higher wages, and this makes possible a continuation of wage differentials. Some productive factors, such as capital, are more highly mobile and may show less geographic differentials in their returns. One effect of trade in commodities is, therefore, partial equalization of factor prices.

DEMAND

An extremely interesting consequence of trade is changes in the demand structure. If goods previously unavailable become available through trade, their presence in the market may reveal a latent demand. Or it may even be economically correct to say that their presence "creates" a demand. Because marketing relationships may make available goods that previously were not available and for which there was no demand, can we say that the newly created demand is a "gain" from trade? Ohlin believes that we cannot call it a "gain" but merely an effect.[7]

Examples of this type of trading effect are numerous. The California Fruit Growers' Exchange set out deliberately to build a demand for oranges through advertising and sales promotion and, given the economic and social environment in which they acted, they

---

[6] See Frank D. Graham, *The Theory of International Values* (Princeton, N.J.: Princeton University Press, 1948), pp. 226-243.

[7] Ohlin, op. cit., pp. 89-90.

succeeded in "creating" a demand. The ready availability of hot dogs and hamburgers on the Champs Elysées in Paris has disturbed the admirers of Parisian cafes and restaurants but illustrates the impact of trading relations on the structure of demand. Few midwesterners in the United States would "demand" southern fried chicken had trade relations of some sort not made knowledge of its qualities available.[8] These are all examples of the diversification and expansion of demand that comes about through trade.

Another by-product of this diversification of demand structure is the *leveling* of demand between trading areas. Geographic specialization is built basically on differences in resources. Trade between production areas may result in the "creation" of a demand in an area where a product was originally not demanded. This means, therefore, that the total effect of these new demands is a leveling of demand among trading nations—a tendency for the demand structure in one area to become more like that of another. The consumption of Espresso coffee, Chianti, Volkswagens, and Toyotas in the United States was precipitated by trade, which has made American consumption patterns more like European or Japanese patterns than would have been true without such trade.

The broader social and cultural effects of these changes may not be without considerable importance. Cultural patterns are manifested to a considerable degree in the kinds of goods and services consumed, for these are media that reflect values and modes of behavior. The diversifying effects of trade on consumption may be "good" or "bad," depending on one's criteria. Most economic criteria would suggest that they are "good" in that total utility is increased when there is greater diversity in what we consume. This is because of declining marginal utility. But there could be "bad" effects if judgment is based on other criteria—if, for example, the greater availability of a wide range of goods stimulates people toward the substitution of material means of achievement for nonmaterial when, on the basis of value judgment, this is regarded as undesirable.

The leveling effects of trade may also be regarded as "good" or "bad," depending again on one's criteria. Some would say they are "good" in that they reduce differences that are the basis for conflict. Others would say they are "bad" in that they minimize interpersonal and intercultural differences that give color, diversity, and stimulation to an otherwise homogeneous culture. Many foreigners criticize the uniformity in American life on grounds like these. This uniformity is at least in part a product of a highly efficient and integrating marketing system.

We raise these questions not because we hope to answer them categorically but because they are important and because they are issues that surround many of the more elementary economic questions with which we shall deal. The demand-creating aspects of marketing cannot be glossed over lightly, for we know not only that marketing has this incidental effect but also that a great deal of marketing effort is deliberately directed toward the achievement of such an effect.

ECONOMIC STRUCTURE

The most important effect of trade on economic structure comes about through the phenomenon of specialization and the creation of a high degree of interdependence

---

[8] This is a good example of demand built on imperfect knowledge. Few of the establishments that serve "southern fried chicken," including Colonel Sanders', approximate the product that originally appeared under that name. The same could be said about French dressing (e.g., "Mrs. Clark's Italian-Style French Dressing"), Russian rye bread, chow mein, German sausage, Hungarian goulash, French toast, Roquefort cheese, Danish rolls, and Swiss cheese.

among economic units. This interdependence results in a higher real income. But it also creates serious problems when part of the system breaks down and forces readjustments in other parts. During such a period of readjustment, there may be a lower real income than would have occurred without prior specialization and trade—"specialization in reverse," as Marsh has called it.[9] During depressions, for example, families who are unemployed may raise gardens, make their clothes, preserve fruits and vegetables, and do similar unspecialized acts of production to raise their real income. Some may return to farming, giving up the possibilities of specialization associated with city life and accepting instead the security of a consistently lower real income through diversified production and close integration between production and consumption.

When one is evaluating the total marketing system and its role in the economy, the potential gains from interdependence must be weighed against the risks and uncertainties which an interdependent economic structure creates. Do the long-run gains of a market economy justify the costs associated with an occasional breakdown? Is it possible to minimize the breakdowns so that we experience the long-run benefits without some of the short-run costs of instability? These are important questions to which we shall return after we have examined in greater detail the functioning of the marketing system.

Measurement of the Gains of Trade

In our discussion of the ways in which trade can affect the economy, we have implied some of the means of measuring the benefits of trade and have also suggested some of the problems of such measurements. In the narrowest possible sense, we might measure the "gains" of trade by computing the total real income of the traders after trade and subtracting from that figure the total real income of the traders before trade. The difference would represent the increase in real income that could be imputed to trade. Empirically, such a procedure is difficult except where trade has just been introduced so that "before" and "after" data are available. Even in these cases, it may take time for the effects to work themselves out fully and be precisely measurable. But the procedure is not practical where trade has been long established and costs must be estimated for a production situation that does not exist. Sometimes such estimates can be made, but they are usually difficult to make.

Ohlin has pointed out another reason for not trying to estimate the "gains" of trade.[10] One of the effects of trade is to modify demands. If, as a result of trade, Parisians learn to demand hot dogs, which they did not want before trade took place, how can we measure this in terms of a "gain"? The introduction of a new product may result in a complete reorganization of preference patterns, but whether such a restructuring is a "gain" or not depends on the criteria by which we judge it. We cannot, within the framework of economics, say categorically that an increase in the variety of goods demanded is an economic gain. Nor can we appraise the effects of a sequence of events, such as increased trade, which leads to increased real income, which leads to increased population, which finally leads to the same real income per capita as before trade. This is a very common short-run effect of increased productivity and trade in less-developed countries. In fact, there may even be a temporary decrease in real income per capita. But this problem of

---

[9] D. B. Marsh, *World Trade and Investment* (New York: Harcourt Brace Jovanovich, 1951), p. 3.

[10] Ohlin, op. cit., pp. 89-90.

identifying and measuring a "gain" from trade does not preclude our recognizing this particular *effect* of trade and *measuring the effect*. The *interpretation* of the effect as a gain or loss will then depend on the criteria we adopt. What we must try to measure is the *effects* of changes in trade.

Another consequence of trade is a change in income distribution. This is difficult to identify as a "gain" or "loss" except in terms of clearly defined welfare criteria. If trade equalizes commodity prices, its general effect is to reduce income differences between traders. On the other hand, if it shifts resource allocation in the direction of utilization of more efficient resources, it may easily increase income inequality, particularly within a single trading unit. There is, therefore, no uniform effect of trade on income distribution, nor can changes in income distribution be categorically identified as "gains" or "losses."

Perhaps therefore we should follow Ohlin's admonition and not worry too much about measuring total gains from trade. Where possible, we can measure the economic effects of trade—the effects on resource utilization, on total real income, on the distribution of income, and on the structure of demand. We can also compute the gains that come from small changes in the volume and direction of trade, particularly where the impact on income can be estimated. But we would be neglecting a significant area of inquiry if we did not point out other, perhaps nonmeasurable, effects of trading patterns and if we did not raise some of the significant questions that this economic phenomenon raises for related disciplines.

LOCATION AND TRADE THEORY

Throughout our discussion we have frequently spoken of trade between "areas." We need now to refine and amplify the concept of area, which is one of the most significant elements of trade.

The Concept of Space

Basic to all trading relations is "space," and "space" consists of a continuum of "points" or locations. We are using space in a very broad sense. There may, for example, be geographic space, and trade in such a space refers to exchange relations between points separated geographically but connected by trade into a single area. When producers in California sell products to buyers in Washington, the states of California and Washington, each comprising a separate cluster of points separated from the other by geographic distance, become a single market area.

There is a second sense in which we use the term *space*. Buyers and sellers are separated in time, and the bridging of temporal space is also a function of marketing. Through marketing, two points in time become parts of a single time "area."

Finally, there is also qualitative space. Producers of differentiated products arrange themselves at points within the complete range of quality possibilities. This is the most complex of our space concepts, for it is not two-dimensional but multidimensional. The number of dimensions is limited only by the qualitative possibilities that physical attributes, technology, consumer perception, and human imagination make possible. Through its integrative functions, marketing makes possible these wide ranges of quality, and marketing is, in turn, enormously influenced in its organization and policies by the kinds and varieties of products available.

When a producer specializes he determines his location in these various types of "space." If he produces high-quality, cotton gray goods in southern mills for sale to converters, he has determined his location in space, time, and quality.

Specialization and Marketing

We have already pointed out that specialization makes marketing necessary and that the existence of marketing facilities makes specialization possible. If we redefine specialization as location in space, using space in the broad sense in which we have used it here, then we can say that the theory of trade and the theory of location are the same. This is, in fact, the approach of Ohlin, Alfred Weber, Walter Isard, E. T. Grether, and others.[11] If we explain why a firm or an industry is located at point x, we can explain trade between that point and other points. If we explain why trade takes place between points x and y, we have explained why buyers and sellers are located at each of those points. The theory of trade becomes, therefore, the theory of location. It is not enough to take the existing economic structure as an assumption and explain marketing organization and behavior within that structure. Because the marketing system is an integral part of that economic structure—both determining and determined—it must be examined in terms of its broader economic function as well as in terms of its relationship to a given economic organization. We shall therefore give attention in this volume to both of these aspects of marketing: (1) the broader economic functions of the marketing system in an economy differentiated and localized in time, space, and quality, and (2) the specific functions and behavior of firms and households in their role as market participants.

---

[11] Ohlin, op. cit., Alfred Weber, *Theory of the Location of Industries,* trans. C. J. Friedrich (Chicago: University of Chicago Press, 1929); August Lösch, *The Economics of Location* (New Haven, Conn.: Yale University Press, 1954); Walter Isard, *Location and Space-Economy* (New York: Wiley, 1956), and *General Theory: Social, Political, Economic, and Regional* (Cambridge, Mass.: M.I.T. Press, 1969); E. T. Grether, "A Theoretical Approach to the Analysis of Marketing," in Reavis Cox and Wroe Alderson, eds., *Theory in Marketing: Selected Essays*, 1st ser. (Homewood, Ill.: Irwin, 1950), pp. 113-123; Bressler and King, op. cit.

3

Risk, Uncertainty, and Marketing Intelligence

It is the certain voice
Of an uncertain moment.

—Edna St. Vincent Millay

The essence of marketing is the meeting of minds that is achieved through the exchange transaction. A buyer and a seller must perceive and accept common terms of trade if a transaction is to be effected, and the marketing system provides the social framework within which this can be accomplished. This framework may itself become a complex network of subsidiary systems, within each of which specific complementary actions occur that contribute to the ultimate exchange of assets that constitutes the marketing transaction. The decisions and actions that precede market participation (or nonparticipation) by buyers and sellers, and market participation itself, involve a variety of risks and uncertainties associated with less than complete and perfect knowledge.

The absence of any information about number and location of vendors, quantities of goods and services available, qualitative attributes of offerings, prices and terms of sale, and vendors' ability and willingness to modify their offerings, prices, or terms are examples of uncertainties that often confront potential buyers. Similarly, lack of any information about the number, location, and attributes of buyers, as well as of buyers' ability and willingness to pay varying prices for varying quantities and qualities of goods or services, are types of uncertainties that may confront potential sellers. On the other hand, few buyers and sellers are completely ignorant of the facts of demand and supply. Sometimes they can calculate precisely or estimate subjectively the probability of specific characteristics of the market situation. Where such probabilities can be established, market uncertainty, which is characterized by no information, is converted into market risk, which is characterized by information formulated in terms of probabilities. Still further movement along the continuum away from uncertainty would bring buyers and sellers to a state of certainty in which information relevant to market decisions and actions would be both accurate and complete. Needless to say, most buyers and sellers would like to operate in a state of certainty but seldom can. Few prefer a state of uncertainty.[1] Most must settle for a market environment in which there is considerable risk, usually coupled with both some certainty and some uncertainty.

THE NATURE OF MARKETING INTELLIGENCE

Marketing intelligence enables the market participant to convert uncertainty into risk and, perhaps, into certainty, although the latter is seldom possible except with respect to

---

[1] While it may seem odd to say that "most buyers and sellers" prefer certainty, and "few" prefer uncertainty, it would be less than realistic to ignore the possiblity that marketing activities *may* be viewed by some as a sport. Even in this case, however, risks are probably preferred to uncertainty.

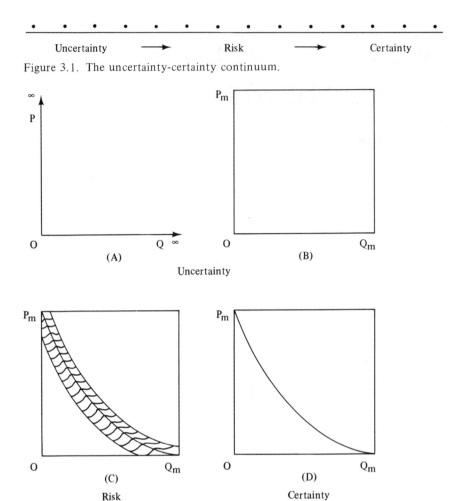

Figure 3.1. The uncertainty-certainty continuum.

Figure 3.2. Uncertainty, risk, and certainty with respect to knowledge of demand.

certain specialized aspects of the market situation. Suppose that a seller knows from past experience, or from market research, that the average income of households to which he is trying to sell his product is $11,450, that they have spent, on an average, $88 per year for this general type of product, that their expenditures range from $0 to $1,984, that the standard deviation of expenditures is $78, that 54 percent of the households spent more than $0 on such items last year, that competitors are offering similar but inferior items for $17 each, and that the advertising expenditure of competing firms is 2.4 percent of their sales. While he cannot face his market with certainty, he can use this and related information to establish with some degree of confidence—in fact, with some specified degree of confidence if his data have been obtained in a manner that so permits—sales probabilities for his product and perhaps also some of the constraints within which his marketing policies will have to be established if he aspires to capture some given share of the market.

Viewing human decisions and action as taking place along a continuum that ranges from a state of uncertainty to one of certainty (see Figure 3.1), we can say that the purpose of marketing intelligence is to make it possible for marketing decisions to be made, and actions to take place, at a point on that continuum farther removed from uncertainty than would have been possible without that intelligence. Figure 3.2 provides another way of viewing uncertainty, risk, and certainty. Assume that a seller is interested in knowing the demand for the generic product that he is producing but has no conception of the relevant price-quantity relationships. Price and quantity could range from zero to infinity. His knowledge is limited to what is shown in section (A) of Figure 3.2. If, however, he knows the minimum price at which zero units will be purchased, and the maximum quantity that will be purchased as price approaches zero, his knowledge would be illustrated by section (B), which shows these two boundaries but nothing in between.[2] If, however, he is able to determine the probabilities of various quantity sales at various prices, his uncertainty becomes risk and is illustrated by section (C). We show there the probability of various quantities of sales at a series of prices, with the probability indicated by the varying height of the probability curve at each price level. Were the seller able to operate with certainty, he would need to know the exact number of units that would be sold at various prices, as illustrated in section (D).

Levels of Marketing Intelligence

We shall define the term *marketing intelligence* to include (1) information about the market situation that is relevant to the decision making that precedes and/or is a part of market participation; (2) understanding of the meaning of that information; and (3) the ability to utilize information in the decision-making process.[3] The distinctions among these three components of "intelligence" as we define it are very important. "Information about" something may consist of an isolated fact or a set of systematically structured facts. The *Census of Business* for retail and wholesale trade contains information about these two major parts of the market structure. Concepts and

---

[2] A seller might not even be interested in these boundaries but in still more constrained limits. He might prefer to know, for example, the maximum quantity that will be purchased at a price that would equal his marginal cost.

[3] This definition of marketing intelligence in terms of three levels of intelligence is closely related to the three levels of communication problems identified by Warren Weaver in his classic exposition of information theory based on Claude E. Shannon's "Recent Contributions to the Mathematical Theory of Communication," in Claude E. Shannon and Warren Weaver, *The Mathematical Theory of Communication* (Urbana: University of Illinois Press, 1949), pp. 95-117. The levels of communication problems identified by Weaver are as follows:

"Level A. How accurately can the symbols of communication be transmitted? (The technical problem.)

Level B. How precisely do the transmitted symbols convey the desired meaning? (The semantic problem.)

Level C. How effectively does the received meaning affect conduct in the desired way? (The effectiveness problem.)"

He points out the overlap between all of the suggested categories of problems.

Information theory has concerned itself primarily with the level A type of problem. It has focused on the quantity of information as a function of the symbols employed, the transmission system, and the processes by which information is transmitted and received. While in this chapter we utilize some of the concepts of information theory, we have attempted to focus much more on the value of information and much less on the technical problems of information transmission. In the appendix to this chapter we have, however, made an attempt to pour marketing institutions and processes into the mold of information theory, thus viewing marketing as an information system.

measurements are the principal ingredients of such information. Sales, establishments, employees, kind of business, method of operation, and firms of varying size are concepts basic to the *Census of Business* reports, and measurements of these are the essence of the reports.

But this is *information*, and it becomes useful only as it takes on *meaning*, the second level of intelligence as we define it. Understanding is a much more advanced level of intelligence than mere "information about." Meaning is based on concepts of "things" and on propositions that describe relationships among concepts and are subject to proof. The information obtained from the *Census of Business* or from the A. C. Nielsen store audits becomes meaningful to marketing management when its various components can be related to one another—for example, changes in number of establishments related to changes in sales per establishment—and, still more important to the marketing firm, when the information and its internal relationships are related to the operating policies of the firm using the information—for example, the relationship between the particular firm's market share and the distribution of sales among all firms (or establishments) in the market in which the particular firm operates. At its most advanced level, understanding of meaning takes the form of theory comprising propositions and theorems structured systematically through the interface of deductive and inductive analysis into increasingly higher levels of generality.

The third level of intelligence is operational—understanding how to utilize information in the conduct of human affairs. Thus marketing management must not only understand the meaning of market data, in terms of theorems about the nature of market relationships, their determinants, and their effects, but it must be able to utilize this understanding in the formulation of *better* policies if management's intelligence is to be meaningful in a functional as well as an intellectual sense. At this level, propositions indicate the operation that will lead to a solution and are therefore problem solving in nature.

The third level raises some interesting questions. By including it as a part of our definition of marketing intelligence, we are forgoing the temptation to define intelligence in the esoteric sense of knowledge for the sake of knowledge. Rather, we are saying that marketing knowledge should be operationally meaningful. We defend this broad, functional concept on the ground that marketing *is* functional. One who seeks knowledge for the sheer pleasure of discovering it might better do so in fields other than marketing. Logic or mathematics would be more fertile areas for indulging in the pursuit of knowledge for the sake of its own intellectual or aesthetic elegance. Marketing has evolved to meet human needs and must be judged in terms of the effectiveness with which it does so. While some market participants doubtless enjoy trading, the basic purpose of trade is to make possible greater utility from the reallocation of goods and services among members of society. Marketing knowledge must therefore lead to conduct in this direction if that knowledge is to have value. We are not interested in marketing information or meaning that cannot affect personal or social conduct.

Each of the three levels of marketing intelligence has both quantitative and qualitative dimensions. Information can vary in both amount and accuracy, as can meaning and effectiveness. Some of the most important questions in marketing research concern reliability, validity, and the trade-off between the amount and validity of findings. An additional observation we should make about the three levels of marketing intelligence is that they are not mutually exclusive but are both complementary and overlapping. Understanding of market information, for example, is in part a function of the quantity and quality of information available, and effectiveness of knowledge is a function of the amount and validity of both the data and the analysis that leads to the understanding of data. The levels are, however, sequential and often circular. Sequence and circularity are characteristic of the acqusition of knowledge by both formal and informal processes. Both are apparent where scientific methods of investigation are employed.

Marketing Intelligence Decisions

The acquisition of marketing intelligence is a problem that confronts all market participants. There are three areas within which decisions have to be made. The first problem is to identify the information needed—the type required for more effective market participation and the amount needed. The second problem is to determine how to acquire the information desired. This involves some kind of search procedure, which entails costs. The third step is information processing—interpreting the data obtained (the second level of intelligence) and making action decisions on the basis of that meaning (the third level).

Of these three decision areas concerning market information—identification, acquisition, and processing—we shall focus in this chapter on the acquisition of information. We shall not ignore problems of identification or processing, since questions such as how much information to obtain and the analytical potential of information have a significant bearing on acquisition, but we shall focus on the acquisition process and the decisions that have to be made concerning whether or not to acquire more or different information. This entire volume on the economics of marketing concerns itself with the analysis of market structure and behavior within the framework of economics. We shall therefore emphasize the data that are needed for analysis and the analysis process itself. Let us now turn to some of the problems associated with getting the information needed for effective market decisions.

The Search Process in Marketing

MARKETING AS A LEARNING PROCESS

One of the principal functions of the marketing system is to transmit information, thereby enabling complementary and competing market participants to make "better" decisions, that is, decisions that yield results closer to those that are theoretically optimal. In this sense, the market can be viewed as a mechanism for enabling buyers and sellers to learn what is possible and, on the basis of that information, to modify their behavior in order to achieve their objectives. A price quotation is very significant information, generally containing many "bits" of information as this would be defined in information theory.[4] Data on sales revenue contain vast amounts of information for a seller. Profits are one of the most important aggregates of information for producers of products. These and many other types of information in the market place inform buyers and sellers of market conditions and serve as a basis for the alteration of decisions in optimal directions. It is in this sense that marketing can be viewed as a learning process and markets as a

---

[4] Robert Dorfman, *The Price System* (Englewood Cliffs, N.J.: Prentice-Hall, 1964), pp. 6-10.

means for transmitting the information essential to learning.[5] The more dynamic the market, the greater the importance of this information communication function, both as a result of the market's dynamic character and as a necessity for equilibrium-inducing forces to be set into operation.

How do buyers and sellers find out about one another and about each other's trading potential? We shall look briefly at the techniques of search and the various forms that it takes in marketing.

METHODS OF SEARCH

One simple way to acquire information about the market is to observe it as it is. This may include such procedures as a buyer's inspecting merchandise on display in a store to determine qualities and prices; a retailer's continuous tabulation of his sales records month by month to detect trends; a wholesaler's classification of his ledger accounts by size of purchase as a basis for clustering his customers; or an automobile manufacturer's collection of data on motor vehicle registrations by state and by make and type of car, on personal income from governmental sources, on characteristics of households from census sources, and on automobile sales from the manufacturers' trade association—all to be used for purposes of multiple regression analysis.

A second method of getting market information is through observation with change introduced. This might be achieved very informally by the ultimate consumer, who, for example, tries out a new shopping center and compares his experience there with that in the center where he has previously made his purchases. More often, however, observation with change is undertaken by the seller, who is usually in a better position than a single consumer to alter the market situation. He might, for example, modify his product quality and closely observe sales after the modification in comparison with those prior to the change. Observation without control is not, however, without interpretive problems. Therefore alteration of marketing policies is often undertaken with controls that will permit the experimenter to filter out with greater validity the effects of the policy change in question.

The third principal method for getting market information is through self-observation. This is, in essence, the survey technique, which is the standby of so much marketing research. Consumers are asked questions; that is, they are asked to report what they have in effect "observed" themselves doing, or what objective or subjective factors the individual has "observed" about himself. Sometimes the consumer is asked to keep a diary of his purchasing, "observing" himself day by day in the act of performing his marketing activities and reporting these observations to the investigator. Kenneth Boulding has compared the survey in the social sciences to the microscope in the biological sciences.[6] Perhaps the survey plus the computer could be compared to the electron microscope. Just as we fail to include the services of housewives in the calculation of real gross national product, so we fail to include the debt of marketing

---

[5] See Kenneth E. Boulding, "The Economics of Knowledge and the Knowledge of Economics," *American Economic Review* 56 (May 1966): 1-13, and Richard H. Day, "Profits, Learning and the Convergence of Satisficing to Marginalism," *Quarterly Journal of Economics* 81 (May 1967): 302-311. See also the appendix to this chapter, in which marketing is viewed as an information system.

[6] Kenneth E. Boulding, *The Impact of the Social Sciences* (New Brunswick, N.J.: Rutgers University Press, 1966), p. 23.

research to patient consumer respondents in the calculation of public and private debt in the United States or in the calculation of gross national product.

The survey is not, of course, restricted to consumers but is also used among other segments of market participants, such as business firms. It is peculiarly effective in consumer research, however, because it offers one of the few tools available for collecting information economically from a large number of market participants, information that is often highly subjective.

TECHNIQUES OF SEARCH

There are countless ways in which buyers and sellers can engage in market search. Ultimate consumers get a great deal of market information from shopping—going to market centers where vendors display merchandise and observing prices and qualities. They can read labels and ask questions of the salespeople. They may try on wearing apparel or may be allowed to take merchandise home on trial. They may consult other consumers before they buy, and they may consult independent parties, such as technical magazines, *Consumer Reports*, or independent business firms (e.g., bankers when looking for a lawyer), and so on. Mail order catalogs, the yellow pages of the telephone book, and technical books may also be consulted in the consumer's search for market information. Advertisements can be consulted with varying degrees of confidence.

The business firm's market search is of two principal types. One has as its goal the finding of sources of goods and evaluation of their offerings.[7] Some of the methods used by ultimate consumers may also be useful to business buyers. This would include visiting central markets, reading advertisements and catalogs, consulting other business users, talking with salesmen of vendors, and trial purchases. A principal difference between the business firm's search and that of the ultimate consumer is the fact that the business firm is likely to find that it can have greater specialization in the performance of its buying function and, hence, more skill in the formulation of a systematic search, as well as decision-making, procedure. The other facet of business "search" is the search for customers, that is, "finding" customers or putting the firm's product in a position where it will be "found" by potential clients. The use of salesmen, advertising, catalogs, and promotional techniques is to attract attention and secure patronage.

ORGANIZATION FOR INFORMATION DISPERSION AND ACQUISITION

A large portion of information dispersion is controlled by sellers. Centralized markets organized by sellers, sellers' auctions, mass displays, advertising, mail order catalogs, and personal salesmanship are examples of seller-controlled means of information dispersal. Consumer buyers may exercise control over market information through publications such as those of Consumers Union and Consumers Research or through consumer cooperatives. Business buyers generally have greater control over market information sources than do consumers, though they, too, may be more inclined to exercise control over information dispersal to their customers than over information acquisition for purposes of better buying. Public control over market information arises largely through regulations concerning standardization, grading, and labeling of products; through

---

[7] We shall restrict our discussion to commodities and not deal with the labor market.

whatever control might be extended to the operation of centralized markets; and through the provision of market information by certain public agencies.

OPTIMUM INFORMATION ACQUISITION

The basic rule governing the decision to search for and acquire market information is not different from that governing all other decisions of the buyer or seller. Information is acquired because of its utility to the party that seeks it. Since its acquisition entails costs, additional costs of information acquisition are justified up to that point where the value of the additional expected benefits to the user equals the additional costs of search. For the marketing firm, this calculation can be based on the marginal cost of information in relation to the marginal return (sales revenue or gross margin, for example) from such information. For the ultimate consumer, the calculation must be in terms of the marginal cost of acquiring information in relation to the marginal benefits of that information vis-á-vis the marginal benefits that would be possible by diverting this expenditure to the best alternative.

If the consumer is interested in searching for the lowest price, it is not difficult to compare the cost of finding the lowest price with the value of the benefits received, since the latter is easily quantified in the same units as the cost of search. If the consumer is interested in searching for the best quality at a given price, it is necessary to assess the value of quality superiority in relation to the cost of getting that information, and this will have to be done in terms of the benefits to be derived from alternative uses of the expenditure for market search. Thus evaluation of information about quality involves a transformation not necessary in the evaluation of information about prices.

The consumer generally wishes to have information about both price and quality. Both of these can often be acquired in the course of a single market search. We shall therefore describe the three most elementary information acquisition models—the search for (1) price information, (2) quality information, and (3) price and quality information.[8]

Information Acquisition Models

A potential market participant will continue to search for additional price information if the reduction in the total expenditure that he expects to realize as a result of the search exceeds the marginal cost of the search. Search will continue, therefore, so long as

$$q \left| \frac{\delta p}{\delta n} \right| > \text{MC}$$

in which q is the quantity purchased or sold,[9] p is the unit price, n is the number of searches, and MC is the marginal cost of the nth search. If the searcher is a buyer, δp will be negative; if the searcher is a seller, δp will be positive.

---

[8] This exposition is adapted from George Stigler, "The Economics of Information," *Journal of Political Economy* 69 (June 1961): 213-225. See also John U. Farley, " 'Brand Loyalty' and the Economics of Information," *Journal of Business* 37 (October 1964): 370-381, especially pp. 370-371.

[9] In order to simplify our exposition, we assume that q remains constant for the buyer or seller regardless of the unit price, although we know that variations in quantity purchased (or sold) as a result of additional price information may be crucial to the user of this market information.

Suppose, however, that we focus on the buyer alone and consider the problem of finding the quality of merchandise that will yield the greatest utility to him. Holding price constant, the buyer will continue to seek additional information about quality, measured in units of utility, so long as

$$q\left(\frac{p\ \delta u}{\delta n}\right) > MC$$

in which u is utility per unit.

Combining these two components of search into a single search objective, the buyer who is seeking information about both price and quality in each search will continue to seek information so long as

$$q\left(\frac{-\delta p}{\delta n}\right) + q\left(\frac{p_o\ \delta u}{\delta n}\right) > MC$$

in which p_o is the original price.[10] This is the same as

$$q\left(\frac{-\delta p + p_o\ \delta u}{\delta n}\right) > MC$$

This is an alternative way of viewing the price-quality search in terms of the change in the price of each unit of utility. In this case, search would continue under the following conditions:

$$\Sigma u \left[\frac{-\delta\left(\frac{p}{u}\right)}{\delta n}\right] > MC$$

So long as the change in the price per unit of utility times the number of units of utility expected from an additional search is greater than the marginal cost of the search, that search is warranted.

In all of the preceding statements, we describe the conditions under which an additional search will be undertaken. If we assume (1) that the search for market information will be directed first toward those sources that will yield the most information and subsequently toward less fruitful sources, and (2) that after some point the cost of each search rises as search is extended, then the combination of declining marginal information from continued search and rising costs of additional search will bring the search conditions into equilibrium when the marginal benefits of the nth search exactly equal the marginal costs of that search. Thus equilibrium will be achieved in the four situations just describe when the left side of the function (the marginal value of the search) equals the right side (the marginal cost of the search).

The value of an expenditure for market information can also be viewed in terms of the price-utility relationship of two market offerings. Equilibrium exists when

$$\frac{pq_1}{\Sigma u_1} = \frac{pq_2}{\Sigma u_2}$$

which may also be stated as

$$\frac{\Sigma u_2}{\Sigma u_1} = \frac{pq_2}{pq_1}$$

---

[10] This would presumably also be the highest price in searches n and n_{-1}.

Table 3.1 Hypothetical Examples of Seven Market Price and Quality (Utility) Alternatives for a Buyer of 100 Units

Alternative	Quantity q	Price per Unit p	Total Price pq	Total Utility Σu	Utility per Unit $\Sigma u/q = u$	Utility per Dollar $\Sigma u/pq = u/p$	Price per Unit of Utility $pq/\Sigma u = p/u$	Value in Relation to Alternative A
A	100	$2.00	$200	100	1.00	.50	$2.00	—
B	100	1.50	150	100	1.00	.67	1.50	+$50
C	100	2.00	200	150	1.50	.75	1.33	+$100
D	100	3.00	300	100	1.00	.33	3.00	-$100
E	100	3.00	300	200	.50	.67	1.50	+$100
F	100	1.50	150	75	.75	.50	2.00	0
G	100	1.50	150	150	1.50	1.00	1.00	+$150

To calculate the maximum economic expenditure, we may use pq_x as the value of pq_2 that will bring the ratios into equality:

$$\frac{\Sigma u_2}{\Sigma u_1} = \frac{pq_x}{pq_1}$$

The difference between pq_x and pq_2 measures the maximum amount that should be spent to acquire the information about p_2 and u_2.

Examples of Economic Search Activity

Table 3.1 illustrates seven possibilities that might confront a buyer who searches for an optimum balance between minimum price and maximum quality.[11] Assume that the information obtained from his first search is alternative A—price per unit is $2, and the total units of utility from the 100 units he plans to buy will be 100. How much would it pay him to spend to find alternative B?

$$q\left(\frac{-\delta p + p_0 \delta u}{\delta n}\right) = 100\left[\frac{-(-\$.50) + (\$2.00)(0)}{1}\right] = \$50.00$$

It would be economical to incur a search cost of up to $50 for this information.

The same result can be arrived at from another of the equations we have given:

$$\Sigma u\left[\frac{-\delta\left(\frac{p}{u}\right)}{\delta n}\right] = 100\left[\frac{-(-.50)}{1}\right] = \$50.00$$

Using the equation that shows the traditional price-utility relationships among alternatives under conditions of equilibrium, we find that

$$\frac{u_2}{u_1} = \frac{pq_x}{pq_1} \quad \text{or} \quad \frac{100}{100} = \frac{pq_x}{150}$$

Since $pq_2 = \$150$, the buyer could afford to spend up to $(pq_x - pq_2) = (\$200\text{-}150) = \$50$ for information about p_2 and u_2.

Were alternative C to be found from the search rather than alternative B, this would be worth $100 search cost. Alternative D is clearly worse than alternative A and should not be sought except under conditions of a negative price greater than $100. Alternative E would be worth an expenditure of up to $100. Alternative F is equal to alternative A, while alternative G is clearly superior to A and to any of the other alternatives. The optimum choice among the seven is alternative G. This is clearly reflected in the price per unit of utility that is lowest when the unit purchase price is $1.50 and the total utility 150 units.

FACTORS INFLUENCING INFORMATION ACQUISITION DECISIONS

The highly simplified model of optimal information acquisition that we have presented obscures many of the complications that arise in the process of making intelligent

---

[11] The example that we give here is hypothetical. Some years ago an interesting experimental game of a similar nature was devised and tested by Alderson and Sessions to determine the extent to which consumers would shop for market information. See "Basic Research Report on Consumer Behavior," mimeographed (Philadelphia, Pa.: Alderson and Sessions, 1957).

decisions concerning whether an individual or firm should or should not seek additional information before making a decision about market participation. We shall consider some of these influencing factors, first as they emerge in any type of information search and particularly as they manifest themselves in the search for marketing information.

Some General Factors

DISPERSION

The amount of search that is necessary to convert uncertainty into risk, or risk into certainty, is in part a function of the dispersion of possibilities. If prices, for example, cluster closely about a particular mean, it takes far less investigation to establish with a high degree of confidence the probability of various price alternatives. For some products, the dispersion of quality alternatives is enormous; for other, more standardized goods, it is a good deal less. Also, the degree of symmetry in the dispersion can affect the amount and cost of the search. Prior information about this dispersion is of great value in structuring an economical search plan, but such information may itself be one of the things sought in the search process. The greater the dispersion of a given amount of information, the less the proportion of all possible information that will be obtained on one contact. Hence, the greater the cost of acquiring a certain amount of information. For example, it is more costly to obtain 25 percent of all possible market information about the prices of women's dresses than to obtain 25 percent of the possible information about the prices of sugar in a given trading center.

INCREASING AND DECREASING RETURNS

Another element that affects the cost of search is the probability of increasing and decreasing returns in the search for information. This can be measured by the amount of information obtained in relation to the search effort (cost). (Note that we refer at this point to the amount of information, reserving for comment at a later point the question of value of information.) The shape of the returns curve will depend in part on the way in which information is distributed throughout the field in which the information seeker must function. For example, information on price variability and quality differences can be obtained by consumers through shopping in retail centers made up of many retail outlets. The amount of information acquired per hour of effort in the shopping process will depend on the amount sought, the amount available in the center, and its dispersion within the center. The greater the amount and variety of information sought per inspection, the more nearly complete is the information available, and the more concentrated that information, the greater the return is likely to be per hour of shopping time. But beyond a certain point decreasing returns are likely to set in as the amount of untapped information is more nearly exhausted.

COST OF ANALYSIS AND CHANNEL CAPACITY

The cost of acquiring information cannot be considered independently of its cost of analysis. Since the cost of knowledge is a combination of both acquisition and analysis costs, the latter must be taken into account in determining acquisition expenditures. In addition, it is important to know how much information the user *can* analyze, for if more information is acquired than the user can incorporate into his decision-making model—that is, he cannot use it at any price—the cost of acquiring this unused portion of data is wasted. In the terminology of information theory, this is a matter of channel capacity.[12] This leads us, therefore, to a consideration of another closely related factor—the value of information to the individual or firm that seeks it.

NONCONSTANT COST-VALUE RELATIONSHIPS

One of the difficulties of analyzing information acquisition procedures within the framework of an economic decision model is the problem of not knowing the value of information before one obtains it. In this respect the seeking of information is like advertising, for the results of neither can be known with certainty prior to the undertaking. As with advertising costs and returns, there is no systematic relationship between search costs and the value of information produced by search. Even though we may assume that systematic search procedures can be established from prior knowledge that will enable someone seeking information to take advantage of possibilities for economics of scale, the opportunity for efficiency is in part a function of information about efficiency-inducing variables or procedures, and the absence of such information is often itself the condition that gives rise to the information-seeking activity. We shall comment later on the ways in which partial information can be employed in marketing research as one guide to search procedures, but even an approach as helpful as that of Bayesian statistics does not fully relate costs to benefits. Only by a sequential process can this relationship be established with sufficient accuracy to be useful in the making of decisions about whether or not to get more data on the market situation.

DIMINISHING UTILITY

Just as we assume that there are possibilities for increasing and decreasing returns in the search for information, there is presumably diminishing utility from increasing amounts of information. However, learning often makes it possible to derive high marginal benefits from small amounts of additional information that complement information already in hand. For example, in marketing transactions many elements may be important in the decision to be or not to be a market participant. Information on basic price, discount rate, credit period, trade-in, and warranty may be substitute components of the fully negotiated price. Absence of information on any one of these could destroy the accuracy of the potential buyer's perception of the terms of the transaction and, thereby, his ability to arrive at the optimal decision. The added information on that one missing component could conceivably yield very high marginal returns to him, returns that might be out of all proportion to the marginal cost. This is not unlike the situation in which a student plods dutifully and painfully through the ramifications of a particular theoretical exposition only to find at last the one small link that makes it all "fall into place."

---

[12] The term *channel* is used here to refer to communication channel rather than to marketing channel. As we shall show in the appendix to this chapter, the marketing channel *can* be viewed as essentially a communication channel. However, since certain activities take place in marketing channels over and above mere communication, we should differentiate between communication channels and marketing channels.

SOCIAL VALUE

We have now come full circle, from the costs of the search to the value of the information that results from search, recognizing that there is no systematic relationship between the two but that some of the factors that affect decisions with respect to other forms of economic activity also apply to this one to the extent that economic considerations—such as diminishing utility and increasing and decreasing returns to scale—are relevant to the decision to use resources for acquiring information that will help in making market decisions. Because reliable and valid market information is necessary to the conversion of uncertainty into risk and to the reduction of market risk, its social value is extremely high. It may be crucial in determining the rate of product and service innovation. It is equally important in affecting the character of competition and, hence, the rapidity with which terms of sale are brought into equilibrium through the elimination of differences due to market imperfections. We shall now turn to some of the special problems of information acquisition in marketing.

The Search for Information in Marketing

One of the functions of the trade channel is to provide a means for the transmission of information that will facilitate the transfer of ownership and the physical movement of goods from the point of physical production to the point of consumption. One criterion, therefore, for evaluating channel efficiency is the amount, reliability, and validity of information transmitted. Some of the procedures and techniques of marketing have been developed specifically for their value in the information-gathering and assimilation process. We shall examine four of these briefly.

MARKETING RESEARCH

No area of marketing endeavor is more closely associated with information than marketing research, which is the systematic search for market information and understanding. It includes both the collection and the analysis of data and differs from other methods of data collection and analysis in marketing because of its objectivity, its logical procedures, and its grounding in the theoretical framework of those disciplines (particularly economics, psychology, sociology, and social psychology) that provide an appropriate framework for understanding marketing phenomena.

Some marketing decisions have to be made under conditions of uncertainty, and various criteria may be employed to guide the decision-making process.[13] Abraham Wald's maxim criterion, for example, would direct the decision maker to calculate the worst possible outcome of alternative courses of action and then choose that which will yield the maximum return. L. J. Savage's minimax regret model would provide for the calculation of the worst possible outcome from alternative courses of action and the choice of that which will minimize the maximum regret that could possibly occur. The

---

[13] The criteria discussed here, and others, are treated in more detail in R. Duncan Luce and Howard Raiffa, *Games and Decisions* (New York: Wiley, 1957). A brief summary can be found in William J. Baumol, *Economic Theory and Operations Analysis*, 2d ed. (Englewood Cliffs, N.J.: Prentice-Hall, 1965), pp. 550-568.

Laplace criterion, on the other hand, assumes that the probability of alternative outcomes is equal and that the best choice is that which will yield the maximum value. Yet in the application of each of these, the decision maker must be able to guess (or, preferably, know) the extremes of outcomes or the complete range of possible outcomes. For this reason, these criteria cannot accurately be applied if there is true uncertainty.

The kind of situation that is most likely to occur in marketing is that in which marketing information is partial. A basis for making decisions under these conditions, which we define as conditions of risk because they are characterized by partial information, usually in the form of probabilities, is to utilize subjective probabilities of alternative outcomes to select that course of action which will yield the maximum probable value. Bayesian analysis provides a framework for determining (1) the expected payoff from alternative courses of action, given partial information (prior analysis); (2) the modification of prior probabilities on the basis of additional information (posterior analysis); and (3) the further modification of expected payoffs in the light of the new information incorporated in step (2) and the choice of optimum strategy with respect to each alternative, including the deduction of the cost of information acquisition to determine net payoff from the total strategy (preposterior analysis).[14]

Most marketing decisions are not based on research findings, nor does most marketing research now employ Bayesian statistics. Nevertheless, research is growing in importance in the marketing field, and Bayesian statistics provide one basis for making better marketing decisions with less than complete information as well as estimating the expected net worth of additional information search efforts.

STANDARDIZATION AND GRADING

The establishment of standards for goods (and sometimes services) and the classification of goods according to these standards is an information-generating function of marketing that greatly facilitates marketing efficiency.

SPECULATION AND HEDGING

Speculative activity in marketing, if undertaken by specialists in risk bearing, can lead to greater efficiency if the speculator brings greater skill to the risk-bearing function through more information, better information, or better information utilization. Part of these efficiencies may be related to economies of scale in obtaining data, and part may be due to the knowledge and skill that result from the amount of experience possible in a highly specialized area of operation. Speculative activity based on imperfect or inaccurate information can have the opposite effect, however, resulting in greater gyrations in prices through time and space due to equilibrium-disturbing effects of imperfections and inaccuracies, rather than the equilibrium-inducing effects of speculation based on better data or better analysis. There is also a possibility of disequilibrating effects from speculation if such speculation is based on expectations that stimulate action that causes the expectations to be realized. For example, if market participants believe that prices will rise and increase their purchases in anticipation of higher prices at a later time, by so doing they can cause prices to rise as a result of the increase in demand. In this type of

---

[14]See, for example, Paul E. Green and Donald S. Tull, *Research for Marketing Decisions*, 2d ed. (Englewood Cliffs, N.J.: Prentice-Hall, 1970), especially pp. 1-68.

situation, specialists in speculation may behave in such a way that a condition of disequilibrium is created and accentuated.

ADVERTISING AND MASS DISSEMINATION OF INFORMATION

One of the purposes of advertising is to convey information to potential buyers. This is not an objective source of information and may be an inferior one under many circumstances. To the extent that it is accurate and complete, providing facts that are relevant to buyers' (or sellers') decisions, it is an economical means of making data available to large numbers of potential clients. When it is used to persuade on the basis of false or incomplete information, it results in biased information, which introduces error into the market decision to the disadvantage of both the individual and the economy as a whole.

Institutional and Social Elements in Marketing Information

ECONOMIES OF SCALE

Some of the unique attributes of marketing information are the result of interactions among the institutions of marketing, the sociopsychological influences on market behavior, and the informational function of marketing. One of the most important institutional factors is the relationship of size of firm to risk. One important source of economies of scale in large firms, and possibly also in large establishments, is the pooling of risks.[15] But the large firm's advantage in risk reduction also rests on its ability to enjoy economies of scale in the acquisition and analysis of marketing information. Data on expenditures for marketing research in the United States show clearly that large firms are the principal generators of marketing information by this means.[16] Only through the pooling of research expenditures—through government support, trade associations, or the use of centralized research facilities—can the small enterprise acquire many kinds of market data on an economical scale.

An excellent example of the possibilities for such pooling are the agricultural research programs sponsored by federal and state governments in land-grant colleges and universities, with the research results dispensed, again at public expense, to the large number of agricultural producers in the country. Since World War II, an extremely large portion of these funds have been devoted to marketing research, in contrast to the form production research that dominated the program before the war. Although not completely ignoring the small marketing firm, the research services of the U.S. Department of Commerce have not served such firms in the same way or to the same degree.

RIGIDITIES AND INFORMATION

This brings us to a second characteristic of market structure that affects the nature of information. Rigidities in institutional arrangements and marketing practices are one

---

[15] See Chapter 10, pp. 269-273, where this is discussed as a factor favoring the large retail firm.

[16] Dik Warren Twedt, *1973 Survey of Marketing Research* (Chicago: American Marketing Association, 1974).

means of increasing the amount of information available to buyers and sellers. As an example, the use of resale price maintenance, with its resulting price uniformity, minimizes the market research necessary to obtain complete price information. Distributors' territories and franchises are additional examples of rigidities that stabilize the market situation in such a way that market participants can know with little effort, and occasionally with certainty, some of the attributes of the market situation. The value of such arrangements in terms of the information they provide is, of course, not a sufficient basis for defending the rigidity. We merely point out that the rigidity does have informational value.

SOCIAL STRUCTURE AND INFORMATION

Sociological studies of the diffusion of information, opinions, and products suggest that social diffusion is essentially an information diffusion process.[17] Diffusion of products among users in both industrial goods and consumer goods markets reflects rates of use and ownership similar to those of learning curves.[18] Most of these have many of the characteristics of biological growth curves. Investigators have studied the role of personal influence in purchase decisions, with particular focus on opinion leaders, and opinion leaders of opinion leaders (the two-step flow of communication). The diffusion of information about market alternatives is a significant element in the diffusion of market participation among the population from whom the effective demand is derived. A cost-benefit analysis of such social processes would provide an economic basis for their evaluation.

BRAND LOYALTY AND THE ECONOMICS OF INFORMATION

A specific problem with which marketing management and research have been concerned is the extent of brand loyalty and the conditions under which it occurs. A brand is useful to buyers and sellers because of the information it conveys. If brands are considered good substitutes for one another, buyers would be expected to seek market information concerning price differentials among alternative brands if the expected price differentials are large enough to matter. If brands are not considered good substitutes for one another, buyers would be expected to seek information not only on prices, if important to the buyer, but also on qualities of alternative brands if these vary greatly and are important to the buyer. If buyers are loyal to a particular brand, however, it would be either because they believe that its combination of price and quality are equal to or better than those of alternatives or because they do not wish to incur the costs of market search. Brand loyalty is the opposite of market search and is therefore a substitute for market search. It must be justified the same way the cessation of market search is justified.

Sometimes, of course, brand loyalty might be the *result* of prior market investigation, occurring after market search has been undertaken and market information assimilated. If

---

[17] See Everett M. Rogers, *Diffusion of Innovations* (New York: Free Press, 1962); Everett M. Rogers and J. David Stanfield, "Adoption and Diffusion of New Products: Emerging Generalizations and Hypotheses," in Frank M. Bass, Charles W. King, and Edgar A. Pessemier, eds., *Applications of the Sciences in Marketing Management* (New York: Wiley, 1968), pp. 227-250; Charles W. King, "Adoption and Diffusion Research in Marketing: An Overview," in Raymond M. Haas, ed., *Science, Technology, and Marketing*, 1966 Fall Conference Proceedings (Chicago: American Marketing Association, 1966), pp. 665-684.

[18] See Chapters 6 and 16.

price and quality differentials are *known* to be small, brand loyalty is a rational approach to a buying decision. If price and quality differentials are *believed* to be small, brand loyalty is also rational. But brand competition is most likely to occur in a dynamic, rather than static, market structure, and differentials are not likely to remain small over time, and still less likely to remain stable. Under these circumstances, the value of market search is higher than it would be under more static conditions, and the value of brands as a source of market information is likely to be less because of the greater diversity of market alternatives than would be true under more static conditions. In this case, the "cost" of brand loyalty to the buyer—in the form of information forgone—is likely to be greater than what it would be under conditions of less vigorous brand competition.

John Farley predicted that "heavy" buyers would be less brand loyal than "light" buyers in cases where brand preferences were not strong.[19] He further predicted that large families would have weaker brand preferences than small families because of the greater importance of price to them. High-income families, however, might be expected to be more brand loyal than low-income families because of the implicit cost of shopping due to the greater value of their time. Empirical tests of these expected relationships were made on the basis of purchases of 199 families among 17 household and grocery products in Chicago in 1957.

Farley found that there was only a moderate positive relationship between the amount bought and the absence of brand loyalty. Nor did large families show any greater brand loyalty than small families. In the case of income, he found that high-income families were more brand disloyal than low-income families, which was the opposite of his predicted relationship. Nevertheless, his data show that some consumers are brand loyal, suggesting that the three characteristics of buyers that he examined are not sufficient to explain brand loyalty. The choice of store, sellers' promotions, and consumers' attitudes toward shopping are some of the alternative factors that he proposes for incorporation into the model for studying brand loyalty.[20]

Scott Cunningham found some evidence to support the thesis that brand loyalty is a function of the amount and seriousness of the risk perceived by the buyer.[21] If all brands are regarded as "safe," brand loyalty will be low. Also, he found that when buyers thought the risk of brand switching was high or medium, buyers who were medium in self-confidence tended to be the most brand loyal. Deviations from this basic pattern appeared to be due to logical mitigating influences.

One of the most interesting findings in brand loyalty studies came from A. S. C. Ehrenberg's analysis of empirical data on repeat purchases of a wide variety of goods in the United Kingdom and the United States.[22] He found systematic relationships between the average number of purchases per buyer of a given brand in a given period and each of the following: (1) the percentage of sales made to repeat buyers during the specified period, (2) the percentage of sales accounted for by buyers who made at least two purchases in the specified period, (3) the percentage of sales accounted for by buyers who made at least three purchases in the specified period, and (4) the percentage of sales

---

[19] See John U. Farley, op. cit.

[20] Ibid., p. 379.

[21] Scott M. Cunningham, "Perceived Risk and Brand Loyalty," in Donald F. Cox, ed., *Risk Taking and Information Handling in Consumer Behavior* (Boston: Harvard University, Graduate School of Business Administration, 1967), pp. 507-523.

[22] A. S. C. Ehrenberg, *Repeat Buying: Theory and Applications* (Amsterdam: North-Holland, 1972).

accounted for by buyers who made an extremely large number of repeat purchases in the specified period. Item (4) was at a lower level than item (3), but the relationship to average number of purchases per buyer was systematic. Each of these relationships could be described by use of a Negative Binomial Distribution and its related Logarithmic Series Distribution. One other interesting finding was that new buyers who appeared in any given period bought nearly the same amount of any brand in any given period regardless of what the product or brand was, how long the period was, or what the average number of purchases was for repeat buyers (which varied, of course, from brand to brand). The consistency of his findings across a wide range of branded food and clothing products in different countries and different parts of a country for different time spans is remarkable. Such findings represent marketing intelligence of the first level—"information about." What remains is to explain *why* the observed patterns obtain and why sales levels differ for different brands of goods.

Brands are, of course, imperfect conveyors of information about product attributes, and their utility as a source of information will vary markedly among potential buyers. Their role in the market information process is therefore unstandardized and dependent on the differential value placed on them by potential buyers. It is within this context that their value and utilization as a source of information would have to be explored.

BUYER INCOME AND MARKET INFORMATION

The cost of obtaining market information differs among buyers. These differences will be a function of the accessibility of information but also a function of the value of alternative uses of the buyer's time. The higher the buyer's income, the greater the cost of search. Thus one would expect low-income families to seek more market information in view of the low value of alternative uses of their time. Some studies of prepurchase planning show, however, that low- and high-income families are those that seek the least information, while middle-income families expend the greatest effort to acquire market information before making a purchase.

Some of the explanations offered for the more limited search of low-income families are that (1) replacement purchases of durables, one of the purchases for which the rewards of search are likely to be greatest, are made by low-income people when their existing stock breaks down, while middle-income buyers may be able to exercise more discretion and use more time in deciding when replacement will occur; (2) medium-income families are more likely to buy a number of items that are not staples and for which price and quality variability are significant variables; (3) middle-income consumers are more likely to have available sources of market information than do low-income consumers. It has also been argued that low-income consumers are constrained to buy in market areas near their place of residence and that these do not offer the variety of prices and qualities to be found in other market centers.[23] The difference between the market search of middle- and high-income families can be explained on the basis of opportunity costs.

---

[23] See, for example, David Caplovitz, *The Poor Pay More* (New York: Free Press, 1963). However, a study in Philadelphia indicated that low-income consumers did not use stores in their residence areas as a source of food except for supplementary purposes and did not, therefore, pay more than higher-income families. See Charles S. Goodman, "Do the Poor Pay More?" mimeographed (Philadelphia: University of Pennsylvania, 1967). A study of chain store pricing of food products in low- and high-income areas by chain stores operating in six cities indicated that while there was some

MACRO ASPECTS OF MARKET INFORMATION

In our discussion to this point, we have concerned ourselves with positive aspects of information acquisition, dealing primarily with the principles underlying decisions of buyers or sellers to acquire and use market information. We have concentrated on the question of whether potential buyers or sellers would find it economical to acquire market information and some of the characteristics of marketing and market information that pose special problems. We turn now to the problem of information as it affects the total economy, and shall touch briefly on some of the normative issues that arise in evaluating the market information system.

Marketing Information in an Affluent Society

The problem of information in affluent societies has dual facets. On the one hand, affluence brings with it an increase in the number and varieties of products, which, in turn, greatly accelerates the need for information. The growth of possible information probably exceeds the growth of income. Also, the increasing importance of services in an affluent society poses special informational problems. It is in services that consumers find it particularly difficult to acquire accurate and reliable information about the quality, and possibly the comparative prices, of market offerings. The importance of word-of-mouth communication has been well established for many consumer products and is especially important in the acquisition of information about services.[24]

On the other hand, affluence increases the opportunity cost of acquiring and processing market information and, at the same time, reduces the relative value of each unit of information. The cost of information acquisition in a high-income economy (or the value of decreased satisfactions resulting from the absence of information) must be assessed in relation to the increased benefits from a higher output. To the extent that these costs are incurred by business enterprises that function in their own behalf or on behalf of consumers as collectors and purveyors of information, they become a part of the gross national product and are included in the value of goods and services. To the extent that these costs are borne by the consumer, they are not reflected in the national income accounts and should be subtracted from the market value of goods and services in arriving at the net value of goods and services to ultimate consumers.

---

variation in pricing by the stores in a chain, there was no systematic relationship between the area and the prices charged. See U.S., Department of Agriculture, *Comparison of Prices Paid for Selected Foods in Chainstores in High and Low Income Areas in Six Cities*, ERS-240 (Washington D.C.: GPO, 1968). A Bureau of Labor Statistics study indicated that food prices were associated with type of store rather than with geographic area. In their purchases of clothing, appliances, and other products, low-income consumers were found to buy quite different items from those purchased by higher-income consumers. See Phyllis Groom, "Prices in Poor Neighborhoods," *Monthly Labor Review* 89 (October 1966): 1085-1090.

A summary of the findings of fifteen comparative pricing studies is in Donald E. Sexton, Jr., "Comparing the Cost of Food to Blacks and to Whites—A Survey," *Journal of Marketing*, 35 (July 1971): 40-46.

[24] Johan Arndt, "Word of Mouth Advertising and Informal Communication," in Donald F. Cox, ed., *Risk Taking and Information Handling in Consumer Behavior* (Boston: Harvard University, Graduate School of Business Administration, 1967), pp. 188-239, and Scott M. Cunningham, "Perceived Risk as a Factor in Information Consumer Communications," in ibid., pp. 265-316.

One additional aspect of marketing information in an affluent society is the problem of keeping such information current in a dynamic market situation. Information useful to both buyers and sellers changes constantly with the introduction of new products and product variations and with shifts in consumer preferences, buying behavior, and ability to buy. Frequency of changes in relevant data will therefore pose special problems for the collectors and users of market information.

Optimum Market Information

There is no doubt that the communication network through which market information flows is an essential, unifying element of the total economic system. Market information is necessary, though not sufficient, to minimize imperfections in the competitive system. There is, however, an optimal amount of total search for a given cluster of buyers or sellers, and not all have to participate in that search for the value of information to be realized by all. If, for example, 10 percent of all buyers are extremely price conscious and obtain considerable information on price variability, it is possible that this will be sufficient to drive all prices to their equilibrium level, so that both information seekers and nonseekers benefit from the search by a few. Thus from a macro point of view the optimum amount of market information is not necessarily the summation of that which is optimum for any individual market participant.[25]

APPENDIX A

MARKETING AS AN INFORMATION SYSTEM

Although information theory has its roots in early work in statistical mechanics, physics, mathematics, cybernetics, and mathematical logic, its formal beginning is generally traced to the article by Claude Shannon that appeared in the *Bell System Technical Journal* in 1948.[1] Since one of the principal functions of the marketing system is to provide a

---

[25] This could be incorporated in a model by including as one of the variables determining the optimal amount of information for a single participant the impact of other market participants on the market alternatives to be considered. If this "external" activity is considerable, so that the range of prices, for example, is reduced to a very low level, then the dispersion of alternatives will be lessened and the individual participant will have less need to incur large expenditures for his market search. To the extent that diversity of alternatives is a reflection of inadequate information on the part of most market participants, this diversity would itself be a good proxy for these "external" influences.

[1] This article has been reproduced in Claude E. Shannon and Warren Weaver, *The Mathematical Theory of Communication* (Urbana: University of Illinois Press, 1949), along with a nonmathematical exposition by Weaver.

Our discussion in this appendix has drawn heavily on Wilbur Schramm, "Information Theory and Mass Communication," in Lee Richardson, ed., *Dimensions of Communication* (New York: Appleton, 1969), pp. 172-191, and Warren Weaver, "Recent Contributions to the Mathematical Theory of Communication," in Shannon and Weaver, op. cit., pp. 95-117. In this brief survey we shall attempt no more than to sketch very broadly some of the components of information theory and to draw analogies between these and certain characteristics of the marketing system. A more advanced melding of marketing and communications theory will have to await increased knowledge and skill of specialists in this area.

communications network for the economy, it seems appropriate to view that system in terms of the principal concepts of information theory.[2]

Systems and Coupling

We shall define a system as a set of related elements that are capable of existing in one or more states. There are three principal subsidiary systems that together make up the economic system—the form production system, made up of business firms in manufacturing, construction, mining, agriculture, forestry, and fishing; the consumption system, consisting primarily of consumers or households and some institutions; and the marketing system, comprising specialized business firms that channel resources to business users and finished goods and services to consumers. The marketing system *couples* the production and consumption systems, which means that the state of production depends to some degree on the state of consumption, and the state of consumption is, in turn, partially dependent on the state of production. In this sense, the marketing system is a communication chain that couples a large number of otherwise separate systems.

A *corresponding system* is one capable of assuming the state of the other. Production and consumption are corresponding systems when the two communicate through the market so that consumers and firms have the same market information and can make mutually accommodating decisions. The marketing system, however, is basically a *noncorresponding system* to the producers and consumers whom it serves, for the marketing system transmits messages without itself changing its state. An exception occurs when the marketing system assumes a positive rather than a passive role by pursuing policies that alter production and/or consumption through market control rather than through the mere transmission of information. When viewed as a noncorresponding system, however, marketing firms are facilitating agencies rather than market participants.

One of the important characteristics of the systems that the marketing system couples is that they are functional rather than merely structural. A *functional system* can learn, while a *structural system* cannot. Buyers and sellers learn through market experience; hence, the parameters that describe their behavior will not be stable over time. The marketing system is also functional in the sense that it, too, can learn and thus alter its message transmission. In so doing, however, it ceases to be a noncorresponding system and becomes a corresponding system to production and/or consumption, to which it adapts.

Information

We turn now to certain aspects of the information that the marketing system transmits, and show how the terminology of communications theory can be applied to market information. All information that is communicated must be *coded* into *messages* and sent over *channels*. The quantity of information in a message is measured in *bits*. A bit is the

---

[2] See, for example, the discussion of the price system as a means for conveying information in Robert Dorfman, *The Price System* (Englewood Cliffs, N.J.: Prentice-Hall, 1964), pp. 6-7.

amount of information obtained when one learns which of two alternatives is true. The amount of information, H, conveyed by a message is

$$H = \log_2 n$$

in which n is the number of equally probable outcomes.

Entropy is the uncertainty or disorganization of a system, while *redundancy* is the opposite—the degree of certainty or predictability in a system. Entropy is measured in terms of the information required to eliminate the uncertainty or randomness from within a system or between two systems. Entropy is at a maximum when all states of the system are equally probable—i.e., when they occur at random. The purpose of information is to reduce entropy. The formula for maximum entropy is the same as the formula for information:

$$H_{max} = \log_2 n$$

in which H_{max} is the maximum entropy or information and n is the number of equally probable outcomes. Thus the closer a buyer and a seller are to a state of complete uncertainty about the desires, intentions, and capacities of the other, the wider the range of probabilities and the greater the amount of information that *can* by conveyed to the other.

Redundancy is the amount of certainty or predictability in a system. Since redundancy is the opposite of entropy, the more redundant a system is, the lower its entropy. Complete certainty means complete predictability. The more stable production and consumption are, the greater the redundancy on the part of either system so long as both systems are functional, that is, capable of learning. Under these circumstances, predictability will be high and little information can be conveyed through the marketing system. The more dynamic production and consumption are, the greater the uncertainty of market participants and the greater the amount of information that can be transmitted through the marketing system.

The amount of information that a communication system transmits is indicated by the *channel capacity*. In the transmission of market information, problems may arise because channel capacity is limited so that sellers and buyers do not obtain as much information as they desire, or the amount of information that the marketing system is capable of transmitting may exceed the amount that the consumer or producer can effectively use. The latter is likely to occur where the consumer has a limited capacity to comprehend and analyze data. The former occurs where adequate channels are not created for the transmission of information.

A serious problem in the transmission of market information arises from *noise*, which is anything in the channel other than that which the communicator puts there. It may come from inside or outside the system. The consumer's perception of a particular advertising message may be contaminated by competing messages, or the results of marketing research may be contaminated by the use of imperfect instruments or incompetent interviewers. Contamination of market information is analogous to noise in technical communication theory. The formula for maximum transmission capacity in the face of noise is

$$C_{max} = W \log_2 \left[\frac{P+N}{N}\right]$$

in which W is band width, P is power of transmission, and N is noise. Thus maximum capacity can be approached by increasing band width, increasing power, or reducing noise. In marketing, increased capacity would result from the use of more channels—for

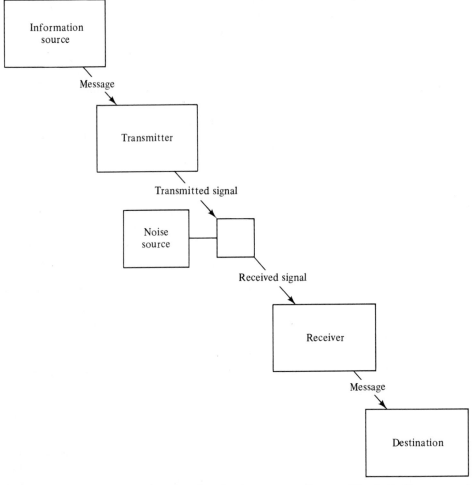

Figure 3A.1. Shannon's general communication system. Source: Claude E. Shannon and Warren Weaver, *The Mathematical Theory of Communication* (Urbana: University of Illinois Press, 1949), p. 5.

example, more outlets—through which information is transmitted (band width) or more powerful or convincing messages, and from fewer opportunities for undesired or irrelevant information to get into the system. If the information presentation is better structured—put into a form that is clearer and less confusing—more information can be transmitted.

The other attribute of information is its *fidelity* or accuracy. In a noiseless communication system, fidelity is largely a function of the code employed, the coding itself, and the decoding. Shannon's diagram of a general communication system is useful. (See Figure 3A.1.)

The Marketing Communication Network

Every system that couples two other systems is a gatekeeper. The marketing system is a gatekeeper in this sense. All the middlemen in the trade channel are performing gatekeeping functions, as are advertising agencies, financial institutions, market research firms, warehouses, and transportation agencies.

There are two important categories of questions to be directed to the marketing system in the performance of its information function. The first concerns the technical efficiency with which marketing institutions perform their gatekeeping function as transmitters of market information. Do they pass on the information that comes to them? How accurately do they reproduce it? How much do they filter out? How much fading and booming do they introduce by changing the emphasis of the message? How much systematic distortion are they responsible for through bias? How much random distortion do they allow by ignorance or lack of effective control?

The second set of questions concerns the social efficiency of the system as an information transmitter in the economy. Part of the system's efficiency as a social network is, of course, dependent on its technical efficiency. But there are other facets of the marketing information system that need to be known if its role in the economic system is to be evaluated. These additional questions concern such matters as how much information the network as a whole handles (traffic), how open or closed the network is (closure), and to what extent all participants participate equally or in different ways (congruence). It is in the latter area that we have many unexplored problems. One, for example, is the fact that so much of the information available to buyers of goods, and particularly to ultimate consumers, is controlled by sellers of goods. This is not to say that it is impossible for buyers, if they choose to do so, to get information from other sources. But to choose to do so usually entails costs, often real as well as monetary, so that the marketing information network that exists is in fact one in which sellers deliver the message and thereby control the amount and content of information. How this market information system is structured depends a great deal on the technical competence of participants in the communication process and on the competitive structure of the marketing system through which the information is transmitted.

Conclusion

This attempt to describe marketing information in terms of some of the concepts of the theory of information in a technical sense is not without its hazards. There is always an intellectual risk in trying to force a particular social phenomenon into the framework of a particular physical phenomenon. It must also be recognized that the concepts that we have lifted from information theory were developed by Shannon and others in dealing with the technical problems of information transmission rather than with the problems of meaning and effectiveness. (The latter are levels B and C in Weaver's hierarchy and levels two and three in ours.) However, Weaver has pointed out that the generality of the theory for level A, from which we have drawn the preceding terminology and discussion, is such that its extension to levels B and C will require only minor additions, including, for example, receivers and noises peculiar to the transmission of meaning rather than just the transmission of symbols. In fact, it is his conviction that Shannon's theory has opened the way for "a real theory of meaning."[3] An engineering theory of communication, he believes, is like a very proper and discreet office employee who accepts a telegram, paying

---

[3] Shannon and Weaver, op. cit., p. 116.

no attention to the meaning but being prepared to handle all messages that come to his or her desk. We know, of course, that most marketing institutions are not like discreet office employees but are more inclined to meddle with the messages they transmit. Meaning and its impact on behavior are surely the important consequences of communication, and we suggest in this brief digression only that there may lie within the technical theory of communication some concepts that may be found useful for a theory of information that includes more significant aspects of the communication process.

ii
The Structure of Demand

4

Consumer Demand and the Macro Consumption Expenditure Function

The infinity which moves us is the sense of multiplicity in uniformity.
Accordingly things which have enough multiplicity, as the lights of a
city seen across water, have an effect similar to that of the stars.
—George Santayana

While the most elementary problem of life is physical survival, its importance is no greater than that of sociopsychological and moral survival. These basic drives, rooted in the nature of man and his culture, manifest themselves in the human desire for a variety of experiences. Some, though not all, of those experiences are made possible through the consumption of goods and services, and much of that consumption is made possible by consumer participation in the market. It is this segment of human activity that will be explored in this and the following chapters. We shall examine the major structural characteristics of consumer demand, using the framework of economics to specify the questions we shall ask and the context within which we shall describe and interpret consumer behavior.

One of the important developments in marketing during the decades following World War II is the redirection of managerial effort toward the interpretation of consumer needs and the analysis of consumer demand for their relevance to the formulation of the firm's production and marketing policies.[1] This has come about primarily because of the nature of competition in the market place and the changing character of the producer's alternatives. Consumer affluence opens opportunities for more diversification but raises the possibility of great difficulty in sustaining the rate of growth in demand. Intensification of competition in the face of an output potential growing at a rate exceeding that of an indigenous consumer demand led to growth in size of firms and in

---

[1] It is unfortunate that marketing has been saddled with an almost illiterate phrase to describe this important development in business management. The orientation of business policies toward the consumer has come to be known as "the marketing concept." It seems to this writer that what appears to be meant by "the marketing concept" is, in fact, "a consumer-oriented concept of marketing" as one means (perhaps the best means) of achieving the firm's objectives. But is this notion really conveyed by the phrase "the marketing concept"?

"Marketing" is itself a concept. One could conceive of a particular firm as essentially a marketing institution. In this sense, then, you could say that the concept of *that* firm is that of a marketing institution, with its processing activities subordinate to its marketing activities. But marketing involves much more than just the consumer. Supply potentials are as important as consumer demand in determining what takes place in the market and what is optimum market performance. "Violin playing" is also a concept. Could one properly say that the commitment of Niccoló Paganini and of Fritz Kreisler to playing the violin was "the violin-playing concept"? We think not.

the amount of integration, and also to increasing attention to market analysis, differentiation, and promotion as means of stimulating demand.

These involve two quite different approaches to a single problem. The problem is how to sell more goods. One way of coping with this is to analyze the demand so precisely that its basic character and shadings are clearly known so that physical processing and distribution of the product through the trade channel will result in certain sales achievements. By tailoring product and marketing to consumer demand, one's competitive advantage is enhanced if this can be accomplished before one's competitors obtain the same information. The other approach is to try to bend consumer demand to the seller's product and marketing procedures by convincing consumers that the cluster of attributes of the product and its accompanying services are both desirable and superior to any alternatives. If a firm has open to it the possibility of both approaches, it is likely to try to integrate the two into a unified set of production and marketing policies. There is good reason why firms are paying more attention to the nature of consumer demand, and particularly to the forces that shape it and to the ways in which it becomes altered over time.

THE CONSUMER DEMAND FUNCTION

We come now to the question of how best to organize what we know and can learn about consumer behavior in such a way that it will help us understand the consumer's role in the functioning of markets. The most useful analytical tool devised in economics for this purpose is the consumer demand function. A demand function shows the relationship between a dependent variable, consumer purchases in units or dollars, and one or more independent variables. Such functions are useful in both describing and understanding the nature of consumer market behavior, for they provide a systematic structure within which important influences, components, results, and proxies can be brought together and their relationships established. Moreover, demand functions can be incorporated into models of the total economic system and, if properly specified, can be combined with production functions to describe and explain much about the functioning of markets.

Multivariate Demand Functions

The concept of demand employed by economists and marketing analysts in recent years is an extension of the classical concept of a price-quantity relationship, and of the Engel-Keynesian concept of an income-expenditure relationship, into a multivariate consumer demand function.[2] The purpose of such a function is to combine these simpler two-variable models into a single model and to extend the function's range still further to include additional economic and social variables that bear a logical relationship to consumer expenditures. The demand for a good, as we shall use the term in our analysis,

---

[2] A useful review of the development of demand theory appears in P. S. George and G. A. King, *Consumer Demand for Food Commodities in the United States with Projections for 1980*, Gianini Foundation of Agricultural Economics, Monograph no. 26 (Berkeley: University of California, California Agricultural Experiment Station, 1971), pp. 3-13. Empirical models of consumer demand are also discussed, pp. 13-33.

is the quantities of that good that are purchased, or the dollar expenditures for that good, within a designated period under specified conditions. We shall describe purchases (in quantities or dollars) as a function, not merely of price or income, but of both of these as well as of other facts and conditions that are related to consumer decisions to buy. The basic model that we shall use contains five independent variables, each of which represents a cluster of factors relevant to consumer purchase decisions:

$$C_i = f(Y, P, T, Q, A)$$

in which C_i is the expenditure (or purchases) of consumers in either physical or monetary units, Y is consumer purchasing power, P is price of the good relative to the price of all other goods, T is tastes (or consumers' "felt needs" or preferences), Q is the attributes (quality) of the good as perceived by consumers, and A is consumer attitudes and expectations.

Purchasing power is the independent variable in the Engel and Keynesian consumption functions, measured in each by income. We shall find that income is itself a very complex concept and that there are many alternative ways of viewing and measuring income. There are, in addition, sources of purchasing power other than income that may be relevant to consumer spending, especially for particular types of goods and services.

Price, the explanatory variable in the Marshallian demand function, should be expanded to include terms of sale as well if these are an important aspect of the transaction. Price is especially important in the demand for a specific good or service. The relative prices of complementary and competing products may necessitate the inclusion of more than one price variable in the estimating function.

The last three variables included in our consumer demand model are those that have only recently been incorporated into demand analysis in any meaningful way. Consumer tastes or preferences often are not well defined and frequently are not visible. Consumers themselves may not even be aware of what their preferences are. These are rooted in physical, psychological, and social needs, and they differ from one consumer to another and from one group to another. They are not stable over time for either a single consumer or a consumer group.

The fourth independent variable, the perceived quality of the product (or service), is almost as elusive as consumer tastes. We know that consumers compare products in terms of the cluster of services (utilities) that they expect to get from each product. A full understanding of consumers' market behavior would require information about (1) what particular attributes of a product they *perceive* (regardless of whether those attributes are in fact present or not) and (2) how they perceive those attributes in relation to their own needs (or preferences). As innovations occur and as product differentiation proceeds, it is extremely useful to know how the consumer views these changes and how he relates these to his own internal preference map.[3] We use the symbol Q for this variable as shorthand for "quality," although we are concerned with perceived attributes rather than some arbitrary quality level determined by a set of standards external to the consumer-buyer.

The fifth variable, consumer attitudes and expectations, is one that has now come to occupy an increasingly important position in demand functions because it has become

---

[3] Kelvin Lancaster has developed a particularly imaginative approach to the use of product attributes, rather than products, as the relevant variable(s) to consider in the analysis of consumer demand. Kelvin Lancaster, *Consumer Demand: A New Approach* (New York: Columbia University Press, 1971).

somewhat amenable to measurement. We include in this the consumer's perception of his present resources and alternatives in relation to those that he expects in the future. This is a matter of the extent to which a specific purchase decision at a specific point in time is optimal in light of the spectrum of options that the consumer *believes* will be open to him in the future. If the future is uncertain, present certainties and risks must be evaluated against that undefinable alternative. For most of us there is usually some expectation that can be established within the bounds of specified probabilities that we have come to know by experience. It is this facet of the consumer's milieu that this variable is designed to represent.

Using this model of consumer demand as a framework within which to explore consumer market behavior, we must (1) determine ways of measuring these five major categories of independent variables and (2) establish the functional relationship between these variables, operating both independently and jointly, and the dependent variable, consumer expenditures for goods and services, which is our focus of interest.

Levels of Aggregation

We shall consider consumer demand at three levels of aggregation. The highest level is aggregate consumption expenditures, in which we analyze total expenditures for all consumer goods and services within the framework of a *macro consumption expenditure function*. At the other extreme are the expenditures of individuals, families, or households. These can be viewed at one moment in time through the use of cross-sectional data, which makes it possible to determine differences in the expenditures of different individuals or households and to relate differences in expenditure patterns to relevant economic, social, and psychological characteristics of the individuals or the environment within which their purchase decisions are made. It is also enlightening to study changes in the consumption expenditures of given families over time, but this has been done less often because of the lack of continuing data from a stable panel. We shall call either of these two types of family expenditure functions *micro consumption expenditure functions*. Another important level of aggregation lies between macro and micro consumption expenditures. At this level, we are interested in the damand for a specific commodity or service. For example, we could analyze the total demand for apples, the total demand for apples in New York State, or the demand for apples by young adults ages 20-29. We shall call these intermediate functions *mini macro consumption expenditure functions*, suggesting that they entail some aggregation but far less than in the macro function.

There are two important reasons why the analysis of aggregate consumption expenditures is significant to marketing analysis. One is the fact that the expenditure on all goods and services not only measures the size of the total market but also indicates, through changes in the aggregate, the vigor of the total economy as evidenced by the rate of growth in this significant market segment. Information about aggregate expenditures is also often used as a basis for evaluating sales activity in particular submarkets. Rates of growth in specialized markets that are greater or less than those in the total economy are useful in pinpointing expanding and contracting segments of the total market. Moreover, information about aggregate expenditures is sometimes used as bench mark data in making forecasts. If there is greater stability in the aggregate than in parts of the aggregate, it may be possible to forecast the aggregate with a higher degree of accuracy than it is the segment. Also, if forecasters of segments have fewer resources for forecasting than do forecasters of aggregates, it is more economical for centralized resources to be used for making forecasts of aggregates, to be shared by all the segment users, and for each segment then to derive, on the basis of expected share of market, the information needed for the specialized market.

In the discussion that follows we shall first consider the basic Keynesian consumption function and the propositions implicit in that function. We shall then review the numerous changes that have been made in the Keynesian function in the form of modifications of its variables and the addition of new variables in an effort to increase the explanatory and predictive value of the function. Finally, we shall make some observations on the present state of the aggregate consumer demand function.

THE KEYNESIAN CONSUMPTION FUNCTION

Keynesian income analysis focused attention on the consumption expenditure and investment functions and laid the groundwork for later theoretical refinement and empirical verification.[4] The basic proposition is that total consumption expenditures are a stable function of income, other objective circumstances, and subjective needs and psychological propensities and habits of consumers. Keynes identified the objective factors that influence the propensity to consume as (1) a change in the wage-unit (i.e., in real income), (2) a change in the difference between income and net income, (3) windfall changes in capital values not considered in calculating net income, (4) changes in the rate of time-discounting (i.e., in the ratio of exchange between present and future goods), (5) changes in fiscal policy, and (6) changes in expectations of the relation between the present and future level of income. Not all of these are truly "objective," however.

Keynes also listed a number of "subjective" factors that would cause individuals *not* to spend their incomes. They might save in order to (1) form a contingency reserve, (2) anticipate future needs, (3) earn interest, (4) enjoy increased expenditures in the future, (5) have independence and power, (6) accumulate working capital, (7) leave a fortune to their heirs, or (8) satisfy "miserliness."

Although these objective and subjective factors vary from period to period, Keynes concluded that it is the aggregate income, measured in terms of the wage-unit, that is the principal variable on which consumption expenditures depend.

The Function

Income has both positive and negative effects on spending. It has a positive effect in the sense that it makes it possible to spend up to the limits of the income. It has a negative effect in the sense that the income limits expenditures beyond that amount. Income is therefore both a *means* and a *constraint*. We would, of course, anticipate a positive relationship between income and expenditures.

If one assumes a straight-line relationship between consumption expenditures and income, the function would be of the form

$$C = a + bY + u$$

in which C is total consumption expenditures, Y is level of total income, u is a random disturbance, and a and b are constants. Hereafter we shall omit the unexplained residual

---

[4] John M. Keynes, *The General Theory of Employment, Interest and Money* (New York: Harcourt Brace Jovanovich, 1935), III, "The Propensity to Consume," pp. 87-131.

(random disturbance). Although some have used national income or income payments as a measure of Y, the income variable most commonly employed is disposable personal income from the national income accounts. In this equation, a is the theoretical expenditure when income is zero, and b is the marginal propensity to spend (consume). Savings, S, are defined as the difference between income and consumption expenditures. Therefore,

$$S \equiv Y - C$$
$$C \equiv Y - S$$
$$Y \equiv C + S$$

The Propositions

The basic proposition of the Keynesian consumption analysis is that consumption expenditures in constant dollars are a constant function of real income. The functional forms most often employed in empirical work of consumption expenditures have been of the following basic types:

$$C = a + bY \quad \text{or}$$
$$\log C = a + b \log Y$$

or sometimes

$$C = a + b \log Y \quad \text{or}$$
$$\log C = a + bY$$

in which C and Y are expenditures and income, respectively, and a and b are constants.

A second proposition in Keynes' analysis was that the marginal propensity to consume (spend) is positive and less than 1. This means, of course, that if income rises or falls, expenditures will also rise or fall, respectively, but by an amount less than the change in income.

Two other propositions are implicit in the Keynesian analysis. One is that the marginal propensity to consume is less than the average propensity to consume. If, for example, the consumption expenditure function is correctly indicated by

$$C = a + bY$$

so long as a is positive, MPC will always be less than APC, since MPC $= b$ and APC $= a/Y + b$.

The final proposition is that the marginal propensity to consume decreases as income increases. If this is true, then a linear arithmetic function does not correctly portray the assumed relationship. A logarithmic function would do so however.

Suppose that we have the function

$$C = aY^b$$

in which C is consumption expenditures, Y is income, and a and b are constants. Calculations of APC and MPC are the same as in the linear function given earlier, except that the functional relations differ:

$$\text{APC} = \frac{C}{Y} = \frac{aY^b}{Y} = aY^{(b-1)} \quad \text{and}$$
$$\text{MPC} = baY^{(b-1)}$$

The constant elasticity of expenditure with respect to income is indicated by b. It is related to APC and MPC as follows:

$$e_{cy} = \frac{\text{MPC}}{\text{APC}} = \frac{ba\,Y^{(b-1)}}{a\,Y^{(b-1)}} = b$$

If b is less than 1, the exponent $(b-1)$ will be negative, and as Y increases, MPC will decrease.

We shall examine these four propositions in terms of what the empirical data show with respect to the income-expenditure relationship, and the modifications of these variables and the addition of new variables that have been found helpful in increasing the explanatory power of this basic aggregate demand function.

SOME PRELIMINARY EMPIRICAL EVIDENCE

If we were to examine national income data for the United States for the years in which we have reasonably good estimates, and were to relate the appropriate income variable to consumption expenditures using a linear estimating equation, we would find that there *is* a linear relationship, that the correlation between the two variables is very high, that the a value is not zero, and that the b value is less than 1.

We have calculated functions for 1929-1940, 1947-1969, and the entire period 1929-1969, omitting the war years 1941-1946, using personal consumption expenditures per capita regressed on disposable personal income per capita, with both variables in 1958 dollars. The results are as follows:

$$C_1 = 215.24 + .76Y_1 \qquad (1929\text{-}1940)$$
$$C_2 = 106.87 + .86Y_2 \qquad (1947\text{-}1969)$$
$$C_3 = 99.48 + .87Y_3 \qquad (1929\text{-}1940, 1947\text{-}1969)$$

For the period 1947-1969 this would mean that, theoretically, the average individual would have spent $106.87 in 1958 dollars had his income been zero. For each additional $1.00 of income, expenditures for all goods and services were increased by $0.86. The b value is below 1.00, as expected, and the a value is positive but not very high, so that the curve for any one of these three functions would be less steep than a 45° line for disposable personal income per capita in 1958 dollars and personal consumption expenditures per capita in 1958 dollars.

Unfortunately, this is not a very meaningful kind of relationship to establish from time series data. In all years except those of World War II, consumption expenditures were a very high percentage of disposable income, and this ratio varied so little that the correlation from time series is bound to be high.[5] If we related savings to disposable personal income, we would subject the function to a more severe test.[6] This is what some economists have done.[7]

---

[5] One problem concealed in our treatment of these data is the fact that we have calculated our functions using per capita figures for both personal disposable income and personal consumption expenditures. Use of a common deflator for both the dependent and independent variables greatly reduces the variance of observed values from the calculated values and leads to a spuriously high correlation between the two. I am indebted to Harry McAllister for this point.

[6] Suppose that the estimating function indicates that consumption expenditures will be 92 percent of DPI, but they turn out actually to be 93 percent. This means that our expenditure estimate is too low by 1.08 percent, while our savings estimate of 8 percent turns out to be too high by 14.29 percent.

[7] For example, Robert Ferber, *A Study of Aggregate Consumption Functions*, Technical Paper no. 8 (New York: National Bureau of Economic Research, 1953), pp. 25-60. This is a dated but excellent

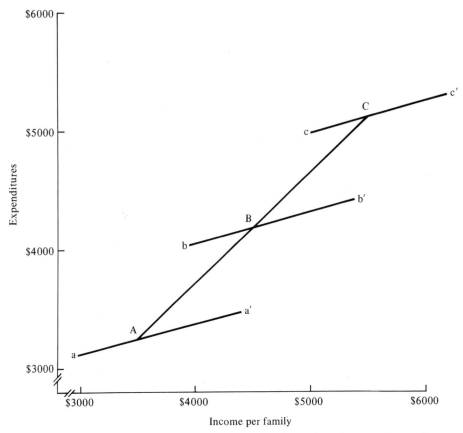

Figure 4.1. Short- and long-run consumption expenditure functions.

One of the amazing characteristics of aggregate consumption expenditures during the period following World War II was their relative stability. In the 1950s and 1960s consumption expenditures as a percentage of DPI varied between a low of 90.1 and a high of 92.9. Only in 1970 and 1971 did the percentage fall below 90.0. This stability was not anticipated by Keynes. If MPC < APC, and if MPC declines as income increases, then this percentage would be expected to fall. It did not do so. Therefore an explanation has to be sought somewhere or the theory has to be changed.

One reasonable explanation that has come out of the postwar analysis of consumption expenditures is that there has been an upward drift of the consumption expenditure function. The "true" function shows a higher *a* value and lower *b* value than does the function derived from observed data. For example, in Figure 4.1 we show a hypothetical upward drift of the entire function from period to period as income and consumption rise, The function to begin with is, let us say, represented by *aa′*. Rising income makes it possible to increase the minimum level of consumption, represented by the intercept, which shows the consumption level below which we are not willing to fall even if income is zero. The new function, *bb′*, is higher than before, and *cc′* is still higher. Actual income and comsumption in the first year is indicated by point *A*. Actual income and

comparison and evaluation of the aggregate consumption functions that had been developed up to the early 1950s. The empirical functions included were, of course, based primarily on data for the period before World War II. The discussion of appropriate variables remains extremely useful.

consumption in the second and third years is indicated by points B and C, respectively. When we fit a line to *observed* income-expenditure data, we get line ABC rather than aa', bb', and cc'. The latter three lines reflect the short-run income-expenditure relationship, while line ABC is indicative of the long-run relationship in which the average propensity to consume equals the marginal propensity to consume. Thus short-run cyclical fluctuations in income do not lead to comparable fluctuations in short-run expenditures. By introducing wealth as a variable in the consumption function, Albert Ando and Franco Modigliani suggest that the function shows the relationship of short-run expenditures to wages, while the upward drift in the level of that function is related to the increasing size of consumers' total savings (hence, income from wealth). According to this analysis, the amount of wealth establishes the a value of the short-run curve and results in long-run stability in the C/Y ratio.[8] Other explanations of the difference between short- and long-run propensities to consume are based on Milton Friedman's permanent income hypothesis and James Duesenberry's relative income hypothesis, which will be discussed later.

Note that we have drawn Figure 4.1 in a very special way. On the horizontal axis, we show disposable income per family in constant dollars. On the vertical axis, we show consumption expenditures per family in constant dollars. At points A, B, and C, personal consumption expenditures are exactly 93 percent of disposable family income. Thus we have a constant expenditure percentage, in keeping with what the aggregate data in the United States approximated during the 1950s and 1960s.

MODIFICATIONS AND EXTENSIONS OF THE KEYNESIAN CONSUMPTION FUNCTION

Most interpretations of the original Keynesian consumption function have been in terms of relating current expenditures for consumer goods and services to current disposable personal income. A number of individuals have, however, corrected these two variables for prices and population, stating both income and expenditures in constant dollars per capita. In this case, the function becomes

$$\frac{C}{NP} = a + b\left(\frac{Y}{NP}\right)$$

in which C is aggregate consumption expenditures in current dollars, Y is aggregate disposable personal income in current dollars, N is population P is a price index, and a and b are constants. This is the formulation that we used earlier in functions for the three periods 1929-1940, 1947-1969, and 1929-1940, 1947-1969.

In an effort to make the Keynesian consumption function more useful in explaining and forecasting aggregate consumption expenditures, a number of modifications have been made in the variables, and occasionally in the functional form, and some new variables have been introduced. The refinements and modifications have been of three principal types: (1) those concerning the concept of income and how income might best be viewed as it relates to personal expenditures, (2) those concerning the introduction of

---

[8] Albert Ando and Franco Modigliani, "The 'Life Cycle' Hypothesis of Savings: Aggregate Implications and Tests," *American Economic Review* 53 (March 1963, pt. I): 55-84. We shall consider later the extension of their analysis to include the relative stability of lifetime consumption expenditures compared with the instability of lifetime income from year to year.

new variables, and (3) those concerning the conceptual framework of the consumption function as evidenced by its assumptions.

Income Refinements

In our discussion of the Keynesian consumption function, the income variable that we have considered is current disposable personal income. Although we prefer the term *current* income, this has also sometimes been referred to as *absolute* income, in contrast to other income concepts, such as *relative* income or *permanent* income. Many of the suggestions for improving the Keynesian function are based on these other income concepts. In some cases, it is proposed that some other measure of income be *substituted* for current disposable income; in others, it is proposed that there be included in the estimating function some other income variable *in addition* to current disposable income.[9]

RELATIVE INCOME

1. *LAGGED INCOME.* In an effort to make the expenditure function more dynamic, some of the consumption functions have incorporated a measure of past income, generally in addition to current income, and occasionally in lieu of current income.[10] Such a function would be of the type

$$C = a + bY + cY_{-1}$$

in which currect expenditures, C, are a function of current disposable income, Y, and last year's disposable income, Y_{-1}.

The reasoning behind the use of lagged income is the assumption that decisions about spending are based on purchasing power available for a period longer than the one in which the expenditure is made. Also, expenditures for durable goods in particular are likely to be planned somewhat in advance.

2. *HIGHEST PREVIOUS INCOME.* Another type of adjustment involving the use of past income was developed by Duesenberry and others to reflect quite a different sort of influence on spending. Duesenberry's version of this was to employ the highest previous income as a variable in the savings function, which, of course, is the inverse of the consumption function, since savings are defined as income that is not spent.[11] The general functional relationship was

$$\frac{S_t}{Y_t} = a + b \left(\frac{Y_t}{Y_o} \right).$$

---

[9] Two excellent treatments of the current status of theoretical and empirical analyses of aggregate consumption expenditures appear in Robert Ferber, "Consumer Economics, A Survey," *Journal of Economic Literature* 11 (December 1973): 1303-1342, and William H. Branson, *Macroeconomic Theory and Policy* (New York: Harper & Row, 1972), pp. 169-197. The former is a survey of theoretical developments, with considerable attention to empirical verification. Branson's treatment is particularly useful as a synthesis and comparison of the absolute, relative, and permanent income hypotheses, in which findings from time series and cross-sectional studies are shown to be theoretically harmonious.

[10] Arnold Zellner, "The Short Run Consumption Function," *Econometrica* 25 (October 1957): 552-567.

[11] James Duesenberry, *Income, Saving, and the Theory of Consumer Behavior* (Cambridge, Mass.: Harvard University Press, 1949). We have made the symbols in Duesenberry's equation consistent with those we have been using.

in which S is savings, Y is income, the subscript t is for the given year, and the subscript o is for that year in which previous income was highest. Davis used a similar idea but substituted C_o for Duesenberry's Y_o.[12] Modigliani used a function similar to Duesenberry's, with the highest previous income as an additional variable rather than a relative variable.[13]

The assumptions that underlie these types of functions in which the previous high income, or high consumption expenditure level, is used are that there is a secular trend in consumption around which there may be cyclical variations, and that the previous high level of consumption, or high level of income, has established a standard from which consumers are reluctant to move. Therefore the highest level of consumption previously experienced becomes a factor in determining future consumption. This implies a lack of symmetry in the income-expenditure relationship.

3. *CHANGES IN INCOME*. Another modification of the income variable employed in time series studies of aggregate consumption expenditures is substitution of income change for current income, and consumption expenditure change for consumption expenditure. Such a function would take the form

$$\Delta C = a + b\,\Delta Y$$

with Δ representing the change in consumption or income from the preceding year or other period.[14]

This kind of function focuses on marginal adjustments. Its logic is based on the assumption that changes in one's income position are more important in determining changes in consumption than is the absolute level of income. Where change in income is considered a variable in addition to current income, the function would become

$$C = a + bY + c\,\Delta Y$$

Although first differences, or some modification of first differences, have not been very useful in the aggregate consumption expenditure function, it should be noted that they have been very useful in disaggregated expenditure functions, especially those for durable goods. There are good reasons for their effectiveness in these functions, and we shall consider these in detail when we discuss the demand functions for specific goods and services.

4. *INCOME DISTRIBUTION*. A fourth relative income refinement is the consideration of income distribution as well as the total level of income. It is recognized that the propensity to spend is not the same for people at all income levels. Therefore if we have information on the distribution of income among members of the economy, it will be possible to make a better estimate of the effect of a given aggregate income on the level of total consumption expenditures. If, for example, the marginal propensity to consume differs among wage earners and salaried workers, among occupational categories, among

[12] T. E. Davis, "The Consumption Function as a Tool for Prediction," *Review of Economics and Statistics* 34 (August 1952): 270-277.

[13] Franco Modigliani, "Fluctuations in the Saving-Income Ratio: A Problem in Economic Forecasting," in *Studies in Income and Wealth*, vol. XI (New York: National Bureau of Economic Research, 1949), pp. 371-443.

[14] Daniel B. Suits, "The Determinants of Consumer Expenditure: A Review of Present Knowledge," Research Study One in Commission on Money and Credit, *Impacts of Monetary Policy* (Englewood Cliffs, N. J.: Prentice-Hall, 1963), pp. 36-39.

income receivers of different geographic areas, and so on, it would be desirable, if data were available, to use an equation of the form

$$C = a + b_1 Y_1 + b_2 Y_2 + \ldots + b_n Y_n$$

in which Y_1, Y_2, ..., Y_n are the total income of each relevant income-receiving group and b_1, b_2, ..., b_n are the respective marginal propensities to consume.

Another refinement would be a correction for income distribution among the total population. The evidence is not clear, however, as to the importance of this. Horst Mendershausen has suggested that income distribution is important, but J.L. Mosak has found that it does not affect the total expenditure for all goods and services, although it does affect expenditures for each of the three disaggregated categories—durable, nondurable, and services.[15]

PERMANENT INCOME

The concept of "permanent income," and the permanent-income hypothesis, were formally developed by Friedman, with versions by others, and have come to occupy a particularly important place in demand functions.[16] Other labels that have been used to describe permanent income or closely related variants are "normal" or "expected" income. The concept is basically that of income that is expected in a given period. Similarly, permanent consumption is consumption that one plans for a given period. The essence of the permanent income hypothesis is that expenditures for permanent consumption are a constant function of permanent rather than current income. These concepts of income and consumption, and the proposition about their relationship, are sufficiently important to warrant our sketching the elements of the permanent income hypothesis.[17]

Income in any given period has two components: permanent income and transitory income. This may be symbolized as

$$Y = Y_p + Y_t$$

in which Y_p is permanent income, Y_t is transitory income, and Y is total income. Permanent income is that income which the consuming unit regards behaviorally as expected on the basis of the consuming unit's evaluation of the current value of the productive potential of its human and nonhuman resources. Transitory income, on the other hand, is income produced by forces that the consumer regards as random. Transitory income may be positive or negative. Unexpected income adversity in a given year may force the consumer to dip into his assets to sustain a desired level of consumption, and this unexpected decline in realized income would be regarded as negative transitory income. If, on the other hand, the consumer wins the Irish sweepstakes, the income from his lottery ticket would be transitory (nonpermanent, unexpected, abnormal) income.

---

[15] Ferber, op. cit., p. 21.

[16] Milton Friedman, *A Theory of the Consumption Function*, National Bureau of Economic Research, General Series no. 63 (Princeton, N. J.: Princeton University Press, 1957).

[17] The permanent-income hypothesis is closely related to the life cycle income hypothesis developed by Ando and Modigliani. Although the life cycle hypothesis can explain aggregate consumption expenditures, it is more easily explained in terms of the behavior of a particular family. We shall therefore reserve our discussion of the life cycle hypothesis for Chapter 5, where we consider micro consumption expenditure patterns. Ando and Modigliani, op. cit.

What determines a consuming unit's permanent income? According to Friedman, this will be a function of (1) the nonhuman wealth of the consuming unit, (2) personal attributes based on training, ability, personality, and the like, and (3) the kind of economic activity the earner(s) of the consuming unit engage in—their location, occupation, work situation, and so on. Thus permanent income is the present discounted value of future income derived from the human and nonhuman assets from which the consuming unit expects to receive future income. The present value of these discounted future income streams can be respresented by

$$x = \sum_j i_j \sum_{r=1}^{\infty} \frac{y_r^j}{(1 + i_j)^{r-1}}$$

in which y_r^j is the expected return from the jth asset during the rth future period, and i_j is the discount rate appropriate for the jth asset.[18]

Transitory income, on the other hand, is determined by accidental or chance factors that may be specific to a particular consumer or consuming unit (the head of the household is fired for repeated infractions of company rules) or to a group of consumers (the head of the household is fired along with other workers of equal skill because of a decline in company profits).

Just as income can be divided into permanent and transitory segments, so consumption can be divided into comparable components. Total consumption is the sum of permanent and transitory consumption:

$$C = C_p + C_t$$

in which C is total consumption and C_p and C_t are permanent consumption and transitory consumption, respectively. Friedman views consumption as we have defined it—to include utilities actually realized rather than merely consumption expenditures. Actual consumption, C, is the value of goods and services consumed, and this includes the value of nondurables plus the rental value of durables plus the value of services used. Permanent consumption, C_p, is the amount of goods and services a consumer plans to consume during that period—that is, the expected level of consumption—while transitory consumption, C_t, is the amount of goods and services consumed that were not planned. C_t may be positive or negative, depending on unexpected developments in the consuming unit's situation.

We focus now on permanent consumption. Friedman hypothesizes that permanent consumption is a function of permanent income, modified by the rate of interest, the ratio of nonhuman wealth to total income, and the consuming unit's preference for consumption in contrast to additions to its wealth that would occur were it to save its income, thereby increasing its assets, instead of using it for current consumption. This can be described as

$$C_p = k(i, w, u)Y_p$$

in which i is the rate of interest, w is the ratio of nonhuman wealth to total income, u is the consumer's preference for current consumption in contrast to additions to wealth, and k is a constant. Presumably w will be positively related to consumption, since if one's

---

[18] From Milton Friedman, "The Concept of 'Horizon' in the Permanent Income Hypothesis," unpublished paper discussed in Franco Modigliani and Albert Ando, "The 'Permanent Income' and the 'Life Cycle' Hypothesis of Saving Behavior: Comparison and Tests," in Irwin Friend and Robert Jones, eds., *Study of Consumer Expenditures, Incomes and Savings: Proceedings of the Conference on Consumption and Saving*, vol. II (Philadelphia: University of Pennsylvania Press, 1960), p. 78.

material wealth is substantial, he is in a position to use income to increase his consumption. If, on the other hand, he loves to amass wealth, u will be low, thus offsetting the high value of w. Let us assume, though, that for a particular family w is high (they have a lot of liquid and fixed assets) and u is high (they love to spend for current consumption). These will both be conducive to current spending. If we think of i as the rate of interest that the consumer pays for funds that he borrows or lends, this affects his ability to consume, through the use of borrowed funds to supplement his income, and/or his desire to invest income instead of spending it. It also affects the rate at which he discounts expected future income as a basis for determining current consumption. Thus permanent income is the important factor in affecting one's spending, modified by one's wealth in relation to one's earning capacity, one's desire for consumption goods, and the rate of interest. The variable u, according to Friedman, depends on the number of consumers in the consuming unit and their characteristics (such as size of family, ages of children, education, etc.), and also on the relative importance of the transitory factors that affect income and consumption to the permanent factors that influence these. The latter might be indicated by the dispersion of the probabilities of transitory versus permanent factors. Since the values of i, w, and u will differ for different consuming units, the value of C_p as an aggregate for all consumers will depend on the distribution of consuming units with respect to different values of i, w, and u.

The essence of the permanent income hypothesis—that permanent (planned, expected, normal) consumption is basically a function of permanent (planned, expected, normal) income—can be shown in three sets of simple correlations that Friedman proposes as true. He assumes that the corrrelation between each of the following three pairs is zero:

$$Y_t \text{ and } Y_p$$
$$C_t \text{ and } C_p$$
$$Y_t \text{ and } C_t$$

The first assumption indicated in this trilogy is simply that one's unexpected income is not systematically related to the size of his permanent income. The second is that one's unexpected (unusual, abnormal) consumption (in some one year, let us say) bears no systematic relationship to his normal consumption pattern. In general, there seems little basis for quarreling with either of these assumptions.

The third assumption gets to the core of Friedman's hypothesis and is less convincing on the surface. What it says is that one's unexpected (transitory) consumption in a particular period bears no consistent relationship to his unexpected (transitory) income. If you get a windfall, let us say, you will not spend it on riotous living. You will go to the bank instead of the bar. Keep in mind that Friedman defined consumption as the value of goods and services *actually consumed* (nondurables + services + rental value of durables). This means that if you spend your windfall on a new car or a yacht, only the imputed rental value of that car or yacht would be counted as your consumption in the year in which you got the windfall. Since expenditures for durables are savings to the extent that their depreciation in the year of their purchase is less than the market value of the durable purchased, then Friedman has left the door open for an expenditure to take place without a commensurate increase in consumption. The reason a person who gets a windfall might *not* want to spend it on current consumption is that it would spoil him for next year. If he builds up consumption habits from his experience, it may be hard to shake them off when times get rough, or even when times return to "normal." The opposite side of the coin is the question of how a consumer would react to an unexpected decline in income—a decline that he thinks will not be permanent. It seems perfectly reasonable to believe that the consumer will try to maintain his consumption as close to the previous level as possible by making an adjustment some other way, perhaps by drawing on his savings, thereby changing the composition of his assets. After consumption takes place both his assets and net worth are reduced.

This brings us to another question on which Friedman has made some observations. What is the planning horizon for an individual—two or three years or a lifetime? Friedman believes that for most people this horizon is about three years,[19] but others have evidence that suggests that this greatly understates the importance of the current year's income in explaining current-year expenditures.[20]

Much empirical work has followed the statement of Friedman's permanent income hypothesis. Friedman himself drew extensively on time series and cross-sectional data to find support for the hypothesis. Others have made empirical tests using data for periods in which there was some clear-cut windfall income that could be isolated and its effects on consumption examined. Others have used standard time series and cross-sectional data from which they have devised a measure of permanent income (usually a projection based on some type of logarithmic declining weighting of income received in prior years), which is then related to expenditures on nondurables.[21] The statistical evidence is mixed. Some investigators have found considerable support for the hypothesis in their empirical studies; others have not.

The problems appear to be both conceptual and empirical. Permanent income needs to be defined in a way that is meaningful in terms of how people perceive and respond to income. What Friedman assumes is that people behave *as if* their income consisted of these two components. If this assumption is correct, the problem then becomes one of sorting out the permanent and transitory components from empirical data on income actually received. Permanent income is not visible; it is conceptual and has to be

---

[19] Friedman, *A Theory of the Consumption Function*, p. 221.

[20] See, for example, Colin Wright, "Estimating Permanent Income: A Note," *Journal of Political Economy* 77 (September-October 1969): 845-850, who found that the current year's income should be weighted closer to .80 than to the .33 that Friedman proposed. On the other hand, Michael Landsberger has found evidence in four savings surveys and one expenditure survey conducted in Israel to support Friedman's contention that the horizon is about three years in length. He found the marginal propensity to consume out of permanent or current income to be several times higher than the propensity to consume out of windfall income. (If his findings are correct, note the possible implications for consumption when personal taxes are on capital gains rather than wages or salaries and when a given change in the personal income tax rate is regarded by taxpayers as a short-term rather than a long-term change in the tax rate.) Michael Landsberger, "Consumer Discount Rate and the Horizon: New Evidence," *Journal of Political Economy* 79 (November-December 1971): 1346-1359.

[21] See, for example, Ronald G. Bodkin, "Windfall and Consumption," *American Economic Review* 49 (September 1959): 602-614; Modigliani and Ando, "The 'Permanent Income' and the 'Life Cycle' Hypothesis of Saving Behavior: Comparison and Tests," pp. 49-174; Mordechai Kreinin, "Windfall Income and Consumption: Additional Evidence," *American Economic Review* 51 (June 1961): 388-390, and "Wind-fall Income and Consumption: A Further Comment," *American Economic Review* 53 (June 1963): 448; Margaret G. Reid, *Housing and Income* (Chicago: University of Chicago Press, 1962); Roger C. Bird and Ronald G. Bodkin, "The National Service Life Insurance Dividends of 1950 and Consumption: A Further Test of the 'Strict' Permanent-Income Hypothesis," *Journal of Political Economy* 78 (October 1965): 499-515. An interesting test of the hypothesis, using international data and an interative estimating technique, is in Balvir Singh and Helmar Drost, "An Alternative Econometric Approach to the Permanent Income Hypothesis: An International Comparison," *Review of Economics and Statistics* 53 (November 1971): 326-334.

computed if it is to be subjected to empirical tests. We know that i, w, and u will be different for different consuming units. When we use aggregate data, therefore, we need to know something about the distribution of consuming units with respect to these determining factors. Thus far income data have not been collected in such a way that isolation of the permanent and transitory components can be done easily or precisely.

Duesenberry has suggested that perhaps the source of income, and the differences in the way people respond to income from different sources, might be a more helpful way to view the general problem that Friedman poses.[22] Certainly the absence of data adequate for testing the hypothesis has been a handicap. There are also questions about the length of the planning horizon and what to do about expenditures for durable goods that involve both saving and current consumption in the year in which the expenditure is incurred.

One interesting assessment of the permanent income and life cycle hypotheses is that of Thomas Mayer, who concluded that the contradictory results of tests of the permanent income and wealth theories of consumption were not necessarily in conflict because the "true" relationship between income and consumption appears to be somewhere in between consumption as a constant proportion of permanent income and a constant proportion of measured income.[23] This would mean, then, that a portion of transitory income is consumed and a portion is invested. Thus the propensity to consume permanent income would not be 1.00 but something less than 1.00, and the propensity to consume transitory income would not be zero but something greater than zero.

In spite of the conceptual and empirical problems, however, the permanent income concept and hypothesis have been found useful in a number of consumer demand functions when attempts have been made to measure permanent income and relate it to consumption expenditures. It is closely related to the life cycle concept of income. The notion of permanent or expected income makes sense as a behavioral concept, and its introduction into economic and marketing analysis has stimulated some very promising probing into the meaning of income and income-expenditure relationships. Perhaps still more exploration will enable us to convert it into an analytical variable useful in a variety of market demand situations.

Other Variables

Another set of adjustments that have been made in the Keynesian consumption function have involved the inclusion of additional variables to measure sources of purchasing power other than income or to measure other factors related to expenditures.

SOURCES OF PURCHASING POWER OTHER THAN INCOME

1. *ASSETS.* There has been considerable discussion by students of demand analysis concerning the relative importance of consumer assets in the aggregate consumption

---

[22] James S. Duesenberry, "Comments," in Friend and Jones, op. cit., p. 189. He also suggests, however, that if we do not have data collected in such a way that permanent income can be measured, perhaps introduction of the permanent income hypothesis will encourage collection procedures that will isolate the permanent and transitory components of income.

[23] Thomas Mayer, *Permanent Income, Wealth, and Consumption: A Critique of the Permanent Income Theory, the Life-Cycle Hypothesis, and Related Theories* (Berkeley: University of California Press, 1972).

expenditure function. Some of the discussion has dealt with total consumer assets or net worth, but most often a special category of assets has been considered as bearing a possible relationship to consumer expenditures. These special types of assets have included liquid assets, money stocks, and changes in the total value of assets, usually identified as capital gains (or losses).

One of the peculiarities in hypothesizing about the relationship between assets and expenditures is the diverse role assets can be viewed as playing in consumers' expenditure decisions. On the one hand, they are an indication of purchasing power, and the more liquid they are, the more readily they can be utilized as purchasing power. They are also an indication of a willingness or unwillingness to spend rather than save, and of a need or lack of need to spend rather than save.

We can formalize these possible relationships into three hypotheses:

1. Current consumption expenditures will be positively related to assets and/or net worth to the extent that the larger the stock of assets,
   a. The greater the purchasing power resulting from their liquidation.
   b. The lower the marginal utility to be derived from additional units of assets.
2. Current consumption expenditures will be negatively related to assets and/or net worth to the extent that the larger the stock of assets, the greater the evidence that consumers prefer asset accumulation to current consumption.

It is possible for the relationship between assets and expenditures to be obscured if they perform two functions that bear opposite relationships to consumption expenditures. These hypotheses refer only to expenditures for current consumption since expenditures for durables would be in part expenditures for nonliquid asset accumulation.

When wealth is used in the aggregate consumption expenditure function, additional problems arise because of the aggregation of consuming units whose asset positions and attitudes toward assets versus consumption will differ. Also, prices have a significant effect on the value of consumer assets, and this may cause consumers' perceptions of the adequacy of their assets to vary as changes in the price level occur.[24]

Most of the empirical studies of aggregate consumption expenditures that incorporate a wealth or liquid asset variable have not indicated that either is particularly helpful. The problem seems to relate to the mixture of possibilities that we have suggested in the hypotheses just given. In addition to those we have mentioned, Daniel Suits has pointed out that some liquid assets may be earning assets that individuals are reluctant to use for current consumption expenditures.[25]

Cross-sectional data indicate this intermixture of consumer attitudes toward liquid assets even more clearly. Some people with large liquid assets continue to add to those assets. Others have reached a saturation level and are no longer inclined to add more to their liquid assets. Many regard liquid assets as a buffer against future declines in income, and in such cases they will draw on those assets to sustain their level of consumption. People with large debts are frequently more likely to spend than people without debts,

---

[24] Price changes and their effects on asset valuation occupy a critical role in the "Pigou effect" and "Keynes effect," which are concerned with consumer response, via consumption expenditures, to changes in asset values through the business cycle. See Gardner Ackley, "The Wealth-Saving Effect," *Journal of Political Economy* 59 (April 1951): 154-161, and *Macroeconomic Theory* (New York: Macmillan, 1961), pp. 369-373, 555-561.

[25] Suits, op. cit., p. 41.

whereas people with large holdings of liquid assets show an inclination to save rather than spend. But the evidence on these matters is not clear-cut, and we are not able to say categorically what the relationship is between assets or wealth and consumer spending.

Michael Evans' very careful study of the role of wealth and liquid assets in the aggregate consumption function, in which he calculated expenditure functions for the United States for the period 1947-1962, using both quarterly and annual data, concludes:

> This study has shown that the time-series evidence gives very little reason to believe that wealth should be included in the consumption function, either implicitly or explicitly. Other studies which have stressed the importance of wealth are found to have biased estimates, unrealistic values of the m.p.c., or non-significant estimates of the wealth-income variables.[26]

A similar conclusion was reached by Suits. His comments add additional insight into the problem:

> The accumulation of conflicting empirical evidence from cross-section studies added to the highly unstable coefficient found for liquid assets in the time series analysis . . . is convincing evidence that the role of liquid assets in the consumption function has not yet been discovered.

> Part of the trouble doubtless lies in the fact that the dollar volume of liquid assets held by the spending unit at any time is the result of the past behavior of the unit. To this extent, the relationship of consumption to liquid asset holdings is the correlation of one aspect of behavior with another. It is hardly correct to speak of an "effect" on consumption of liquid balances that are deliberately saved up to be spent. (One might just as well hold Christmas clubs responsible for the December retail boom.)[27]

It appears, therefore, that at this point, on both theoretical and empirical grounds, we have little basis for assigning a specific and unequivocal role to liquid assets or other measures of consumer wealth in aggregate demand analysis. However, there is some evidence that liquid assets can be useful in studying the demand for durable goods, that capital gains may bear some relationship to consumer spending, and that the expenditures of particular families may be peculiarly sensitive to these variables, since the distribution of wealth within the population is highly skewed.[28] We shall therefore return to some wealth variables when we consider expenditures for specific goods, particularly durables, and cross-sectional expenditure patterns among families.

2. *CREDIT.* The other important nonincome variable that can have an effect on consumer purchasing power is credit. Changes in the terms of credit (interest rate, down payment requirement, and length of repayment period) and in the availability of credit

---

[26] Michael K. Evans, "The Importance of Wealth in the Consumption Function," *Journal of Political Economy* 75 (August 1967. Pt. 1): 349 © 1967 by the University of Chicago. One interesting detail that Evans found in his analysis was the extremely low correlation between the ratio of liquid assets to income and wealth to income. The correlation for the years 1946-1964 was .055, indicating that year-to-year variations in liquid assets differ markedly from those for wealth. His wealth data were net worth values estimated by Albert Ando. Ibid., p. 341.

[27] Suits, op. cit., p. 43.

[28] Ferber, "Consumer Economics, A Survey," pp. 1312-1313.

(ease or difficulty of acquiring it, regardless of terms) has been regarded as significant in certain consumer goods markets. Because of important differences between mortgage credit and other forms of consumer credit, these two are generally treated separately. For the purposes of this discussion, we shall consider only consumer credit, but most of the generalizations that we shall make could also be translated into similar inducements or constraints for the housing market.[29]

One of the important effects of credit is through the timing of purchases. The availability of credit on favorable terms makes it possible for consumers to buy those goods for which credit is an appropriate transaction medium (usually durables) earlier than they would otherwise have acquired them. This could have a positive influence on the long-run pattern of consumption by establishing a consumption habit. If credit makes it possible to acquire durables earlier or more easily, thereby making it unnecessary to acquire more expensive substitutes (a washing machine vs. a laundry; a vacuum cleaner vs. domestic service), it would be conducive to an increase in the propensity to spend. On the other hand, the extension of credit is negative saving for the borrower, while its repayment is positive saving for the individual. Thus negative saving must be followed by positive saving. If consumers would never save in advance of the time they acquire consumer goods, then credit enforces saving. In the long run these two would cancel out, so that the average long-run propensity to spend is not affected except to the extent that the cost of credit has to be met. But if the repayment of debts were to establish a habit of saving that would otherwise not have occurred, it could reduce the average long-run propensity to spend.

Probably the greatest effect of credit on aggregate consumer spending comes from the fact that changes in credit terms and availability can cause people to bunch purchases at one time or another, following this by repayment of debts. This possibility has induced some people to suggest that consumer credit might be used as a countercyclical force. There is not much evidence that credit can fulfill such a role effectively any more than can investment credit. During recessions and depressions, both consumers and lenders are reluctant to enter into credit transactions. During periods of expansion, both are willing because of the outlook, and this may well have an accelerating effect on the expansion. During the contraction, the opposite is likely to result, at least at that point when everyone is convinced that the downturn is a reality. Like toothpaste in a tube, consumer credit moves in one direction more readily than another at a given time.

Credit affects the kinds of goods consumers buy, since credit can more appropriately be used for durables than nondurables and services. Its impact is therefore quite selective. One market in which the impact of consumer credit on demand has been most noticeable is the automobile market. (Were we also discussing mortgage credit, we would, of course, include the housing market.)

So far as aggregate consumption expenditures are concerned, it would appear at this point that there is not convincing evidence that consumer credit is an important influence. Its influence in particular markets suggests that it should be considered as an

---

[29] However, it should be noted that expenditures for new housing construction that result in an equity are regarded as savings in the national accounts rather than consumption expenditures. A similar type of differentiation for consumer durables would greatly enhance our ability to analyze consumer decisions in these markets, but the difficulty of making such an adjustment has not yet been overcome. Therefore we continue to classify expenditures for durables, other than housing, as current consumption expenditures even though their consumption may extend over a period much longer than one year.

independent variable in demand functions for particular items where its importance can be established.[30]

OTHER EXPLANATORY VARIABLES

1. *RELATIVE PRICES*. Over time there will, of course, be disproportionate shifts in the prices of different goods; some items will rise in price, others will fall in price, and some will remain the same. There are two ways of viewing aggregate consumption expenditures so far as this phenomenon is concerned. One is to assume that consumers will tend to spend x percentage of their income, or x percentage plus a constant amount. If the prices of some goods rise, they will buy less of those (unless, of course, the rise in price *reflects* an increase in demand). If preferences remain the same, we can assume that less of the more expensive good will be bought and more of the good whose price has not risen. This assumes that consumers spend all of their budgeted income, adjusting to price changes as they must. This would mean, therefore, that real consumption expenditures are a stable function of real income.

The other view is that consumers do not necessarily react to price changes in this way. Assume that there are only two goods. One rises in price relative to the other. If consumers *do* spend all their total budgeted allocation for consumption, they are likely to shift some of their expenditures from the higher-priced good to the one that is stable in price. But suppose that the one that is stable in price is food and the one that rises in price is durables. Will they eat a lot more food in order to avoid paying for higher-priced durables? This is not likely. They have another option, and that is to increase their savings.

Gardner Ackely and Daniel Suits have developed the second approach theoretically, but it has not been tested empirically.[31] We shall leave the matter, therefore, as a question that should be introduced in considering the structure of the aggregate consumption expenditure function.

2. *TIME*. Another variable that has been incorporated into some aggregative demand functions is time. This may be in addition to a correction for population or, some-

---

[30] A curious phenomenon is the lack of very much solid economic analysis of consumer credit. Two decades ago the Board of Governors of the Federal Reserve System sponsored a series of studies that appeared under the title *Consumer Instalment Credit*, pts. 1-4 (Washington, D.C.: GPO., 1957). This included papers from the 1956 Conference on Regulation sponsored by the National Bureau of Economic Research, *The Problem of Consumer Credit Regulation, Consumer Instalment Credit*, pt. II, vols. 1 and 2. One of the earlier studies of interest is Avram Kisselgoff, *Factors Affecting the Demand for Consumer Instalment Sales Credit*, Technical Paper no. 7 (New York: National Bureau of Economic Research, 1951). The National Bureau of Economic Research also sponsored a series of studies published as *Studies in Consumer Instalment Financing*. Most of these appeared in the 1940s, with only three in the 1960s. The latest was Geoffrey H. Moore and Philip A. Klein, *The Quality of Consumer Instalment Credit*, National Bureau of Economic Research, Studies in Consumer Instalment Financing no. 13 (New York: Columbia University Press, 1967). Other recent studies have focused on the effect of credit on the demand for specific goods. See Janet A. Fisher, "Consumer Durable Goods Expenditures, with Major Emphasis on the Role of Assets, Credit and Intentions," *Journal of the American Statistical Associationsm, 58 (September 1963)*: 648-657; Maw Lin Lee, "Income, Income Change and Durable Goods Demand," *Journal of the American Statistical Association* 59 (December 1964): 1194-1202; James Duesenberry et al., *The Brookings Model: Some Further Results* (Chicago: Rand-McNally, 1969).

[31] Gardner Ackely and Daniel B. Suits, "Price Changes and Consumer Demand," *American Economic Review* 40 (December 1950, pt. 1): 785-804.

times, in lieu of such correction. Because population usually shows some regularity in secular trend over time, use of a time variable instead of a population variable yields some of the same results. A time variable can also be used to take into account secular shifts in consumption patterns.

There are different ways of handling the time variable in the estimating function. One is to make it a separate additive variable, as in the following:

$$C = a + bY + ct$$

in which t is the year–1, 2, . . . , n or sometimes (year – 1950) or some other base year. Another functional form is the following:

$$C = a_0 + a_1 + b_0 Y + b_1 Y$$

in which a_0 and a_1 are intersects for two periods, and b_0 and b_1 are the marginal propensities to spend for two periods. Still another possibility is to include a dummy variable for different periods with clearly demarcated levels of expenditure. In the equation

$$C = a + bY + d$$

d could be a dummy variable, carrying the value of zero during certain years, the value of 1 during other years, and the value of 2 during still other years. The effect, of course, is to make the a intersect equal to a during the first period, equal to $(a + 1)$ during the second, and equal to $(a + 2)$ during the third. The marginal propensity to consume, b, would be the same for all periods.

There is some question about the desirability of using a time variable to remove secular changes in expenditures. If it is desirable to isolate the relation of these secular changes to consumption expenditures, it is preferable to do it by more direct measures if such measures can be found. Use of a trend variable is a little like factor analysis in that secular shifts are recognized and filtered out, with the explanation for their occurrence dependent on further analysis.

Alan Powell, Tran Van Hoa, and R. H. Wilson used a trend variable in their estimating equations for their disaggregated consumption functions for nine categories of expenditures during the postwar period, 1949-1963.[32] Their observations on the trend factor are relevent:

> The final puzzle which cannot go without comment, is the question of how one should interpret estimated trends. [The data show] that apparently autonomous trends in consumption have been, for the most part, quantitatively important; moreover, except in the cases of *Food, Public Transportation,* and *Miscellaneous Non-Durables,* trend coefficients are statistically "significant" under classical tests. These shifts range in size from 3 percent per annum in *favour* of *Housing* through 4 percent *against Public Transportation.* It is fair criticism to claim that an approach which "explains" observed consumer behavior in terms of unexplained, autonomously occurring, changes in consumer habits, does not explain consumer behavior at all. . . .

> But we do hasten to point out that any attempt to suppress trends makes interpretation of the data, in terms of economic constructs, almost impossible. *Clothing* is a case in point. Suppressing trends in equations attempting to explain *Clothing* consumption in the post-war period leads to results which simply cannot be squared at all with

---

[32] Alan A. Powell, Tran Van Hoa, and R. H. Wilson, "A Multi-Sectoral Analysis of Consumer Demand in the Post-War Period," *Southern Economic Journal* 35 (October 1968): 109-120.

cross-sectional data. . . . what remains to be done in the dynamics of consumer response, clearly is immense.[33]

3. *DEMOGRAPHIC AND SOCIOLOGICAL ATTRIBUTES*. Population and household characteristics of an economy have an important bearing on the expenditures of that economy. For example, age distribution of the population influences the total level of consumption expenditures. Similarly, stage in the family life cycle and size of household are important. Cyclical variations in birthrate, marriage rate, rate of household formation, and similar factors have an important influence on expenditures at the time the variation occurs and often also at a later time.

Demographic factors have most often been examined as variables explaining expenditures for specific goods and services and interfamily differences in expenditures. These have been found to be particularly useful in the analysis of demand for specific categories of commodities. For example, R. Agarwala and J. Drinkwater considered four socioeconomic variables—married female participation in the labor force, eductional composition, age composition, and degree of urbanization—and finally concentrated their empirical study on married female labor force participation, which was found to be useful in explaining expenditures for durables and semidurables (not for nondurables or services).[34] Vernon Lippitt also found that information from cross-sectional data on family expenditures on house furnishings and equipment helped explain some of the observations from aggregate data for this category of expenditure. He says:

It does seem clear that shifts in the distributions of households by various characteristics have a significant influence on aggregate expenditures for house furnishings and equipment. . . . These distributional effects will need to be allowed for in long-term forecasts. Their importance in short-term forecasting rests on the consideration that the influence of the combined distributional effect needs to be allowed for in the historical time series before unbiased estimates of the influence of the time-series variables can be obtained.[35]

An example of the use of demographic and personal characteristics in the study of aggregate behavior is the savings model developed by W. H. Somermeyer and R. Bannink.[36] What they sought to do was to eliminate some of the simplifying assumptions

[33] Ibid., pp. 119-120. Reprinted from the *Southern Economic Journal*, Vol. 35, No. 2, October 1968, Chapel Hill, North Carolina. See also Powell's study of demand in Australia, in which the same type of function was employed: Alan A. Powell, "A Complete System of Consumer Demand Equations for the Australian Economy Fitted by a Model of Additive Preferences," *Econometrica* 34 (July 1966): 661-675. One conclusion in the latter study was: "Very large trends are evident and no explanation has been offered for their sign or their magnitude. Investigation of this puzzle certainly offers a challenge to further theoretical and empirical work connected, in its way, with the problem of economic development." Ibid., p. 674.

[34] R. Agarwala and J. Drinkwater, "Consumption Functions with Shifting Parameters Due to Socio-Economic Factors," *Review of Economics and Statistics* 54 (February 1972): 89-96. See also a study by W. H. Somermeyer and R. Bannink. *A Consumption-Savings Model and Its Applications* (Amsterdam: North-Holland, 1972), in which age, sex, occupation, and other demographic variables are analyzed along with economic variables as determinants of expenditures and savings.

[35] Vernon G. Lippitt, *Determinants of Consumer Demand for House Furnishings and Equipment*, Harvard Economic Series, Vol. CX (Cambridge, Mass.: Harvard University Press, 1959), pp. 136-137.

[36] Somermeyer and Bannink, op. cit.

of the traditional life cycle model by including not only the "hard core" economic variables—current income, capitalized expected future income, personal wealth, and rate of interest—in the savings model but also sociological and psychological variables—family composition, age, occupation, sex, and intelligence and other psychic factors. These underwent transformation to generate specific variables that would reflect expected income, expected rate of interest, initial wealth, desired final wealth, possible future expenditures, and utility function to yield optimal consumer expenditures and optimal current savings. Not all of these could be quantified in their empirical analysis of data for the Netherlands for the years 1949-1966, but they included many measures of sociopsychological attributes as well as the more common stock and flow variables.

The relationship between socioeconomic characteristics of families or households and aggregate consumption expenditures for all goods and services is likely to be less clear-cut than when expenditures for specific categories of goods and services are being considered. Nevertheless, significant changes in family and household composition and the distribution of social attributes is bound to affect the aggregate if that attribute bears a relationship to a specific expenditure that is not perfectly compensated for by an opposite relationship to some other expenditure. For this reason, cross-sectional data on social attributes might be found useful in explaining deviations from estimated aggregate expenditures in certain situations. Further exploration of these relationships on a disaggregated expenditure basis may throw additional light on the nature of the relationship to aggregate expenditures.[37]

4. *PSYCHOLOGICAL FACTORS.* The most important psychological factors that have been considered in demand functions are consumer attitudes and expectations.[38] Hypotheses concerning the influence of these and empirical measurement of their impact have been centered in the work of the Survey Research Center at the University of Michigan. Under the direction of George Katona, Eva Mueller, and others, the Survey Research Center has created an index of consumer sentiment (formerly called the index of consumer confidence) based on data obtained from its annual and quarterly surveys. Responses to five questions are averaged:

1. We are interested in how people are getting along financially these days. Would you say that you and your family are better off or worse financially than you were a year ago?
2. Now looking ahead—do you think that a year from now you people will be better off financially, or worse off, or just about the same as now?
3. Now turning to business conditions in the country as a whole—do you think that during the next twelve months we'll have good times financially, or bad times, or what?
4. Looking ahead, which would you say is more likely—that in the country as a whole we'll have continuous good times during the next five years or so, or that we will have periods of widespread unemployment or depression, or what?

---

[37] See, for example, D. J. Laughhunn, *On the Predictive Value of Combining Cross-section and Time-series Data in Empirical Demand Studies* (Urbana: University of Illinois, Bureau of Economic and Business Research, 1969).

[38] A discussion of the ways in which psychological factors affect aggregate consumer spending and saving responses to inflation, recession, or increased assets and inventories is in George Katona, "Psychology and Consumer Economics," *Journal of Consumer Research* 1 (June 1974): 1-8.

5. About the big things people buy for their homes—such as furniture, house furnishings, refrigerator, stove, television, and things like that. For people in general, do you think now is a good or a bad time to buy major household items?[39]

The index is calculated by taking the percentage of respondents who give a favorable or optimistic response to each question, subtracting the percentage who give an unfavorable or pessimistic response, and adding 100. There is then a score for each of the five questions. These five relative scores are averaged and adjusted to the base, February 1966 = 100.

There is no assurance that each of these questions is equally important, nor that their importance is the same at all points in time. The approach is simple and straightforward, and the collection of responses to a *consistent* set of questions over a period of time gives an opportunity to test the usefulness of the index against market experience.[40] The fifth question is a clue to the expenditure that has been found most closely related to the index—expenditures for durable goods.[41] The index of consumer sentiment has been used in the Brookings economic model, and refinements may open opportunities for incorporating it as a variable in other aggregate models.

It is not too difficult to perceive of Katona's concept of consumer sentiment as closely related to the Friedman concept of permanent income (although Katona would doubtless disclaim any relationship). Permanent income is expected income, and expectations are a function of one's experience, the resources at his disposal, the environment within which he produces and consumes, and his perception of what the future will bring in needs and opportunities. When we incorporate a measure of consumer sentiment into a demand function that also contains income, we are saying that the individual is playing a more active role in making his expenditure decisions than the traditional Keynesian consumption function assumed. The consumer assesses the situation with which he is confronted and makes a decision as to whether he will or will not make an expenditure at that moment. That assessment will be affected by his expectations. If one looks at questions 2, 3, and 4 in the five-question sequence used in calculating the index of consumer sentiment, it is clear that the designers of this index gave considerable weight to consumer expectations.

Consumer sentiment is not identical to the permanent-income concept, but it is much closer than most have recognized. The index of consumer sentiment is an attempt

[39] George Katona, Lewis Mandell, and Jay Schmiedeskamp, *1970 Survey of Consumer Finances* (Ann Arbor: University of Michigan, Institute for Social Research, Survey Research Center, 1971), pp. 247-248.

[40] A factor analysis of the components of the index is summarized in Richard T. Curtin, "Index Construction: An Appraisal of the Index of Consumer Sentiment," in Lewis Mandell et al., eds. *Surveys of Consumers, 1971-72* (Ann Arbor: University of Michigan, Institute for Social Research, 1973), pp. 253-261.

[41] See Eva Mueller and George Katona, "The Function of Expectational and Motivational Data," in *1960 Survey of Consumer Finances* (Ann Arbor: University of Michigan, Institute for Social Research, Survey Research Center, 1961), pp. 171-185, and George Katona et al., *1968 Survey of Consumer Finances* (Ann Arbor: University of Michigan, Institute for Social Research, Survey Research Center, 1969), pp. 129-140. In each of these, the effect of attitudes on expenditures for durables is measured. In S. W. Burch and H. O. Stekler, "The Forecasting Accuracy of Consumer Attitude Data," *Journal of the American Statistical Association* 64 (December 1969): 1225-1233, it was found that while the inclusion of attitudinal variables in regression equations to explain durable goods consumption yielded high R^2s, the errors were generally larger than those of naive models.

to measure the degree of confidence that consumers have in their present and expected situation. In this sense, it supplements the permanent income concept by indicating a probability. It seems reasonable to believe that the usefulness of the permanent-income concept would be enhanced if a measure of confidence in the expectation were incorporated, because the probability distribution of consumers' expectations is not necessarily constant, and that distribution is bound to influence their concept of their permanent income at any point in time.[42]

One other variable that is closely related to the attitude variable we have described is expressed buying intentions or plans. This is not "psychological" in the same sense as the attitude variable, for it combines attitudes, inclinations, and/or decisions. To get an indication of buying intentions, individuals can be asked if they plan to buy specific goods within the next three or six months. This information has been found most useful in explaining and forecasting the demand for consumer durables, but it is less useful than the index of consumer sentiment. In a study of the demand for consumer durables, however, Thomas Juster and Paul Wachtel found that they were able to substitute purchase expectations and consumer sentiment for income. With appropriate adjustments for lags, the expectations and sentiment variables were found to be as reliable as income in explaining purchases.[43]

A New Approach to the Income-Expenditure Function

In the original Keynesian consumption function, consumption expenditures are viewed as a *response* to income. The two are positively related, but the relationship that is implied is that income serves as a constraint on expenditures. Only if it increases will expenditures rise. If it decreases, expenditures will fall in *response* to the change in income. The implication is that the level of expenditures is caused by the level of income. Underlying this conception of cause-and-effect relationships is the assumption that the determination of income lies beyond the control of the individual, while consumption expenditures lie within his control. Income, determined externally, constrains expenditures, which are determined "internally" by the consuming unit.

The modifications of the original consumption function that we have discussed thus far do not change this conception of income as an externally determined variable to which the individual adjusts his expenditures. What the modifications have done is to suggest different ways of perceiving the income variable or to introduce other variables that, in addition to income, would influence expenditure decisions. Some of the additional variables do suggest, however, that the consumer is not quite so passive as the Keynesian function implies. The attitude variable, for example, has been introduced to show that consumers willfully adjust expenditures in accordance with their assessment of the situation at that moment. But even in this case, income is taken as a datum, as it is in all demand functions.

This view of the consumer as a passive market entity, adjusting his expenditures to his

---

[42] Friedman discussed the shifting level of an individual's permanent income at different ages, based on his income experience up to that point and the probability distribution of his expectations. See Friedman, *A Theory of the Consumption Function*, pp. 23–25.

[43] F. Thomas Juster and Paul Wachtel, "Anticipatory and Objective Models of Durable Goods Demand," *American Economic Review* 62 (September 1972): 564–579.

income, has been challenged in a very interesting hypothesis. This hypothesis is that the consumer *controls* his income to fit his desires for expenditures.[44] This does not mean that he has complete control, nor is that control possible in all phases of the business cycle, such as during depressions and periods of extensive unemployment. But the focus is on a consumer enterprise, functioning in many respects like a business enterprise.[45] Decisions are made, not only with respect to the use of income, but also with respect to the use of the human and nonhuman resources available to the consumer enterprise.

There are many avenues by which this control can be exercised. To the degree that a consuming unit has choices with respect to training and education, occupation, migration, number of hours worked, number of earners in the consuming unit, and the utilization of nonhuman resources (e.g., home ownership, investments), it can affect its income. For example, in a study for 1959 James Morgan and his colleagues found that one-third of the variation in hourly earnings of spending unit heads was "accounted for by factors which relate directly to the individual—mobility and attitudes, education and achievement motivation. To this extent, the individual has some control over his wage rate."[46] In a much more detailed study of cross-sectional data for 1965, Morgan, Ismail Sirageldin, and Nancy Baerwaldt found that a composite index that they developed to represent "concern with progress," comprising measures of four major subgroups (ambition and aspiration, planning and time horizon, achievement orientation, and receptivity to change), was positively related to hours of work for money and that it was "an important variable in explaining total productive effort, even after allowing for basic constraints and opportunity factors."[47]

Other evidence of the positive role individual choices may play in determining the size of family income is in the extent to which married women participate in the labor force. In 1970, for example, 43 percent of all women in the United States were gainfully employed, and 41 percent of women who were married and living with their husbands were employed.[48] Of all women employed, over 40 percent said they worked because of "financial necessity," while an additional 15 percent said that they worked to earn "extra money."[49] Another evidence of this kind of choice making is the number of individuals who hold multiple jobs. In 1973, for example, 5.1 percent of all employed people had two or more jobs. Multiple jobholding was more common among men, with 6.6 percent, than among women, with 2.7 percent.[50]

The extent to which the individual *can* control his own income has not, of course, been

---

[44] One of the best expositions of this idea is in Ruth P. Mack, "Trends in Consumption and the Aspiration to Consume," *American Economic Review* 66 (May 1956): 55-68.

[45] Ibid., p. 65.

[46] James N. Morgan et al., *Income and Welfare in the United States* (New York: McGraw-Hill, 1962), p. 69.

[47] James N. Morgan, Ismail Sirageldin, and Nancy Baerwaldt, *Productive Americans: A Study of How Individuals Contribute to Economic Progress*, Survey Research Center Monograph no. 43 (Ann Arbor: University of Michigan, Institute for Social Research, 1966), p. 359.

[48] Elizabeth Waldman and Anne M. Young, "Marital and Family Characteristics of Workers, March 1970," *Monthly Labor Review* 94 (March 1971): 46-50.

[49] Carl Rosenfeld and Vera C. Perella, "Why Women Start and Stop Working: A Study in Mobility," Special Labor Force Report no. 59 (Washington, D.C.: U.S. Department of Labor. Bureau of Labor Statistics, 1965).

[50] "Multiple Jobholding, May 1973," Special Labor Force Report (Washington, D.C.: U.S. Department of Labor, Bureau of Labor Statistics, December 1973), p. 3.

clearly established, nor does the theoretical framework yet exist for systematically exploring this aspect of behavior. But the evidence is highly suggestive, and it would seem that the possibility of a cause-and-effect relationship among the variables of the traditional consumption function opposite to that commonly assumed needs more careful study. If it is found to be a reality, the problem then becomes one of trying to assess its importance as a dynamic factor in the determination of income levels and its impact on expenditures. Marketing people have long believed that individuals can learn to want more and more and thereby be driven to work more in order to fulfill these expanding desires. The economic analysis of this phenomenon is not yet complete.

AN EXAMPLE OF A DYNAMIC AGGREGATE DEMAND FUNCTION

H. S. Houthakker and Lester Taylor have undertaken one of the most comprehensive analyses of consumer demand ever done in the United States. They have developed a dynamic model that takes into account the influence of total consumption expenditures in the preceding year, the change in total expenditures from the preceding year to the given year, the effect of the stocks of goods at the beginning of the period, prices, and the rate at which stocks depreciate in explaining expenditures for a specific item. The model was used in estimating short- and long-run price and expenditure elasticities, as well as stock coefficients and rates of depreciation, for 82 categories of personal consumption expenditure, using data from the national income accounts for the years 1929-1964.[51] These were commodity demand functions, and we shall refer to the important findings for the major expenditure categories in the following chapter. Our interest in their analysis at this point is in the aggregate demand function that they calculated, using the same basic concepts, with parameters estimated for total expenditures for goods and services. We reproduce their findings based on annual data for the United States for the periods 1929-1941 and 1947-1964.

The Houthakker-Taylor Aggregate Function

The basic equation was of the form

$$q_t = A_0 + A_1 q_{t-1} + A_2 \Delta x_t + A_3 x_{t-1}$$

in which q_t is the total amount spent in 1958 dollars in year t, x is disposable personal income in 1958 dollars, and the subscript t is the given year. The values of A_0, A_1, A_2, and A_3 are a function of the stock coefficient and the rate of depreciation of the stock.

$$A_0 = \frac{\alpha \delta \tau^2}{1 - \frac{\tau}{2}(\beta - \delta)}$$

$$A_1 = \frac{1 + \frac{\tau}{2}(\beta - \delta)}{1 - \frac{\tau}{2}(\beta - \delta)}$$

[51] H. S. Houthakker and Lester D. Taylor. *Consumer Demand in the United States: Analyses and Projections*, Harvard Economic Studies, vol. CXXVI, 2d enl. ed. (Cambridge, Mass.: Harvard University Press, 1970). The material presented here is adapted by permission of the authors and publisher from pp. 9-24, 281-303.

$$A_2 = \frac{\gamma(1 + \frac{\tau\delta}{2})}{1 - \frac{\tau}{2}(\beta - \delta)}$$

$$A_3 = \frac{\gamma\delta\tau}{1 - \frac{\tau}{2}(\beta - \delta)}$$

In these α is the intercept, δ is the depreciation rate, τ is the period ($\tau = 1$ for one year, $\tau = \frac{1}{4}$ for one quarter), β is the stock coefficient, and γ is the short-run coefficient of total expenditure (short-run MPC).

The values of α, γ, β, and δ are related as follows for annual data:

$$\alpha = \frac{2A_0 (A_2 - \frac{1}{2}A_3)}{A_3 (A_1 + 1)}$$

$$\beta = \frac{2(A_1 - 1)}{A_1 + 1} + \frac{A_3}{A_2 - \frac{1}{2}A_3}$$

$$\gamma = \frac{2(A_2 - \frac{1}{2}A_3)}{A_1 + 1}$$

$$\delta = \frac{A_3}{A_2 - \frac{1}{2}A_3}$$

On the basis of annual data for the period 1929-1941 and 1947-1964, the estimated parameters were

$$q_t = 9.871 + .659q_{t-1} + .607\Delta x_t + .287x_{t-1}$$
$$(21.385) \ (.177) \qquad (.057) \qquad (.157)$$

$$\alpha = 18.81 \quad \beta = .26 \quad \gamma = .55 \quad \gamma' = .94 \quad \pi = .62$$
$$R^2 = .997 \quad S_e = 18.10 \quad \text{D.W.} = 2.39$$

The variable γ' is the long-run coefficient of total expenditure. D.W. is, of course, the Durbin-Watson coefficient. All of the parameters shown here are only estimates; we have, however, suppressed the hats.

The apparent marginal propensity to consume (spend) is indicated by A_2 and is .607. But the values of γ and γ' are more important, because these break the marginal propensity to spend into its short- and long-run components. From these we see that the short-run MPC is .55 and the long-run MPC is .94. Houthakker and Taylor concluded that since the coefficients of Δx and x_{t-1} are very close to each other, a static equation would have been equally satisfactory.

The authors also calculated equations for the postwar period, 1947-1964, using both annual and quarterly data. None of the equations, including the one just presented, gave completely satisfactory results. They attempted, therefore, to compute an estimating function for savings, which is the complement of total consumption expenditures, approaching savings as expenditures for a nondepreciating asset. This was further adjusted to include prices and the rate of interest, but again completely satisfactory results were not realized. We have presented some of these findings as an example of one of the more highly refined approaches to the problem of structuring and estimating the parameters of the consumption expenditure function. It is apparent that this problem has not yet been resolved. Better empirical results must await better theory.

5

Family Expenditures: Micro Consumption Expenditure Functions

Never ask of money spent
Where the spender thinks it went.
Nobody was ever meant
To remember or invent
What he did with every cent.

—Robert Frost

A great deal can be learned about the size and composition of aggregate demand by examination of the demands of different families and by analysis of the structure of demand in specific and small market situations. In this chapter we shall focus on family expenditure patterns, and specifically on interfamily differences in expenditures, for their value in understanding the structure of aggregate and commodity consumption expenditure functions.

THE MULTIVARIATE FAMILY EXPENDITURE FUNCTION

In the analysis of family expenditures, we shall use the multivariate approach proposed in the preceding chapter. The basic function is

$$C_{ij} = f(Y_i, P_j, T_i, Q_j, A_i)$$

in which C_{ij} is the expenditure by family i for item j, Y_i is the purchasing power of family i, P_j is the price of item j relative to all other goods, T_i is tastes ("felt needs" and relative preferences) of family i, Q_j is relative quality of item j (i.e., utility as perceived by family i), and A_i is attitudes and expectations of family i.

In Table 5.1 we have outlined the variables that we shall consider and the direct or indirect factors by which they can be measured. This is similar to Table 6.1 in the following chapter, which shows the variables used in studying the market demand for specific commodities or services. There are, however, certain elements contained in Table 5.1 for families that are not so useful for the study of market demand unless some measure of central tendency or dispersion can be applied to family data to arrive at a meaningful market measure. For example, the family's stage in its life cycle may explain why that particular family does or does not buy furniture. Unless there are changes in the number of people in the population who are at those stages in their life cycle when they are normally heavy buyers of furniture, this information whould not be nearly so useful in studying market demand. On the other hand, some variables that are useful in studying market demand may not have much bearing on interfamily differences in spending. For example, prices may change from season to season and from year to year, thereby affecting consumer purchases. But if we are looking at different families that are buying in the same markets in which price alternatives are essentially the same for all buyers, price will not play the same role in the analysis. Only to the extent that different families

Table 5.1. Concepts and Measures of the Independent Variables in a Family Consumption Expenditure Function

PURCHASING POWER (Y)	TASTES ("FELT NEEDS" OR PREFERENCES)(T)
Income:	**Family Status:**
Current disposable personal income (DPI)	Stage in family life cycle
Past income	Size of family
Income from previous period(s)	
Highest past income	**Social Status:**
Changes in income	Location
Relative position in income distribution	Stratum
Permanent (normal) Income	Social group
Discretionary income	
	Ownership Status:
Assets:	Existing stocks of durables
Liquid assets	Family stocks
Nonliquid assets	Others' stocks
Credit	Market stocks
	Psychological stocks of
	nondurables (habits)
	Personality Attributes

PRICES (P)	ATTITUDES (A)
Market Prices	**Present Situation**
Terms of Sale	**Expected Future Situation**

PRODUCT QUALITY (PERCEIVED UTILITY)(Q)

Product Itself ("Own" Attributes)
Alternative Products

make different decisions about which price they will choose from the alternatives available to them will price be important in explaining interfamily differences in expenditures.

The items detailed in Table 5.1 are those that are relevant to family expenditure patterns. Since we have treated several of these in our discussion of macro expenditure functions, we shall not repeat those observations unless there is something unique about the way the variable enters the family expenditure function. This would apply, for example, to such matters as the use of disposable personal income versus permanent income. We shall focus instead on those variables that are particularly valuable in explaining interfamily differences in expenditure, such as the economic and social characteristics of one family in comparison with others.

Most of the information on which family expenditure analyses rests is cross-sectional, showing how, in one period of time, families differ with respect to their expenditure patterns. This is basically a static social situation, in which we observe inter-family differences as they are manifested at one point in time.

Family Income-Expenditure Relationships

As in most demand functions, family expenditures have been found to be very closely tied to family income. Many studies have related current income to current consumption expenditures, but the same reasons that would justify the use of more refined income variables—past income, changes in income, relative income, and permanent income—could apply to the family as well as to all consumers. Most of the studies we shall cite, however, are those in which current expenditures are related to current personal disposable income, or in which current expenditures for specific goods and services are related to total current consumption expenditures.

Engel Functions

These functions have come to be known as Engel functions, named after Ernst Engel, a mining engineer who had been a student of LePlay and was director of the Statistical Bureau of Saxony. In 1857 Engel published data that showed the expenditures of 153 working families in Belgium.[1] On the basis of these data, which had been collected by Ducpetiaux, plus additional data previously published by LePlay, Engel formulated the generalization that has since become known as Engel's "law": "The poorer a family, the greater the proportion of its total expenditure that must be devoted to the provision of food."[2]

Engel's study was followed in 1868 by a study by Hermann Schwabe, director of the Berlin Statistical Bureau, in which he observed that "the poorer anyone is, the greater the amount relative to his income that he must spend for housing."[3] In 1875, while head of the Bureau of Labor Statistics of Massachusetts, Carroll Wright contributed further to the development of the full set of Engel "laws" through a publication in which he analyzed Engel's findings in combination with information about workingmen's families in Massachusetts. A later study, undertaken under his direction as commissioner of labor statistics of the United States, was published by Wright in 1901.[4]

Out of this sequence have come the five propositions known as "Engel's laws," although Engel stated only the one about food, while Schwabe and Wright contributed the others in a formal sense. We present these as two basic propositions, with the first consisting of four subsidiary parts:

1. As family income increases, the percentage of total consumption expenditures that goes for
   a. food   — decreases.
   b. rent, fuel, light   — decreases.
   c. clothing   — increases.
   d. other goods and services   — increases.

---

[1] Ernst Engel, "Die Productions- und Consumptionsverhältnisse des Königreichs Sachsen," originally in *Zeitschrift des Statistischen Bureaus des Königlich Sächsischen Ministerium des Inneren*, nos. 8 and 9 (November 22, 1857); reprinted in *Bulletin de l'Institut International de Statistique*, IX (1895). See George J. Stigler, "The Early History of Empirical Studies of Consumer Behavior," *Journal of Political Economy* 42 (April 1954): 98-100.

[2] The translation is that of Stigler, op. cit., p. 98.

[3] Hermann Schwabe, "Das Verhältmiss von Miethe und Einkommen in Berlin," in *Berlin und seine Entwickelung für 1868* (Berlin, 1868), pp. 264-267, as quoted in Stigler, op. cit., p. 100.

[4] Massachusetts Bureau of Labor Statistics, *Sixth Annual Report of the Bureau of Labor Statistics* (Boston, 1875), p. 385, as quoted in Stigler, op. cit., p. 100. There was considerable confusion between Engel and Wright in the interpretation of their published papers. For the history of this, see Stigler, op. cit., pp. 98-101.

2. As family income increases, the percentage of income that goes for saving — increases.

Note that in the first proposition each of the subgroups is related to total consumption expenditures rather than income, while in the second proposition saving is related to total income. When these relationships are expressed in the form of a mathematical function, they are known as Engel functions, and we shall refer to any relationship between family income (or total expenditures) and either savings or the expenditure for a specific item as an Engel function.

After Engel, Wright, and Schwabe, empirical work on consumption expenditures and the search for regularities in expenditure patterns proceeded at an off-and-on pace. In the United States the collection of data on family income and expenditures has been tied closely to revisions in the Consumer Price Index. Carroll Wright's 1901 study was used to establish the food components of the Consumer Price Index. Subsequent large-scale investigations were made in 1918, 1934-1936, 1941, 1950, 1960-1961, and 1972-1974.

The principal data that we shall employ in this discussion are from the 1960-1961 study of consumption expenditures by families and individuals in the United States.[5] Until data from the 1972-1974 study are available, these are the most recent comprehensive statistics that we have on this subject.

Empirical Findings

In the discussion that follows we shall try to determine to what extent there are or are not patterns of total expenditure-specific expenditure (or income-expenditure) relationship that are meaningful in terms of consumers' market behavior and, hence, of sellers' marketing policies. We shall look first at total expenditures and their relationship to income. We shall then explore the relationship between expenditures for specific goods and services and total expenditures.

TOTAL EXPENDITURES

In Table 5.2 we show that for urban consuming units expenditures exceeded after-tax income for the average family or individual with an income less than $4,000. The

---

[5] Out of an estimated 55,306,253 consumer units in the universe, usable schedules were obtained from 13,728. Some families were interviewed in 1960 and some in 1961. Both urban and rural families were included, but much of the analysis in this chapter will focus on the 9,476 urban families surveyed. The results were published in U.S., Bureau of Labor Statistics, *Survey of Consumer Expenditures, 1960-61*, BLS Report 237, nos. 1-93 (Washington, D.C.: U.S. Department of Labor, 1962-1966), and U.S., Agricultural Research Service, *Consumer Expenditures and Income*, USDA Consumer Expenditure Survey Reports nos. 1-30 (Washington, D.C.: U.S. Department of Agriculture, 1962-1966). Publications of the Department of Agriculture cover the rural population; publications of the Bureau of Labor Statistics cover the urban and rural nonfarm population. A review of the survey procedures is in U.S., Bureau of Labor Statistics, *Consumer Expenditures and Income: Survey Guidelines*, Bulletin no. 1684 (Washington, D.C.: GPO, 1971).

Data for 1950 appeared in U.S., Bureau of Labor Statistics and Wharton School of Finance and Commerce, University of Pennsylvania, *Study of Consumer Expenditures, Incomes, and Savings*, vols. I-XVIII (Philadelphia: University of Pennsylvania Press, 1957). The principal study intervening between the 1950 and 1960-1961 studies was Alfred Politz Research, *Life Study of Consumer Expenditures*, vols. I-VII (New York: Time, 1957-1958). For a history of consumption expenditure studies, see Carolyn S. Bell, *Consumer Choice in the American Economy* (New York: Random House, 1967), pp. 5-48, 77-125.

Table 5.2 Total Expenditures for Current Consumption by Urban Families and Single Individuals with Respect to Money Income After Taxes, 1960-1961

Income After Taxes	Average Propensity APC = C/Y	Marginal Propensity MPC = ΔC/ΔY	Elasticity $e_{c,y} = \dfrac{\Delta C/C}{\Delta Y/Y}$
Less than $1,000	1.999		
		.537	.380
$ 1,000-$ 1,999	1.170		
		.914	.823
2,000- 2,999	1.067		
		1.031	.974
3,000- 3,999	1.057		
		.793	.774
4,000- 4,999	.999		
		.746	.767
5,000- 5,999	.954		
		.811	.866
6,000- 7,499	.928		
		.705	.778
7,500- 9,999	.879		
		.707	.824
10,000- 14,999	.831		
		.490	.675
15,000 and over	.674		

Source: Calculated from U.S., Bureau of Labor Statistics, *Survey of Consumer Expenditures, Consumer Expenditures and Income, Urban United States, 1960-61,* Bureau of Labor Statistics Report no. 237-38 (Washington, D.C.: U.S. Department of Labor, 1964).

break-even point occurred between $4,000 and $5,000. As family income increased, the amount spent for goods and services also increased, but not in proportion to income. The average propensity to spend declined markedly as income increased. But there was not the systematic decline in the marginal propensity to spend or in income elasticity that we might expect. The marginal propensity to spend increased up to an income level of about $3,000, and it rose again at about $6,000. Both the MPC and income elasticity figures in Table 5.2 suggest that there were strong pressures for increased expenditures up to this first peak, at an income level of approximately $3,000, and a secondary peak, at about $6,000. At the $10,000 level there was a slight increase in the income elasticity and also in the MPC. Perhaps these are threshold levels at which a certain type of consumption satisfaction is experienced. We shall explore this in more detail as we examine specific expenditures.

EXPENDITURES FOR MAJOR PRODUCT GROUPS

The data we have discussed thus far are expenditures by urban families and individuals. In Table 5.3 we show average expenditures for all families classified by place of residence and race. Not only did the levels of expenditure differ, but also the breakdown of expenditures by product and service group. Explicit expenditures by urban families for shelter were more than twice those by farm families. Blacks spent proportionately more for housing and clothing than did whites. "Other" races (Japanese, Chinese, Indians, and others who were classified as neither white nor black) spent almost $200 more per family

Table 5.3 Average Annual Expenditures for Current Consumption by Families in the United States by Residence and Race, 1960-1961

Item	All Families	Residence			Race		
		Urban	Rural		White	Negro	Other
			Nonfarm	Farm			
Total estimated number of families (in thousands)	55,307	40,131	11,663	3,512	49,392	5,321	593
Percentage	100.0	72.6	21.1	6.3	89.3	9.6	1.1
Total expenditures	$5,047	$5,390	$4,296[a]	$3,594[a]	$5,219	$3,465	$4,900
Food	1,235	1,311	1,083	866	1,269	886	1,454
Prepared at home	989	1,036	905	728	1,015	728	1,121
Other	246	275	178	138	254	158	333
Tobacco	91	95	85	64	93	75	67
Alcoholic beverages	78	90	50	27	79	65	76
Housing	1,461	1,588	1,189	917	1,507	1,061	1,233
Shelter	658	748	453	310	677	488	572
Owned dwelling	354	385	300	178	379	145	187
Rented dwelling (inc. other shelter)	304	363	153	132	298	343	385
Other expenses[b]	803	840	736	607	830	573	661
Clothing and personal[c]	1,003	1,068	828	843	1,034	736	883
Recreation and education[d]	298	326	233	187	312	169	312
Transportation	770	793	737	613	808	419	756
Other	111	119	91	77	117	54	119
Percentage of total	100.0	100.0	100.0[a]	100.0[a]	100.0	100.0	100.0
Food	24.5	24.3	25.2	24.1	24.3	25.6	29.7
Prepared at home	19.6	19.2	21.1	20.3	19.4	21.0	22.9
Other	4.9	5.1	4.1	3.8	4.9	4.6	6.8
Tobacco	1.8	1.8	2.0	1.8	1.8	2.2	1.4
Alcoholic beverages	1.5	1.7	1.2	0.8	1.5	1.9	1.6
Housing	28.9	29.5	27.7	25.5	28.9	30.6	25.2
Shelter	13.0	13.9	10.5	8.6	13.0	14.1	11.7
Owned dwelling	7.0	7.1	7.0	5.0	7.3	4.2	3.8
Rented dwelling (inc. other shelter)	6.0	6.7	3.6	3.7	5.7	9.9	7.9
Other expenses[b]	15.9	15.5	17.2	16.8	15.9	16.5	13.5
Clothing and personal[c]	19.9	19.9	19.3	23.4	19.8	21.3	18.1
Recreation and education[d]	5.9	6.0	5.4	5.2	6.0	4.9	6.4
Transportation	15.3	14.7	17.1	17.1	15.5	12.1	15.4
Other	2.2	2.2	2.1	2.1	2.2	1.6	2.4

[a] 1961 only.

[b] Fuel, light, refrigeration, water, house furnishings and equipment, and household operations.

[c] Includes clothing materials and services, personal care, and medical care.

[d] Includes reading matter.

Source: U. S., Bureau of Labor Statistics, Consumer Expenditures and Income, Total United States, Urban and Rural, 1960-61, Report no. 237-93 (Washington, D.C.: U.S. Department of Labor, 1966).

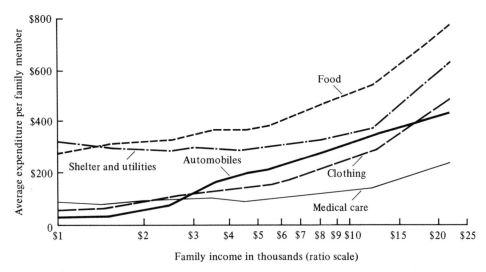

Figure 5.1. Average annual expenditure per urban family member for major categories of goods and services at different after-tax income levels, 1960-1961. Both families and single consumers are included. Source: Kathryn R. Murphy, "Contrasts in Spending by Urban Families," *Monthly Labor Review* 87 (November 1964): 1411.

for food than white families and more than $500 more than the average black family. They also spent almost as much as whites for transportation.

In Figure 5.1 we present data for all families and individuals, urban and rural, and show these converted into an expenditure per family member. This conversion removes some of the differences in expenditures that are due to family size.[6] Note the stability in expenditures for shelter and utilities between $2,000 and about $6,000 income. In fact, there was not much difference between $2,000 and $10,000. Medical care was likewise quite stable within these income limits. Clothing, food, and automobiles showed much more sensitivity to changes in income. These differences are extremely important in understanding market behavior of consumers and market responses of sellers, and we shall now explore them in more detail.

Table 5.4 shows the average propensity to spend for 19 categories of goods by families and individuals in 10 different income classes in 1960-1961.

THE ENGEL "LAWS"

Are the four generalizations that we have identified as the Engel functions supported by the data for 1960-1961 in the United States?

The proposition about food is obviously verified.

The proposition about shelter and utilities is essentially verified, although there is a tiny increase in percentage spent for these combined items in the $5,000-6,000 income level and at income levels greater than $15,000. Shelter is more of an outlet for expenditure by higher-income groups than the Schwabe generalization would lead one to believe. Expenditures for owned dwellings become increasingly significant as income rises. There

---

[6] We do not remove all differences related to family size, however, since Figure 5.1 is based on averages for different income levels corrected by average number of family members of each income class. Thus intraclass variation is not taken into account.

Table 5.4 Average Propensity for Families and Single Consumers at Various Income Levels in the United States to Spend for Specific Goods and Services with Respect to Total Consumption Expenditures, 1960-1961[a]

Money Income After Taxes	Total Expenditures For Current Consumption Amount	Total Expenditures For Current Consumption APC	Food Total	Food Prepared at Home	Food Away from Home	Tobacco	Alcoholic Beverages
			APC	APC			
Under $1,000	$ 1,276	1.000	.290	.242	.048	.017	.005
$ 1,000-$ 1,999	1,781	1.000	.299	.261	.038	.020	.010
2,000- 2,999	2,670	1.000	.282	.235	.047	.022	.011
3,000- 3,999	3,636	1.000	.262	.215	.047	.022	.013
4,000- 4,999	4,428	1.000	.254	.208	.046	.021	.015
5,000- 5,999	5,172	1.000	.250	.208	.041	.020	.015
6,000- 7,499	6,125	1.000	.242	.196	.046	.019	.016
7,500- 9,999	7,416	1.000	.238	.186	.052	.017	.016
10,000- 14,999	9,521	1.000	.221	.164	.057	.013	.018
15,000 and over	14,208	1.000	.191	.130	.061	.010	.018
Total	$ 5,047	1.000	.245	.196	.049	.018	.015

Money Income After Taxes	Housing Total	Housing Shelter Total	Housing Shelter Rented Dwelling	Housing Shelter Owned Dwelling	Housing Shelter Other	Housing Fuel, Light, Refrigeration, Water	Housing Household Operations	Housing House Furnishings, Equipment	Clothing, Clothing Services
Under $1,000	.362	.176	.103	.067	.006	.092	.056	.038	.062
$ 1,000-$ 1,999	.351	.171	.115	.053	.003	.081	.059	.040	.067
2,000- 2,999	.317	.153	.097	.053	.003	.065	.055	.044	.083
3,000- 3,999	.300	.139	.087	.048	.004	.055	.056	.049	.090

Money Income After Taxes									
4,000- 4,999	.287	.131	.076	.051	.004	.051	.054	.051	.095
5,000- 5,999	.291	.132	.061	.066	.005	.051	.054	.055	.098
6,000- 7,499	.287	.129	.041	.081	.007	.048	.055	.055	.105
7,500- 9,999	.275	.122	.034	.080	.007	.044	.055	.055	.112
10,000- 14,999	.271	.116	.024	.081	.011	.040	.060	.055	.119
15,000 and over	.296	.125	.017	.088	.020	.034	.083	.054	.123
Total	.289	.130	.053	.070	.007	.049	.057	.053	.103

Money Income After Taxes	Personal Care	Medical Care	Recreation	Reading	Education	Transportation			Other Expenditures
						Total	Automobile	Other Transportation	
Under $1,000	.025	.102	.021	.009	.011	.067	.053	.014	.029
$ 1,000-$ 1,999	.029	.088	.021	.009	.003	.078	.063	.015	.025
2,000- 2,999	.032	.082	.027	.009	.004	.110	.094	.016	.021
3,000- 3,999	.031	.073	.033	.009	.006	.143	.128	.015	.018
4,000- 4,999	.029	.066	.036	.008	.006	.164	.150	.014	.018
5,000- 5,999	.030	.066	.037	.009	.008	.160	.148	.011	.017
6,000- 7,499	.029	.065	.041	.009	.010	.158	.146	.012	.020
7,500- 9,999	.029	.063	.044	.009	.011	.165	.151	.014	.021
10,000- 14,999	.027	.063	.049	.009	.019	.165	.146	.019	.025
15,000 and over	.024	.062	.047	.009	.028	.144	.112	.032	.049
Total	.029	.067	.040	.009	.010	.153	.137	.015	.022

[a] Average propensity to spend is (c_{ij}/c_{tj}), in which c_{ij} is the average expenditure on item i by income group j and c_{tj} is the average total expenditure on all goods and services by income group j.

Source: U.S., Bureau of Labor Statistics, *Survey of Consumer Expenditures, Total United States, Urban and Rural, 1960-61*, BLS Report no. 237-93 (Washington, D.C.: GPO, 1965), p. 11.

are three elements that may account for this. A technical factor is the nature of the housing expenditure data. Payments for rental housing are usually explicit, while payments for owned dwellings include taxes, insurance, interest, repairs, and other current operation expenditures of homeowners. Payments on mortgage principal are excluded. Therefore, if repairs and maintenance do not equal depreciation, explicit payments counted in arriving at these averages for owner-occupied housing would not reflect imputed rental value if there were no mortgage or if no repairs were made. Another factor, of course, is that it has been public policy to encourage home ownership. At the same time, however, consumer preferences, unfettered by policy, may be reflected in the data. In general, we can say that as income increases, the percentage spent for shelter and utilities together is a declining percentage of income. But we should watch carefully what happens to this among the highest-income groups, for there is some evidence that housing is regarded as a "superior" superior good. We shall return to this later.

The proposition about increasing proportionate expenditures for clothing as income increases is substantiated by our data. It is interesting to note, however, that when clothing expenditures are related to income rather than to total consumption expenditures, the percentage spent is nearly the same at all income levels. In our discussion, however, we are using total consumption expenditures as our base.

The last proposition about commodity expenditures is that the proportion of total expenditures that goes for miscellaneous goods and services increases as income increases, and this is substantiated by the data in Table 5.4.

We have to go back to Table 5.2 to find data concerning the proposition about the percentage of income that is saved. From that table it is clear that the percentage of income that is saved increases as family income increases. Below the $4,000-5,000 group dissaving occurs, and saving rises sharply as income increases beyond that point.

CONSTANT (SINGLE) EXPENDITURE ELASTICITIES

The coefficient of expenditure elasticity is one of the most useful measures that we have in the analysis of family expenditure patterns. It can be employed as a means of classifying items according to the relationships described by the Engel functions. Those items with a high elasticity coefficient are ones for which expenditures show great sensitivity to changes in the total expenditure level, while those with low elasticity would show the least sensitivity to changes in the family's aggregate expenditure level. Food, for example, would, in keeping with Engel's "law," presumably have a low elasticity coefficient, while clothing and miscellaneous items would have high elasticity coefficients.

In Table 5.5 the elasticities of expenditure for a number of specific items are given.[7] These were derived from the 1960-1961 family expenditure data rather than from a time series and show the relationship between the relative change in expenditure for a specific

---

[7] This table and others that we shall discuss are based on data from H. S. Houthakker and Lester D. Taylor, *Consumer Demand in the United States: Analyses and Projections*, Harvard Economic Studies, vol. CXXVI, 2d enl. ed. (Cambridge, Mass.: Harvard University Press, 1970), pp. 237-280. This is one of the most comprehensive analyses of the 1960-1961 survey of consumer expenditures. Studies based on the 1950 survey of expenditures appear in Irwin Friend and Robert Jones, eds., *Study of Consumer Expenditures, Incomes and Savings: Proceedings of the Conference on Consumption and Saving*, vols. I and II (Philadelphia: University of Pennsylvania, 1960).

Table 5.5 Elasticity of Expenditure for a Number of Specific Items with Respect to Total Expenditure for All Goods and Services from BLS Cross-Sectional Data for Families in the United States, 1960-1961[a]

Item	Elasticities with Respect to		
	Total Personal Consumption Expenditure[b]	Family Size[c]	F-Ratio[d]
Food, alcohol, tobacco	.513	.322	.49
Alcohol	1.541	-.429	1.86
Food purchased	.578	.293	3.33
Purchased meals	1.400	.005	8.42
Farm produced food	-1.566	1.457	1.14
Tobacco	.635	.047	2.71
Clothing	1.021	.338	6.05
Shoes, clothing, jewelry	1.098	.403	5.69
Clothing upkeep	1.194	-.251	2.15
Personal care	.832	.079	3.62
Toilet articles	.704	.280	3.37
Personal care services	1.032	-.164	2.14
Housing	1.041	-.244	1.46
Owned dwelling	1.486	-.377	7.57
Rented dwelling (nonfarm)	.433	-.293	4.88
Lodging away from home	2.113	-.537	.67
Household operation	.918	-.086	1.79
Furniture	1.482	-.179	1.53
Appliances	.889	.068	.63
Housewares	1.411	-.081	1.52
Other furnishings	1.065	-.086	.41
Cleaning preparations	.763	.103	.79
Household utilities	.515	.048	5.21
Electricity, gas	.501	.056	4.50
Water	1.022	-.191	6.22
Fuel	.384	.083	1.59
Telephone	1.134	-.530	3.39
Medical	.697	-.187	3.90
Drugs	.610	-.307	7.44
Ophthalmic and medical supplies	.818	-.309	11.22
Physicians paid directly	.746	-.151	3.15
Dentists	1.418	-.053	2.79
Other professional services	.888	-.615	1.21
Hospital expenses (direct)	.693	-.317	(e)
Medical insurance	.918	-.309	.72
Transportation	1.470	-.190	4.49
User operated transportation	1.523	-.151	4.20
Automboile purchase	2.456	-.099	(e)
Accessories and parts	.815	.107	2.78

Table 5.5 cont.

Item	Elasticities with Respect to		
	Total Personal Consumption Expenditure[b]	Family Size[c]	F-Ratio[d]
Auto repair	1.247	−.204	2.55
Auto insurance	1.395	−.394	1.42
Recreation	1.120	.092	3.24
Books	1.444	.755	3.37
Toys, participant sports	1.427	.563	8.50
Radio and TV	1.224	.011	.68
Spectator sports	1.574	.163	7.20
Private education	2.458	.769	2.42
Religious and welfare	1.142	−.352	2.49

[a]Most of these elasticities were derived directly from the Bureau of Labor Statistics data tape containing information on the expenditures of individual households. For some of the items, however, the data were not available on the tape. In these cases, the average expenditure for households in that income group was assigned from the printed tabulation in order to derive elasticities in this table. Consult the original for a complete explanation of this adjustment process.

[b]Based on 17 total expenditure classes.

[c]Based on 5 household size classes. One-person households were excluded because of extremely low expenditures in a number of item categories. The smallest household size on which these elasticities were based is a 2-person household; the largest is a household of 6 or more.

[d]The F-ratio was derived from an analysis of covariance in which the separate equations for the five household size classes were compared with the pooled regression. Each equation was based on 17 group means and had 2 parameters, yielding 15 degrees of freedom. The pooled regression was based on 85 group means and had three parameters, yielding 82 degrees of freedom. For $F(15,82)$ the 5 percent level is 2.15 and the 1 percent level is 3.00.

[e]F-ratios for private hospitals and new cars were not computed; it is evident from the small standard errors that they would be very large.

Source: Adapted by permission of the authors and publisher from H.S. Houthakker and Lester D. Taylor, *Consumer Demand in the United States: Analyses and Projections*, Cambridge, Mass.: Harvard University Press, 1970, pp. 255-265.

item and relative change in total expenditures. On an average, a family whose total is 1.000 percent higher than that of another family will spend .578 percent more for food than will the other family.

Private education, automobile purchases, and lodging away from home all had elasticity coefficients greater than 2.00. A large number of items were clustered in the 1.40-1.60 range. Included in this range were several recreation-related items (spectator sports, alcohol, and toys and sports equipment). Purchased meals might sometimes also be a recreation-related item. Three were related to housing (owned dwellings, furniture, and housewares), but most housing items were closer to 1.00 or below 1.00 (floor coverings and blankets, household appliances, household cleaning supplies), and two had extremely low coefficients (utilities and rented dwellings). Housing in the sense of shelter averaged out slightly above 1.00 (1.04), with owned housing and lodging away from home showing a higher coefficient and rented housing a very low coefficient. Household operation, furnishings, and equipment as one group were slightly below 1.00 (.92). The only inferior good indicated in Table 5.5 is farm-produced food.

The major group elasticities show the important areas in which an expenditure growth is likely to come as family incomes increase: transportation (automobile purchases in particular), recreation, and housing (owner-occupied housing in particular). The least growth is likely to occur in food and tobacco. Whether or not the elasticity for medical expenditures remains at its low level of .70 will probably depend on public policy and the responsiveness of suppliers and consumers of medical services to changing needs and opportunities. If medical service is made available to all as needed, it will show little expenditure elasticity.

VARYING (MULTIPLE) EXPENDITURE ELASTICITIES

The expenditure elasticities in Table 5.5 are constant (single) elasticities. These are accurate so long as the appropriate estimating function for the data is a double logarithmic function. If, however, there is a curvilinear relationship between total expenditures of various families and their expenditures for specific items, a single elasticity coefficient does not accurately reflect the response of families to changes in their total expenditure level.

Table 5.6 offers an opportunity to explore these elasticities more carefully to determine whether it is correct to assume that the elasticity is the same at all income levels, or whether it is more appropriate to think in terms of varying elasticity coefficients as income level varies. The elasticities shown in this table for families at different income levels are very crude, for they are merely arc elasticity coefficients calculated from the weighted means for ten income classes. Nevertheless, they give additional insight into the

Table 5.6 Elasticity of Expenditure of Urban Families and Single Consumers at Various Income Levels in the United States for Specific Goods and Services with Respect to Total Consumption Expenditures, 1960-1961[a]

Money Income After Taxes	Total Expenditures for Current Consumption	Food			Tobacco	Alcoholic Beverages
		Total	Prepared at Home	Away from Home		
						Elasticity Coefficient
Under $1,000	$ 1,307					
	)	1.222	1.524	−0.215	1.379	2.520
$ 1,000-$ 1,999	1,770					
	)	0.882	0.757	1.501	1.339	1.205
2,000- 2,999	2,675					
	)	0.724	0.672	0.940	1.046	1.635
3,000- 3,999	3,716					
	)	0.887	0.930	0.712	0.852	1.359
4,000- 4,999	4,501					
	)	0.914	1.115	0	0.735	0.834
5,000- 5,999	5,240					
	)	0.816	0.633	1.631	0.682	1.397
6,000- 7,499	6,229					
	)	0.960	0.780	1.647	0.423	1.103
7,500- 9,999	7,534					
	)	0.698	0.493	1.337	−0.062	1.287
10,000- 14,999	9,744					
	)	0.643	0.421	1.168	0.396	0.971
15,000 and over	1 4,475					

Table 5.6 cont.

Money Income After Taxes	Housing								Clothing, Clothing Services
	Total	Shelter				Fuel, Light, Refrigeration, Water	Household Operations	House Furnishings, Equipment	
		Total	Rented Dwelling	Owned Dwelling	Other				
			Elasticity Coefficient						
Under $1,000	0.862	0.658	1.007	0.103	-3.322	0.777	1.315	1.533	1.798
$ 1,000-$ 1,999	0.677	0.627	0.502	0.900	1.637	0.499	0.789	1.147	1.667
2,000- 2,999	0.745	0.506	0.461	0.533	1.674	0.475	1.042	1.590	1.294
3,000- 3,999	0.728	0.569	-0.013	1.645	1.586	0.826	0.677	1.193	1.965
4,000- 4,999	0.984	0.817	-0.549	2,580	1.532	1.109	0.823	1.511	1.105
5,000- 5,999	0.901	0.778	-1.455	2.314	2.900	0.654	1.074	1.251	1.252
6,000- 7,499	0.723	0.591	-0.037	0.845	1.376	0.652	0.964	0.846	1.409
7,500- 9,999	0.908	0.740	-0.529	1.000	2.704	0.570	1.088	1.018	1.241
10,000- 14,999	1,219	1.151	0.244	2.382	2.264	0.687	1.009	0.966	1.082
15,000 and over									

Money Income After Taxes (Under $1,000)	Personal Care	Medical Care	Recreation	Reading	Education	Transportation — Total	Transportation — Automobile	Transportation — Other Transportation	Other Expenditures
					Elasticity Coefficient				
Under $1,000) $1,000-$1,999	1.485	0.507	0.805	1.072	-3.797	1.397	2.314	0.195	0.332
$1,000-$1,999) 2,000-2,999	1.267	1.053	1.577	0.893	1.637	2.040	2.404	1.091	0.427
2,000-2,999) 3,000-3,999	0.869	0.676	1.582	0.818	1.784	2.195	2.522	0.604	0.800
3,000-3,999) 4,000-4,999	0.670	0.226	1.474	0.977	0.872	1.839	2.026	0.449	1.083
4,000-4,999) 5,000-5,999	1.132	1.202	1.083	0.758	2.635	1.017	1.162	-0.372	0.552
5,000-5,999) 6,000-7,499	0.658	0.995	1.775	1.238	2.368	0.948	0.916	1.273	2.212
6,000-7,499) 7,500-9,999	1.022	0.872	1.361	0.850	1.905	1.241	1.216	1.477	0.939
7,500-9,999) 10,000-14,999	0.785	0.872	1.392	1.311	3.088	1.085	0.966	2.049	1.926
10,000-14,999) 15,000 and over	0.681	1.031	0.798	0.712	1.786	0.669	0.333	2.133	2.384

[a] Arc elasticity coefficients are computed by the formula

$$e_{c_i} = \frac{c_{ij} - c_{i(j-1)}}{c_{ij} + c_{i(j-1)}} \div \frac{c_{tj} - c_{t(j-1)}}{c_{tj} + c_{t(j-1)}}$$

in which e_{c_i} is the elasticity of the expenditure for item i with respect to total expenditure; c_{ij} and $c_{i(j-1)}$ are the total expenditures on all goods and services by income groups j and $(j-1)$, respectively; and c_{tj} and $c_{t(j-1)}$ are the total expenditures on all goods and services by income groups j and $(j-1)$, respectively.

Source: U. S. Bureau of Labor Statistics, *Survey of Consumer Expenditures, Urban United States, 1960-61*, BLS Report no. 237-38 (Washington, D.C.: GPO. 1964).

way consumers respond with respect to specific expenditures when there is a change in their total expenditure level. By combining this information on elasticity at different income levels with information about the average and marginal propensities to spend for various items, it is possible to group the items in the consumer budget into four categories. (See Table 5.7.)

1. *PRIMARY EXPENDITURES*. These are characterized by (1) a low single (average) expenditure elasticity and (2) a tendency for the APC, MPC, and elasticity to decline as income increases. These are items that are bought *first* in the sense that if income is low, these items take priority over others. They are also items for which *saturation* can set in fairly quickly. Included in this group are food at home, tobacco, personal care, and rented dwelling.

Payments for rental housing deserve special comment. Rental housing was an inferior good (service?) for families at income levels of $4,000 to $15,000. But for very high-income families—those with incomes greater than $15,000—it became a superior good again. Not only were the negative elasticities for rental housing in the $4,000-15,000 bracket accompanied by positive elasticites for owner housing, but by extremely high elasticities for owner housing in most income levels. It was within these brackets, and especially in the $5,000-7,500 bracket, that home ownership became extremely important. The shift in the rental elasticity coefficient from negative to positive at $15,000 income was probably due to the fact that where such families rented rather than owned housing it was a matter of preference or of the kind of housing available. High-income families that rent are most likely to do so in large metropolitan areas where multiunit housing makes ownership more difficult unless a cooperative or condominium arrangement is possible. It is clear that the reasons for renting were quite different among low-income families than among high-income families.

Although we normally think of food expenditures as showing the most sluggish growth with rising family income, it is interesting to observe the extent to which they did respond to changes in total expenditure level. In Table 5.4, for example, we can see that the highest-income group spent about $14,000 for all goods and services, which was about 12 times as much as the lowest-income group spent. Yet the food expenditures for home consumption by that average high-income family were 6 times as much as those of the lowest-income group. The expenditure elasticity for families between the $4,000 group and the $5,000 group was greater than 1.00. The break-even level for all expenditures occurred between $4,000 and $5,000, and it is clear that when this was reached families showed their eagerness to get more and/or better food.

2. *SECONDARY EXPENDITURES*. The second category of expenditures we show in Table 5.7 are for items with an average expenditure elasticity close to 1.00 (except medical care, .70) and with little evidence of a distinctive peak in elasticity. For the three items in this group—medical care, household operation, and reading—it appears that while elasticities differed at different income levels, they hovered fairly closely around the overall average elasticity, so that the relationships between total expenditure and expenditures for these items tended to be linear. Over time, medical care may move from this group into the primary group if medical services are made available to all irrespective of income, or if there are tendencies in that direction. Table 5.5 indicates that of the various medical services available, services of dentists were those most likely to be related to total expenditure level. Drugs and hospital expenses paid directly by the patient were least income sensitive.

3. *TERTIARY EXPENDITURES*. These are goods characterized by one dominant characteristic: Although expenditure for them expands as income increases, there appears to be a saturation achieved at some income level beyond which increased total expenditures cause increased expenditure for these items but not in proportion to the addditional rise in total outlay. For these goods, the marginal propensity to spend and expenditure elasticities rose up to a certain income level and then decreased as income continued to increase. Expenditure elasticities peaked at higher income levels than was true for primary expenditures.

Those items that are in group A include automobiles, house furnishings and equipment, alcoholic beverages, and clothing. For these, there was a major peak in elasticities at about the $3,000 or $4,000 level and a lesser peak at the $5,000-7,500 level. Group B includes household utilities, recreation, and food away from home, which had their principal peak in elasticity at the $5,000-7,500 level and a lesser peak at $2,000-3,000. These are products that meet physical needs, but they offer opportunities for expansion of consumption as income increases. If income rises, consumers eagerly buy more of these goods up to some point. For most of these items, the constant expenditure elasticity is greater than 1.00.

One item in group B seems somewhat out of place. Household utilities—fuel, light, refrigeration, and water—would, offhand, appear to fit better with the primary expenditures. For example, if we look at the average propensity to spend in Table 5.4, it fell considerably and almost consistently for this group of items. But the MPC peaked between $4,000 and $6,000. Rising family income between the $3,000 and $6,000 levels brought about a disproportionate increase in expenditures for this item. This could be associated with electrical needs of additional appliances; increased use of water for air conditioners, dishwashers, and clothes washers; and possibly more expensive fuels.

4. *QUATERNARY EXPENDITURES*. These expenditures are those for which demand continues to expand as family income increases. Most are double peaked, with one of the peaks at the highest or next-highest income level. They represent, therefore, those items for which there is a growing demand among families at higher income levels.

Items included in group A of the quaternary expenditures are those for which the highest elasticity peak occurred at about $5,000 or $6,000, with another peak occurring at the $10,000 or $15,000 income levels. This was characteristic of expenditures for owned dwelling and other shelter. Even though its primary peak occurred at the $10,000 income level, education is included in group A because its secondary peak was at $5,000, suggesting that there was not the unlimited expansion of expenditures beyond the $10,000 income level that characterizes items in group B. There was, in effect, a point of inflection below the highest income level beyond which expenditures for education did not continue to expand proportionately as much as they did up to that point. Group B includes items for which the highest elasticity occurred at the highest income level; there is no evidence of saturation of demand for these items, as is true of the tertiary expenditures. The two categories that meet this characteristic are "other" expenditures and "other" transportation. "Other transportation" includes all transportation except automobile purchases, operation, and maintenance. It would include such things as taxi fares, bus and trolley fares, airline and railroad travel, and car pools. "Other expenditures" include interest on personal loans, funeral expenses, legal expenses, bank service charges, money lost or stolen, allowances to children, all-expense tours, and any other nonallocable expenditures. There are within these categories considerable opportunities for increased physical consumption and more costly consumption.

Table 5.7 Classification of Expenditures by Urban Families and Single Consumers in the United States on the Basis of Income Elasticity at Different Family Income Levels, 1960-1961

Basic Pattern	Group and Item	Elasticity with Respect to Total Consumption Expenditure[a]	After-Tax Income Level at Which Elasticity of Expenditure[b] Was	
			Highest	Next Highest[c]
	PRIMARY			
	Food at home	.578	$ 1,000	$ 5,000
	Tobacco	.635	1,000	–
	Personal care	.832	1,000	5,000
	Rented dwelling	.433	1,000	–
	SECONDARY			
	Medical care	.697	(d)	(d)
	Household operation	.983	(d)	(d)
	Reading	.936	(d)	(d)
	TERTIARY			
	Group A:			
	Automobile	1.592[e]	3,000	–
	House furnishings, equipment	1.269[e]	3,000	5,000
	Alcoholic beverages[f]	1.541	3,000	7,500
	Clothing	1.021	4,000	6,000
	Group B:			
	Household utilities	.515	5,000	–
	Recreation	1.120	6,000	3,000
	Food away from home	1.400	7,500	2,000

c_p vs y; c_s vs y; c_t vs y

QUATERNARY

Group A:			
Owned dwelling	1.486	5,000	15,000
Other shelter	2.113	6,000	10,000
Education	2.458	10,000	5,000
Group B:			
Other expenditures	1.079^e	15,000	6,000
Other transportation	2.189^e	15,000	—

[a]Calculated from a double logarithmic function fitted to data for 17 expenditure classes except as indicated by footnote e. (See Table 5.5)

[b]Based on arc elasticity coefficients calculated from 10 urban income classes. (See Table 5.6) The income level indicated is the midvalue between the two expenditure levels used in calculating the arc elasticity coefficient.

[c]The criteria for identifying a "next highest" were as follows: (1) The income level had to be at least one class removed from that identified for the highest elasticity; (2) the elasticity coefficient in at least one of the income levels between the highest and next highest had to be lower than at each peak; and (3) the elasticity coefficient at the next-highest peak had to be within 25 percent of that at the highest peak.

[d]Although there was some variation in elasticity coefficients at different income levels, for all of the products in this group the elasticities were very nearly the same at several income levels. It would be misleading to identify any one income level as conspicuously higher than all others. Therefore the table does not indicate either a point of highest elasticity or the several points at which elasticities were high and nearly equal.

[e]Calculated from a double logarithmic curve fitted to the weighted means for 10 urban income classes.

[f]The elasticity between the two lowest income groups was excluded in classifying this item.

Source: Tables 5.5 and 5.6 and calculations based on data from which these tables were compiled.

With owner-occupied housing, income over a period is more likely to be a relevant factor in determining the type and quantity of housing consumed and the family's willingness to spend for it. Margaret Reid has found, in fact, that there is a very high income elasticity in housing expenditures when something that approaches the "permanent" income concept is used in place of short-term income, which usually shows very low income sensitivity.[8]

Owner housing was a tertiary good for those families that actually owned their own homes, but a quaternary good for families as a whole. The latter was due to the fact that the incidence of ownership increased as family income rose. Housing as a whole (owner *and* rental) was almost a secondary good, as evidenced by the relatively stable elasticity coefficients in Table 5.6 for all income levels up to $15,000 and the constant elasticity coefficient of 1.04 in Table 5.5.

MULTIPLE EXPENDITURE ELASTICITIES: ANOTHER VIEW

In order that we can see more clearly the kinds of adjustments consumers make in their expenditure patterns as their income varies, we have "collapsed" the nine elasticity coefficients for each product in Table 5.6 to a total of five by averaging each of the first four pairs for successively higher income levels and retaining the coefficient for income levels of $10,000 or more. This is a very crude type of adjustment, but it reduces the variability at various income levels sufficiently to show the direction of change more sharply. The results of this are shown in Table 5.8. In Figure 5.2, the collapsed elasticity coefficients are graphed according to the primary, secondary, tertiary, and quaternary expenditure classes that we have described; in Figure 5.3, they are graphed according to five important categories.

From a marketing point of view, we can say that as families move through different income levels in their family life cycle their expenditure patterns will not remain the same. Moreover, as the average income rises and the portion of the total population in higher-income groups increases, expenditure patterns will change. Not all products will share proportionately in rising incomes.[9] Quaternary expenditures contain more *proportionate* growth potential than other expenditures. The elimination of poverty would probably affect tertiary expenditures the most, for this would put a larger portion of the population in what is now the "middle"-income groups, where sensitivity to income level is particularly great for the several items of this type.

Expenditure Elasticities and Product Quality

One of the methods by which consumers adjust to changes in income is to shift to different price lines. Higher and lower price lines are likely to be positively associated

---

[8] See Margaret Reid, "Capital Formation in Residential Real Estate," *Journal of Political Economy* 66 (April 1958): 131-153, and "Comments," in Friend and Jones, op. cit., vol. I, pp. 474-476. See also Richard F. Muth, "The Demand for Non-Farm Housing," in Arnold C. Harberger, ed., *The Demand for Durable Goods* (Chicago: University of Chicago Press, 1960), pp. 29-96.

[9] Note the difference between sharing "equally" and sharing "proportionately." The comparative size of the APC for different products shows the extent to which different expenditures share (equally or unequally) in a *given* income. The comparative size of the MPC for different products shows the extent to which different expenditures share in a given *increase or decrease* in income. The

with higher and lower quality and, in this sense, may be regarded as entailing "more" or "less" of the good quantitatively. The use of aggregate expenditure data, and even the use of dollar aggregates of family expenditure data, may conceal important information about quantities consumed.

PRICE VARIABILITY

For some products the price variability in a given market permits considerable adjustment to be made to differences in income according to the price lines. For example, in one study in a midwestern city it was found that the highest price line for women's and misses' dresses available in 22 department and specialty stores was 30 times that of the lowest price line.[10] Price data reported by Consumers Union for 1965 and 1966 showed that infants' blanket sleepers ranged in price from $2.50 to $10.00; men's dress slacks from $9.50 to $40.00; 8mm movie cameras from $37.95 to $225.75; compact phonograph systems from $189.95 to $459.00; washing machines from $178.88 to $339.95; clothes dryers from $138.88 to $300.00; kitchen blenders from $16.95 to $49.99; and finishing sanders from $15.95 to $39.95.[11] Therefore one way for consumers to adjust to changes in income level is to change the price line, and presumably the quality, of the product they purchase. Quality is not, however, perfectly correlated with price line and must be examined as a separate variable.

QUALITY ELASTICITY

In Table 5.9 we show the results of an interesting attempt to estimate quality elasticity for various food products. P. S. George and G. A. King used the 1965 survey of consumers' food purchases to make estimates of quality elasticity.[12] They had information about family income, dollar expenditures for various food products, and the quantities purchased of each. From these data, it was possible to determine the elasticity of dollar expenditure for various food products with respect to income and also the quantity elasticity with respect to income. They then assumed that the expenditure elasticity was the sum of the quantity elasticity and the quality elasticity. Elasticity coefficients for quality were therefore imputed by subtracting the quantity elasticity from the expenditure elasticity. The results of their study are of interest from the viewpoint of both fact and method.

Of the 43 products, 13 showed negative expenditure elasticities, indicating that these

---

comparative size of the income elasticity coefficient shows the extent to which different expenditures share proportionately in a 1 percent change in income. (In our calculations, of course, we use an expenditure elasticity coefficient instead of an income elasticity coefficient, and this shows the extent to which different expenditures share proportionately in a 1 percent change in total expenditures.)

[10] Mary Ellen Roach, "Problems of Sizes of Women's Ready-Made Dresses as Reflected in Alteration Costs," M. S. thesis, Iowa State College, 1948, p. 23.

[11] *Consumer Reports* 30 (March, May, November 1965): 116, 126-127, 234, 546, and 31 (June, August, September, October 1966): 273, 387, 432, 448, 480, 488-489.

[12] P. S. George and G. A. King, *Consumer Demand for Food Commodities in the United States with Projections for 1980*, Giannini Foundation Monograph no. 26 (Berkeley: University of California, Division of Agricultural Sciences, Giannini Foundation of Agricultural Economics, 1971), p. 74. Their cross-sectional data were obtained from U.S., Department of Agriculture, Agricultural Research Service, *Household Food Consumption Survey 1965-66*, Reports 1-5 (Washington, D.C.: GPO, 1968).

Table 5.8 Expenditure Elasticities at Different Income Levels for Urban Families and Single Consumers in the United States as Evidenced by Collapsed Arc Elasticity Coefficients of the Expenditure for Particular Items with Respect to Total Expenditures, 1960-1961[a]

	Income Level[b]								
Less Than $3,000		$2,000-5,000		$4,000-7,500		$6,000-15,000		$10,000 or more	
Item	e_{ij}	Item	e_{ij}	Item	e_{ij}	Item	e_{ij}	Item	e_{ij}
Automobile	2.36	Automobile	2.27	Education	2.50	Education	2.50	Owned housing	2.38
Alcohol	1.86	Other housing	1.63	Owned housing	2.45	Other housing	2.04	Other expenditures	2.38
Clothing	1.73	Clothing	1.63	Other housing	2.22	Other transportation	1.76	Other housing	2.26
Personal care	1.38	Reac	1.53	Recreation	1.43	Food away	1.49	Other transportation	2.13
Tobacco	1.36	Recreation	1.50	Home furnishings and equipment	1.38	Other expenditures	1.43	Education	1.79
Home furnishings and equipment	1.34	Alcohol	1.39	Other expenditures	1.38	Recreation	1.38	Food away	1.17
Recreation	1.19	Home furnishment	1.33	Clothing	1.18	Clothing	1.33	Clothing	1.08
Food at home	1.14	Education	1.09	Alcohol	1.12	Alcohol	1.20	Medical care	1.03
Education	1.08	Owned housing	0.95	Medical care	1.10	Automobile	1.09	Household operation	1.01
Household operation	1.05	Tobacco	0.94	Automobile	1.04	Reading	1.08	Alcohol	0.97
Reading	0.98	Other expenditures	0.90	Reading	1.00	Household operation	1.03	Home furnishings and equipment	0.97
Medical care	0.78	Reading	0.86	Household operation	0.95	Home furnishings and equipment	0.93	Recreation	0.80
Rented dwelling	0.75	Household operation	0.83	Personal care	0.90	Owned housing	0.92	Reading	0.71
Food away	0.64	Food away	0.80	Fuel, light, refrigeration	0.88	Personal care	0.90	Fuel, light, refrigeration	0.69
Other transportation	0.64	Food at home	0.77	Food at home	0.87	Medical care	0.87	Personal care	0.68
Fuel, light, refrigeration	0.61	Personal care	0.65	Food away	0.82	Food at home	0.64	Food at home	0.42
Owned housing	0.50	Fuel, light, refrigeration	0.53	Tobacco	0.71	Fuel, light, refrigeration	0.61	Tobacco	0.40
Other expenditures	0.38	Other transportation	0.45	Other transportation	0.45	Rented dwelling	0.29	Automobile	0.33
Other housing	-0.84	Medical care	0.22	Rented housing	-1.00	Tobacco	0.18	Rented dwelling	0.24
		Rented dwelling							

[a]The "collapsed" expenditure elasticities given in this table are an average of the two expenditure elasticities for each successive pairs of income groups and are calculated by averaging the elasticity coefficients in Table 5.6. For example, in Table 5.6 the first two elasticity coefficients for automobiles are 2.314 and 2.404. The first of these is the expenditure elasticity for income groups under $1,000 and $1,000-1,999, and the second is for income groups of $1,000-1,999 and $2,000-2,999. The average of these is (4,718/2), or 2.359. Because of the crudeness of the data and of this approach, we have rounded this to 2.4 in reporting the "collapsed" (or averaged) expenditure elasticity. Income levels included in the calculation of this coefficient were all those less than $3,000. The next collapsed coefficient for automobiles represents the average of the two expenditure elasticities in Table 5.6 for income levels $2,000-2,999 and $3,000-3,999, and income levels $3,000-3,999 and $4,000-4,999. The elasticities in Table 5.6 are 2.522 and 2.026, respectively, which average out to 2.3 (4.548/2 = 2.274). This method of averaging accounts for the fact that the overlap in the income levels is twice as much as for those in Table 5.6.

[b]Note that the elasticity coefficients are elasticity of expenditure for a specific item with respect to total expenditures for all items, while the families and single consumers are grouped by income level rather than total expenditure level.

Source: Calculated from Table 5.6.

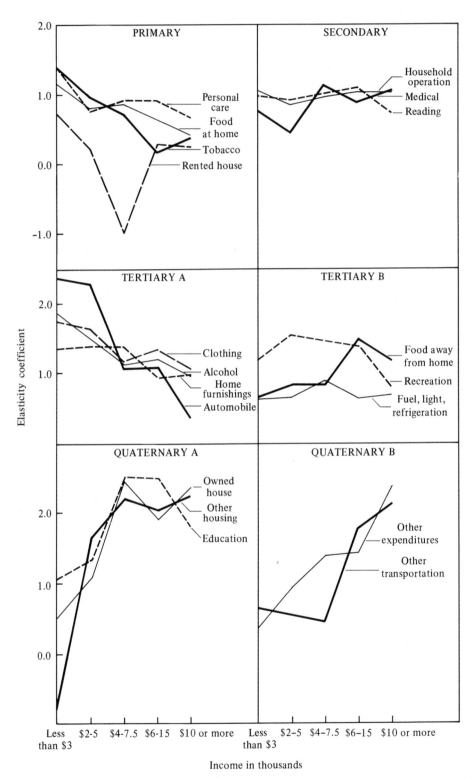

Figure 5.2. Expenditure elasticities at different family income levels for consumer goods and services based on collapsed arc elasticity coefficients. Source: Table 5.8.

were inferior goods. The items were eggs, lard, shortening, evaporated milk, sweet potatoes, sugar, corn syrup, dry fruits, fresh beans, dry vegetables, wheat flour, rice, and corn meal. Apparently shortening, however, was not an inferior good, because the quantity elasticity was positive, indicating that if the income of a family were 10 percent higher, the amount of shortening consumed would be nearly 3 percent greater. For all the other inferior items, however, both quantity and expenditure elasticities were negative.

The imputed quality elasticities raise some interesting questions. Some of them seem strange. For 12 of the items, the so-called quality elasticity is negative. This would suggest that families with higher incomes bought lower qualities of these items. On the other

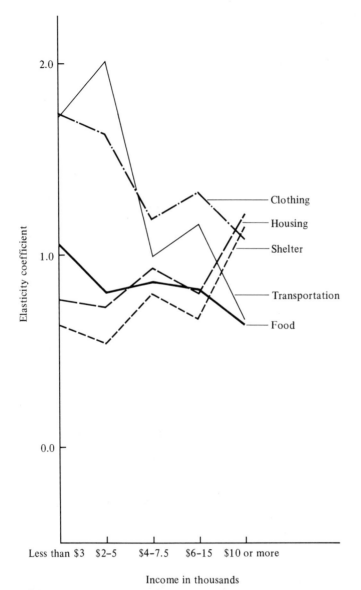

Figure. 5.3. Expenditure elasticities at different family income levels for five major groups of goods and services based on collapsed arc elasticity coefficients. Source: Calculated from Table 5.6.

Table 5.9 Elasticities of Expenditure, Quantity, and Quality for Food Products with Respect to Family Income, 1965

Product	Elasticity with Respect to Income of		
	Expenditure	Quantity	Quality[a]
Beef	.380	.270	.110
Veal	.698	.551	.147
Pork	.130	.008	.122
Lamb and mutton	.576	.591	−.015
Chicken	.056	−.034	.090
Fish	.140	−.060	.200
Turkey	.869	.768	.101
Eggs	−.016	−.072	.056
Butter	.274	.269	.005
Lard	−1.236	−1.297	.061
Shortening	−.040	.029	−.069
Margarine	.051	−.006	.057
Salad dressing	.401	.284	.117
Fresh milk	.349	.367	−.018
Evaporated milk	−.640	−.610	−.030
Cheese	.241	.227	.014
Ice cream	.335	.323	.012
Potatoes	.036	.016	.020
Sweet potatoes	−.293	−.504	.211
Sugar	−.178	−.169	−.009
Corn syrup	−.569	−.706	.137
Apples	.207	.142	.065
Oranges	.192	.227	−.035
Bananas	.140	.135	.005
Canned peaches	.009	.012	−.003
Canned pineapples	.475	.408	.067
Dry fruits	−.037	−.031	−.006
Fresh tomatoes	.278	.161	.117
Fresh beans	−.431	−.481	.050
Onions	.022	.005	.017
Carrots	.268	.313	−.045
Lettuce	.348	.424	−.076
Canned peas	.110	.043	.067
Canned corn	.065	.054	.011
Canned tomatoes	.151	.165	−.014
Dry vegetables	−.641	−.818	.177
Frozen vegetables	.619	.577	.042
Wheat flour	−.611	−.631	.020
Rice	−.319	−.605	.286
Breakfast cereals	.195	.056	.139

Table 5.9 continued

Product	Elasticity with Respect to Income of		
	Expenditure	Quantity	Quality[a]
Corn meal	−1.013	−1.059	.046
Coffee	.011	.047	−.036
Soup	.228	.216	.012

[a]It is assumed that the expenditure elasticity is the sum of the quantity and quality elasticities. Therefore the quality elasticity in this column is imputed by subtracting the explicit quantity elasticity coefficient from the explicit expenditure elasticity coefficient.

Source: P. S. George and G. A. King, *Consumer Demand for Food Commodities in the United States with Projections for 1980,* Giannini Foundation Monograph no. 26 (Berkeley: University of California, Division of Agricultural Sciences, Giannini Foundation of Agricultural Economics, 1971), p. 73.

hand, for most items the quality index, as indicated by this procedure, produced meaningful positive values. For example, beef showed an expenditure elasticity of .380, meaning that if a family's income were 10 percent higher than the average, let us say, its expenditures for beef would be 3.8 percent greater. More than two-thirds of this increased expenditure (.270/.380) was for greater quantity and less than one-third for better quality. With fish, however, the expenditure elasticity was only .140. With a rise in income the quantity of fish purchased declined, but the quality increased substantially more than the amount spent.

In order to see if this imputed quality index correlated with price, George and King made a second table in which they cross-tabulated the actual price differential between what high-income families and low-income families paid per unit for each of these food items (determined by dividing the family's expenditure by the quantity purchased) and the quality index in Table 5.9. The results showed clearly a positive relationship between the quality index and the price differential.[13]

QUANTITY-QUALITY ALTERNATIVES

An increase in income opens three possibilities for a consumer unit: a greater range of goods, more of previously consumed goods, and an "increase" in the quality of previously consumed goods, Dorothy Brady has described an interesting use of coefficients of income elasticity as a basis for selecting that point at which consumers shift from "more and more" and to "better and better."[14] This point is where a rising income elasticity coefficient ceases to rise and begins to decline.[15] The reasoning is that if the number of

---

[13] George and King, op. cit., p. 74.

[14] Dorothy S. Brady, "The Use of Statistical Procedures in the Derivation of Family Budgets," *The Social Service Review* 23 (June 1949): 141-157.

[15] This would occur where the second derivative of the estimating equation for income-expenditure relationship is equal to zero. In the case of the Bureau of Labor Statistics family budget study cited by Brady, this point was established from a more direct estimate of income elasticities based on the differences of the logarithms of quantities purchased at different income levels relative to the differences of the logarithms of income. Since these ratios showed clearly an increase and then a decrease with rising income, the maximum was determined at the point where lines fitted to the rising and falling segments intersected. Ibid.

units purchased rises more rapidly than income, it reflects an "eagerness" to consume that has been latent until income permitted. When the display of "eagerness" slows, it can be interpreted as an indication that a certain level of satiety has been achieved. Beyond this point, the increase in dollar expenditures may continue to rise very rapidly, but units purchased do not increase so rapidly as consumers shift their emphasis from quantity to quality.

This adjustment process is illustrated in a study by Arthur Okun, in which he compared new passenger car registrations as reported by R. L. Polk with stated intentions to purchase made by spending units in the *Surveys of Consumer Finances*. With number of new cars as the dependent variable, r^2s of .40, .49, and .38 were obtained. In correlating the median planned expenditure with actual dollar expenditure, however, he obtained r^2s of .66, .67, and .66, indicating a closer relationship between planned dollar expenditures and actual expenditures than between planned number of units purchased and actual number purchased.[16]

Expenditure Variations Within an Income Group

A characteristic of expenditure patterns is their variation (and variance) for different families and for families of a given income level. Unfortunately this problem has not been explored to the degree that its importance would appear to warrant. One of the best of the studies is that of Ruth Mack, based on data for white wage and clerical workers for six large cities, 1934-1936. Her findings are given in Table 5.10. Approximately two-thirds of the families covered had total expenditures within about 33 percent of the mean for all families. For clothing expenditures the variance was even higher: About two-thirds of the families included had expenditures roughly ±63 percent of the mean, and for furnishings and equipment two-thirds fell within about ±137 percent of the mean. The items in column (1) have been arrayed from those with the lowest variation through those with the highest variation about the sample mean. In general, the more nearly essential expenditures had the lower coefficient of variation.

Obviously some of the variation observed in column (2) could have been accounted for by differences in income. Column (3) indicates the average coefficient of variation for each $300 income class; the average coefficient for all items was 17, meaning that about two-thirds of the families in each $300 income group deviated from the group mean by 17 percent. With two exceptions, the coefficients in column (3) increase as we go down the column. Even when we allow for different income levels, there is still considerable diversity in expenditures patterns about the mean for any given income group. In column (4), the difference between columns (2) and (3) is shown as a percentage of column (2), indicating the percentage by which the coefficient of variation in column (2) is reduced

---

[16] Arthur M. Okun, "The Value of Anticipations Data in Forecasting National Product," in *The Quality and Economic Significance of Anticipations Data*, Universities-National Bureau Committee for Economic Research (Princeton, N.J.: Princeton University Press, 1960), pp. 407-460. The estimating equations for units used the number of new passenger car registrations as the dependent variable. The first equation employed the fraction of spending units intending to buy a new car as the independent variable and was fitted to data for 11 periods. The second employed the fraction of spending units intending to buy any car as the independent variable and was also fitted to data for 11 periods. The third was the same as the second equation but was fitted to data for 13 periods. Unit sales were in millions. Dollar sales were derived by multiplying the proportions planning to buy by the median planned expenditure on new cars.

Table 5.10 Coefficients of Variation (V) of Money Disbursements of White Wage and Clerical Workers Averaged for Six Large Cities, 1934-1936

Item (1)	Coefficient		Percentage by Which V for Total Sample Is Reduced When Data Are Grouped by Income Class— (col. 3 − col. 2)/(col. 2) (4)
	For Total Sample (2)	Average for Each $300 Income Class (3)	
All items	33	17	48
Food	33	24	27
Housing	35	30	14
Personal care	55	43	22
Clothing	63	48	24
Recreation	75	61	19
Other household items	74	60	19
Surplus	101	83	18
Deficit	107	105	2
Transportation	108	91	16
Medical care	128	119	7
Furnishing and equipment	137	135	1
Other items	149	124	17
Gifts and contributions	172	142	17

Source: Based on data from Faith M. Williams and Alice C. Hanson, *Money Disbursements of Wage Earners and Clerical Workers in Eight Cities in the North Central Region 1934-36,* U.S. Bureau of Labor Statistics Bulletin 636, Table 24 (A and B), as given in Ruth Mack, "Economics of Consumption," ed. Bernard F. Haley, *A Survey of Contemporary Economics,* vol. II (Homewood, Ill.: Irwin, 1952), p. 44.

when income level is taken into account. While the variation in expenditures for all items was reduced 48 percent by taking into account income class, only one item—food—showed a reduction of more than 25 percent. The effectiveness of income in "explaining" the variation was particularly low for furnishings and equipment, medical care, and housing. It is obvious, therefore, that other factors, such as social relationships, individual values and tastes, the availability of purchasing power other than money income, and possibly supply conditions affected expenditure patterns.

There are some very important implications for marketing in these variations and variances. Averages can easily conceal aspects of demand that may represent market potentials for meeting demand more effectively. From a social point of view, the implications are also of considerable importance. Are consumers becoming more alike in their expenditure patterns, or are they diverging? One would expect greater divergence under affluence than under conditions in which incomes tend to be low, but is this the case? What is the effect of expenditure variances on economies of scale in production? We need a great deal more information, currently and historically, in order to determine the social impact of changes in demand over time and to formulate sound marketing policies.

International Comparisons of Expenditure Functions

Does the expenditure behavior observed in the United States hold for other countries, or do countries at different stages of economic maturity exhibit different expenditure patterns? Several studies made in recent years permit us to make some international comparisons, although comparisons involving studies of different periods must be interpreted with some care.[17]

Most of the studies involving international comparisons show similarities among various countries. Some of the principal findings are as follows:

1. The average expenditure elasticity for food is less than 1.0, confirming the validity of Engel's law. The range is substantial, however. H. S. Houthakker's summary shows an average elasticity coefficient of 0.731 for working-class families in Poland in 1927 and 0.344 for middle-class families in the United Kingdom in 1938-1939. U.S. elasticity coefficients appear to be high compared with those of other countries. This may be due to price influences in the coefficients, although this is not completely clear from the data.

2. Elasticities for clothing with respect to total expenditure are generally greater than 1.0 and less than 1.5.

3. Housing expenditures, including fuel and light but excluding furnishings and equipment, generally show expenditure elasticities less than 1.0, adding support to Schwabe's law. Differences are considerable, however, both between and within countries. Houthakker points out that the elasticity coefficient is highest in the United States for families living in suburbs and least for residents of large cities.

   Irving Kravis, however, finds some difficulty in discerning clear patterns of total expenditure-housing expenditure relationships and attributes this difficulty to the existence of rent control and to the problems of estimating equivalent rental values. He does, however, find a tendency for the rent as a ratio of total consumption expenditures to rise with real per capita consumption. Home expenses other than rent show considerable stability relative to total consumption expenditures, with only domestic services declining in relative importance as consumption rises.

4. Elasticity coefficients for all other expenditures as a whole are above 1.0, usually at a level greater than 1.4. It is interesting that it is in the Netherlands, Canada, and the United States that the "all other" category is less than 1.4. Houthakker attributes this to the fact that transportation, which shows considerable sensitivity to income levels in other countries, is probably regarded as more of a "necessity" in the United States and Canada.

Houthakker summarizes his findings of empirical expenditure relationships as follows:

> ... if no data on the expenditure patterns of a country are available at all, one would not be very far astray by putting the partial elasticity with respect to total expenditure at .6 for food, 1.2 for clothing, .8 for housing, and 1.6 for all other items combined.[18]

---

[17]See H. S. Houthakker, "An International Comparison of Household Expenditure Patterns, Commemorating the Centenary of the Engel's Law," *Econometrica* 25 (October 1957): 532-551; Faith Williams, "International Comparisons of Patterns of Family Consumption," in Lincoln Clark, ed. *Consumer Behavior: Research on Consumer Reactions* (New York: Harper & Row, 1958), pp. 270-307; Irving Kravis, "International and Intertemporal Comparisons of the Structure of Consumption," in ibid., pp. 308-337; Colin Clark, *The Conditions of Economic Progress* (London: Macmillan, 1951), pp. 350-394.

[18]Houthakker, op. cit., p. 550.

These are derived from equations that also include family size as a variable.

Kravis examines the influence of price on consumption patterns by comparing two countries with different price levels at two periods of time. Coefficients of rank correlation suggest that from one-third to one-half of the variance in ranks of the quantity ratios is accounted for by prices alone. If this is correct, we must, in analyzing secular and intermarket differences in expenditure patterns, recognize that supply, and hence price, may be one important determinant of expenditure patterns. The evidence available suggests, however, that for broad categories of consumer spending international comparisons can be made and show similarities in expenditure behavior between countries.

OTHER VARIABLES IMPORTANT IN MICRO EXPENDITURE FUNCTIONS

Thus far in this chapter we have sketched very broadly the patterns of relationship between family expenditures for goods and services and total family expenditures for all goods and services. Family expenditures have also been related to such things as income, family size, stage in the family life cycle, age of head, age of children, number of wage earners, debt, assets, race, education, occupation, and residence (urban, rural, etc.). In general, it has been found that the ability of income to explain expenditures is greatest when it is considered alone, and that its explanatory power declines as the number of additional variables increases. This suggests that income serves as a proxy for other factors when those other factors are not included in the analysis. Age of family head and education, for example, are correlated with income.

Although most studies show that income, or total expenditure, is the most important single variable in explaining family expenditures for most commodities, it is seldom sufficient to explain even one-half of the variance in expenditures of different families. H. S. Houthakker and Lester Taylor found, for example, in their principal components analysis of the 1960-1961 survey data, that the most important component, which they identified as total family expenditures, was able to explain 27 percent of the total variance in specific family expenditures.[19] It appears that variables other than income are important in "explaining" interfamily differences in consumption expenditures. From the list of determinants that we have presented, we shall discuss three: demographic characteristics of the family, number of earners, and family assets.

Demographic Characteristics

Size of family (or spending unit), family life cycle, and ages of family members have been found to be related to family expenditures. In his discussion of family expenditures, Engel introduced family size as a relevant variable and invented the term *quet* (after Quételet, a Belgian statistician whose work Engel admired) to describe the value of food consumed by a child less than one year old, from which equivalent adult values could be determined. Age of family members and stage in the family life cycle had long been recognized by sociologists as relevant in studies of family behavior but were incorporated into economic and market analyses nearer the middle of the 20th century. The

---

[19] Houthakker and Taylor, op. cit., pp. 225-259.

1935-1936 studies of consumer expenditures were the first empirical surveys to include detailed information about family types and stages in the family life cycle. Janet Fisher, Dorothy Brady, John B. Lansing, and James N. Morgan were among the pioneers in the analysis of age and life cycle in relation to family expenditures.[20] Franco Modigliano and R. E. Brumberg, in their pioneering study that preceded publication of Friedman's permanent income hypothesis, employed the concept of "total life resources" rather than current income in their analysis of expenditures.[21]

FAMILY SIZE

Houthakker and Taylor incorporated family size in their estimating functions for various family expenditures. Their findings are particularly useful because their estimating function also included total consumption expenditures, which made it possible to isolate the effect of family size with the effect of total expenditures removed.[22] Their findings are summarized in Table 5.5.

There are several interesting facts about these elasticities. One is their relatively small size compared with the total expenditure elasticities, indicating that interfamily differences in expenditure are more closely related to interfamily differences in total consumption expenditures than they are to family size. Another fact is that expenditures for housing, house furnishings, medical care, transportation, and religious and welfare purposes are negatively related to family size. This appears to be a result of the strong pressure that family size puts on the budget for food, clothing, and educational expenditures, and especially for food, since this is the largest item of expenditure. The only family size elasticity greater than 1.00 is that for farm food. This is one means by which farm families can increase their real income without increased expenditures in the market.

The relationship between family size and expenditures is important in analyzing the market demand for specific items, especially when there are changes in the birthrate and, hence, in the distribution of families by size. Between 1940 and 1973, for example, the average population per family in the United States declined from 3.76 to 3.48. Average population per household declined even more—from 3.67 to 3.01—as a result of the undoubling that occurred and the creation of more households headed by primary

---

[20] The volume in which some of the first empirical studies appeared was Lincoln H. Clark, ed., *Consumer Behavior*, vol. II, *The Life Cycle and Consumer Behavior* (New York: New York University Press, 1955). See also Janet Fisher, "Income, Spending, and Saving Patterns of Consumer Units in Different Age Groups," in *Studies in Income and Wealth*, vol. XV (New York: National Bureau of Economic Research, 1962), pp. 75-102, and Dorothy S. Brady, "Influence of Age on Saving and Spending Patterns," *Monthly Labor Review* 78 (November 1955): 1240-1244.

[21] Franco Modigliani and R. E. Brumberg, "Utility Analysis and the Consumption Function: An Interpretation of Cross Section Data," in K. K. Kurihara, ed., *Post-Keynesian Economics* (New Brunswick, N.J.: Rutgers University Press, 1954), pp. 388-436. Some empirical tests of the permanent income and life cycle hypotheses appear in Franco Modigliani and Albert Ando, "The 'Permanent Income' and the 'Life Cycle' Hypothesis of Saving Behavior: Comparison and Tests," in Friend and Jones, op. cit., vol. II, pp. 49-174, and "Tests of the Life Cycle Hypothesis of Savings," *Bulletin of the Oxford University Institute of Statistics* 19 (May 1957): 99-124.

[22] This is important because income (hence, total consumption expenditure) increases as family size increases up through families of six. In 1970 for example, median income for families of increasing size was: two, $7,786; three, $9,997; four, $11,167; five, $11,501; six, $11,513; seven or more, $10,619. U.S., Bureau of the Census, "Income in 1970 of Families and Persons in the United States," *Current Population Reports*, ser. P-60, no. 80 (Washington, D.C.: GPO, 1971), p. 40.

Table 5.11 Clothing Expenditures per Urban Person by Age and Sex in the United States, 1960-1961

| Age Group[a] | Males | | Females | | |
| | Amount | Percentage of Lowest Age Group | Amount | Percentage of | |
				Lowest Age Group	Males of Same Age Group
2 to 5	$ 67	100	$ 74	100	110
6 to 11	104	154	115	155	111
12 to 15	144	213	187	253	130
16 to 17	173	257	247	334	142
18 to 24	185	273	255	345	138
25 to 64	169	250	212	287	126
65 and over	77	114	98	132	127

[a]Average expenditure for boys and girls under 2 years of age was $38.

Source: Ann Erickson, "Clothing the Urban American Family: How Much for Whom?" *Monthly Labor Review* 91 (January 1968): 16.

individuals rather than head of family.[23] If in the years ahead the declining size of family continues, this alone could have a substantial effect on the demand for specific products.

AGE

It is well known that there are substantial differences in demand according to the age of the potential user. Demand analysis for perambulators, elementary textbooks, baseball bats, household appliances, automobiles, bifocals, dentures, and hearing aids all show patterns related to the age of consumers. This would affect original (new) demand as well as the time at which replacement (of durables) occurs.

One of the items for which age variables are particularly important is clothing. In Table 5.11 clothing expenditures per urban consumer in 1960-1961 are shown for males and females in different age groups. The elasticity of demand with respect to age is particularly high for females between the ages of 12 and 24. Clothing expenditures per person for both men and women is lowest before the age of 6 and at the age of 65 or more.

Table 5.11 is, however, deceiving in one respect. We have classified per person clothing expenditures by age and sex, not taking into account income or any other variables that might enter into the picture. As the age of the head of household increases, the income tends to increase up to age 45 or 55.[24] The presence of 16-year old sons and daughters in the household is likely to begin when the head is about 40.[25] Therefore the increase in

[23]U.S., Bureau of the Census, "Household and Family Characteristics: March 1971," *Current Population Reports*, ser. P-20, no. 233 (February 1972), p. 1.

[24]In 1970 median income was related to age of family head as follows: 14-24 years, $7,037; 25-44, $9,853; 35-44, $11,410; 45-54, $12,121; 55-64, $10,381; 65 and over, $5,053. U.S., Bureau of the Census, "Income in 1970 of Families and Persons in the United States," pp. 33-35.

[25]The median age at the first marriage in 1970 was 23.2 years for men and 20.8 years for women. U.S. Bureau of the Census, *Statistical Abstract of the United States: 1971*, 92d ed. (Washington, D.C.: GPO, 1971), p. 60.

clothing expenditures by individuals in their late teens is related to *both* the increase in family income and the changing pattern of preferences. Clothing is, of course, only one of many items that show age-related preference patterns.

STAGE IN THE FAMILY LIFE CYCLE

A refinement of the age variable that has been quite useful in consumer demand analysis is stage in the family life cycle. This can be a fairly simple stratification of families according to age of head and number of children, or it can be a much more complicated intermixture of marital status, age of adults, number of children, and age of children. This could be arrived at through a multivariate analysis or, as in Table 5.12, through the clustering of families by stages that are assumed to represent meaningful demarcations between different preference patterns.

In Table 5.12 is shown the extent to which families at different stages in the family life cycle deviated from the average family in their expenditures for durables over a 4-year period. The unadjusted deviation is the percentage of income spent for durables by the average family in that stage from the mean expenditure of 8.4 percent for all families. The adjusted deviation is the difference between the percentage of income spent by the average family in that group from the mean after adjustment has been made for the income effect. The adjusted deviation therefore has the effect of holding income constant.

It is clear that the highest expenditure occurs among young married families and, within that group, among young married families with no children. There is, however, a secondary peak for families whose youngest child is 6 or more. This is probably a replacement demand, reflecting the wearing out of household durables as the children grow older.

Both family income and family needs vary through the family's life cycle but not by the same amounts at each stage. Consumption rises secularly as the family matures, but the rise in consumption levels is not necessarily steady. Income, on the other hand, rises rapidly, peaks when the age of the head is 45-60, and then declines rapidly. Needs tend to exceed purchasing power when the family is young, and dissaving through the use of consumer credit is likely to be highest for newly established households. During the years of later middle age when family income is highest and the pressure of growing family demands has begun to subside, savings are likely to be positive and large. Dissaving recurs after the age of 65 through asset liquidation and dissolution. Note, for example, in Table 5.12 the tremendous impact of stage in family life cycle on the amount of instalment debt relative to income. The mean for all families was 10.0 percent, while the adjusted mean for young families with no children was 12.2 percent, declining to 7.6 percent for husband-wife families with no children at home.

Number of Earners

The increase in the number of working women in families has had a considerable effect on family income. In the course of two decades, from 1950 to 1970, the percentage of married women who were living with their spouse and who were gainfully employed outside the home increased from less than 25 percent to more than 40 percent. Most wives who work do it because they find it necessary to do so if they are to maintain the level of consumption that they believe is necessary or to achieve a higher level than they would otherwise have.[26] In 1966, among families in which both husband and wife were present and working the median family income was $9,200. In families where the wife did not work it was $7,100.[27] Wives who worked full time contributed 37 percent of the family income. The higher the family income up to $15,000, the greater the probability that the wife was employed.

There is, however, another side to the coin, and that is the effect of the presence of two wage earners in a family on family expenditures. In 1960-1961, total food expenditures differed little between one- and two-worker urban families, with the two-worker family spending more away from home and less at home than the one-worker family. The two-worker family spent less for shelter and medical care and more for clothing and transportation. Home furnishings expenditures were about the same for both.[28] These comparisons conceal some of the differences between the two families in terms of number of children, age of children, and stage in the family life cycle. Wives are more likely to work before they have children or when the children are older. These effects would show in the family expenditures. However, some of the differences are associated with the life style of two-employee families.

Assets

LIQUID ASSETS

We have already made some comments about cross-sectional differences in family expenditures associated with liquid assets. The largest expenditures on durables occur among those whose liquid assets have increased slightly during that period or decreased substantially. The amount of liquid assets owned by a family is positively related to income, age, and education. A family whose head was under 45 years of age was much more likely to have an instalment debt (a negative liquid asset) than one with an older head. Also, the incidence of instalment debt in 1970 was greatest among those with incomes of $10,000 to $15,000, although three or four years before that the incidence was highest for those in the $5,000-7,500 group.[29] But a single-variable approach to this

---

[26] In one survey women were asked to state the most important reason why they took a job. Of the married women, 42 percent indicated that it was "financial necessity," 17 percent said that they wanted "to earn extra money," and 7 percent indicated that their husbands had lost their jobs. These different "reasons" are ambiguous. If we combine them, we can say that two-thirds of working wives indicated that they worked because of their need or desire for the income. Not quite 20 percent indicated that it was primarily for their own personal satisfaction. The others gave assorted reasons: They had finished school, there was a change in the family's status, someone offered them a job, and the like. Carl Rosenfeld and Vera C. Perrella, "Why Women Start and Stop Working: A Study in Mobility," U.S. Bureau of Labor Statistics, Special Labor Force Report no. 59 (Washington, D.C.: U.S. Department of Labor, 1965).

[27] U.S., Department of Labor, Women's Bureau, "Working Wives—Their Contribution to Family Income," release, November 1968.

[28] Based on U.S., Bureau of Labor Statistics, *Consumer Expenditures and Income, 1960-61*, BLS Report 237-38, supp. 2, pt. A, (Washington, D.C.: GPO, 1966) pp. 73-74.

[29] George Katona, Lewis Mandell, and Jay Schmiedeskamp, *1970 Survey of Consumer Finances* (Ann Arbor: University of Michigan, Institute of Social Research, Survey Research Center, 1971), pp. 19-33, 95-122.

Table 5.12 Deviation of Proportion of Income Spent on Major Durables from Proportion for Sample Mean and Deviation of Ratio of Outstanding Instalment Debt to Income from Ratio for Sample Mean Among Families Classified by Life Cycle Attributes, 1966-1969

Group	Deviation of Proportion of Four-Year Income Spent on Major Durables from Proportion for Sample Mean[a]			Deviation of Ratio of Outstanding Instalment Debt to Four-Year Income from Ratio for Sample Mean[b]		
	Number of Families	Unadjusted Deviation[c]	Adjusted Deviation[c]	Number of Families	Unadjusted Deviation[d]	Adjusted Deviation[d]
Stage in Family Life Cycle[e]						
Young, single	58	0.0	-1.3	63	.1	-2.4
Young, married, no children	84	1.8	1.6	85	2.1	2.2
Young, married, youngest child under 6	412	.3	.3	409	1.9	1.7
Young, married, youngest child 6 or older	208	.6	.6	207	1.4	1.3
Older, married, children at home	266	.1	.2	267	-1.0	-.7
Older, married, no children at home	212	-.5	.1	210	-3.0	-2.4
Older, single	82	-2.4	-2.0	84	-3.9	-2.9
Any age, single, with children	84	-1.7	-2.0	84	-.2	-1.0
Major Change in Life Cycle						
Got married	48	1.6	3.2	54	4.2	5.6
Became single	54	-1.5	-1.6	57	.5	.5
Last child left home	71	.8	.7	70	.1	1.0
No children to having children	44	2.1	.2	44	2.2	-.7
More than one change in marital status	21	1.1	1.5	21	.5	1.4
No major change	1168	-.1	-.1	1163	-.3	-.3

[a]The dependent variable is the percentage of four-year income spent on major durables. The mean of the dependent variable was 8.4. The dependent variable was regressed on average annual income (not shown in this table), stage in family life cycle, and major change in life cycle. The R^2 was .057. There were 1406 families in the major durables expenditure analysis. They had 1406 families for whom they had sufficient data to make the major durables analysis and 1409 families for the instalment debt analysis.

[b]The dependent variable is the ratio (in percent) of outstanding instalment debt to four-year income. The mean of the dependent variable was 10.0. The dependent variable was regressed on average annual income (not shown in this table), stage in family life cycle, and major change in life cycle. The R^2 was .091. There were 1409 families in the instalment debt analysis.

[c]Unadjusted deviations are univariate subgroup means expressed as deviations from the sample mean of 8.4. The adjusted deviations are dummy variable regression coefficients simultaneously adjusted for income level. In the equations by which adjusted deviations were calculated, the sample mean of the dependent variable, 8.4, was the constant term.

[d]Unadjusted deviations are univariate subgroup means expressed as deviations from the sample mean of 10.0. The adjusted deviations are dummy variable regression coefficients simultaneously adjusted for income level. In the equations by which adjusted deviations were calculated, the sample mean of the dependent variable, 10.0, was the constant term.

[e]"Young" is less than 45 years of age; "old" is 45 or more years of age.

Source: Gary Hendricks, Kenwood C. Youmans, and Janet Keller, *Consumer Durables and Installment Debt: A Study of American Households* (Ann Arbor: University of Michigan, Institute for Social Research, Survey Research Center, 1973), pp. 55, 60 © 1973 by the University of Michigan.

kind of analysis is very deceiving. If the effect of stage in the family life cycle is held constant, the incidence of outstanding instalment debt is greatest for those with an income of $5,000-5,999, but with those in the $8,500-9.999 group showing nearly as great a debt volume.[30]

In a few cross-sectional studies, liquid assets have been found to be useful in analyzing family expenditures, especially durables but also nondurables in some cases.[31] However, until we are able to ferret out the reasons why people hold liquid assets—that is, the consumer's perception of his assets as a reserve for contingencies, for future consumption, or for unanticipated opportunities—the relationship between liquid assets and expenditures will not be clearly established.

HOUSEHOLD STOCKS

Nonliquid assets can be very useful in studying cross-sectional expenditure patterns, but they are often not used because we do not have good data on a cross-sectional basis. Only recently have we begun to get a time series on consumer holdings of durables. If families can be identified as owners or nonowners, and if we can know something about the size and condition of the stock held by individual families, then this information could be incorporated into the family expenditure function. The presence of a durable—such as a car—would suggest two possibilities. If it is in good condition, it may preclude another purchase until it needs replacement. On the other hand, its ownership by a family may indicate that family's tendency to acquire such goods and suggest further pruchases. This is the Houthakker-Taylor stock of goods-stock of habit dichotomy, which we shall discuss in the following chapter.

DISTRIBUTION OF ASSETS

A study of consumers' wealth on a cross-sectional basis was sponsored by the Board of Governors of the Federal Reserve System in 1962.[32] One of the useful findings of this survey was the degree of inequality in the holding of wealth by consuming units and the patterns of expansion that were followed as wealth of a household increased. Inequality in the distribution of wealth among consuming units is shown in Figure 5.4, which is adapted from one presented by Dorothy Projector and Gertrude Weiss. The left axis indicates the percentage of consuming units that held less than the amount of wealth indicated on the horizontal axis, and the numbers on the right indicate the percentage of spending units at or above the wealth level indicated. For example, about 60 percent of the consuming units had up to $10,000 wealth, and about 40 percent had $10,000 or more. Wealth as defined in this study included homes, automobiles, businesses or professions, liquid assets (checking and saving accounts and U.S. savings bonds),

---

[30] Gary Hendricks and Kenwood C. Youmans, *Consumer Durables and Instalment Debt: A Study of American Households* (Ann Arbor: University of Michigan, Institute for Social Research, Survey Research Center, 1973), p. 60.

[31] See, for example, Janet A. Fisher, "Consumer Durable Goods Expenditures, with Major Emphasis on the Role of Assets, Credit and Intentions," *Journal of the American Statistical Association* 58 (September 1963): 648-657, and Pao L. Cheng, "Consumption of Nondurable Goods and Contractual Commitment of Disposable Income," *Review of Economics and Statistics* 45 (August 1963): 254-263.

[32] Dorothy S. Projector and Gertrude S. Weiss, *Survey of Financial Characteristics of Consumers*, Federal Reserve Technical Paper (Washington, D.C.: Board of Governors of the Federal Reserve System, 1966).

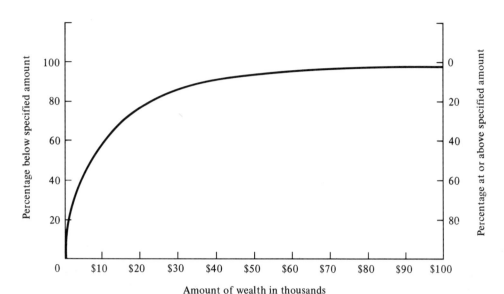

Figure 5.4. Distribution of consumer units by amount of wealth, December 31, 1962. Source: Dorothy S. Projector and Gertrude S. Weiss, *Survey of Financial Characteristics of Consumers,* Federal Reserve Technical Paper (Washington, D.C.: Board of Governors of the Federal Reserve System, 1966), p. 6.

investment assets (mainly marketable securities, investment real estate, and mortgages), and a miscellaneous group consisting largely of assets held in personal trusts. From the total value of these items was subtracted a consuming unit's debts that were secured by any of the designated assets.

ELASTICITIES OF OWNERSHIP

Table 5.13 shows the elasticities of ownership for specific items of wealth with respect to total wealth. In the Federal Reserve study three elasticities were calculated, of which we have taken two. The first one, $E_{1(y, w)}$, is a constant elasticity calculated from a simple double logrithmic function with specific wealth (y) as a function of total wealth (w). The third function in their study, which is the other one we give in Table 5.13, is also a constant elasticity and is a combination of two components. The first component, $E_{31(p, w)}$, reflects the impact of the growth in the proportion of consuming units that own that kind of wealth. The second component, $E_{32y(H), w(H)}$, reflects the effect of the growth in the value of ownership of that particular asset.

The two items among the five wealth components identified that are of particular importance in marketing are owned homes and automobiles. Note the relatively low elasticities for automobiles, reflecting the fact that most will tend to own one. As age increases up to 65, most heads of households apparently put their money into better automobiles or more frequent replacement. The desire for better housing is strongest among the youngest heads and weakens as age increases. Liquid assets show a relatively low elasticity, increasing slightly as age increases.

NEED FOR ASSET ANALYSIS

This type of approach to demand analysis is very badly needed. We need to know more about what people own and how they add to and subtract from those assets. Durable

Table 5.13 Elasticities of Wealth Components at the Point of Mean Wealth by Age of Head of Consuming Unit

Wealth Component	$E_{1\,(y,\,w)}$	$E_{3\,(y,\,w)} = E_{3\,1\,(p,\,w)} + E_{3\,2\,y\,(H),\,w(H)}$
		Head under 35
Own home	1.47	$1.02 = .14 + .88$
Automobile	.41	$(a) = (a) + .37$
Business, profession	1.68	$1.73 = .83 + .90$
Liquid assets	.73	$.70 = .03 + .67$
Investment assets	1.18	$1.46 = .56 + .90$
		Head 35-54
Own home	1.18	$.75 = (b) + .75$
Automobile	.44	$.41 = .02 + .39$
Business, profession	1.39	$1.72 = .72 + 1.00$
Liquid assets	.78	$.70 = .02 + .68$
Investment assets	1.43	$1.65 = .57 + 1.08$
		Head 55-64
Own home	.91	$.63 = (b) + .63$
Automobile	.47	$.44 = .09 + .35$
Business, profession	1.53	$1.63 = .61 + 1.02$
Liquid assets	.83	$.74 = .01 + .73$
Investment assets	1.17	$1.61 = .53 + 1.08$
		Head 65 and over
Own home	.97	$.55 = (b) + .55$
Automobile	.56	$.64 = .26 + .38$
Business, profession	1.62	$1.67 = .50 + 1.17$
Liquid assets	.79	$.82 = .08 + .74$
Investment assets	1.82	$1.87 = .67 + 1.20$

[a]Not available.

[b]Value between −.005 and +.005.

Source: Dorothy S. Projector and Gertrude S. Weiss, *Survey of Financial Characteristics of Consumers,* Federal Reserve Technical Papers (Washington, D.C.: Board of Governors of the Federal Reserve System, 1966), p. 83.

goods are obvious candidates for study along these lines, and cross-sectional analysis of ownership and of changes in ownership would enrich our marketing data in a way that would make possible new insights into the patterns that emerge from consumers' choices. F. G. Pyatt did some pioneering work in formulating an approach to this kind of problem in his study of priority patterns for durables.[33] Until recently we have had little data on

[33]F. G. Pyatt, *Priority Patterns and the Demand for Household Durable Goods,* University of Cambridge, Department of Applied Economics, Monograph no. 11 (Cambridge: Cambridge University Press, 1964).

consumers' holdings of various durables. If quarterly surveys of consumer stocks of various durables, such as that contained in *Consumer Buying Indicators*, a discontinued publication of the U.S. Bureau of the Census,[34] could be continued and supplemented with additional information from specialized studies, such as the now outdated but thorough study of clothing inventories by Margaret Brew,[35] we might begin to make consumer stocks a more meaningful source of information for consumer demand analysis.

Concluding Note

We have by no means exhausted all the possibilities for finding variables to include in our estimating functions. We have not even touched upon the more complex but important problem of whether we want to settle for a single equation or whether we should seek a system of equations that will enable us to involve more variables, and more sets of the relationships that lie behind or enter into market relationships. We have, however, enumerated some of the other influences, or proxies for influences, that are appropriate to use in specific situations—occupation, education, attributes of one's place of residence, race, social class. These are used extensively and with varying degrees of success. As is true with the demographic variables we have discussed, most of these are proxies for what we are really interested in knowing. We want some way to identify who will and who will not buy in terms of the probability of their doing so or not. Ideally we would like to have a way to probe the minds of consumers so that we could classify each correctly in terms of probable behavior. Lacking that, we shall probably continue to use the easy, conspicuous ways of identification if we succeed in establishing a significant relationship between the existence of these conspicuous characteristics and the buying behavior in which we are interested. The potential for creative research in this field is still enormous.

---

[34] The last issue was U.S., Bureau of the Census, "Consumer Buying Indicators," *Current Population Reports*, Series P-65, no. 46 (July 1973). The Bureau of the Census indicated at that time that it would "continue to collect data periodically on ownership and purchases" but would not continue to issue the *Survey of Consumer Buying Expectations*, which was part of the *Consumer Buying Indicators* series. The expectation series was based on consumers' stated buying intentions for the next six months. The series was terminated because of serious questions concerning the predictive value of the data.

[35] Margaret L. Brew et al., *Family Clothing Inventories and Purchases—With an Analysis to Show Factors Affecting Consumption*, U.S. Department of Agriculture, Agricultural Research Service, Household Economics Research Branch, Agriculture Information Bulletin no. 148 (Washington, D.C.: GPO, 1959).

6

Product and Service Demands: Mini Macro Consumption Expenditure Functions

Where the telescope ends, the microscope begins.
Which of the two has the grander view?

—Victor Hugo

In Figure 6.1 we have set forth some of the influences that are important in determining whether or not a market transaction takes place. At the top of the diagram we show the supply variables. The boxes that are double lined at the bottom and to the left of the diagram indicate the important demand factors. For each of the three major determinants of consumer demand—wants, consumption resources, and consumer knowledge—we have indicated its essential nature and the evidence, or proxies, that we use to estimate it. It is these that comprise the independent variables of the demand function.

One of the things that this diagram makes clear is the important role that human and subjective factors play in the structure of demand. While resources are important, both as means and constraints to consumption, choices about their utilization are greatly influenced by the structure of wants and preferences and by the consumer's perception of his needs and alternatives.

Many of the variables that we have used in the analysis of aggregate and family consumption expenditures are applicable in the analysis of specific demands. But because a specific good is one of a large variety of alternative products, its availability is a function of many production alternatives, and the demand for it is affected by demand alternatives. For these reasons, a variable may bear a unique relationship to expenditures for a particular product, and additional variables can often be useful in explaining commodity sales. We turn now to a consideration of the relevance of variables that we have already discussed to the demand for specific goods and services, and shall pay particular attention to new variables that bear a unique relationship to the demand for particular items.

THE BASIC DEMAND FUNCTION

At this point, it is appropriate to return to our basic demand function, introduced in Chapter 4, in order to see how it can be used to understand the attributes of consumer behavior with respect to specific goods and services. The function that we proposed and shall use is

$$C_i = f(Y, P_i, T_i, Q_i, A)$$

in which C_i is the consumption expenditure for item i; Y is purchasing power; P_i is the relative price of item i; T_i is consumer tastes or preferences for product i in relation to

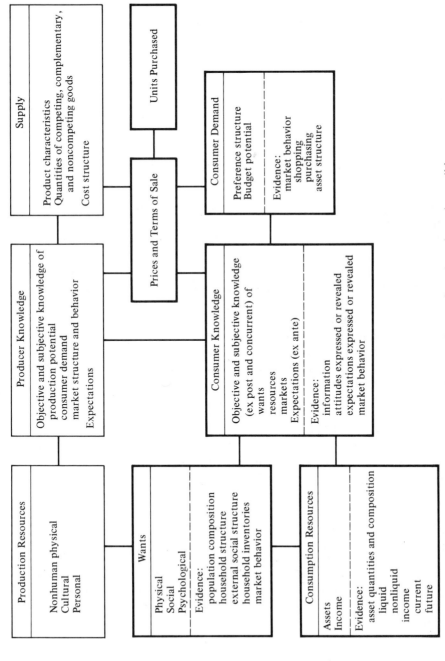

Figure 6.1. Selected factors that affect consumer purchases of a selected good, possible bases for their measurement, and their relationship to other market forces.

Table 6.1 Concepts and Measures of the Independent Variables in a Commodity Demand Function

PURCHASING POWER (Y)	PRODUCT QUALITY (ATTRIBUTES) (Q)

Income:
  Current disposable personal income (DPI)
Past Income:
  Income from previous period (s)
  Highest past income
Changes in income
Income distribution
Permanent (normal) income
Discretionary income
 	
Assets:
  Liquid assets
  Nonliquid assets
  Credit
	Product Itself ("Own" Attributes)
	Alternative Products
	
	─────────────
	Tastes (Preferences) (T)
	─────────────
	Diffusion
	
	Stocks:
	  Durables: physical stocks
	    New demand
	    Replacement demand
	  Nondurables psychological stocks (habits)

PRICES (P)	ATTITUDES (A)
Product Itself ("Own Price) **Competing (Substitute) Product (s)** **Complementary Products**	**Present Situation** **Expected Future Situation**

substitute and complementary items; Q_i is consumers' perception of the relative quality of product i, that is, its perceived attributes; and A is consumer attitudes and expectations. C_i can be thought of as an expenditure in monetary units, or it may be viewed as purchases in quantity units. These five variables are those that have a bearing on consumption expenditures. Our problem becomes that of trying to hypothesize about the nature of the relationship between each of these and expenditures for specific goods and of devising means of measuring each so that it can be incorporated into an estimating function if it is found to be relevant.

In Table 6.1 we have outlined the most important concepts or measures that have been developed for making each of these variables empirically viable. This is comparable to Table 5.1, in which the relevant variables for family expenditures are indicated. We shall, in the discussion that follows, examine a number of variables and show how they would theoretically be related to specific consumption expenditures. We shall also show in a number of cases the empirical evidence of their usefulness in explaining demand.

PURCHASING POWER

Most consumers derive most of the purchasing power that they exercise in a given period from the income flow during that or some previous period. For this reason, income has been found to be by far the most important of the purchasing-power variables. The other source of purchasing power is the reserves, or assets, that a consuming unit owns or can acquire through credit.

Income

We have reviewed the use of income in the aggregate consumption expenditure function and the use of income, or total consumption expenditures, in the Engle function, and have considered the relative merits of current income, past income, previous high income, changes in income, income distribution, and permanent income as alternative ways of viewing the income flow relevant to consumer spending. Each of these is also relevant to the demand for specific goods and services, and the choice of a particular income measure is of considerable importance in determining the usefulness of the resulting function. We shall concentrate in this discussion on two aspects of the income-expenditure relationship that are important in analyzing the demands for different types of products: (1) interproduct differences in expenditure elasticities and (2) the concept of discretionary purchasing power and its usefulness in analyzing the demand for certain types of products.

THE HOUTHAKKER-TAYLOR EXPENDITURE ELASTICITIES

We show in Table 6.2 the short- and long-run elasticity coefficients with respect to total expenditures for goods and services that were calculated by Houthakker and Taylor from national income time series data for the years 1929-1941 and 1946-1964. Several different models were employed in an attempt to get the best explanation of expenditure behavior over the span of years studied. It was found that a dynamic model that incorporated not only information about the current year but also information about previous years was particularly effective for a number of functions. The dependent variable was per capita personal consumption expenditure for the specific item in year t in 1958 dollars.

The functional relationships studied included these variables:

$$q_t = f(q_{t-1}, \Delta q_t, x_t, x_{t-1}, \Delta x_t, p_t, p_{t-1}, \Delta p_t)$$

with the following meanings:

q_t = per capita personal consumption expenditure for the item in year t in 1958 dollars

Δq_t = $q_t - q_{t-1}$

x_t = total per capita personal consumption expenditures in year t in 1958 dollars

Δx_t = $x_t - x_{t-1}$

p_t = relative price of item in year t (implicit price deflator for item divided by implicit price deflator for all consumption expenditures)

Δp_t = $p_t - p_{t-1}$

Occasionally a dummy variable was used to separate the pre-World War II period from the postwar period. Not all variables were used in the equations for all products. Where calculations using ordinary least squares indicated the presence of autocorrelation, a three-pass least squares method of estimating parameters was used. Frequently, however, the dynamic model made the three-pass least squares estimation unnecessary so that the ordinary least squares was employed.

From these equations, it was possible to determine short- and long-run values for the marginal propensity to consume, elasticity of expenditure with respect to total

Table 6.2 Short- and Long-Run Elasticity of Consumption Expenditures for Specific Items with Respect to Total Expenditures for All Items, United States, 1929-1941, 1946-1969

Item	Elasticity with Respect to Total Expenditures	
	Short-Run	Long-Run
Airline travel	5.87	—
New cars & net purchases of used cars	5.46	1.07
Radio & television receivers, records and musical instruments	4.20	2.99
Expenditures in U.S. by foreign residents	3.71	—
Gas (household utility)	3.11	—
Elementary & secondary education	2.77	—
Other intercity transportations	2.71	—
Furniture	2.60	.53
Semi-durable house furnishings	2.23	.65
Higher education	2.15	—
Other durable house furnishings	2.09	1.18
Domestic services	1.89	—
Religious and welfare expenditures	1.85	—
Expenditures abroad by U.S. Govt. personnel (military & civilian)	1.73	—
Books and maps	1.67	1.42
Purchased meals (excluding alcoholic beverages)	1.61	—
Space rental value of tenant-occupied housing	1.53	—
Stationery	1.52	1.83
Commercial participant amusements	1.42	1.91
Tires, tubes, accessories, and parts	1.40	1.93
Wheel goods, durable toys, sports equipment, boats & pleasure aircraft	1.37	3.72
Other professional services	1.33	—
Ophthalmic products & orthopedic appliances	1.29	1.39
Pari-mutuel receipts	1.28	2.28
Other housing	1.27	—
Other recreation	1.21	2.15
Kitchen & other household appliances	1.18	—
Expense of handling life insurance	1.16	—
Taxicabs	1.15	—
Clothing, including luggage	1.14	.51
Rental value of farm houses	1.13	—
Flowers, seeds, and potted plants	1.03	3.32
Jewelry and watches	1.00	1.64
Cleaning & polishing preparations, and miscellaneous household supplies & paper products	.99	1.66

Table 6.2 continued

Item	Elasticity with Respect to Total Expenditures	
	Short-Run	Long-Run
Other clothing, accessories, etc.	.95	1.17
Shoes and other footwear	.94	—
Automobile repair, greasing, washing, parking, storage, and rental	.94	.90
Clubs & fraternal organizations, except insurance	.87	5.44
Water	.87	.59
Barbershops, beauty parlors, & baths	.87	1.36
Net personal cash remittances to foreign countries	.86	1.20
Motion pictures	.81	3.41
Other fuel and ice	.75	—
Legitimate theater and opera	.74	1.26
Street & electric railway and local bus	.72	1.38
Medical care & hospitalization insurance	.69	2.02
Other personal business expenditures	.69	—
Food furnished government (including military) and commercial employees	.68	1.03
Funeral and burial services	.65	—
Clothing unkeep and laundering in establishments	.65	—
Radio and television repair	.64	5.20
Drug preparations and sundries	.62	3.04
Services furnished without payment of financial intermediaries	.62	1.07
Nondurable toys	.59	2.01
Other household operation	.56	1.27
Gasoline and oil	.55	1.36
Shoe cleaning and repairs	.52	.72
Food purchased for off-premise consumption (excluding alcoholic beverages)	.50	.71
China, glassware, tableware & utensils	.47	.77
Legal services	.43	—
Bank service charges, trust services, and safe-deposit-box rental	.40	—
Newspapers and magazines	.38	—
Dentists	.38	1.00
Private hospitals & sanitariums	.37	3.71
Auto insurance premiums, less claims paid	.37	1.26
Other educational expenditures	.35	1.13
Telephone, telegraph, & wireless	.32	—
Alcoholic beverages	.29	.62

Table 6.2 continued

	Elasticity with Respect to Total Expenditures	
Item	Short-run	Long-Run
Physicians	.28	1.15
Toilet articles and preparations	.25	3.74
Foreign travel by U.S. residents	.24	3.09
Tobacco products	.21	.86
Intercity bus	.17	1.89
Bridge, tunnel, ferry, and road tolls	.17	4.48
Electricity (household utilities)	.13	1.94
Space rental value of owner-occupied housing	.07	2.45
Spectator sports	.05	1.07
Food produced and consumed on farms	− .67	−
Brokerage charges & investment counseling	−2.96	−

Source: Adapted by permission of the authors and publisher from H.S. Houthakker and Lester D. Taylor, *Consumer Demand in the United States: Analyses and Projections*, Cambridge, Mass.: Harvard University Press, 1970, pp. 161-163, 166-167.

expenditure, and price elasticity for most (but not all) items. One of the most useful values that could be determined from these equations was a stock coefficient, which we shall discuss later in considerable detail.

In Table 6.2 commodities and services have been arrayed according to the short-run expenditure elasticities. In a number of cases it was not possible to calculate the long-run expenditure elasticity, either because a static model was used or because the assumptions underlying the function did not indicate a long-run adjustment different from the short-run adjustment. Note in this table the items that had extremely high short-run expenditure elasticities:

Transportation, travel, automobiles
Airline travel, new and used cars, tires and tubes, other intercity transportation, taxicabs

Home furnishings
Radio and TV, furniture, semi- and other durable housefurnishings, kitchen and household appliances

Education
Elementary and secondary, higher, books and maps

Recreation
Purchased meals, participant amusements, sports equipment, parimutuel, other recreation

If we also consider additional items that had quite high long-run expenditure elasticities, the list would be expanded to include the following:

Transportation, travel, automobiles
Foreign travel, tolls, intercity bus

Home furnishings

Radio and TV repair, flowers and plants, household supplies, electricity

Recreation

Clubs and fraternal organizations, motion pictures, sports equipment, other recreation, nondurable toys, commercial participant amusements

Medical

Drugs, private hospitals, medical care and hospital insurance

As would be expected, food purchased for off-premise consumption showed low coefficients for both the short and long run. Clothing showed moderate elasticity in the short run (1.14) and a much lower value for the long run (.51). Housing is quite mixed, reflecting a moderately high elasticity for rental housing in the short run (1.53), which hardly seems plausible. Perhaps this was influenced by postwar developments in the rental market. Owner-occupied housing, however, shows almost no sensitivity to the short-run changes in total expenditures (.70) but a substantial sensitivity to long-run changes (2.45), which seems reasonable.[1] House furnishings as a group showed fairly high elasticities in the short run but much lower coefficients in the long run. Generally, durable goods had higher expenditure elasticities than did nondurables or services.

Table 6.3 presents similar data for 11 broad groups of commodities. The 81 items in Table 6.2 are combined in Table 6.3 in terms of their functional relationship.

Were we to generalize about Tables 6.2 and 6.3, we could say that the unmet desires of consumers in the United States appear in the short run to be

Strongest for	*Moderately strong for*	*Least strong for*
Automobiles, travel, transportation	Clothing	Food
Education	Accessories	Tobacco
Home furnishings and equipment	Personal care	Personal business services
Recreation		Alcohol
		Medical care

In the long run, however, unmet desires appear to be

Strongest for	*Moderately strong for*	*Least strong for*
Radio, TV, recreation	Automobiles	Clothing
Medical care	Accessories and personal care	Transportation
Owner-occupied housing	Personal business services	Food
Toilet articles		Alcohol
		Tobacco

Where both short- and long-run elasticities could be established, the long-run coefficient was generally greater than the short-run coefficient, suggesting that in these cases the responsiveness was subject to a considerable time lag. In a few cases (e.g., clothing,

---

[1] It is important to note that owner-occupied housing "expenditures" in the national income accounts, from which these elasticities were determined, is the imputed rental value of owner-occupied housing. It does not include maintenance costs or new housing construction except to the extent that such expenditures are reflected in the value of housing quarters occupied in a given year.

Table 6.3 Stock Coefficients and Short- and Long-Run Coefficients of Price Elasticity and of Elasticity of Expenditure with Respect to Total Consumption Expenditures for 11 Major Commodity Groups, United States, 1929-1941, 1946-1964[a]

| | | Elasticity of Expenditure with Respect to | | | |
| | Beta | Total Expenditure | | Price | |
Group	Coefficient	Short-Run	Long-Run	Short-Run	Long-Run
Automobiles and parts	−.6128	5.06	1.07	−	−
Furniture and household equipment	−.3992	2.23	1.49	−	−
Other durable goods	.5512	.88	2.27	−.56	−1.45
Food and beverages	.0225	.72	.85	−	−
Clothing and shoes	−.1710	1.20	.35	−	−
Gasoline and oil	.3236	.48	1.69	−.14	−.48
Other nondurable goods	.1483	.81	1.18	−	−
Housing	1.0229	.12	1.68	−.05	−.66
Household operation[b]	.0869	.62	5.53	−.39	−3.44
Transportation	.2097	.41	.47	−.82	−.95
Other services	.2687	.53	.94	−	−

[a]Based on a state-adjustment model.

[b]Presumably this group would include cleaning and polishing preparations, miscellaneous household supplies and paper products, stationery, utilities, telephone and telegraph, and domestic services. The long-run elasticity coefficient of 5.53 seems unduly high. This may have been due to the high long-run coefficients for cleaning supplies (1.66), stationery (1.83), and electricity (1.94). Household gas had a very high short-run elasticity of 3.11. But none of these alone could account for a long-run elasticity for the group greater than 5.00. The coefficients for this group when expenditures were related to income rather than total expenditures are .32 and .33 for the short and long run, respectively (Houthakker and Taylor, p. 190). The latter two figures seem far more reasonable.

Source: Adapted by permission of the authors and publisher from H.S. Houthakker and Lester D. Taylor, *Consumer Demand in the United States: Analyses and Projections*, Cambridge, Mass.: Harvard University Press, 1970, pp. 186-187.

furniture), the short-run elasticity was greater, indicating that short-term adjustments to total expenditure changes were made for these products but no comparable once-for-all long-run adjustment.

DISCRETIONARY INCOME

In a pioneering study of the demand for automobiles made during the late 1930s, Charles Roos and Victor von Szeliski introduced the concept of "supernumerary income," which they used as the income variable in their estimating equation. This was defined as that portion of disposable income left over after meeting "necessitous living costs."[2] It was calculated by subtracting from an estimate of disposable income an amount that it was estimated would be adequate to cover necessary living costs, using the value of $200 per capita per year for 1923 as the base and adjusting this by the National Industrial Conference Board index of the cost of living for other years.

[2]Charles F. Roos and Victor von Szeliski, "Factors Governing Changes in Domestic Automobile Demand," in General Motors, *The Dynamics of Automobile Demand* (New York, 1939), pp. 21-95.

Since the work of Roos and von Szeliski, the Conference Board (formerly the National Industrial Conference Board) has developed and publishes at regular intervals measures of "discretionary purchasing power," "discretionary saving," and "discretionary spending." Through these measures, the Conference Board is attempting to provide income variables that would be more useful than disposable personal income in explaining consumption expenditures, particularly those for durable goods and "luxuries" that might be dispensable under certain circumstances but highly attractive expenditure outlets under other circumstances.[3] The relationship among the principal concepts with which they deal are described as follows:

Disposable Personal Income

+ net household credit
+ credits from government insurance
+ other adjustments

= Aggregate Consumer Purchasing Power

  − net contractual saving
  − essential expenditures
  − fixed commitments
  − imputed income and income in kind

= Discretionary Purchasing Power

  − discretionary saving

= Discretionary Spending

The idea is to construct an income series that will delete relatively stable expenditures that are considered basic by most families so that the residual income will reflect more closely what consumers regard as that portion of income not committed to more or less regular expenditures. This adjustment process is detailed in Table 6.4.

The most controversial component of this adjustment process is the "essential" expenditure category. To define what is "essential" requires some measure of what consumers conceive as "adequate" or "essential." We do not know what the social consensus on this is. Therefore the Conference Board devised a procedure for arriving at a rough estimate of this that would include an adjusting standard to reflect rising standards associated with rising levels of consumption. For food and clothing it used the average per capita consumption during the preceding three years in real units, converted into current year values based on prices for the current year, and into total current year expenditures based on the population for the current year. In order to avoid a negative essential outlay in any year in which, in the process of cyclical adjustment, consumers spent less than the average of the preceding three years, the Conference Board used the expenditure for the current year as the minimum standard. Transportation expenses incurred for getting to and from work and for medical purposes were regarded as "essential."[4]

---

[3] Morton Ehrlich, "Discretionary Spending," Technical Paper no. 17 (New York: The Conference Board, 1966).

[4] The estimate by the Bureau of Public Roads for 1963 shows that 44 percent of total vehicle miles traveled was for earning a living, while travel for social purposes was about 37 percent of total mileage. The other 19 percent would be for shopping and for education, civic, and religious activities. U.S., Bureau of Public Roads, Public Roads (December 1963), as quoted in Ehrlich, op. cit., p. 17.

Table 6.4 The Conference Board Method of Estimation of Aggregate Consumer Purchasing Power, Discretionary Purchasing Power, and Discretionary Spending from Disposable Personal Income

Principal Component and Additions or Deletions	Detail
Disposable Personal Income	
+ Net household credit (mortgage, consumer, bank, other)	Net change in all forms of household credit (mortgage, consumer, bank, other)
+ Credits from government insurance	Credits from government life insurance and retirement funds
+ Other adjustments	Capital gains dividends paid by investment funds to households
= *Aggregate Consumer Purchasing Power*	
− Net contractual saving	Household payments into public and private life insurance and pension equities less benefit receipts
− Fixed commitments	Home ownership expenses (taxes, interest, insurance) Tenant rent Health and accident insurance Auto liability insurance Interest paid by consumers Personal transfer payments to foreigners
− Imputed income and income in kind	Food furnished employees Proprietors' income Standard clothing issued to military personnel Employees' lodging Imputed net rent of owner-occupied nonfarm dwellings Services furnished by financial intermediaries without compensation
− Essential expenditures	Deducted in full: Medical care, excluding health insurance, and death expenses Household utilities (electricity, gas, water, other fuels, ice) Telephone and telegraph Maintenance and repair of owner-occupied housing Legal services Tobacco Deducted in part as indicated: Food—Annual expenditure per capita during the three preceding years adjusted for changes in prices and population (if

Table 6.4 continued

Principal Component and Additions or Deletions	Detail
	expenditure so calculated is greater than that incurred in the given year, the given year expenditure is used)
	Clothing—Annual expenditure per capita for purchased clothing and footwear (not jewelry, accessories or maintenance) during the three preceding years adjusted for changes in prices and population
	Transportation
	Local transportation:
	streetcars, local buses, railway commutation not taxicabs)
	User-operated transportation (new cars, net purchases of used cars, tires, tubes, accessories, parts, auto repair, greasing, washing, parking, storage, rental, tolls—bridge, tunnel, ferry, road—auto insurance premiums less claims paid): proportionate share of total mileage estimated by Bureau of Public Roads which was for "earning a living" and "medical purposes"
Discretionary Saving—Discretionary Purchasing Power	
	Changes in household holdings of demand deposits and currency, savings, accounts, credit and equity market instruments (corporate stock, U.S. Government securities, corporate and foreign bonds, and mortgages)
	Net financial investment in noncorporate businesses
– Discretionary Spending	

Source: The Conference Board (formerly National Industrial Conference Board), *Discretionary Spending,* Technical Paper no. 17 (Washington, D.C.: The Conference Board, 1966).

It is clear that there are many problems in arriving at an estimate of what consumers might generally regard as "discretionary purchasing power." Some of the decisions that the Conference Board made in arriving at this estimate are necessarily arbitrary, reflecting its judgment as to how best to deal with an income concept not amenable to quantification given the kind of income data available. The expenditures that are included in "discretionary spending" are those for liquor, that part of food expenditures in excess of calculated "essential" amounts, that part of clothing expenditures in excess of the calculated "essential" amount, all jewelry, watches, and miscellaneous clothing services, personal care, transient hotels and motels, residential construction, furniture and house furnishings, personal business (brokerage charges, bank service charges, employees' payments to unions and associations, expenses of handling life insurance), transportation not covered by the "essential" categories, recreation, private education and research, religious and welfare activities, foreign travel, and plant and equipment purchases by nonprofit organizations (which the national income accounts include under the personal expenditure category).[5] These are the expenditures that one would expect to be most closely related to the discretionary purchasing power as calculated in this series. Most of these are durable goods and a selected group of services.

Discretionary purchasing power is much more volatile from quarter to quarter and year to year than aggregate consumer purchasing power. In spite of the crudeness of its estimation, it is probably a more useful series to employ in analyzing expenditures for durables, where the consumer has a greater range of options in terms of choosing when he will make a given purchase, and certain services, which consumers may regard as more easily dispensable when income constraints are greatest.

Assets

In our discussion of the aggregate consumption-expenditure function, we pointed out the ambiguity in the possible relationships of assets to consumption expenditures. Assets may be an indication of purchasing power. They may also be an indication of willingness or unwillingness to spend. They can, in addition, be an indication of the need to spend or not to spend. We wish to view assets at this point *only* as a source of purchasing power. We shall consider the second and third possibilities when we discuss the role of consumer stocks.

LIQUID ASSETS

It is reasonable to believe that some consumers might spend more willingly if they have liquid assets to draw upon, or if the presence of liquid assets makes them more willing to use current income for purchases rather than saving. Where liquid assets have been included in consumer demand functions, they have most often been used in analyzing the demand for consumer durables. There is not very much clear evidence that the size of liquid assets, or changes in liquid assets, are related to expenditures for durables in any significant way. Some evidence, however, has appeared in cross-sectional data showing expenditure patterns of families with different asset positions.

CREDIT

The other asset variable of possible importance in consumer spending is credit. In terms of aggregate expenditures it appears that consumer credit does not have very much influence. The net change in the total amount of credit outstanding in any one year is the difference between the amount extended and the amount repaid. Although this net amount has tended to be positive for a number of years, it is usually a small amount relative to the total amount of consumer disposable income. In the sale of automobiles, however, consumer credit is particularly important. In 1969, for example, only 39 percent of the families buying household durables used credit, while 66 percent of new

---

[5] Ibid., pp. 23-26.

car purchasers and 45 percent of used car purchasers used instalment or other credit.[6] In his demand function for automobiles, Daniel Suits deflated his price variable by the average number of months for which credit contracts ran on automobile purchases.[7]

The other market in which credit is of tremendous importance is housing. Use of some kind of credit variable is almost essential in structuring a demand function for new housing construction and for used housing. The amount of down payment, the interest rate, and the length of amortization period are all significant influences. Interest rates are generally a less powerful determinant than down payment requirements and amortization period. Interest rates interact with the down payment requirements and amortization period to determine the size of the monthly payment, and it is this that probably has the greatest impact on cunsumer decisions to buy new or used housing. Since housing purchases usually entail the accumulation of equities, "buying" decisions in this market are only partially consumption expenditures. They are more saving than spending to the extent that the monthly mortgage payment exceeds the imputed rental value of the dwelling.

PRICES

Another market characteristic of great importance in explaining consumer purchases is, of course, price, and particularly price of a given good in relation to that of all other goods. The general level of prices can be taken into account in demand functions by a price-deflating variable or by a separate variable.

Price Elasticity

OWN ELASTICITY

A demand function that includes a price variable makes it possible to measure price elasticity, which we define as the relative change in the quantity sold associated with a relative change in price. It is symbolized as

$$e_{q,p} = \frac{dq/q}{dp/p} = \frac{dq}{dp} \cdot \frac{p}{q}$$

in which $e_{q,p}$ is the elasticity of demand with respect to price, and p and q are price and quantity, respectively. Except for inferior goods, the elasticity coefficient will be negative, reflecting the inverse relation between the price of a good and the quantity purchased. By definition, an elasticity coefficient greater than -1.00 is elastic, a coefficient equal to -1.00 is unit elasticity, and one less than -1.00 is inelastic. Elasticity is a function of the urgency of the consumer's need for the good, the availability and price of substitutes, the price of complementary goods, the consumer's saturation level,

---

[6] George Katona, Lewis Mandell, and Jay Schmiedeskamp, *1970 Survey of Consumer Finances* (Ann Arbor: University of Michigan, Institute for Social Research, Survey Research Center, 1971), pp. 59, 75.

[7] Daniel B. Suits, "The Demand for Automobiles in the United States, 1929-56," *Review of Economics and Statistics* 40 (August 1958): 273-278.

the product's durability, and the relative level of the price of a unit of the product. Sometimes there will be the same elasticity at all points on the demand curve, but ususaly the elasticity is not the same at all prices.

CROSS-ELASTICITY

It may be possible to improve the estimate of purchases by including a price variable for closely related products, such as competing or complementary goods. There should be a positive relationship between the price of a competing good and purchases of the good whose sales are being estimated. For example, a rise in the price of fuel oil would be expected in the long run to be associated with an increase in the sale of gas for domestic heating. On the other hand, we would expect a negative relationship between the price of a jointly demanded product and the units sold of the product whose sales are being estimated. Cross-elasticity of demand between two products can be symbolized by

$$e_{q_i, p_j} = \frac{dq_i/q_i}{dp_j/p_j} = \frac{dq_i}{dp_j} \cdot \frac{p_j}{q_i}$$

in which e_{q_i, p_j} is the cross-elasticity of demand for product i with respect to the price of product j, and q_i and p_j are the quantity of item i and the price of item j, respectively. The cross-elasticity of demand between two products is not reversible, that is, not symmetrical. If products are competing or substitute products, consumers may prefer one to the other, and this will affect their willingness to substitute one for the other. Hence, the cross-elasticity will not be the same in both directions. Where there is a joint demand, that item which is higher in price will be more influential in determining whether or not buyers purchase the two items that are used together. Therefore a change in the price of the more costly item will have a greater effect on the sales of the other item than will a change in the price of that item (the lower-priced one) have on the quantity sold of the higher-valued item in the pair.

SHORT- AND LONG-RUN PRICE ELASTICITIES

In Table 6.5 we have arrayed in order the "own" price elasticity coefficients calculated by Hendrik Houthakker and Lester Taylor from time series data for the United States for the period 1929-1941 and 1946-1964. Both short- and long-run elasticity coefficients were calculated where possible. In some cases the long-run elasticity could not be established separately from the short-run coefficient. In seven cases neither short- nor long-run coefficients differed significantly from zero.

The most striking thing about this array is the fact that so few items show up as having an inelastic demand with respect to price in the short run. Those that do have a high price elasticity are not significant in total dollar volume relative to total expenditures. Clothing, shoes, sports equipment, motion pictures, and tires and tubes had an elasticity close to −1.00. All other items showed inelasticity in the short run, and some showed extremely great inelasticity.

The long-run price elasticity was generally greater, as might be expected. The highest elasticities in the long run wére for china and glassware, intercity railway, motion pictures, flowers and plants, radio and television repair, intercity bus, and toilet articles.

PRICE VERSUS INCOME ELASTICITIES

One would expect a similarity between expenditure elasticity and price elasticity, since there is a complementary relationship between a change in price and a change in income.

Table 6.5 Short- and Long-Run Elasticity of Expenditure for Specific Items with Respect to Price, 1929-1941, 1946-1964

Item	Elasticity with Respect to Price	
	Short-Run	Long-Run
Expenditures in U.S. by foreign residents	-5.56	—
Purchased meals (excluding alcoholic beverages)	-2.27	—
Other personal business expenditures	-1.94	—
China, glassware, tableware & utensils	-1.54	-2.55
Intercity railway	-1.42	-3.19
Shoe cleaning and repairs	-1.31	-1.81
Religious and welfare expenditures	-1.02	—
Clothing upkeep and laundering in establishments	- .93	—
Shoes and other footwear	- .91	—
Wheel goods, durable toys, sports equipment, boats, and pleasure aircraft	- .88	-2.39
Motion pictures	- .87	-3.67
Tires, tubes, accessories, and parts	- .86	-1.19
Flowers, seeds, & potted plants	- .82	-2.65
Other fuel and ice	- .73	—
Railway (commutation)	- .72	- .91
Domestice services	- .66	—
Taxicabs	- .63	—
Kitchen and other household appliances	- .63	—
Street and electric railway and local bus	- .62	-1.20
Rental value of farm houses	- .60	—
Other recreation	- .57	-1.01
Bank service charges, trust services, and safe-deposit-box rental	- .53	—
Other educational expenditures	- .52	-1.65
Radio and television repair	- .47	-3.84
Stationery	- .47	- .56
Tobacco products	- .46	-1.89
Newspapers and magazines	- .42	—
Jewelry and watches	- .41	- .67
Automobile repair, greasing, washing, parking, storage, and rental	- .40	- .38
Ophthalmic products & orthopedic appliances	- .37	- .40
Legal services	- .37	—
Medical care & hospitalization insurance	- .31	- .92
Nondurable toys	- .30	-1.02
Other professional services	- .27	—
Telephone, telegraph, & wireless	- .26	—
Intercity bus	- .20	-2.17

Table 6.5 (cont)

Item	Elasticity with Respect to Price	
	Short-Run	Long-Run
Water	− .20	− .14
Toilet articles and preparations	− .20	−3.04
Legitimate theater & opera	− .18	− .31
Space rental value of tenant-occupied housing	− .18	−
Foreign travel by U.S. residents	− .14	−1.77
Electricity (household utility)	− .13	−1.89
Other household operation	− .13	− .29
Space rental value of owner-occupied housing	− .04	−1.21

Source: Adapted by permission of the authors and publisher from H.S. Houthakker and Lester D. Taylor, *Consumer Demand in the United States: Analyses and Projections*, Cambridge, Mass.: Harvard University Press, 1970, pp. 161-163, 166-167.

If the price of a given product falls, consumers can spend more on it because this is the equivalent to a rise in income, which, had they had such a rise, would have resulted in some additional sales of the product (unless it is an inferior good). But in addition, buyers may purchase still more of this product that has suddenly become cheaper, substituting it for other goods that have not fallen in price. Both an income effect and a substitution effect can result from the decline in price. Similarly, a rise in the price of a good will discourage people from buying it, partly because the rise in price reduces their real income and has, therefore, an income effect on their expenditures, and because the rise in price causes them to seek cheaper alternatives, resulting in a substitution effect.

It is clear from Tables 6.2 and 6.5 that total consumption expenditure is a far more important variable than price in explaining the expenditure for any particular item. In only two of the items studied was total consumption expenditure excluded as an explanatory variable. These were "commuting by railway" and "intercity railway travel." Prices, on the other hand, were found useful in only 44 of the 81 equations, and 26 of these are classified as services in the national income accounts.[8]

In a study of Swedish expenditures for the period 1931-1958 by Taylor, it was found that prices were more important in explaining particular expenditures than was income. In 64 of the equations calculated for items of expenditure in Sweden, price appeared in 46.[9] Sweden's per capita income during this span of years was about half that of the United States. Therefore it appears that price is more important in affecting expenditures in economies with lower income levels but becomes less important as income increases.

PRICE AND INCOME ELASTICITIES FOR FOOD PRODUCTS

More empirical work has been done in the analysis of agricultural prices and markets than in any other area of economics. This is due largely to the considerable amounts of

[8] Hendrik S. Houthakker and Lester D. Taylor, *Consumer Demand in the United States: Analyses and Projections*, Harvard Economic Studies, vol. CXXVI, 2d enl. ed. (Cambridge, Mass.: Harvard University Press, 1970), p. 165.

[9] Lester D. Taylor, "Personal Consumption Expenditures in Sweden, 1931-1958," *Review of the International Statistical Institute* 36, no. 1 (1968): 19-36, as discussed in Houthakker and Taylor, op. cit., pp. 164-165.

research money that the federal government has poured into support for this proportionately small segment of economic activity. Probably no agricultural product has escaped some scrutiny of its price and income elasticity at the farm, wholesale, or retail market level. One of the more comprehensive studies of agricultural prices is that of P. S. George and G. A. King, in which they analyzed the demand for various agricultural products using time series data for the period 1946-1965 and cross-sectional data from the 1955 and 1965 surveys of food consumption.[10]

We have reproduced some of the findings from this excellent study in Tables 6.6 and 6.7. Both income and price elasticities for a number of food products at retail are shown in Table 6.6. Notice how low the income elasticities are. For all food it was .18, compared to 1.24 for all nonfood items. For only five items was the income elasticity greater than .50. These were turkey (.77), frozen fruits (.66), frozen vegetables (.62), veal (.59), and lamb (.57). Lard is the only item that appears from the time series analysis to be an inferior good, with an income elasticity of -.05.[11]

Price elasticities were also quite low. For food as a whole the price elasticity was -.24, compared to -1.02 for all nonfood items. Only five items were greater than -1.00, and one item was exactly -1.00. These were lamb (-2.63), veal (-1.72), turkey (-1.56), frozen vegetables (-1.03), and frozen fruits (-1.00)—exactly the same items that had the highest income elasticities—plus shortening (-1.02).

CROSS-ELASTICITIES FOR FOOD PRODUCTS

We have included Table 6.7 to show some of the interesting cross-elasticities that George and King found for food products. One would expect the substitutability of food products for one another to be sufficiently high to cause cross-elasticities to be much higher than own-price elasticities. We have deliberately selected for inclusion in Table 6.7

Table 6.6 Elasticity of Demand for Food Products at Retail with Respect to Price and Income in the United States[a]

| Product | Elasticity with Respect to | | |
	Own Price	Income	Price of All Foods
Beef	- .6438	.2899	- .3896
Veal	- 1.7177	.5911	- .7943
Pork	- .4130	.1335	- .1793
Lamb and mutton	- 2.6255	.5712	- .7675
Chicken	- .7773	.1785	- .2398
Turkey	- 1.5553	.7684	- .9262
Fish	- .2300	.0040	- .0054
Eggs	- .3183	.0549	- .0737
Butter	- .6524	.3181	- .4274
Shortening	- 1.0158	.0291	- .0391
Lard	- .4100	- .0500	.0672
Margarine	- .8465	.0000	.0000
Salad dressing	- .6944	.2849	- .3828

[10] P. S. George and G. A. King, *Consumer Demand for Food Commodities in the United States with Projections for 1980*, Giannini Foundation Monograph no. 26 (Berkeley: University of California, Division of Agricultural Sciences, Giannini Foundation of Agricultural Economics, 1971).

[11] Cross-sectional data do, however, give evidence of inferior items among food products.

Table 6.6 (continued)

Product	Elasticity with Respect to		
	own Price	Income	Price of All Foods
Fresh milk	− .3455	.2036	− .2736
Evaporated milk	− .3198	.0000	.0000
Cheese	− .4601	.2489	− .3344
Ice cream	− .5276	.3313	− .4452
Potatoes	− .3086	.1166	− .1567
Sugar	− .2419	.0321	− .0432
Apples	− .7200	.1399	− .1880
Bananas	− .6150	.1393	− .1871
Oranges	− .6632	.2605	− .3500
Canned peaches	− .7592	.3407	− .3992
Canned pineapples	− .8262	.4473	− .5241
Dried fruits	− .6553	.3153	− .3694
Frozen fruits	− 1.0000	.6614	− .8888
Lettuce	− .1414	.1470	− .1723
Tomatoes	− .3846	.1703	− .2288
Beans	− .2550	.0000	.0000
Onions	− .2500	.0047	− .0063
Carrots	− .4971	.3194	− .4291
Canned peas	− .1850	.0321	− .0431
Canned corn	− .2550	.0236	− .0318
Canned tomatoes	− .1760	.1734	− .2032
Frozen vegetables	− 1.0344	.6161	− .8279
Rice	− .3200	.0555	− .0746
Wheat flour	− .3000	.0831	− .1117
Breakfast cereals	− .2200	.0577	− .0775
Bread and other cereals	− .1500	.0000	.0000
Coffee	− .2522	.0472	− .0635
Soup	− .4500	.2364	− .3176
All food	− .2368	.1763	− .2368
Nonfood	− 1.0179	1.2432	− .2253

[a]Based on a time series, 1946-1965, adjusted by cross-sectional food consumption data, 1955 and 1965.

Source: P. S. George and G. A. King, *Consumer Demand for Food Commodities in the United States with Projections for 1980*, Giannini Foundation Monograph no. 26 (Berkeley: University of California, Division of Agricultural Sciences, Giannini Foundation of Agricultural Economics, 1971), pp. 46-51.

Table 6.7 Demand Elasticity Matrices for Selected Food Products at Retail[a]

Meats & Fish

	Beef	Veal	Pork	Lamb	Chicken	Fish
Beef	-.6438	.0280	.0826	.0454	.0676	.0031
Veal	.3593	-1.7177	.1977	.0660	.1736	.0032
Pork	.0763	.0141	-.4130	.0602	.0353	.0046
Lamb	.5895	.0661	.8914	-2.6255	.2336	.0028
Chicken	.1971	.0436	.1208	.0546	-.7773	.0037
Fish	.0209	.0022	.0266	.0021	.0068	-.2300

Fats

	Butter	Margarine
Butter	-.6524	.1605
Margarine	.4245	-.8465

Milk

	Fresh Milk	Evaporated Milk
Fresh milk	-.3455	.0100
Evaporated milk	.2147	-.3198

Fresh Fruits

	Apples	Bananas	Oranges
Apples	-.7200	.1246	.2558
Bananas	.2136	-.6150	.0005
Oranges	.1613	.0000	-.6632

Canned Vegetables

	Canned Peas	Canned Corn	Canned Tomatoes
Canned peas	-.1850	.0472	.0340
Canned corn	.0590	-.2550	.0001
Canned tomatoes	.0564	.0000	-.1760

Beverages

	Coffee	Other Beverages
Coffee	-.2522	.0273
Other beverages	.0330	-.4387

All Goods

	All Food	Nonfood
All food	-.2368	.0606
Nonfood	-.2253	-1.0179

[a]Matrix format: Products

	1	2		n
1	e_{11}	e_{12}	$\cdots$	e_{1n}
2	e_{21}	e_{22}	$\cdots$	e_{2n}
.	.	.		.
.	.	.		.
.	.	.		.
n	e_{n1}	e_{n2}	$\cdots$	e_{nn}

in which

$$e_{12} = \frac{dq_1}{dp_2} \cdot \frac{p_2}{q_1}$$

Source: P. S. George and G. A. King, *Consumer Demand for Food Commodities in the United States with Projections for 1980,* Giannini Foundation Monograph no. 26 (Berkeley: University of California, Division of Agricultural Sciences, Giannini Foundation of Agricultural Economics, 1971), pp. 46-51.

those food products that might be expected to have high cross-elasticities. The items listed horizontally across the top are those whose price is changed; those listed vertically down the left side are those for which changes in quantity purchased are related to the price change of the item in the column indicated. Own-price elasticities are negative and are indicated by the diagonals.

The elasticity of demand for beef with respect to its own price is -.64. The elasticity of demand for beef with respect to the price of chicken is .07; that is, if chicken prices decline 1.00 percent, the pounds of beef purchased will decline 0.07 percent. But if chicken declines 1.00 percent in price, the quantity of chicken purchased in pounds will increase 0.78 percent. If beef declines 1.00 percent in price, purchases of chicken will decline 0.20 percent. Thus chicken purchases are more greatly affected by the price of beef than beef purchases are affected by the price of chicken.

There are some interesting relationships revealed in this table. Purchases of veal are more greatly affected by the price of beef than purchases of beef are affected by the price of veal. Lamb prices have the most effect on purchases of lamb itself and very little on purchases of other meat, poultry, or fish. Changes in fish prices have very little effect on purchases of meats or poultry. Nor are fish purchases very much affected by prices of meat or poultry. However, fish purchases are more affected if the price of beef or pork changes than if the price of veal, lamb, or chicken changes. Changes in the price of chicken have the most effect on veal and lamb sales of the substitutes shown. Why do people buy lamb? Apparently they buy it when it is cheap enough or when beef and pork prices increase. Why do consumers buy fish? It must be because they like it, because it is cheap, or because they feel they must.

The price elasticity of margarine is greater than that of butter. Changes in the price of butter have some effect on margarine purchases, while changes in the price of margaine have little effect on butter purchases. Changes in the price of fresh milk have a slight effect on purchases of evaporated milk, while changes in the price of evaporated milk have practically no effect on purchases of fresh milk. Changes in the price of oranges have more effect on the quantity of apples bought than on the quantity of bananas bought, while changes in the price of apples have more effect on banana purchases than on orange purchases.

Are canned peas, canned corn, and canned tomatoes substitutes? Not to any great extent. To the small extent that they are substitutes, corn and tomatoes appear to be equally good substitutes for peas, but corn and tomatoes are not substitutes for each other. The demand for coffee is quite inelastic, as one might expect. Other beverages are poor substitutes for coffee.

The last matrix in Table 6.9 reveals a very interesting fact about food and nonfood items. The demand for food is quite inelastic; the demand for nonfoods has an elasticity slightly greater than unity. Note, however, what happens when food prices change. If food prices rise, purchases of nonfoods decrease. If food prices fall, purchases of nonfoods rise. This reflects the unwillingness of consumers to move outside the upper and lower limits of what they regard as their consumption needs. On the other hand, if the price of nonfoods falls, little of this increased purchasing power goes into foods. Most of it goes into nonfoods. If the price of nonfoods rises, food consumption is not affected very much, while purchases of other things are greatly affected.

BUYERS' PRICE PERCEPTIONS

In economic literature, and throughout this discussion, we have assumed that there is a negative relationship between unit price and the number of units sold. A number of empirical studies have been undertaken to determine the validity of this assumed relationship. These findings have been summarized by Kent Monroe as follows:

> Despite the evidence available from specific effect of price on choice studies, the evidence available from the absolute and differential price threshold research suggests we know very little about how price affects a buyer's perceptions of alternative purchase offers, and how these perceptions affect his response. Perception is one intervening variable between a stimulus and a response, and as suggested by adaptation-level theory, the stimulus context is indeed an important variable affecting perception. . . . Because of the seemingly heavy reliance on the inverse price-demand function by price setters, it should be realized that a number of psychological and other contextual factors may lead to a perception of price by the buyer that is different from the perception assumed by the price setter.[12]

Empirical studies on price-quality relationships do not yield consistent results, although a positive relationship is indicated for some products over at least a range of prices. Consumers are frequently unaware of the last price they paid for a purchase. Moreover, when they do compare prices, their judgment and behavior are affected by the range of prices offered, the reference price, and the "end" (high and low) prices.[13] Buyers' price perceptions should therefore be incorporated into any realistic model of buyers' market behavior.

CONSUMER PREFERENCES

In Table 6.1 we have included two factors that are an indication of consumers' tastes or preferences—diffusion and stocks. These two alone are not a very satisfactory treatment of the concept of "tastes" or "preferences" as an explanatory variable in a commodity demand function. Ideally we would like to have some indication of how strongly consumers desire a certain product, or at least some scalar indication of the relative strength of their desire for one product versus alternatives. While there has been some success in developing scaling devices for measuring the strength of desires, the refinement of this approach to demand analysis must await the development of better techniques for translating consumer preferences into a measure that can be summed across all consumers to arrive at an aggregate index of degree of preference.

What we propose in Table 6.1 is the use of two factors that reflect the growth of consumer demand. At least one of the two has resulted in greatly improved commodity demand functions. We shall discuss, first, the concept of diffusion, and second, the concept, measurement, and analysis of stocks as they are relevant to both durable and nondurable goods markets.

Diffusion

It is known that most products move through some kind of life cycle, embracing periods of introduction, early growth in demand, rapid growth in demand, stabilization of

---

[12] Reprinted from Kent B. Monroe, "Buyers' Subjective Perceptions of Price," *Journal of Marketing Research* 10 (February 1973): 78, published by the American Marketing Association.

[13] Ibid., pp. 75-77.

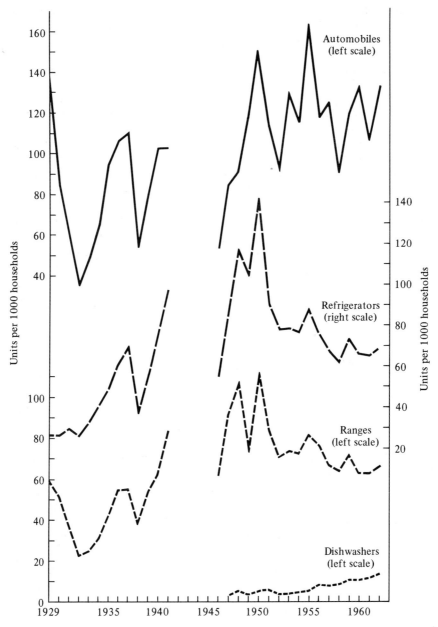

Figure 6.2. Number of automobiles, refrigerators, ranges, and dishwashers sold by manufacturers each year per 1000 households in the United States, 1929-1941, 1947-1962. (Refrigerators include only electric; ranges include both electric and gas. Automobiles include domestically produced passenger cars and imported passenger cars, with the latter estimated for the years prior to 1935 by applying the import-domestic ratio for 1936-1940 to data on domestic production for the years 1929-1935.) Sources: Based on data *Merchandising Week* (formerly *Electrical Merchandising*), Annual Statistical and Marketing Issue, 1930-1963: Automobile Manufacturers' Association, *Automobile Facts and Figures,* 1948 and 1963 eds. (Detroit, 1948 and 1963): U.S. Bureau of the Census, *Current Population Reports, Population Characteristics,* Series P-20, No. 92, p. 4: No. 140, p. 6 (Washington, D.C.: GPO, 1959 and 1965).

demand, and perhaps decline, either to stabilization at a lower level of sales or to complete extinction. In spite of marked cyclical fluctuations in sales, a portion of the product life cycle for each of four durable goods is apparent in Figure 6.2. If one could devise a measure of the level of market maturity in terms of consumer acceptance and incorporate this into either the long- or short-run demand function for the product in question, it would greatly increase the estimating and forecasting value of the function.

A number of individuals have analyzed these growth patterns and attempted to incorporate them into sales functions. Arne Rasmussen, for example, has employed an asymptotic growth curve to describe the secular growth of sales in certain industries.[14] He has computed theoretical sales volumes for goods of various degrees of durability and has made empirical analyses of Danish sales trends in radios, automatic food dispensers, telephones, and silk stockings, as well as trends for household appliances in the American market.

F. Graham Pyatt has structured a basic model, involving priority and probability patterns, to describe the growth in demand for household durables, and has shown how consumers' priorities change over time and how the various patterns of household preferences might be aggregated for use in market analyses.[15] Although his model lacks the support of empirical data, it is an imaginative approach to the analysis of preference patterns and the growth of demand that may eventually lead to more meaningful demand functions. In an analysis of air passenger traffic, William Wallace observed regularities in the growth of traffic volume associated with a particular type of aircraft. The introduction of a new aircraft brought the volume level to a point approximately 50 percent above the previous peak.[16] Biological growth models have frequently been employed to describe sales through the product life cycle. For example, Frank Bass used an epidemic model to forecast sales of new household appliances.[17] On the basis of sales data from the first few years after the product was introduced, it was possible to forecast sales in subsequent years until replacement demand became significant.

Another, but closely related, approach is that of Dorothy Brady and F. Gerard Adams, who have studied the impact of the rate of diffusion of new products on consumption expenditures.[18] They employ a model to explain the growth of product usage in terms of the number of users and nonusers and the rate of purchases by each of these at various points in time, from which a diffusion function can be calculated. They examine

---

[14] Arne Rasmussen, *Pristeori eller parameterteori,* Skrifter fra Instituttet for Salesorganisation og Reklame, nr. 16 (Copenhagen: Einer Harcks Forlag, 1955), particularly pp. 93-136.

[15] F. Graham Pyatt, *Priority Patterns and the Demand for Household Durable Goods,* University of Cambridge, Department of Applied Economics, Monograph no. 11 (Cambridge: Cambridge University Press, 1964).

[16] William M. Wallace, "An Analysis of Air Traffic Growth," *Review of Economics and Statistics* 45 (February 1963): 89-100.

[17] Frank M. Bass, "A New Product Growth Model for Consumer Durables," *Management Science* 15 (January 1969): 215-227.

[18] Dorothy S. Brady and F. Gerard Adams, "The Diffusion of New Products and Their Impact on Consumer Expenditures," Report on a Study Prepared at the Economics Research Services Unit, Department of Economics, University of Pennsylvania, for the U.S. Bureau of Labor Statistics, mimeographed (Philadelphia: University of Pennsylvania, 1962). See also F. G. Adams and D. S. Brady, "The Diffusion of New Durable Goods and Their Impact on Consumer Expenditures," *Proceedings of the Business and Economics Statistics Section, American Statistical Association,* (Washington, 1963), pp. 76-88.

Table 6.8 Purchase and Ownership Rates for New and Used Cars by Economic Group for Selected Years, 1918-1960

Item and Year	Economic Group			
	I Lowest	II Second	III Third	IV Highest
Purchase Rate **(New and Used)**	Percentage of Families			
1918	2.0	10.6	17.0	30.1
1941	11.1	25.8	34.1	36.8
1950	14.8	30.9	40.6	52.6
1955	21.9	34.9	35.6	43.5
1960	20.2	31.2	36.7	41.0
Ownership Rate				
1935-36	28.0	52.4	67.3	79.0
1950	36.8	70.8	81.9	88.7
1960	61.6	89.8	94.3	95.5

Source: Dorothy S. Brady and F. Gerard Adams, "The Diffusion of New Products and Their Impact on Consumer Expenditures," Report on a Study Prepared at the University of Pennsylvania, Department of Economics, Economics Research Services Unit, for U.S. Bureau of Labor Statistics, mimeographed (Philadelphia: University of Pennsylvania, 1962), p. 38.

ownership and purchase data for various products, including nondurables such as foods and durables such as household appliances and automobiles.

A portion of the data that Brady and Adams assembled from cross-sectional studies of automobile purchases and ownership for selected years during the period 1918-1960 are reproduced in Table 6.8. The economic groups are income groups classified into quartiles. Reading rows horizontally, we see the extent to which higher-income groups exceeded lower-income groups in rate of purchase and ownership in any given year, and we can see that the dispersion among the income groups narrowed over the years. For example, in 1941 the purchase rate for the highest income group was about three times that for the lowest, while by 1960 it was only twice that of the lowest group. We can also view the trend vertically by columns, which show the change in rate of purchase or ownership within a given income group over time. For example, between 1941 and 1960 the purchase rate for the lowest income quartile doubled, while that for the highest income group increased a little more than 10 percent. Interestingly enough, the purchase rate for the highest group declined after 1950.

Stocks play an unusually important role in the demand for durables. In addition, it has been found that the concept of stocks is relevant not only to durable goods but also to nondurable goods. We shall therefore consider this facet of consumer demand analysis and then show how diffusion rates and stock accumulation can be integrated into the consumer demand function.

Stocks

We are again turning our attention to assets and their role in consumer demand, but this time we are viewing assets not as a source of purchasing power but as an indication of consumer needs or preferences. Before we examine the two basic assumptions that underlie the use of this variable in the demand function, we should define what we mean by consumer stocks.

The concept of consumer stocks is simply the aggregate units of goods owned by consuming units. If these units are homogeneous, they may be specified as a total number, such as the number of refrigerators, the number of automobiles, or the number of cans of soup owned. If the product is heterogeneous, aggregates would have to be specified in monetary values, preferably in constant dollars if a time series is used. If the refrigerators, automobiles, or cans of soup to which we have referred are not identical, monetary values would make possible their aggregation. Ideally the condition of these stocks should be considered if the utility of the stock is to be taken into account. This requires some estimation of quality in terms of depreciated value, age, or some other indication of condition.

STOCK-FLOW RELATIONSHIPS

The two important elements of stocks are implicit in the concept set forth previously: cumulative acquisitions and depreciation. Stocks are built up from flows of goods. If the flow results in an accumulation—that is, inflow > outflow—a stock is created or increased. If the flow results in a decumulation—that is, outflow > inflow— a stock is decreased.[19] If the inflow is positive and goods never wear out, stock accumulation would occur. But most goods do wear out. Therefore the critical factors are the rate of inflow and the rate of outflow. In consumer goods markets these are indicated by (1) sales (from the point of view of sellers) or purchases (from the point of view of buyers) and (2) depreciation.

STOCK-PURCHASE RELATIONSHIPS

There are two assumptions that underly the use of a stock variable in a demand function. The first is that ownership of goods can signify the propensity to build stocks, hence, the propensity to buy. The second is that ownership of goods can signify the absence of a need to buy since stocks are already available. These two seemingly contradictory propositions are in fact both plausible.

The first merely says that if people have built up stocks in the past, it shows a tendency on their part to buy goods rather than to save their income. We are saying, for example, that if consumers add to their stocks in one year, they are likely to want to add to their stocks in a subsequent year. Or if one family builds its stocks of goods while another tends not to do so, we can say that the first family has shown a greater propensity to add to its stocks than has the other and may continue doing so, in contrast to the second family, which shows the opposite disposition.

The second proposition, however, says that if we desire stocks in order to use those stocks, once the stocks are built up there is less need to add to them. If all consumers aspire to have two cars per family, there will be a tendency for them to buy more cars so long as they *do not* have two cars per family, and a tendency for them to stop buying cars once they *do* have two per family. We shall return to these two sides of the consumer stock coin in the course of our discussion of the stock variable.

---

[19] We assume that there cannot be negative stocks. There are ways of handling this possibility—for example, through the use of credit—but we do not wish to introduce these complexities at this point.

THE HOUTHAKKER-TAYLOR BETA COEFFICIENT

We have drawn heavily upon the theoretical and empirical work of Houthakker and Taylor in our discussion of commodity demand functions. We do so again in order to discuss specifically the stock coefficient, which they have utilized with great effectiveness in explaining the demand for both consumer durables and nondurables.[20] The basic function with which they worked was as follows:

$$q_t = \alpha + \beta s_t + \gamma x_t + \eta p_t + u_t$$

in which q_t is the consumption expenditure for a given item in year t, s_t is the stock of that item at the beginning of year t, x_t is total expenditure for all goods and services in year t, p_t is relative price of the item, and u_t is an error term. The meaning of α, β, and γ. is the same as in their aggregate consumption function.[21] The estimating equation derived derived from this, which they used in calculating expenditure functions, was

$$q_t = A_0 + A_1 q_{t-1} + A_2 \Delta x_t + A_3 x_{t-1} + A_4 \Delta p_t + A_5 p_{t-1} + v_t$$

The meaning of A_0, A_1, A_2, and A_3 is the same as in their aggregate consumption expenditure function.[22] The meaning of A_4 and A_5 is as follows:

$$A_4 = \frac{\eta\left(1 + \frac{\delta}{2}\right)}{1 - \frac{1}{2}(\beta - \delta)} \quad \text{and} \quad A_5 = \frac{\eta\delta}{1 - \frac{1}{2}(\beta - \delta)}$$

The error term is v_t.

The stock coefficient, β, is

$$\beta = \frac{2(A_1 - 1)}{A_1 + 1} + \frac{A_3}{A_2 - \frac{1}{2}A_3}$$

and the depreciation rate, δ, is

$$\delta = \frac{A_3}{A_2 - \frac{1}{2}A_3} \quad \text{or} \quad \delta = \frac{A_5}{A_4 - \frac{1}{2}A_5}$$

where an interactive technique is used to choose between the two calculations of the depreciation rate.

We shall use their estimating function for food and clothing to illustrate the meaning of the stock coefficient and depreciation rate. The estimating equation for food expenditures for off-premise consumption (excluding alcoholic beverages), based on data for the years 1929-1941, 1946-1964, was

$$q_t = 31.76 + .5695q_{t-1} + .1029x_t + .0580x_{t-1}$$
$$(11.81) \quad (.1545) \quad\quad (.0186) \quad\quad (.0212)$$

from which the following estimates can be derived:

$$\alpha = 51.56 \quad \beta = .2365 \quad \gamma = .0942 \quad \gamma' = .1348$$
$$(18.09) \quad\quad (.2774) \quad\quad (.0251) \quad\quad (.0065)$$

$$\eta = .4972 \quad \eta' = .7115 \quad \delta = .7851$$
$$(.4780)$$

---

[20] Houthakker and Taylor, op. cit., pp. 17, 23.

[21] See p. 100.

[22] See pp. 99-100.

These are estimates, but we have suppressed the hats.[23] The short- and long-run MPCs are .09 and .13, respectively. The short- and long-run elasticities of expenditure with respect to total expenditures are .50 and .71, respectively. Price does not appear because its influence was statistically insignificant. It is the stock coefficient, β, .24, and the depreciation rate, δ, .79, in which we are primarily interested at this point.

Unfortunately the large standard error for the β coefficient makes an interpretation of its importance doubtful. However, we shall ignore the standard error for the moment and merely focus on the positive value of β. If $\beta > 0$, this indicates that past purchases have influenced present purchases. Food is not, of course, something that consumers store to any extent. Therefore Houthakker and Taylor interpret this as a "psychological stock of food-buying habits."[24] This value is much lower than the β value for tobacco products, which is .90, indicating that habit has a much stronger influence on tobacco consumption than on food consumption.[25] For a nondurable, therefore, the concept of stock is not that of a physical stock but of a psychological stock.

The depreciation rate, δ, shows the rate at which this stock (habit) is depreciated. With a δ value of .61, it is clear that this relatively weak habit is eroded quite rapidly.

One of the interesting findings of the Houthakker-Taylor study is the estimating equation for clothing (including luggage), which was as follows:

$$q_t = 11.594 + .7599q_{t-1} + .0862 \Delta x_t + .0100x_{t-1}$$
$$(7.181) \quad (.1152) \quad\quad (.0152) \quad\quad (.0050)$$

with the following estimates for the important parameters:

$$\alpha = 107.48 \quad \beta = -.1503 \quad \gamma = .0923 \quad \gamma' = .0415$$
$$(53.58) \quad\quad (.0844) \quad\quad (.0160) \quad\quad (.0082)$$

$$\eta = \quad 1.1423 \quad \eta' = .5131 \quad \delta = .1226$$
$$(.0807)$$

Relative price was unimportant when included in the equation.[26]

If $\beta < 0$, it indicates that the product is a durable good, that is, that if purchases are high in one year, they will not be so high in a subsequent year because stocks have already been added to; and if purchases are low in one year, they will be higher in a subsequent year because of stock depletion. The equation just presented shows that clothing is a durable good, evidenced by the β value of -.15. Not all items of clothing would be durable, of course, but the durable components outweigh the nondurable components. Houthakker and Taylor observe that the depreciation rate of .12 seems much too low, for clothing is surely not that durable. The short-run MPC is .09 and the long-run MPC .04. The expenditure elasticity is 1.14 in the short run and .51 in the long run.

The impact of habit formation on food expenditures and of stock accumulation and depletion on clothing expenditures in the Houthakker-Taylor model is illustrated in

---

[23] Adapted by permission of the authors and publisher from Houthakker and Taylor, op. cit., p. 62. As in their aggregate consumption expenditure function. γ is the short-run coefficient of total expenditure. η is the short-run elasticity with respect to total expenditure, and η' is the long-run elasticity with respect to total expenditure.

[24] Ibid., p. 17.

[25] The standard error for the β value for tobacco is, however, quite high: 1.13. Ibid., p. 66.

[26] Ibid., p. 69.

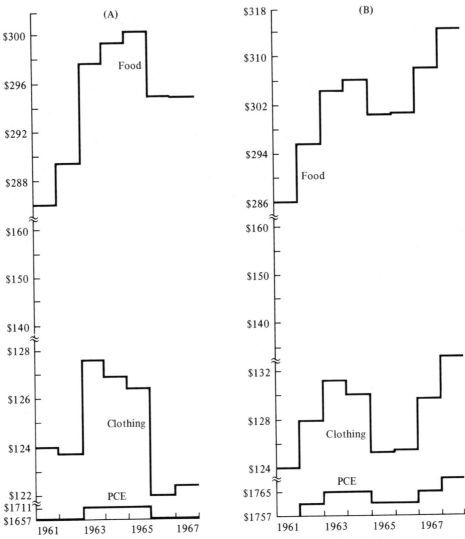

Figure 6.3. Changes in food and clothing expenditures per capita in relation to changes in total personal consumption expeditures per capita in 1958 dollars. Source: Adapted by permission of the authors and publisher from H.S. Houthakker and Lester D. Taylor. *Consumer Demand in the United States,* Cambridge, Mass.: Harvard University Press, 1970, p. 22.

Figure 6.3, which we have taken from their study.[27] Assume that total personal consumption expenditures are the same in 1961 and 1962, as indicated in part (A) of Figure 6.3, rise to a slightly higher level in 1963-1965, then drop back to their previous level in 1966 and 1967. Food expenditures would tend to rise during the first two years

---

[27]Ibid., p. 22. It should be noted that the estimating equations that we have given for food and clothing are from the second edition (1970) and are based on data for the period 1929-1941, 1946-1964. The graphs that we have reproduced in Figure 6.3 also appear in the second edition but were taken without change from the first edition. They are therefore based on equations *slightly* different from the ones we have given here, since the data were for the years 1929-1941, 1946-1961, some of which have been slightly revised. These small differences do not affect the basic relationships that we are discussing, however.

owing to habit. They would rise still more the next year not only because of habit but also because of the increase in total expenditures. They would continue to rise but at a slower rate as they get closer to a long-run equilibrium level. The decline in total expenditures in 1966 would bring about a decline in food expenditures. Psychological stocks (habit) cause expenditures not to decline very much in 1967.

Clothing expenditures, on the other hand, are affected inversely by stock accumulations in previous periods. Clothing expenditures in the second year are less than in the first, even though total expenditures are the same. The reason is that consumer inventories have been built up and continued buying is not necessary. The rise in income in 1963 causes a marked rise in clothing expenditures, and they remain high during that higher expenditure period but decline slightly each year. Having built up their stocks during this period of heavy spending, consumers then drop spending markedly with a decline in total personal consumption expenditures—down to a level lower than that in 1961 and 1962.

Section (B) of the graph shows the relationship between food and clothing expenditures and total personal consumption expenditures when total expenditures fluctuate even more than in part (A). The influence of habit on food expenditures causes them to rise and fall with each change in total expenditures but to rise less rapidly as food consumption reaches higher and higher levels. Clothing expenditures, on the other hand, are relatively more responsive to changes in income than are food expenditures, but because of the building up of stocks during those periods of higher income, clothing expenditures decline in subsequent periods.

It is helpful to recall the short- and long-run expenditure elasticities for these two and their beta coefficients:

	Food	*Clothing*
Expenditure elasticity		
Short-run	.50	1.14
Long-run	.71	.51
Beta coefficient	.24	- .15

There were 81 items for which expenditure functions were calculated in the Houthakker-Taylor study. Stock coefficients were calculated for 61 functions and were assumed to be zero for an additional 4 functions.[28] Of the 61 functions, 46 had positive values and 15 had negative values. These are arrayed in Table 6-9.

Since a positive value is interpreted as evidence of habit formation and a negative value as evidence of inventory adjustment, it is apparent that habit formation dominates consumption in the United States. Houthakker and Taylor have indicated that the 46 categories reflecting habit formation by this criterion accounted for 61 percent of total expenditures in 1964 (in 1958 dollars), while those subject to inventory adjustment accounted for 28 percent.[29] They further state:

In a similar study of 64 categories of consumer expenditure in Sweden for the period 1931-1958, Taylor (1968) found habit formation to be much less pervasive, accounting

---

[28] The four items for which it was assumed that $\beta = \sigma = 0$ were bank service charges; funeral and burial expenses; other personal business expenditures (for labor unions, employment agencies, professional associations, money order fees, etc.); and newspapers and magazines. The remaining 16 functions in their study for which there are no β coefficients include 14 in which the model used did not have a stock coefficient and 2 for which β coefficients were not calculated—remittances to foreigners and expenditures by foreigners in the United States.

[29] Houthakker and Taylor, op. cit., p. 164.

Table 6.9 Specific Items of Personal Consumption Ranked According to the Size of the Stock Coefficient (β) in the Expenditure Function, 1929-1964

Item	β
Space rental value of owner-occupied housing	1.94[a]
Bride, tunnel, ferry, and road tolls	1.93[a]
Electricity (household utility)	1.92
Spectator sports	1.92[a]
Toilet articles and preparations	1.87[a]
Foreign travel by U.S. residents	1.85[a]
Physicians	1.52[a]
Private hospitals & sanitariums	1.09
Alcoholic beverages	1.07[a]
Nondurable toys	1.01
Tobacco products	.90
Intercity bus	.88
Auto insurance premiums, less claims paid	.86
Services furnished without payment by financial intermediaries	.84[a]
China, glassware, tableware, and utensils	.79[a]
New cars and net purchases of used cars	.64
Dentists	.63
Wheel goods, durable toys, sports equipment, boats and pleasure aircraft	.54
Other educational expenditures	.51
Radio and television repair	.50
Pari-mutuel receipts	.46
Other household operation	.46
Commerical participant amusements	.45
Motion pictures	.43
Telephone, telegraph and wireless	.40[c]
Medical care and hospitalization insurance	.37
Food furnished government (including military and commercial) employees	.36
Jewelry and watches	.36
Legitimate theater and opera	.34
Cleaning and polishing preparations and misc. household supplies and paper products	.33
Drug preparation and sundries	.27
Food purchased for off-premise consumption (excluding alcoholic beverages)	.24
Barbershops, beauty parlors and baths	.22
Intercity railway	.22
Clothing upkeep and laundering in establishments	.22[c]
Stationery	.18

Item	β
Gasoline and oil	.17
Other recreation	.17
Tires, tubes, accessories and parts	.15
Shoe cleaning and repairs	.15
Net personal cash remittances to foreign countries	.11
Flowers, seeds and potted plants	.10
Street and electric railway and local bus	.09
Other clothing, accessories, etc.	.09
Railroad (commutation)	.05
Ophthalmic products and orthopedic appliances	.04
Other fuel and ice	$-.01^b$
Automobile repair, greasing, washing, parking, storage, and rental	$-.02$
Purchased meals (excluding alcoholic beverages)	$-.03^b$
Shoes and other footwear	$-.04^b$
Domestic services	$-.05^b$
Taxicabs	$-.07^b$
Other durable house furnishings	$-.08$
Books and maps	$-.10$
Other intercity transportation	$-.11^b$
Radio and television receivers, records and musical instruments	$-.12$
Furniture	$-.14$
Clothing, including luggage	$-.15$
Expenditures in U.S. by foreign residents	$-.18^b$
Water	$-.21$
Semi-durable house furnishings	$-.53$

$^a\delta = 2.$
$^b\delta = 0.$
$^c\delta = \beta.$

Source: Adapted by permission of the authors and publisher from H. S. Houthakker and Lester D. Taylor, *Consumer Demand in the United States: Analyses and Projections,* Cambridge, Mass.: Harvard University Press, 1970, pp. 161-163.

for only about 40 percent of total Swedish consumption expenditure in 1958. Since incomes in Sweden over the period were roughly half those in the United States, these two results suggest that the strength of habit formation may be a positive function of the level of income.[30]

[30] Ibid. Taylor's study was "Personal Consumption Expenditures in Sweden, 1931-1958."

They hypothesize that this relationship can be explained in terms of two factors. One is that since every stock coefficient combines the influence of inventory adjustment and habit, and since as income grows a smaller percentage of income is allocated to durable goods, for which the inventory adjustment is a dominant factor, the importance of habit formation in consumption is likely to increase. The second factor is that as income rises the mix of goods demanded changes so that the larger proportions are allocated for those goods and services that are subject to habit formation. In the United States in 1939, for example, they find that the goods subject to habit dominance accounted for only 52 percent of total expenditures (compared to 61 percent in 1964). Services tend to rise in relative importance as income increases, and the consumption of these tends to be a function of habit, since they cannot be held in consumer stocks.

In the analysis of the demand for durables, it is often advisable to break the total demand into two components: the demand for replacement and the new demand. The need for replacement will be evidenced by the age and condition of consumer stocks. But one of the problems in forecasting the volume of demand arises out of the fact that the consumer often has some discretion in choosing *when* the replacement will be made. He cannot do this, of course, if the product collapses and is unrepairable. But for most consumer durables there is usually some discretion possible about when they will be replaced. The more affluent consumers are, the more discretion they can exercise. As consumers use this opportunity to choose the time of replacement, it means that consumer stocks are much more stable over time than purchases of durables.

The unique contribution of the Houthakker-Taylor stock coefficient is, however, that it opens the way for introducing a "stock" variable into the demand for consumer nondurables. The concept of "psychological stocks" is both theoretically and empirically appealing, and we hope that its role in consumption expenditures can be explored more fully.

THE DYNAMICS OF STOCK ADJUSTMENTS

Before we leave the question of consumer stocks and their role in consumer spending, we shall describe briefly the accelerator principle as it is manifest in consumer goods markets. This is particularly appropriate for the analysis of demand for durables, for it is concerned with the difference between rates of change in sales vis-à-vis rates of change in the stocks of goods from which consumers derive utilities.

Many of the peculiarities of the demand for consumer durables are related to the durability of the goods. Because they are consumed over a period of time, such goods are purchased at intervals. The longer the interval, the more important replacement sales become as a portion of total sales. As we have indicated, replacement sales inject a timing problem into the consumer's decision, for he can choose when replacement will be made. Thus his buying behavior for durables is not circumscribed in quite the same way as it is for nondurables, which are purchased for frequent replacement. He may continue to consume a durable if he still has some of it in stock and await the most propitious time for replacing it. *Not* replacing it at a given time does not necessarily preclude its use, provided that what remains in his stock is indeed usable.

Now if we superimpose upon this replacement option the additional possibility that new users enter the market in varying numbers at different points in time, we have a much more complicated situation than in nondurable goods markets. Let us isolate the latter possibility and explore it more fully.

In Table 6-10 we show hypothetical figures for the housing inventory of a community.

Table 6.10 The Accelerator Principle Illustrated: Number and Percentage Change in Housing Inventory and Constructuion Volume in Five Periods

| Period | Ending Inventory | | Construction | | | |
| | Number | Percentage Change from Preceding Period | Replacement | New Demand | Total | |
			Number	Number	Number	Percentage Change from Preceding Period
1	10,000	—	100	0	100	—
2	10,100	+ 1.00	100	100	200	+ 100.00
3	10,200	+ 0.99	100	100	200	0.00
4	10,220	+ 0.20	100	20	120	− 40.00
5	10,220	0.00	100	0	100	− 16.67

We assume that in period 1 the community had 10,000 housing units and that its construction each year was solely for replacement. We have assumed that approximately 1 percent of the existing units were being replaced each year, amounting to 100 housing units constructed per year. Suppose that a new industry moves into the town, causing people to move to this community. The number of housing units needed by the old and new residents is 10,100, as is shown for period 2. This is an increase in the total housing inventory of 1.00 percent. Let us see what effect this has on the housing construction industry. If the industry continues to build 100 housing units for replacement, and if it also builds 100 additional housing units to add to the total stock, this will result in a total output in this year of 200 units. Thus there is a 100.00 percent increase in production to take care of the 1.00 percent increase in total inventory. It is possible, of course, that the housing construction business is not able to expand by this amount in a single year and will therefore slow its replacement construction in favor of construction to care for new demand. Nevertheless, were the industry able to expand, it would experience this increase in total output.

Let us assume further that the movement of 100 new families into the community is continued in the year that follows. In period 3 the total number of housing units desired is 10,200. This is an increase of 0.99 percent in the total number of units in use. If the housing construction industry continues to build 100 units for replacement demand and also meets the new demand of 100 units, its total construction will be 200 units per year, exactly the same as in the preceding year. Thus we have a situation in which a 0.99 percent increase in the total number of units in use results in a 0.00 percentage change in the number of units constructed. The industry, having achieved its expansion during period 2, is able to sustain the same amount of growth in the total stock without any change in the level of output.

Now let us move to period 4. We have assumed that the rate of inflow of new families has now declined so that only 10,220 houses are demanded, reflecting the inflow of 20 new families. If the new demand is met, and if replacement of deteriorated houses continues at the same rate, the total number of housing units to be put in place will be 120, which is a 40.00 percent decrease from the number constructed in the preceding period. This is a case where there was a 0.20 percentage *increase* in the number of units in use, but this resulted in a 40.00 percent *decrease* in the output of the industry.

We now enter period 5 with 10,220 houses. Assume that no more new families move into this community. The number of houses needed remains at 10,220. Since the 220 houses built during these years have probably not yet deteriorated to the point where they will need replacement, the construction industry reverts to its usual replacement of 100 units. No new demand must be met. Output falls from 120 units in period 4 to 100 units in period 5—a decline of 16.67 percent in order to adjust to a 0.00 change in units needed in stock.

This is a demonstration of the accelerator principle. This was first stated in terms of the relationship between changes in income and changes in the volume of investment. It is also applicable, however, to consumer durables, which have some of the attributes of capital goods, since their purchase makes possible future consumption; that is, they involve saving to some degree. In the example we have given in Table 6-10, we have shown a positive change in inventory with which a greater positive increase in output was associated, a positive change in inventory and a zero change in output, a positive change in inventory and a negative change in output, and a zero change in inventory and a negative change in output. All the movements in the construction output were markedly greater than those in the inventory segment. We could generalize these relationships in terms of a sales-production accelerator principle(s) as follows:

1. A change in the number of units of a durable good in consumer inventories can result in
   a. a greater positive change in the sales of the industry producing the good
   b. no change in the sales of the producing industry
   c. a negative change in the sales of the producing industry
2. A zero change in the number of units of a durable good in consumer inventories can result in
   a. a positive change in the sales of the industry producing the good
   b. no change in the sales of the producing industry
   c. a negative change in the sales of the producing industry

We have illustrated 1a, 1b, 1c, and 2c in Table 6-10. Situations 1a and 1b are not illustrated there but could be. It is unlikely, of course, that the illustration we have given in Table 6-10 would be actually experienced within, let us say, a period of five years. What is more likely to happen is that replacement demand would not be met in years when new demand is very strong, while replacement demand would take up the slack in years in which new demand is not so strong. It is often possible to postpone replacement where there are pressures on the industry to meet other stronger demands. This can be accomplished through price increases. However, we often observe the tendency for replacement demand in durable goods markets to be strong in the same periods when new demand is also strong, for both are related to other economic and social factors that influence consumer decisions to buy or not to buy.

The consumer goods industries affected by this phenomenon are those producing durable goods. Those most affected produce in a single year a relatively small percentage of the total number of units in use. The housing industry is an example, as are the automobile industry, the household appliance industry, and even industries producing semidurables such as heavy wearing apparel. The importance of cyclical fluctuations in these industries is demonstrated in Figures 6-2 and 6-4.

In Table 6-11 we show the number of passenger cars registered in the United States on December 31 of each year during the 1950s and the 1960s. The availability of accurate data on consumer stocks is one reason for the large number of studies made of the demand for automobiles and the incorporation of a stock variable in such functions. Note

Figure 6.4. Annual expenditures for durable goods per household in the United States in 1954 dollars, 1929-1962. Sources: U.S. Department of Commerce, *U.S. Income and Output* (Washington, D.C.: GPO, 1958); *Survey of Current Business,* 1959-1963; U.S. Bureau of the Census, *Current Population Reports, Population Characteristics,* Series P-20, No. 92, p. 4; No. 140, p. 6 (Washington, D.C.: GPO, 1959 and 1965).

especially the relatively small percentage change in number of registrations from year to year. Because of the lack of production during the period of World War II, the high income during the postwar period, and the relatively large cache of liquid assets that many consumers had accumulated during the war years, the rate of change in sales from 1950 to 1955 was higher than during subsequent years. After 1955, the change in the size of the stock was never greater than 4 percent. Factory sales of U.S. manufacturers, however, fluctuated markedly from year to year, not only from 1950 to 1955 but also during the next decade and a half, rising and falling in accelerated response to changes in the total stock. Part of the problem facing domestic manufacturers during this period was the rising volume of imports, which reached a level greater than 1 million in 1967 and 2 million in 1970. The percentage change in total sales (domestic sales and imports) also reflects the accelerator effect of relatively small changes in the number of registrations.[31]

PRODUCT QUALITY

Producers sometimes introduce technological or style changes in order to stimulate new demand and to encourage more rapid replacement of existing stocks. To the degree that

---

[31] Because we are concerned only with consumer demand in this discussion, we have not, of course, given any consideration to the demand for industrial goods. However, it is appropriate to point out that the accelerator principle is even more important in the markets in which industrial goods are bought and sold, particularly for industries in which a considerable amount of capital equipment is used. As indicated earlier, the accelerator principle developed out of the analysis of income-investment relationships, and purchases of capital equipment are evidence of new investment or maintenance of an existing level of investment. Therefore changes in aggregate income are likely to lead to an accelerated change in expenditures for capital goods. We shall consider this more specifically in our discussion of derived demand.

Table 6.11 Motor Vehicle Registrations of Passenger Cars and Factory Sales, 1950-1970

| | Registrations December 31 | | Sales | | | | | |
| | | | Domestic Factory Sales | | Imports | | Total | |
Year	Number (Thousands)	Percentage Change[a]	Number (Thousands)	Percentage Change[a]	Number (Thousands)	Percentage Change[a]	Number (Thousands)	Percentage Change[a]
1950	40,339	+11	6,504	+31	21	+182	6,525	+31
1951	42,683	+ 6	5,068	−22	24	+ 11	5,092	−22
1952	43,818	+ 3	4,149	−18	33	+ 40	4,182	−18
1953	46,422	+ 6	5,926	+43	30	− 12	5,956	+42
1954	48,461	+ 4	5,350	−10	35	+ 17	5,385	−10
1955	52,145	+ 8	7,661	+43	57	+ 65	7,718	+43
1956	54,211	+ 4	5,610	−27	108	+ 88	5,718	−26
1957	55,918	+ 3	5,935	+ 6	259	+140	6,195	+ 8
1958	56,891	+ 2	4,122	−31	431	+ 66	4,553	−27
1959[b]	59,454	+ 4	5,469	+33	668	+ 55	6,137	+35
1960	61,682	+ 4	6,525	+19	444	+ 66	6,969	+14
1961	63,417	+ 3	5,394	−17	279	+ 63	5,773	−17
1962	66,108	+ 4	6,743	+25	375	+ 34	7,118	+23
1963	69,055	+ 4	7,433	+10	409	+ 9	7,842	+10
1964	71,983	+ 4	7,543	+ 1	537	+ 31	8,080	+ 3
1965	75,251	+ 4	9,092	+20	559	+ 4	9,651	+19
1966	78,123	+ 4	8,326	− 8	913	+ 63	9,239	− 4
1967	80,414	+ 3	7,055	−15	1,021	+ 12	8,076	−13
1968	83,592	+ 4	8,390	+19	1,620	+ 59	10,010	+24
1969	86,861	+ 4	7,786	− 7	1,847	+ 14	9,633	− 4

Table 6.11 (continued)

| | Registrations December 31 | | Sales | | | | | | |
| | | | Domestic Factory Sales | | Imports | | Total | | |
Year	Number (Thousands)	Percentage Change[a]	Number (Thousands)	Percentage Change[a]	Number (Thousands)	Percentage Change[a]	Number (Thousands)	Percentage Change[a]
1970[c]	89,861	+ 3	6,171	–21	2,013	+ 9	8,184	–15

[a]From preceding year.
[b]The addition of Alaska and Hawaii to the registration count in 1959 accounted for 236,000 total additional registrations.
[c]Preliminary.
Source: Automobile Manufacturers Association, *Automobile Facts and Figures*, 1957 and 1971 ed. (Detroit, 1957 and 1971).

this influences consumer purchases, it too would constitute an independent variable that influences the volume of sales.[32] Quality variables, however, have rarely been included in demand functions because of the difficulties of quantifying them and of measuring their impact on sales. Were quality attributes quantifiable, there would still remain the question of knowing what their relation to sales is likely to be, since it is unlikely that this relationship will be stable over time. The important thing is how consumers perceive and assess the quality attribute in terms of the product's ability to meet their desires. The presence or absence of a particular characteristic is therefore far less important than the consumer's sensitivity and reaction to its presence or absence.

Quality and Price Indexes

Since the measurement of consumers' perception of product attributes is a sticky wicket, would it be possible to measure objectively determined physical attributes as a proxy for the more meaningful perception of attributes? Most of the empirical work in this area of economics has been done in connection with price indexes where price changes for products are determined over a period of time. The quality question is obviously critical to the calculation of such an index, for a price index is supposed to measure changes in prices of the same goods and services and not changes in prices of changing goods and services. If quality is changing at the same time that prices are changing, this has to be taken into account or the price index ceases to be a measure of price changes associated with changes in the demand for and/or supply of a specified bundle of goods.

COURT'S HEDONIC PRICE INDEX

An interesting attempt made several years ago to incorporate quality variables into a price index was reported by A. T. Court of the Automobile Manufacturers Association.[33] He experimented with such variables as car weight, wheelbase, and horsepower as indications of automobile quality. Other quality factors for which he obtained data were comfort—indicated by tire section, front spring period, wheel base, and front seat width; performance—top speed, deceleration, and acceleration; durability and dependability —horsepower per pound of car weight, tire section per pound of car weight, percentage surviving five years, resale price when three years old, resale price when five years old. Also, he obtained certain operating cost indexes such as gasoline gallons per mile, total operating cost per mile, repair expense per mile, and tire expense per mile. However, a number of these were not available on a basis that made comparability between manufacturers possible. His purpose was to try to build a hedonic price index that would measure the change in price from one year to the next for a product comparable in utility from year to year rather than one comparable merely in name.

THE GRILICHES AND TRIPPLETT EXTENSIONS

Zvi Griliches used Court's approach to develop a hedonic automobile price index for the 1950s, using as variables advertised brake horsepower, shipping weight, overall length,

---

[32] See Wroe Alderson, "Consumer Reaction to Product Innovation," in *Consumer Behavior—Research on Consumer Reactions*, ed. Lincoln H. Clark (New York: Harper & Row, 1958), pp. 3-9. See also Eva Mueller, "The Desire for Innovations in Household Goods," in ibid., pp. 13-37, and A. C. Nielsen, Jr., "Consumer Product Acceptance Rates," in ibid., pp. 40-49.

[33] A. T. Court, "Hedonic Price Indexes," in General Motors, op. cit., pp. 99-119.

number of cylinders, hardtop or not, automatic transmission as standard equipment or not, power steering as standard equipment or not, power brakes as standard equipment or not, and compact or not.[34] Using regression analysis to determine the relationship between prices and these various quality characteristics, he concluded that between 1937 and 1950 about one-third of the 83 percent rise in the wholesale price of automobiles could be explained by quality improvements, and that between 1954 and 1960 nearly all of the 20 percent rise in price could be explained by quality changes.

Jack Tripplett did a replication of Griliches' study to determine what happened during the 1960-1965 period.[35] He found that the quality index deteriorated by about 8 percent between 1960 and 1962 and remained at about that level through 1966. Thus the relative stability in automobile prices in this period concealed an increase in the "real" price of cars if one assumes that the hedonic price index does in fact enable one to calculate the "real" price. But Tripplett goes on to show that the use of these particular automobile attributes may not be a good measure of quality. Weight, for example, was important in both the Court and Griliches indexes, but Tripplett points out that weight may be increased in order to accommodate other quality improvements, and this would mask its importance for its own sake. Also, changes in the casting process and in the types of materials used have resulted in a reduction in weight without necessarily any decrease in quality. This suggests, therefore, the considerable problems that are associated with creating a measure of quality and the need to have such measures developed by individuals fully aware of technological aspects of the product and its production as well as what is useful and desirable to consumers.

THE DHRYMES INDEX

Phoebus Dhrymes used a similar approach to develop a quality index for refrigerators.[36] The variables he employed were cubic footage capacity, freezer compartment cubic footage, height, width, depth, and whether or not the refrigerator had a meat drawer, egg shelf, butter shelf, shelves on freezer door, shelves in freezer compartment, ice ejector, sliding shelves, swing-out shelves, semiautomatic defrosting, automatic defrosting, automatic defrosting in freezer section but not in fresh foods section, completely frostless in freezer and fresh-foods section, and two doors. He found substantial quality improvements during certain years and especially during the period 1963-1965, the last 3 years of his 15-year time series.

QUANTIFICATION OF QUALITY

While a quality index can enter the demand function as a price deflator, it can be more useful as a separate variable whose relationship to sales can then be determined. The main problem, however, is to devise meaningful measures of quality. The engineering measures used by Griliches and Tripplett are extremely crude.

The problem of quality measurement for purposes of demand analysis is a dual one.

---

[34] Zvi Griliches, "Hedonic Price Indexes for Automobiles: An Econometric Analysis of Quality Change," Staff Paper no. 3 in *The Price Statistics of the Federal Government*, a Report to the Office of Statistical Standards, Bureau of the Budget, by the National Bureau of Economic Research, General Series no. 73 (New York: National Bureau of Economic Research, 1961), pp. 173-196.

[35] Jack E. Tripplett, "Automobiles and Hedonic Quality Measurement," *Journal of Political Economy* 77 (May-June 1969): 408-417.

[36] Phoebus J. Dhrymes, "On the Measurement of Price and Quality Changes in Some Consumer Capital Goods," *American Economic Review* 57 (May 1967): 501-518.

One problem is to determine the specific attributes consumers see in a product or service. This is itself a complex matter. An attribute may need to be defined in terms of its intensity as well as in terms of whether it is present or not. Moreover, an attribute set, rather than a single attribute, may be the relevant variable. A loaf of bread, a jug of wine, and thou may *each* bring the consumer happiness, but when they are *all* present at once the effect is something quite different. Once attributes are identified, the problem is to determine the value that consumers place on them.

CONSUMER ATTITUDES, EXPECTATIONS, AND BUYING PLANS

In our discussion of the aggregate consumption-expenditure functions, we included consumer attitudes as an explanatory variable and described the index of consumer sentiment of the Survey Research Center (SRC) as a simplified approach to measurement of relevant aspects of consumer attitudes. As we pointed out, the index has been found most effective in increasing the explanatory power of the demand function for consumer durables. There has, however, been less than unanimity in the opinion of demand analysts concerning the utility of data on consumer attitudes and purchase intentions in demand models for durable goods.

In an early study of the effectiveness of attitudes and buying intentions in explaining and/or forecasting consumer quarterly purchases of major household durables and automobiles over the years 1952-1961, Eva Mueller found that the Index of Consumer Attitudes, as it was then called, performed consistently well in the time series test and added to the predictive power of estimating equations that also included income as an explanatory variable.[37] While consumer buying intentions appeared to make a net contribution to the forecast in some of her regression equations, these were primarily equations that excluded the attitudes index. When both attitudes and buying intentions were included, buying intentions performed erratically as a predictive variable.

On the basis of this success, a quarterly survey of consumer buying intentions (QSI) was undertaken by the U.S. Department of Commerce for the years 1960-1966, and of consumer buying expectations (CBE) for the years 1967-1973. One of the unique characteristics of the information obtained in the quarterly CBE survey was the indication by the consumer of the probability of his making a purchase. F. Thomas Juster was one of the first to propose the use of probability measures in conjunction with buying plans in order to refine information about buying intentions so that it would be more useful in forecasting sales.[38]

The Department of Commerce found that buying plans appeared to be a useful variable in durable-goods demand functions for the period 1959-1966 but that they were not useful for the period 1957-1973, apparently because of the considerable variability in consumers' stated buying plans. Figure 6.5 shows the deviation of actual purchases from

---

[37] Eva Mueller, "Ten Years of Consumer Attitude Surveys: Their Forecasting Record," *Journal of the American Statistical Association* 58 (December 1963): 899-917. See also her earlier article, "Effects of Consumer Attitudes on Purchases," *American Economic Review* 44 (December 1957): 946-965.

[38] F. Thomas Juster, *Consumer Buying Intentions and Purchase Probability: An Experiment in Survey Design*, National Bureau of Economic Research, Occasional Paper no. 99 (New York: Columbia University Press, 1966). See also his earlier study, *Consumer Expectations, Plans, and Purchases: A Progress Report*, National Bureau of Economic Research, Occasional Paper no. 70 (New York: National Bureau of Economic Research, 1959).

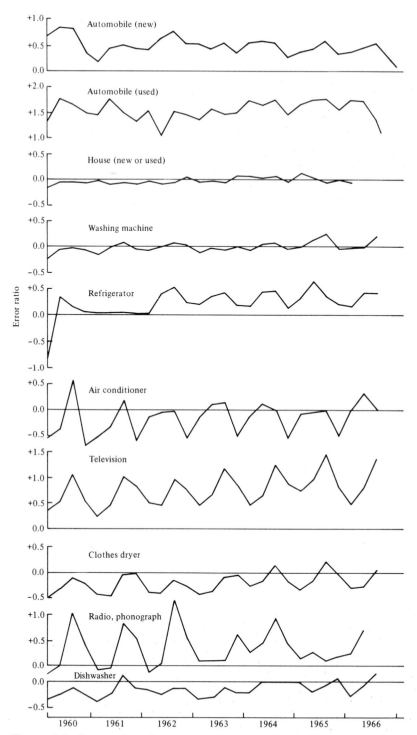

Figure 6.5. Error ratio of actual purchases to planned purchases of various durables reported by households, 1960-1966. The value plotted is [(percentage of households making purchases)-(percentage of households planning purchases)]/(percentage of households making purchases)]. Except for houses, planned purchases were for the next 6 months. For houses, planned purchases were for the next 12 months. Sources: "Quarterly Survey of Consumer Buying Intentions," *Federal Reserve Bulletin,* 1960-1962; U.S. Bureau of the Census, *Current Population Reports,* "*Consumer Buying Indicators,*" Series P-65, Nos. 1-20 (Washington, D.C. GPO, 1963-1967).

Table 6.12 Number and Percentage of Spending Units Reporting Automobile Buying Intentions for 1956 Compared with Actual Buying Activity During 1956

Stated Intention to	Bought a New Car		Bought a Used Car		Did Not Buy a Car		Total		
	Number	Percentage	Number	Percentage	Number	Percentage	Number	Percentage	
Buy a new car	32	48	8	12	27	40	67	100	(9)
Buy a used car	2	6	16	52	13	42	31	100	(4)
Buy no car	69	10	86	13	520	77	675	100	(87)
Total	103	13	110	14	560	73	773	100	(100)

Source: Reprinted from the September 21, 1957 issue of *Business Week*, p. 132, by special permission. © by McGraw-Hill, Inc.

expected purchases as reflected in the Department of Commerce data for each quarter, 1960-1966. Most items had a positive deviation, indicating actual purchases greater than expected purchases, but the extent of deviation differed among various durable products. Because of the high variability in consumer responses for the years after 1966, the Department of Commerce ceased publication of its *Survey of Consumer Buying Expectations* after the April 1973 survey.[39]

Other research organizations that were undertaking the measurement of consumer attitudes and buying intentions during the late 1960s and early 1970s encountered similar difficulties. These included Sindlinger's firm and the Conference Board, both of which produced findings that business firms found of dubious value in explaining actual behavior.[40]

In a study covering the years 1953-1967, Juster and Paul Wachtel found that models that employed anticipatory data alone—including (1) attitudes, from the SRC index, and (2) buying plans, from the SRC (1953-1959) and from the QSI and CBE surveys of the Department of Commerce (1960-1967)—were as good as a fully specified objective model that included measures of income, prices, credit terms, stocks, and unemployment.[41] The substitutability of the simple two-variable anticipatory model for the objective model was greatest "when both purchase expectations and consumer sentiment can be measured with reasonable precision.... The evidence [of substitutability] is markedly less convincing when purchase expectations are measured with relatively large sampling errors."[42] In the latter situation it appeared that a significant part of the objective model should be included in the demand model. Juster and Wachtel were particularly convinced of the need for including a price measure in either type of demand function.

It appears, therefore, that both consumer attitudes and buying plans should not yet be dropped from consideration as candidates for inclusion in demand functions, particularly

[39] The last issue was U.S., Department of Commerce, *Current Population Reports*, Series P-65, *Consumer Buying Indicators*, no. 46 (July 1973).

[40] "A Loss of Faith in Pollsters," *Business Week*, June 1, 1974, p. 25.

[41] F. Thomas Juster and Paul Wachtel, "Anticipatory and Objective Models of Durable Goods Demand," *American Economic Review* 62 (September 1972): 564-579.

[42] Ibid., p. 578.

in functions for consumer durables. Not all people can (or will) report accurately what their behavior will be in the future, but it appears that aggregates of such estimates are more nearly correct than specific responses. (See Table 6.12.) Technical refinements in the measurement itself, combined with additional research on the validity of responses to such questions, will have to determine if information of this type will some day be of real value in explaining and forecasting buying behavior.

7

The Structure of Derived Demand

The last thing you get to know,
Pascal had said, is what comes first.

—Howard Nemerov

In the preceding chapters we considered the characteristics of consumer demand for goods and services and some of the variables related to demand. Goods and services in their final form consist of a large number of attributes, which become incorporated into the final product through a series of productive activities. These successive productive activities are coordinated through markets, and the demand for goods and services by consumers filters down through these layers of markets and makes its influence felt in wholesale markets, which are far removed in function, time, and space from the retail markets in which consumers actively participate. The demand for goods in wholesale markets then filters back into factor markets, where real estate and other natural resources, investment capital, labor, and business management are made accessible to business firms. The result is a series of vertically related markets. Each has its own demand and supply structure, but each demand and each supply bears a relationship to the demands and supplies above and below it.

We shall here examine some of the characteristics of derived demand, that is, the demand for goods in wholesale markets, which is derived from the demand in retail markets, and the demand for productive factors, which is derived from the demand in all markets through which goods move in the productive process.

THE MARSHALL-ROBINSON PROPOSITIONS

Alfred Marshall formulated four propositions concerning the relationship between the elasticity of demand for a finished good and that of a demand derived from it.[1] To these four we shall add a fifth proposition based on the analysis of imperfect competition by Joan Robinson.[2] In stating these propositions we shall refer to the ultimate consumer demand as the *final demand* and to all others as *derived demands*.[3]

The Propositions

PROPOSITION ONE

A demand derived from a final demand that shows considerable inelasticity will tend also to be inelastic.

---

[1] Alfred Marshall, *Principles of Economics*, 8th ed. (London: Macmillan, 1920), pp. 383-388.

[2] Joan Robinson, *The Economics of Imperfect Competition* (London: Macmillan, 1933), pp. 253-264.

[3] Alfred Marshall identified those goods that are ready for immediate use as "goods of the first order" or "consumers' goods" and those used as factors of production for other goods as "goods of the second order" or "producers' goods." Marshall, op. cit., pp. 381-382.

186

Suppose, for example, that we find that the demand for cotton shirts is inelastic. An increase in price from $10 to $11 decreases the number purchased from 2100 to 2000. A decrease in supply that comes about, let us say, from an increase in wage rates of workers causes the new equilibrium price to become $11 per shirt. There will be a drop in number purchased and a corresponding drop in the amount of cotton purchased. But because the drop in the number purchased is not proportionate to the increase in price, neither will the decrease in the amount of cotton consumed by the shirt industry be equal to the proportionate increase in price. The elasticities of the two demand curves will tend, therefore, to be positively related, although not necessarily identical, as we shall show later.

Similarly, sellers of productive resources or raw materials used in products that have an elastic demand will be subject to fluctuating sales as supply conditions in those industries change, causing variations in sales volumes and positively related variations in the demand transmitted to other, related markets.

PROPOSITION TWO

For a good with more than one cost component, that component whose value represents the smallest proportion of the total will ususlly have the most inelastic derived demand.[4]

If the price of nails goes up, it does not affect the number purchased for housing construction to any noticeable degree, for the cost of nails is a very small percentage of the total cost of a house and will not influence housing costs and, hence, the volume of housing construction. Components whose price represents a large proportion of the total value of a consumer good will, on the other hand, show an elasticity more closely related to that of the final good.

Martin Bronfenbrenner has indicated that this proposition is probably true in most cases. He has shown, however, that there may be cases in which a productive service has the largest weight in the total cost of a commodity but not the most elastic derived demand.[5] These exceptions depend on the relative size and signs of the elasticity coefficients for the final commodity, for the substitution between two productive services, and for the supply of cooperant and substitute services. Using σ as the elasticity of substitution between two productive services, η as the elasticity of demand for the final product, and e as the elasticity of supply of cooperant and substitute services, he has shown that the proposition is valid if (1) $\eta - \sigma$ and e are positive; (2) $\eta - \sigma$ is positive, e is negative, and $\sigma > e < \eta$; or (3) $\eta - \sigma$ is negative, e is negative, and $\eta > e < \sigma$. The proposition is not valid, for example, if supply elasticities are positive and/or sufficiently large. It seems unlikely, however, that these exceptions would often occur.

PROPOSITION THREE

A derived demand will tend to be more inelastic when the technical substitutability of other factors for it is very low.[6]

---

[4] An alternative way to state this proposition would be as follows: Under certain conditions the smaller the proportionate cost that is accounted for by a single component, the greater the difference between the elasticity of demand for the final good and that for the component. See Joan Robinson, op. cit., pp. 254-256.

[5] M. Bronfenbrenner, "Notes on the Elasticity of Derived Demand," *Oxford Economic Papers,* N.S., 13 (October 1961): 254-261. See also J. R. Hicks, "Marshall's Third Rule: A Further Comment," ibid., pp. 262-265, and D. H. Robertson, "Another Comment," ibid., p. 266.

[6] This could also be stated as follows: A derived demand will be more inelastic the lower the elasticity

This parallels the general proposition that the elasticity of any demand is reduced as substitutions become easier to make. The demand for a particular fiber for clothing is affected by the price and availability of substitute fibers. The more readily substitutions can be made, the greater the elasticity of derived demand. Weekly earnings of bituminous coal miners in the United States increased from an average of $24 in 1940 to $148 in 1966, an increase of 517 percent. If we convert 1966 weekly earnings into their equivalent in 1940 dollars, they become $64. Real earnings, therefore, increased 167 percent during this quarter century. During this period mechanization in the industry proceeded very rapidly, and employment in the industry declined from 425,000 in 1940 to 113,000 in 1966, a decrease of 73 percent.[7] According to our third proposition, had capital been a less ready substitute for labor, employment would have declined less than it did. But according to our first proposition, elasticity of demand for coal, which is greatly influenced by the availability of heating substitutes, would have been reflected in the elasticity of demand for coal miners' wages.

PROPOSITION FOUR

If a good with a derived demand is used jointly with other goods, the more inelastic the supply of the other goods, the more inelastic the derived demand for the first good.

This involves a more complicated set of relationships than some of the other propositions. Amplifiers and speakers are components of stereo systems. Therefore the demand for each is derived from the demand for stereo systems. If the price of speakers rises, the increased cost can be borne by either consumers of the total system or those who produce complementary components such as amplifiers. If the supply of amplifiers is quite inelastic, then their price will fall sharply with even a small decrease in the quantity bought. Hence there will be little effect on the number of speakers purchased as a result of the rise in their price, reflecting an inelastic derived demand. If, on the other hand, the supply of amplifiers were quite elastic, it would take a large decrease in output to enable amplifiers to absorb all of the necessary price adjustment, and this would, in turn, cause the demand for speakers to be much more elastic.

PROPOSITION FIVE

A fifth proposition concerning derived demand was developed by Robinson and concerns demand relationships under conditions of imperfect competition.[8]

Derived demand will be inelastic when purchasers operate under imperfect competition and pursue a policy of maintaining stability in their selling prices.

---

of substitution. Elasticity of substitution is the proportionate change in the ratio of the amounts of the factors employed in production divided by the proportionate change in the ratio of their marginal physical productivities. The latter will be equal to the ratio of prices under conditions of pure competition. See Robinson, op. cit., pp. 256-257, 330.

[7] United States of Labor Statics, *Employment and Earnings Statistics for the United St tes, 1909-67*, Bulletin no. 1312-5 (Washington, D.C.: GPO, 1967), pp. 18-19.

[8] Robinson, op. cit., pp. 267-304.

If buyers succeed in holding fairly rigid sales prices on their products, changes in raw material prices will bear little relationship to changes in final consumer goods prices. If, on the other hand, buyers of a product attempt to pass on to consumers of the final product each cost change that occurs, sales of the final good will fluctuate sharply, and so will sales of goods whose demand is derived.

Interrelations of Propositions

These five propositions concern two-variable relationships: If one condition prevails, another follows. In real market situations, however, many conditions determine the character of a particular market, and many relationships exist between two vertically related markets. It is possible, therefore, that one condition that makes derived demand inelastic is neutralized by another that is conducive to greater elasticity. If, for example, there is a derived demand for a good that represents a very small proportion of the total cost of the final good, this would be conducive to an inelastic derived demand because of the relative unimportance of the cost of the item in the final good. But if, at the same time, there are ready substitutes available for the good with the derived demand, this would be conducive to considerable elasticity of the derived demand, for if the price of the ingredient goes up, a substitute will be used.

The demand for asbestos shingles on new houses would be inelastic if these represented the only available form of roofing, for other costs are more important in determining whether people will or will not buy houses. Once they have decided to acquire housing, they will not forgo the new house because the shingles cost too much. But if there are good substitutes for asbestos shingles, such as tile, wood, slate, or plastic, buyers of new housing will substitute these for asbestos shingles if the price of the asbestos product becomes too high.

If the elasticity of substitution is greater than the elasticity of demand for an ingredient whose cost is a small portion of total cost, the substitution effect will be greater than the complementary effect.[9] Likewise, if the elasticity of substitution is greater than the elasticity of demand for complementary goods, then again the substitution effect will be greater than the complementary effect.

A further qualification of the Marshallian derived demand propositions concerns economies of scale. Assume that a raw material that enters into a final product represents such a small percentage of the total price of the product that it would show, by this criterion, a very inelastic demand. If there are possibilities that lower costs can be achieved by large-scale production, it may be desirable to buy more and more of a given good if, when used in combination with other goods, total costs are reduced through the expansion of output. One might, for example, expect the demand for steel used in automobiles to be more inelastic than the demand for automobiles. But if more steel is bought because its price has declined, and more automobiles are produced, it is possible that other components of automobile cost will drop enough, because of large-scale production, to make the demand for steel by the automobile industry of equal or greater elasticity than the demand for automobiles by consumers.[10]

---

[9] This hybrid proposition is developed in ibid., pp. 258-260.

[10] Ibid., pp. 262-264.

GRAPHIC ANALYSIS OF FINAL
AND DERIVED DEMAND RELATIONSHIPS

Marshall stated the "law" of derived demand as follows:

> The price that will be offered for any thing used in producing a commodity is, for each separate amount of the commodity, limited by the excess of the price at which that amount of the commodity can find purchasers, over the sum of the prices at which the corresponding supplies of the other things needed for making it will be forthcoming.

> To use technical terms, the demand schedule for any factor of production of a commodity can be *derived* from that for the commodity by subtracting from the demand price of each separate amount of the commodity the sum of the supply prices for corresponding amounts of the other factors.[11]

He used familiar supply and demand curves to show (1) the relationship between the final demand for a good and the derived demand for one of its components, and (2) the relationship between the difference between final and derived demand, on the one hand, and the difference between the supply of the total product and of its components, on the other.

Suppose that we are considering the demand for shoe tops and shoe soles. Let us assume that these are the only two parts for each pair of shoes. Although neither is useful without the other, we shall examine specifically the demand for shoe soles, recognizing that they are complementary to shoe tops. In Figure 7.1 *DD'* is the demand for shoes, including tops and soles. *SS'* is the supply of shoes, including raw materials, labor, capital, and profits necessary for production. Given these conditions and a competitive market situation, *OQ* shoes will be sold at price *P*.

The curve *ss* represents the supply of soles; the higher the price, the greater the number produced and offered on the market. When the price of a pair of soles is *RX, OR* soles will be produced. When tops sell for *VX* per pair, *OR* tops will be produced. Therefore when the completed pair of shoes sells for *RV, OR* soles and *OR* tops will be produced. For purposes of simplification we have assumed that the supply of soles is less than perfectly elastic and that the supply of tops is perfectly elastic.

Now let us examine the derived demand for soles. If *OR* shoes are offered on the market, consumers are willing to pay *RZ* for them. At this output level *VX* is the supply price for that many tops. If, therefore, consumers pay *RZ* for these shoes, they must pay *VX* of this price to get the tops. *RZ* - *VX* is the amount they are willing to pay for the soles. The line *dd'* is drawn so that it is the same distance below *DD* as *ss'* is below *SS*. *RT* is, in other words, the excess of *RZ* over *VX*. The line *dd'* represents the derived demand for soles, and *ss'* is their supply. The equilibrium quantity will be *OQ*, and the equilibrium price for soles alone will be *Op*.

This is an oversimplified explanation, for if one part of a final product changes in price, it is unlikely that all other parts will remain undisturbed. The partial and total supply curves may not be so neat as those we have described here. Simple linear relationships may not exist among components of a product, and substitutions among components may take place if price changes are very marked. Moreover, in our example we have assumed that the supply of one component is perfectly elastic. Rising marginal costs

---

[11] Marshall, op. cit., p. 383.

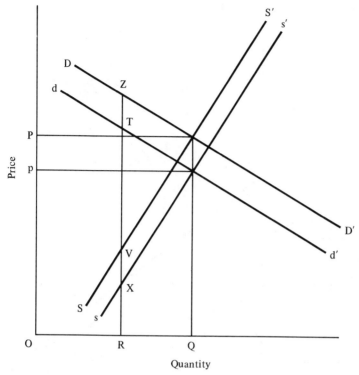

Figure 7.1. Derived demand and supply.

would make this unlikely in most industries. It is more reasonable to expect a less than perfectly elastic supply for both soles and tops. Finally, we should note that we have assumed in our example that consumers pay what they must for tops and that any excess that they are willing to pay for the pair of shoes as a whole accrues to the soles. Whether this is the way the pot is divided will depend, of course, on the competitive structure of the top and sole segments of the industry.

Despite these complications, however, it is useful to see that the amount consumers are willing to pay for one component depends on the amount they are willing to pay for the total product less the amount they *must* pay for the other components. They will not buy a component by itself, nor will they buy it if the combination of all prices of all components exceeds the limits set by their demand. This principle has important implications for the combination of marketing and nonmarketing costs and the relationship of that total to the consumer demand for goods and services.

MARKETING MARGINS AND DEMAND ELASTICITIES: PURE COMPETITION

Vertical demand relationships in the marketing system are most apparent where the total production and marketing process has been segmented into units performed by specialized firms connected by a series of vertically related markets. Wholesalers buy from manufacturers and sell to retailers, who, in turn, sell to consumers. Agricultural products may move through a myriad of market levels on their way from farm to consumer. By combining the graphic analysis of final and derived demand relationships of Marshall and the propositions concerning the relative elasticities of the two demands, and by making

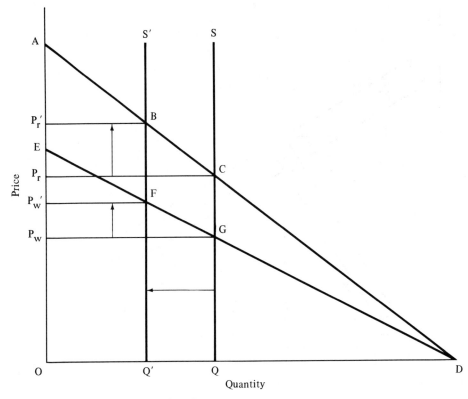

Figure 7.2. Derived demand: Case I.

certain assumptions about the relationship of marketing margins to the aggregate volume of sales, we can set up three useful models that will demonstrate the elasticity relationships that will prevail under different types of market situations. As our empirical data on market characteristics increase, we can modify these pure models in the direction of ones built on more realistic assumptions concerning market conditions. We shall structure all of our models in terms of the relationship between the demands in retail and wholesale markets, although the same patterns of relationship would prevail were we concerned with demand relationships in any other vertically related markets.[12]

---

[12] The exposition of vertical demand relationships in this and the section that follows owes much to Neil T. Houston, "Methods of Efficiency Analysis in Marketing," Ph.D. dissertation, Harvard University, 1948. Other discussions can be found in U.S. Temporary National Economic Committee, *Large-Scale Organization in the Food Industries*, Monograph no. 35 (Washington, D.C.: GPO, 1940), and Edward R. Hawkins, "Vertical Price Relationships," in Reavis Cox and Wroe Alderson, eds., *Theory in Marketing*, 1st ser. (Chicago: Irwin, 1950), pp. 179-191.

While we have chosen to employ a graphic approach in this presentation, an algebraic exposition has been used in a number of analyses of vertical demand relationships for agricultural products. See, for example, Richard J. Foote, *Analytical Tools for Studying Demand and Price Structures*, U.S. Department of Agriculture, Agriculture Handbook no. 146 (Washington, D.C.: GPO, 1958), pp. 100-110, and P. S. George and G. A. King, *Consumer Demand for Food Commodities in the United States with Projections for 1980*, Giannini Foundation Monograph no. 26 (Berkeley: University of California, Division of Agricultural Sciences, 1971), pp. 53-67. Other treatments, both theoretical and empirical, of margins for agricultural products are in Dana G. Dalrymple, *On the Nature of Marketing Margins*, Agricultural Economics Report no. 824 (East Lansing: Michigan Agricultural Experiment Station, 1961); Clifford Hildreth and Francis G. Jarrett, *A Statistical Study of Livestock Production*

Case I: Constant Percentage Margin

The marketing margin as a percentage of retail price remains constant as volume of sales increases. For this to be possible the dollar margin per unit decreases as sales increase. Figure 7.2 illustrates this type of price relationship. The line *ABCD* is the demand for a good at retail. The line *EFGD* is the demand at wholesale. The difference between the two, represented, for example, by *BF* and *CG*, is the marketing margin, which is a constant percentage of the retail price. The two demand curves converge at point *D*. If the supply is perfectly inelastic and is represented by *SQ*, the price at retail will be P_r, of which *CG* represents the retail margin. If the supply decreases to $S'Q'$, a new retail price of P_r' is established, of which *BF* is the new retail margin, and this new margin is the same percentage of P_r' as *CG* was of P_r. The percentage increase in the wholesale price is the same as the percentage increase in the retail price. The elasticity of demand at retail is exactly equal to the elasticity of demand at wholesale for any given quantity.[13]

Case I in Table 7.1 shows an arithmetic example in which retail margins are a constant percentage of the retail price.[14] Assuming a margin of 40 percent, we can see that if the retail price rises from $80 to $100, or 25 percent, the wholesale price will also rise 25 percent (from $48 to $60) if the 40 percent margin is retained. If the quantity bought and sold is the same in both retail and wholesale markets, it is apparent that the elasticity of demand is the same in both markets for any given quantity-price relationship.

One implication of such a demand relationship is that changes in supply conditions will cause the same relative changes in retail and wholesale markets. If, on the other hand, dollar margins rather than percentage margins are relatively rigid, price fluctuations will not be the same in the two types of markets.

Case II: Increasing Percentage Margin

The marketing margin as a percentage of retail price increases as volume of sales increases. This may be possible under different conditions with respect to dollar margins: Dollar margins may remain constant (Case IIA); they may increase (Case IIB); and they may decrease (Case IIC).

CASE IIA: CONSTANT DOLLAR MARGIN

Figure 7.3 illustrates Case IIA, in which the dollar margin remains constant regardless of volume. The retail margin is represented by the difference between the line *ABCD*, the demand at retail, and line *EFGH*, the demand at wholesale. *BF* equals *CG*; that is, the retail margin per unit is the same regardless of the volume of transactions. If supply is represented by *SQ*, the retail price will be P_r and the wholesale price P_w. If supply

---

and Marketing, Cowles Commission Monograph no. 15 (New York: Wiley, 1955); Anthony S. Rojko, *The Demand and Price Structure for Dairy Products*, U.S. Department of Agriculture, Technical Bulletin no. 1168 (Washington, D.C.: GPO, 1957); Frederick V. Waugh, *Demand and Price Analysis*, U.S. Department of Agriculture, Economic Research Service, Technical Bulletin no. 1316 (Washington, D.C.: GPO, 1964).

[13] See Appendix A of this chapter for a geometric proof of this and succeeding propositions.

[14] These are crude estimates in which the smaller value is used as the base.

Table 7.1 Arithmetic Examples of the Relationship of Retail and Wholesale Margins Under Varying Conditions

Case Number	Retail Margin Behavior as Quantity Purchased Increases		Quantity Purchased	Per Unit					
				Retail Price		Wholesale Price		Retail Margin	
	Percentage of Retail	Dollar Amount Per Unit		Amount	Percentage Difference[a]	Amount	Percentage Difference[a]	Amount	Relative to Retail Price
I	Constant	Decreases	100	$100		$60		$40	40%
			200	80	25%	48	25%	32	40
			300	60	33	36	33	24	40
			400	40	50	24	50	16	40
IIA	Increases	Constant	100	100		80		20	20
			200	80	25	60	33	20	25
			300	60	33	40	50	20	33
			400	40	50	20	100	20	50
IIB	Increases	Increases	100	100		90		10	10
			200	80	25	65	38	15	19
			300	60	33	40	63	20	33
			400	40	50	15	167	25	63

Table 7.1 (continued)

Case Number	Retail Margin Behavior as Quantity Purchased Increases		Quantity Purchased	Per Unit					
	Percentage of Retail	Dollar Amount Per Unit		Retail Price		Wholesale Price		Retail Margin	
				Amount	Percentage Difference[a]	Amount	Percentage Difference[a]	Amount	Relative to Retail Price
IIC	Increases	Decreases	100	100		80		20	20
					25		29		
			200	80		62		18	23
					33		41		
			300	60		44		16	27
					50		69		
			400	40		26		14	35
III	Decreases	Decreases	100	100		80		20	20
					25		18		
			200	80		68		12	15
					33		26		
			300	60		54		6	10
					50		42		
			400	40		38		2	5

[a]The percentage difference is computed with the smaller dollar value as the base.

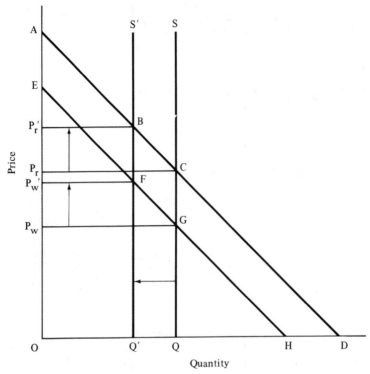

Figure 7.3. Derived demand: Case IIA.

decreases to $S'Q'$, the total price rises to P_r' and the wholesale price to P_w'. Since each price rises by the same amount, the proportionate change in the wholesale price is greater than in the retail price. This means that the elasticity of demand at retail is greater than the elasticity of demand at wholesale.

Part IIA of Table 7.1 illustrates this type of situation arithmetically. A retail margin of $20 exists for all price-quantity relationships. Such a margin is an increasing percentage of the retail price as quantity of sales increases and unit price decreases. But the relationship in which we are particularly interested is the relative change in retail price compared with that in wholesale price. When the retail price moves, for example, from $60 to $80, an increase of 33 percent, the wholesale price moves from $40 to $60, an increase of 50 percent. If the quantity bought and sold is the same in both retail and wholesale markets, it is apparent that the elasticity of demand is greater in the retail market, since the relative price adjustment is much greater in the wholesale market.

Case IIA may be a significant one. If we find that the cost of marketing—in this case, the cost of retailing—is almost a constant amount per unit sold regardless of volume of transactions, changes in supply conditions will be reflected in sharper movements in wholesale prices than in retail prices. There is some evidence that dollar margins in retailing are in fact fairly rigid with changing sales volume, particularly in the short run, and this may be a major factor in the greater fluctuations in wholesale prices through time than in retail prices.

CASE IIB: INCREASING DOLLAR MARGIN

Another type of situation, Case IIB, involves an increasing margin percentage and also an increasing dollar margin as volume of sales increases. Illustrated by Figure 7.4 and part

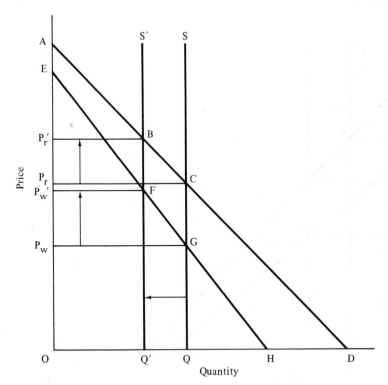

Figure 7.4. Derived demand: Case IIB.

IIB of Table 7.1, this is a case where retailing would presumably experience increasing costs. As the industry grows, cost of retailing per unit sold increases, giving rise to a derived demand for goods at wholesale that is far more inelastic than the demand for the same goods at retail. In Figure 7.4 the increase in the wholesale price from P_w to P_w' is greater absolutely than the corresponding increase in retail price from P_r to P_r' and obviously greater as a percentage of the base price. Section IIB of Table 7.1 shows the same principle arithmetically where, for example, an increase in the retail price from $60 to $80, or 33 percent, has associated with it an increase in wholesale price of 63 percent. The demand for goods at retail is therefore more elastic than the demand at wholesale. Also, the difference between retail and wholesale price elasticities in Case IIB is greater than in Case IIA.

This particular situation will occur only if retailing proves to be an industry of increasing costs, or if it is, at a given time, experiencing increasing costs as the size of the industry grows. If the total unit cost of retailing rises as volume of sales increases, the situation described by Case IIB will be representative.

CASE IIC: DECREASING DOLLAR MARGIN

Case IIC is more likely to occur than Case IIB if there are increasing returns to scale in marketing industries. In this situation, percentage margins increase, but dollar margins decrease as volume of sales expands with a lowering of prices. Figure 7.5 illustrates these relationships by showing a retail demand curve, $ABCD$, and a wholesale demand curve, $EFGH$, related by narrowing dollar margins but never reaching the point where retail and wholesale prices are equal with positive values. Part IIC of Table 7.1 shows a simplified arithmetic relationship between relative price changes in these two markets. Assuming the

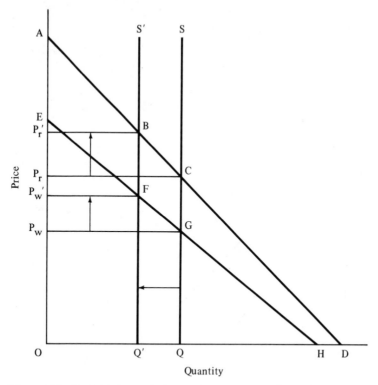

Figure 7.5. Derived demand: Case IIC.

same percentage change in quantity in both markets, we can see that an increase in retail price from $40 to $60, or 50 percent, has associated with it an increase in the wholesale price of 69 percent, thereby showing greater elasticity of demand in the retail market than in the wholesale market.

Case III: Decreasing Percentage Margin

Let us assume that the marketing margin as a percentage of retail price decreases as retail price decreases and quantity sold increases. In order for this to occur, the dollar margin must also decrease. If the percentage margin decreases, a point is reached where, with positive values for price and quantity, the margin becomes zero; beyond this point, an extrapolation of the same functions would show a negative margin, with wholesale prices higher than retail prices. It is not reasonable that vertically related firms will operate beyond this point of zero margin, since to do so would involve losses because the retail margin has become negative. Were firms to operate beyond that point, retailers would be subsidizing consumers. Up to this point, however, we find that the decreasing percentage margin throws a greater burden of price adjustment on the retail market and a relatively greater quantity adjustment on the wholesale market. For example, in Figure 7.6, as the retail price moves from P_{rw} to P_r', sales decline from OQ to OQ'. At the same time wholesale price rises from P_{rw} to only P_w'. The percentage change in quantity is the same for both wholesale and retail markets, while the percentage change in price is much greater for the retail market than for the wholesale market. We can say, therefore, that the elasticity of demand is greater in the wholesale market than in the retail market.

Part III of Table 7.1 illustrates this arithmetically. When the retail price rises from $40

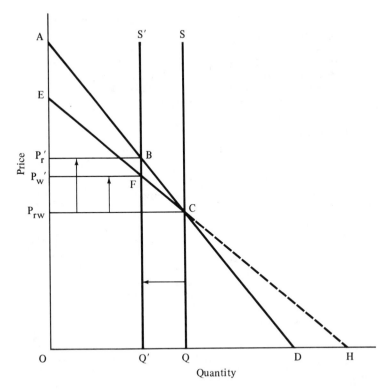

Figure 7.6. Derived demand: Case III.

to $60, or 50 percent, the wholesale price rises only 42 percent, showing that the quantity adjustment in the wholesale market relative to the price adjustment is greater than in the retail market.

If retailing or other marketing segments show signs of decreasing costs as volume of transactions increases, Case III provides an appropriate framework for analysis of the probable changes in retail and wholesale prices under conditions of changing supply. In this situation, wholesale prices will show less sensitivity than retail prices. As margins narrow with increasing output, a point is finally reached where margins become zero, and further expansion of the industry is unlikely because selling prices will not equal total costs.

Summary

Table 7.2 summarizes the price relationships that we have described in retail and wholesale markets. Because the structure of costs at various levels of the trade channel determines the supply of processing and marketing services, we shall reserve further generalizations about vertical price relationships until after we have explored some aspects of cost structure in various types of markets.

MARKETING MARGINS AND DEMAND ELASTICITIES: IMPERFECT COMPETITION

Up to this point, we have considered short-run demand relationships among vertically related markets of pure competition with increasing, decreasing, and constant costs in

Table 7.2 Summary of the Comparative Elasticities of Final and Derived Demands Under Differing Marketing Margins

Case Number	Margin Characteristics as Retail Price Decreases and Quantity Sold Increases	Graph	Relative Demand Elasticities
I	percentage margin constant; dollar margin decreases		$\eta_{AC} = \eta_{DC}$
II	percentage margin increases;		
A	dollar margin constant		$\eta_{AC} > \eta_{DF}$
B	dollar margin increases		$\eta_{AC} > \eta_{DF}$
C	dollar margin decreases		$\eta_{AC} > \eta_{DF}$
III	percentage margin decreases; dollar margin decreases		$\eta_{AC} < \eta_{DF}$

retailing. We shall now consider demand relationships among *firms* that are vertically related in the trade channel, and shall assume that these firms are operating in markets of imperfect competition, that is, markets in which the demand facing a particular firm is less than perfectly elastic. If consumers, for example, have a strong enough preference for a particular brand or retail outlet, some of them will be willing to pay more than the prevailing price in order to buy the good or buy from that firm, and additional customers can be attracted to this brand or store by a lower price. Under such circumstances the average revenue curve has a negative slope.

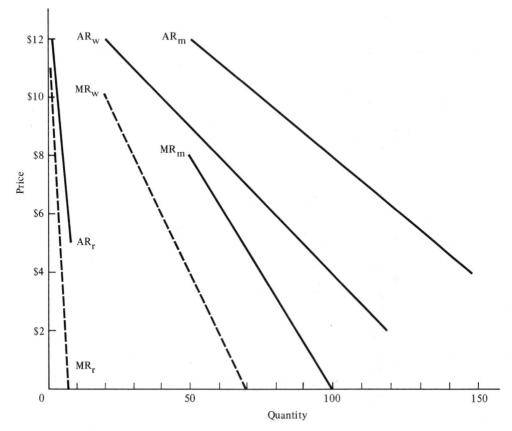

Figure 7.7. Average and marginal revenue for each of 100 retail firms, 5 wholesale firms, and 2 manufacturing firms, each operating under conditions of imperfect competition. Source: Table 7.3.

Vertical Demand Relationships

Table 7.3 and Figure 7.7 illustrate this situation. We describe here a situation in which each of 100 retail firms is operating with a demand curve that is less than perfectly elastic. There are 5 wholesale firms, which average one-fifth of the total volume of sales to retail firms. Wholesale firms are, in turn, serviced by two manufacturing firms. Since each retailer's sales are affected by his prices, his marginal revenue becomes in effect his demand price for goods at wholesale. Wholesale and retail firms are larger on an average than wholesale firms, and sales per firm will be larger but subject to the declining average revenue curves of their customers. The average-revenue curve for a firm at any level in the trade channel is the aggregate of the marginal revenue curves of its customers. This is demonstrated in Figure 7.7, where the AR_w curve for a single wholesaling firm is assumed to be 20 times the MR_r curve for its retail customers, and each manufacturing firm has an average revenue curve twice the MR_w curves of its wholesale customers.

In Figure 7.8 we have converted the data from Table 7.3 and Figure 7.7 into average revenue and marginal cost per unit sales per retailer. What we show here is how the demand curve facing *a single retailer* who is operating under conditions of imperfect

Table 7.3 An Example of Price and Quantity Relationships in Retail, Wholesale, and Manufacturer Markets Under Conditions of Imperfect Competition in Each Market

Retail Price per Unit P_r	Quantity Sales per Retailer Q_r	Total Revenue per Retailer P_rQ_r	Marginal Revenue per Retailer $\Delta(P_rQ_r)$	Wholesale Price per Unit P_w	Quantity Sales to all Retailers $100Q_r = \Sigma Q_w$	Quantity Sales per Wholesaler $\Sigma Q_w/5$	Total Revenue per Wholesaler P_wQ_w	Marginal Revenue per Wholesaler Per 20 Units $\Delta(P_wQ_w)$	Per Unit $\Delta(P_wQ_w)/20$
$12	1	$12	$12	$12	100	20	$240	$240	$12
11	2	22	10	10	200	40	400	160	8
10	3	30	8	8	300	60	480	80	4
9	4	36	6	6	400	80	480	0	0
8	5	40	4	4	500	100	400	-80	-4
7	6	42	2	2	600	120	240	-160	-8
6	7	42	0	0	700	140	0	-240	-12
5	8	40	-2		800				

Manufacturer's Price per Unit P_m	Quantity Sales to All Wholesalers $100Q_r = \Sigma Q_r = \Sigma Q_w = \Sigma Q_m$	Quantity Sales per Manufacturer $\Sigma Q_m/2$	Total Revenue per Manufacturer $P_m Q_m$	Marginal Revenue per Manufacturer Per 50 Units $\Delta(P_m Q_m)$	Per Unit $\Delta(P_m Q_m)/50$
$12	100	50	$600	$600	$12
8	200	100	800	200	4
4	300	150	600	-200	-4
0	400	200	0	-600	-12

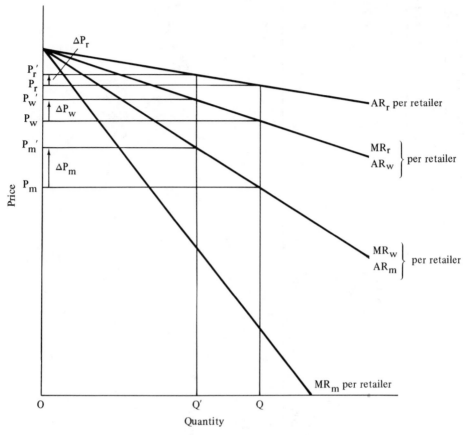

Figure 7.8. Derived demand per retailer: imperfect competition.

competition filters through the trade channel to become *a portion* of the total demand for wholesalers and manufacturers who supply him with goods and services. If we added together such curves from all retailers, we would then have the total demand facing wholesalers and manufacturers.[15] Let us examine in detail the meaning of the successive curves in Figure 7.8.

The AR_r curve is the average revenue for a good offered at retail *by one firm*. If Q quantity is placed on the market, the retail price will be P_r. The marginal revenue curve to the retailer is represented by MR_r. Because added quantities can be sold only if the price is lowered on all units, the marginal revenue declines twice as rapidly as the average revenue. A retailer will not, therefore, be willing to purchase Q quantity at a price higher than the marginal revenue he would obtain from that quantity. The retailer's marginal revenue then becomes *his* demand curve, that is, the wholesaler's AR *for sales to that one customer*. If the wholesaler aggregates the MR curves for all his customers, this then becomes his own AR_w curve, which we show in Figure 7.7. The retailer's MR_r for a given quantity is the wholesaler's P_w. If all retailers have the same AR curves, P_w is the highest

---

[15] Failure to see the relationship between what is shown in Figures 7.7 and 7.8 has caused confusion and some misinterpretation of vertical price movements. An example of this confusion is D. F. Dixon, "Demand Relationships in Marketing Channels," *Mississippi Valley Journal of Business and Economics* 6 (Spring 1971): 15-31.

price any one of them will be willing to pay for Q quantity, since this is the price that will exactly equal the marginal revenue each retailer can obtain when he sells this quantity at P_r. Thus MR_r, the retailer's marginal revenue, is also AR_w, the wholesaler's average revenue for that one customer. The total of these AR_w curves for all the wholesaler's customers will give the wholesaler his aggregate AR_w curve. A wholesaler selling to a retailer under conditions of imperfect competition cannot sell at a price higher than the marginal revenue of the retail firm. Given these conditions, the demand for goods at wholesale will be more inelastic than that for the same goods at retail.

The same analysis can apply when we are considering the relationship between the wholesaler's average revenue per retail customer, AR_w, and the manufacturer's average revenue per retail customer, AR_m. The wholesaler's declining average revenue as volume increases forces his marginal revenue per customer, MR_w, to decline even more rapidly, and he will not purchase Q quantity from the manufacturer at a price higher than P_m, which is the marginal revenue he will obtain from the purchase and resale of the last unit. MR_w is therefore the manufacturer's average revenue per retailer—the unit price at which the manufacturer can sell various quantities. The manufacturer's marginal revenue per retailer, MR_m, will, in combination with marginal cost, determine the output at which he will maximize profits. This is a case in which the elasticity of demand is greater the closer the market is to the ultimate consumer.

Note that in this discussion of imperfect competition we are not taking into account costs of operation for retailers, wholesalers, or manufacturers. We are speaking only of the effect of a less than perfectly elastic demand at one level of the trade channel on the elasticity of demand and prices at successive levels. This is the impact only of conditions of imperfect competition on price differentials in the trade channel. We would also need to know the costs of operation at different levels of the channel and the relation between costs and quantity sold to know fully what price differentials would actually prevail in vertical market relationships. We shall introduce cost variables in a later treatment of vertical price relationships.[16]

Effects of Changes in Demand and Supply

Up to this point, we have assumed that demand is given and have compared marketing margins with different margin policies. What effect would changes in demand have on the margins we have described? Under these conditions, changes in demand will not cause wholesale price fluctuations to be greater absolutely than price movements in retail markets, but they will cause relative price changes in wholesale markets to exceed those in retail markets.

Figure 7.9 illustrates the effect of an increase in demand on wholesale and retail prices. The original demand at retail is represented by DE, while DF is the marginal revenue for the retail firm and the average revenue for the wholesale firm. An increase in demand causes a shift of the demand curve to the right so that AB becomes the new average revenue curve at the retail level and AC the corresponding marginal revenue curve at retail and the average revenue per retailer at wholesale. If the supply is perfectly inelastic and is represented by KQ, the effect of the increase in demand is to raise the retail price from P_r to P_r' and the wholesale price from P_w to P_w'. ΔP_r will exactly equal ΔP_w: The absolute

---

[16] See Chapters 12 and 15.

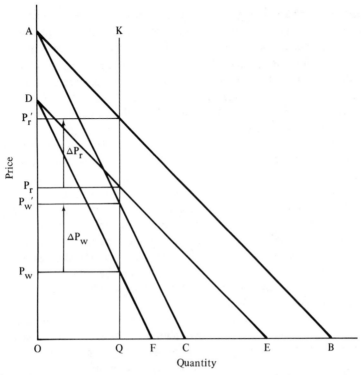

Figure 7.9. A change in demand and retail and wholesale margins: imperfect competition.

amount of price change will be the same in both markets. But because the wholesale price is lower than the retail price, the percentage change will be greater in the wholesale market.[17]

If we have described correctly the relationships among demands at three vertically related levels in the trade channel under conditions of imperfect competition, we can demonstrate the effect of a change in supply conditions on price movements in the three markets. In Figure 7.8, if there is a decrease in supply so that Q' instead of Q quantity is sold through all levels of the trade channel, prices in the retail market will rise from P_r to P_r', in the wholesale market from P_w to P_w', and in the manufacturer's market from P_m to P_m'. Not only is the absolute amount of price increase greatest in the manufacturer's market and least in the retail market, but the relative (percentage) change in price is greatest in the manufacturer's market and least in the retail market. In successive markets of imperfect competition, demand will not only be less than perfectly elastic in all markets but will become increasingly inelastic as markets become further removed from the ultimate consumer. One consequence of this pattern of demand relationships is that price fluctuations with changing supply conditions will be greatest, both absolutely and relatively, in markets furthest removed from the retail level.

ADDITIONAL VARIABLES AND DERIVED DEMAND

Consumer demand analysis began as a simple formulation of quantities purchased as a function of price and then developed into a multivariate analysis of consumption

---

[17] See Appendix B of this chapter for a geometric proof of this proposition.

expenditures in which a number of economic, demographic, social, and psychological variables were included and their parameters estimated. Our discussion of derived demand has, however, been limited almost exclusively to the measurement of relative price elasticities for linear demands at different market levels. It is appropriate to suggest at this point some of the additional factors that influence derived demand, which may eventually be incorporated in the models of derived demand relationships.

Dynamic Demand Conditions and Inventory Speculation

An additional complication that affects the transmission of demand changes through the trade channel is the variability of demand at any level in the channel. Variations in demand throw upon the marketing firm the need for adapting buying and inventory policies to the probable variation in sales. Let us examine the effects of demand variability on speculative inventory accumulation.

If retail firms are faced with marked variations in consumer demand through time, they will find it desirable to maintain larger average inventories than they would were the demand less variable so long as the probable value of sales revenue that they would lose, were those inventories not held, exceeds the marginal cost of maintaining additional stocks. The possibility of speculative inventory accumulation and decumulation modifies the way in which demand is transmitted from one market to another. If sales or price increases are expected, retailers may buy not merely for replacement of anticipated stock depletions but also for anticipated price increases, thus transmitting to the wholesale level a demand greater than would have occurred under more stable demand conditions. Likewise, anticipated price or sales decreases may cause inventory decumulation and decreased derived demand in more remote markets.

It would appear, therefore, that the more dynamic the demand situation at a given market level, the greater the probability that shifts of demand will be transmitted with exaggeration to the next market level. But this will not always occur, for marketing firms have to weigh two different factors against each other. Variability of demand makes it possible to engage in speculative inventory accumulation and decumulation. But the greater the variability of demand, the greater the risks associated with such speculation. The reaction of a marketing firm to such a situation will depend on its assessment of the probability of gain versus the probability of loss. From the firm's point of view, there is likely to be an optimum amount of demand variability for speculative inventory policies to be attractive. Too little variability may make speculation not worthwhile; too much may increase the risks beyond those the firm is willing to assume.

Elasticities at Various Output Levels

We have not considered the fact that elasticities are likely to vary at different output levels. When we say, for example, that a derived demand is likely to be more inelastic than a final demand, we should recognize that the differences in elasticities will vary according to the level of output at which firms of the industry are functioning. On linear demand curves elasticities decline as sales volume increases.

In the examples we have given, we have assumed that demand functions are linear. This may not be a realistic picture of particular markets. While nonlinear functions would not modify the basic logic underlying our analysis of demand relationships, they would alter the amount and variation in elasticity coefficients at various output levels. Were we to include in our analysis the influence of costs and consider the effects of curvilinear cost functions, this too would modify our conclusions concerning the optimum output.

Competitive Structure at Various Levels of the Trade Channel

Our examples involve assumptions concerning similar competitive conditions at all levels of the trade channel. It is possible that a high degree of competition at, let us say, the retail level may be associated with monopolistic control at another level. In the automobile industry, for example, a manufacturing industry characterized by oligopoly services a retail industry in which the physical product itself shows the same degree of differentiation but in which the number and variety of alternative retail outlets is so great that manufacturers have, through the franchise, deliberately established policies that would control the use of competitive devices among retail dealers. Such differences in competitive structure in vertically related markets are often conducive to vertical integration or disintegration.

It is quite likely that there may also be situations in which the kinked demand curve may better represent the structure of consumer demand. In markets characterized by both monopolistic competition and oligopoly, a firm has a less than perfectly elastic demand for its own brand and may attract additional customers by lowering its price and detract some customers by raising its price. But if the firm's price is raised above the general level prevailing in the industry, it is probable that its loss of clientele may be substantial because of the availability of reasonably good substitutes in the form of other brands. This therefore causes the firm's demand curve to "kink" or bend at the point of its prevailing price. A price reduction attracts additional customers but not so many as are repelled by a price increase. Under these circumstances, the derived demand curve will take on a special character, which complicates our analysis.

The absolute amount of elasticity and the differences between elasticities in retail and wholesale markets will depend, therefore, not only on the amount of goods bought and sold but also on the degree to which buyers and sellers can behave independently of competing buyers and sellers.

Long-Run Versus Short-Run Demand

An additional condition of considerable import in understanding relative elasticities of demand is the time dimension within which elasticities are established. Most studies suggest that long-run demand elasticity is greater than short-run demand elasticity, and because of the interrelationship of final and derived demand, long-run derived demand would be expected to show greater elasticity than short-run derived demand.

Another facet of these relationships rests on the possibility that vertically related demands may not represent the same time periods. It is possible, for example, that short-run fluctuations in consumer demand at the retail level may not be transmitted back to the wholesale level in terms of demand derived specifically and precisely from the short-run final demand but, rather, in the form of an accumulation of short-run demands over a period of time, with the retailer absorbing the differences between the two. We have alluded to these in our discussion of inventory speculation. A retailer can assume time functions and substitute his skills of anticipation for those of the consumer. If his competence in foresight exceeds that of the average consumer, he will behave in such a way that he transmits to the wholesaler a demand more like the cumulative short-run demands of consumers. This is reflected in the market place in a difference in the scale and frequency of market participation by firms at various levels of the trade channel.

It is interesting to note, however, that the market behavior of small-scale manufacturing firms is often similar to that of households. They may depend on marketing firms to perform functions associated with variations through time in supply and demand. Wherever in the trade channel there is a locus where time functions are performed, there is likely to be transmitted from that point a demand more elastic than would occur were the firm's activities primarily those of responding to its customers' short-run demands. If, for example, wholesalers "collect" a cluster of retail demands and anticipate future clusters by buying in large quantities and storing goods against future demand, the demand they transmit back to the manufacturer is likely to be more elastic than that transmitted by the retail firms. The retailers' demands are short run and the wholesaler's demand is long run. Likewise, if wholesalers of industrial goods serve an industry in which manufacturing is performed by many small, decentralized firms, it is likely that the demands transmitted by wholesalers into factor markets, where such things as machinery, labor, and raw materials are being purchased, would be more elastic to the extent that the wholesalers are performing time functions, which makes wholesale demands more elastic than those of the wholesaler's customers. Time functions may apply to anticipations of short-run demand fluctuations "above" the firm or short-run supply fluctuations "below" the firm. In either case the transmitted demand is more elastic than it would be without the performance of the time function. These observations bring us to a summary generalization concerning derived demand.

Factors Peculiar to Particular Market Situations

Each trade channel has characteristics peculiar to itself. Demand and supply conditions vary not only between industries but between horizontally related markets and particularly between vertically related markets. Therefore the patterns we have described in our discussion are highly generalized and are subject to extensive modifications when they are applied to particular market situations at different levels of a trade channel. Manufacturer-wholesaler-retailer relationships in farm machinery differ markedly from those in food, electrical equipment, or textiles, and only a careful consideration of the market conditions peculiar to each industry and each market level can reveal the variables that need to be studied and suggest their probable import in the demand structure.

Appendix A

ELASTICITY OF DEMAND IN VERTICALLY RELATED RETAIL AND WHOLESALE MARKETS

In each of the following cases, the average revenue at retail is AC and the average revenue at wholesale DF. When sales are OQ the retail price is QB, the wholesale price QE, and the retail margin EB.

Case I (Figure 7A.1)

Conditions: As the quantity purchased increases, the percentage margin is constant and the dollar margin per unit decreases.

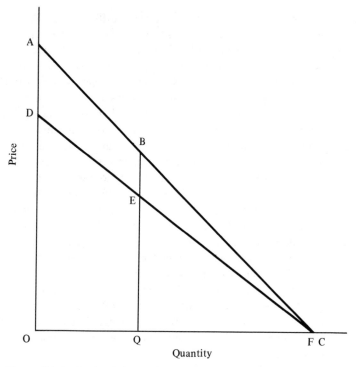

Figure 7A.1. Derived demand: Case I.

Proof that $\eta_B = \eta_E$:

$$\eta_B = \frac{BC}{AB}$$

$$\eta_E = \frac{EC}{DE}$$

$$\frac{BC}{AB} = \frac{QC}{OQ}$$

since a line parallel to the base of a triangle divides the other sides proportionally.

Also, $\dfrac{EC}{DE} = \dfrac{QC}{OQ}$

Therefore

$$\frac{BC}{AB} = \frac{EC}{DE} \quad \text{and} \quad \eta_B = \eta_E$$

Case IIA (Figure 7A.2)

Conditions: As the quantity purchased increases, the percentage margin increases and the dollar margin per unit is constant.

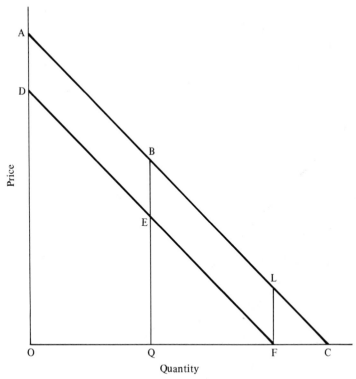

Figure 7A.2. Derived demand: Case IIA.

Proof that $\eta_B > \eta_E$:

$$\eta_B = \frac{BC}{AB}$$

$$\eta_E = \frac{EF}{DE}$$

$$AB = DE$$

Draw $LF \parallel BEQ$ and ADO.
$$EF = NL$$
Therefore
$$BC > BL$$
Since
$$\frac{BC}{AB} > \frac{EF}{DE} \quad \text{then} \quad \eta_B > \eta_E$$

Case IIB (Figure 7A.3)

Conditions: As the quantity purchased increases, the percentage margin increases and the dollar margin per unit increases.

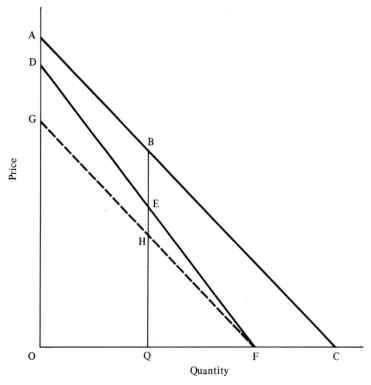

Figure 7A.3. Derived demand: Case IIB.

Figure 7A.4. Derived demand: Case IIC.

Proof that $\eta_B > \eta_E$:
   Draw *GHF* || *ABC.*
        $\eta_E = \eta_H$ (from Case I)
        $\eta_B > \eta_H$ (from Case IIA)
   Therefore

$$\eta_B > \eta_E$$

Case IIC (Figure 7A.4)

Conditions: As the quantity purchased increases, the percentage margin increases and the dollar margin per unit decreases.

Proof that $\eta_B > \eta_E$:
   Draw *GHF* || *ABC.*
        $\eta_E = \eta_H$ (from Case I)
        $\eta_B > \eta_H$ (from Case IIA)
   Therefore

$$\eta_B > \eta_E$$

Case III (Figure 7A.5)

Conditions: As the quantity purchased increases, the percentage margin decreases and the dollar margin per unit decreases.

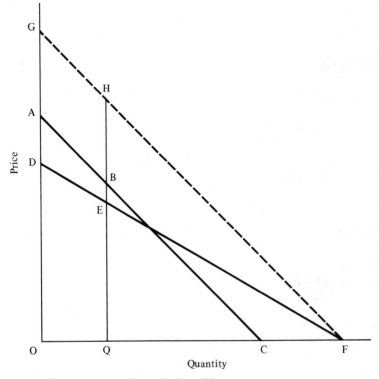

Figure 7A.5. Derived demand: Case III.

Proof that $\eta_B < \eta_E$:
   Draw $GHF \parallel ABC$.
     $\eta_H = \eta_E$ (from Case I)
     $\eta_H > \eta_B$ (from Case IIA)
   Therefore
     $\eta_B < \eta_E$

Appendix B

EFFECT OF CHANGES IN DEMAND ON CHANGES IN RETAIL AND WHOLESALE PRICES UNDER IMPERFECT COMPETITION

See Figure 7B.1.

DE is the original average revenue at retail.

DF is the original marginal revenue at retail and the original average revenue at wholesale.

AB is the new average revenue at retail and is parallel to DE.

AC is the new marginal revenue at retail and the new average revenue at wholesale.

GL is parallel to OB and intersects DE and AC at point J.

By definition $OF = FE$ and $OC = CB$.

RW is parallel to OB.

With the increased demand the retail price rises from M to K and the wholesale price from P to N.

Proof that $HJ = ST$:
   By definition
     $GH = HJ$
     $GH + HJ = JL$
   If HJ is substituted for GH
     $HJ + HJ = JL$
   Therefore

$$HJ = \frac{JL}{2}$$

   Since
     $JL = VW$ then $HJ = \dfrac{VW}{2}$

   Also by definition,
     $RS = ST + TV$
     $RS + ST = TV + VW$
   Therefore
     $ST = TV + VW - RS$
   If $ST + TV$ is substituted for RS,
     $ST = TV + VW - (ST + TV)$
   Therefore
     $ST = VW - ST$
    $2ST = VW$
     $ST = \dfrac{VW}{2}$

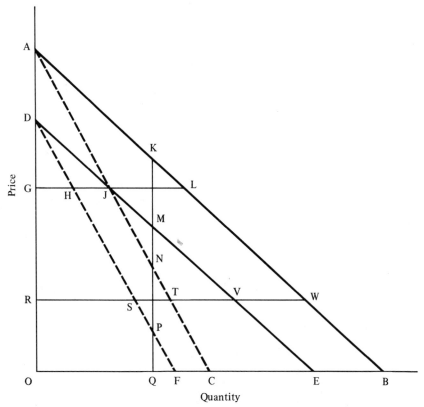

Figure 7B.1. A change in demand and retail and wholesale prices: imperfect competition.

$HJ = ST$
$AC \parallel DF$

Proof that $PN = MK$:
 $KQ \parallel AO$
 $AB \parallel DE$
 $AC \parallel DF$
Therefore
 $PN = AD$
 $MK = AD$
 $PN = MK$

iii

The Structure of the Marketing Industry

8

Organization of The Marketing System

Nature hides her secrets through
her intrinsic grandeur, but not
through deception.

—Albert Einstein

We began our discussion of the economics of marketing by delineating the economic functions of marketing, showing how the marketing system is related to the total economic structure and how the activities carried on within the system are a part of the broad complex of economic activities. We then turned our attention to the structure of demand. We considered in some detail the characteristics of consumer demand and then examined the relationship between consumer demand and derived demand in wholesale markets.

The principal focus of Part III will be on the supply of marketing services—the institutional structure and functional relationships that make up the organized marketing system. We use the term *system* to indicate that there is an institutional and functional framework within which the behavior of individual decision-making entities is unified in the course of their participation in the market as buyers, sellers, and/or facilitators of buying and selling.

The marketing system as a whole has the broad function of coordinating specialized economic units of society through transactions. In so doing it fills gaps between decision-making entities—gaps of intelligence, time, and space. These broad economic functions can be translated into specific business functions of buying, transporting, selling, and storing. In physical terms these would be assembling, mixing, holding, and dispersing. Each of these functions may be performed under conditions of certainty, risk (probability), or uncertainty. Any one of these could be further broken into numerous subfunctions. Buying, for example, involves evaluation of needs, formulation of specifications, acquisition of marketing information, evaluation of market choices, negotiation, and financing.

THE TRADING FIRM

A marketing, or trading, firm specializes in the performance of marketing functions. If it is a highly specialized firm—such as a food broker—it performs a limited number of marketing functions. Generally, however, we reserve the term *marketing firm* (or trading firm) for the firm whose principal functions are buying, selling, and holding stocks of merchandise. In addition, the typical marketing firm performs auxiliary functions associated with its primary functions of moving and maintaining stocks and buying and selling goods and services. Speculation may or may not be a primary part of the firm's activities. The pure marketing firm does not process goods physically; therefore its net income is a function of the buying, selling, transportation, and storage activities around which its operation revolves.

It is not too difficult to observe and measure the output of firms in some industries. Firms in the automobile industry are producing passenger cars, trucks, buses, and parts, and these can usually be described in physical terms and counted in real and monetary units. Agricultural output is measurable in units that indicate its weight, bulk, or value. Transportation output can be measured in such units as ton miles. The output of the trading firm, however, is services. In this respect, the trading firm is much like a service business. Services are often ambiguous, difficult to describe with precision, and almost impossible to isolate and measure in real terms. It is also difficult to place a monetary value on marketing services, for they are rarely separated from the physical product with which they are associated and cannot be valued empirically as a separate entity unless the physical product can be priced both with and without the services. The customer of a retail store or wholesale firm buys from the retailer or wholesaler not goods but services, such as the retailer's anticipation, transaction services, product mix, financing, delivery, and information. In considering the services of marketing, it is helpful to distinguish between those necessary to complete the production process and those auxiliary services that are not necessary to complete the production of a good but have utility to buyers or sellers.

PRODUCTION-COMPLETING SERVICES

Services that are essential to the completion of production must be performed, or the utility of an item to the consumer or industrial user is zero or negative. With such services the utility of the item is positive. For example, meat in the packer's warehouse has no utility to a consumer who has neither physical nor legal access to it. A retail firm that performs functions necessary to transfer the product physically and legally to the consumer's possession is completing the production process for that good. While the consumer might have performed these services himself, the retail firm specializes in such functions. These services, or functions, are those of type I, simple coordination, and type II, competitive speculation, identified in Figure 1.3. They are passive or neutral and are utility creating. A very large share of the services rendered by the typical retailer or wholesaler is of this type.

AUXILIARY SERVICES

At the other end of the continuum are auxiliary services. If these are performed, they have utility for the buyer or seller. If they are not performed, their absence does *not* reduce the utility of the good to which they are complementary to zero or a negative value but instead merely causes the positive value of the good to be less than it would have been had such services been rendered. Auxiliary services may be either marketing or nonmarketing services. If marketing, they are of type IV, creative speculation.[1] If nonmarketing, such services are in the nature of form production, such as, for example, repairs and alterations. Retailing is full of examples of both types of auxiliary services: alteration of ready-made wearing apparel to obtain better fit; provision of restaurants, clubrooms, and bridge lessons to attract patronage; maintenance of bureaus of general

---

[1] Because they do not create social utility, type III functions, monopolistic speculation, are not considered a "service" of marketing. Socially this type of function is a disservice. This does not preclude the possibility of its having value to an individual, however, for restriction of output can increase the exchange value of a product to its owner.

information; advertising and sales promotion. Although wholesaling also provides auxiliary services, it is less frequently concerned with such services than is true is retailing.

Why does a retailer or wholesaler, who is primarily a marketer of goods, provide auxiliary services? Clearly these additional functions are designed to increase profits. So long as the added cost of the service is less than the added revenue from it, the firm is justified in adding the service, But the cost-revenue calculus may be complicated by the fact that the added revenue cannot always so obviously be related to the added cost. In marketing, perhaps more than any other field or business endeavor, the effect of a particular activity on *total* revenue is the critical question. For example, some department stores show a profit on their restaurant, but many do not. Such a service can be justified even at a loss if it can be shown that it increases the revenue of the store more than it increases the store's total cost of operation. It may provide convenience and attraction to the customer and keep him in the store for a longer time, thereby exposing him to a larger number of buying appeals. Similarly, the cost to the wholesale firm of time and effort of its salesmen to help resolve the day-to-day business problems of the firm's customers may add to the firm's long-run revenue far more than it adds to short-run costs. The complex structure of merchandising and service operations in retailing and wholesaling, characterized by large numbers of joint demands and considerable cross-elasticity of demand, makes it probable that such firms appraise services in terms of their indirect effects on total profits.

An additional complication in the analysis of the output of marketing firms arises because the utility of some of the services rendered accrues to the seller rather than to the buyer. Advertising, for example, which is directed toward increasing demand, presumably yields benefits to buyers who become informed or persuaded, but not all the benefits of advertising expenditures are garnered by the buyer. If they had the option, some buyers would choose not to pay for their pro rata share of advertising. This injects, therefore, an additional dimension into the analysis of the marketing firm's operation. We shall explore this more thoroughly when we consider the problem of efficiency in marketing.

INSTITUTIONAL STRUCTURE OF THE MARKETING SYSTEM: VERTICAL

The Trade Channel

A trade channel consists of specialized marketing institutions that relate to each other as buyers and sellers. Just as marketing functions can be grouped broadly into those concerning the transfer of title and those concerning physical supply, channels can also be described as (1) the institutions through which title moves from raw material to intermediate consumer and from intermediate to ultimate consumer, or (2) the institutions that perform transportation and storage functions as products move through time and space to consumers. (See Figure 8.1.) Some marketing firms, such as agents, perform only one of these two sets of functions. Others, such as merchant wholesalers, perform both. The flow of title is between successive owners and involves a two-way flow, that is, the exchange of title to a specific good for a title to goods in general, or generalized purchasing power. An equality is achieved in each transaction. On the other hand, the physical flow of goods is in one direction only, and institutions in the physical marketing channel are holders or movers of stocks but not necessarily of title. Each institution in a trade channel performs a function that is essential in the sequence of functions necessary to complete the production process, and each is unique in the time

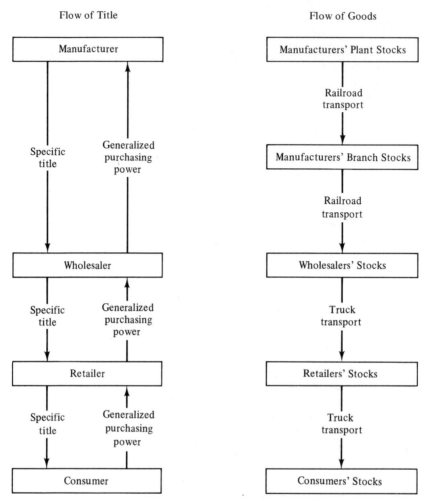

Figure 8.1. Flow of title and flow of goods between manufacturer and consumer.

when it performs its functions. Functions are often realigned among marketing firms as cost structures and competitive patterns change.

Two of the basic problems in trade channel analysis are determining (1) the optimum number of firms for the flow of product title between producer and ultimate consumer, and (2) the optimum number of establishments for facilitating the transfer of title and for performing physical marketing functions. These problems of channel structure cannot be isolated from those of horizontal market relationships. Whether or not, for example, a wholesaler is most efficient in holding and transfering title and in moving, storing, and mixing goods depends in large measure on his volume of business, and this, in turn, depends on the number of competitors with whom he shares these kinds of functions. Questions of specialization or integration both vertically and horizontally are interrelated.

Determinants of Trade Channels

Figure 8.2 outlines the major conditions that are conducive to long or short trade channels. The length of channel is a function of the characteristics of the product, of its

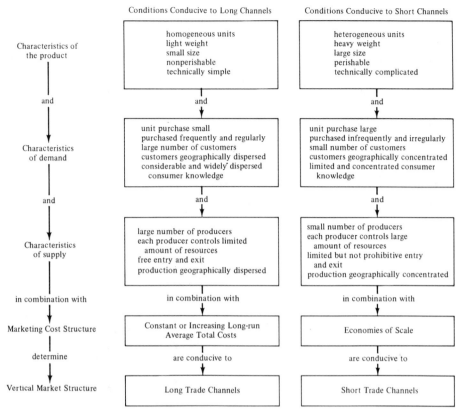

Figure 8.2. Determinants of trade channel length.

demand, of its supply, and of the cost structure of the marketing firms that integrate demand and supply. These factors are also determinants of competitive structure.

Each of these influences is, in turn, a result of certain other conditions. For example, the characteristics of demand that determine trade channel length concern the size of unit purchase, the frequency and regularity of purchase, the number of customers and their geographic distribution, and the amount and dispersion of buyer knowledge. These are basically matters of *dispersion* of the aggregate demand through time and space. Similarly, the characteristics of the product that are identified in Figure 8.2 are a matter of qualitative dispersion physically, technically, and functionally. Finally, the characteristics of supply are also matters of dispersion of the aggregate output institutionally and geographically.

Market organization, including trade channel length, is greatly affected by the costs of marketing firms. If the costs of marketing firms are constant as size of firm increases, there is no incentive for the firm to be large or small unless it faces a declining average revenue. It is not likely, though, that marketing costs are constant as scale of operations increases. Even though firms may show fairly stable costs as volume of sales increases within certain limits, increased sales beyond a certain point usually entail a widening of market areas and, with that, an increase in the costs of the firm or in the buying costs incurred by the customer. If, on the other hand, a marketing firm experiences economies of scale, it will seek these lower unit costs by increasing the scale of operations, thereby reducing the number of such firms horizontally and shortening the channels of distribution.

Seldom does a product or the market situation in which it is produced and sold fit precisely all the characteristics of either of the extremes on any one continuum. Some characteristics of a market situation may be conducive to long channels; others may be conducive to short ones. A fairly homogeneous product, such as cement, is very bulky and involves large transportation costs. Automobiles are sold to customers widely dispersed geographically, yet are produced by a small number of firms whose plants are geographically concentrated. These divergent forces sometimes cancel out, sometimes do not. It is the net effect of all the divergent forces that determines where along the continuum the channel(s) for a particular product will fall.

INSTITUTIONAL STRUCTURE OF THE MARKETING SYSTEM: HORIZONTAL

The Concept of Competition

Economic theorists have devoted considerable attention to the delineation of various types of competitive models and to the analysis of the behavior of firms and consumers in these situations. The basic issue is whether the nature of the product and the number and behavior of buyers and sellers is such that ultimate consumers are assured of (1) prices close to the lowest possible unit cost, (2) an optimum variety of goods and innovations to meet the diversity of consumer demand, and (3) realization of the productive potentials of the economy's physical and nonphysical resources. Starting from the concept of pure competition and monopoly, they have defined and analyzed deviations from these with respect to numbers of buyers, numbers of sellers, and product homogeneity. In addition, the concept of perfect competition has been introduced, and variations with respect to the extent of knowledge on the part of market participants and of freedom of entry into and exit from markets have been introduced as additional variables influencing market structure and behavior.[2] Those models of greatest interest to the marketing economist are modifications of pure and perfect competition and of pure monopoly. Some are deviations from the pure and perfect types; others are hybrids.

EFFECTIVE COMPETITION

Building on the work of Joan Robinson and Edward H. Chamberlin, John M. Clark has raised important questions about the usefulness of the traditional concept of competition viewed as a mechanism of equilibrium rather than as a dynamic process. He has emphasized what he calls "effective competition," in which competition is regarded as an

---

[2] The marketing student will find some of the important developments in value and price theory in Alfred Marshall, *Principles of Economics,* 8th ed. (London: Macmillan, 1890); Edward H. Chamberlin, *The Theory of Monopolistic Competition*, 7th ed. (Cambridge, Mass.: Harvard University Press, 1956); Edward H. Chamberlin, *Toward a More General Theory of Value* (New York: Oxford University Press, 1957); Joan Robinson, *The Economics of Imperfect Competition* (London: Macmillan, 1933); William Fellner, *Competition Among the Few* (New York: Knopf, 1950); Robert Triffin, *Monopolistic Competition and General Equilibrium Theory* (Cambridge, Mass.: Harvard University Press, 1940). A summary of traditional theory is in E. A. G. Robinson, *The Structure of Competitive Industry*, rev. ed. (Chicago: University of Chicago Press, 1959). See also the review volume by Robert E. Kuenne, ed., *Monopolistic Competition Theory: Studies in Impact* (New York: Wiley, 1967).

activity rather than a state of hypothetical equilibrium. At one point he refers to competition as "a sequence of moves and responses."[3]

Clark defines competition between business units as "the effort of such units, acting independently of one another (without concerted action), each trying to make a profitable volume of sales in the face of the offers of other sellers of identical or closely similar products."[4] It is action designed to improve the *relative* position of a market participant. Such action may be aggressive, to enhance the seller's or buyer's position, or it may be defensive, to prevent or minimize encroachment by other firms on the market position of the firm that undertakes the activity.

COMPETITIVE CONDITIONS, ACTIVITIES, AND PRESSURES

Clark distinguished among competitive conditions, competitive activities, and competitive pressures. The *conditions* of competition are the market structure, its mores, and the structure of industry. Competitive *activities* can take several forms. They may concern the product itself, the amount and quality of selling effort, or the price, including all terms of the transaction. Firms undertake these activities either as initiators or in response to actions of other firms in the same market, and such actions may be aggressive or defensive. Competitive *pressures* result from both current and potential conditions and activities. These are the forces that impel a firm to additional action. At no other point does the difficulty—and impossibility—of isolating "marketing" from "economics" become more clearly apparent.

Some of the most critical marketing decisions in our economy concern competitive actions that a firm can and should undertake and that, from a social point of view, have an impact on resource utilization and allocation and, hence, on consumer welfare. Also, both the marketing specialist and the economist are greatly concerned with competitive conditions and pressures and their effects on market participants. Although socially ideal economic decisions in a nonmarket economy would theoretically be the same as socially ideal decisions in a market economy, given the same objectives, it is unlikely that correct decisions could be made in the absence of markets without the use of synthetic market analysis. It is this basic identity of interest that behooves economists and marketing specialists to open wider the intellectual trade channels between their fields in order that both may benefit.

Determinants of Competitive Structure

In our discussion of the determinants of trade channel length, we identified four determining factors: the characteristics of the product, those of the demand, those of supply, and those of the structure of marketing costs. (See Figure 8.2.) Many of the

---

[3] See his original exposition, "Toward a Concept of Workable Competition," *American Economic Review* 30 pt. 1 (June 1940): 243-244, and especially his more recent *Competition as a Dynamic Process* (Washington, D.C.: Brookings, 1961). Other discussions of Clark's concept of workable (effective) competition can be found in George Stigler, "Extent and Bases of Monopoly," *American Economic Review* 32, pt. 2, supp. (June 1942): 2-3; Jesse Markham, "An Alternative Approach to the Concept of Workable Competition," *American Economic Review* 40 (June 1950): 349-360; Corwin D. Edwards, *Maintaining Competition* (New York: McGraw-Hill, 1949), pp. 9-10.

[4] Clark, *Competition as a Dynamic Process*, p. 13.

conditions that underlie these attributes of markets are also determinants of competitive structure.

THE PRODUCT

Product homogeneity is essential to a purely competitive market situation. If the number of possible product variations is considerable, it is likely that these quality differences will be reflected in a modified competitive situation. Simplicity of a product is also critical, for product complexity increases the difficulty of obtaining full information on the part of the consumer. Similarly, covert product characteristics make it more difficult for buyers to be fully informed. The technical attributes of a good are therefore of considerable importance in determining what kind of market situation can, and is likely to, develop.

STRUCTURE OF DEMAND

There are three facets of demand that influence competitive structure. First, the greater the variability in buyer preferences, the greater the opportunities for product and service differentiation in marketing. Income distribution, patterns of social influence and behavior, and the range in personal tastes and capacities determine the range in quantities and qualities of goods desired by consumers. These influences filter down to determine derived demand. It is within this preference space that marketing institutions locate themselves. Heterogeneous marketing firms are in part a reflection of heterogeneity of demand.

A second demand condition that influences the nature of horizontal market structure is the extent to which a derived demand is large enough to support specialized production units. The number of sawmills in operation will be determined by the demand for lumber from lumberyards and by the contractors who place orders directly with wholesalers or manufacturers. If the demand for lumber declines, the number of sawmills will also decline, but equally important, there is likely to be increased vertical integration in the industry if sawmilling becomes unprofitable as a specialized business operation but continues to be necessary to the more profitable wood-processing industry. Changes in demand or supply conditions filter through to the intermediate marketing firms and modify the competitive structure by changing the number of firms or by encouraging increased vertical integration or disintegration.

Finally, the amount and dispersion of buyer knowledge of products and market alternatives greatly influences demand. The greater the amount of market knowledge on the part of buyers, the greater will be the possible influence of buyers on the market behavior of selling firms. There are often substantial differences between retail and wholesale markets in the level of buyers' knowledge. These differences are reflected in the comparative competitive structure of markets at these two levels.

It is of some interest to consider the proportion of buyers who must be informed for this factor to serve as an effective market thermostat. Must all buyers be informed, or need only a portion be knowledgeable? It would appear that a relatively small percentage of consumers need to be highly informed, and the greater the number with *some* information, the less information each needs to have so long as their information is not duplicated. Suppose, for example, that a supermarket is sensitive to the possibility of losing customers through improper price or merchandise policies. Only marginal customers would be affected by a change in policies. Under conditions in which uniform policies and prices are applied to all customers, sensitivity of marginal customers to the firm's actions will keep the firm in line for the benefit of all consumers. This assumes, of course, that all customers have similar demands. Unique demands by a single consumer cannot be protected by this method.

There is an optimum amount of buyer information that needs to be made available, and there is indeed an optimum dispersion of that information among consumers. In view of the relatively high cost of technical consumer education, this fact may be of considerable importance in maximizing social returns from a given public or private expenditure for consumer education.

CHARACTERISTICS OF SUPPLY

Supply characteristics that determine competitive structure include the quantities and qualities of resources available, the freedom of entry into and exit from the industry, the number and economic proximity of sellers, the potentials for creating differentiated goods and services, and possibilities for economies of scale. Marketing firms are particularly sensitive to possibilities for achieving competitive advantages through an optimal mix of imitation and differentiation. What the firm will seek is optimal differentiation with respect to (1) price and terms of sale; (2) physical, aesthetic, and functional attributes of its products and product mix; and (3) services, ranging from tangible services such as delivery, repair, and maintenance to intangibles such as information, anticipation of demand through time and space under conditions of risk and uncertainty, and the assumption for buyers of postpurchase risk and uncertainty. When combined with advertising and promotion, these means of differentiation become the basis upon which retail and wholesale firms determine their marketing mix and, hence, their identity, which can be viewed as a location on the product, service, and price surfaces of the marketing system. It is these options and decisions that will comprise the subject matter of Part IV.

Concentration in Retail and Wholesale Trade

One of the important evidences of the competitive structure in marketing is the degree of concentration among firms and establishments in retailing and wholesaling. We shall utilize some standard techniques for showing relative concentration among marketing establishments and firms, and comment on some important trends in concentration.

LORENZ CURVES AND GINI COEFFICIENTS

One of the most useful measures of relative concentration is the Gini coefficient, derived from the Lorenz curve, which shows graphically the concentration of a distribution.[5] If retail stores, for example, are arrayed according to their size, from smallest to largest (see Table 8.1), and the cumulative percentage of total retail sales and the cumulative

[5] M. O. Lorenz, "Methods of Measuring the Concentration of Wealth," *Quarterly Publications of the American Statistical Association* 9, n.s., no. 70 (June 1905): 209-219. See also James Morgan, "The Anatomy of Income Distribution," *Review of Economics and Statistics* 44 (August 1962): 270-283, especially pp. 281-282; Mary Jean Bowman, "A Graphical Analysis of Personal Income Distribution in the United States," *American Economic Review* 35 (September 1945): 607-628.

Table 8.1 The Distribution of Total Retail Sales Among Total Retail Establishments in the United States Classified by Sales Volume of Establishment, 1967[a]

Sales per Establishment	Number of Establishments	Sales (Add 000)	Percentage of		Cumulative Percentage of	
			Total Establishments	Total Sales	Total Establishments	Total Sales
Less than $5,000	89,030	$ 277,209	5.33	.09	4.33	.09
$ 5,000- 9,000	130,776	900,927	7.83	.30	13.16	.39
10,000- 19,000	201,506	2,908,004	12.06	.97	25.22	1.36
20,000- 29,000	161,679	3,947,104	9.68	1.32	34.90	2.68
30,000- 49,000	226,823	8,769,334	13.58	2.93	48.48	5.61
50,000- 99,000	322,761	22,887,829	19.32	7.64	67.80	13.25
100,000-299,000	358,570	60,290,397	21.46	20.14	89.26	33.39
300,000-499,000	73,702	28,109,627	4.41	9.39	93.67	42.78
500,000-999,000	55,400	38,463,767	3.32	12.84	96.99	55.62
More than $1,000,000	50,323	132,875,627	3.01	44.38	100.00	100.00
Total	1,670,570	$299,429,825	100.00	100.00		

[a]Includes only establishments operated entire year.

Source: U.S., Bureau of the Census, *Census of Business, 1967*, vol. I, *Retail Trade–Summary Statistics*, pt. 1 (Washington, D.C.: GPO, 1971), p. 2-1.

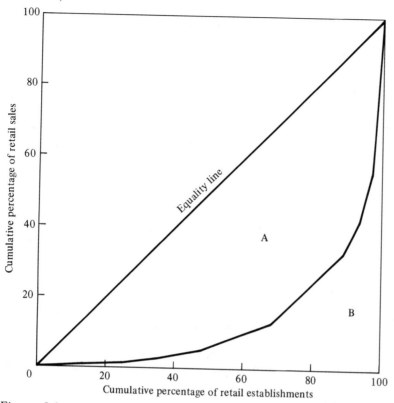

Figure 8.3. Lorenz curve of cumulative percentage of retail establishments that accounted for a cumulative percentage of retail sales in the United States in 1967. Source: Table 8.1.

percentage of retail stores are plotted against each other, as in Figure 8.3, where we show the distribution of total retail sales in the United States in 1967, the larger the gap between the equality line and the curve, the greater the inequality in the distribution of sales among retail establishments, that is, the larger the percentage of total retail sales accounted for by the few largest stores. The Gini coefficient, a measure of relative degree of inequality, is the ratio of area A in Figure 8.3 to the total area $(A + B)$. It can range from 0.00, perfect equality, to 1.00, perfect inequality. Thus the larger the coefficient, the greater the degree of inequality in the distribution of sales among establishments.[6]

---

[6] The distribution curve can be described by

$$\log N = \delta \log Y - \log c$$

in which N measures the number of units among which the variable is distributed (in our example, number of establishments) in which the distributed variable (in our example, retail sales) for each is greater than a given amount, z, and Y measures the aggregate of the distributed variable above z. The Gini coefficient is δ.

This is closely related to the Pareto coefficient derived from the formula

$$\log N = \log A - a \log x$$

in which N is the number of units in which the distributed variable is at least as large as x, and A is a constant. The Pareto coefficient, a, is a measure of the degree of inequality in the distribution: The higher its value, the greater the concentration of the distribution. The Gini N is a function of S, the total of the distributed variable above z, while the Pareto N is a function of z itself.

See *International Encyclopedia of the Social Sciences*, s.v. "Income Distribution: Size."

Table 8.2 Gini Coefficients for the Distribution of Sales Among All Retail Establishments and Among Retail Establishments in Nine Major Kinds of Business, 1948-1967[a]

Kind of Business	1948	1954	1958	1963	1967
Total, all establishments	.6771	.6849	.6979	.7071	.7327
Food stores	.6470	.6780	.7223	.7315	.7403
General merchandise stores	.8300	.8147	.8355	.8042	.8098
Apparel, accessory stores	.6310	.5922	.5958	.5850	.6018
Furniture, home furnishings, equipment stores	.5767	.6107	.6244	.6019	.6361
Automobile dealers	.5956	.6608	.6639	.6960	.7133
Gasoline service stations	.4435	.4288	.4104	.3880	.4216
Eating, drinking places	.5149	.5105	.5391	.5559	.5975
Drug, proprietary stores	.4534	.4421	.4458	.4426	.4985
Lumber, building materials, farm equipment, hardware dealers	.5509	.5873	.6015	.5840	.6196

[a]Based only on establishments operated entire year.

Source: Data for 1948-1963 from Steven M. Brilling, "Concentration of Sales in Retail Establishments in the United States, 1948 to 1963," M.B.A. Paper, Washington State University, 1967, pp. 15, 26, 37, and 47, based on U.S., Bureau of the Census, *Census of Business: 1963*, vol. I, *Retail Trade—Summary Statistics*, pt. 1 (Washington, D.C.: GPO, 1966), pp. 2-2 and 2-3; data for 1967 based on U.S., Bureau of the Census, *Census of Business: 1967*, vol. I, *Retail Trade—Subject Reports* (Washington, D.C.: GPO, 1971), pp. 2-1-2-7.

Using grouped data from the *Census of Business*, we have calculated the Lorenz coefficients for retail and wholesale trade by establishments and firms for selected census years. The calculation of coefficients from grouped data, particularly where only ten groups are detailed, yields only a rough estimate of the true coefficient.

1. *RETAIL TRADE.* Lorenz coefficients for retail trade are shown in Table 8.2 for the census years 1948-1967. It is clear that there is a high degree of concentration in retail trade and that there was a tendency for concentration to increase over these two decades. Gasoline service stations and drugstores showed the least concentration, while general merchandise stores and food stores showed the most. Since sales of general merchandise and food stores accounted for over one-third of total retail sales, they greatly influenced the coefficient for total retail trade. Over this period, concentration in all lines of trade increased, except for general merchandise stores, gasoline service stations, and apparel stores. The largest percentage increase in the concentration ratio between 1948 and 1967 was for automobile dealers and food stores.

From the viewpoint of the national market, concentration of sales in retailing depends more on the size of firm then on the size of establishment.[7] Multiunit firms in retailing (those with two or more stores) accounted for 40 percent of all retail sales in 1967, and firms with 11 or more stores for 29 percent. The average single-unit store had sales of about $110,000 in 1967, the average small chain (2-10 stores) had sales of about

---

[7]Louis P. Bucklin, *Competition and Evolution in the Distributive Trades* (Englewood Cliffs, N.J.: Prentice-Hall, 1972), p. 133.

$275,000 per store, and the average large chain (11 or more stores) has sales of about $700,000 per store.[8]

In order to gain additional insight into the size structure of retailing firms, we have calculated Gini coefficients for retail firms and establishments arrayed by number of establishments in the firm. (See Table 8.3.) These Gini coefficients are not, of course, the same as those shown in Table 8.2, where establishments were arrayed by sales volume. The Gini coefficients in Table 8.3 for the distribution of sales by all single-unit and multiunit firms arrayed by number of establishments show the extent to which sales were concentrated in multiunit firms. Compare, for example, the close relationship between the Gini coefficients in column 4 with those in column 3, where multiunit sales as a percentage of total sales are indicated. However, if we examine column 6, which shows Gini coefficients for multiunit firms only, we get a clue concerning the extent to which large chains dominated the total sales of all chains. Large chains appear to have been most important in general merchandise and food chain retailing, somewhat less important in drug chain retailing, and least important among automobile dealer, furniture and equipment, and lumber and hardware chain firms.

Columns 5 and 7 show additional information about the size of stores maintained by firms, which have been arrayed by the number of stores in the firm. According to column 5, there was practically no difference in the size of single-unit stores and multiunit stores in automobile retailing, gasoline service stations, and lumber and hardware retailing, all of which were fields of operation in which chains were relatively unimportant. There was slightly more difference, but not much, for eating and drinking places, furniture and home furnishings stores, apparel stores, and drugstores. The biggest difference between the size of stores owned by single-unit firms and those owned by multiunit firms was in general merchandise and food retailing.

If we exclude the single-unit firms and focus exclusively on the multiunit firms, do we find much difference between the sales volume per store of the large chains versus the small chains? Some clues to this are apparent in column 7. In drug retailing, chains accounted for 39 percent of the total retail volume, and large chains tended to have somewhat bigger stores than small chains. Chain stores were not very important among eating and drinking places, accounting for only 18 percent of the total volume for this type of retail outlet. Where chains did exist the outlets of very large chains tended, on an average, to be slightly larger than those of small chains, but only slightly larger. The same was true of food stores, where chains were, of course, much more important, accounting for 58 percent of total volume, but with stores owned by large chains only slightly larger, on an average, than those owned by small chains. For most kinds of retail businesses, column 7 indicates that large chains seldom had stores that were, on an average, much larger than those of small chains.

There are, however, three negative values in column 7: automobile dealers, lumber and hardware dealers, and furniture and equipment stores. This suggests that in these fields large chains tended to have a slightly smaller sales volume per store than small chains. Note the nature of the product and the markets in which these firms operate. All entail heavy and bulky products, which limit the size of the retail trading area, with automobile market areas further constrained by the franchise system, and all are selling products that entail considerable personal selling service for certain portions of their volume. The

---

[8] Calculated from U.S., Bureau of the Census, *Census of Business: 1967*, vol. I, *Retail Trade—Subject Reports* (Washington, D.C.: GPO, 1971), pp. 4-8.

Table 8.3 Distribution of Sales Among Retail Firms and Establishments in Nine Major Kinds of Business in the United States with Firms Arrayed by Number of Establishments, 1967[a]

| Kind of Business | Multiunits as Percentage of All | | | Gini Coefficient for Distribution of Sales of | | | |
| | | | | Single and Multiunit Firms Among | | Multiunit Firms Only Among | |
	Firms (1)	Establishments (2)	Sales (3)	Firms (4)	Establishments (5)	Firms (6)	Establishments (7)
Total Retail trade	2.2	12.5	39.8	.3832	.2814	.7920	.1627
Food stores	1.6	14.9	58.0	.5719	.4384	.8445	.0860
General merchandise stores	3.7	32.9	86.7	.8572	.5422	.8584	.0173
Apparel, accessory stores	5.4	26.3	48.3	.4468	.2268	.6785	.0533
Furniture, home furnishings, equipment stores	3.7	14.0	28.1	.2497	.1393	.4918	−.0510
Automobile dealers	2.2	9.5	10.9	.0883	.0130	.4774	−.1024
Gasoline service stations	1.8	10.8	16.6	.1496	.0585	.7095	.0330
Eating, drinking places	1.4	7.0	18.4	.1714	.1158	.6662	.1057
Drug, proprietary stores	3.6	16.5	39.0	.3657	.2412	.7981	.2453
Lumber, building materials, farm equipment, hardware dealers	2.8	13.0	21.2	.1872	.0800	.5225	−.0773

[a]Based only on firms and establishments operated entire year.

Source: U.S., Bureau of the Census, *Census of Business: 1967*, vol. I, *Retail Trade—Subject Reports* (Washington, D.C.: GPO, 1971), pp. 4-8-4-29.

effectiveness of the large chain in these fields of retailing is probably greatest where the merchandise sold is fairly well standardized, making possible opportunities for economies arising from quantity buying, buying skill, and standardized methods of operation and control. This could occur, for example, in selling used cars, where sales volume per transaction would be lower than for new cars, and low-margin furniture, furnishings, and equipment. Lumber, hardware, and farm equipment are less likely to lend themselves to these low-service, standardized types of operation. In these cases, the large chain can profitably service fairly remote, thinly populated areas even though average sales per store are not so large as is true for the smaller chain. The markets serviced by these large chains, or at least by some of the units of large chains, can be economically serviced only through large, multiunit firms in which the marginal cost of some smaller additional units is low enough to make them economical.

2. *WHOLESALE TRADE*. Information about concentration ratios for wholesaling, similar to that presented for retailing, is given in Tables 8.4, 8.5, and 8.6. Sales were much more concentrated among wholesale establishments than among retail establishments. While concentration in retail trade increased considerably during the 1960s, data for wholesale merchants indicate only a very slight increase in concentration of sales among establishments. Concentration ratios in 1967 were greatest for manufacturers' sales offices and branches, and least for merchandise agents and brokers.

While multiunit firms accounted for about 60 percent of all wholesale establishments, they accounted for about 30 percent of total sales, in contrast to retailing, where multiunit retailing firms accounted for only 12.5 percent of all retail establishments but 40 percent of sales. Multiunit firms dominated wholesaling for manufacturers' sales branches and offices and other types of wholesaling. They were important, but less so, in merchant wholesaling and agent and brokerage operations. Where multiunits existed in wholesaling, large chains tended to have slightly larger establishments than did small chains for all types except "other types."

3. *A NOTE ON INTERNATIONAL DIFFERENCES IN CONCENTRATION OF TRADE*. We do not have good measures of concentration ratios for marketing in various countries. Observations made from inspection of census data indicate, however, that retailing is more concentrated among establishments in the United States than in some countries with lower per capita income.

For example, in the United States in 1954, the largest 3 percent of retail stores accounted for 43 percent of retail sales. In Norway in 1952, the largest 3 percent of stores accounted for 15 percent of retail sales.[9] While the smallest 40 percent of stores in each country did about the same proportionate share of that country's total retail trade (about 6 percent in the United States and 8 percent in Norway), retail trade in the United States was more greatly affected by the presence of a small number of extremely large stores.

But this difference was not true of wholesaling in the two countries. Wholesaling was far more concentrated in Norway than in the United States in this period. For example,

---

[9] Computed from U.S., Bureau of the Census, *United States Census of Business: 1954*, vol. I, *Retail Trade—Summary Statistics* (Washington, D.C.: GPO, 1957), pp. 2-6, and *Bedriftstelling i Norge* (Census of Business Establishments in Norway), vol. 2, Norges Offisielle Statistikk, XI, 287 (Oslo: Statistisk Sentralbyrå, 1958), pp. 46-47.

Table 8.4 Distribution of Sales Among Wholesale Establishments in the United States Classified by Sales Volume of Establishment, 1967[a]

Sales per Establishment	Number of Establishments	Sales (Add 000)	Percentage of		Cumulative Percentage of	
			Total Establishments	Total Sales	Total Establishments	Total Sales
Less than $100,000	55,860	$ 2,997,764	18.40	.67	18.40	.67
$100,000- 199,999	49,340	7,172,334	16.25	1.61	34.65	2.28
200,000- 299,999	32,830	8,066,793	10.81	1.81	45.47	4.08
300,000- 499,999	40,813	15,876,772	13.44	3.56	58.91	7.64
500,000- 999,999	49,611	35,188,795	16.34	7.88	75.25	15.52
1,000,000- 1,999,999	34,824	48,713,784	11.47	10.91	86.72	26.43
2,000,000- 4,999,999	25,153	76,857,936	8.29	17.22	95.01	43.65
5,000,000- 9,999,999	8,564	58,843,454	2.82	13.18	97.83	56.83
10,000,000-14,999,999	2,665	32,371,485	.88	7.25	98.71	64.08
15,000,000-19,999,999	1,268	21,754,987	.42	4.87	99.12	68.95
20,000,000 and over	2,663	131,612,408	.88	31.05	100.00	100.00
Total	303,591	$446,456,512	100.00	100.00		

[a]Includes only establishments operated entire year.

Source: U.S., Bureau of the Census, *Census of Business: 1967*, vol. III, *Wholesale Trade—Subject Reports* (Washington, D.C.: GPO, 1971), p. 2-1.

Table 8.5 Wholesale Sales by Four Types of Operation and Gini Coefficients for the Distribution of Sales Among All Establishments and Among Establishments of Each Type in the United States, 1967[a]

Type of Operation	Number of Establishments	Sales (Add 000)	Gini Cooefficient
Total all types	303,591	$446,456,512	.7680
Merchant wholesalers	206,577	199,001,955	.7288[b]
Manufacturers' sales offices, sales branches	30,366	154,200,203	.7616
Merchandise agents and brokers	25,824	59,233,065	.6693
Other types	40,824	34,021,289	.6784

[a]Based only on establishments operated entire year.

[b]The comparable coefficient for 1958 was .7212. Based on U.S., Bureau of the Census, *Census of Business: 1958*, vol. III, *Wholesale Trade–Summary Statistics and Public Warehousing* (Washington, D.C.: GPO, 1971), p. 2-1.

Source: U.S. Bureau of the Census, *Census of Business: 1967*, vol. III, *Wholesale Trade–Subject Reports* (Washington, D.C.: GPO, 1971), p. 2-1.

the largest 5 percent of wholesaling establishments accounted for about two-thirds of Norway's wholesale trade in 1952, compared with about one-half of the United States' wholesale trade in 1954.[10] The geographic distribution of population in Norway, where more than 3 million people were spread over 125,000 square miles, probably accounts for the dispersion of retail establishments, and the comparatively smaller scale of the total economy would account for the concentration of wholesaling in those few wholesale firms that were large enough to realize some economies of scale. In the United States, the mobility of population, due to greater reliance on automobile travel, would make large-scale retailing units economical, as would the larger number of large population centers. Also, the larger total volume of output in the United States would make it possible for proportionately more establishments in wholesaling to operate at economic levels, thereby dispersing wholesale trade among more wholesaling outlets.

Decentralization of retailing and wholesaling has also been noted in Japan. Despite the emergence of industrialization and market orientation among manufacturing firms following World War II, the Japanese marketing system remained essentially unchanged, with large numbers of small retail and wholesale firms and extremely long channels of distribution. By 1969, however, mass merchandising retail firms had developed that accounted for about 12 percent of total retail sales.[11]

4. *IMPLICATIONS OF SALES CONCENTRATION RATIOS.* The importance of these sales concentration ratios in retailing and wholesaling centers on two principal questions:

[10]U.S., Bureau of the Census, *United States Census of Business: 1954*, vol. III, *Wholesale Summary* (Washington, D.C.: GPO, 1957), p. 12, and *Bedriftstelling i Norge*, op. cit., pp. 14-15.

[11]M. Y. Yoshino, "Marketing Developments in an Emerging Mass Consumption Society: The Case of Japan," in George Fisk, ed., *New Essays in Marketing Theory* (Boston: Allyn & Bacon, 1971), pp. 389-405.

Table 8.6 Distribution of Sales Among Wholesale Firms and Establishments in Four Major Types of Operation in the United States with Firms Arrayed by Number of Establishments, 1967[a]

Type of Operation	Multiunits as Percentage of all			Gini Coefficient for Distribution of Sales of			
				All Single and Multiunit Firms		Multiunit Firms Only	
	Firms	Establishments	Sales	Firms	Establishments	Firms	Establishments
Total all types	5.7	61.1	29.7	.5598	.3132	.7759	.1067
Merchant wholesalers	5.5	17.2	39.4	.2336	.3502	.4926	.1596
Manufacturers' sales offices, sales branches	63.6	96.4	97.1	.8167	.1140	.7603	.1042
Merchandise agents and brokers	3.8	8.2	21.6	.1813	.1364	.3318	.1293
Other types	10.4	58.3	66.5	.6185	.0827	.8340	.0034

[a]Based only on establishments and firms operated entire year.

Source: U.S., Bureau of the Census, *Census of Business: 1967*, vol. III, *Wholesale Trade–Subject Reports* (Washington, D.C.: GPO, 1971), p. 2-127.

(1) Has the distribution of retail and wholesale sales among firms and establishments resulted in firms and establishments of optimum size from the viewpoint of internal operating efficiency? (2) Has the distribution resulted in an optimal market structure as reflected in the interfirm and interestablishment relations both horizontally and vertically? Not only are we interested in efficiency of the particular marketing institution, but we are also interested in efficiency of the system as it fulfills its role in the total economy. Efficiency in the latter sense means, of course, that the benefits of efficiency accrue to consumers as well as to investors in the marketing industry. We shall consider both of these questions in more detail at a later point.

SALES AND THE RANK-SIZE RULE

1. *THE RANK-SIZE RULE*. Pareto's law of income distribution has been adapted by several students of population and location to describe concentration in the distribution of population among cities of a country. The relationship between population of a city and its rank in population among all cities can be stated as follows:

$$S_R = \frac{S_1}{R}$$

in which S_1 is the size of the largest city, R is the rank of a given city, and S_R is the size of the city having the rank of R. This is the Pareto cumulative greater-than frequency distribution applied to city size. A more generalized statement of the relationship is

$$\log R = -q \log P + \log k$$

in which R is the rank of a city in population, P is its population, and q and k are constants.[1,2]

If we plot population rank on the horizontal axis of a double logarithmic graph and population on the vertical axis, the observations yield approximately a straight line. The distinctive characteristic of empirical estimates of the constants of the function fitted to these empirical observations is that q is generally 1.00. The higher the value of q, the greater the degree of concentration of population among cities.

2. *APPLICABILITY OF THE RANK-SIZE RULE TO MARKETING*. If we examine retail sales instead of population and compare cities by rank, does the same regularity observed with respect to population and rank hold? In Figure 8.4 we show on a double logarithmic graph the distribution of 180 metropolitan areas of the United States according to their retail sales rank in 1958 on the horizontal axis and their 1958 retail sales volume on the vertical axis. It is apparent that a linear function would not describe

---

[1,2] Summaries and examples of the rank-size rule applied to population and to other economic and social phenomena can be found in Rutledge Vining, "A Description of Certain Spatial Aspects of an Economic System," *Economic Development and Cultural Change* 3 (January 1955): 147-195; Martin J. Beckman, "City Hierarchies and the Distribution of City Size," *Economic Development and Cultural Change* 6 (April 1958): 243-248; George Kingsley Zipf, *Human Behavior and the Principle of Least Effort* (Cambridge, Mass. Addison-Wesley, 1949). See also John Q. Stewart, "Potential of Population and Its Relationship to Marketing," in Reavis Cox and Wroe Alderson, eds., *Theory in Marketing* (Chicago: Irwin, 1950), pp. 19-40. There is an interesting intercountry comparison of the concentration of retail sales among establishments in R. Bellamy, "The Changing Pattern of Retail Distribution," *Bulletin of the Oxford University Institute of Statistics* 8 (August 1946): 237-260.

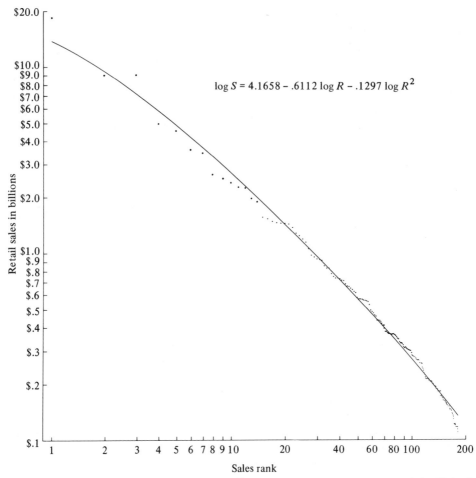

Figure 8.4. Total retail sales and retail sales rank of 176 metropolitan areas of the United States, 1958. S = total retail sales; R = sales rank. Source: Calculated from U.S. Bureau of the Census, *United States Census of Business: 1958*, vol. 1 (Washington, D.C.: GPO, 1961).

this relationship accurately. Therefore a second-degree curve was fitted to the logarithms of sales volume and sales rank. The equation was

$$\log S = 4.1658 - .6112 \log R - .1297 \log R^2$$

in which S is retail sales volume and R is rank. This is equivalent to a fourth-degree curve fitted to the arithmetic values of S and R.

In order to calculate a constant slope, S, the 180 metropolitan areas were broken into three segments, and a straight line was fitted to the logarithms of sales and rank for each of these three segments. The equation that we have used to describe the sales-rank relationships for each segment is

$$\log S = \log a + b \log R \quad \text{or} \quad S = aR^b$$

in which S is volume of sales, a is a constant, R is sales rank, and b is a constant and the slope of the curve. The results when this function was fitted to three segments of the metropolitan areas ranked according to total retail sales are shown in the first section of Table 8.7. For the first 54 metropolitan areas, the slope of the line was -.87, and for the next 55 it was $-.98$. For the balance the slope was -1.52, which is much higher than the value of -1.00 hypothesized by the rank-size rule. For these data, it would appear that the rank-size rule held for retail sales and rank of metropolitan areas at this point in time, with a slope of approximately -1.00 until the metropolitan area's sales fell to about $240 million.

In Table 8.7 we have included similar calculations for different kinds of retail businesses. In addition, we have made calculations for selected services in the 185 metropolitan areas and for wholesale sales in the 50 largest centers. In each case the metropolitan areas were clustered on the basis of judgment concerning breaking points and, hence, the appropriateness of a linear function in describing the sales-rank relationship. From these calculations, certain observations can be made about the rank-size rule as it applies to marketing establishments:

1. For those metropolitan areas ranking among approximately the first 100, the slope (the value of b) for both retail trade and services was very close to -1.00. This means that the second-ranking metropolitan area had sales of about one-half those of the first-ranking area, the third-ranking areas had sales of about one-third those of the first, the fourth-ranking area had sales of about one-fourth those of the first, and the twentieth-ranking area had sales of about one-twentieth those of the first. It would appear, therefore, that the rank-size rule, which has been found to hold for population size and rank, also tended to hold for retail and service sales and rank.
2. Wholesaling showed the highest degree of sales concentration among metropolitan areas. Services were second and retailing third. The degree of concentration is indicated by the b value—the exponent of R. The higher the exponent of R, the higher the degree of concentration. Although the fitting of a second-degree curve to four observations, as we have done for the top four ranking areas in wholesale sales, is not justified because of the degrees of freedom lost, this was done because these four centers did not appear to fall logically into the pattern of sales-rank relationship of the metropolitan areas that were next in volume of sales. A coefficient of -1.30 reflects the high concentration of sales among these four areas. The next 19 areas showed much less concentration, but those that followed again showed high concentration. If the optimum size for wholesale establishments and wholesaling centers is much greater than that for other types of enterprises, concentration of sales is likely also to be much greater in this type of trade.

   Services showed greater concentration than retailing, with concentration coefficients greater than -1.00 for all groups selected for the fitting of linear functions to the logarithms. Since services are rendered on a personal basis and do not lend themselves readily to economies related to mechanization and large-scale organization of retailing, why do they show a higher degree of concentration? There are probably two reasons. First, because they are so personal in nature, they can be highly differentiated, lending themselves to specialized and, hence, unique production in certain marketing centers. Second, the income elasticity of demand for some services is higher than that for goods, thus increasing their sales potential disproportionately in larger centers.
3. The data in Table 8.7 show that retail, wholesale, and service sales are correlated with population size, but not perfectly. Exceptions are particularly apparent in wholesaling, where factors other than city size have an important bearing on the advantages of a given center for performing wholesaling functions. For example, Denver, Colorado, was smaller than Buffalo, New York, yet had a larger wholesale volume. Thus while wholesale sales were clearly related to population size, other factors somewhat

Table 8.7 Estimating Equations of Retail, Wholesale, and Service Sales in Metropolitan Areas of the United States as a Function of Sales Rank, 1958

Type of Establishment	Group	Sales Rank	Metropolitan Area	1960 Population in Thousands	1958 Sales in Millions	Parameters Log a	b
			Highest and Lowest Ranking Areas in Group				
Retail total	A	1	New York, N.Y.-Northeastern N.J.	14,759	$18,489.8	4.2629	-.8746
		54	Jacksonville, Fla.	455	522.6		
	B	55	Fresno, Calif.	366	491.8	4.4082	-.9772
		109	Rockford, Ill.	210	253.4		
	C	110	Atlantic City, N.J.	161	240.3	5.5130	-1.5201
		176	Lynchburg, Va.	111	108.0		
Retail food	A	1	New York, N.Y.-Northeastern N.J.	14,759	4,955.6	3.6615	-.8802
		49	Toledo, Ohio	457	147.2		
	B	50	Allentown-Bethlehem-Easton, Penn.-N.J.	492	137.7	4.0234	-1.0973
		121	Greenville, S.C.	210	50.3		
	C	122	Augusta, Ga.-S.C.	217	48.6	3.9542	-1.0765
		144	Winston-Salem, N.C.	189	42.1		
	D	145	Lubbock, Tex.	156	40.6	6.2984	-2.1546
		168	Wichita Falls, Tex.	130	31.1		
	E	169	Pueblo, Colo.	119	30.4	13.5604	-5.3910
		184	San Angelo, Tex.	65	19.0		

	A					
Retail department stores	1	New York, N.Y.-Northeastern N.J.	14,759	$ 1,332.3	3.1436	-.7692
	22	Indianapolis, Ind.	698	126.7		
B	23	Kansas City, Mo.-Kansas	1,039	111.3	3.5751	-1.0989
	60	Wichita, Kansas	343	40.3		
C	61	Phoenix, Ariz.	664	39.3	3.6388	-1.1539
	105	West Palm Beach, Fla.	228	20.6		
D	106	Columbus, Ga.	218	19.5	4.3553	-1.4979
	154	Springfield, Mo.	126	12.3		
E	155	Fall River, Mass.-R.I.	138	10.6	19.4526	-8.3581
	175	Kenosha, Wisc.	101	3.8		
Retail women's clothing and specialty A	1	New York, N.Y.-Northeastern N.J.	14,759	853.6	5.8396	-.9993
	124	Wheeling, W.Va.-Ohio	190	5.6		
B	125	Baton Rouge, La.	230	5.3	8.6742	-2.3377
	176	Bay City, Mich.	107	2.5		
C	177	San Angelo, Tex.	65	2.3	35.8471	-14.3722
	185	Terre Haute, Ind.	108	1.2		
Wholesale total A	1	New York, N.Y.-Northeastern N.J.	14,759	$ 54,700.8	4.7230	-1.3028
	4[c]	Philadelphia, Pa.-N.J.	4,343	8,826.5		
B	5	Detroit, Mich.	3,762	8,252.0	4.4994	-.8211
	23	Denver, Colo.	929	2,408.5		
C	24	Buffalo, N.Y.	1,307	2,386.2	5.7637	-1.7210
	48	San Diego, Calif.	1,003	696.0		

Table 8.7 continued

Highest and Lowest Ranking Areas in Group

Type of Establishment	Group	Sales Rank	Metropolitan Area	1960 Population in Thousands	1958 Sales in Millions	Parameters[b] Log a	b
Selected services	A	1	New York, N.Y.-Northeastern N.J.	14,759	6,459.0	3.6927	-1.0335
		26	Portland, Oreg.-Wash.	822	166.9		
	B	27	Indianapolis, Ind.	698	146.7	3.6328	-1.0043
		56	Charlotte, N.C.	272	72.5		
	C	57	Norfolk-Portsmouth, Va.	579	68.0	3.9322	-1.1951
		101	Greensboro-High Point, N.C.	247	34.5		
	D	102	Columbia, S.C.	261	33.8	5.5014	-1.9555
		174	Pittsfield, Mass.	74	11.5		
	E	175	San Angelo, Tex.	65	11.4	12.5340	-5.1168
		185	Laredo, Tex.	65	4.7		

[a]The 1958 Census of Business listed 191 standard metropolitan statistical areas. Two of these were omnibus metropolitan areas, comprising more than one of the other metropolitan areas included among the 191. The New York City and northeastern New Jersey standard consolidated area included the following standard metropolitan statistical areas: New York, N.Y.; Newark, N.J.; Jersey City, N.J.; Paterson-Clifton-Passaic, N.J.; and also Middlesex and Somerset Countries, N.J. The Chicago and Northwestern Indiana standard consolidated area consisted of two standard metropolitan areas: Chicago, Ill., and Gary-Hammond-East Chicago, Ind. In this table, the New York and Chicago consolidated areas have been used. Therefore there were 185 metropolitan areas from which sales data could be analyzed. The total number actually included in the functions for retail trade ranged between 175 for department stores and 185 for women's clothing and specialty stores. Sales data were not analyzed for a few smaller metropolitan areas where a new grouping would have been required or for areas where the data were not reported by the Bureau of the Census because it would reveal individual operations. This latter situation obtained primarily for retail department stores sales. Service sales were analyzed for all 185 metropolitan areas. Wholesale sales were analyzed for only the 50 areas with the largest volume of sales.

[b]$S = aR^b$, in which S = sales and R = sales rank.

[c]Rank 2–Chicago, Ill.-Northwestern Ind.; Rank 3–Los Angeles-Long Beach, Calif.

Source: U.S., Bureau of the Census, United States Census of Business: 1958, vols. I, III, V (Washington, D.C.: GPO, 1961), and Current Population Reports, Series P-23, no. 2 (November 1962).

different from those operating in retail centers were important. In his factor analysis of wholesale market structure in 1963, Louis Bucklin identified one set of these relevant factors as "market center." Wholesale sales per capita and the wholesaler-retail sales ratio were both loaded highly on this factor.[13] There were also discrepancies between population size and service sales. Charlotte, North Carolina, was about one-half the size of Norfolk-Portsmouth, Virginia, yet had higher service sales. Greensboro-High Point, North Carolina, was smaller than Columbia, South Carolina, but had a higher service volume.

In some cities department stores were important, while in others specialty stores were more important. For example, department store sales were greater in Indianapolis than in Kansas City, although Kansas City was larger. But sales by women's clothing stores in Kansas City ranked 15th, compared to 47th in Indianapolis. It would appear that historical factors played a part in this. The type of retail institution that was becoming dominant at the time a city was reaching its economic maturity probably occupied a particularly important role in the city's marketing structure at that time. Once firmly entrenched but, at the same time, sufficiently flexible to survive new developments in marketing, such firms may have been able to retain positions of considerable importance in the retail trade structure of cities where they existed, even though this type of firm would not have been chosen by new entrepreneurs at a later time. Witness, for example, the survival of the traditional department store during eras when specialized chain stores, discount houses, and suburban shopping outlets have been developed. This survival has been due in part to the fact that such stores had an entrenched position in the communities in which they were established that new types of retail outlets could usurp only at great cost. But it was also due to the adaptability of such firms to new methods of organization and merchandising.[14]

4. Generally the rate of concentration increased as the size of the metropolitan area decreased. In most cases concentration was least among the largest centers and highest among the smaller areas. One important exception was in wholesaling, where concentration was high among the largest four areas, although the number of centers on which this statement is based is too small for a generalization to be made. There was some slight decline in concentration of service sales between the first group of metropolitan areas and the next 30, but for centers with sales of less than about $70 million concentration increased as size of center decreased.

---

[13] Bucklin, op. cit., pp. 237-238.

[14] One evidence of ability to survive and to adapt is change in proportionate share of retail sales. Between 1948 and 1958, department store sales declined from 7.3 percent of total retail sales to 6.7 percent. But by 1967, their proportionate share had risen to 10.4 percent. Although these shares, based on *Census of Business* data, are not precisely the same as the retail sales data reported for noncensus years from the Bureau of the Census in its *Annual Retail Trade Report*, the latter data for the years 1967-1970 indicate that department store share continued to increase. Part of this increase in relative share of sales during the 1960s was a result of the fact that some stores that were originally specialty stores found it expedient to diversify their lines of merchandise sufficiently to become department stores. The combination of adaptation on the part of "old" department stores and the entrance of "new" department stores is reflected in the sales position of this type of retail outlet. The following publications of the U. S. Bureau of the Census contain the relevant data: *United States Census of Business: 1948*, vol. I, *Retail Trade–General Statistics* (Washington, D.C.: GPO, 1952); *United States Census of Business: 1958*, vol. I, *Retail Trade–Summary Statistics* (Washington, D.C.: GPO, 1961); *Annual Retail Trade Report*, 1969-1971.

Table 8.8 Approximate Population and Sales Volume of Metropolitan Areas in Which Sales Concentration Ratios Shifted from About 1.00 or Less to More Than 1.00, 1958[a]

Type of Establishments	Population	1958 Sales
Total retail	200,000	$250 million
Retail food stores	200,000	40 million
Retail department stores	200,000	20 million
Retail women's clothing and specialty stores	200,000	5 million
Selected services	250,000	35 million
Total wholesale	2,000,000	2 billion

[a]These are rough estimates based on rounded figures read from Table 8.7.

5. Retail and service sales concentration ratios increased sharply in centers of about 200,000 or less population, while wholesale concentration ratios increased among areas of about 2 million or less population. Although we have pointed out that population and sales are not perfectly related, nevertheless this pattern shows considerable consistency among the few types of establishments whose sales data we have examined. Table 8.8 indicates roughly the breaking point between concentration ratios of 1.00 or less and those greater than 1.00 and the approximate sales volumes associated with these breaking points. Because breaking points were determined by inspection and curves were fitted to the segments so chosen, there is, of course, an arbitrary element in these data.

George Zipf has examined certain other empirical regularities in the marketing system. He has found a positive linear relationship of approximately 1.00 between the logarithm of city population in 1940 and that of the number of retail stores in 1939. The relationship between the logarithm of population and that of the number of different kinds of retail stores does not yield such a close fit, possibly because of certain crudities inherent in census classifications of kinds of enterprises.[15]

3. *REASONS FOR THE RANK-SIZE RULE IN MARKETING.* The distribution of retail, wholesale, and service sales reveals a systematic order. Why does this exist? No coherent theory of sales allocation has been developed that fully explains the observed relationships. It appears, however, that such a theory would explain the fairly precise balance effected between the power of a city to attract residents, customers, industries, and other participants in its economic and social activity, on the one hand, and its inability to do so as distance from it increases. In addition, economies of scale are conducive to large enterprises concentrated in large centers. Diseconomies are conducive to smaller, dispersed enterprises.

Walter Isard has discussed some of the possible reasons for the rank-size rule as it applies to cities, and the considerations that he raises are particularly appropriate to our consideration of retail and wholesale sales.

According to one possible line of reasoning, modern cities have become increasingly centers of numerous market-oriented activities, each activity tending to have a defined sales area. Since the size of a city is positively associated with the number of activities which locate within it and since economies of scale and other factors preclude the

---

[15] Zipf, op. cit., pp. 376-377.

presence of each activity in each city, cities of different sizes emerge. Further, one can expect the longer (and a larger volume of) population and commodity flows to be generally associated with the larger cities which have been fortunate in usurping those functions wherein economies of scale are marked and with which the larger market areas are linked. Still more, economies of scale have varying significance for different commodities and activities; when they are most dominant, the commodity produced (or service rendered) tends to be national, being supplied to all market points from one location. Hence, that city which captures the largest amount of these "national market area activities" and which concomitantly engages in all other activities whose market areas are of lesser geographic scope tends to be largest in size. It tends to be a terminal point of the longest average population and commodity flows and of the largest volume of such flows, *ceteris paribus*. And that city which captures the next largest amount of these national activities, while at the same time being a center of all "non-national" activities, would tend to be second in size and to rank second in average length (and volume) of population and commodity flows, *ceteris paribus*. And in like fashion, the third, fourth . . . nth largest city would tend to rank third, fourth . . . nth in average length (and volume) of flows, *ceteris paribus*, the progression of activities from those with national markets to those with major regional markets to those with minor regional markets . . . to those with only local markets being duly taken into account. As a consequence, a statistically regular hierarchy of average length and volume of flows emerges. Thus regularity of flows over distance and regularity in the spatial patterning of cities can come to be associated with a statistically regular hierarchy of cities, *ceteris paribus*.[16]

Ceteris paribus indeed!

ALEXANDERSSON'S MEASURE OF INTERCITY TRADE DIFFERENCES

Gunnar Alexandersson has devised a technique for measuring intercity differences in retail and wholesale trade by determining the importance of these industries in a city's total economic structure.[17] Using 1950 census data, he computed the percentage of each city's total employment accounted for by retail and wholesale trade. All cities were then arrayed from those with the lowest employment ratios to those with the highest ratios.

On the basis of 864 cities for which he analyzed data, he then selected the employment ratio for city 9, which was 1 percent below the lowest ratio, and city 43, which was 5 percent below the lowest. These he designated as the k_1 and k ratios, respectively. The k ratio for other retail trade (excluding food and eating and drinking), for example, was 8.0 percent. This he interpreted as an assumed minimum employment essential to provide "other" retail services for a city's own residents. An employment ratio higher than this was assumed to show that retailing was a *city-forming* activity, in contrast to a *city-serving* activity. The reason for selecting 5 percent instead of a lower percentage was to eliminate extremes. The k value for retail trade of 8.0 percent was less than the national average of 9.2 percent retail employment, and the difference can be explained by the greater weight given in the national average by those cities in which retail trade represented a higher-than-average percentage.

This array and its median provide a basis for comparing retail trade with other economic activities as a city-forming activity, and for comparing cities of different sizes

---

[16]Walter Isard, *Location and Space Economy* (New York: Technology and Wiley, 1956), pp. 57-58.

[17]Gunnar Alexandersson, *The Industrial Structure of American Cities* (Lincoln: University of Nebraska Press, 1956), pp. 96-108.

and cities of different regions in the importance of retail trade to the city's total economic structure. In general, he concluded that retail trade did not rank as a leading city-forming activity, although it was a major city-forming activity in a majority of towns west of the Mississippi. He further found that all cities of more than 1 million population, and a majority of those of 250,000 or more, had a retail employment below the median for all 864 cities. There was a high negative correlation between the percentage employed in other retail trade and the percentage employed in manufacturing. Nearly all the towns in the prairie states (roughly, North Dakota south through Texas) had above-average retail trade employment, while towns in the northeast had a below-average percentage.

There was a positive relation between employment in retail trade and employment in wholesale trade and an inverse relation between employment in wholesale trade and employment in manufacturing. More than two-thirds of the cities in the prairie and western states (excluding mountain areas) had above-average employment in wholesale trade, but regional differentials were not so pronounced as in retail trade. Those cities with the largest wholesale "surplus" tended to be a belt through the Midwest and South. The highest wholesale percentages were in small cities serving areas of intensive agricultural production (Corona, Santa Paula, Salinas in California; Mercedes, San Benito, Edinburg in the Rio Grande Valley; Sanford, Fort Pierce in Florida; Suffolk in Virginia).

The Interrelationship of Horizontal and Vertical Structure

In considering the characteristics of vertical and horizontal market structure in this chapter, we have frequently noted how horizontal characteristics are a result of, or contribute to, vertical characteristics, and how vertical attributes are, in turn, related to horizontal structure. The interrelationship of these two dimensions of the marketing system will become increasingly clear as we describe additional attributes of the system. Just as Cormoran of Cornwall's viability as an organism was a function of *both* his height and the width of his bones, particularly his leg bones, so is the survival of the marketing system a function of both its vertical and horizontal dimensions.

9
The Retail Firm

Because a man has shop to mind
  In time and place, since flesh must live,
Needs spirit lack all life behind,
  All stray thoughts, fancies fugitive,
  All loves except what trade can give?

—Robert Browning

A retail firm specializes in the performance of those marketing functions that, in the sequence of the production process, lie closest to the ultimate consumer. It is the unique qualities of the demand for its services that distinguish the retail firm from all other marketing institutions. Wtihin the constraints set by the nature of its output, the technology of its production, and the competitive milieu within which it operates, the retail firm is structured in response to the character of consumer demand. In this chapter, we shall consider (1) those aspects of consumer demand that determine and comprise the demand for retail services as a component of the total demand for goods and services and (2) the distinguishing characteristics of retailing firms as evidenced by their capital and cost structure.

THE DEMAND FOR RETAIL SERVICES

While the principles that underlie the operation of a retail firm or store and its relationship to its customers are the same as those basic to the operation of any marketing institution, the specific character of retail policies is shaped by a demand quantitatively and qualitatively decentralized and rooted in the complexities of human desires and choices. Characteristics of consumer demand that impinge especially strongly on the retail firm are the heterogeneity of products and services demanded by a single consuming unit, smaller unit transactions than are found in many market situations (although there are important exceptions), and a demand based on a calculus rooted in subjective values.

The Demand Complex

The demand for retail services involves a number of interrelated demands, for there are numerous possibilites for competing and complementary relationships to arise.

DERIVED DEMAND

Since the demand for a product includes the demand for the retailing services essential to complete its production, the demand for retailing is a derived demand. Because retailing costs are less than the combination of all other costs of production, the demand for retailing services is likely to be more inelastic than the demand for the fully produced good. But retailing is the largest single segment of total marketing cost, and for this reason the demand for it is likely to be more elastic than that for any other single functional segment of marketing.

COMPLEMENTARY (JOINT) DEMAND

Both product-completing and auxiliary retailing services are complementary to other production services that consumers demand. Since production-completing services are essential for any utility to be realized by consumers, their joint relationship to other productive activities is closer than in the case of auxiliary services.

The rendering of auxiliary services is, however, a particularly important possibility in retailing, and certain kinds of retail stores have made this an important part of their total output. Historically this has been an important function of department stores, for example. The extent to which such services are a profitable component of the retail firm's output is in part a function of their costs and in part a function of consumer response to such services. That response is, in turn, related to consumer income, the relative price of such services, and their importance to consumers vis-á-vis other goods and services that might be consumed instead. This possibility for choice making on the part of the consumer suggests a third demand relationship important to retailing.

COMPETING DEMANDS

Auxiliary services are not essential to complete the production of the good with which they are associated. The consumer can choose more or less of such services and by so doing allocate more or less to alternative services. He can spend more for shopping comfort and less for the services embodied in the good purchased. Because of their dispensability auxiliary services probably have a more elastic demand with respect to both price and income than product-oriented services if we assume that auxiliary services are more nearly "luxuries" than is commonly true of product-oriented services. Such services provide the retail firm with a production alternative of considerable flexibility, for the more elastic their demand, the greater the possibility of influencing the amount of sales by price changes.

Figure 9.1 is a family of indifference curves drawn to illustrate this assumed relationship between the demand for product-oriented services and auxiliary services. Assume that I_1, I_2, and I_3 are indifference curves that indicate the consumer's relative preferences for goods and product-oriented retailing services, on the one hand, and auxiliary services, on the other, with the marginal rate of substitution between these shown by the slope of the curves. The consumer's budget line, based on purchasing power and market prices, is AC. The consumer will select the combination of OG goods, with product-oriented services "built in," and OL auxiliary services. If, however, the price of auxiliary services were to fall so that he could buy OB services were he to spend all his budget on auxiliary services, he will shift his consumption to point K on his new indifference curve, I_3, consuming OM services and only OJ goods. The proportionate increase in services bought is greater than the proportionate decrease in the price of auxiliary services, reflecting a demand for services that is elastic with respect to price, indicated by the negatively sloping HK line. But if goods and their built-in retailing services had fallen in price with no change in the price of auxiliary services, so that a new consumption possibility line, DC, emerged, a new consumption pattern would have resulted. The consumer would buy OQ goods (instead of the original quantity, OG) and OR auxiliary services (instead of the original, OL). But the consumption of goods would

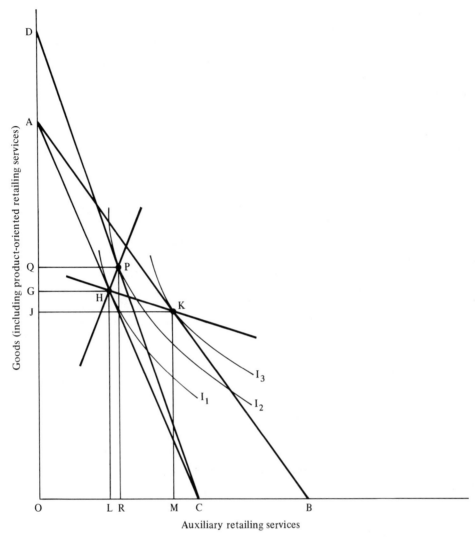

Figure 9.1. Consumer preferences for and prices of product-oriented and auxiliary retailing services.

not have increased in proportion to the change in the price of goods, since the demand for goods is inelastic with respect to price, as reflected in the positively sloping HP line. Increases in income would probably also have had a greater effect on the demand for auxiliary services than on the demand for goods.

Empirical data on the demand for retailing services are rather limited, and such data do not separate the demand for auxiliary services from that for product-related services. David Schwartzman's estimate that the elasticity of demand for retailing services in general is about -1.0 with respect to price and about 1.0 with respect to income conceals any internal differential that may exist between elasticity of demand for the two components of service we have identified.[1] It seems reasonable to believe, however, that

---

[1] David Schwartzman, The Decline of Service in Retail Trade, Washington State University, College of Economics and Business, Bureau of Economic and Business Research, Study no. 48 (Pullman: Washington State University, 1971), pp. 183-186.

the average price elasticity of –1.0 may well consist of an elasticity greater than –1.0 for dispensable services and less than –1.0 for essential services. The problem is a critical one for management, for it lies at the heart of the firm's decision about the cluster of services that it will offer consumers and the prices to be charged for those services.

There is yet another aspect of competition among retailing services, and this is the possibility that consumers may choose more of one service and less of another, for example, more delivery and less credit. This brings us to the matter of cross-elasticity of demand, the fourth aspect of demand for retailing services that we shall consider.

CROSS-ELASTICITY OF DEMAND

This is a measure of the effect of a change in the price of a good on the quantity of another good or service that is purchased. We shall consider cross-elasticity only as it manifests itself within the firm rather than between firms. Substitute products have a positive cross-elasticity: When one rises in price, sales of the other will increase. Complementary products have a negative cross-elasticity: When one rises in price, sales of the other decrease. The complementary good that has the larger price relative to the other has the dominant influence in this cross-relationship.

As an assembler and mixer of a variety of goods and services, a retail store is peculiarly sensitive to the interrelationships of prices and sales of *all* goods handled and services provided. The use of leaders and the selection of particular items for special promotion reflect retailers' awareness of these interrelationships.

SUMMARY

The importance of the demand relationships that we have described is that the formulation of retail policies must be made within a complex market situation where no item or service can be regarded in isolation from others. These relationships are not peculiar to retailing, but in no other market is their complexity and impact so clearly demonstrated.

The Interrelationship of Costs and Demand

We have dealt thus far with demand as though it were independent of cost. We shall now explore two aspects of retailing costs and their relationship to the structure of the demand for retailing services.

SELLING COSTS

Because a store normally devotes many of its resources to the creation of demand, one of the determinants of demand is selling costs. There are many means by which retailers can influence consumer demand—advertising, sales promotion, window displays, interior displays, the provision of auxiliary services, communication between salespeople and customers, and merchandise selection. There is, however, no rigid relationship between expenditures for these and the resultant change in consumer demand, for much of the effectiveness of such policies depends on *how* the dollars are spent. All of these activities are designed to create good will for the *store*, and consumers appear to be willing to pay for the creation of this good will.[2] Although this interrelationship is not peculiar to retailing, it is most clearly demonstrated in retail operation. We have identified this function of marketing as "creative speculation"—the use of productive resources to create a demand. (See Chapter 1.)

From an analytical point of view, this interrelation of demand and cost complicates the problem of determining how big a retail firm should be if it is to maximize its profits or achieve some other financial objective.[3] If a demand function is independent of a firm's cost function, we may lay the two side by side and determine the optimum size of firm.[4] But if a given quantity of inputs in a firm bears either an unstable or an unknown relationship to output, it is not possible to reach categorical conclusions about the optimum size of firm. It is particularly troublesome when the output is a function of the *quality* of inputs, as, for example, where sales are influenced by the *form* that a given advertising expeniture takes. A manufacturer of furniture can know with some precision how much additional cost he will incur in manpower, raw materials, and capital equipment if he increases his production of furniture. Given knowledge of the sales revenue possibilities from the additional output, he can arrive at a reasonable estimate of the most profitable size for his firm. A furniture retailer can make similar calculations to a certain extent, for he knows that if he wishes to increase sales, he must increase the number of manhours hired and his investment in inventory and space. But the retailer has a wide range of additional opportunities for increasing his expenditures for sales promotion and advertising, and from these he expects increased sales but may not know how much increase.

This means that positive price theory needs considerable amplification if it is to serve as a realistic model for determining optimum output and price. It will be necessary to know what the relationhip is likely to be between selling costs and sales, and to incorporate this parameter into the model. In other words, we have an additional nonstable, and frequently unprecise, variable that has been introduced into the environment within which the retail firm's decisions are made.

CUSTOMER BUYING COSTS

A second factor that bears directly upon the demand for the services of the retail firm is consumer buying costs. Were we considering retailing in its broadest sense, we would regard the monetary and real outlays of consumers in shopping as a cost factor and not as a demand factor. But here we are considering the demand for the services of the retail firm, and customer buying costs are like a tax on consumers that decreases their demand

---

[2] Margaret Hall has suggested a logical basis for consumer willingness to pay for advertising and sales promotion whose purpose is persuasion. By surrendering control over demand and accepting the indoctrinating effects of advertising, the consumer no longer finds it necessary to make a decision. Thus he forgoes the cost of decision making and will choose to do so if the satisfaction-cost ratio of a "rational" (or deliberate) consumer choice is less than the satisfaction-cost ratio of indoctrinated choice. See Margaret Hall, *Distributive Trading* (London: Hutchinson's University Library, 1949), pp. 76-78.

[3] See the discussion of this by Joel Dean, "Department-Store Cost Functions," in Oscar Lange et al., *Studies in Mathematical Economics and Econometrics* (Chicago: University of Chicago Press, 1942), especially pp. 222-225.

[4] This assumes that there is a unique solution.

for the services of the retailer. For this reason, they are one of the determinants of demand.

Any firm in a trade channel has open to it the possibility of shifting some of the marketing functions forward to customers or back to manufacturers. Small retail stores often buy on credit from wholesalers, shifting much of the financing function back to the wholesaler, and provide little to consumers in the way of services such as credit, delivery, or merchandise selection. Such firms should show low costs, for the range of services is not great. But it is possible that the cost at which they perform the services they do perform may be quite high.

Customer shopping is not costless. The acquisition of market information is particularly time consuming; movement to a shopping center involves both the use of time and the incurring of transport costs; the provision of means of payment involves interest cost; the assumption of risk and uncertainty involves an imputed cost of reserves against contingencies; and the movement of the purchased product from retail store to the consumer's residence involves transport cost and probably time costs. If these costs are paid by consumers, they decrease the ability of the consumer to pay for retail services. It is quite possible that some of these "costs" may be regarded by consumers as the price of "admission" paid for the "entertainment" aspects of shopping,[5] but this calculus does not obliterate their existence. Nor does the quaint custom of excluding the value of housewives' services from our national income accounts justify exclusion of customer buying costs from our analysis of marketing costs or from our consideration of forces that shape the demand for the services of the retail firm.

One of the important effects of customer buying costs on retailing is that it limits the size of the store. Let us assume that retail stores show decreasing unit costs as the size of the store increases, with no observable point at which unit costs increase. This would imply that stores will continue to become bigger and bigger in order to obtain the advantages of lower unit costs. But in order to become bigger, a store must increase its sales, and this means more intensive penetration of the demand within its usual trading area or an increase in the size of the area. Either consequence involves additional costs. More intensive penetration of demand within its usual selling area must be achieved by price competition, which reduces gross margins, or by nonprice competition, which increases costs of operation. An increase in the size of the selling area will probably involve higher operating costs for the store in order to attract the new customers, and it will definitely increase the customers' buying costs because they shop at a greater distance. Such costs serve, therefore, to limit the size of the retail *store*. They do not, however, have the same effect on the optimum size of the retail *firm*, for one way to circumvent higher customer buying costs as the size of the individual store's trading area increases is to establish additional outlets, thereby preserving economies of scale associated with buying and management but avoiding higher customer buying costs.

CHARACTERISTICS OF RETAIL FIRMS

We turn now to a consideration of the supply of retailing services, which we shall treat in terms of the characteristics of the institutions in retailing. We shall focus first on the

---

[5] R. Bellamy, "Private and Social Cost in Retail Distribution," *Bulletin of the Oxford Institute of Statistics* 7 (November 1946): 351.

attributes of the retail firm, reserving for later consideration the retail establishment and the matter of multiunit firms.

Legal Form of Organization

In Table 9.1 we show the percentage of firms and the percentage of sales accounted for by proprietorships, partnerships, and corporations in nine industrial groups in 1967. The distribution of firms in retailing was typical of industry as a whole, with about three-fourths proprietorships. In mining, manufacturing, wholesaling, and finance, the relative importance of proprietorships was less. Proprietorships in retailing accounted for 25 percent of the total volume of retail trade. Only in agriculture and services were they more important than that. Corporations in retailing increased their proportionate share of retail trade during the 1960s—from 53 percent in 1957 to 69 percent in 1967.[6]

Assets and Liabilities

The most distinctive attributes of the asset structure of retail firms are the very high percentage (33) of assets devoted to inventories and the large percentage (24) in notes and accounts receivable. (See Table 9.2.) Only corporations in construction and finance had a larger percentage of their assests in the form of notes and accounts receivable. The holding of merchandise stocks and the extension of credit to buyers are clearly principal functions of retailing. But the extension of credit by retail firms was partially offset by a very high accounts payable ratio—18 percent compared to an industry average of 6 percent. Only construction corporations had a higher accounts payable percentage. On the other hand, the equity of corporate owners in retail firms was equal to 43 percent of their total assets (or liabilities). This ratio was somewhat above the average for all industries, although mining, manufacturing, and transportation had higher equity ratios.

Income and Balance Sheet Relations

Table 9.3 shows that the average retail corporation had sales in 1968 of nearly $800,000, a net income of $21,000, assets of $285,000, and a net worth of $122,000. Sales in agriculture, construction, finance, and services tended, on an average, to be smaller than those in retailing. Sales per corporate firm were particularly high for general merchandise stores, food stores, and automobile and truck dealers. (See Table 9.4.) Food stores and automobile and truck dealers had the lowest ratio of net income to sales. Sales per firm were quite low for eating and drinking places, liquor stores, other retail stores, and gasoline service stations. Three of these—gasoline service stations, eating and drinking places, and liquor stores—had the highest ratio of net income to net worth.

Retailing is distinctive in the low ratio of net income to sales. As is apparent in Table 9.2, its net worth relative to assets was higher than average for industries in general. Its net income relative to net worth was about the same as in mining, manufacturing, and wholesaling; considerably higher than in agriculture, transportation, and finance; and lower than in construction or services.

---

[6] See Table 9.1 and U.S., Department of the Treasury, Internal Revenue Service, *Statistics of Income: 1957-58, United States Business Tax Returns* (Washington, D.C.: GPO; 1960), pp. 7, 11, 14.

Table 9.1 Number of Firms in Major Industries and Percentage of Firms and Sales Accounted for by Proprietorships, Partnerships, and Corporations in the United States, 1967[a]

Industry	Number of Firms (Thousands)	Firms Percentage of Total[b]				Sales Percentage of Total[b]			
		Total	Proprietorships	Partnerships	Corporations	Total	Proprietorships	Partnerships	Corporations
Agriculture, forestry, fisheries	3,358	100.0	95.5	3.6	.9	100.0	72.2	10.3	17.4
Mining	69	100.0	62.3	18.8	18.8	100.0	7.6	6.1	86.3
Construction	839	100.0	79.0	6.0	15.0	100.0	19.8	7.6	72.6
Manufacturing	397	100.0	43.3	8.3	48.4	100.0	1.0	.9	98.1
Transportation, communication, electric, gas	367	100.0	77.9	4.1	18.0	100.0	5.3	1.1	93.6
Wholesale trade	453	100.0	59.2	7.1	33.8	100.0	8.7	4.7	86.7
Retail trade	2,113	100.0	76.8	8.3	14.9	100.0	24.9	6.7	68.5
Finance, insurance, real estate	1,222	100.0	42.2	24.5	33.3	100.0	4.7	5.7	89.5
Services	2,795	100.0	85.5	6.3	8.2	100.0	36.1	16.0	47.9
Total, all industries[c]	11,613	100.0	78.9	7.9	13.2	100.0	12.5	4.5	83.0

[a]Based on a stratified sample of income tax returns filed for accounting periods ending July 1967 through June 1968.

[b]Details do not always add to total because of rounding.

[c]Includes businesses not allocable to individual industries.

Source: U.S., Bureau of the Census, *Statistical Abstract of the United States, 1970,* 91st ed. (Washington, D.C.: GPO, 1970), p. 468; from U.S., Department of the Treasury, Internal Revenue Service, *Statistics of Income: 1967, Business Income Tax Returns* (Washington, D.C.: GPO, 1971).

Table 9.2 Specific Assets and Liabilities as a Percentage of the Total in Corporate Firms in Major Industries in the United States, 1968[a]

Item	Total	Agriculture	Mining	Construction	Manufacturing	Transportation	Finance	Services	Wholesale and Retail		
									Total	Wholesale	Retail
Assets					Percentage of Total[b]						
Cash	6.8	5.9	6.7	9.8	4.3	3.8	8.5	8.6	7.3	7.4	7.3
Notes and accounts receivable	22.5	11.4	13.8	32.5	21.0	8.4	26.0	16.8	28.5	33.8	24.3
Inventories	7.4	13.1	5.4	12.7	19.6	1.9	.1	5.0	31.5	29.1	33.4
Government securities and other current assets	10.7	3.5	4.6	9.7	4.6	4.5	16.2	4.2	2.9	3.0	2.8
Loans and other investments	27.5	8.1	15.9	9.1	13.1	9.6	41.8	13.8	8.2	9.8	7.0
Depreciable and depletable assets	20.9	30.9	47.0	18.9	31.9	67.4	4.3	40.5	16.2	12.7	19.0
Land	1.8	23.6	2.0	3.1	1.8	1.0	1.5	5.6	2.5	1.8	3.1
Other assets	2.4	3.5	4.8	4.2	3.8	3.4	1.6	5.6	2.9	2.6	3.1
Total assets	100.0	100.0	100.0	100.0	100.0	100.0	100.0	100.0	100.0	100.0	100.0
Liabilities					Percentage of Total[b]						
Accounts payable	5.6	6.2	7.3	22.5	10.1	5.3	1.5	9.6	20.6	24.0	17.9
Other current liabilities	39.6	21.8	13.7	22.2	14.1	10.6	60.7	19.6	19.9	20.5	19.4
Long-term loans, mortgages, notes, etc.	13.6	27.5	17.5	15.5	16.9	35.5	6.2	32.2	13.9	12.2	15.4
Other liabilities	11.1	3.4	4.9	10.6	4.5	5.4	16.8	5.3	3.4	2.2	4.4
Capital stock and surplus	30.1	41.2	56.7	29.3	54.5	43.2	14.8	33.4	42.2	41.1	42.9
Total liabilities	100.0	100.0	100.0	100.0	100.0	100.0	100.0	100.0	100.0	100.0	100.0

[a]Based on a stratified sample of corporation income tax returns filed for accounting periods ending July 1968 through June 1969.

[b]Details do not always add to total because of rounding.

Source: U.S., Department of the Treasury, Internal Revenue Service, *Statistics of Income: 1968, Corporation Income Tax Returns* (Washington, D.C.: GPO, 1972), pp. 14-19.

Table 9.3 Number, Receipts, Net Income, Assets, and Net Worth of Corporate Firms in Major Industries in the United States, 1968[a]

Industry	Number of Firms	Per Firm				Net Incomes to Receipts[b]	Ratio of	
		Receipts[b]	Net Income (In Thousands)	Assets	Net Worth		Net Worth to Assets	Net Income to Net Worth
Agriculture, forestry, fisheries	31,248	$ 32.0	$ 16.0	$ 267.0	$ 109.9	.502	.412	.146
Mining	12,813	1,135.7	153.8	1,546.3	876.1	.135	.567	.176
Contract construction	125,999	573.5	180.4	2,849.2	83.6	.033	.294	.223
Manufacturing	191,915	3,381.5	244.8	2,608.3	1,421.1	.072	.545	.172
Transportation, communication, electric, gas, sanitary services	65,554	1,717.5	174.0	3,639.3	1,620.3	.101	.445	.107
Wholesale and retail trade	471,987	957.4	25.0	343.5	144.8	.026	.422	.173
Wholesale trade	153,117	1,354.9	32.6	466.2	191.7	.024	.411	.170
Retail trade	314,605	767.4	21.4	284.9	122.3	.028	.429	.175
Finance, insurance, real estate	407,199	360.8	41.7	498.3	437.9	.116	.148	.095
Services	228,904	223.0	13.5	206.3	68.9	.060	.334	.196
Total, all industries	1,541,670	$ 978.0	$ 61.7	$1,437.6	$ 432.4	.063	.301	.143

[a]Based on a stratified sample of corporation income tax returns filed for accounting periods ending July 1968 through June 1969.

[b]Total receipts include sales receipts plus other income.

Source: U.S. Department of the Treasury, Internal Revenue Service, *Statistics of Income: 1968, Corporation Income Tax Returns* (Washington, D.C.: GPO, 1972), pp. 8-11.

Table 9.4 Number, Receipts, Net Income, Assets, and Net Worth of Corporate Retail Firms by Kind of Business in the United States, 1968[a]

Kind of Business[b]	Number of Firms	Per Firm				Ratio of		
		Receipts[c]	Net Income (in Thousands)	Assets	Net Worth	Net Income to Receipts[c]	Net Worth to Assets	Net Income to Net Worth
Gasoline service stations	9,366	$ 386.5	$ 10.4	$ 98.4	$ 44.6	.027	.453	.233
Eating and drinking places	58,289	224.9	7.8	92.1	34.7	.035	.377	.226
Liquor stores	7,656	271.6	6.6	77.0	31.4	.024	.407	.211
Other automotive dealers	13,442	414.1	12.2	184.0	59.7	.030	.324	.205
Apparel and accessory stores	34,430	400.0	18.0	176.8	92.4	.005	.523	.194
Drug, proprietary stores	17,238	497.0	15.1	170.4	77.9	.030	.457	.194
Food stores	22,577	2,367.1	40.6	446.7	218.2	.017	.489	.186
General merchandise stores	16,615	3,068.6	131.9	1,758.2	742.7	.043	.422	.178
Other retail stores	48,094	311.5	11.7	160.3	71.6	.038	.446	.163
Automobile and truck dealers	28,516	1,726.7	20.7	400.0	136.5	.012	.341	.152
Furniture, home furnishings, equipment stores	29,099	400.4	12.5	196.4	84.3	.031	.429	.148
Building materials, hardware, farm equipment stores	29,283	492.5	16.3	243.7	116.6	.033	.479	.140
Total retail	314,605	$ 767.4	$21.4	$ 284.9	$122.3	.028	.429	.175

[a]Based on a stratified sample of corporation income tax returns filed for accounting periods ending July 1968 through June 1969.

[b]Ranked according to ratio of net income to net worth.

[c]Total receipts include sales receipts plus other income.

Source: U.S., Department of the Treasury, Internal Revenue Service, Statistics of Income: 1968, Corporation Income Tax Returns (Washington, D.C.: GPO, 1972), pp. 10-13.

Table 9.5 Summary Operating Statement for 314,605 Active Retail Corporations for the Year 1968[a]

Item	Amount (Billions)	Percentage of	
		Business Receipts	Gross Margin
Business receipts	$241.4	100.0	
Cost of goods sold	170.7	70.7	
Gross margin	$ 70.7	29.3	100.0
Compensation of officers	4.4	1.8	6.3
Rent	4.8	2.0	6.8
Taxes paid	3.5	1.5	5.1
Interest paid	1.9	.7	2.2
Amortization, depreciation, depletion, and repairs	3.4	1.4	4.8
Advertising	3.6	1.5	5.1
Other deductions	43.5	18.0	61.5
Total expenses	64.9	26.9	91.8
Net income	$ 5.8	2.4	8.2

[a]Based on a stratified sample of income tax returns filed for accounting periods ending July 1968 through June 1969.

Source: U.S., Department of the Treasury, Internal Revenue Service, *Statistics of Income: 1968, Corporation Income Tax Returns* (Washington, D.C.: GPO, 1972), p. 17.

In Table 9.4 we have arrayed the various kinds of retail businesses according to net income relative to net worth. While the average ratio for retail corporations as a whole was .175, the range was from .140 for building materials and hardware stores to .233 for gasoline service stations. Those with high rates of return tended to be firms with a high stockturn and, in many cases, limited inventories, while those with a low rate of return on investment required large inventory investments and generally had a much lower rate of stockturn.

Operating Expenses

Retail corporations had an average gross margin of 29 percent of sales in 1968, an average expense ratio of 27 percent, and a profit ratio of slightly more than 2 percent of sales.[7] (See Table 9.5.) Expense ratios varied widely according to the kind of business. (See

[7]We should point out that the value of "sales" that we used in making these calculations is "total receipts" rather than "business receipts." In retailing, the difference between the two amounted to about 2 percent of total receipts in 1968. In general, business receipts were gross receipts from sales and operations less returns and allowances. This would therefore have been the value most closely related to sales revenue for retail corporations. Total receipts include, in addition to business receipts, income from investments, such as interest, rents, royalties, and dividends, and capital gains from the exchange of capital assets. Since we are comparing retailing with other industries, we chose to use total receipts rather than business receipts as the base in order that those industries in which interest represents a large share of receipts (e.g., finance) would be comparable. See the section entitled "Law and Terminology" in U.S., Department of the Treasury, Internal Revenue Service, *Statistics of Income: 1968, Business Income Tax Returns* (Washington, D.C.: GPO, 1972),pp. 249-257.

Table 9.6 Abbreviated Operating Statement for Corporate Retail Firms by Kind of Business in the United States, 1968[a]

Kind of Business	Gross Receipts per Firm (Thousands)	Percentage of Sales				
		Gross Sales	Cost of Goods Sold	Gross Margin	Operating Expenses	Net Profit
Food	$2,367.1	100.0	78.5	21.5	19.9	1.5
General merchandise	3,068.6	100.0	59.1	40.9	36.7	4.1
Apparel	400.0	100.0	62.5	37.5	33.5	4.0
Furniture, furnishings	400.4	100.0	63.7	36.3	33.9	2.4
Automobile and truck	1,726.7	100.0	85.1	14.9	13.9	1.0
Gasoline service stations	386.5	100.0	75.5	24.5	22.2	2.3
Other automobile dealers	414.1	100.0	71.4	28.6	26.5	2.1
Eating and drinking	224.9	100.0	44.6	55.4	53.3	2.1
Building materials, hardware	492.5	100.0	74.5	25.5	22.7	2.8
Drug	497.0	100.0	69.0	31.0	28.4	2.7
Liquor	271.6	100.0	78.0	22.1	20.4	1.7
Other retail trade	311.5	100.0	65.3	34.7	31.7	3.0
Total	$ 767.4	100.0	70.7	29.3	26.9	2.4

[a]Based on a stratified sample of income tax returns filed for accounting periods ending July 1968 through June 1969.

Source: U.S., Department of the Treasury, Internal Revenue Service, *Statistics of Income: 1968, Corporation Income Tax Returns* (Washington, D.C.: GPO, 1972), pp. 17-18.

Table 9.6.) They were quite low for food stores and automobile dealers and quite high in eating and drinking places, general merchandise stores, furniture and furnishings stores, and apparel stores. Intertype differences are related to such things as the amount and kind of services rendered with each transaction, the amount of personal selling effort required, the importance and cost of location, the degree of standardization in merchandise and operating methods, the amount of capital used, the importance and volume of advertising, the volume of sales per establishment and per firm, the size of the average transaction, and the amount and character of competition at the retail level. Since retailing is the most costly of marketing activities, we shall examine some of the components of these costs.

WAGES AND SALARIES

This is the largest single cost category in the retail firm. In department stores, for example, it accounted for about half of the gross margin. (See Table 9.7.) Of the amount spent for wages and salaries in department stores, not quite half was for salespeoples' wages and the balance was for nonselling labor costs. In retail corporations, compensation of officers was about 6 percent of the gross margin. The balance of the nonselling wage costs would be for services such as office work, advertising and promotion, and merchandise handling and delivery.

An estimation of wage costs in noncorporate retail enterprises is difficult to arrive at because of the confounding of wages of management, wages of labor, and return on equity investment. In 1968 payroll costs in retail partnerships were reported to be about 40 percent of total operating expenses, and this would presumably include wage

Table 9.7 Gross Margin and Operating Expenses of Department Stores, 1970

Item	$1 to $2 Million		$2 to $5 Million		$5 to $10 million		$10 to $20 Million		$20 to $50 Million		$50 Million or More	
	Sales	Gross Margin	Sales	Gross Margin	Sales	Gross Margin	Sales	Gross Margin	Sales	Gross Margin	Sales	Gross Margin
	Percentage of											
Gross margin	37.3	100.0	35.8	100.0	36.9	100.0	36.0	100.0	36.4	100.0	37.8	100.0
Payroll	20.4	54.7	18.7	52.2	19.0	51.5	18.4	51.1	19.9	54.7	18.9	50.0
Salespeoples' salaries	9.4	25.2	8.9	24.9	9.0	24.4	8.6	23.9	8.9	24.5	8.5	22.5
Other payroll	11.0	29.5	9.8	27.4	10.0	27.1	9.8	27.2	9.0	24.8	10.4	27.5
Real estate costs	2.6	6.9	2.3	6.5	2.9	8.0	2.7	7.5	2.7	7.3	2.4	6.3
Advertising	2.5	6.6	2.8	7.9	2.6	7.0	2.9	8.0	2.5	7.0	2.2	5.7
Other expenses	9.2	24.7	8.2	23.0	8.9	24.2	9.1	25.2	8.4	23.0	8.5	22.6
Total expenses	34.7	92.9	32.1	89.6	33.5	90.6	33.1	91.8	33.5	92.0	32.0	84.7

Source: National Retail Merchants Association, Controllers Congress, *Financial and Operating Results of Department and Specialty Stores of 1970* (New York, 1971), pp. 10-49.

Table 9.8 Abbreviated Operating Statement for Retail Proprietorships, Partnerships, and Corporations in the United States for the Year 1968[a]

Item	Proprietorships		Partnerships		Corporations	
	Amount in Billions	Percentage of Sales	Amount in Billions	Percentage of Sales	Amount in Billions	Percentage of Sales
Total receipts	$85.5	100.0	$23.2	100.0	$241.4	100.0
Cost of goods sold	63.2	73.9	16.6	71.6	170.7	70.7
Gross margin	$22.3	26.1	$ 6.6	28.4	$ 70.7	29.3
Operating expenses	16.6	19.3	4.9	21.2	64.9	26.9
Wages and salaries	$ 5.7	6.6	$ 2.0	8.6	(b)	(b)
Other expenses	10.9	12.7	2.9	12.6	(b)	(b)
Net income	$ 5.8	6.8	$ 1.7	7.2	$ 5.9	2.4

[a]Based on a stratified sample of income tax returns filed for accounting periods ending July 1968 through June 1969. Details may not add to total because of rounding.

[b]Not available. Officers' salaries alone ammounted to $4.4 billion, or 1.8 percent of sales.

Source: U.S., Department of the Treasury, Internal Revenue Service, *Statistics of Income: 1968, Business Income Tax Returns* (Washington, D.C.: GPO, 1972).

payments to partners, but not necessarily in all cases. In proprietorships, wages and salaries were about 30 percent of operating expenses. In the latter case earnings of proprietors would be included in profits, which were equal to about one-third of operating expenses, contrasted with about one-fourth for partnerships and less than one-tenth for corporations. The relevant data are shown in Table 9.8. It seems clear that some of the wages of management in both proprietorships and partnerships are included in the firms' net income figure.

Payroll costs for retail establishments were reported in the *Census of Business* for 1967.[8] These would not include managerial wages and salaries for stores that did not separate these out as explicit labor costs, but they provide an additional check on our wage cost data for retailing. For stores that were operated the entire year, payroll was 11.7 percent of sales, 39.9 percent of the estimated gross margin, and 43.4 percent of the estimated operating expenses, based on the gross margin and operating expense ratios in Table 9.5.[9] It seems reasonable to conclude therefore that wages and salaries represented about 45 percent of the retail operating costs of all retail stores and about 50 percent for department stores.

Wage rates in retailing are among the lowest to be found in any industry. Jules Backman has offered six reasons for the low wages in retail trade:[10]

1. Low capital investment per worker. In retailing, investment is largely in inventories and space rather than machinery, and this form of investment does not add much to labor productivity.

---

[8]U.S., Bureau of the Census, *United States Census of Business: 1967*, vol. I, *Retail Trade—Subject Reports* (Washington, D.C.: GPO, 1971).

[9]The relevant data are as follows: sales of stores operated entire year, $299,430 million; payroll, $34,986 million; estimated gross margin (29.3 percent of $299,430 million), $87,733; and estimated operating expenses (26.9 percent of $299,430 million), $80,547 million.

[10]Jules Backman, "Why Wages are Lower in Retailing," *Southern Economic Journal* 23 (January 1957): 295-305.

2. High labor costs in relation to total costs, a condition commonly associated with low wage rates.
3. A stable relationship between retail trade employment and total employment.
4. Low productivity per worker, as evidenced by income produced per employee. Moreover, over the years, productivity has increased less in retail trade than in other industries.
5. The younger age of the average retail employee, reinforced by the large number of part-time employees.
6. A low level of unionization.

While some of these six factors may be regarded as *causes* of low wage rates in retailing, others are conditions *associated* with low wages, reflecting the basic productivity condition that gives rise to low wages.

PHYSICAL PLANT AND EQUIPMENT

The second-largest expense in retailing is the cost of physical plant and equipment. Rent alone accounted for about 7 percent of the corporate retail firm's gross margin. If we add to this the costs of amortization, depreciation, depletion, and repairs, most of which would be concerned with store buildings, warehouses, and equipment, the total would be about 12 percent of gross margin. Department stores reported real estate costs ranging between 6 and 8 percent of gross margin. (See Table 9.7.) These costs would be equivalent to rent and would not include other expenses related to the maintenance of physical equipment.

Since rents are more price determined than price determining, and since retail stores are among the most important bidders for sites, it is possible for us to regard real estate costs as partly a reflection of the value of the store's monopoly of its site.[11] Large stores show a lower real estate cost ratio than smaller stores, indicating that sales increase more rapidly than space costs. However, differences between stores in their leasing and ownership of real estate will affect the location of space costs in the firm's accounts, and we must be careful when basing generalizations on explicit rents.

INVENTORY COSTS

Retail firms are inventory-carrying institutions, and the cost of maintaining stocks of goods is an important variable in the firm's operations. The annual cost of this investment consists of interest, space and necessary maintenance, protection against the predictable risks of physical deterioration, and the "normal" profit required to bear the uncertainty of market obsolescence. Imputed interest on inventory investment would be represented by $i(I)$, in which

$$I = \frac{S}{T}$$

The annual rate of interest is represented by i, I is the average inventory at cost, S is cost of goods sold, and T is stockturn at cost. Sales of $10 million at retail, with a gross margin of 30 percent, would have a cost of sales of $7 million. An average stockturn of 3.5 would indicate an average inventory investment of $2 million at cost. At a 10 percent rate of interest, this would be a cost of $200,00 per year, or approximately 6.7 percent of the firm's gross margin ($200,000/$3,000,000). If we add to this the costs of risk and

---

[11] R. Bellamy, "Size and Success in Retail Distribution," *Bulletin of the Oxford University Institute of Statistics* 8 (October 1946): 324-339.

Table 9.9 Advertising Expenses as a Percentage of Business Receipts in Wholesale and Retail Trade and Seven Other Industries in the United States, 1968[a]

Industry	Advertising Expenses as Percentage of Total Receipts
Agriculture, forestry, fisheries	0.36
Mining	0.14
Contruction	0.20
Manufacturing	1.34
Transportation, communication, electric, gas	0.56
Wholesale trade	0.49
Retail trade	1.50
Food	1.21
General merchandise	2.52
Apparel, accessories	1.89
Furniture, home furnishings	2.73
Automobiles, filling stations	0.88
Eating, drinking places	1.23
Building materials, hardware	0.72
Other	1.30
Finance, insurance, real estate	0.75
Services	1.83
Total, all industries	1.08

[a]Based on a stratified sample of income tax returns filed for accounting periods ending July 1968 through June 1969.

Source: U.S., Department of the Treasury, Internal Revenue Service, *Statistics of Income: 1968, Corporation Income Tax Returns* (Washington, D.C.: GPO, 1972), pp. 14-19.

uncertainty, the total inventory cost would probably exceed real estate costs for the typical store. Part of the space costs of the retail firm should be imputed to inventories, and part of the wages and salaries of the firm are for inventory maintenance, but we shall not attempt to estimate either of these.

Because large firms show higher stockturn rates, inventory costs do not rise so rapidly as sales. This gives the large firm a cost advantage. Moreover, the higher stockturn rates of large firms may themselves stimulate sales through greater merchandise selection.

SELLING COSTS

We have already observed that the retail firm is peculiarly affected by the interrelationship of selling costs and revenue. Is it possible to estimate the size of this group of costs, that is, costs incurred to influence the position and slope of the demand curve? Even if we could isolate certain functions as purely "selling" activities, we would probably not be able to isolate their costs with complete accuracy. Nevertheless, it is instructive to observe the importance of certain cost elements that most closely reflect the retail firm's selling activities.

Data from the Internal Revenue Service show that retail corporations in 1968 had advertising expenditures of 1.50 percent of sales and 5.11 percent of gross margins. (See Tables 9.5 and 9.9.) These were highest for furniture and home furnishings, general merchandise, and apparel stores, and lowest for building materials and hardware stores. No other type of industry among the nine groups into which the Internal Revenue Service classified reporting firms showed such a high expenditure in relation to sales, although services and manufacturing did have high ratios. Those industries whose output was closest to form production used advertising far less than those whose output was farthest from form production. Within retail trade itself, sellers of shopping goods, where price and nonprice competition are keen, were the heaviest users of advertising relative to sales.

If we were to total all costs that we call "selling cost," we would include advertising and a sizable portion of the retail firm's wage costs. We cannot, however, do more than estimate the proportion of labor costs that should be classified as "selling." Suppose, however, that we take one-half of the payroll cost, which would be about 22-25 percent of the gross margin of retail corporations, and add to this advertising costs of about 6 percent. These two together would account for 28-31 percent of retail margins. It would not appear unreasonable to say that one-fourth to one-third of the average store's margin is probably for "selling cost," that is, costs directed toward changing the demand. This does not include costs of window display, interior display, and numerous services that might also reasonably be classified as "selling costs."

In an interesting study completed several years ago. Max Kjær-Hansen attempted to estimate the cost in Scandinavian countries of what he called "retail store advertising," defined to include window and interior displays, neon signs, and other point-of-sale methods of attracting sales, plus, of course, printed advertisements, film and slide advertising, outdoor advertising, exhibitions, other media, and advertising management.[12] Of the total estimated advertising expenditures in Sweden, Denmark, Norway, and Finland in 1953, between 32 and 41 percent were for "retail store advertising."[13] Using his estimates of retail gross margins in these four countries, we find that his estimated interior display advertising expenditures accounted for 4-7 percent of the gross margin of retailing in those four countries.[14] It is possible that the absence of radio and television advertising in those countries in that year plus the differences in advertising customs would result in different media patterns in Scandinavia and in the United States. Nevertheless, Kjær-Hansen's figures suggest that in-store advertising can be an important part of the total advertising bill and a significant element of retail costs.

THE COST COMPLEX

The control of costs in retail stores is complicated by the character of the cost-output relationship, by the indivisibility of certain costs, and by limitations on the extent to which management can control the rate of hourly output. We have already considered the problem of cost-output relationships and have shown that demand may itself be a function of cost allocation and that this functional relationship is rarely precise or predictable. Let us examine the other aspects of the retail firm's cost complex—the indivisibility of certain costs and the inability of management to control the rate of output.

1. *JOINT COSTS.* The cost structure of retailing is complicated by the existence of a large number of joint costs. While certain costs can be allocated to particular items and/or

---

[12] Max Kjær-Hansen, *Salgs- og reklameomkostningerne i Norden*, Nordisk Salgs- og Reklameforbunds Skriftserie Nr. 1 (Copenhagen: Einar Harcks Forlag, 1956), especially pp. 46-48.

[13] In Sweden, 32.2 percent; in Norway, 32.4 percent; in Denmark, 38.0 percent; in Finland, 41.3 percent. Ibid., p. 98.

[14] In Norway, 4.34 percent; in Finland, 4.38 percent; in Sweden, 5.26 percent; in Denmark, 7.14 percent. Computed from ibid., pp. 20, 26, 28, 29, 40, 56, 68, 79.

particular transactions, many are not separable. Labor and management costs are difficult to allocate, particularly in the nondepartmentized store. Inventory and space costs are allocable, although allocation of the latter usually involves use of arbitrary bases. Perhaps the most significant effect of joint costs is on the retail store's pricing procedures. The one cost most easily and accurately allocable to a specific item of merchandise is the cost of the merchandise. This therefore is likely to be the variable cost that the retailer will use most often in determining the minimum resale price for a product. In the short run the bulk of his operating costs will be fixed, and he will price individual products in such a way that he maximizes the gross margin of the entire store.

2. *RATE OF HOURLY OUTPUT*. Cost control in retailing is further complicated by the inability of management to control the rate of hourly output. A retail store must adapt itself to consumers' decisions about when they will shop and buy. These decisions often create an unsteady flow of customers through time, with large numbers of shoppers in certain periods. Not only are there seasonal patterns, but also weekly and daily variations in sales and, within a single day, hourly differences. The retailer's defense against these fluctuations is to anticipate and prepare for them or to retain within his organization flexibility in the use of personnel and capital so that peak demand can be met by shifting resources from one activity, such as stock handling, to another, such as selling. He may also use promotional methods to shift demand from peak periods to periods of normally low demand, or price differentials that will yield an optimum revenue-cost relationship for the entire period.

This phenomenon is particularly apparent in supermarkets. In a study of Kroger stores, for example, it was found that 55 percent of the week's sales were made on Thursday and Friday and an additional 20 percent on Saturday.[15] (At the time of this study, most of the stores were not open on Sunday.) This concentration of sales appears to be in part a result of consumer preferences for shopping on those days, associated with paydays and the weekly pattern of family activities. But it is also encouraged by supermarket operators, who concentrate their use of price leaders and sales promotion on those days. While it would appear that competition between supermarkets forces all of them to carry special promotions on similar days to minimize the loss of sales to competing stores, it would also appear that a monopoly would behave similarly if it could derive more benefits from each promotional dollar near weekends than earlier in the week. This assumes that the character of demand is different near the weekend and is more responsive to promotion than is true earlier in the week. It is probably cheaper to increase an expanding demand still further than to increase a contracting or stable demand.[16]

Even department and specialty apparel stores have a high weekly concentration of sales. In one week in the spring of 1970, for example, department and specialty stores did 41 percent of their total weekly volume on Friday and Saturday, and in one week in the fall, 42 percent. Branch stores alone did 44 percent on Friday and Saturday in both the spring week and fall week.[17]

---

[15] *Consumer Dynamics in the Super Market* (New York: Progressive Grocer, n.d.), p. 104. (This was published about 1965.)

[16] See, for example, Neil H. Borden, *Economic Effects of Advertising* (Chicago: Irwin, 1942), pp. 422-438.

[17] National Retail Merchants Association, Controllers Congress, *Financial and Operating Results of Department and Specialty Stores of 1970* (New York, 1971), p. xx

10

Size and Efficiency of Retail Institutions

Keep thy shop, and thy shop will keep thee.
Light gains make heavy purses.

—George Chapman,

Our discussion of retailing up to this point has focused on retailing as a whole or on the average firm or establishment. Louis Bucklin has pointed out that in national markets the relative importance of chains and independents is critical, while in local markets it is the size of establishments (i.e., stores) in relation to the size of the total market that is the important issue.[1] The chain store organization has been particularly important in retailing, for this has been one avenue by which the advantages of the relatively small retail store have been combined with those of the large retail firm. Modifications of the corporate chain, in the form of voluntary and cooperative chains, have further extended opportunities for horizontal integration in retailing, although the looseness of the voluntary chain has limited its ability to benefit from all of the potential advantages of horizontal and vertical integration in retailing.

Between 1958 and 1967 the number of retail firms reporting to the Internal Revenue Service increased only slightly, from 1,990,000 to 2,046,209.[2] The number of proprietorships declined slightly, from 1,552,566 to 1,543,999; the number of partnerships declined markedly, from 250,629 to 186,629; and the number of corporations increased markedly, from 186,405 to 315,581. In spite of the growth in population and volume of retail trade, the number of firms in retailing increased only 2.8 percent, indicating that sales per firm increased considerably. Data on retail stores likewise show a tendency toward consolidation. There were 1,794,700 retail stores in 1958 compared with 1,763,300 in 1967, a decline of 1.8 percent.[3] The tendency has been to have slightly fewer and much larger stores and slightly more firms and much larger ones.

It is appropriate, therefore, to consider some of the issues associated with the size of retail firms and establishments. One question is why small firms and stores continue to survive in view of the considerable advantages of large retailing institutions. We shall also explore the important question of whether optimum size has been achieved in retailing institutions from the viewpoint of internal operating efficiency. We shall reserve for later consideration the impact of the size of firms and establishments in retailing on interfirm relations and consumer welfare.

---

[1] Louis P. Bucklin, *Competition and Evolution in the Distributive Trades* (Englewood Cliffs, N.J.: Prentice-Hall, 1972), p. 133.

[2] U.S., Department of the Treasury, Internal Revenue Service, *Statistics of Income: 1967, Business Income Tax Returns* (Washington, D.C.: GPO, 1972), pp. 370-379.

[3] U.S., Bureau of the Census, *United States Census of Business: 1958* and *1967*, vol. II, *Retail Trade—Area Statistics*.

THE SMALL RETAIL STORE

Retailing is often pointed to as an example of an industry in which there is considerable ease of entry, a large number of small firms and establishments, and a tendency toward overcapacity.[4] There is, of course, evidence of inefficiency in retail trade in many local markets, and this is particularly true in retailing in underdeveloped countries.[5] But the overall evidence on retailing operations in the United States does not indicate that this is an industry that is characterized by any more inefficiency than are a number of other industries. The rate of return on capital investment, as shown in Tables 9.3 and 9.4, is actually above the average for all coporations. The percentage of retail corporations that showed a loss in 1968 was no greater than in industry as a whole.[6] Nor do the limited data available on mortality rates indicate that retailing is plagued by a higher failure rate than other forms of business.[7] On the basis of the incidence of operating deficits, return on investment, and mortality rates, we simply do not find sufficient basis for regarding retailing *as a whole* as being a more inefficient segment of the economy than other industries.

The Problem of the Small Store

This is not to say, however, that all retail firms and stores are efficient. In 1967, for example, out of a total of 1,700,000 retail stores in the United States that were operated for the entire year, more than 800,000 had sales of less than $50,000. A store with sales of $50,000 would have a gross margin of about $12,000 or $13,000 to cover wages and salaries, rent, advertising, all other operating expenses, and the return on investment. Consider further the plight of the nearly 600,000 stores that, in that year, had sales of $30,000 or less. Gross margin for these stores is unlikely to exceed about $8,000, and for most of them it would be less. But the importance of these small stores is not great in terms of the total volume of retail trade. Stores with sales of less than $50,000 accounted

---

[4] See, for example, the discussions by Henry C. Smith, *Retail Distribution—A Critical Analysis* (London: Oxford University Press, 1937); and Margaret Hall, *Distributive Trading* (London: Hutchinson's University Library, n.d., ca. 1949).

[5] See Chapter 21.

[6] In 1968, for example, 66 percent of the retail corporations filing income tax returns had a positive net income, compared with 73 percent in wholesaling, 70 percent in manufacturing, and 65 percent in all industries. Calculated from U.S., Department of the Treasury, *Statistics of Income: 1968, Business Tax Returns*, pp. 261-276.

[7] Unfortunately we do not have very good information on this, and comprehensive time series are seriously lacking. Dun and Bradstreet's data, based on firms listed in the July issue of the *Dun and Bradstreet Record Book*, seem to show that even though retailing firms accounted for 40 to 50 percent of the failures for which they have data over the period from 1955 to 1971, the failure rate (failures per 10,000 active firms) was not higher than in other industries. In 1970, for example, the rate for all industries was 44. Among various kinds of retail businesses, most showed a failure rate less than that, with a higher than average rate in women's ready-to-wear apparel (77), furniture and furnishings (74), cameras and photographic supplies (67), infants' and children's wear (57), books and stationery (57), men's wear (52), and appliances and TV (45). Other types of retail businesses showed rates as low as 14 for women's accessories and 15 for groceries and meats. See Dun and Bradstreet, *The Failure Record through 1970* (New York, 1971), p.5, and U.S., Bureau of the Census, *Statistical Abstract of the United States: 1972* (Washington D.C.: GPO, 1972), p. 485.

for only 5.6 percent of total retail volume in 1967.[8] Most of these stores were probably too small to be efficient. (We know also, of course, that some stores of larger size were inefficient.)

Reasons for Suboptimal Small Stores

The presence of a large number of relatively small stores in retailing is due to two facts: (1) They offer certain retailing services desired by consumers, such as locational convenience near their customers and a personalized type of operation that some consumers prefer, and (2) their owners prefer to remain in this kind of business rather than to invest in some other enterprise or to seek alternative employment. We are particularly interested in the reasons why small stores of less than optimum size continue to exist.

PERSONAL FACTORS

From the consumer's point of view, the small retail store may offer a convenient, personalized type of service that he prefers over that available from a large establishment. From the viewpoint of the store owner, however, retailing shares with agriculture and service businesses some characteristics that account for the presence of a number of stores and firms of suboptimal efficiency. One is that personal and business finance are often melded for owners of many small retail enterprises. A family that owns and operates a small retail store may use it as a source of supply for the goods that they acquire at wholesale prices quite as much as they use it as a source of employment. This means that although the firm shows a loss as a business enterprise, it constitutes a valuable source of real income for the family. Another possibility is that a retail store owner may place a high premium on being his own boss and does not aspire to a "normal" profit. Still another possible reason for the existence of small uneconomic retail outlets is that the owner may not even know his operation is unprofitable.

DISGUISED UNEMPLOYMENT

In many cases retail firms employ marginal workers, as evidenced by the low wage rates in the industry. If there are certain segments of the labor force that are less productive than the going wage rate, it is desirable that there be opportunities for these people to be employed at occupations in which they would be most efficient. Since many retailing tasks require a relatively low level of skills, retail firms can provide some employment opportunities for individuals who might otherwise be unemployable. Increased mechanization and increased efficiency in work organization in retailing tend, of course, to reduce possibilities for using retailing as a medium for this type of disguised unemployment.

SIZE OF MARKET AREA

The problem of the small retail store is further affected by the size of retail market areas. Suppose, for example, the optimum retail drug store needs a clientele of 8,000

---

[8] U.S., Bureau of the Census, *United States Census of Business: 1967*, vol. I, *Retail Trade–Subject Reports* (Washington, D.C.: GPO, 1971).

consumers. A small town with a population of 2,500 is not able to support such a store. One alternative will be for some other kind of store to handle drug products, but these will have to be restricted to proprietary drugs. Another possibility is for residents of the small community to use the drugstore facilities of a larger retail center. This, however, entails additional costs of transportation, inconvenience, and possibly even hazards in the case of emergencies. Hence, the small store may survive in the small community, charging its customers higher prices than would be possible in a larger outlet in a larger trading center, because the cutomers derive sufficient marginal utility from the accessibility of the small store to warrant their paying such prices.

Another problem arises in the small market center that is able to support only one establishment of a kind. Not only is there a question of whether that establishment will be of optimal size but it is doubtful whether, in the absence of competition, such an establishment will have sufficient incentive to operate efficiently. If the residents of the community have access to other market centers, this overlapping of areas will broaden the effective competitive area in which the one-store community operates.

In order for a store in a small market center to increase its volume, it is necessary to draw additional customers from a greater distance. This, however, increases consumer buying costs, if consumers pay such costs explicitly, or the cost of retailing if the retail store pays all or a portion of delivery costs. If these costs are proportional to distance, they cause the lowest-unit-cost point for the retail firm, or the point of equilibrium between marginal cost and marginal revenue, to shift to the left, resulting in lower volume and higher prices. There are therefore important limitations on the ability of a retail store in a small center to increase its volume to an optimum level.

In a large retail trading center, however, because of the presence of large numbers of customers for whom buying costs are quite low because of their proximity to the center, it is much more likely that optimum size can be achieved. In addition, the presence of a far larger number of competing establishments tends to push the retail store to achieve a volume and price level closer to the socially optimum. Ease of entry and excessive numbers of stores in such centers could, on the other hand, result in overcapacity in the retail industry and operation at a level lower than optimum—that is, on the declining portion of the store's average cost curve. We should also note that the large market center generates its own consumer buying costs as a result of proliferation of inventories and shopping congestion.

THE LARGE RETAIL STORE AND FIRM

In spite of the large number of retail stores in the United States, the 50,000 large retail establishments with sales of $1,000,000 or more in 1967 accounted for 48 percent of the total retail volume in that year.[9] Small stores continue to survive because they have the capability of rendering certain unique services to consumer buyers, but large stores have certain operating advantages over small stores. The same thing is true of retail firms: We have a large number of small retail firms and a small number of large firms, with the latter dominating the total volume of retail trade. We shall now consider the large retail store and retail firm.

---

[9] Ibid.

Means of Growth

A retail store can become larger by an increase in its stock depth in a given merchandise line, in its stock width, or in both. This would be accompanied by an increase in physical plant and facilities and in the size of the store's selling and nonselling labor force. Average store size in the United States has increased markedly in the decades since World War II. While this has entailed considerable increase in stock depth, the increase in stock width has been especially important.

If a retail firm maintains only one establishment, growth of the store and growth of the firm are one and the same. But retail firms can also grow by establishing new retail stores or acquiring existing stores, as well as by having the store or stores they own increase in size. Thus the retail firm can be much larger than the store. One of the distinctive characteristics of retail institutions is the discrepancy between optimum size of firm and optimum size of establishment. In no other industry except services is this difference so great. The chain store method of operation has made it possible to have the desired (not necessarily optimum) size of establishment within a much larger managerial unit. Voluntary and cooperative chains provide similar possibilities within a looser federation of retail establishments and centralized firm.

Multiestablishment firms are very important in retailing. Chains of four or more stores accounted for 34 percent of the total retail volume in the United States in 1967. They were particularly important for limited-price variety and department stores, where they accounted for 82 percent and 91 percent of sales, respectively. They accounted for slightly more than half of the sales of shoe stores and food stores and were least important among gasoline service stations, furniture and home furnishings stores, and building materials and hardware outlets, where they did less than 20 percent of the total retail volume.[10]

Advantages of Large Retail Institutions

Let us examine some of the advantages of large retail stores and firms. In some cases, the advantages of large stores and large firms are the same. In other cases, the advantages are peculiar to one or the other. We shall consider those common to both and indicate those that are relevant only to the multiunit firm.[11]

COST ADVANTAGES

The large retail unit can buy in larger quantities and enjoy the cost benefits of quantity discounts. This is known as the *principle of bulk transactions*: The larger the firm, the greater the volume of goods per transaction and the lower the transactional cost per unit. It is relevant to retailing in the buying of goods far more than in the selling of goods, since the average sales transaction is much smaller than the average buying transaction. Just as important as quantity purchases, however, is the possibility of greater buying skill in the large retail institution, with the cost spread over a larger volume of sales.

---

[10] Ibid.

[11] See George J. Stigler, *The Theory of Price*, 3d ed. (New York: Macmillan, 1966), pp. 146-160, 221-225; R. Bellamy, "Size and Success in Retailing," *Bulletin of the Oxford University Institute of Statistics* 8 (October 1946): 324-339; Hall, op. cit., pp. 80-81.

Operating costs can also be lower in large units to the extent that specialization of labor, capital, and management is possible; capital equipment can be effectively utilized; financing costs are reduced owing to the volume and the stability that results from diversification; and standardized operating methods can be devised and implemented.

In addition, managerial skill can be much higher in the large firm. According to the principle of proportionality, if resources are available only in discontinuous units, that resource whose minimum unit is largest will determine the minimum size of the firm. In retailing, lumpiness of resources is far less than in manufacturing, where the minimum amount of capital equipment may be the important factor in determining the minimum size of firm. The one resource that is extremely lumpy in retailing is management, and superior managerial competence and a superior managerial organization often give the large firm a distinct cost advantage. One reason managerial competence is likely to be greater in the large store or firm is that successful little stores tend to grow into big stores. Another reason is that a large retail firm can afford to hire better management, since the cost per unit is low.

Knowledge of merchandising methods, sources of supply, pricing and promotion policies, and the nature and needs of consumers gives competent retail management a real advantage in an expanding market. Also, the availability of capital to the successful retail firm is far greater than to the small store that is not so profitable. Not only can capital be acquired in the market at lower interest cost, but the successful firm is likely to generate capital for expansion. Much of the capital used for the expansion of chain stores in the 1920s came from within the firms rather than from capital markets. Existing firms have real advantages in undertaking further expansion.

Customer buying costs can also be reduced in the large store to the extent that size makes possible merchandise diversification and reduced buying time for the consumer.

PROMOTIONAL ADVANTAGES

The large store and the large firm can spread the cost of advertising over a much larger volume of sales. Since it is known that the impact of advertising is in part a function of how much is spent on it, this can be a critical factor. In this respect, the chain store has tremendous advantages. One advertisement, for example, can service 10 stores in one city, or 1,000 stores if the advertising is national. Chain supermarkets and general merchandise chains are greatly benefited by the economies of scale that they realize in the use of advertising.

One student believes that retail advertising has been much more informative than that of manufacturers.[12] Point-of-purchase displays, store image resulting from the sheer size of the plant, and retailer brands are likewise economically acquired advantages of the large retail institution. There are also many example of retailer-owned brands that are priced at levels below those owned by manufacturers. It is likely that this development has had a net favorable effect on consumers.

REDUCED RISK AND UNCERTAINTY

According to the *principle of pooled uncertainty*, the larger the firm, the greater the effectiveness of any resource employed to protect against contingencies. The predict-

---

[12] W. Arthur Lewis, "Competition in Retail Trade," *Economica*, n.s., 12 (November 1945): 218.

ability of a single event is less than that of the incidence of occurrence of a group of similar events. The pooling of uncertainties can make it possible to convert them into risk; that is, the probability of their occurrence can be established. In retailing, stocks are held against probable demand. The larger the firm, the greater the sales that a given inventory will support. This will show up in a higher sales-stock ratio for the large firm.

The large store also has some advantage over the small store through reduced risks associated with merchandise diversification and its ability to experiment with innovations. Still more possibilities for risk reduction accrue to the chain through horizontal integration and the spreading of risks; through vertical integration, which assures the retail unit of merchandise availability and greater market control; through opportunities for innovations affecting merchandise, promotion, and operating methods; and through research ensuring better managerial decisions with respect to operating policies.

A related aspect of risk reduction is the desire on the part of some entrepreneurs to secure their market position for purposes of self-perpetuation of the firm. Some writers have considered this not in terms of the longevity of the firm's life but in terms of the psychic income of the entrepreneurs. It is very difficult to assess the importance of this particular factor in American marketing. Nevertheless, it would appear that one of the reasons why existing firms continue to expand by establishing more and more stores is the desire on the part of management to see its control more firmly entrenched in the market in which it functions, or even to see its name spread more widely. Surely J. C. Penney found satisfaction in seeing his name in a greater and greater number of communities in the United States. Some of these underlying psychological factors may be just as important as more objective profit-making factors in explaining the expansion of retailing (and other) institutions.

Disadvantages of Large Retail Institutions

In each of the three areas that we have identified—cost, promotion, and risks—there are also limitations that constrain retail stores and firms from expanding size indefinitely.

COST DISADVANTAGES

Beyond a certain size level stores and firms will experience increasing unit costs. These arise from diminishing returns in the use of its resources and policy alternatives because of increasing cost of coordination and control as establishment or firm size increases.

The amount of communication required to coordinate a given number of communicators increases exponentially by the number of communicators. Because of the personal service character of retail selling, the number of individuals involved in receiving and transmitting messages is likely to be quite large. Every salesperson receives information from the firm, transmits information to the customer, receives information from the customer, and transmits information to the firm. Moreover, communication between two salespeople can flow in either of two directions. This complication is not peculiar to retailing, but it differs from the situation in many industries because the salesperson is the strategic liaison between firm and customer in retailing. Employees in a factory do not perform a comparable function. Other scale economies in retailing likewise become exhausted at some point. There is therefore a sales volume beyond which the cost of administrative coordination in retailing exceeds the benefits of centralization of management.

Consumer buying costs are especially important in limiting the size of the retail store. The larger the store, the larger its trading area must be and the larger the stocks of merchandise that it handles. The larger the trading area, the more it costs consumer buyers at the fringes of the area to come to the store to shop. Also, the larger the stocks in the store, the more the consumer has to wade through to find what he wants. Up to a point, the consumer will benefit by having more choices; beyond that point, he finds it too costly to search for the item he wants. He desires *optimum* depth and width rather than *maximum* depth and width. The shopping center itself can provide diversification without sacrificing the merchandising and promotional advantages of the small, specialized store.

PROMOTION DISADVANTAGES

Standardization of operation, which is an advantage in terms of controlling operating procedures and costs, can rebound to the disadvantage of the store and retail firm if consumers are seeking differentiation and diversification. Also, the size of the store and the firm may deny the consumer buyer the pleasures he finds in personal contact with the retail management.

INCREASED RISKS

The larger the store and the larger the retail firm, the greater its commitment to its area of operation and the greater the loss if the expected potentialities of that atea of operation are not realized. A&P and Montgomery Ward are testimony to the problems some firms have had in adapting to changing market conditions. Inflexibility is not inherent in large stores and firms, but a large retail unit can easily develop rigidities as a result of standardization of its operating methods.

There is scant evidence, however, that small retail units are optimally flexible. Hardening of the arteries can be seen in both large and small retail firms. One would indeed expect it less often in the large firm, since successful managers of small firms are likely to see their firms grow into big ones. But *if* inflexibility occurs and bad managerial decisions are made, the size of the commitment in the large store or retail firm is great, and the loss will be proportional.

Also, the bigger the firm, the more impact its policies will have on the actions of competitors. If the large firm makes an error and attempts to correct that error, the market may react in such a way that the correction is impossible. This is particularly true if horizontal integration has taken place in order to take advantage of an imperfectly competitive market situation. The imperfect competitor finds that his market power has increased, and his impact on the market in which he operates is much greater.

SOME EMPIRICAL EVIDENCE ON THE OPTIMUM SIZE OF RETAIL FIRMS

What do our studies show with respect to the structure of retailing costs and the relation of these to operating efficiency? Although some of the empirical studies that we shall cite are based on costs incurred in retail stores of various sizes, we shall be concerned mainly with costs of retail firms.

Short-Run Costs of the Retail Establishment

Since the largest percentage of the cost of retail services is joint costs not imputable to a particular product, the marginal cost of a particular item or bundle of items will be regarded by the retailer as the cost of the merchandise. Unless a single firm is an oligopsonist or monopsonist, therefore, it is likely that its short-run cost curve will be very flat, showing only a very slight decline after the increased efficiencies from initial expansion have been realized. Empirical studies substantiate this expectation.[13] This suggests that the average and marginal cost curves of retail stores drop very sharply as sales increase from those of a very small store to one of intermediate size, but that these curves will be very elastic over the entire intermediate sales range.

Short-and Long-Run Costs of the Retail Firm

We have assembled the principal components of the income statement for retail corporations for 1957.[14] From this, we have calculated operating expenses as a percentage of sales; net operating profit and compiled net profit as a percentage of capital stock and surplus;[15] and the elasticity of operating expenses, cost of goods sold, and capital stock and surplus with respect to sales.

RETAIL COST ELASTICITY COEFFICIENTS: MEANING AND MEASUREMENT

The costs of retailing are the outlays for productive resources used in creating and transmitting its services to consumer buyers. These would include the cost of merchandise, wages and salaries, locational costs, costs of capital investment, and entrepreneurial cost. If we were to examine changes that occur in the relationship of any one of these costs to sales revenue as volume of sales is varied, we would be measuring the elasticity of that cost with respect to sales. This could be shown by the following formula:

$$e_{c_i, s} = \frac{\delta c/c_i}{\delta s/s_i} = \frac{\delta c}{\delta s} \frac{s_i}{c_i}$$

[13] See, for example, Joel Dean, "Department Store Cost Functions," in Oscar Lange, ed., *Studies in Mathematical Economics and Econometrics* (Chicago: University of Chicago Press, 1942), pp. 222-254; and Bob R. Holdren, *The Structure of a Retail Market and the Market Behavior of Retail Units* (Englewood Cliffs, N.J.: Prentice-Hall, 1960), particularly pp. 27-66. Other examples of empirical cost studies in retailing include S. C. Bakkenist and D. E. Beutick, "An Investigation into the Costs of Distribution in the Grocery Retail Trade in the Netherlands," European Productivity Agency, *Productivity Measurement Review*, Special Number (July 1957); F. M. Bass, "Expense and Margin Functions in Drug Stores," *Journal of Marketing* 20 (January 1956): 236-241; R. Bellamy, "Private and Social Cost in Retail Distribution," *Bulletin of the Oxford University Institute of Statistics* 7 (November 1946): 345-351; Leonard Cohen, "Costs of Distribution in Department Stores," *Manchester School of Economic and Social Studies* 20 (May 1952): 139-173; Joel Dean and R. W. James, *The Long Run Behavior of Costs in a Chain of Shoe Stores: A Statistical Analysis,* Studies in Business Administration, vol. 12, no. 3 (Chicago: University of Chicago Press, 1942); John K. Galbraith and Richard H. Holton, *Marketing Efficiency in Puerto Rico* (Cambridge, Mass.: Harvard University Press, 1955); Margaret Hall and John Knapp, "Gross Margins and Efficiency Measurement in Retail Trade," *Oxford Economic Papers*, n.s., 7 (October 1955): 312-326; Margaret Hall and John Knapp, "Productivity in Distribution with Particular Reference to the Measurement of Output," European Productivity Agency, *Productivity Measurement Review* (February 1957): 22-38; James B.

in which $e_{c_i,s}$ is the elasiticity of cost i with respect to sales, δc is an infinitesimally small change in cost i at cost level c_i, s_i is the sales volume at cost level c_i, and δs is an infinitesimally small change in sales at sales volume s_i.

If this coefficient is 1.00, it means that a change in sales of 1 percent had associated with it a change in cost of exactly 1 percent. A coefficient greater than 1.00 is elastic, reflecting a greater percentage change in cost than in the associated change in sales, while a coefficient less than 1.00 is inelastic, reflecting a smaller percentage change in cost than in sales. If we could describe all specific costs as a function of sales, we could then determine at what sales levels an increase in output is related to a greater or less than proportionate change in costs.

It would not suffice, however, to measure this for a single cost. We have already indicated the large range of substitution possibilities in retail trade, and we must recognize that an increase in one cost may often make possible a decrease in another. Therefore any conclusion about the desirability of a particular expansion or contraction policy must be made with due consideration to the total structure of costs of the firm. For example, by spending more on buyers' salaries a retail firm may increase its operating costs. If, however, this increase in operating costs results in greater buying skill and lower buying prices, the firm may have increased its overall operating efficiency in terms of total-cost-total-revenue relationships. By examining these components of the total cost and their relationship to sales, we may discover some of the important sources of efficiency in retailing.

EMPIRICAL COST ELASTICITY COEFFICIENTS

The operating statement for retail food corporations for 1959 is summarized in Table 10A.1, and elasticity coefficients for each of the three years 1957-1959 are shown in Table 10A.2. We show graphically findings for 1957 for retail food, general merchandise, apparel, furniture and home furnishings, and drug corporations in Figures 10.1-10.5, where cost and profit ratios are related to the logarithm of sales. In Tables 10.1 and 10.2 we have summarized our findings with respect to the critical points for these types of retail corporations as well as for four other types—building materials and hardware, automotive and filling stations, eating and drinking, and other.

Jeffreys et al., *Productivity in the Distributive Trade in Europe* (Paris: Office of European Economic Cooperation, 1954); F. R. J. Jervis, "Profits in Large-Scale Retailing," *Manchester School of Economic and Social Studies* 21 (May 1953): 165-175; A. Plant and R. F. Fowler, "The Analysis of Costs in Retail Distribution," *Economica*, n.s., 6 (May 1939): 121-155; S. Pollard and J. D. Hughes, "Retailing Costs: Some Comments on the Census of Distribution, 1950," *Oxford Economic Papers*, n.s., 102 (February 1955): 71-93; S. Pollard and J. D. Hughes, "Retailing Costs: A Reply," *Oxford Economic Papers*, n.s., 7 (October 1955): 327-328; Fred M. Wiegmann et al., *Comparison of Costs of Services and Self-Service Methods in Retail Meat Departments*, Research Bulletin 422 (Ames: Iowa Agricultural Experiment Station, 1955).

[14] Much of the data and results reported here first appeared in Edna Douglas, "Size of Firm and the Structure of Costs in Retailing," *Journal of Business* 35 (April 1962): 158-190. The calculations in this section are based on U.S., Department of the Treasury, Internal Revenue Service, *Statistics of Income: 1956-57, 1957-58, 1958-59, Corporation Income Tax Returns* (Washington, D.C.: GPO, 1959, 1960, 1961).

[15] Compiled net profit includes net operating profit plus "other income" from nonmerchandising operations.

Table 10.1 Comparison of Sales Volume at Which Retail Food and General Merchandise Corporations Broke Even; Had Low Elasticity Coefficients for Cost of Sales, Operating Expenses, and Capital Investment; and Had High Net Profit Ratios, 1957-1959

Item	Type of Firm and Year					
	Food			General Merchandise		
	1957	1958	1959	1957	1958	1959
Sales Volume			Thousands of Dollars			
Break-even point (based on compiled net profit)	300	145	330	140	135	200[a]
	Millions of Dollars					
Points of low elasticity coefficients[b] (*Lowest coefficient)						
Cost of goods and sales	1.2 / 10.5 / 96.8 / 401.1*	2.5 / 22.2 / 409.1*	6.6 / 24.6*	0.1 / 0.5* / 9.9 / 86.9	0.1 / 0.5 / 2.1 / 10.1 / 46.7*	0.7 / 21.4* / 762.5
Operating expenses and sales	0.3 / 5.3 / 49.6 / 239.6* / 1,510.3	0.3 / 11.5 / 45.5 / 224.1* / 1,643.2	0.3 / 46.9 / 279.3* / 1,580.1	4.9 / 86.9* / 772.2	0.3 / 2.1 / 22.3 / 86.0 / 787.9*	0.6 / 10.1 / 43.2*

Millions of Dollars and Associated Variables[e]

(Capital stock + surplus) and sales	2.5	0.3	0.3	9.9	1.1	21.4
	49.6	5.3	3.0	47.7*	10.1	188.7*
	239.6*	96.8*	100.7*	172.0	175.9*	
	1,510.3	1,643.2	1,580.1			
Points of high compiled net profits (relative to capital stock + surplus)[c] (*Highest profit ratio)	7.4	7.3	4.1	1.4	0.4	0.8
	(1) CI	(1) CI	(1) CI	(1) CG	(1) OE	(1) CG
	(2) OE	(2) CG	(2) CG		(2) CG	
and	62.8	62.4	62.9	28.6	2.9	13.3
	(1) CI	(1) OE	(1) CG	(1) CG	(1) CG	(1) CG
	(2) OE	(2) CG	(2) OE		(2) OE	
	348.6*	317.0*	420.1*	107.1	13.8	112.2
Variables associated with each profit optimum (ranked in order of importance)[d]	(1) OE	(1) OE	(1) CI	(1) OE	(1) CI	(1) CG
	(2) CI		(2) OE	(2) CG	(2) CG	
			(3) CG		(3) OE	

Table 10.1 Continued

2,570.0	2,785.3	2,587.0	1,307.6*	109.3	1,259.7*
(1) CI	(1) CI	(1) CI	(1) OE	(1) OE	(1) OE
(2) OE	(2) OE	(2) OE	(2) CI	(2) CG	(2) CI

1,333.4*
(1) CI
(2) OE

[a]Losses were incurred for some asset groups up to a sales volume of about $5 million, and a small profit was made by that asset group whose sales averaged $100,000 per firm.

[b]Sales volumes identified are those at which elasticity coefficients reached a low point and were less than 1.00. The lowest coefficient occurred at that sales volume indicated by *, excluding sales volumes less than $500,000.

[c]Sales volumes identified are those at which compiled net profit ratios reached a high point. The sales volume with the highest ratio is indicated by *. Since all computations are based on group averages, it should be noted that the sales figures used to identify points of high profits are not exactly the same as those used where sales volumes are related to elasticity coefficients. Figures in the net profit row are derived from operating data for a single group of retail firms, and the sales volume given is the average of that one group. Elasticity coefficients, however, are related to the midpoints between two groups of retail firms, and the sales volumes identified are the average sales of the two groups.

[d]Based on elasticity coefficients less than 1.00, ranked in order of deviation from 1.00.

[e]OE = operating expenses; CG = cost of goods sold; CI = capital investment.

Source: Part of these data are from Edna Douglas, "Size of Firm and the Structure of Costs in Retailing," *Journal of Business* 35 (April 1962): 180, © 1962 by the University of Chicago. All coefficients are based on data from U.S., Department of the Treasury, Internal Revenue Service, *Statistics of Income: 1956-57, 1957-58, 1958-59, Corporation Income Tax Returns* (Washington, D.C.: GPO, 1959, 1960, 1961).

Table 10.2 Sales Volumes at Which Various Types of Retail Corporations Broke Even; Had Low Elasticity Coefficients for Cost of Sales, Operating Expenses, and Capital Investment; and Had High Net Profit Ratios, 1956-1957

Item	Total[a]	Apparel and Accessories	Furniture and House-Furnishings	Drugs	Building Materials and Hardware	Automotive and Filling Stations	Eating and Drinking Places	Other
				Type of Firm				
Break-even point (based on compiled net profit)				Thousands of Dollars — Sales Volume				
	75	75	150	(c)	125	525	75	75
Points of low elasticity coefficients[b] (*Lowest coefficient)				Millions of Dollars				
Cost of goods and sales	5.9	0.2	0.2	0.2	0.5	9.2*	0.2	0.5
	59.2	4.8	1.4	0.3	1.9*		7.3*	2.0
	235.8*	50.1*	6.0*	3.4				9.9*
				31.0*				
Operating expenses and sales	0.2	*0.1	0.1	1.5	0.1	0.2	0.3	0.3
	25.5	26.8*	15.0*	15.5*	7.2*	16.5*	1.1	1.1
	132.8*			68.4			12.3*	4.0*
	1,008.4							
(Capital stock + surplus) and sales	0.8	1.0	0.7	1.5	0.5	16.5*	7.3*	9.9*
	132.8*	11.2*	3.1*	15.5*	4.0			
	1,008.4		14.8	68.4	12.5*			

Table 10.2 Continued

Item	Type of Firm							
	Total[a]	Apparel and Accessories	Furniture and House-Furnishings	Drugs	Building Materials and Hardware	Automotive and Filling Stations[e]	Eating and Drinking Places	Other
	Sales Volume							
	Millions of Dollars and Associated Variables[e]							
Points of high compiled net profits (relative to capital stock + surplus[d]) (*Highest profit ratio)	182.3 (1) OE (2) CI	0.3 (1) CG	0.3 (1) CG	0.9 (1) OE (2) CG	16.0* (1) CI	23.2* (1) CI (2) OE (3) CG	11.0* (1) CI (2) CG	14.3* (1) CI (2) CG
and	1,727.4* (1) CI (2) OE	62.7* (1) CG	0.9 (1) CG (2) CI	21.3 (1) CI (2) OE				
Variables associated with each profit optimum (ranked in order of importance[f])			22.0* (1) CI (2) OE	96.1* (1) CI (2) OE (3) CG				

[a]Includes food and general merchandise corporations detailed in Table 10.1, plus firms of the seven types detailed in this table.

[b]Sales volumes identified are those at which elasticity coefficients reached a low point and were less than 1.00. The lowest coefficient occurred at that sales volume indicated by *, excluding sales volumes less than $500,000.

[c]Average corporations of all groups showed a positive profit rate.

[d]Sales volumes identified are those at which compiled net profit ratios reached a high point. The sales volume with the highest ratio is indicated by *. Since all computations are based on group averages, it should be noted that the sales figures used to identify points of high profits are not exactly the same as those used where sales volumes are related to elasticity coefficients. Figures in the net profit row are derived from operating data for a single group of retail firms, and the sales volume given is the average of that one group. Elasticity coefficients, however, are related to the midpoints between two groups of retail firms, and the sales volumes identified are the average sales of the two groups.

[e]OE = operating expenses; CG = cost of goods sold; CI = capital investment.

[f]Based on elasticity coefficients less than 1.00, ranked in order of deviation from 1.00.

Source: Edna Douglas, "Size of Firm and the Structure of Costs in Retailing, *Journal of Business*, 35 (April 1962): 181 © 1962 by the University of Chicago.

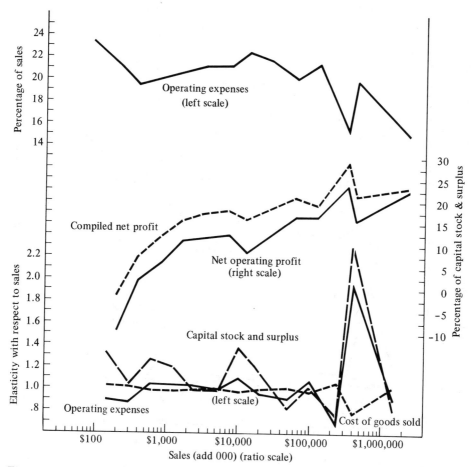

Figure 10.1. Retail food corporations. Operating expenses as a percentage of sales; net operating profit and compiled net profit as a percentage of capital stock and surplus; and elasticity of cost of goods sold, operating expenses, and capital investment with respect to sales. Source: Edna Douglas, "Size of Firm and the Structure of Costs in Retailing," *Journal of Business* 35 (April 1962), 175, © 1962 by the University of Chicago.

Firms have been grouped according to increasing volume of assets. Assets are only one indication of size of firm. Others that might have been used are sales, transactions, store area, and number of employees. Since assets were the basis for size classification in the reports of the Internal Revenue Service, we have used the average gross sales of firms grouped according to total assets as an indication of relative size. Thus our ranking of groups of firms by average gross sales per corporation is derived from a classification of firms by assets.

Our analysis is concerned with the three main elements of the operating statement: cost of goods sold, operating expenses, and capital stock and surplus. The latter is assumed to represent the cost of capital investment, although it is recognized that some capital costs may be included in operating expenses (e.g., interest on long-term debt).

If our data provide a reasonable approximation of these three important costs and their relation to sales, what is the meaning of our elasticity coefficients, and what light do they throw on the operation of retail firms? If we examine Figure 10.1 closely, we can see a number of important characteristics of the cost elasticity coefficients for retail food corporations in 1957. When, for example, gross sales were about $10 million, captial stock increased much more, relatively, than sales. Operating expenses also increased

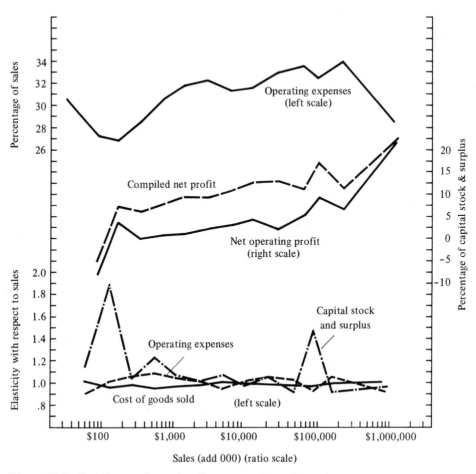

Figure 10.2. Retail general merchandise corporations. Operating expenses as a percentage of sales; net operating profit and compiled net profit as a percentage of capital stock and surplus; and elasticity of cost of goods sold, operating expenses, and capital investment with respect to sales. Source: Edna Douglas, "Size of Firm and the Structure of Costs in Retailing," *Journal of Business* 35 (April 1962), 176, © 1962 by the University of Chicago.

relatively more than sales. While the increase in the cost of goods was slightly less than in sales, the difference was not sufficient to offset the considerable upward shift in capital investment and operating expenses. Therefore profits as a percentage of sales declined sharply at that volume level compared with sales volumes slightly smaller or slightly larger. According to Table 10.1, retail food corporations had their best profit ratio in 1957 at a sales volume of nearly $400 million, and this was associated primarily with a favorable operating-cost ratio and secondarily with efficient use of capital.

COST RELATIONSHIPS AND PROFITABILITY

It is not our purpose here to discuss the many problems of empirical cost analysis and the complications of interpreting such data.[16] Rather, we shall summarize some of the broad

[16] Problems of empirical cost analysis of cross-sectional data are discussed in George M. Borts, "The Estimation of Rail Cost Functions." *Econometrica* 28 (January 1960): 108-131; Milton Friedman, "Comment" (on study by Caleb Smith), in *Business Concentration and Price Policy*, Universities-

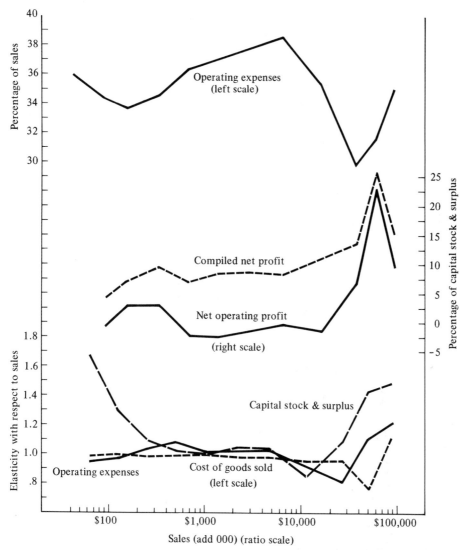

Figure 10.3. Retail apparel and accessories corporations. Operating expenses as a percentage of sales; net operating and compiled net profit as a percentage of capital stock and surplus; and elasticity of cost of goods sold, operating expenses, and capital investment with respect to sales. Source: Edna Douglas, "Size of Firm and the Structure of Costs in Retailing," *Journal of Business* 35 (April 1962), 177, © 1962 by the University of Chicago.

patterns of cost-sales relationship for what light they may throw on the operation of the retail firm.

1. It is apparent from an examination of Figures 10.1-10.5 that operating expenses alone are not a sufficient basis for judging efficiency in retailing. Although often used as a

National Bureau of Economic Research (Princeton, N.J.: Princeton University Press, 1955), pp. 230-238; J. Johnston, "Statistical Cost Functions: A Reappraisal," *Review of Economics and Statistics* 40 (November 1958): 339-350; J. Johnston, *Statistical Cost Analysis* (New York: McGraw-Hill, 1960). These problems are summarized in Douglas, op. cit., pp. 159-163.

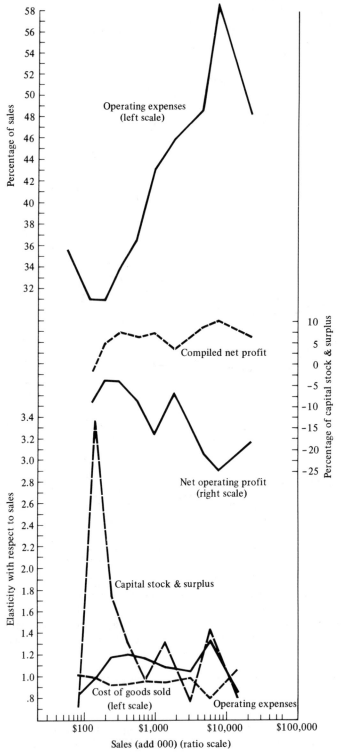

Figure 10.4. Retail furniture and housefurnishings corporations. Operating expenses as a percentage of sales; net operating profit and compiled net profit as a percentage of capital stock and surplus; and elasticity of cost of goods sold, operating expenses, and capital investment with respect to sales. Source: Edna Douglas, "Size of Firm and the Structure of Costs in Retailing," *Journal of Business* 35 (April 1962), 178, © 1962 by the University of Chicago.

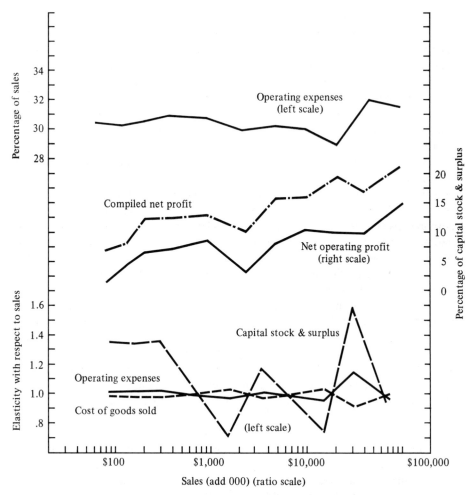

Figure 10.5. Retail drug corporations. Operating expenses as a percentage of sales; net operating profit and compiled net profit as a percentage of capital stock and surplus; and elasticity of cost of goods sold, operating expenses, and capital investment with respect to sales. Source: Edna Douglas, "Size of Firm and the Structure of Costs in Retailing," *Journal of Business* 35 (April 1962), 179, © 1962 by the University of Chicago.

   measure of efficiency, operating costs should be evaluated in combination with buying costs and capital investment.

2. In only a few cases did the lowest coefficient occur at the same sales volume for cost of goods sold, operating expenses, and capital investment. Sometimes the operating-expense coefficient was high while the capital investment coefficient was low. At some sales volumes buying advantage was dominant while expense and investment coefficients were far less favorable. These shifting coefficients give some insight into the nature of resource substitution in retailing. Increased capital investment may make possible operating efficiencies, which are reflected in lower operating costs. Or perhaps by increasing operating expenses it may be possible to lower the cost of goods sold. Inverse relations between these coefficients were particularly apparent among firms with large sales volumes. The large retail corporation has a wide range of substitution possibilities because the total resources allocated to any one phase of its operations are large enough to make additions or subtractions to one allocation economical.

3. While there was an optimum size, as measured by return on capital investment, for each of the nine types of retail firms studied, there were also other sizes of high relative efficiency. There is, in fact, an interesting similarity between the short- and long-run cost relationships of economic theory and those implied by our three cost estimates and the logarithm of sales. However, careful consideration of the forces that determine empirical cost functions compels us to be very wary of interpreting the curves that we have obtained from empirical data as representing the short- and long-run cost curves of economic theory. There are many reasons why empirical coefficients can be larger or smaller than the theoretical coefficients. Our data and curves show best the *direction* in which cost-sales relationships moved rather than their exact level.

4. It would appear that there were economies of scale in retailing but that in many lines the most efficient size was less than the largest firm existing. In four lines the largest corporations reported the highest profit ratio relative to capital: building materials and hardware, general merchandise, furniture and housefurnishings, and drugs. In all others—food, apparel and accessories, eating and drinking, automobile and filling stations, and others—the largest corporations had lower profit ratios than corporations of somewhat smaller size.

5. The most profitable firms varied in size from one line of trade to another. The most profitable general merchandise corporations were very large, with nearly $1.5 billion in sales. The most profitable food corporations had less than $0.5 billion in sales. Next were the medium-sized corporations—apparel and accessories and drug—with "best" sizes about $50 million to $100 million. Finally, the other types—furniture and house furnishings, building materials, automobiles and filling stations, eating and drinking, and other—tended to be small, with maximum profits at sales volumes of $10 million to $25 million.

    The basic nature of retailing is clearly revealed in these data. Retailing is an operation that is highly dispersed geographically. There is a limit to the optimum size of a given store in terms of accessibility of the store and its merchandise to customers. Large firms may develop, however, in those merchandise lines where multistore ownership and/or vertical integration offer sufficient economies or other marketing advantages. The differences in estimated optimum size that we have noted would seem to be related to the extent to which the particular line of business would or would not lend itself to economies related to specialized management; standardization of merchandise and operating procedure; skill and scale in buying; and the relative sales appeal of greater quality, price, and stock diversification. It is interesting that the only type of firm that reached its maximum profit at a sales volume greater than $1 billion was characterized by the greatest amount of merchandise diversification.

6. Since we have used profit ratios as a percentage of capital investment as an indication of efficiency, it is not surprising that highest profit ratios were most often associated with favorable capital investment elasticity coefficients. Occasionally, however, high profit ratios were associated with favorable expense or cost-of-goods coefficients.

7. Because a firm's profitability is a result of the combined effect of its total merchandising efforts, it is not necessary that the most profitable firm be the most efficient with respect to any one phase of its operations. For example, the most profitable size for general-merchandise corporations was the very largest group, with average sales of $1.3 billion. But this was not the sales volume at which cost of goods sold, operating expense, or capital investment elasticity coefficients were lowest. However, these coefficients were sufficiently low that the *total* impact of these three phases of the firm's operation resulted in the largest profit ratio for all firms.

8. There were differences among the various types of firms in the stability of their coefficients at various sales volumes. Capital investment was the most variable for all types of firms, suggesting the existence of a "lumpiness" in investment required at a certain sales volume.

CONCLUSIONS

While conclusions from our empirical evidence must be regarded as tentative, it appears that it is the mixture of resources and policies that is the ultimate determinant of retail profitablitity and that there may be many alternative mixes. The ability to estimate the optimum proportioning of resources for a given size of firm and the ability to determine and to achieve the optimum size among all possible sizes are the tests of retail managerial efficiency. While we have assumed that the profit-capital ratio is an adequate measure of this accomplishment, we must recognize that market structure also influences the profitability of a firm's operations and the extent to which its efficiencies or inefficiencies are transmitted to consumers through price and quality of products sold. Differences in profits among firms of various sizes may have reflected the competitive situation in which they functioned as well as the efficiency of management.

Appendix A

OPERATING STATEMENT, CAPITAL STOCK AND SURPLUS, AND ELASTICITY COEFFICIENTS FOR RETAIL FOOD CORPORATIONS

Table 10A.1 Operating Statement and Capital Stock and Surplus of Retail Food Corporations Imputed from Reports to the Internal Revenue Service, July 1958-June 1959

Item	Total	Total Assets per Corporation (Add 000)					
		Under $25	$25 and Under $50	$50 and Under $100	$100 and Under $250	$250 and Under $500	$500 and Under $1,000
Asse t group		(1)	(2)	(3)	(4)	(5)	(6)
				Number			
Number of corporations	10,979	3,620	1,919	2,059	2,054	732	271
				Dollars (Add 000)			
Average gross sales per corporation	2,403	99	210	450	961	1,936	4,114
Capital stock and surplus per corporation	230	5	16	29	69	159	325
				Ratio			
Gross sales / Capital stock + surplus	10.46	19.56	13.09	15.68	13.87	12.17	12.65
				Percentage of Gross Sales			
Gross sales	100.00	100.00	100.00	100.00	100.00	100.00	100.00
Cost of goods sold	81.17	77.83	78.55	81.45	82.66	82.13	81.90
Gross margin	18.83	22.17	21.45	18.55	17.34	17.87	18.10
Operating expenses	17.42	23.26	21.77	18.30	16.81	16.99	17.50
Net operating profit	1.41	-1.09	- .32	.25	.53	.88	.60
Other income	.56	.32	.27	.39	.66	.55	.97
Compiled net profit	1.97	- .77	- .05	.64	1.19	1.43	1.57
				Percentage of Capital Stock and Surplus			
Net operating profit	14.78	-21.23	-4.24	3.84	7.33	10.63	7.57
Compiled net profit	20.64	-15.08	- .75	10.01	16.55	17.33	19.84

Table 10A.1 continued

Total Assets per Corporation (Add 000)							
$1,000 and Under $2,500	$2,500 and Under $5,000	$5,000 and Under $10,000	$10,000 and Under $25,000	$25,000 and Under $50,000	$50,000 and Under $100,000	$100,000 and Under $250,000	$250,000 or more
(7)	(8)	(9)	(10)	(11)	(12)	(13)	(14)
Number							
185	48	37	29	11	6	5	3
Dollars (Add 000)							
9,040	18,337	30,949	62,860	138,502	420,103	573,214	2,587,043
757	1,719	3,917	8,149	15,229	37,943	72,023	235,847
Ratio							
11.95	10.67	7.90	7.71	9.09	11.07	7.96	10.97
Percentage of Gross Sales							
100.00	100.00	100.00	100.00	100.00	100.00	100.00	100.00
81.26	81.05	79.87	79.22	79.12	81.18	81.57	81.65
18.74	18.95	20.13	20.78	20.88	18.82	18.43	18.35
18.06	18.70	19.29	19.27	19.39	16.67	16.88	16.11
.68	.25	.84	1.51	1.49	2.15	1.55	2.24
.76	1.28	1.40	1.08	.50	.58	.90	.06
1.44	1.53	2.24	2.59	1.99	2.73	2.45	2.30
Percentage of Capital Stock and Surplus							
8.17	2.75	6.65	11.64	13.47	23.85	12.36	24.58
17.27	16.38	17.72	19.95	18.12	30.21	19.52	25.22

Source: Calculated from U.S., Department of the Treasury, Internal Revenue Service, *Statistics of Income: 1958-59, Corporation Income Tax Returns* (Washington, D.C.: GPO, 1961).

Table 10A.2 Arc Sales and Net Investment Elasticity Coefficients for Retail General Merchandise Corporations Reporting to the Internal Revenue Service for the Years ending June 30, 1957, 1958, 1959

Item	Year	(1) and (2)	(2) and (3)	(3) and (4)	(4) and (5)	(5) and (6)	(6) and (7)	(7) and (8)	(8) and (9)	(9) and (10)	(10) and (11)	(11) and (12)	(12) and (13)	(13) and (14)
								Dollars (add 000)						
Average gross sales	1957	63	133	266	548	1,088	2,266	4,912	9,938	20,893	47,693	86,938	172,000	772,243
	1958	71	134	269	548	1,067	2,143	4,596	10,071	22,292	46,667	85,962	175,929	787,942
	1959	70	142	284	568	1,120	2,354	5,050	10,070	21,414	43,248	84,557	188,675	762,452
								Elasticity Coefficients[b]						
Gross margin and sales	1957	.955	1.108	1.033	1.099	1.056	1.032	.978	1.028	1.023	1.047	1.061	1.008	.997
	1958	.942	1.116	1.056	1.090	1.017	1.053	.980	1.031	.963	1.116	1.047	1.010	.998
	1959	.855	.947	1.027	1.090	.985	1.017	1.040	1.131	.834	1.160	1.064	.990	.987
Operating expenses and sales	1957	.900	1.016	1.060	1.089	1.050	1.019	.966	1.011	1.049	1.019	.928	1.053	.931
	1958	.758	1.087	.978	1.130	1.076	.995	1.047	1.025	.990	1.060	.953	1.050	.937
	1959	.783	.947	1.027	1.077	1.021	1.023	1.000	1.101	.859	1.146	1.164	1.022	.934
Cost of goods sold and sales	1957	1.016	.960	.987	.957	.974	.984	1.011	.986	.988	.975	.966	.995	1.002
	1958	1.013	.952	.992	.961	.993	.974	1.009	.985	1.018	.939	.974	.994	1.001
	1959	1.053	1.034	.989	.953	1.007	.996	.980	.928	1.083	.917	.963	1.006	1.007
(Operating expenses + cost of goods sold) and sales	1957	.984	.975	1.007	.997	.998	.996	.996	.994	1.008	.990	.953	1.015	.979
	1958	.940	.991	.988	1.013	1.020	.981	.992	.998	1.009	.980	.966	1.014	.980
	1959	.967	1.008	1.000	.992	1.011	1.005	.987	.988	1.010	.994	1.025	1.012	.984
(Capital stock + surplus) and sales	1957	1.147	1.888	1.043	1.228	1.068	1.010	1.066	.976	1.050	.916	1.469	.919	.959
	1958	1.780	1.420	1.032	1.186	.979	1.170	1.070	.932	1.009	1.047	1.325	.896	.971
	1959	1.776	1.177	1.100	1.260	1.022	1.106	1.122	1.063	.874	1.170	1.209	.839	.994

Asset Group[a]

Compiled net profit and (capital stock + surplus)	1957	− .418	2.900	1.608	2.198	1.249	.993	1.168	1.211	1.006	.822	1.508	.458	1.234
	1958	1.234	−3.327	2.259	.952	.120	1.643	.867	1.338	.995	1.047	1.268	.691	1.318
	1959	−4.586	1.221	1.183	1.299	.984	.918	1.057	1.206	.750	.871	1.508	.632	1.218

[a] Asset groups are identified in Table 10A.1.

[b] The elasticity of gross margin relative to sales is computed by the formula $E_{gm,s} = \dfrac{(GM_2 - GM_1)/(GM_1 + GM_2)}{(S_2 - S_1) \; / \; (S_1 + S_2)}$

in which $E_{gm,s}$ = the Elasticity of Gross Margin with respect to sales, GM = Gross Margin, and S = Gross Sales. The subscript 2 is for the group with the larger average sales volume and subscript 1 for the group with the smaller average sales volume. All other elasticity coefficients are computed by similar methods.

Source: Data for 1957 and 1958 from Edna Douglas, "Size of Firm and the Structure of Costs in Retailing," *Journal of Business* 35 (April 1962): 174, © 1962 by the University of Chicago. All coefficients are calculated from U.S., Department of the Treasury, Internal Revenue Service, *Statistics of Income: 1956-57, 1957-58, 1958-59, Corporation Income Tax Returns* (Washington, D.C.: GPO, 1959, 1960, 1961).

Appendix B

THE RELATIONSHIP OF NET PROFIT, SALES, AND CAPITAL IN RETAILING

R. Bellamy has shown the relationship of profit as a percentage of capital invested and profit as a percentage of sales, and the elasticity coefficients of profit with respect to capital invested and profit with respect to sales.[1] His first proposition is that

$$\frac{P}{C_i + C_o} = \frac{P/S}{\dfrac{1}{S/C_i} + \dfrac{1}{S/C_o}}$$

in which P is profit, S is sales, C_i is inventory capital, and C_o is other capital. Since

$P/(C_i + C_o)$ = profit as a percentage of total capital invested
$\quad P/S$ = profit as a percentage of sales
$\quad S/C_i$ = stock turnover
$\quad S/C_o$ = other-capital turnover

the proposition states that profit as a percentage of total capital invested equals the ratio of profit as a percentage of sales to the sum of the reciprocals of stock turnover and other-capital turnover.

The proof is as follows:

$$\frac{P}{C_i + C_o} = \frac{P/S}{(C_i + C_o)/S}$$

Since

$$\frac{C_i + C_o}{P} = \frac{C_i}{S} + \frac{C_o}{S} = \frac{1}{S/C_i} + \frac{1}{S/C_o}$$

then

$$\frac{P}{C_i + C_o} = \frac{P/S}{\dfrac{1}{S/C_i} + \dfrac{1}{S/C_o}}$$

The elasticity coefficient of the profit-capital percentage with respect to sales is related to the elasticity of the profit-sales percentage with respect to sales and the elasticity of the sales-capital percentage with respect to sales as follows:

$$e_{(p/c),s} = e_{(p/s),s} + e_{(s/c),s}$$

in which $e_{(p/s),s}$ is the elasticity of profit as a percentage of total capital invested with respect to sales, $e_{(p/s),s}$ is the elasticity of profit as a percentage of sales with respect to sales, and $e_{(s/c),s}$ is the elasticity of sales as a percentage of total capital invested with respect to sales. The identity just indicated shows that the elasticity of the profit-capital ratio with respect to sales equals the sum of the elasticity of the profit-sales ratio with respect to sales and the elasticity of the sales-capital ratio with respect to sales.

---

[1] R. Bellamy, "Size and Success in Retail Distribution," *Bulletin of the Oxford University Institute of Statistics* 8 (October 1946): 324-339.

The proof is as follows:

$$\frac{P}{C_i + C_o} = \frac{P}{S} \frac{S}{C_i + C_o}$$

and

$$\log \left(\frac{P}{C_i + C_o}\right) = \log \left(\frac{P}{S}\right) + \log \left(\frac{S}{C_i + C_o}\right)$$

Therefore

$$\frac{\delta \log \left(\frac{P}{C_i + C_o}\right)}{\delta \log S} = \frac{\delta \log \left(\frac{P}{S}\right)}{\delta \log S} + \frac{\delta \log \left(\frac{S}{C_i + C_o}\right)}{\delta \log S}$$

and

$$e_{(p/c),s} = e_{(p/s),s} + e_{(s/c),s}$$

Bellamy points out that

it is difficult to estimate $[e_{(s/c)}]$ precisely, but since about 40 per cent of the capital employed in retail trade represents stocks, and since the ratio of stocks to sales is a decreasing function of sales volume, and since "other" capital remains in a fairly constant ratio to sales, . . . it can be said with some assurance that total capital will be a smaller proportion of sales as sales increase. Empirical evidence enables us to give an approximate value [to $e_{(s/c),s}$ of] +0.3.[2]

He further estimates that $e_{(p/s),s}$ in department stores in the United Kingdom is about +0.25. The value of this elasticity coefficient depends on whether increasing selling costs, which are necessary to maintain an increasing volume of sales, are offset by a decrease in other operating expenses.

He concludes that even with fixed retail prices and gross margins, larger enterprises obtain a larger net profit because of their lower operating costs (net of selling costs), which enable them to spend more on advertising and other means of promotion. Thus there appear to be important monopolistic advantages that are the result of economies of scale.

---

[2] Ibid., p. 332.

11

The Wholesale Firm

"How is your trade, Aquarius,
This frosty night?"
"Complaints is many and various,
And my feet are cold," says Aquarius.

— Robert Graves

The distinguishing characteristic of wholesaling is that its sales are made to business buyers. One important group of buyers is engaged in form production and obtains raw materials, fabricated materials and parts, and capital equipment from wholesale firms. Such buyers also use wholesale firms, or maintain their own wholesaling outlets, to sell their finished products to other firms for further processing or for resale. Firms that buy from wholesalers for resale are therefore a second important group of customers. Wholesalers sell, then, to firms that are processing goods, to firms that resell to processors of goods, and to firms that resell consumer goods.

Wholesale firms can be classified in many different ways according to the types of customers to whom they sell, the kind of merchandise they handle, the number and kinds of marketing functions that they perform, the size of firm and the number of establishments that they operate, the geographic area they serve, their pricing and promotional policies, and any other characteristic of wholesaling operations. We shall not attempt to give a comprehensive picture of wholesaling but shall focus instead on some of the distinctive characteristics of wholesaling—those that set it apart from other industries and particularly those that set it apart from retailing, with which it shares many common characteristics.

THE DEMAND FOR WHOLESALING SERVICES

We have pointed out that the customers of wholesaling are business firms that purchase goods for processing or resale. To firms from which wholesalers buy, however, the wholesaler is a selling firm, performing the marketing functions necessary to move the goods of manufacturers or middlemen through the trade channel into the hands of processors or other middlemen. The demand for wholesaling services is a derived demand, and because of the wholesaler's position in the trade channel, the demand he faces is likely to be more inelastic with respect to price than is true at the retail level. The important effect of greater inelasticity of demand is that wholesale firms will, in general, be subjected to greater cyclical fluctuations in demand and in their selling prices than occurs in retailing. Greater inelasticity does not mean, however, that wholesale prices will reflect monopolistic pricing behavior to a greater extent than in other types of markets, for the level of prices in wholesale markets will be a function of the kind of competition that exists in those markets.

The average wholesale transaction is larger than the average retail transaction, since the clientele of wholesaling are business firms. This is likely to give rise to somewhat more specialization in wholesaling than in retailing. The extent of product diversification (i.e., the lack of product specialization) depends on the product mix required by the wholesaler's customers and on the degree to which product heterogeneity makes possible certain economies in wholesaling operations and provides the wholesaler with selling and promotional advantages.

The revenue-cost calculus of the wholesaler's customers is different from that of the retailer's customers. Since wholesaling transactions involve goods that will eventually be resold, either as they are or after further processing, the buyer should make a careful calculation of their cost in relation to their revenue-producing potential. Customer buying costs and transportation costs, for example, are likely to be determined with considerable care by the customers of wholesale firms. This is not to negate the importance of such cost to customers of the retail store but, rather, to make clear the difference in the kind of calculation that is possible where dollars to be paid out are related to dollars received rather than satisfaction received. Complementary or joint demands, competing demands, and cross-elasticities of demand are likely to be calculated with quite as much care by the wholesale firm as by the retail firm, and even more carefully if the pencils of his customers are very slightly sharper than are those of customers of retail stores, who, unlike those in wholesale markets, are not specialists in buying.

CHARACTERISTICS OF WHOLESALE FIRMS

Some of the data we shall use in this discussion appeared in the interindustry comparisons made in Tables 9.1, 9.2, and 9.3.

Legal Form of Organization

In Table 9.1, for example, we show that nearly 60 percent of the wholesaling firms in 1967 were proprietorships, compared to more than 75 percent of the retailing firms. But corporations dominate the wholesale field, accounting for only 34 percent of the firms but for 87 percent of the total sales volume. The importance of corporations in wholesaling increased between 1958, when their share of sales was 76 percent, and 1967, when their share was 87 percent.[1]

Assets and Liabilities

The most distinctive characteristics of wholesaling firms indicated in their balance sheets were the large proportion of assets in notes and accounts receivable, reflecting the importance of their financing function. (See Table 9.2.) About two-thirds of this was offset by their accounts payable, and to this extent they were serving as a financial aperture, both receiving and extending credit. The other one-third represents a positive increase in credit through their operation. Inventories were the second largest asset. Accounts receivable and inventories together accounted for nearly two-thirds of their assets and reflect the importance of their merchandising and financing functions. The equity investment in wholesaling firms was about the same, proportionately, as in retailing and higher than the average for all industries.

---

[1] The 1958 value was calculated from U.S., Department of the Treasury, Internal Revenue Service, *Statistics of Income: 1957-58, United States Business Tax Returns* (Washington, D.C.:GPO, 1960), pp. 7, 11, 14.

Table 11.1 Number, Receipts, Net Income, Assets, and Net Worth of Corporate Wholesale Firms by Kind of Business in the United States, 1968[a]

Kind of Business	Number of Firms	Per Firm (in Thousands)				Ratio of		
		Receipts[b]	Net Income	Assets	Net Worth	Net Income to Receipts[b]	Net Worth to Assets	Net Income to Net Worth
Motor vehicles, automotive equipment	11,617	$ 890.1	$34.5	$308.9	$133.0	.039	.431	.259
Electrical goods	8,926	1,249.8	43.7	445.4	182.6	.035	.410	.240
Dry goods, apparel	7,732	1,246.0	37.8	502.8	188.9	.030	.376	.200
Alcoholic beverages	4,614	2,641.4	27.6	383.7	156.9	.021	.409	.199
Groceries, related products	16,555	2,400.8	31.6	448.6	181.9	.031	.406	.174
Other wholesale	38,243	937.4	25.1	394.2	146.2	.027	.371	.172
Drugs, chemicals, allied products	6,909	1,400.6	43.3	600.6	255.1	.031	.425	.170
Metals, minerals (except petroleum, scrap)	3,569	2,179.8	68.2	978.3	405.7	.031	.415	.168
Lumber, construction materials	7,780	1,227.4	29.0	394.3	172.7	.024	.439	.168
Paper and its products	3,587	1,510.3	29.7	430.9	193.1	.020	.448	.154
Hardware, plumbing, heating equipment	7,925	1,196.5	35.8	489.0	254.3	.023	.520	.141
Petroleum, petroleum products	7,354	1,533.7	33.5	703.2	306.5	.022	.436	.109
Farm goods–raw materials	5,419	2,991.8	25.7	830.2	316.8	.009	.382	.081
Total wholesale	153,117	$1,354.9	$32.6	$466.2	$191.7	.024	.411	.170

[a]Based on a stratified sample of corporation income tax returns filed for accounting periods ending July 1968 through June 1969.

[b]Total receipts include sales receipts plus other income.

Source: U.S., Department of the Treasury, Internal Revenue Service, Statistics of Income: 1968, Corporation Income Tax Returns (Washington, D.C.: GPO, 1972), pp. 10-11.

Income and Balance Sheet Relations

The average wholesale firm had sales of $1,400,000 in 1968, compared to $800,000 in retailing. (See Table 9.3.) Only manufacturing and transportation had firms of larger average size. Also, the average wholesale firm was much larger than the average retail firm in volume of assets, which were nearly $500,000 per firm in wholesaling compared to nearly $300,000 in retailing. But both of these were far below the average for all industries—$1,400,000. Net worth per wholesaling firm was about $190,000, compared with $120,000 for retailing and $430,000 for all industries.

The net income of wholesale firms was only 2.4 percent of sales, compared with 2.8 percent in retailing and 6.3 percent in industry as a whole. But net income was 17.0 percent of net worth, and this compares quite favorably with retailing and other industries. Only contract construction and services were noticeably higher in net return on investment. (See Table 9.3.) Not all kinds of wholesale businesses shared in this average. In Table 11.1 we have arrayed wholesale corporations by kind of business, showing that net income to net worth ranged from a high of 25.9 percent for wholesalers of motor vehicles and automotive equipment to 8.1 percent for wholesalers of farm products sold as raw materials. The most profitable by this measure were those wholesalers handling high-value and/or highly processed industrial equipment or consumer goods. Drugs and chemicals are the only group that would meet these criteria but did not show a high net-income-to-net-worth ratio, possibly because of their relatively high net-worth-to-assets ratio. In general, raw materials and bulky processed goods showed low net income ratios. These data do not indicate the extent to which firms might have had access to borrowed funds, which, if available, would have permitted considerable leverage and therefore a higher net profit in relation to equity investment.

Operating Expenses

Table 11.2 shows the gross margin and some of the principal operating expenses of wholesale firms in 1968. The gross margin of wholesaling firms was about 18 percent, compared to 29 percent in retailing. Total operating expenses were about 16 percent, compared to 27 percent in retailing. (See Table 9.5.) Gross margin, a crude estimate of the value added by a firm, indicates that retail firms added a far greater percentage of their total sales volume than was true of wholesaling. Table 11.3 shows that operating expense ratios were particularly high for machinery and equipment, hardware and plumbing, electrical goods, drugs and chemicals, and motor vehicles and automotive equipement, but were quite low for many raw materials or semifabricated goods. Groceries and farm products sold as raw materials had especially low expense ratios. These differences would be related to such things as the size and frequency of purchases, the dollar value of the average transaction, the importance of special plant and equipment for storage and transportation, the quantity and quality of services rendered by the wholesaler, the degree of product standardization, the stability of purchases and the amount of risk, and the importance of locational convenience.

WAGES AND SALARIES

A comparison of Table 11.2 for wholesaling with Table 9.5 for retailing shows that the compensation of corporate officers represented a far higher percentage of gross margin in wholesaling than in retailing. The figure for wholesaling was 10 percent and for retailing 7 percent. A still better comparison of wages and salaries in these two types of marketing

Table 11.2 Summary Operating Statement for 153,117 Active Wholesale Corporations for the Year 1968[a]

Item	Amount (Billions)	Percentage of Business Receipts	Percentage of Gross Margin
Business receipts	$207.5	100.0	
Cost of goods sold	170.8	82.3	
Gross margin	$ 36.7	17.7	100.0
Compensation of officers	$ 3.6	1.7	9.7
Rent	1.3	.6	3.4
Taxes paid	2.4	1.2	6.5
Interest paid	1.1	.6	3.1
Amortization, depreciation, depletion, repairs	1.9	.9	5.1
Advertising	1.0	.5	2.8
Other deductions	21.0	10.1	57.3
Total expenses	32.3	15.6	87.9
Net income	$ 4.4	2.1	12.1

[a]Based on a stratified sample of income tax returns filed for accounting periods ending July 1968 through June 1969.

Source: U.S., Department of the Treasury, Internal Revenue Service, *Statistics of Income: 1968, Corporation Income Tax Returns* (Washington, D.C.: GPO, 1972), p. 17.

Table 11.3 Abbreviated Operating Statement for Corporate Wholesale Firms by Kind of Business in the United States, 1968[a]

Kind of Business	Gross Receipts per Firm (Thousands)	Gross Sales	Cost of Goods Sold	Gross Margin	Operating Expenses	Net Profit
Motor vehicles and automotive equipment	$ 890.1	100.0	79.0	21.0	17.4	2.6
Drugs, chemicals	1,400.6	100.0	79.4	20.6	17.7	3.0
Dry goods, apparel	1,250.8	100.0	81.3	18.7	16.0	2.7
Groceries	2,400.8	100.0	87.3	12.7	11.6	1.1
Farm products (raw materials)	2,991.8	100.0	91.8	8.2	7.6	0.6
Electrical goods	1,249.8	100.0	78.9	21.1	17.9	3.2
Hardware, plumbing, heating	1,196.5	100.0	77.4	22.7	19.9	2.8
Machinery, equipment, supplies	835.1	100.0	75.2	24.8	21.9	2.9
Metals and minerals	2,179.8	100.0	84.0	16.0	13.1	2.9
Alcoholic beverages	2,641.4	100.0	82.1	17.9	15.9	2.0
Petroleum and petroleum products	1,533.7	100.0	82.1	17.9	15.9	1.9
Lumber, construction materials	1,227.4	100.0	83.3	16.8	14.6	2.1
Paper and paper products	1,510.3	100.0	82.3	17.8	16.0	1.7
Other wholesale trade	937.4	100.0	80.3	19.7	17.4	2.3
Total	$1,354.9	100.0	82.3	17.7	15.5	2.1

[a]Based on a stratified sample of income tax returns filed for accounting periods ending July 1968 through June 1969.

Source: U.S., Department of the Treasury, Internal Revenue Service, *Statistics of Income–1968, Corporation Income Tax Returns* (Washington, D.C.: GPO, 1972), pp. 10-12.

Table 11.4 Payroll Costs of Retail and Wholesale Establishments in the United States as a Percentage of Sales, Gross Margin, and Operating Expenses, 1967

Item	Retail[a] Dollars (Thousands)	Retail[a] Percentage	Wholesale Dollars (Thousands)	Wholesale Percentage
Total sales	$299,430	100.0	$459,476	100.0
Gross margin	87,733	29.3[b]	81,327	17.7[b]
Operating expenses	80,547	26.9[b]	71,678	15.6[b]
Payroll	34,986	11.7	23,992	5.2
Gross margin		100.0		100.0
Payroll		39.9		29.4
Operating expenses		100.0		100.0
Payroll		43.4		33.4

[a]Based only on establishments operated the entire year.

[b]Gross margin and operating expenses calculated by applying the gross margin and operating expense ratios in Tables 9.5 and 11.2 to census sales data.

Source: Sales and payroll from U.S., Bureau of the Census, *Census of Business: 1967*, vol. I, *Retail Trade–Special Subjects*, and vol. IV, *Wholesale Trade–Area Statistics* (Washington, D.C.: GPO, 1971).

institutions can be made from the *Census of Business* data for 1967 shown in Table 11.4. Payrolls for that year were about 40 percent of gross margin in retailing, compared to nearly 30 percent in wholesaling. Wage rates per hour are higher for wholesale workers than for retail workers, and this is a reflection of the higher productivity per worker. Ratios from 1958 census data were higher and were about the same for both wholesaling and retailing. The declining ratio for wholesaling relative to retailing suggests that there was considerable increase in productivity in wholesaling during the 1960s, probably associated with mechanization.

PHYSICAL PLANT AND EQUIPMENT

Rent and depreciation was 11.6 percent of retail margins compared to 8.5 percent for wholesaling. Wholesaling plants tend to be quite large, but their location need not be in the high-rent area as is true in retailing. Also, wholesaling corporations that function as agents or sales offices would not carry stocks and would therefore not need storage space, while nearly all retail corporations would carry stocks and, except for such establishments as mail order offices, would require display space. Still another possible difference is that the common practice of leasing retail sites would cause rent costs to appear in the operating statement, while wholesale firms that own their physical plant would not show rent as an explicit cost unless, for example, they were paying interest on it. Even with these qualifications it would appear that the cost of plant and equipment is proportionately lower in wholesaling than in retailing.

INVENTORY COSTS

Since inventories represent nearly 30 percent of the total assets of wholesale corporations (See Table 9.2), this would be a substantial component in their operating costs. As in retailing, such costs would include imputed interest on investment, space costs, maintenance and handling costs, and the positive or negative costs of depreciation-appreciation.

SELLING COSTS

The two big difference between wholesaling and retailing with respect to selling costs are the higher percentage of gross margin that goes for advertising in the retail firm and the higher prcentage of margin in retailing for salespeople. The wholesaler's salesmen are an important part of his operation, but it does not appear that total wages and salaries in wholesaling are as large as in retailing, relative to total gross margin, reflecting the higher productivity of the sales force as well as the goods-handling labor force.

Profits

We have already noted that the wholesale firm has net income relative to sales and to capital investment that is about the same as that in retailing. A comparison of Tables 9.5 and 11.2, however, reveals a very interesting and significant difference between these two types of corporations. In the average wholesale corporation net income was 12 percent of gross margin, compared to 8 percent in retailing. The wholesale firm had a lower gross margin than the retail firm and a larger capital investment, though not larger in relation to its sales. In order for the wholesale firm to get approximately the same return on its capital investment as the retail firm, the share of its gross margin that was net income had to be greater than in retailing. Part of this net income was the cost of capital, and this would be a larger share of wholesaling costs than of retail costs. Retailing is a more service-oriented marketing institution, while wholesaling is oriented more toward physical or logistical functions.

Multiunits in Wholesaling

In 1967 multiunit wholesale establishments accounted for about 40 percent of the total volume of wholesale trade.[2] This included firms with two or more establishments. As Louis Bucklin has pointed out, however, the large chain is far more important in retailing than in wholesaling, where multiunit firms tend to have far fewer branches than chain retailing firms have stores. One reason he cites for this difference is that one wholesale establishment can cover a whole city or metropolitan area, while comparable coverage in retailing would require many establishments. Also, economies of branch operation in retailing are much greater than in wholesaling. Advertising, for example, is an important advantage of retail chains but of much less importance in wholesaling.[3]

COMPETITIVE FACTORS IN WHOLESALING

The wholesale firm uses many of the same resources as the retail firm—labor in the form of a sales force, goods-handling employees, and office workers; capital and land in the

---

[2] U.S., Bureau of the Census, *United States Census of Business: 1967*, vol. I, *Retail Trade–Subject Reports* (Washington, D.C.:GPO, 1971).

[3] Louis P. Bucklin, *Competition and Evolution in the Distributive Trades* (Englewood Cliffs, N.J.: Prentice-Hall, 1972), pp. 256-261.

form of inventories, plant, and physical facilities; and management. Both wholesaling and retailing are multiproduct, multiservice marketing institutions. Both have a large number of joint costs, although wholesaling probably has greater opportunities for segregating and allocating costs by customer and product line than does the retail store. Other similarities between retailing and wholesaling are related to economies and diseconomies of scale that arise in both types of institutions. Many of these are related to the technology of the firm. The technology of retailing and wholesaling are similar to the extent that both are centered around the receiving, holding, and dispersing of goods, and in the performance of the transactional functions necessary to complete the marketing process.

In spite of these similarities, however, there are distinctive characteristics of wholesale markets that modify policy alternatives of the firm and are reflected in the competitive structure of the markets in which wholesaling takes place. We shall comment briefly on five attributes of wholesale markets that affect the character of competition.

1. Since the demand for wholesaling services is a derived demand and therefore is more inelastic than the demand for retailing services, the wholesale firm is subjected to the probability of greater cyclical fluctuations in the demand for its services and in its prices than occurs in retailing. Declining sales are likely to set in operation very strong forces for price competition.

2. There is likely to be greater imperfection in the typical wholesale market than in the typical retail market because of the larger average size of transaction, fewer establishments and firms, and the greater degree of specialization that is possible. One would expect these factors to enhance the wholesaler's opportunities for nonprice competition. However, these imperfection-inducing forces are offset to a considerable degree by other attributes of wholesale markets that are more conducive to price competition.

3. Customers of wholesale firms are more likely to have considerable market information than customers of retail firms because of the specialized buying skill probable among such customers and because of the objective bases on which their purchase decisions can be made. While some retail customers are well informed, it seems unlikely that the number of well-informed customers will be as great among consumer buyers as among business buyers. This can give rise to both price and nonprice competition in wholesale markets.

4. The demand for wholesale services is not based on a utility-price calculus on the part of the customer but on a revenue-cost calculus, which is more precisely measurable. This implies a behavior pattern that is conducive to more price competition and less nonprice competition.

5. Wholesaling is a more goods-oriented phase of marketing than is retailing. The importance of selling, promotion, and auxiliary services in retailing, which are reflected in the retail firm's margins, resource utilization, and mode of operation, make it qualitatively quite different from wholesaling. In commenting on the source of economies of scale in wholesaling, Bucklin has pointed out the importance of the wholesaler's physical functions: "In general, it appears that scale economies are more important whenever inventory and processing costs are greater than those of selling and service."

---

[4] Ibid., p. 253.

SOME EMPIRICAL EVIDENCE ON THE OPTIMUM SIZE
OF WHOLESALE FIRMS

In our discussion of retail firms we introduced the concept of cost elasticity coefficients and showed how these could be measured, using empirical data from operating statements and balance sheets of retail firms.[5] We have calculated similar coefficients for wholesaling, and from these it is possible to get some indication of the relative importance of cost of goods sold, operating expenses, and capital investment as elements of wholesale costs and to relate these to the profitability of wholesale operations.

We have utilized data from the Bureau of Internal Revenue for the years 1957, 1958, and 1959 for all wholesale corporations. Arc sales and net investment elasticity coefficients are summarized in Table 11A.1 for the three years 1957-1959, and operating data are shown in Table 11A.2 for 1959. Because firms were classified by size on the basis of assets rather than sales, and because there were so few firms in the three top size groups, we must be very careful about drawing strong generalizations from our data. We shall, however, summarize our findings.

1. Elasticity coefficients for cost of goods sold with respect to sales reached their optimum points at approximately $30 million and $300 million sales in 1959, with the lowest coefficient at the larger sales volume. These coefficients were consistently high, falling slightly above or below 1.000 at most sales volumes. They showed little variation at different sales volumes until sales exceeded about $200 million. Except for extremely large wholesale firms, therefore, it would appear that any buying advantages that occurred were, more often than not, offset by decreases in margins. In general, it appears that this was not an important source of wholesale profits, except for the average firm among the 13 that were next to the largest in size, and these firms also reported the highest net-profit-to-investment ratio.
2. Operating-expense elasticity coefficients were fairly consistently below 1.000 except for the few firms with the highest sales volumes. There was little variation from one sales volume to another in these coefficients. However, the lowest coefficients occurred at sales volumes of $400,000 and $250 million-300 million in 1957 and 1959. Although operating expenses did not appear to play a major role in the profitability of the largest, most profitable corporations in wholesaling, they were of first or second importance in the profit pattern of smaller wholesale firms that showed high profit ratios relative to total capital investment.
3. The elasticity coefficient for capital stock and surplus was most conspicuously low for sales volumes ranging from about $130 million to $225 million in the three years whose experience we have examined. Up to that sales level there was a general tendency for the elasticity coefficients to fall. Beyond that point, however, capital investment coefficients rose to very high levels. There was, however, a very efficient use of capital among firms that, in 1959, had sales of about $350 million, for the return on capital investment was higher for these firms than for any of the other asset groups. But the very largest wholesale corporations, with capital investment elasticity coefficients of 4.5-6.8, showed an extremely low return on capital investment, indicating that they were not using this investment as efficiently as many other wholesale corporations.

---

[5] See Chapter 10.

4. The most profitable wholesale corporations were those whose sales were slightly smaller than the largest firm reporting to the Internal Revenue Service in 1959. Thirteen firms reporting an average sales volume of slightly more than $350 million in 1959 had the highest net profit relative to total capital investment. This was associated with a very favorable cost of goods sold elasticity coefficient. The largest five firms had average sales of slightly more than $400 million in 1959 but very low profit ratios relative to capital investment. Their compiled net profit ratio was one of the lowest.

5. The most favorable elasticity coefficients for operating expenses, cost of goods sold, and capital occurred at approximately the same sales volumes for both wholesale and retail firms, taking all retail firms as a whole. (See Table 11.5.) Cost-of-goods-sold elasticity coefficients were most favorable at approximately $250 million in sales in 1957. Operating-expense coefficients were most favorable at approximately $130 million. Capital stock and surplus coefficients were also most favorable at approximately $130 million. But using net profit ratio relative to capital stock and surplus as our criterion of profitability, we find that wholesale firms were most efficient at sales volumes slightly more than $300 million in 1957, while retail firms reached their highest profit ratio at a sales volume of about $1.7 billion.

Only six wholesale firms in 1957, and only five in 1959, had sales as high as $400 million, while the three largest retail corporations had sales of about $2.5 billion. It is clear that the constraints on large firms in wholesaling are much greater than in retailing. Multiunit wholesaling has fewer advantages than multiunit retailing since it is through multiunits that most large firms can evolve in marketing. This is probably due to the fact that so many of the wholesaler's functions are physically oriented, where diminishing returns can set in much more quickly, whereas in retailing the large firm has more promotional advantages.

6. If we compare the profit ratios of retail and wholesale corporations for 1957, we find that wholesale corporations had consistently higher net profit ratios than retail corporations of comparable sales volumes up to $200 million.[6] The highest profit ratio in wholesaling was earned by the 12 firms whose sales averaged slightly more than $300,000 and whose rate of return on investment was 21.59 percent. The highest profit ratio in retailing, however, was realized by the 9 largest retail corporations with average sales of $1.7 billion and a profit ratio of 23.14 percent. These differences reflect not only the extent to which economies of scale can be realized in these two types of markets but also the competitive structure of retailing and wholesaling and its impact on numbers of firms and efficiency in resource utilization.

---

[6] This is based on all retail corporations, not just food and general merchandise firms, which were the only ones discussed in detail in Chapter 10.

Table 11.5 Comparison of Sales Volumes at Which Retail and Wholesale Corporations Broke Even; Had Low Elasticity Coefficients for Cost of Sales, Operating Expenses, and Capital Investment; and Had High Net Profit Ratios, 1957

Item	Type of Firm	
	Wholesale	Retail
	Sales Volume	
	Thousands of Dollars	
Break-even point (based on compiled net profit)	155	75
	Millions of Dollars	
Points of low elasticity coefficients[a] (*Lowest coefficient)		5.9
Cost of goods and sales	58.5	59.2
	255.3*	235.8*
Operating expenses and sales	0.2	0.2
	1.8	25.5
	15.5	132.8*
	133.9*	1,008.4
(Capital stock + surplus) and sales	33.2	0.8
	133.9*	132.8*
		1,008.4
	Millions of Dollars and Associated Variables[d]	
Points of high compiled net profits relative to (capital stock + surplus)[b] (*Highest profit ratio)	10.4 (1) OE	182.3 (1) OE (2) CI
and	45.8 (1) CI (2) OE	1,727.4* (1) CI (2) OE
Variables associated with each profit optimum (ranked in order of importance[c]	314.0* (1) CG	

[a]Sales volumes identified are those at which elasticity coefficients reached a low point and were less than 1.00. The lowest coefficient occurred at that sales volume indicated by *, excluding sales volumes less than $500,000.

[b]Sales volumes identified are those at which compiled net profit ratios reached a high point. The sales volume with the highest ratio is indicated by *. Since all computations are based on group averages, it should be noted that the sales figures used to identify points of high profits are not exactly the same as those used where sales volumes are related to elasticity coefficients. Figures in the net profit row are derived from operating data for a single group of retail firms, and the sales volume given is the average of that one group. Elasticity coefficients, however, are related to the midpoints between two groups of retail firms, and the sales volumes identified are the average sales of the two groups.

[c]Based on elasticity coefficients less than 1.00, ranked in order of deviation from 1.00.

[d]OE = operating expenses; CG = cost of goods sold; CI = capital investment.

Source: Calculated from U.S., Department of Treasury, Internal Revenue Service, *Statistics of Income: 1956-57, Corporation Income Tax Returns* (Washington, D.C.: GPO, 1959).

Years Ending June 30, 1957, 1958, 1959

Item	Year	Asset Group[a] (1) and (2)	(2) and (3)	(3) and (4)	(4) and (5)	(5) and (6)	(6) and (7)	(7) and (8)	(8) and (9)	(9) and (10)	(10) and (11)	(11) and (12)	(12) and (13)	(13) and (14)
							Dollars (add 000)							
Average gross sales	1957	105	224	445	910	1,772	3,560	7,587	15,470	33,191	58,540	133,892	255,270	351,577
	1958	106	222	436	899	1,751	4,481	7,472	15,072	30,615	60,847	224,508	370,092	396,798
	1959	102	215	436	878	1,662	3,264	7,341	15,681	29,422	61,805	175,447	313,271	388,778
							Elasticity Coefficients[b]							
Gross margin and sales	1957	.905	.787	.911	.910	.887	.991	.941	.852	.943	.957	.710	1.892	.652
	1958	.922	.782	.881	.906	.917	.947	.909	.941	1.047	.891	.479	(c)	1.311
	1959	.856	.828	.849	.896	.903	.942	.913	.924	1.130	.824	.435	3.746	– .070
Operating expenses and sales	1957	.905	.758	.868	.907	.866	.926	.915	.839	.933	1.017	.771	1.710	1.630
	1958	.822	.735	.853	.895	.902	.916	.883	.941	.965	.905	.494	(c)	2.535
	1959	1.028	1.009	.997	.998	.999	.995	.999	.999	.993	1.002	1.009	.896	1.227
Cost of goods sold and sales	1957	1.026	1.050	1.008	1.059	1.020	1.002	1.010	1.022	1.008	.983	1.032	.885	1.057
	1958	1.027	1.052	1.026	1.018	1.014	1.011	1.014	1.009	.993	1.016	1.035	(c)	.951
	1959	1.046	1.047	1.031	1.020	1.017	1.009	1.013	1.011	.981	1.024	1.043	.644	1.181
(Operating expenses + cost of goods sold) and sales	1957	1.000	.995	.982	1.011	.998	.992	.998	1.001	1.000	.987	1.010	.969	1.127
	1958	.981	.990	.996	.999	.998	.998	.998	1.001	.990	1.004	1.005	(c)	1.146
	1959	1.028	1.009	.997	.998	.999	.995	.999	.999	.993	1.002	1.009	.896	1.227
(Capital stock + surplus) and sales	1957	1.517	1.156	1.201	1.003	1.071	1.068	1.041	1.035	.894	1.949	.347	2.002	4.513
	1958	1.640	1.318	1.158	1.019	1.061	1.099	1.041	1.023	1.058	1.323	.375	(c)	6.790
	1959	1.672	1.203	1.124	1.100	1.089	1.087	.993	.954	1.254	1.057	.525	2.849	6.831
Compiled net profit and (capital stock + surplus)	1957	2.956	1.135	1.330	1.021	1.037	1.219	1.055	.987	1.151	.865	1.344	.504	.102
	1958	–	1.644	1.017	1.007	1.143	1.085	1.112	.751	1.425	.803	1.223	1.055	.172
	1959	-7.299	1.332	1.013	1.018	1.000	1.178	1.072	.918	1.121	1.297	– .815	1.872	.043

[a] Asset groups are identified in Table 11A.1.

[b] The elasticity of gross margin relative to sales is computed by the formula $E_{gm,s} = \dfrac{(GM_2 - GM_1)/(GM_1 + GM_2)}{(S_2 - S_1)/(S_1 + S_2)}$

in which $E_{gm,s}$ = the Elasticity of Gross Margin with respect to sales, GM = Gross Margin, and S Gross Sales. The subscript 2 is for the group with the larger average sales volume and subscript 1 is for the group with the smaller average sales volume. All other elasticity coefficients are computed by similar methods.

[c] Not computed because sales of Asset Group 13 for 1958 were only 3.82 percent higher than those of Asset Group 12, thus invalidating the use of asset size as a basis for classifying firms by volume of sales, which was the base for the elasticity coefficients.

Source: U.S., Department of the Treasury, Internal Revenue Service, *Statistics of Income: 1956-57, 1957-58, 1958-59, Corporation Income Tax Returns* (Washington, D.C.: GPO, 1959, 1960, 1961).

Table 11A.2 Operating Statement and Capital Stock and Surplus of Wholesale Corporations Imputed from Reports to the Internal Revenue Service, July 1958-June 1959

Item	Total	Under $25	$25 and Under $50	$50 and Under $100	$100 and Under $250	$250 and Under $500	$500 and Under $1,000
				Total Assets per Corporation (Add 000)			
Asset Group		(1)	(2)	(3)	(4)	(5)	(6)
				Number			
Number of corporations	98,842	19,842	12,931	16,813	24,629	12,833	6,591
				Dollars (Add 000)			
Average gross sales per corporation	1,108	56	147	283	589	1,166	2,158
Capital stock and surplus per corporation	185	2	16	36	83	176	346
				Ratio			
Gross sales / Capital stock + surplus	5.99	23.58	9.11	7.89	7.13	6.62	6.23
				Percentage of Gross Sales			
Gross sales	100.00	100.00	100.00	100.00	100.00	100.00	100.00
Cost of goods sold	85.87	74.94	78.60	81.04	83.15	84.38	85.33
Gross margin	14.43	25.06	21.40	18.96	16.85	15.62	14.67
Operating expenses	13.73	28.26	21.92	18.79	16.53	15.16	14.19
Net operating profit	.70	−3.20	−.52	.17	.32	.46	.48
Other income	1.09	1.87	1.27	1.01	.99	.98	1.05
Compiled net profit	1.79	−1.33	.75	1.18	1.31	1.44	1.53
				Percentage of Capital Stock and Surplus			
Net operating profit	4.20	−75.31	−4.78	1.34	2.32	3.05	2.98
Compiled net profit	10.73	−31.38	6.77	9.28	9.39	9.53	9.53

Table 11A.2 continued

Total Assets per Corporation (Add 000)							
$1,000 and Under $2,500	$2,500 and Under $5,000	$5,000 and Under $10,000	$10,000 and Under $25,000	$25,000 and Under $50,000	$50,000 and Under $100,000	$100,000 and Under $250,000	$250,000 or More
(7)	(8)	(9)	(10)	(11)	(12)	(13)	(14)
Number							
3,560	931	417	210	51	19	13	5
Dollars (Add 000)							
4,370	10,311	21,051	37,794	85,815	265,078	361,463	416,092
750	1,758	3,464	7,311	17,496	30,309	77,593	220,799
Ratio							
5.83	5.87	6.08	5.17	4.90	8.75	4.66	1.88
Percentage of Gross Sales							
100.00	100.00	100.00	100.00	100.00	100.00	100.00	100.00
85.96	87.08	87.82	86.78	88.70	94.25	84.32	86.51
14.04	12.92	12.18	13.22	11.30	5.75	15.68	13.49
13.21	12.02	11.20	11.83	10.05	5.76	12.45	13.41
.83	.90	.98	1.29	1.25	− .01	3.23	.08
1.08	1.14	.87	1.02	1.54	.58	1.07	3.82
1.91	2.04	1.85	2.41	2.79	.57	4.30	3.90
Percentage of Capital Stock and Surplus							
4.85	5.28	6.00	7.18	6.14	− .02	15.05	.15
11.14	11.95	11.26	12.46	13.68	5.06	20.04	7.34

Source: U.S., Department of the Treasury, Internal Revenue Service, *Statistics of Income: 1958-59, Corporation Income Tax Returns* (Washington, D.C.: GPO, 1961).

12

Vertical Market Structure

The future enters into us,
in order to transform itself in us,
long before it happens.

—Rainer Maria Rilke

We have defined marketing as a particular cluster of activities necessary to achieve an exchange relationship, and a market as the exchange relationship itself. Usually many buyers and sellers participate in the purchase and sale of a particular kind of good. The activities of these various participants tend to impinge upon each other so that the character of a particular market is determined by the influence of all buyers and sellers and of all buyer-seller relationships. These are known as the horizontal relationships of marketing and have received considerable attention from both economists and marketing specialists. We have noted numerous aspects of these horizontal relationships in the preceding chapters.

A second aspect of market structure is its vertical relationships. Such relationships determine the nature of a trade channel, which consists of the institutions or individuals through which the title to a product moves from original producer to ultimate consumer. Vertical market realtionships are closely related to horizontal relationships. For example, the optimum number of institutions operating at any one level in the trade channel has an important bearing on the optimum number of levels in the trade channel. Similarly, the optimum functional mix for a marketing institution operating at any one level in the trade channel is related to the functional mix of vertically related institutions.

The focus of this chapter is on vertical market relationships. We shall first consider the case of vertically related firms in which the price and output of one firm at one level in the trade channel bear an important relationship to the price and output of successive firms in the channel. We shall then examine the conditions under which vertical integration occurs where a single firm or decision-making entity replaces the market as a control mechanism.

DETERMINATION OF PRICE AND OUTPUT AMONG VERTICALLY RELATED FIRMS

We shall use the wholesaler-retailer segment of a manufacturer-wholesaler-retailer channel as the basis for our discussion of price and output among vertically related firms. An important consideration that enters into the analysis of vertical price and output relationships is the relative volumes of vertically related firms. A retailer normally sells to many consumers. He is therefore concerned with his aggregate demand—that is, the summation of the demands of his individual customers—from which he can derive his marginal returns, which he can then relate to his costs. Similarly, a single wholesaler is concerned with *his* aggregate demand, which is the summation of the demands of his individual retail customers, and this is then related to *his* costs. The wholesaler may sell to many small retail firms so that his total demand is greater than that of any one of his retail customers. Sometimes, however, the wholesaler is an assembler in a sequence of assemblies in which very large retail firms undertake the final collection of outputs from many wholesale firms. In order to standardize our analysis of various types of market situations, we shall concentrate on the case in which the wholesale firm is larger than either of the manufacturing firms from which it buys or the retail firms to whom it sells. It assembles goods from many manufacturers and resells them to many retail firms.

We shall consider the determination of price and output in retail and wholesale markets in the following types of market situations:

1. Pure and perfect competition with a perfectly elastic retail demand, increasing costs of retailing, and a perfectly elastic wholesale supply
2. Imperfect competition with an inelastic retail demand and increasing cost of retailing
   a. Constant costs of wholesaling and
      (1). wholesaler dominance or
      (2). retailer dominance
   b. Decreasing costs of wholesaling and
      (1). wholesaler dominance or
      (2). retailer dominance
   c. Increasing costs of wholesaling and
      (1). wholesaler dominance or
      (2). retailer dominance

To simplify the analysis we have assumed linear cost and revenue functions but shall modify this assumption at the end of the analysis,

The following symbols will be used:

AGR = average gross revenue (selling price per unit)
$AVCO$ = average variable cost of operations (excluding cost of merchandise)
ANR = average net revenue ($AGR - AVCO$)
MNR = marginal net revenue
ACG = average cost of goods
MCG = marginal cost of goods
AC = average cost ($ACG + AVCO$)
MC = marginal cost
P = price
Q = quantity

The subscript r will stand for all the retail firms that are actual or potential customers of the wholesale firm. This could be a large number of retail firms in a purely competitive market or a single retail firm if there is bilateral monopoly. The subscript w will stand for the wholesale firm. The manufacturing firm(s) from whom the wholesaler buys will be indicated by the subscript m.

Pure Competition

Figure 12.1 describes the cost and revenue structure for retail firms operating under conditions of pure and perfect competition and buying in a purely competitve wholesale market. AGR_r is the summation of the average gross revenue curves of each retail firm that patronizes a given wholesaler. We assume that all retail firms are alike. Therefore to derive the AGR_r curve for any one retailer we would merely divide the quantity in Figure 12.1 by the number of retailers. The AGR_r curve is not the same as an aggregate demand

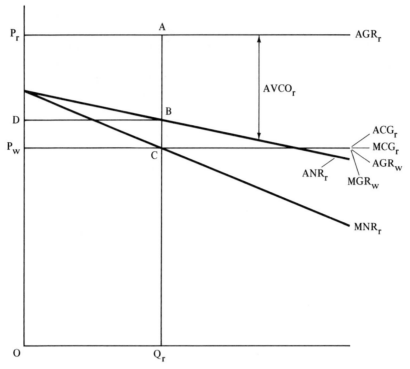

Figure 12.1. Pure competition in retailing and wholesaling.

curve for these retailers, for such a curve would show a negative slope. What we are showing here is that each retailer is in a highly competitive market situation in which the price is set by the market, and he is able to sell an unlimited quantity at that prevailing price. He views his own demand curve, therefore, as perfectly elastic, and all of his competitors do likewise. If we sum all these individual demand curves, each of which is perfectly elastic, we have AGR_r, which differs from the average gross revenue curve for a single retailer only in the greater quantities associated with the prevailing retail unit price where all the individual curves are summed.

ACG_r is the average cost of goods to all the retail firms. Since these retail firms are buying in a competitive wholesale market, this is also the marginal cost of goods to them, indicated by the MCG_r curve, which is identical to the ACG_r curve. Because the wholesaler is selling in a competitive market, the average cost of goods to the retailers, ACG_r, is the same as the average gross revenue of the wholesaler, AGR_w. Since the wholesale market is also purely competitive, $AGR_w = MGR_w$. Thus we have the retail price indicated by the average gross revenue of the retailers and the wholesale price indicated by the average gross revenue of the wholesaler, which is also the average cost of goods to the retail firms.

A further assumption that we have made in creating Figure 12.1 is that the average variable cost of operation of each retail firm is increasing and that is $AVCO_r$. This is shown on our graph as the difference between the average gross revenue of the retail firms, AGR_r, and the average net revenue of the retail firms, ANR_r. Because we have assumed that the average variable cost of operation is increasing for each firm, the average net revenue of each retail firm and of all firms summed is decreasing with increasing volume of sales. Thus while the retail firms have perfectly elastic average gross revenue curves, reflecting pure competition in the retail market, their average net revenue is declining as a result of the increasing average variable cost of operation. If the retailer's average net revenue, ANR_r, is declining, his marginal net revenue, MNR_r, is declining twice as rapidly. We show this relationship in the summations, ANR_r and MNR_r, in Figure 12.1.

This combination of demand and cost conditions will cause this group of retail firms to buy Q_r from the wholesaler at a price of P_w to be retailed at a price of P_r. AB represents the average variable cost of operation for each firm. Since P_w (or CQ_r) is the average cost of merchandise to each retail firm, BC represents the revenue per unit that the retail firm may apply toward fixed costs of operation over and above variable costs and the cost of merchandise. Total revenue of *all* the retail firms is represented by OQ_rAP_r, total cost of merchandise by OQ_rCP_w, total variable cost of operation by $DBAP_r$, and total revenue to be applied toward fixed costs by P_wCBD. To calculate these values for *each* firm, each of these totals would have to be divided by the number of retail firms.

If the retail market is purely and perfectly competitive, as we have assumed, the retail firm will make only sufficient profits at this level of operation to permit it to remain in business. Profits in excess of an amount necessary and sufficient to keep its operation intact will attract competing retail firms, thus driving AGR_r down to a level which brings profits to the necessary and sufficient level. Profits less than that will drive enough firms out so that AGR_r rises until profits have again returned to the required level.

Were we to assume a constant average variable cost of operation for the retail firm, or a decreasing average variable cost, it would be impossible, of course, to reach a point at which equilibrium would be achieved between the retail and wholesale firms with the perfectly elastic demand that we have assumed. But this will not be the case if diminishing returns set in at some point. When this happens, increasing average variable costs of operation will eventually set a limit on the expansion of the retail firms and determine the optimum volume.

The example introduced in Figure 12.1 is highly simplified, assuming not only pure and perfect competition but also linear cost and revenue functions. We have used it primarily to introduce the concepts of average gross revenue and average and marginal net revenue, and to show how increasing unit costs operate to limit the volume of purchases that competing retail firms will make from a wholesale firm.

Imperfect Competition

The important difference between a retail firm that sells under pure competition and one that sells under conditions of imperfect competition is the elasticity of the firm's average gross revenue. Under imperfect competition the average gross revenue declines as the volume of sales increases. We shall consider three different sets of cases, and in each we assume that there is (1) imperfect competition in the retail market, (2) increasing operating costs in retailing, and (3) pure competition in the markets in which wholesalers buy goods for resale. The first assumption means that each individual retailer's demand curve is less than perfectly elastic and that the sum of these demand curves for a single wholesaler will be less than perfectly elastic. The second assumption means that the elasticity of an individual retailer's average net revenue curve is greater than that of his average revenue curve, and this will also be true for the summation of these individual curves as they are viewed by the individual wholesaler. The third assumption means that the average cost of goods sold for the wholesaler will be represented by a perfectly elastic ACG_w curve.

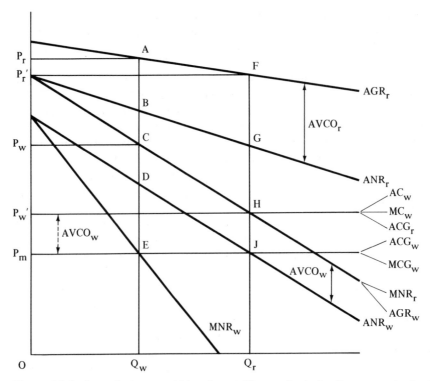

Figure 12.2. Imperfect competition in retailing and wholesaling: constant wholesaling costs.

We shall consider three different types of situations with respect to the wholesaler's costs: constant operating costs, decreasing operating costs, and increasing operating costs. In each case we shall consider two situations: one in which the wholesaler is dominant and a second in which the retail customer(s) is (are) dominant, with the dominant trader able to exercise some control over the resulting price and volume.

CASE A1: CONSTANT COSTS OF WHOLESALING WITH WHOLESALER DOMINANCE

In the first case we shall consider, the wholesaler is the dominant trader. He assesses the market situation and is able to set the price and thereby determine the volume of sales that will be to his greatest benefit.

In Figure 12.2 we show the summation of the retailers' gross revenue curves as AGR_r, from which the ANR_r curve is derived. Increasing costs of operation for the retail firm are demonstrated by the increasing size of the gap between the AGR_r curve and the ANR_r curve as volume increases. $AVCO_r$ is the average cost of operation of one firm when it sells its share of the wholesaler's total volume of Q_x. The marginal net revenue for the retail firm represents the maximum that the retail firm is willing to pay for additional quantities of merchandise. It is therefore the retail firm's demand curve when that firm is operating in a market of imperfect competition. Hence, the marginal net revenue for all the retail firms added together constitutes the average gross revenue for the wholesale firm, AGR_w. Since ANR_r declines, the wholesaler will find that his average gross revenue curve, AGR_w, declines twice as rapidly because $AGR_w = MNR_r$.

One of the assumptions we made in this case was constant costs of operation of the wholesale firm, and these are shown by the difference between the wholesale firm's AGR_w and its ANR_w. The distance between these two lines in Figure 12.2 is constant. We now have the wholesale firm's ANR_w, from which we can derive its marginal net revenue, shown by the MNR_w line in Figure 12.2.

We have assumed that manufacturing firms from whom the wholesaler is buying are selling in markets of perfect competition. This is evidenced by the average cost of goods to the wholesale firm, ACG_w, which is perfectly elastic at the prevailing manufacturer's price. The average cost of goods to the wholesaler, ACG_w, and the marginal cost of goods to the wholesaler, MCG_w, are identical in Figure 12.2. The wholesaler will sell, and therefore wish to purchase, that quantity of goods at which his marginal net revenue exactly equals the marginal cost of those goods to him, and this occurs in the situation illustrated in Figure 12.2 at the quantity OQ_w. At this volume, the purchase price to the wholesaler will be OP_m, the selling price to the retailer will be OP_w, and the retailer will, in turn, sell these at price P_r.

Let us examine the allocation of the wholesaler's average revenue, OP_w. This is equal to $Q_w C$ in Figure 12.2. Of this revenue per unit, $Q_w E$ goes to the manufacturer as the cost of goods. EC represents the wholesaler's gross margin per unit, of which CD goes to cover his average variable costs of operation and DE covers all other costs of operation, including the profit per unit. Similarly, the retail selling price of $Q_w A$ per unit, which is equivalent to OP_r in Figure 12.2, is divided between the wholesaler and the retailer. The wholesaler and manufacturer have absorbed $Q_w C$. The retailer uses AB to cover his variable operating costs, and BC goes to cover unit fixed costs and profit per unit.

One of the important facts demonstrated in Figure 12.2 is that under conditions of imperfect competition in vertically related markets, the revenue curve becomes increasingly inelastic as we move from the retail market back into primary markets. The effect of this is to encourage restriction of output as inelasticity increases and to cause price changes in primary markets to be transmitted sluggishly and imperfectly into retail markets. Price changes in retail markets are transmitted with exaggerated effects into wholesale markets. Even though there is perfect competition at one level of the trade channel, as in the primary market in this case, nevertheless, imperfections in other segments of the trade channel impose restrictions on the level of output that is possible in the competitive market. In addition, increasing costs of operation in one level of the trade channel transmit their effects to other levels, as is demonstrated by the increasing costs of operation in retailing compared to constant costs of operation, which are assumed to prevail in wholesaling. The higher the constant unit costs of operation in wholesaling in this example, the greater will be the difference between the elasticities of the average net revenue of the retail firm and the average net revenue of the wholesale firm.

CASE A2: CONSTANT COSTS OF WHOLESALING WITH RETAILER DOMINANCE

In our explanation of the determination of price and output in Case A1, we assumed that the first determination was made by the wholesaler and that this was done in a way that would maximize his profits. Suppose, however, that we have an extreme case of imperfect competition in which there is only one retail firm buying from one wholesale firm. This would be an example of bilateral monopoly. In this case, the retail customer of the wholesaler is only one firm, and the subscript r stands for that one firm.

Under these circumstances, it would depend on the relative bargaining strength of wholesaler and retailer as to which determines the level of transactions between the two. If the wholesaler were dominant, he would behave as described in Case A1. If the retailer

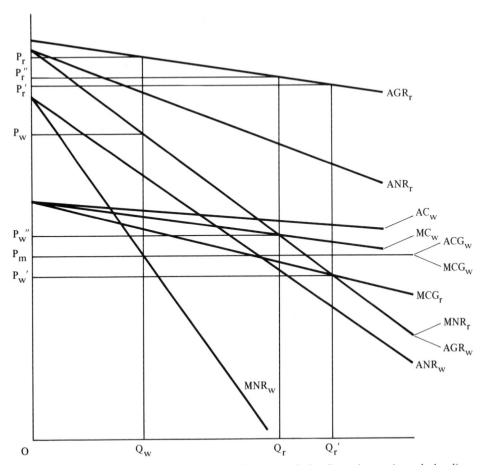

Figure 12.3. Imperfect competition in retailing and wholesaling: decreasing wholesaling costs.

is dominant, however, the level of output would be OQ_r in Figure 12.2. This would be so because a dominant retail firm would be able to force the buying price of its product down to the point where the marginal costs of the wholesaler, MC_w, are just covered. At volume level Q_r, the wholesale price becomes P_w', and this exactly equals the marginal net revenue of retail buyers, MNR_r. The retail price will then become P_r', the retailer's unit margin will be FG, and GH will be the contribution to the retailer's overhead and profit per unit. The wholesaler covers the cost of merchandise, ACG_w, plus the unit operating cost, $AVCO_w$. The wholesaler can remain in business in the short run but not in the long run if he has fixed costs over and above $AVOC_w$.

Under bilateral monopoly it is impossible to say where between Q_w and Q_r the actual level of output will fall. This will depend on the relative strength of the retail and wholsale firms. We have shown the range within which the output will tend to fall and the range within which the retail and wholesale prices will tend to move. It is of some interest to note that the possible range of wholesale prices, P_w P_w', is much greater than that of retail prices, P_r P_r'. This is consistent with our earlier observations about the effect of greater elasticity of demand in many retail markets on price fluctuations in those markets compared with fluctuations in wholesale markets.

It is unlikely that cases of bilateral monopoly will occur in real markets. It is not impossible, however, to see cases of bilateral oligopoly between retail and wholesale firms, or between retail firms and manufacturing firms. In the absence of a mature theory of bilateral oligopoly, we are utilizing the theory of bilateral monopoly to indicate the range within which the actual price and output will tend to fall.

It is appropriate to add one further note about the difference between the output determined under conditions of wholesale domination compared with retail domination. In our example we have shown that the output under retail domination will be larger than would be true under wholesale domination and also that prices will be lower. Although it is reasonable to believe that this condition will tend to obtain in many market situations, we shall show in a later discussion that there may be certain circumstances under which wholesaler domination would result in a lower price than would retailer domination. It is the relative elasticity of revenue and cost that will determine whether one or the other form of domination operates to the benefit of consumers.

CASE B1: DECREASING COSTS OF WHOLESALING WITH WHOLESALER DOMINANCE

The next case that we shall consider under imperfect competition is that in which wholesaling costs are decreasing as the level of output increases. In other respects the circumstances of this market relationship are similar to those found in Case A1. The costs of retailing are rising as level of sales increases, and manufacturers are selling in a competitive market. Figure 12.3 illustrates the conditions that we have specified for this market situation. The average gross revenue for each retail firm is declining; therefore the AGR_r for all firms is negatively sloping. From this is derived the ANR_r, which declines even more rapidly, reflecting the rising average variable costs of operation for the retail firm. The marginal net revenue of each retail firm declines twice as rapidly as the average net revenue, and the sum of these marginal net revenues is MNR_r, which is, of course, the average gross revenue of the wholesale firm, AGR_w.

We have assumed that manufacturers are selling in competitive markets, and for this reason the average cost of goods as well as the marginal cost of goods to the wholesaler, ACG_w and MCG_w, are perfectly elastic, represented by the horizontal line at price P_m. The new condition that we have introduced is that the average variable cost of operation of the wholesaler is declining, and this accounts for the declining average cost curve for the wholesale firm, AC_w, which we see in Figure 12.3. The gap between this line and the average cost of goods to the wholesaler, ACG_w, is the average variable cost of operation of the wholesaler, $AVCO_w$. Because AC_w is declining, the marginal cost for the wholesale firm, MC_w, is declining twice as rapidly. If the wholesaler is able to determine the level of output through the entire trade channel, he will choose that at which his marginal net revenue is exactly equal to his marginal cost of merchandise, and this occurs at quantity OQ_w. (Note that the marginal net revenue has taken into account marginal costs). At this volume, it is possible to sell at a wholesale price of P_w and for the retailer to resell at price P_r. The allocation of the unit revenue, P_r, as described in connection with Figure 12.2, is also relevant to the allocation of the situation described in Figure 12.3. We shall not repeat that breakdown.

We do not know, of course, how much profit or loss the wholesaler receives at this sales level, for we do not know what his fixed costs are. All we can say is that if his volume of sales is less than we have indicated, he receives less contribution toward his overhead than he could were he to expand sales up to that point. Were he to exceed the indicated level of sales, he would reduce the revenue available to cover fixed costs. Therefore this is the volume level at which total short-run profits will be maximized or losses minimized.

CASE B2: DECREASING COSTS OF WHOLESALING WITH RETAILER DOMINANCE

Suppose that the situation we describe in Figure 12.3 is one of bilateral monopoly in which the retail firm is dominant. The retailer will choose that level of output at which the marginal cost of goods to him, MCG_r, equals the marginal net revenue of the retail firm, MNR_r. Let us explain the process by which the retail firm arrives at this decision.

First, we shall review the wholesaler's costs. ACG_w is the average cost of goods to the wholesaler, or the price per unit paid by the wholesaler to the manufacturer. Since the wholesaler can buy any quantity at a constant unit price, $ACG_w = MCG_w$. AC_w is the wholesaler's total cost per unit, including both cost of goods and operating costs. Because we are assuming that the operating costs per unit decline as volume increases, AC_w is negatively sloping. MC_w is the marginal cost curve related to AC_w, and it, of course, has an even greater slope. We can consider the MC_w curve as the wholesaler's supply curve.

How, then, does the retailer view this MC_w curve, which, if the wholesaler calls the tune in the market, is, in effect, the retailer's ACG_r curve? We have already noted that $ACG_r = MCG_r$ if the cost of goods per unit is constant. But in Figure 12.3 MC_w is declining. This means, therefore, that the marginal cost of goods to the retailer, MCG_r, will be declining even more rapidly, since the marginal cost to the retailer will be affected by the declining MC_w. We show the MCG_r curve in Figure 12.3 as marginal to the MC_w curve. This is the marginal cost of goods to the retailer. If the retailer wishes to maximize profits or minimize losses in the short run, he will choose that volume at which the marginal cost of goods equals his marginal net revenue, and this occurs at Q_r'. At this quantity level, the retail price will be P_r' the wholesale price will be P_w', and the manufacturer's price, of course, P_m.

Note, however, that this is a very unsatisfactory state of affairs for the wholesaler, because the wholesale price of his merchandise, P_w', is less than the price of merchandise he buys, P_m. This is therefore an unstable situation. If the wholesaler's retail customer were to try to force this on the wholesaler, one alternative for the wholesaler would be to take over the retailing function through integration. If he did this, he would reduce output to Q_r (instead of Q_r'), raise the wholesale price to P_w'', and raise the retail price to P_r''. Under these conditions, the integrated firm would receive a marginal net revenue at retail that would cover the marginal costs of the wholesale operation ($MNR_r = MC_w$). At a later point we shall consider this and other cases in which integration of retail and wholesale firms would affect level of output and retail and wholesale prices.

In the example we have given here, the quantity bought and sold will be considerably greater when the retailer is dominant than when the wholesaler is dominant. If neither is dominant, the two will negotiate, and the quantity actually traded may fall somewhere between Q_w and Q_r', with corresponding adjustments in P_r and P_w.

CASE C1: INCREASING COSTS OF WHOLESALING
WITH WHOLESALER DOMINANCE

We turn now to what is likely to be the more common situation—increasing costs of wholesaling. It is unlikely that wholesale firms will operate under conditions of constant costs at all levels of output. It is also unlikely that decreasing costs will prevail forever. At some point volume will reach a level at which diminishing returns set in, and this will show up in a rising average cost curve. If there is excess entry into the wholesaling industry, firms may, of course, operate at output levels at which they are experiencing decreasing costs. In the absence of excessive entry, however, firms are likely to be

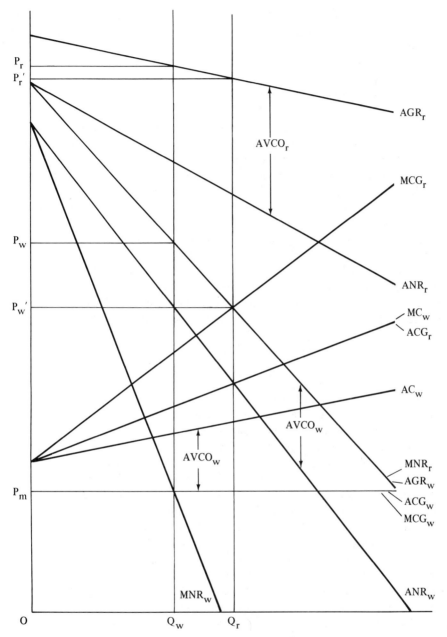

Figure 12.4. Imperfect competition in retailing and wholesaling: increasing wholesaling costs.

operating on the rising portions of their average cost curves. We have made this assumption throughout so far as retail firms are concerned. We shall now extend the same assumption to wholesale firms and examine the vertical relationships that result.

In Figure 12.4 we show a constant manufacturer's selling price at all volume levels so that ACG_w and MCG_w are perfectly elastic. But we assume that the wholesaler's average variable cost of operation, $AVCO_w$, is rising as volume increases. When the average variable cost of operation is added to the average cost of goods, the average total cost curve, AC_w, rises. Therefore MC_w also rises, but even more rapidly.

The MNR_w curve is derived from the retailer's AGR_r curves, as developed in our previous analysis. If the wholesaler is able to control the price and output level, he will elect Q_w, since that is the volume at which his $MNR_w = MCG_w$. The retail price will be P_r, the wholesale price will be P_w, and of course, the manufacturer's price will be P_m.

CASE C2: INCREASING COSTS OF WHOLESALING WITH RETAILER DOMINANCE

If the situation we describe in Figure 12.4 is one in which the retailer is dominant rather than the wholesaler, the retailer will view the wholesaler's MC_w curve as the wholesaler's offer curve. In other words, that will represent the average cost of goods to the retailer and becomes, therefore, the retailer's ACG_r curve. From this, he can calculate the marginal cost of goods, and this we show as MCG_r. To maximize his retail profits, or to minimize his losses, he will elect quantity Q_r, if he has the power to do so, with a retail price of P_r' and a wholesale price of P_w'.

Again we observe a case in which the volume bought and sold will be greater under retailer dominance than under wholesaler dominance. However, the output is not always greater under retailer dominance than under wholesaler dominance. Whether it will be greater under one or the other depends on the relative elasticities of revenue and cost. We shall now review our findings up to this point and then consider briefly some extensions that will permit us to generalize about the locus of market power and its effect on the level of output and prices.

RECAPITULATION

Our basic approach to the analysis of vertical price and output relations under imperfect competition in Cases A, B, and C has been to show that where the wholesaler is dominant his calculations will involve the determination of his average gross revenue, from which his cost of operations will be subtracted, yielding his average net revenue. From this, he will determine marginal net revenue and relate this to his marginal costs, including marginal cost of goods plus marginal variable costs of operation. If the retailer has the greater market power, however, he will attempt to push the price of the goods he buys from the wholesaler down to the point where marginal cost of goods to the retail firm is equal to the retail firm's marginal net revenue, which is its marginal gross revenue less its marginal cost of operations.

In each of the three pairs of examples we have given, we have assumed different cost situations in wholesaling. Case A involved constant wholesale costs, Case B involved decreasing wholesale costs, and Case C involved increasing wholesale costs. In each we showed a situation in which the output and prices would be higher with wholesaler dominance than with retailer dominance. It is necessary now to show that this is not always the case.

COST AND REVENUE ELASTICITIES

The effect of domination by either retailer or wholesaler on the volume of goods bought and sold and the level of prices will depend on the relative elasticity of revenue and cost in all of the vertically related markets. Joan Robinson has described many of these relationships.[1] We describe two of these in Figure 12.5. In order to simplify the

[1] Joan Robinson, *The Economic of Imperfect Competition* (London: Macmillian, 1950), pp. 60-82.

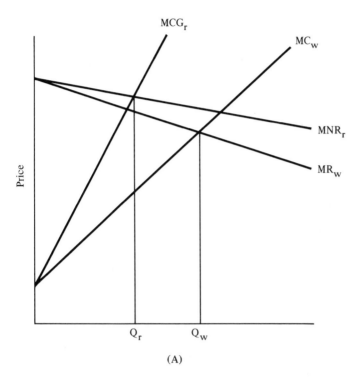

(A)

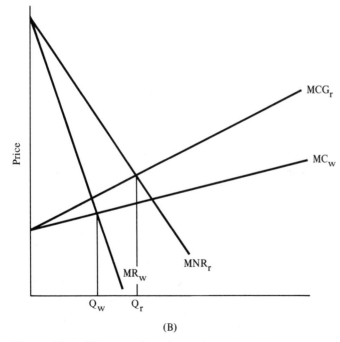

(B)

Figure 12.5. Volume of trade under bilateral monopoly with retailer or wholesaler dominance.

presentation, we have introduced the wholesaler's marginal return, MR_w, which is simply the marginal return of the wholesale firm from the marginal net revenue curve for all his retail customers, MNR_r. Since $MNR_r = AGR_w$, MR_w is the marginal return from AGR_w. It is not the same as the wholesaler's marginal net revenue, MNR_w, in Figures 12.2, 12.3, and 12.4, since these involved the deduction of the wholesaler's operating costs from his gross revenue. The other curves in Figure 12.5 are identical to those we used in other graphs.

Different elasticities are possible at different levels of the trade channel. We shall compare only two. In part (A) of Figure 12.5, we show a situation in which the level of output that would be effected under retailer domination, Q_r, is less than under wholesaler domination, Q_w. In this case, retail and wholesale prices would be higher under retailer domination than under wholesaler domination. We do not indicate prices in Figure 12.5, but they could be imputed from the marginal revenue curves shown.

In part (B) of Figure 12.5, we show a situation in which the optimum output, were it determined by the wholesaler, would be less than that determined by the retailer. In the example we give, the short-run output under competitive conditions would be considerably more than under either wholesaler or retailer domination.

The differences between the effects of wholesaler and retailer domination observed in parts (A) and (B) of Figure 12.5 are dependent on the relative elasticities of revenue and cost. In general, if revenue is more elastic than costs, wholesaler domination results in greater volume. If the cost is more elastic than revenue, retailer domination results in greater volume. If wholesalers' costs, for example, are rising quite sharply as volume increases, compared to the rate at which revenues decline with rising volume, it behooves retailers, where they are in a position to control price and volume, to restrict volume to lower levels where the differential between costs and revenue will be greater. If, on the other hand, costs of goods to retailers (based on wholesalers' purchase price and cost of operations) are rising rather slowly as volume increases, while revenues are declining at the same rate as before, retailers with any degree of market control will elect to buy and sell larger volumes of goods. Wholesalers, on the other hand, are more sensitive to declining revenues, for they use the marginal return on the retailer's marginal net revenue curve as their MNR_w curve. If they have the power to do so, they will curtail output more sharply if returns are inelastic than if costs are inelastic. Higher relative inelasticity of the wholesaler's costs bears more heavily on the retailer, encouraging him to restrict volume; higher relative inelasticity of retail demand bears more heavily on the wholesaler, encouraging him to restrict volume.

As marketing costs become a higher percentage of the total price of goods paid by consumers, the discrepancy between the elasticity of demand at the retail level and that at lower levels in the trade channel is likely to be greater. This is one of many factors that has a bearing on the effects of market control at one level of a trade channel on output and prices throughout the channel. If at one level of the trading channel marketing costs are relatively high, and particularly if they show a tendency to increase rapidly with increasing volume of sales, greater market power at that level will result in greater volume and lower prices than if power is concentrated at other levels. This may be one of the reasons why chain stores have been able, during periods of rising retailing costs, to be an effective force in keeping prices down and volume up. Wholesaling costs during the 1920s and 1930s were by no means rising as rapidly as retailing costs, and this pattern has continued, particularly during the 1950s and 1960s. This created a situation in which the large chain was able to bring into play in the marketplace its considerable bargaining power to suppress prices and sustain volume. In one sense it was the vulnerability of the retail firm vis-á-vis its wholesale suppliers that forced it to assume a less vulnerable character by institutional restructuring and, in effect, becoming itself a more formidable bargainer with the firms from whom it purchased.

In our discussion of vertical price and output relations under conditions of imperfect competition, we have focused on the upper and lower limits of price and output, depending on whether the retailer or the wholesaler has the greater power in bargaining under conditions of bilateral monopoly. Neither retailers nor wholesalers will be content for long to buy at the highest price or to sell at the lowest price they can bear. Moreover, we seldom find bilateral monopoly. We are far more likely to find oligopoly, oligopsony, or bilateral oligopoly. Under these circumstances, the relative bargaining strength of the market participants would have to be established to know where the volume and price levels will fall between the extremes we have indicated. This is likely to differ from market to market and from time to time in any given market. In the long run, of course, fixed costs will also enter into the calculations of both buyers and sellers, for fixed costs must be recovered if firms are to remain intact over time as processing or marketing entities. In view of the tendency in American markets for firms to integrate both horizontally and vertically, and for product and service differentiation to be prevalent, vertical market realtionships are more likely to be related to what we have described under conditions of imperfect competiton than under those of pure competition.

Curvilinear Cost Functions

Throughout our discussion of vertical price and output relationships, we have assumed linear revenue and cost functions. Before we leave this analysis, we should consider briefly the effect of curvilinear cost functions on the net revenue position of vertically related firms. We shall assume that both the wholesale firm and the retail firm (or firms) experience decreasing and then increasing costs of operation as their volume of sales increases.

We shall use two examples. In Figure 12.6 we assume that the retail firms are operating under conditions of pure competition and have a perfectly elastic demand at the prevailing market price, indicated by AGR_r, which, of course, is equal to MGR_r. While the quantities shown are summed for all retail firms, these could be converted to a per firm basis by dividing the total quantities by the number of retailers, leaving prices intact. We have introduced in Figure 12.6 the notion of gross margin, which is simply the difference between the selling price per unit and the cost of goods sold. Since we are assuming that the wholesale firm from which these retail firms purchase their goods undergoes decreasing and then increasing costs as sales increase, we see that the per unit cost of goods sold is quite high if each firm's volume is small, that unit cost decreases as sales increase up to a total level of 80,000 units for all stores, and that it increases as volume increases beyond that level. Subtracting average cost of goods, ACG_r, from average gross revenue, AGR_r, we derive the average gross margin, AGM_r, curve, which rises up to a total volume of 80,000 units and then declines.

To determine the unit profit for retail firms, AP_r, we subtract the average variable costs of operation, $AVCO_r$, from the average gross margin. Since again we are assuming first decreasing and then increasing unit costs, the curve for AP_r rises and falls even more than the AGM_r curve. According to our graph, unit operating costs of retail stores were minimized at a total volume for all stores of 90,000 units. The marginal profit of retail firms is indicated by the MP_r curve, which is derived from the AP_r curve by the usual process.

We are now in a position to say what the retail firm would do were it making its

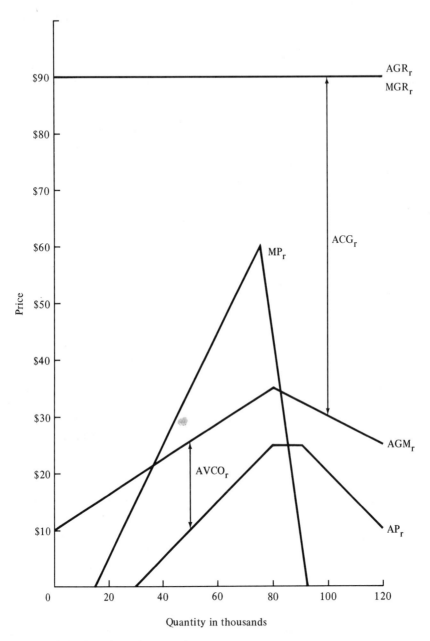

Figure 12.6. Retail purchases under pure competition.

purchase decisions in this case. Let us assume that the quantities indicated are for 100 stores and that each store is alike. We merely divide the quantities shown on the horizontal axis by 100 to determine quantities per retail firm. The profit per unit for each store is highest at 800 or 900 units. Its marginal profit is highest at 750 units. But because it continues to add to its profits beyond 750 units, it will purchase up to 900 units. At 900 units the average retail firm's selling price will be $90.00, its unit cost $57.50, its operating cost per unit $7.50, and its unit profit $25.00. Total profit will be $22,500 ($25 × 900). If 800 units were bought, total profit would be $20,000. If 1,000 units were

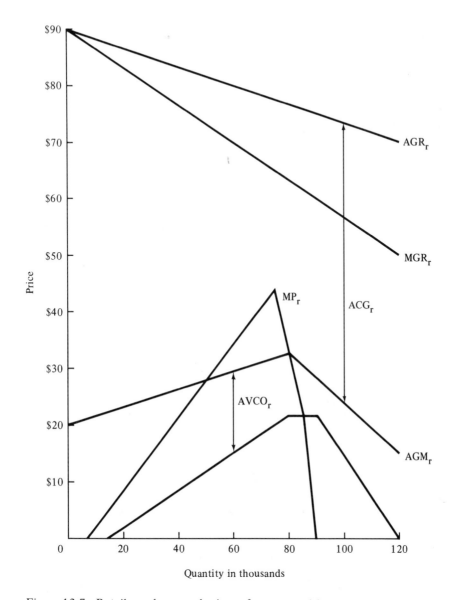

Figure 12.7. Retail purchases under imperfect competition.

bought and sold, total profit would be $20,000. Thus at 900 units total profit is maximized.

Figure 12.7 shows graphically a similar type of calculation, involving retail firms operating under conditions of imperfect competition with a negatively sloping AGR_r curve. In this case, the MGR_r declines more rapidly than the AGR_r. Although the revenue and cost data used as a basis for Figure 12.7 are different from those in Figure 12.6, the point of maximum profits turns out to be 900 units in Figure 12.7, just as it did in Figure 12.6.

While curvilinear cost and revenue functions complicate the calculations necessary to arrive at a solution to problems involving the determination of optimum vertically related prices and quantities, the two examples we have just cited involving curvilinear cost functions suggest that the approach appropriate in the analysis of curvilinear functions is basically the same as that we employed in analyzing linear functions

VERTICAL INTEGRATION AND DISINTEGRATION

In the preceding discussion we have assumed the existence of independent but vertically related business firms and have examined the determination of price and output among such firms. We now turn to questions of integration and disintegration. We shall be primarily concerned with the conditions under which independent firms will forgo their independence and integrate vertically, and the conditions under which vertically integrated business firms will tend to disintegrate, breaking their functions up among a series of vertically related firms.

Means of Integration

The ways in which business firms tend to integrate either vertically or horizontally will depend on the legal and social sanctions of the society in which they function as well as on the technological and economic bases for integration. In a relatively free market society, the tightest form of integration occurs through outright ownership of one firm by another. If a retail firm buys complete control of a wholesale firm, this results in vertical integration by ownership. Ownership may be partial if a firm buys a controlling interest in a vertically related firm. Creation of a trust or holding company makes it possible for a combination to be achieved through a somewhat different ownership structure. A holding company that controls automobile manufacturing can, for example, buy a controlling interest in sources of supplies and in distributive agencies. The effect of this is very much the same as that of outright ownership.

Independent business action is also modified when two firms overtly or tacitly agree to behave as a single firm, with no outright ownership or control. We have numerous examples in our economy of overt and tacit agreements of this sort. One form that this may take is control through contract, as, for example, among voluntary chains sponsored by wholesale firms that agree to provide certain services for retail firms in return for certain assurances concerning patronage and the pursuit of specified merchandising policies. Other more rigid franchise arrangements are common in the marketing of various goods and services, for example, automobiles, gasoline, fast foods, automotive products, and convenience groceries.[2]

A special case of control by contract has arisen under resale price maintenance laws, which have legally sanctioned price maintenance contracts between manufacturers or other owners of branded merchandise and wholesalers and retailers who resell such merchandise under the condition that a specified resale price or resale margin will be maintained. Although such contracts have in recent years been greatly weakened legally, they have played an important role in selected vertical market relationships in a number of countries.

A form of interfirm control of a somewhat different sort is the domination of one firm by another through the exercise of market leadership. Often such leadership is price leadership, but it need not be restricted to this. It could pertain to product quality or promotional policies. Although market leadership is more likely to arise in order to achieve horizontal integration than vertical integration, its effects on vertical market structure can be considerable.

---

[2] U.S. Department of Commerce, Bureau of Domestic Commerce, *Franchising in the Economy, 1969-1971* (Washington, D.C.: GPO, 1971).

These examples show that integration can be achieved through means ranging all the way from outright and complete ownership of one firm by another to a loose federation or cooperative effort of two firms. In between are various modification such as partial ownership or control by contract.

Conditions Conducive to Vertical Integration

The impetus for vertical integration can occur at any level in the trade channel. Forward integration, also referred to as downstream integration, refers to the tendency for a primary producer to move into wholesaling or for a wholesaler to move into retailing. Backward integration starts nearer the retail level and goes toward the wholesaling and form production levels. Forward integration arises either because suppliers of goods have the most to gain from integration or because they have something to gain, though not necessarily more than others in the trade channel, and they alone have the resources necessary to undertake the integration, from which they expect to receive returns in excess of the costs to be incurred. Backward or upstream integration arises because buyers of goods have the most to gain from integration or command the resources to undertake profitable integration. E. A. G. Robinson has identified still another form of integration—mutual integration.[3] This arises because the need is equally strong on the part of both parties who join to become the integrated firm.

What are the specific conditions under which a given firm will integrate forward or backward? We shall consider this question in terms of two broad sets of factors: (1) economies of integration and (2) market imperfections. In considering these two sets of factors we shall by inference also be considering the forces that are conducive to disintegration, for it is the absence of integration-inducing forces, or the shift away from such forces, that causes the disintegration of vertically related functions into separate productive entities.

ECONOMIES OF INTEGRATION

There are three kinds of situations under which a vertically integrated firm will find that it is able to operate at a cost level lower than would be possible were its functions broken up among a number of independent firms.

1. *FUNCTIONAL EFFICIENCY.* The first concerns the optimum scale for the performance of a series of vertically related functions. Suppose, for example, that a retail store has been buying from a wholesale firm. As the retail firm increases in size, its scale of operations becomes closer to that of the wholesale firm. When the two reach a point at which their scales of operation are equal, integration may occur. This may involve a few functions or many. If a retail firm uses the services of an independent wholesaler because the wholesaler performs certain tasks for the retailer more cheaply than the retail firm can perform them for itself, it may find that, as its own size increases, it can then begin to perform those services efficiently for itself.

George Stigler has explained vertical integration in terms of a slightly more complex

---

[3] E.A. G. Robinson, *The Structure of Competitive Industry*, 2d rev. ed. (Chicago: University of Chicago Press, 1958), pp. 112-113.

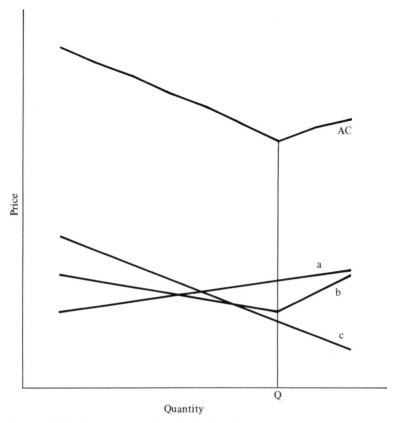

Figure 12.8. Average cost of each of three functions and average total cost.

clustering of functional costs.[4] A business firm performs a series of productive activities; each of these has a cost function. For example, in Figure 12.8 we describe three possible cost functions for a firm. Function (a) is one that entails increasing costs as the scale of output is increased. Function (c), on the other hand, reflects decreasing unit cost as level of output increases, and function (b) shows first decreasing and then increasing cost after a certain level of output has been reached. All of these together give the aggregate average cost curve for the firm, which is shown as AC. The firm experiences, on the whole, decreasing unit costs up to the output level Q. Thereafter average cost of production increases. Average cost comprises all of the costs of functions (a), (b), and (c) in combination.

If an industry is small, firms in the industry may likewise be small, often operating at less than their most efficient level of output. This will mean that each firm performs many functions, since the scale of operations for the entire industry is too small to support specialized producers. As the industry increases in size, however, the output of all firms increases sufficiently that certain functions with decreasing average unit costs are taken over by new firms that spring up to specialize in the production of those outputs. Function (c), for example, would be a likely candidate for absorption by an independent producer when the scale of output in the entire industry becomes sufficiently high to make possible low unit costs of production even by a specialized producer. The growth of

---

[4] George G. Stigler, "The Division of Labor Is Limited by the Extent of the Market," *Journal of Political Economy* 59 (June 1951): 185-193.

the industry would have the effect, therefore, of stimulating production of certain functions by specialized firms, which take advantage of the declining average cost of performing a single function that is a part of the total complex of functions necessary to complete the production process.

Other functions may be performed at increasing cost, however. Thus function (a) shows a rising cost as level of output increases. This therefore becomes a second function that may be absorbed by specialized producers who operate on a smaller scale of production and experience a lower unit cost than is possible for the expanding integrated firm. It is quite possible, however, that the firm that originally performed function (a) will continue to produce at least a part of the output of this particular function, enjoying the low unit costs that are possible with a low level of production but disbursing production among other producers once it experiences increasing average unit cost.

A firm will not give up the performance of a particular function unless it can buy the output or service at a price at least as low as that at which it could produce the same output.[5] Therefore the specialized producer who develops within a vertically related industry is held in check by the possibility of the reabsorption of his function by the original producer.

From an historical viewpoint, the general effect is that young and small industries are likely to show a high degree of vertical integration, while large and mature industries are likely to show a higher degree of vertical disintegration. A contracting industry will show an increasing amount of vertical integration as its demand declines and its level of output decreases. The specialized firm will find it increasingly difficult to maintain output at a low unit cost level in the face of the decrease in the demand for its product. Thus its functions may again be absorbed by the major firm among a series of vertically related institutions.

The functions performed by a typical marketing institution include buying, financing, selling, maintenance of inventories, transportation, and general management. Some of the data that we have presented give an indication of the structure of certain functional costs in retailing and wholesaling.[6] Empirical data and judgment suggest that management, buying, and financing show decreasing costs fairly continuously up to rather substantial sizes. Unit selling costs, on the other hand, probably show an increase at a somewhat smaller sales level. This is particularly true of personal selling. There is considerable evidence, however, that certain types of retail firms enjoy very great promotional advantages as a result of their large scale of operations. Inventory costs and transportation costs probably show the decline and increase in unit levels that are generally assumed in many economic analyses. It is unlikely, however, that any functions that are performed by marketing institutions can go on with decreasing unit costs indefinitely, and even where this is possible, increasing customer buying costs would offset the economies effected by decreasing marketing costs by the business firm.

2. *OPTIMUM MANAGERIAL AND TECHNICAL UNITS.* If the optimum managerial unit is larger than the optimum technical unit for production, integration will be encouraged. Suppose, for example, that the most efficient size for a retail store is not great enough to absorb fully the talents of good retail management. In this case, management could be utilized to full capacity by extending its operations over a

---

[5] An exception to this would occur if the firm's resources are limited and it realizes even greater differential efficiencies in the performance of other functions.

[6] See Chapters 10 and 11.

wholesale firm. Such a differential in the optimum units of production could, of course, lead to horizontal integration as well as to vertical integration. Because managerial talent is likely to be more easily transferred horizontally than vertically, it is likely that this is the direction in which this economy will evolve. If, however, possibilities for horizontal dispersion are limited, vertical integration may result.

3. *COORDINATION*. A third economic reason for integration is to achieve coordination among vertically related firms. An integrated firm effects coordination by administrative action, while nonintegrated firms are coordinated through the market. There may be certain circumstances under which administrative coordination is more effective than market coordination. This would arise where it is important that two functions be close together or in rapid succession. The economic effect is that information is transmitted more readily and the degree of uncertainty in the operation of vertically related enterprises is decreased. Also, transactional costs are avoided.[7]

MARKET IMPERFECTIONS

The existence of vertical integration can also be related to market imperfections. Vertically integrated firms are sometimes a result of market imperfections that existed in the past and led to the creation of integrated firms, which, once created, tend to perpetuate themselves. In other cases vertical integration is designed to correct market imperfections, to take advantage of such imperfections, or to generate additional profit-making imperfections.

1. *INTEGRATION AS A RESULT OF IMPERFECTIONS*. We have pointed out that a newly developing industry frequently demonstrates a high degree of vertical integration. As the industry grows, the firms within it slough off those functions that can be performed more efficiently by independent firms as the scale of operation increases. Sometimes, however, a firm that has initially undertaken a part of the production process continues to perform this process, either because of rigidities or imperfections in the markets, or because the firm is able to devise ingenious administrative procedures by which it retains the advantages of vertical control without the inhibiting effects that might normally arise. The large holding company, for example, which is made up of a large number of relatively independent components held together by the threads of financial control, may achieve certain economies, particularly in large-scale financing and management, that will not be possible for the small firm. At the same time, each of the independent units may operate very much as an independent firm. New firms and new capital may not be able to flow into the industry for the simple reason that the large firm got there first and has no incentive to move out of that phase of its production.

In our marketing economy there is nothing that ensures the entry of new firms except (1) the opportunity for making profits and (2) the perception of that opportunity by those who have a desire to obtain those profits. The more complex industrial organizations become, the more likely it is that rigidities and imperfections will develop at various points to discourage new entrants. If this is coupled with a deliberate policy on the part of existing firms of keeping out new entrants, it can be very difficult for new firms to penetrate the industry.

---

[7] See Chapter 24, where the relative advantages of market and intrafirm coordination are explored more fully.

Another set of circumstances derived from historical facts that may give rise to vertical integration is the availability of capital among existing firms, coupled with restriction on entry for firms that are vertically related to the existing ones. For example, if large wholesale outlets that are seeking sources of supply find that there is a limitation on the number of firms that are now producing that product, and difficulty on the part of potential producers in getting into the field, the wholesale firm may, if it has available the capital necessary for creating the enterprises to produce the goods it is seeking to buy, find it advantageous to go into production itself. Similarly, if there is sluggishness of wholesale markets, which prevents existing wholesalers or potential wholesalers from providing the services sought by retail firms, this would encourage existing retail firms to provide wholesaling functions so long as they have the capital available for doing so.

2. *INTEGRATION TO INCREASE MARKET CONTROL.* A second condition that tends to encourage the creation of vertically integrated firms is the desire on the part of the firm to achieve a greater degree of market control. Richard Heflebower refers to this as the firm's desire to round out its control.[8]

This form of integration can give the firm a greater possibility for the profits of monopoly or of monopolistic competition. It can also make possible a certain flexibility of policy where competition is shifting very rapidly. Flexibility arises out of the fact that a vertically integrated firm is able to transfer competition from a vulnerable level to one that is less vulnerable. If, for example, competition in retail markets is extremely intense, while competition in wholesale markets is much less intense, the integrated firm can take advantage of the lower degree of competition in wholesale markets to compensate for the much higher degree of competition that exists in retail markets. A good example of this would be the firm that is able to practice price discrimination at different levels of the trade channel. Many of the prices within an integrated firm are accounting prices and can therefore be spurious. The integrated firm has more possiblities for price discrimination at various levels of the trade channel than nonintegrated firms. The flexibility of policy made possible by this fact is therefore a real advantage, particularly where competitive relations are shifting rapidly.

Vertical integration can also result from a combination of reasons involving both the existence of market imperfections, which it seeks to correct, and the desire to exploit the profit-making opportunities created by market imperfections. If, for example, markets are not cleared at the point where marginal costs are equal to the marginal value product, there may be a tendency for integration to occur. If production is greater than consumption, forward integration may take place. If consumption, on the other hand, is greater than production, there will be a tendency for backward integration to occur. Sometimes during periods of shortages, for example, wholesalers have to scout around for supplies. Under these circumstances, the wholesaler may find it advantageous to set up his own manufacturing plant. Or if at any time manufacturers have difficulty in obtaining loyal wholesale and retail customers, they may find it advantageous to set up their own wholesale and retail outlets. Thus market imperfections can encourage the movement of firms into production or marketing, thereby making it possible to substitute a market imperfection more favorable to the integrating firm for the existing imperfection, which the integration is designed to counteract.

---

[8] Richard B. Heflebower, "Monopoly and Competition in the United States of America," in Edward H. Chamberlain, ed., *Monopoly and Competition and Their Regulation*, (New York: Macmillan, 1954), pp. 110-140.

3. *INTEGRATION TO ELIMINATE MARKET IMPERFECTIONS.* A third major reason for vertical integration is to eliminate the constraints resulting from monopolistic or semimonopolistic behavior of firms with which the integrating firm deals in the trade channel. In Figure 12.5, for example, we showed that under bilateral monopoly a retail firm and a wholesale firm are not likely to arrive at the same decision concerning the optimum volume of sales (and hence of prices). If one or the other is dominant, it will tend to make decisions favorable to its own trading position. Under such circumstances the firm that is left in the less favorable position will have a strong inducement to assume the trading functions of the other through vertical integration. It does not follow, of course, that under integration the retailer would choose exactly the same level of output as he would under a bilateral monopoly in which he is the dominant party in a market transaction. We shall show in a later section that his decision under integration will be different from the decision that would be made by either trader in the market. He can, however, use vertical integration as a means of reducing the negative impact of vertical market power on his profit position.

EXAMPLES OF VERTICAL INTEGRATION

There are numerous examples of vertical integration that have occurred in the United States and other countries for one or more of the various reasons we have described. Many chain stores have undertaken the performance not merely of wholesaling functions but also of manufacturing activities. While some of these production decisions may have been rooted primarily in the desire to achieve operating economies, it would appear that on a number of occasions the objective was to achieve control over a monopolistic output or to penetrate the lethargy of an imperfectly competitive market in which such firms were buying. Evidence of this lies in the fact that the chain stores have chosen certain fields of manufacturing but have very carefully avoided entrance into other fields. For example, A&P has been active in the canning of milk, the production of roasted coffee, and the manufacture of bread. It has not, however, entered the meatpacking business. It would appear that one of the reasons is that the effectiveness of "competition" among firms in this industry of oligopoly has been such that there was little to gain by the entrance of chain stores into that field.[9]

In certain European countries cooperatives have performed many of the same functions economically that chain stores have in the United States. One of the large cooperative in Finland does about 25 percent of its own manufacturing. The policy that it follows is largely one of manufacturing those things that it can produce more cheaply than it can obtain them in the market. This is clearly a case of using this particular technique for breaking up any monopolistic control that occurs.

Chain stores in the United States and cooperatives in many countries undertake the production and sale of goods under their own brand names where the margins obtained by manufacturer-controlled brands are larger than necessary in order to keep resources in the production of that particular product. Often, also, this particular technique is used not merely to obtain the profits of monopoly but also to ensure the availability of products of a given quality. Many of the chains have wished to obtain canned and packaged goods, household appliances, and soft goods of given qualities not available on the free market. By engaging in their own manufacturing, or through purchase by specification, they were able to control product quality.

---

[9] Richard B. Heflebower, "Mass Distribution: A Phase of Bilateral Oligopoly or of Competition?" *American Economic Review* 47 (May 1957): 274-285.

Other examples of market control achieved through vertical integration can be observed in manufacturers' sales branches and sales offices, the use of franchising in the retailing of food specialties and services, the use of exclusive agencies and selective selling, and the declining importance of independent retail outlets in the marketing of most types of goods and services.

Effects of Vertical Integration on Consumer Welfare

If marketing firms integrate vertically, does this work for or against consumers' interests? There is, of course, no single answer to this question, for it depends on the conditions giving rise to the integration, the effect of the integration on the revenue and cost structure of the producing firms, and the resulting competitive struture of the markets in which the integrated firms function.

In general, integration designed to achieve economies of scale is likely to result in cost reduction with lower prices and increased output. If cost reductions are realized, the extent to which they will benefit consumers will depend to a large degree on the competitive structure of the markets in which the integrated firm markets its output. To a large extent it is *horizontal* market relationships that govern the impact of efficiency-induced vertical integration on consumer welfare. Many students of industrial organization have found convincing evidence that backward vertical integration has frequently resulted in lower prices for consumers, although there is some evidence and opinion to the contrary.[10]

Let us examine the case in which integration is undertaken not to realize economies of scale but to break market control at some level in the trade channel. In Figure 12.9 we show three situation in which we shall assume that there is bilateral monopoly between wholesaler and retailer.[11] Two of these are similar to the examples shown in Figure 12.5. In part (A) we show that retailer control over the bargaining situation would result in a lower level of output (and correspondingly higher prices) than would wholesaler control. In part (B), we show that retailer control would result in a higher level of output (and lower prices) than would wholesaler control.

In both cases, however, we can see that if there were vertical integration, and if the integrated firm brought the marginal revenue of the wholesaling operation, MR_w, into equality with the marginal cost of wholesaling, MC_w, as would be expected, the output level, Q_i, would exceed the output level of either retailer or wholesaler if either were able to control the terms of the transaction. In these two cases, therefore, we can say that vertical integration would benefit consumers through greater output and lower prices.

But in part (C) of Figure 12.9 we show a case in which wholesaling has decreasing

---

[10] See, for example, John K. Galbraith, "Countervailing Power," *American Economic Review* 44 (May 1954): 1-6; George J. Stigler, "The Economist Plays with Blocks," *American Economic Review* 44 (May 1954): 7-14; Richard B. Heflebower, "Mass Distribution: A Phase of Bilateral Oligopoly or of Competition?" op. cit., A particularly good summary of the "iffy" issues associated with counter-vailing power and vertical integration is in F. M. Scherer, *Industrial Market Structure and Economic Performance* (Chicago: Rand McNally, 1970), pp. 239-252.

[11] See William Fellner, *Competition Among the Few* (New York: Knopf, 1949), pp. 244-251, where the determination of output and price under conditions of joint profit maximization in bilateral monopoly is developed. Our Figures 12.5 and 12.9 are modifications of Fellner's Figure 15, p. 244. We have changed Fellner's notation to be consistent with our notation of retail and wholesale revenue and margins.

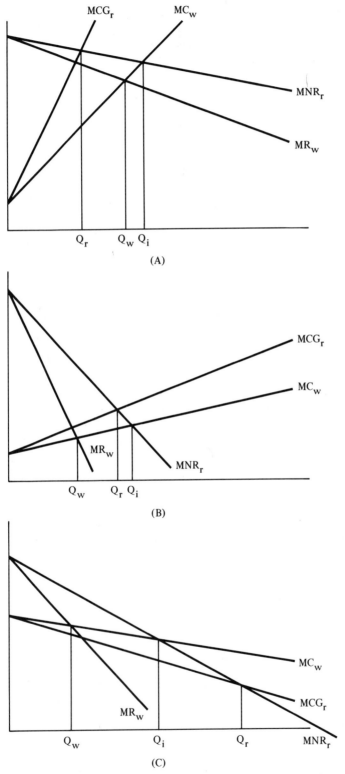

Figure 12.9. Volume of trade under bilateral monopoly with retailer dominance, wholesaler dominance, or retailer-wholesaler integration.

costs. Under these circumstances, retail control would be to the best interests of consumers, for the retailer would drive prices down, and output would rise to the level Q_r. Were the retailer to integrate vertically and take advantage of the profit-making opportunities inherent in the wholesaling operations of the integrated firm, he would restrict output to Q_i, resulting in less goods for consumers and higher prices. But case (C) in Figure 12.9 is unlikely, for firms will rarely be operating on the decreasing cost portion of their average cost curves unless the industry is immature and minimum cost points have not yet been reached, or unless there is excess capacity in the industry. In general, it is reasonable to conclude that integration undertaken to eliminate the deleterious effects of monopolistic control in the trade channel is likely to benefit consumers, with the exceptions we have noted.

Where the purpose of vertical integration is to achieve for the integrated firm a high degree of market control and the flexibility of policy that makes it possible for the firm to take advantage of price discrimination and other profit-generating practices at various levels of the trade channel, it is likely that consumer welfare is not increased but, rather, decreased. If such control results in greater equalization of the competitive structure horizontally, however, it is possible that certain benefits will accrue to consumers. Suppose, for example, that we have a firm that is operating in competition with sellers of similar products. Let us assume that these other sellers have integrated forward in order to achieve greater market control over outlets' selling policies and other factors that affect the sales and prices of their outputs. A firm confronted with such competition may, in the interest of increasing its own market control, integrate forward, as its competitors have. The effect of this is to achieve greater equality of bargaining power horizontally in the market place. This may lessen possibilities for monopolistic control that might be exercised by another firm or a small number of other firms that are enjoying the monopolistic benefits of vertical integration.

This argument is somewhat analagous to Galbraith's thesis concerning countervailing power, in which he argued that *horizontally* integrated firms at one level of the trade channel could hold in check equally powerful horizontally integrated firms at other levels. The argument we present here is that *vertically* integrated firms may hold other vertically integrated firms in check horizontally, thus mitigating the possibly unfavorable effects such firms are likely to have on consumer welfare. This type of balance is not without tremendous hazards for consumers, for there is no *assurance* that two equally powerful vertically integrated firms will exactly balance each other, or that they will choose to use their power in ways that will contribute to consumer welfare. There are, however, potential benefits in such a case, and this possibility should not be ignored.

A NOTE ON LONG-RUN EQUILIBRIUM IN VERTICAL MARKET STRUCTURE

Up to this point, our analysis has been largely in terms of short-run market adjustments. The Stigler thesis, however, suggests the directions in which long-run adjustments will be effected, depending on the cost structure for various functions involved in the production process. Economics of scale that are made possible by vertical rather than horizontal integration can prevail for a long period and, so long as they do, will determine the optimum size of firms vertically. Similarly, changes in the conditions under which economies are effected vertically will encourage a greater or less degree of vertical integration. For example, improved methods of internal control, such as might occur with the use of computers and other electronic data-processing equipment, could stimulate a movement toward vertical integration with the substitution of administrative control for market control. On the other hand, increased uncertainty in the market situation might make internal control a good deal more hazardous in the sense that the large-scale firm is subject to a multiplier effect from its errors if the scope of its decisions is quite large.

Long-run changes in the optimum technical unit may also have a bearing on the directions in which integration will tend to move. If the optimum managerial unit remains quite large in the face of a relatively small technical unit, it is likely that vertical integration will occur in an attempt to equalize the optimum size of these two units. But if innovations cause an increase in the optimum size of the technical unit, it is probable that vertical disintegration will occur with no loss in economy, owing to the ability of the technical unit to support an efficient managerial unit.

The economic factors making for long-run integration or disintegration lie partly in the technology of production and partly in the level of demand. As the level of output increases and demand expands, this affects the optimum size of the industry and of the firms within the industry. As technology expands, it can open up opportunities that make it possible for the integrated firm to achieve certain efficiencies that the nonintegrated firm cannot achieve through market relationships. Technology is not merely physical technology; it can also be organizational and social. Although recent progress has been greatest in those decision areas of marketing that most closely resemble the physical world—for example, inventory and location—much of the technology of marketing introduced during the past quarter-century has been the product of the social and behavioral sciences rather than the natural sciences. The complexity of the subject matter of these sciences far exceeds that of the natural sciences. But if progress continues in these fields, it may have a significant impact on the optimum size of the marketing firm, both horizontally and vertically. The slowness of progress in these fields is probably one of the reasons for the continued survival of the small marketing unit with its unique role in both horizontal and vertical market relationships. On the other hand, increased uncertainties in the market situation may, in some cases, give rise to greater dependence on the market and its self-correcting mechanism or, in other cases, to integration of production in order to minimize the uncertainty associated with the achievement of equilibrium between the supply and demand.

Market imperfections can be short or long run, depending on their origin and effects. Rigidities that arise out of historical patterns of industrial organization are more likely to be long-run imperfections; those that arise out of the inability of the production system to adapt itself rapidly and completely to changes in consumer demand are more likely to be short-run imperfections. Each situation must be assessed in terms of both the causes and effects of existing and potential vertical market relationships.

THE RELATIONSHIP OF VERTICAL AND HORIZONTAL STRUCTURE

Up to this point, we have discussed vertical and horizontal market structure separately as though the choice were between one or the other. However, these two aspects of market organization are very closely related.[12]

---

[12] See, for example, an interesting treatment of the relationship of costs and assortments in different channel structures in Louis P. Bucklin, "Macro Models of Vertical Marketing Systems," in Louis P. Bucklin, ed., *Vertical Marketing Systems (Glenview, Ill.: Scott, Foresman, 1970), pp. 158-174.*

Vertical and Horizontal Scale Relations

If large retail firms are more efficient than small ones, it is likely that they will encourage the existence of large wholesale outlets. It is also possible, however, that large retail firms will integrate vertically and take over the functions of the large wholesale firms rather than having those performed by specialized independent wholesalers. If, on the other hand, wholesaling in this particular line of business is more efficiently performed by smaller firms than that necessary to provide the entire quantity of goods utilized by the retail firm, the vertical integration will be only partial, and the retail firm will continue to buy a portion of its products from other sources. It will not attempt to equalize the size of wholesale and retail operations unless this could be done economically on such a scale.

Small retail outlets often encourage the existence of large mechant wholesale firms. This is because the scale of operations that is most efficient for wholesale firms is much larger than for retail firms, making it more economical to have a few specialized wholesalers servicing a large number of widely dispersed small retail stores than to maintain either small retail firms and small wholesale firms or large wholesale firms and exclusively large retail firms.

One of the functions of the market is to make possible the existence of the optimum size of firm at each level in the trade channel and in each market and to coordinate those production units that differ in optimum size. Although there are cases where large scale at one level begets large scale at another, there are numerous cases where small- and large-scale firms exist in a vertical relationship.

Imperfect Competition

Where scale of operations, and particularly integration either horizontally or vertically, occurs for reasons of imperfect competition, it is quite possible that this will induce a comparable development elsewhere in the market. For example, horizontal integration undertaken for purposes of obtaining semimonopolistic marketing advantages may induce competing firms to undertake a similar type of integration. On the other hand, horizontal integration on the part of one firm may force another firm into vertical integration in order to get certain compensating advantages from this type of market control. If horizontal integration encourages a firm also to undertake vertical integration, a similar action may be taken by a competing firm. Thus horizontal integration leading to vertical integration by a particular firm, can in turn lead to horizontal integration and eventually vertical integration by another firm. It is unlikely that conditions of imperfect competition are alone sufficient to induce extensive integration vertically or horizontally unless there are also present certain economies that are possible to the integrated firm. But it does appear that integration of a particular sort may occur because of a desire on the part of the integrating firm to entrench its market position.

Circular Integration

A slightly more complicated type of integration occurs where there is an intermixture of vertical and horizontal integration. If a firm integrates vertically, this may open up possibilities for increased horizontal integration, either at the level at which it was originally operating or at the new vertical level into which it has moved. For example, a retail firm may integrate horizontally and then acquire certain wholesaling facilities. Having acquired wholesale facilities, it decides to increase its integration horizontally at the wholesale level. Thus the initial integration was horizontal, the second stage was vertical, and then the third stage of integration was again horizontal but at a different level in the trade channel.

It is unlikely, although possible, for a firm to integrate in what we might call a diagonal fashion. This would occur if a retail firm acquires a wholesale firm handling merchandise outside the retail firm's usual line of activity. Another example would be where a manufacturing firm acquires wholesale facilities that are designed to handle merchandise unlike the merchandise it normally sells. A possible advantage of integration of this sort is diversification. On the other hand, the disadvantages also rest on the diversification, for the firm is moving into (1) a commodity area quite different from that in which its technical competence exists and (2) a level in the trade channel in which it has not yet had experience. Therefore it is much more likely that circular integration will occur rather than diagonal integration. Such an operation greatly broadens the base of operations for the integrating firm and carries with it the advantages and disadvantages of extensive product and service diversification.

Partial Integration

We have spoken as if horizontal or vertical integration involves the complete absorption or control of the acquired firm by the integrating firm. This is not necessarily true. If, for example, a manufacturing firm wishes to acquire wholesaling facilities, it may find that the most economical scale of operation for such outlets is smaller than that which is required to handle its entire output. Under these circumstances, the wholesale firm could use its integrated warehouse facilities for a portion of its output but continue to sell the balance of its output through independent wholesalers or other middlemen. An opposite situation would occur where the manufacturing firm has a total output less than that which is optimal for the wholesale branch. Under these circumstances, vertical integration could occur, but the manufacturing firm would have to utilize that portion of its unused plant and equipment in the warehouse for the outputs of other manufacturers.

The marketing system offers numerous examples of these differences in scale of operation that are handled effectively through partial integration. Many firms, for example, manufacture a portion of their materials but buy another portion. Other firms handle not only their own output but also the products of competing producers. The attempt in all cases should be to try to operate each unit of activity and each function at its optimum scale. These possibilities give the integrated firm increased flexibility along with the opportunity to take advantage of efficiencies associated with increased integration either vertically or horizontally.

A Concluding Note on Vertical and Horizontal Market Structure

It is important to recognize that the institutional structure of marketing is merely the framework within which decisions are made and actions occur. Structure alone does not determine what the behavior of individual firms or of consumer participants will be. It can influence that behavior, for market structure helps channel behavior into one avenue or another. In this sense it may be conducive to certain forms of behavior or it may limit certain forms of behavior, but it cannot alone determine what that behavior will be. In the end we must utilize a behavior test in attempting to evaluate the desirability of a given market structure. One of the greatest benefits to result from a discussion of the structural characteristics of markets is the identification of structural attributes that are related to the behavior of market participants.

It is for this reason that our presentation in this volume includes (1) a study of market structure and (2) a study of marketing policies. Policies define the behavior pattern, while structure defines the institutional framework within which that behavior takes place. Structure must be evaluated in terms of how well it provides a favorable or unfavorable social framework within which the activities of businessmen and consumers are carried out.

iv
Marketing Policies

13

Horizontal
Price Relationships

Greet prees at market maketh deere ware,
And to greet cheepe is holde at litel prys;
This knoweth every womannen that is wys.

— Geoffrey Chaucer

The nature of market structure and the processes by which prices and levels of output are determined in markets with differeing attributes is the central subject matter of microeconomics. Students of marketing have been quite critical of pricing theory, pointing to its lack of "realism" and its failure to provide "useful" guidelines for decision making in the marketing firm.

The purpose of theory is not, however, to *mirror* reality, with all its myriad details, but to show the underlying structure of reality. To do this, it describes and explains a simplified system. It is a *map* of reality rather than a detailed portrait.[1] A road map, for example, does not show every hill, every curve, every intersection, or even every road. But it is *valid* if it describes accurately the system of roads, and it is *useful* if it enables a driver to get from one place to another. It is even more useful if it enables him to get from one place to another in the least possible time, via the most scenic route, or on the best possible roads.

By analogy, a realistic price theory will describe and explain how prices are determined. If such a description is useful, not only will it make it possible to understand the price-determining process, but it will also provide guidelines for policy making where a buyer or seller has sufficient market power to exercise some degree of control over price.

Price determination under pure and perfect competition has had a prominent place in economics and is the most highly developed area of value theory. But pure and perfect competition rarely exist, while markets of oligopoly and monopolistic competition abound. Yet the theory of price determination in either of these latter, or in the two combined, is far from adequate. In these respects, therefore, the criticism of price theory as a guide for policy making is partially justified. Until a theory of the firm is evolved that explains the determination of the *total* cluster of policies, of which pricing is one, under market conditions in which varying numbers and sizes of firms are competing in the sale of differentiated products by differentiated marketing methods, the marketing manager will not find in economic theory all of the directives that he needs in the formulation of effective policies. What we shall attempt to do, however, is to show that even a less than perfect theory can be useful in indicating a way of thinking about the price-determining process.

It will be our objective to focus specifically on those aspects of pricing of greatest concern to the marketing firm, that is, where the marketing firm has open to it some

---

[1] Kenneth E. Boulding, *Economic Analysis*, vol. I, *Microeconomics*, 4th ed. (New York: Harper & Row, 1966), pp. 12-13.

pricing options. In this chapter, we shall review very briefly the current state of the theory of pricing under conditions of oligopoly and under conditions in which price discrimination occurs. In the two chapters that follow, we shall consider, first, pricing in the multiproduct marketing firm, and second, vertical pricing policy in the trade channel. Because price determination in markets of monopolistic competition cannot be considered in isolation from product quality, sales promotion, and other aspects of nonprice competition, our principal treatment of pricing under conditions of monopolistic competition will appear in two subsequent chapters, which are concerned with nonprice competition.

PRICING IN A MARKET OF OLIGOPOLY

An oligopoly is characterized by the presence of relatively few sellers in a market. The critical question then becomes, how "few" must the number of sellers be? This has usually been specified in terms of a number sufficiently small so that each takes into consideration the reaction of his rivals when formulating policy. Thus interaction among rivals becomes a critical attribute of oligopolistic markets. Sellers not only watch their rivals; they are also aware that their rivals are, in turn, watching them, and they structure their policies accordingly.[2]

William J. Baumol defines oligopoly much more loosely as "any comparatively large company that produces commodities some of which are identical with, or very similar to, the output of other firms."[3] Thus he excludes consideration of interdependence on the ground that management often is not concerned with elements of interdependence, particularly in its day-to-day decisions. He believes that the objective of the firm operating in such a market situation is not merely to maximize profits, nor even to "satisfice"—that is, attain some acceptable and feasible goal[4]—but, rather, to achieve some given size or scale of operations along with some specified level of minimum profits.

In this discussion, we shall define *oligopoly* as the existence of a relatively few firms selling to meet the demand in a given market. We shall assume not only that these rival firms are free to differentiate their products and marketing methods, but that the advantages of doing so are strong enough to make such differentials highly probable. Where the products sold by oligopolists are different but imperfect substitutes for each other, we have a case of *differentiated oligopoly*, which is in contrast to a *homogeneous oligopoly*, in which the products of the oligopolists are identical. We shall consider the processes of price determination in the light of three conditions: (1) where the price-making firm expects a given pricing reaction from his rivals, (2) where there is interaction among rivals in the making of price, and (3) where price determination by the oligopolist is independent of rivals' expected reactions.

An oligopolist will formulate policies concerning the physical attributes of his product, its price, promotional methods, channels of distribution, and all the other facets of his manufacturing and marketing activities. Let us assume for the moment that his product quality, promotional methods, and so on are similar to those of rival producers but

---

[2] See, for example, Fritz Machlup, *The Economics of Sellers Competition*, (Baltimore: Johns Hopkins Press, 1952), pp. 97-102.

[3] William J. Baumol, *Business Behavior, Value and Growth*, rev. ed. (New York: Harcourt Brace Jovanovich, 1967), p. 13.

[4] See Herbert A. Simon, "Theories of Decision-Making in Economics," *American Economic Review* 49 (June 1959): 262-264.

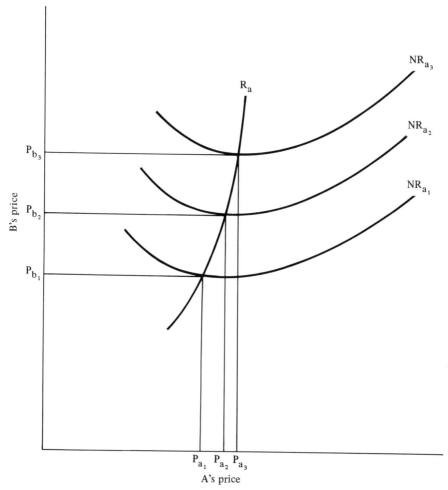

Figure 13.1. Derivation of A's reaction curve from the relationship of A's and B's prices to A's net revenue.

sufficiently different to distinguish his output and to evoke some degree of customer loyalty. Holding these variables constant, we shall examine the process of price determination by firms operating in markets of oligopoly, dealing first with the action and interaction of two firms and later with the interactions of more than two firms.

The Firm's Reactions Curve

The first case we shall examine is that of *duopoly*, which is a special case of oligopoly.[5] The profits that one firm receives are a function of the prices charged by that firm and by its rival. In Figure 13.1 we show the net revenue that firm A will receive, given various

---

[5] The classical treatment of this problem appears in Augustin Cournot, *Researches into the Mathematical Principles of the Theory of Wealth*, 1838, trans, Nathaniel T. Bacon (New York: Augustus M. Kelley, 1960), pp. 79-89. See also William Fellner, *Competition among the Few* (New York: Knopf, 1949), and Baumol, op. cit., pp. 15-33.

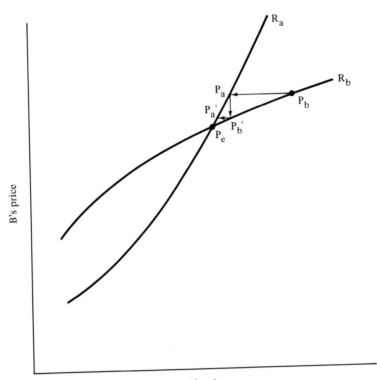

Figure 13.2. Reaction curve of firm A and firm B.

combinations of prices of A and B. Each net revenue indifference curve shows a combination of prices that will yield equal net revenues. The level of revenues on the indifference curve NR_{a_1} is lower than that on higher indifference curves. If B's price is specified, A will react by charging a price equal to that which will enable the firm to reach the highest net revenue indifference curve. Thus, if B adopts price P_{b_1}, A will respond with price P_{a_1}, which is the only price that will enable the firm to reach the net revenue indifference curve NR_{a_1}. Higher prices for firm B will provoke higher prices for firm A. A's reaction curve is then described by the curve R_a. The assumption underlying this reaction curve is that A knows the price charged by B and reacts to it, but B does not counterreact to A's price. The optimum price for A is that which makes it possible to achieve the highest net revenue given the price decision of B.

Figure 13.2 shows the reaction curve not only of A but also of B. B's reaction curve will be determined by the shape of its net revenue indifference curves and by the price charged by A. B's and A's prices establish point P_e, which represents the only price combination that will provide temporary equilibrium. But neither firm will yearn to stay at this point unless it happens also to coincide with the point of maximum net revenue for both, and this is unlikely. If B's maximum net revenue is at point P_b, it will set its price there. A will react by setting a price of P_a, and this provokes B to set a price of P_b', to which A again reacts by setting a price of P_a'. While the movement to point P_e is clear, neither seller will willingly stay at point P_e if he has greater profit possibilities at some other price. The result is likely to be a highly unstable situation.

This brief examination of reaction curves and the assumptions underlying their use in pricing anlysis indicates the relative sterility of this approach to the understanding of realistic pricing processes. It is not reasonable to assume that one firm alone reacts, and

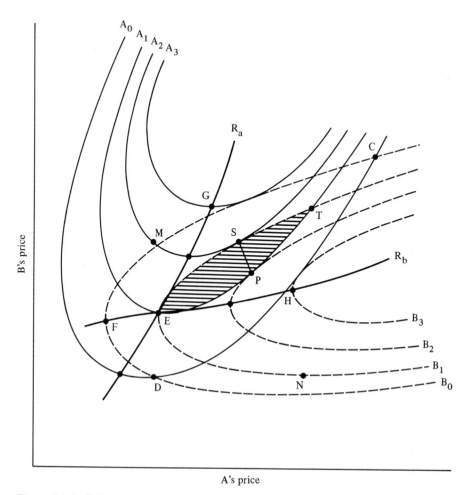

Figure 13.3. Pricing interaction between firm A and firm B.

we see that if the reactions of two firms do not yield a price that is optimum for both, there is no basis for expecting stability to be achieved. The absence of any true equilibrium point, except by chance, suggests the need for a somewhat more sophisticated approach to price determination in the kind of rivalry situation with which we are now dealing. In the next section we focus more sharply on the implications of interaction among the sellers in a given market.

Pricing Interaction

Figure 13.3 shows the isorevenue curves for firms A and B that are associated with various combinations of prices. A_0 and B_0 are the minimum revenues acceptable to A and B, respectively. A_3 is the maximum revenue that A could obtain, and B_3 is the maximum for firm B. But neither of these is a possibility, as our examination of price determination will show.

In Figure 13.3 we show the price combinations for products of firm A and firm B that will yield equal net revenues for each firm at four revenue levels. We also show the reaction curves for both A and B. At point E we have what is known as the Cournot equilibrium point. These are the prices at which the reaction curves of A and B intersect. But both firms can do better than this by moving into the shaded area bounded by *ESTP.* At point *S*, firm B is no better off than at point *E*, but A is on a higher net revenue contour. At point *P*, A is no better off than at *E*, but B will be on a higher net revenue indifference curve. Revenue for the two firms at point *T* is exactly the same as at point *E*. Therefore both firms would benefit were they able to arrive at some combination between *S* and *P*. The *SP* line is the Edgeworth contract curve, or the Pareto optimum.[6] Where between these two points the prices are set will depend on the way in which the firms interact and arrive at a pricing decision. Operation at point *S* would give B low profits and A high profits; operation at point *P* would give B high profits and A low profits. By a process of experimentation, interaction, and accomodation, A and B *could* arrive at some intermediate point on this line. Would there not, however, still be some inducement to A and B to change the price and try to drive the other firm out of existence? Let us examine the possibilities.

EXTINCTION

We shall consider first the possibility of extinction. Suppose that point *S* is arrived at by experimentation. Would it be possible for A, which is operating on a relatively high net revenue curve, to change its prices and drive B out of existence? Suppose that A moves to point *M*; that is, it lowers its price from *S* to *M*, while B's price remains the same as it was at *S*. This is now outside of B's reaction surface, for it throws B to an indifference curve below its minimum acceptable profit. Thus B would be forced out of business; it cannot accommodate itself to such a low price for firm A's product.

Is there any reason why A will not take this step and drive B out of business? Apart from legal reasons, perhaps the principal economic reason why A might not behave in this way is that B has the power to do the same thing to A. Suppose, for example, that instead of A's moving from *S* to *M*, B decides to move from *S* to *N*. Its profits would be the same as formerly, but B's price would be so low that A could not even achieve its required minimum.

Thus it is quite possible that each will avoid extinguishing the other, though there is no assurance that one may not choose to gain market control via a blitzkrieg pricing action against the other. The more limited the area of overlap between B's minimum isorevenue contour, B_1, and A's minimum isorevenue contour, A_1, the stronger the forces for extinction are.

COEXISTENCE

The area of coexistence for A and B will be that bounded by the lines that go through *CDF*. Within these bounds, both firms can earn at least the minimum necessary for survival. But movement toward some point intermediate between *S* and *P* is desirable, for B wants to be as close to B_3 as possible and A wants to be as close to A_3 as possible. Mutual accommodation can *best* be achieved on line *SP*. If the two firms make their initial movements from their reaction curves, R_a and R_b, the area to the northeast of *GEH* is that within which prices will be established. As *reaction* is resolved into *interaction*, prices will be established within the area *ESP*.

Suppose the firms settle at point *S*. Will they want to move to point *T*? B is as well off

[6] See Baumol, op. cit., p. 21, and Boulding, op. cit., pp. 595-597.

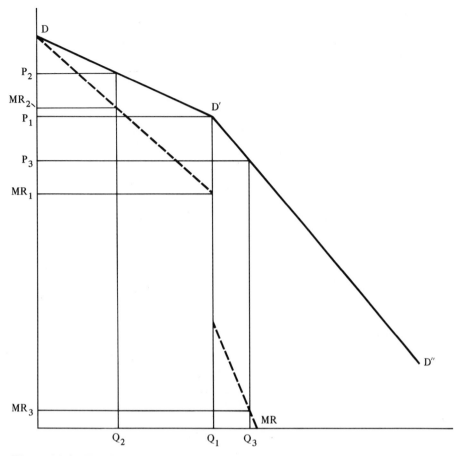

Figure 13.4. The kinked demand and marginal revenue curves of a firm operating in a market of oligopoly.

at point T as it is at point S, but A is worse off than at S, for it has dropped from its A_2 profit curve to its A_1 profit curve. Therefore A would have an incentive to manipulate its prices in order to get back to its higher profit contour. Similarly, if the two firms arrive at point P, A could move to point T with no loss, for its profits would be the same. But point T places B on a lower profit curve, and B would be induced to cut its prices in order to get to a higher profit contour. It is not impossible that the firms will settle at some point within the area ESP of Figure 13.3, never reaching line SP, for they may not be sure where SP lies. Or they may not be sure what kind of reaction a price change might evoke from the rival firm, preferring a known satisfactory net return to an unknown rate that might be higher or lower.

Suppose, however, that they do reach a point at which inducements to experiment further with price are minimal. Will this be a stable equilibrium? Not necessarily, though one approach has been developed that suggests that there may be considerable stability if firms anticipate fairly strong reactions to price changes on the part of both consumers and rivals. The device by which this is illustrated is the kinked demand curve in Figure 13.4. The prevailing price for an oligopolist is P_1, and his sales are Q_1. If he were to raise his price, a few consumers would remain loyal to him, but many would move to rival sellers. Thus a rise in price from P_1 to P_2 would result in a sizable reduction in sales, from Q_1 to Q_2. Marginal revenue would be affected particularly, rising from MR_1 to MR_2. If the quantity demanded at prices above the prevailing market price shows considerable elasticity, an oligopolist will have little incentive to raise his price.

The effect of a price reduction by the oligopolist is to evoke similar price cuts by his rivals. Rivals may not match a price increase, but they may feel forced to match or

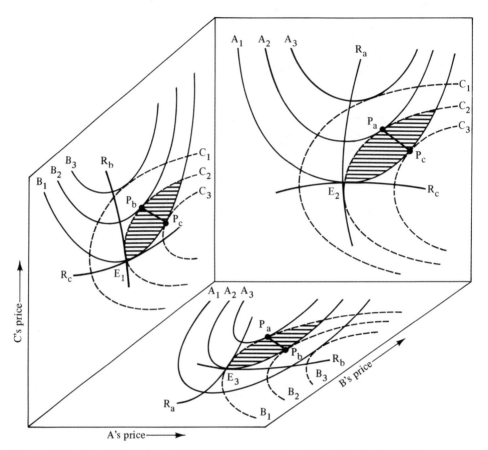

Figure 13.5. Possibilities for pricing interaction among oligopolists A, B, and C.

surpass a price decrease. Such a response is quite likely where the cost of recovering former customers is believed to be higher than the cost of retaining them. Under these circumstances, an oligopolist who cuts his price will find that he is dealing with a demand far more inelastic than that above the prevailing price. Thus his marginal revenue drops sharply. In Figure 13.4 a decrease in price from P_1 to P_3 would result in an increase in sales from Q_1 to Q_3. Although the decrease in price from P_1 to P_3 equals the increase from P_1 to P_2, the effect on quantity sold is far greater in the case of the increase than in the case of the decrease. Moreover, with the price decrease marginal revenue drops from MR_1 to MR_3, falling almost to zero.

This does not explain how the price P_1 was first established. In the preceding discussion we have suggested that this is based on a feeling out of the demand potential and of rivals' reactions until some relatively satisfactory pricing level is reached below or up to the Pareto curve. Once this is achieved Figure 13.4 implies that the firm may wish to retain that price, believing that the demand above and below that level has different elasticities that would cause the firm to be worse off were it to raise or lower its prices.

More Than Two Firms

Up to this point, our analysis has been in terms of two firms. The relationships are essentially the same when more than two firms are considered, but there is increased

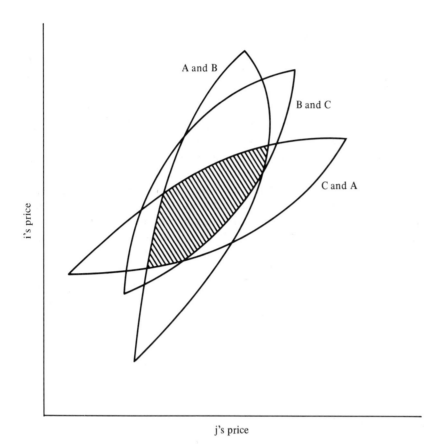

Figure 13.6. Coexistence pricing zone for oligopolists A, B, and C.

complexity arising from greater possibilities for interaction. In Figure 13.5 we extend our consideration of interaction to include three firms and show the total revenue contours for each firm in relation to each of the others. For each pair we indicate the Cournot equilibrium (E_1, E_2, and E_3) and the Pareto optimum (P_bP_c, P_aP_c, and P_aP_b). The shaded area is that which the two firms will prefer over point E. It extends beyond the Pareto optimum to indicate that there may exist other intermediate net revenue curves not shown on the graph. In Figure 13.5 we show how the shaded areas to the northeast of E could be superimposed to indicate the possibilities for absolute or conditional coexistence or for extinction to occur. Figure 13.6 shows the overlap of these three areas and indicates, by shading, their common parts, within which the pattern of prices must be established if all three firms are to survive. But this may be a very unstable situation, for any two of the firms can survive outside this area of commonality. The temptation to manipulate prices to points beyond these confines will therefore be strong.

Dynamic Equilibrium

How is stability achieved in an oligopolistic market? One method could be through overt collusion among rivals, were this a legally viable alternative. Another method could be through tacit collusion—mutual recognition by market participants that the probability of increased revenues from changing prices is less than the probability of decreased returns. Once this is mutually accepted there will be no price maneuvering. But this kind of "understanding" can be very unstable. If one party changes its mind, the stability is destroyed.

In some industries techniques for calling the signals have been developed.[7] One is to use backlog orders and inventories as short-term buffers to allow time for short-term fluctuations in pricing to "settle" before corrective action is taken by manipulating output. Another is price leadership, in which decision making is centralized in one firm. Or pricing rules can be used. If these become a part of the folklore of the industry, they can result in conformity in pricing action. These would include such practices as using a uniform markup on cost; focal point pricing (odd prices, customary prices, or price lines); or not reducing prices because of fear of "spoiling the market."

In spite of these techniques for achieving price stability in the type of market situation we have described, changes in cost or demand conditions bring strong pressures on sellers and may, where entry has been excessive and fixed costs are high, give rise to frequent and severe price wars that either drive rivals out or bring all to economic exhaustion, encouraging a return to prices that yield a level or profits more satisfactory to all parties and a calmer life for all.

It seems reasonable therefore to believe that where interaction effects are strong there is no such thing as a true equilibrium position. Rather, there would appear to be zones of mutual accommodation within which rivals array themselves in some fashion that will permit all to achieve satisfactory returns and not provoke destructive action by one or more of the participants. Within such a zone there may be moderate movements undertaken cautiously to maximize one's minimum payoff, or minimize rivals' maximum returns.[8]

Independent Action

William J. Baumol argues that most firms pay little attention in their day-to-day decisions to the actions of competitors but behave as if their own actions are independently arrived at. The reasons that he cites are the complexity of most organizations, which is not conducive to rapid action, reaction, and hence, interaction; to the use of rules-of-thumb, which, as we have noted, reduce competitive give and take; and to what he calls the "desire for the quiet life."[9] This is not to say, however, that competitors' actions are not taken into account but, rather, that a firm's pattern of policies is structured in such a way that it takes into account the broad pattern of policies likely to be evolved by rival firms.

---

[7] An excellent treatment of these and related aspects of pricing under oligopoly can be found in F. M. Scherer, *Industrial Market Structure and Economic Performance* (Chicago: Rand McNally, 1970), pp. 131-252.

[8] In our discussion we have adhered to a more nearly classical treatment of oligopolistic interaction. A more recent approach, evolving from the creative framework of von Neumann and Morgenstern is in terms of game theory, with the choice of strategy based on minimax-maximin expectations. A strategist will either maximize his own minimum expected return or minimize his rival's maximum expected return. Equilibrium, or saddle, points will be sought using pure or mixed strategies. See John von Neumann and Oskar Morgenstern, *Theory of Games and Economic Behavior*, 2d ed. (Princeton, N.J.: Princeton University Press, 1947), and R. Duncan Luce and Howard Raiffa, *Games and Decisions* (New York: Wiley, 1957). A very brief but clear treatment of the relevance of game theory to oligopolistic behavior can be found in William J. Baumol, *Economic Theory and Operations Analysis*, 2d. ed. (Englewood Cliffs, N.J.: Prentice-Hall, 1965), pp. 529-549.

[9] Baumol, *Business Behavior, Value and Growth, pp. 27-33.*

At those strategic times when a marketing firm reviews its policy structure—for example, its changing share of market and the factors associated with it—it is surely taking into account broadly, if not minutely, the impact of its rivals' behavior on its own position.

It is probably wrong to try to construct a theory of market behavior by the oligopolistic firm in terms purely of reactions to rivals' behavior. It is also unreasonable to believe that pricing policy in such situations can be fully understood apart from related market policies, particularly those that are often alternatives—such as advertising, promotion, and product differentiation. Pricing must be viewed as a part of the total marketing mix.

The principal thrust of our discussion of oligopolist pricing is the importance of *zones* of action and interaction among rival firms that establish boundaries for pricing decisions. Although this approach is not so intellectually satisfying as that provided by the marginal revenue-marginal cost calculus, it does provide a reasonable, and probably realistic, framework within which to view the "feeling out of the market" that all firms must do from time to time. We should not, however, claim too much for a theory that provides so few useful solutions to a marketing firm's actual problems. Rather, we have pinpointed the area within which management can move *one* of its chips, and shall examine other determinants of the firm's play in subsequent chapters.

PRICE DISCRIMINATION

Price discrimination is sometimes defined as the sale of a homogeneous product at two or more prices.[10] This assumes that each unit sold is identical to all other units sold and that discrimination among buyers is effected by price differentials. For example, suppose that the demand for a seller's product is shown by DD' in section (A) of Figure 13.7. Such a curve has the effect of arraying all the units demanded according to the maximum price at which each successive unit can be sold. If the seller does in fact sell each unit at that maximum price, his total revenue will be indicated by the shaded area $DD'QO$. Each buyer pays the maximum price he is willing to pay for each of the units that he purchases, and there is no consumer surplus. This kind of discrimination will result in maximum profits for the seller only if the lowest price charged equals the marginal cost of production at that level of output.

Complete discrimination of this sort is known as *first-degree discrimination.*[11] It refers to pricing in which every buyer is charged the maximum amount he is willing to pay for

---

[10] The classical treatment of price discrimination is in Joan Robinson, *Economics of Imperfect Competition* (New York: Macmillan, 1933), bk. V. Good discussions can also be found in Arthur R. Burns, *The Decline of Competition* (New York: McGraw-Hill, 1936), pp. 273-371; George J. Stigler, *The Theory of Price,* 3d ed. (New York: Macmillan, 1966), pp. 209-214; W. J. L. Ryan, *Price Theory*, (London: Macmillan, 1960), pp. 286-289. One of the most complete empirical treatments, along with an analysis of the conditions necessary to, and reasons for, price discrimination, is in the series of articles by Ralph Cassady, Jr., "Some Economic Aspects of Price Discrimination under Non-Perfect Market Conditions," *Journal of Marketing* 11 (July 1946): 7-20; "Techniques and Purposes of Price Discrimination," *Journal of Marketing* 11 (October 1946): 135-150; "Legal Aspects of Price Discrimination: Federal Law," *Journal of Marketing* 11 (January 1947): 258-272; and "Legal Aspects of Price Discrimination: State Law," *Journal of Marketing* 11 (April 1947): 377-389.

[11] The concepts of first-, second-, and third-degree price discrimination were developed by A. C. Pigou; see *The Economics of Welfare*, 4th ed. (London: Macmillan, 1960), pp. 275-289.

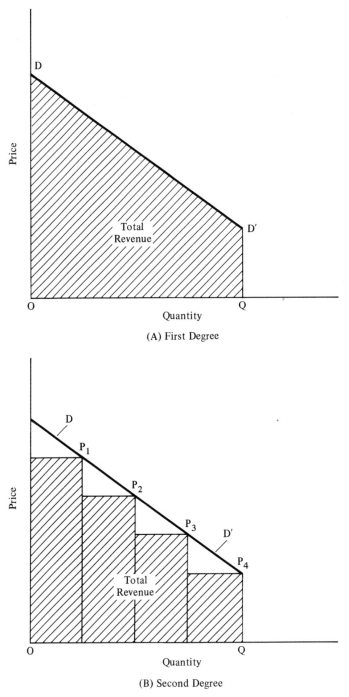

Figure 13.7. First- and second-degree price discrimination.

every unit that he purchases, obliterating all consumer surplus. Second-degree discrimination occurs when the units demanded are arrayed according to the maximum price buyers are willing to pay for each of those units, and the array is then broken into groups, with all the units of each group priced at the lowest maximum price of that group. If, for example, the seller had broken the *DD'* curve in section (A) of Figure 13.7 into four segments and charged each segment the maximum price for the marginal unit of that segment, some units would be bought at prices lower than buyers would be willing to pay. Thus some of the consumer surplus would be retained by buyers and some would be absorbed by the seller. Second-degree price discrimination is illustrated in section (B) of Figure 13.7.

Third-degree discrimination occurs when a total market can be segmented into two or more parts, with a different price in each part. Thus some units will be sold in one segment at a given price, but in another segment there will be no units sold at that particular price. Third-degree discrimination is the most common form, and our discussion will focus on this type.

One other attribute of price discrimination in practice is the fact that it often accompanies product differentiation. That is, sellers of products charge different prices to different buyers but sweeten their higher prices by making the quality, time of availability, or services surrounding the product's sale and use a little bit better. Our definition of price discrimination should therefore be modified to take into account this fairly common case. Dropping the constraint of product homogeneity, we shall say that price discrimination exists when the ratio of the selling price to the marginal cost differs for various units of similar goods and services.[12] This defines price discrimination by the inequality

$$\frac{P_a}{MC_a} \neq \frac{P_b}{MC_b}$$

in which P_a and P_b are the prices that a given seller charges customers a and b, respectively, and MC_a and MC_b are the marginal costs of production (including selling costs) for sales to customers a and b, respectively.

Conditions of Price Discrimination

Why will a seller wish to discriminate in price among his customers, and under what conditions will he be able to do so? A profit-maximizing firm will want to discriminate if it results in increased net profits. We should, however, also consider some additional cases, not uncommon in certain kinds of markets, where sellers may discriminate among customers for noneconomic reasons. Doctors, for example, frequently lower their "standard" fees for patients with low incomes. While this sometimes results in profit maximization for the physician, it may just as often spring from the physician's sense of responsibility to his clients. One might in fact view such discounts from selling prices as a "cost," that is, the cost of adherence to the Hippocratic oath. We shall focus our discussion, however, on price discrimination that rests on an economic decision.

MONOPOLY POWER

Pure price discrimination can, of course, persist as a policy only if the seller controls the supply of the product. In the absence of monopoly power, competitors would enter the

---

[12] We could strike the word *similar* and include all goods and services sold by a single seller. The differential is clearer, however, as well as more meaningful in terms of horizontal price relationships, if we restrict our analysis to "similar" goods and services.

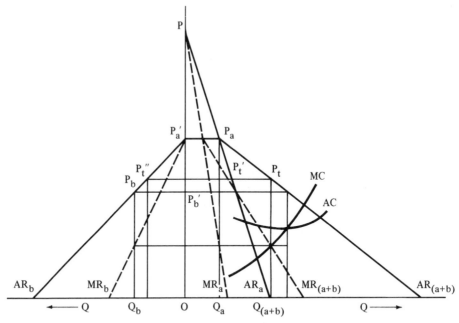

Figure 13.8. Third-degree price discrimination in markets A and B.

industry and drive the price down to the point where all would find it necessary to charge a single price that, in the long run, would cover the lowest average cost.

But less than perfect discrimination may be possible for a firm that has less than complete monopoly control over the output of the industry. This possibility occurs under monopolistic competition where a firm may be able to build up sufficient brand loyalty to engage in price discrimination. Additional possibilities for price discrimination may arise from subdifferentiation within the differentiated line, that is, by establishing various quality levels within a branded line of merchandise. The more secure one's monopoly position, the more extensive price discrimination can be and the longer it can persist without erosion from sellers of similar products. If product differentiation develops in an oligopolistic market situation, any one seller may have considerable opportunity to utilize quality and promotional differentials as vehicles for implementing some degree of price discrimination. It is essential, however, that some monopoly control exist for even a small degree of price discrimination to occur.

DISCRETE MARKETS

A second requisite for price discrimination is the separation of potential buyers into at least two markets without the possibility of their movement from one market to another. Thus the seller functions in both (or all) markets, while buyers do not have equal mobility. If this were not true, buyers who are charged the higher price would move into the market where buyers are being charged a lower price, thus destroying all possibility for discrimination.

A theater can charge adults one price and children another, because most adults cannot easily pretend to be children, though some may try (and even succeed by all criteria except age). Utilities can charge business firms and housholds different rates, since each can be classified according to its principal function and one cannot shift into the other market. Obstetricians can charge students one fee for a birth and nonstudents another with confidence that students will not resell the service they obtain to nonstudents at a rate higher than that which students were required to pay. The telephone company charges less for long-distance calls at night than during the day. Though some frugal souls will defer their call till nighttime, most business calls must be made during the daytime. Most such customers are not likely to shift to the nighttime market.

Preferably total, but at least partial, separation of markets must be possible for a seller to discriminate in price successfully. Without this, either buyers shift into the lower-priced market or buyers in such markets find it worthwhile to buy at low prices and resell to customers who would otherwise have patronized the high-priced market.

DIFFERENCES IN DEMAND ELASTICITIES

In the two or more markets that provide the setting for price discrimination, the demand elasticities must be different for price discrimination to be worthwhile from the seller's point of view. If the demands are the same in two markets, the most profitable price in one will be the same as the most prifitable price in the other. This assumes, of course, that the seller's costs are the same in the two markets, or that marginal costs in the two do not differ. If marginal cost differs among different markets, price discrimination exists if there is *not* a difference in prices charged in the two markets, for without price differences equality in the price/marginal cost relationships in the two markets cannot be achieved.[13]

Price Determination with Discrimination

We turn now to the question of how prices are established under conditions that make discrimination possible.

DEMAND DIFFERENCES IN TWO MARKETS

In Figure 13.8 we show AR_a, the demand in market A; AR_b, the demand in market B; and $AR_{(a+b)}$, the sum of these two demands. Note that the left section of the graph, where we show market B's demand, is reversed, with quantity increasing from zero as we move to the left. $MR_{(a+b)}$ is the sum of the marginal revenues, MR_a and MR_b. The monopoly firm that is selling in these two markets will maximize its profits by producing that quantity at which its marginal cost equals its marginal revenue. This will be $Q_{(a+b)}$. Without price discrimination in the two markets, the price in each will be P_t (which is equal to P_t' in market A and P_t'' in market B).

If, however, the monopolist discriminates in price, he will do so by equating marginal cost at output level $Q_{(a+b)}$ to the marginal revenue in each of the two markets. This is accomplished in market A at the quantity level Q_a and in market B at the quantity level Q_b. Thus in market A the selling price will be P_a and in market B it will be P_b. Total

---

[13] This is the basis for the stipulation under the Robinson–Patman Act that price differences related to differences in costs of producing or selling a product to different buyers are not evidence of price discrimination. The law does not, however, specify marginal cost, and it is this alone that could serve as a sound theoretical basis for price differentials related to cost.

revenue from market A will be $P_a P_a'$ OQ_a, and in market B, $P_b P_b'$ OQ_b. Total profit with discrimination will be greater than total profit without discrimination only if the elasticity of demand between points P_t' and P_a in market A is less than the elasticity of demand between points P_t'' and P_b in market B. If price is increased in the market in which the demand is more inelastic and is decreased in that in which the demand is more elastic, total revenue increases. Since cost per unit is the same, profits will be higher with discrimination than without.[14]

DISCRIMINATION AS A REQUISITE TO SALES

Figure 13.9 shows a different case from that in Figure 13.8. The demand in market A differs in amount and elasticity from that in market B, but the monopolist has costs of production, shown in section (C), that cannot be recovered at any level of output by treating markets A and B as a single market with a single price. Under these circumstances, price discrimination makes it possible for the monopolist to increase his total revenue to the point where it will exceed costs of production. Following the same principle as in the previous case, he would equate marginal revenue in each market with marginal cost at that point where marginal cost equals marginal revenue in the two markets combined. The price in market B would be P_b, and in market A it would be P_a. The average price of the seller would be P', which is $[(OP_a)(OQ_a) + (OP_b)(OQ_b)]/(OQ_t)$ and in this case is higher than the average cost of production at output level OQ_t. Thus price discrimination would make it possible for the firm to produce; without price discrimination the firm could not exist.

Use of price discrimination for the purposes described here has the net effect of utilizing the market system to impose a tax on those buyers whose demnnd is more inelastic in order to subsidize those whose demand is more elastic. The consequences of

---

[14] These relationships can be shown algebraically.

$$R = P_a Q_a + P_b Q_b - CQ_t$$

in which R is total profit; P_a and P_b are the unit price in markets A and B, respectively; Q_a and Q_b are quantities sold in A and B, respectively; C is average cost; and Q_t is the sum of Q_a and Q_b, or total quantity sold. When total profit is maximized,

$$\frac{\Delta(P_a Q_a)}{\Delta Q_a} = \frac{\Delta(P_b Q_b)}{\Delta Q_b} = \frac{\Delta(CQ_t)}{\Delta Q_t}$$

This means, of course, that $MR_a = MR_b = MR_t = MC$, where MR_a, MR_b, and MR_t are marginal revenue in market A, market B, and both markets combined, respectively, and MC is the marginal cost for the firm.
Since

$$MR_a = P_a\left(1 - \frac{1}{e_a}\right) \quad \text{and} \quad MR_b = P_b\left(1 - \frac{1}{e_b}\right)$$

in which e_a and e_b are elasticities of demand in markets A and B, respectively, then

$$P_a\left(1 - \frac{1}{e_a}\right) = P_b\left(1 - \frac{1}{e_b}\right)$$

Therefore,

$$\frac{P_a}{P_b} = \frac{1 - (1/e_b)}{1 - (1/e_a)}$$

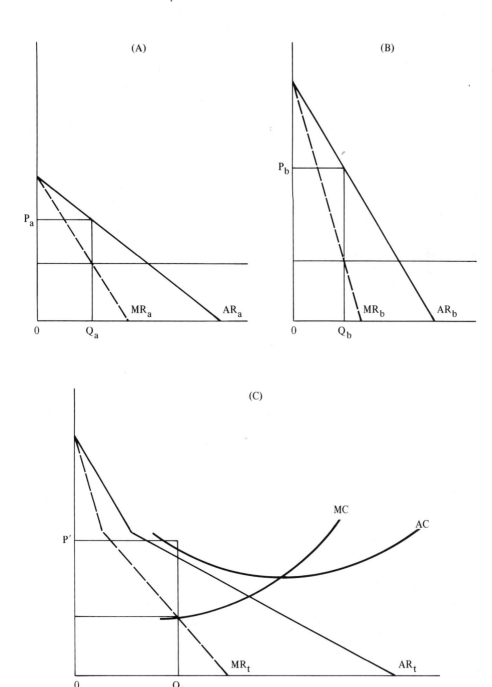

Figure 13.9. Price determination where sales would be zero without discrimination.

this are of highly dubious value on economic grounds, for more resources go into this industry than would otherwise be the case, and the impact is felt on other industries to whom these resources would otherwise be cheaper or whose clientele have been absorbed by this substitute offering under price discrimination. The only ground on which this could be justified would have to be that the social benefit from the production of this good exceeds the sum of its costs, including social costs.

PRICE DIFFERENTIALS WITHOUT DISCRIMINATION

If a firm is able to sell in one market at a price that is lower than in another market, it can employ price differentials without discrimination so long as the price in each market bears a stable relation to the marginal cost in each market. If the demand in each market is the same, cost differentials necessitate price differentials if discrimination is to be avoided. This is the basis on which buyers of large quantities are often given lower unit prices than buyers of small quantities. Functional discounts to wholesalers related to the value of functions that they perform in the marketing channel may, if utilized consistently for all buyers, be evidence of nondiscrimination. Where differences in costs exist, therefore, it is necessary that price differentials be employed if price discrimination is to be avoided. It is possible, however, for such markets to exhibit discriminatory pricing if the differentials are not in equal ratio to differentials in marginal cost The Robinson-Patman Act, which requires that price differences be related to cost differentials, errs in that it fails to designate marginal cost rather than full cost as the basis for such a determination.

Techniques of Discrimination

It is not difficult to envision possibilities for price discrimination to exist where markets are separated physically so that sellers are free to take advantage of differences in the structure of demand in the separate markets in order to increase revenue and profits. But discrimination is more likely to occur in company with some kind of product differentiation that separates buyers in a given market into discrete groups, each of which responds to some type of product or service difference.

MARKET SEGMENTATION AND PRICE DISCRIMINATION

Market segmentation is in part an attempt to demarcate submarkets in which differentials can be employed for the purpose of achieving the firm's objectives with respect to profits, sales, return on investment, or other goals. Policy differentiation may be realized through the adaptation of the product's physical attributes to differences in demand in the two markets, or it may concern service differentials. Price is often an important medium for effecting differentiation between markets, and if it is unrelated to differentials in measurable marginal costs, it is discriminatory. Although monopolistic competition may lead in the long run to an equilibrium that eliminates profits, it is not impossible for a highly flexible set of policies directed toward the sale of a continually modified product and cluster of services to offer a means of maximizing long-run profits. Price discrimination may be one of the methods by which this is accomplished.

Examples of this form of price discrimination are common in the markets in which such products as automobiles, household appliances, furniture, books, clothing, drugs, and cosmetics are sold. Not all price differences within a line of products are examples of price discrimination, of course, for some are related to differences in cost. But where they are demand based, reflecting differences in demand elasticity in various market segments, they are a means of price discrimination. Cadillacs, Buicks, Oldsmobiles, Pontiacs, and Chevrolets array themselves along a price spectrum with much overlapping. (See Figure 13.10.) Within each of these makes there is a wide range of prices. While each division of General Motors may be expected to realize a given volume of sales or a specified return on investment, all are not necessarily equally profitable, and certainly within a single line

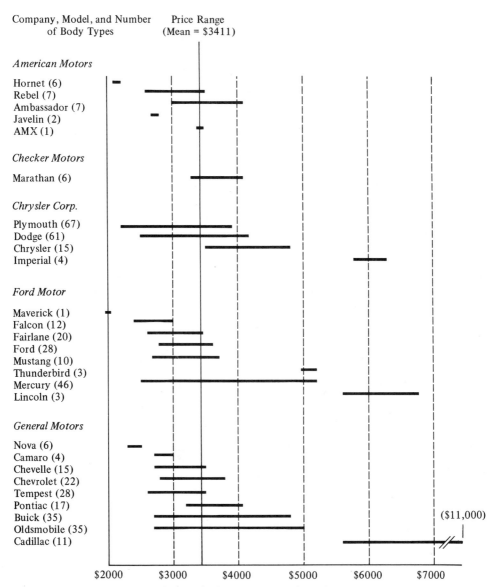

Figure 13.10. The range of suggested retail prices for 1970 U.S. passenger cars. The suggested retail price is for cars with standard equipment and includes federal excise taxes and dealer preparation and conditioning charges. Transportation charges, state or local taxes, finance charges, and optional equipment are extra. Source: "1970 Passenger Car Prices, Weights and Body Types," *Automotive Industries* 142 (March 15, 1970): 101-102.

not all show equal returns in either sales or profits. So long as some buyers respond to price changes among makes and models in a fashion different from the response of other customers, price discrimination can accompany product differentiation.

CYCLICAL AND SEASONAL PRICE DISCRIMINATION

Another form of product or service differentiation that provides a vehicle for the achievement of price discrimination is the timing of purchases. Sellers of style merchandise frequently place a higher price on their merchandise at the beginning of the season. Buyers who purchase at the close of the season may receive sizable discounts from the beginning-of-season price. A swimsuit bought in August is not identical to one bought in June in terms of current utility and the timeliness of its style. If the ratio of the sale price to marginal cost differs from that of merchandise sold at the beginning of the season, price discrimination has been effected through the segmentation of customers into early- and late-season buyers.

Similar examples of this kind of pricing can be observed in first-run versus later-run movies and hardback versus paperback editions of books. Not totally different in charcter is the new-product pricing policy that is geared to skimming, with successive price reductions taken after the maximum possible return from a higher price has been realized. By scooting down his demand curve over time, such a seller maximizes total revenue by segmenting his clientele on the basis of the timing of their acquisition in the product's history.

Social Implications of Price Discrimination

Price discrimination is not possible without some degree of monopoly control. Discrimination could not persist unless there were restrictions on freedom of entry into the industry. In this sense, therefore, price discrimination is a symptom of monopolistic control. On the other hand, price discrimination can sometimes result in greater output than under a one-price monopoly policy, resulting in more efficient use of resources. But this is not always true, and the opposite can be true, as, for example, with the use of a basing-point system of pricing.

Since price discrimination results in a redistribution of income, the effect of this on social welfare must be made on the basis of value judgments. Unsystematic price discrimination *can* be used to increase competition by forcing down monopoly prices in one market segment. But systematic price discrimination is more likely to reflect, and perhaps reinforce, market power.[15]

---

[15] Scherer, op. cit., p. 272.

14

Pricing in the Multiproduct Marketing Firm

Bring me bread
Bring me butter
Bring me cheese
And bring me jam
Bring me milk
And bring me chicken
Bring me eggs
And a little ham.[*]

—Gertrude Stein

It is the purpose of this chapter to concentrate on those aspects of price determination that are peculiar to, or made most clearly apparent in, the behavior of the marketing firm, that is, the firm whose primary activities center around the buying and selling of goods, the maintenance of stocks, and the physical transfer of those goods without changing their physical form. Thus we shall focus on the formulation of pricing policy within the retail and wholesale firm.

From the buyer's point of view, the price is the total amount he pays for a unit of goods and services. From the viewpoint of the marketing firm, however, an additional and more critical concept of price would be the dollar margin over and above the cost of merchandise, an amount comparable to the value added by a processor. This portion of total price imputed to the marketing firm is the payment received by the firm for the services it renders. In this sense, it is the "price" that the buyer pays for the output of the marketing firm. It equals the amount the firm pays to the owners of the resources that it uses. In a retail firm, for example, it is the difference between the selling price to the consumer and the cost of goods sold. The latter includes invoice cost plus inward transportation less any discounts applicable to the store's invoice cost, inlcuding advertising and promotional allowances. This is the same as the gross margin of the marketing firm.[1]

It is customary in retailing and wholesaling to express the gross margin as a percentage—usually a percentage of net sales and occasionally a percentage of cost of goods sold. Although there are many occasions when such relative values are useful, we shall focus on the margin measured in dollars (or other monetary units). Table 14.1 shows the wide range in gross margins in both dollars and percentages among various product types sold in one supermarket chain.

---

[1]The gross margin is computed by subtracting *all* merchandise costs from net sales and includes the the deduction of cash discounts.

Table 14.1 Weekly Sales per Store, Average Unit Selling Price, and Average Margin of 52 Selected Products Sold by Six Colonial Stores during Eight Weeks of 1963

Product	Weekly Sales		Unit Selling Price in Cents	Gross Margin	
	Units	Dollars		Total Dollars	As Percentage of Sales
Total store[a]	118,283	$44,379.79	37.5¢	$8,865.30	20.0%
Baby food (strained vegetables)	264	27.16	10.2	3.00	11.0
Baking powder	45	8.23	18.2	2.15	26.1
Beer	981	573.52	58.4	68.75	12.0
Cake mix (white)	46	16.62	36.1	2.91	17.5
Candy	1,584	428.45	27.0	116.48	27.2
Catsup	427	105.35	24.6	29.12	27.6
Cereals (cold)	1,239	381.40	30.7	72.65	19.0
Cereals (hot)	405	84.41	20.8	19.79	23.4
Cigarettes	1,184	2,255.79	191.0	130.85	5.8
Coffee (regular)	899	631.98	70.2	65.23	10.3
Cooking utensils	51	30.34	59.4	9.94	32.8
Dog food	1,505	305.80	20.3	64.52	21.1
Eggs	1,729	931.65	53.8	130.44	14.0
Floor wax	123	96.78	78.6	29.43	30.4
Flour (family)	514	298.41	58.0	35.97	12.1
Gelatin	736	84.53	11.4	11.68	13.8
Green beans (canned)	479	98.48	20.5	27.11	27.5
Green beans (frozen)	111	30.88	27.8	9.11	29.5
Ice cream	361	213.67	59.1	51.24	24.0
Laundry detergent (package)	989	492.41	49.7	60.52	12.3
Light bulbs	265	70.06	26.4	33.88	48.4
Luncheon meats (canned)	147	64.90	44.1	12.14	18.7
Macaroni	235	35.32	15.0	8.18	23.2
Magazines & books	731	240.89	32.9	52.01	21.6
Meat	13,689	10,689.96	78.1	1,860.34	17.4
Meat dinners (frozen)	247	120.78	48.9	32.95	27.3
Milk	2,215	846.77	38.2	76.25	9.0
Milk (canned)	2,247	292.57	13.0	32.52	11.1
Orange juice (canned)	202	55.62	27.5	16.66	30.0
Orange juice (frozen)	918	282.37	30.7	84.89	30.1
Oven cleaners	17	11.49	67.6	5.77	50.2
Paper towels	677	203.20	30.0	43.99	21.5
Peaches (canned)	533	137.22	25.7	34.77	25.3
Peaches (frozen)	1	0.15	15.5	0.03	20.0
Peanut butter	312	139.61	44.7	32.43	23.2
Peas (canned)	917	182.80	19.9	38.96	21.3
Peas (frozen)	135	47.16	34.9	12.88	27.3
Pickles	473	157.47	33.2	46.59	29.6
Pies (fruit)	394	145.91	37.0	40.88	28.0
Potato chips	694	236.57	34.1	57.53	24.3

Table 14.1 (Continued)

Product	Weekly Sales		Unit Selling Price in Cents	Gross Margin	
	Units	Dollars		Total Dollars	As Percentage of Sales
Produce, fresh	13,488	3,018,38	22.4	856.68	28.4
Salad dressings	382	133.01	34.8	30.81	23.2
Salt	281	32.63	11.6	7.04	21.6
Shampoos	183	121.95	66.6	48.90	40.0
Soaps, hand & facial	1,339	219.08	16.3	36.06	16.5
Soft drinks	1,169	610,21	52.2	111.53	18.3
Soup (canned)	2,556	418.75	16.3	67.60	16.1
Sugar (granulated)	871	476.27	54.6	44.60	9.4
Toothpaste	463	223.87	48.3	70.22	31.3
Tooth brushes	80	25.52	31.9	14.67	57.5
Tuna fish (canned)	230	76.20	33.1	17.02	22.3
Vitamins	13	14.96	115.0	6.61	44.1

[a]Detail does not add to total, since the detail covers only 52 products while the total is based on 577 products.

Source: Progressive Grocer, *Colonial Study* (New York: Progressive Grocer, [1964]), pp. C-21-C-40.

A second attribute of price in the marketing firm is the character of the unit of sale. A retail transaction often involves the transfer of title to more than one good and embraces a cluster of associated retailing services. It is helpful, therefore, to distinguish among three kinds of retail margins when discussing the price of retailing: the margin on the smallest possible transaction, that is, on the price of one unit of a physically identifiable item; the aggregate margin on a cluster of transactions, that is, on a "market basket" of physically identifiable items; and the aggregate margin that the retail firm receives from all transactions with all customers, that is, the firm's total gross margin.[2] If the objective of the firm is the maximization of total profit, the aggregate margin and aggregate costs will become the focus of analysis. Hence, optimum behavior with respect to item margins and "market basket" margins will depend on the relationship of these to aggregate gross margin. The unit of transaction from the viewpoint of both consumer and retailer is usually the market basket rather than a single physical component of that basket. The consumer is interested in the total price of his market basket. The retailer, on the other hand, is interested in the gross margin on each basket times the number of market baskets sold, or the store's total gross margin. It is the latter that constitutes the store's sales revenue, out of which it must pay fixed and variable operating costs. In our analysis we shall use the market basket as our point of departure and examine the relationship between the size and composition of the basket and the margins on specific components of the basket, as well as the role of item prices in determining the number of market baskets sold. Thus the concept of unit price in retailing (or wholesaling) is quite different

---

[2]It is this feature of retailing that was not incorporated in one of the best of the early theoretical studies of retail pricing. See Arthur Smithies, "The Theory of Value Applied to Retail Selling," *Review of Economic Studies* 6 (June 1939): 215-221. The multiproduct nature of retailing was, however, considered in John F. Due, "A Theory of Retail Price Determination," *Southern Economic Journal* 7 (January 1941): 380-397.

from that employed in traditional price theory, for the composition of the "item" sold—that is, the market basket—may differ for every customer.

We shall begin our analysis with a consideration of the pricing process in the retail supermarket, where the typical transaction involves the purchase of a market basket of goods and the market structure is generally oligopolistic. Much of what we can say about supermarket pricing is applicable to other types of retail firms, and we shall point out similarities and differences between supermarket pricing and that in certain other types of retail institutions. Finally, we shall consider how our analysis of pricing in the marketing firm would be modified were we to apply it to the merchant wholesaler, who is also handling a wide range of goods but whose customers are business firms rather than ultimate consumers.

ELEMENTS OF A THEORY OF RETAIL PRICE DETERMINATION: THE SUPERMARKET CASE[3]

Characteristics of Retailing That Influence Pricing

Many of the important characteristics of the retail firm that distinguish it from other firms are relevant to its pricing policies and practices.

THE STRUCTURE OF COSTS

A large percentage of retail supermarket costs are joint costs not allocable to a particular physical item or transaction. The most important variable cost of the retail store is the cost of goods sold. This includes invoice cost, plus inward transportation, less any discounts from the invoice price, less advertising allowances granted by the manufacturer for the promotion of particular items. This net cost figure is the one that the retail firm can allocate with least error to a specific transaction.[4]

It is extremely difficult to allocate other costs of retailing on an item or market basket basis. Only in special cases is it possible to allocate wages and salaries to particular transactions. Space costs can be more precisely established, but even these are complicated by differences in the relative values of different portions of the total space controlled by the firm. The cost of investment in, and maintenance of, inventory may be determined by products, but less reasonably so by transactions. Advertising and certain other selling costs, such as displays, have limited allocability. The cost of advertising space or time—that is, the cost of resources employed within space or time—can often be assigned to a specific commodity or group of commodities, but it can seldom be allocated

---

[3] One of the best discussions of supermarket pricing, and one on which we have relied heavily in the development of this presentation, is Bob R. Holdren, *The Structure of a Retail Market and the Market Behavior of Retail Units* (Englewood Cliffs, N.J.: Prentice-Hall, 1960). A history of theories of retail price determination is in Donald L. Shawver, *The Development of Theories of Retail Price Determination in England and the United States,* Illinois Studies in the Social Sciences, vol. XXXIX (Urbana: University of Illinois Press, 1956).

[4] We consider here only explicit cost without taking into account opportunity costs. For instance, by stocking item A a store may forgo revenue from item B. If the net revenue from item B is greater than that from item A, the difference could be considered an opportunity cost imputable to item A. This complication will not be introduced in this analysis in connection with costs. It will, however, enter the analysis via the market basket approach to pricing, which we shall utilize. We shall also employ the alternative cost concept more directly when we introduce the approach of Richard H. Coase and Richard H. Holton (see pp. 384-390).

to specific transactions. This is true even for costs related to the advertising of specific commodities, for the effects of advertising are often institutional in nature, spilling over into sales of other goods and services of the firm and sometimes of the industry. Except for the highly specialized retail firm, and often one combining traditional "retailing" with some kind of form production—for example, tailoring—it is very difficult to allocate most of the costs of retail operation to a particular product or a particular transaction.

Nevertheless, some significant efforts have been made by Robert D. Buzzell and others[5] to show that retail operating costs can be allocated to specific products. Costs for which they have developed logical bases for allocation include labor for unloading, price marking, shelving, and checkout; supplies for wrapping and bagging; warehousing and transportation; trading stamps; insurance and taxes on inventory; and imputed interest on inventory. Deduction of these additional costs from an item's gross margin yields "direct product profit" (DPP). One example that they cite for a food chain in 1961 shows that the firm's gross margin of 21.28 percent is reduced to a direct product profit of 12.04 percent through the estimation and elimination of these additional product costs.[6] Much of this exploratory study is devoted to the estimation of these "product costs." Confronted with the problem of estimation, the authors formulate the "accuracy trade-off principle," by which an attempt is made to balance off the value of a higher degree of accuracy in arriving at estimates against the cost of the higher degree of accuracy.[7]

In the analysis that follows we shall take the position that the one variable cost of retailing that can be established with greatest precision is the cost of the merchandise. It is likely that this will bear a fairly stable relationship to sales within rather wide sales volume limits, dropping to lower percentage levels only when quantity discounts or bargaining power become important enough to influence the average purchase price for several items. We shall assume that costs other than the cost of goods sold are largely fixed in the short run. Thus store margins rather than item margins become the focus of attention. The concept of a "market basket margin" becomes a device for converting store margins into meaningful transaction units.

THE DEMAND FOR RETAILING SERVICES

The demand for output of the retail firm is the demand for a market basket of goods and services. A customer buys not goods alone but goods with their associated retailing services. There is considerable variability possible in the purchases of different customers. This may be in the size of the total basket as well as in the components of the basket. Seldom does a supermarket sell one unit of merchandise to a customer, and even when it does the transaction involves the melding of physical good and physical and nonphysical services necessary to complete the transaction. Usually the consumer purchases a variety of goods and services. The retailer's pricing objective will be, therefore, to try to achieve a

---

[5] Robert D. Buzzell, Walter J. Salmon, and Richard F. Vancil, *Product Profitability Measurement and Merchandising Decisions* (Boston: Harvard University, Graduate School of Business Administration, Division of Research, 1965). See also the several studies by McKinsey in which methods of cost allocation were developed for different types of marketing institutions and products. For example, *The McKinsey Meat Study*, Paper presented at the Management Clinic of the National Association of Food Chains and the American Meat Institute, Hollywood Beach, Florida, February 24, 1964; *McKinsey-Lever Brothers Study* (New York: Lever Brothers, 1964); *McKinsey-General Foods Study* (White Plains, N.Y.: General Foods, 1963).

[6] Ibid., p. 36.

[7] Ibid., pp. 38-40.

set of prices that, in combination, will maximize his gross margin from all customers, each of whom has his own cluster of purchases. He must be mindful that consumers are more sensitive to the prices of some goods and services than to those of others and that his ability to attract patronage to one item may affect his ability to obtain patronage for another. Further, he is aware that price is only one of several variables that he can control in order to influence quantity purchased. This multiproduct, multiservice aspect of retailing demand is another reason for emphasis on store margins rather than item margins. If the retailer can achieve the proper combination of selling prices, his total revenue will be optimized, and the difference between it and variable costs will be maximized in the short run.

COMPETITIVE STRUCTURE

In addition to the structure of costs and of demand, the retail firm must make its decisions and see them exercised subject to the possibilities and constraints of the market environment. If there are large numbers of firms selling similar items and offering similar retailing services, the area of discretion becomes highly limited. If there are not large numbers of similar firms but there is freedom of entry, the range of choice is similarly restricted. In the absence of these conditions, pricing discretion is widened, and this will be reflected in both the level and the diversity of pricing practices.

But whatever the range of competitive structure, every retail store has an opportunity to achieve differentiation with respect to such things as its location, which in the narrowest sense is unique; its services; its promotional efforts and techniques; and the quantity, quality, and diversity of its stock. Choices among these will therefore have a bearing on pricing policies and practices.

The Supermarket Pricing Problem

THE ROLE OF GROSS MARGIN

If we assume that the retail firm's objective is maximization of profits, in the long run it will pursue a pricing policy that will maximize the difference between its total net revenue and its total costs. In the short run, however, its policy will be structured to maximize the difference between total net revenue and total variable costs. If the firm believes that it will not be able to cover its variable costs, it will be unwilling to incur them. But it will seek to do more than merely cover variable costs. It will also wish to maximize the difference between those costs and net sales revenue.

It is helpful to visualize the retailer's gross margin as an aggregate of margins at three successive levels. The gross margin to be maxmized is the dollar gross margin of the firm. Because most retail customers buy more than a single item from the firm, the aggregate gross margin is a summation of the gross margins on all market baskets. But the margin of each basket is a summation of the margins on the individual items in the basket. Let G represent the aggregate gross margin for the retail firm, g_b the gross margin on the market basket, and g_i the gross margin on the individual item in the basket. There are m market baskets sold and n items in each basket. The following identities obtain:

$$g_b = \sum_{i=1}^{n} g_i \quad \text{and} \quad G = \sum_{i=1}^{m} g_b$$

If some items in the basket are duplicates, the gross margin on the market basket could also be considered as the sum of the gross margin on each unique item, i', weighted by the quantity of each, q', with the total number of unique items in the basket represented by n'.

$$g_b = \sum_{i'=1}^{n'} (g_{i'} \, q_{i'})$$

SALES AS A FUNCTION OF PRICE AND NONPRICE VARIABLES

The quantity of any one item that is sold is a function of both price and nonprice variables, including price and nonprice characteristics of other items available in the store. Thus how many pounds of bacon a supermarket sells is a function not only of the price of bacon but also of the price of other goods in the store, of the variety and quality of the other merchandise offerings, and of the various promotional and service aspects of the store's operation. In order to focus attention on the role of prices in consumer choice, we shall lump all the nonprice factors that influence purchases of a given item into a single variable, which we shall designate s_i. The price of a particular item will be represented by p_i, and the quantities of various items purchased by q_i. Choices will be made from among the n items available in the store:

$$q_1 = f(p_1, p_2, p_3, \ldots, p_n, s_1, s_2, s_3, \ldots, s_n)$$
$$q_2 = f(p_1, p_2, p_3, \ldots, p_n, s_1, s_2, s_3, \ldots, s_n)$$
$$q_3 = f(p_1, p_2, p_3, \ldots, p_n, s_1, s_2, s_3, \ldots, s_n)$$

$$\vdots$$

$$q_n = f(p_1, p_2, p_3, \ldots, p_n, s_1, s_2, s_3, \ldots, s_n)$$

Let us for the moment consider only the role of price variability in the retailer's decisions, reserving nonprice factors for later consideration. The management will attempt to set the prices of various items in the store in such a way that the *combination* will attract, from the total potential patronage, that quantity and quality of patronage which will maximize the firm's gross margin. This brings us to the center of the retailer's pricing problem.

Supermarket Pricing Procedures

What the retailer would like to do is to cut the price (from his point of view, the margin) on those items that will attract to his store patronage that will result in the largest possible gross margin for the entire store. Price reductions on some items will draw more patronage than those on other items. But patronage alone is not enough; the patronage must also have the desired effect on gross margins. Let us consider these dual aspects of the supermarket pricing problem. We shall first introduce certain concepts basic to our analysis and then consider possible sales and net revenue effects of alternative pricing decisions.

BASIC CONCEPTS

An important measure of achievement of the retail firm is the volume of sales. A change in the dollar volume of sales resulting from a change in any other variable is called a *sales effect*. A sales effect can result from internal or external causes—for example, from a change in the firm's policies, such as advertising, location, merchandise mix, or services; from a change in consumers' preferences or buying decisions; or from a change in competitors' actions. In this discussion, we shall focus first on the sales effect of price changes in the retail supermarket. If a change in price causes the dollar volume of sales to rise, there is a positive sales effect. A positive sales effect can result from either an increase or a decrease in the unit price of the product, and we shall consider on which products price decreases would appear appropriate and on which products increases would be preferred. Also, one often finds that a positive change in a merchandising or selling practice is associated with a positive sales effect. This would tend to be true, for example, with most advertising expenditures if they are employed effectively.

Since a store's sales equal consumer expenditures in the store,[8] the *sales effect* is the same as the *consumer expenditure effect*. Thus we distinguish between two sources of the sales effect. When a supermarket reduces the price of one or more items, its sales may increase (1) because consumers, without spending more in total, transfer their patronage, or expenditures, from some other store to the supermarket that has reduced its price(s), and/or (2) because consumers react to reduced prices by increasing the total amount that they budget and spend for all goods and services, either by saving less or by dissaving. The first of these reactions is the *transferred expenditure effect*, and the second is the *budgeted expenditure effect*.[9] The difference is whether the increased (or deceased) sales arise from consumers' spending more in all stores or from their merely spending more of a fixed total in one store.

It is the transferred expenditure effect that is most critical to the management of the retail supermarket, for the ability of one or all supermarkets to increase consumers' total spending is extremely limited, while a single firm can, through proper manipulation of its price structure, attract patronage from competing firms and must, because of the competitive structure of the market in which it sells, react to similar tactics on the part of competing firms. Throughout this discussion we shall therefore assume that the aggregate budgets of consumers do not vary—that is, that the budgeted expenditure effect is zero—but that consumers will sometimes shift their patronage from store to store in response to price changes—that is, that the transferred expenditure effect can be greater than zero.

One of the possible effects of a price reduction is that the increase in sales volume that results may occur in products other than those whose price was reduced. The prices of some products have an unusually high transferred expenditure effect, not only with respect to their own sales but also with respect to sales of other goods. Such products are

---

[8] Consumer expenditures are payments for goods and services to be used by the purchaser. They do not include sales taxes collected by the retail store at the time of purchase.

[9] We are indebted to Bob R. Holdren for the terms *transfer effect* and *budget effect*, from which our concepts *transferred expenditure effect* and *budgeted expenditure effect* are derived. The reason for the transformation of Holdren's terminology is to make clear the fact that we are referring to dollar sales (or expenditures) rather than to quantities sold (or purchased). Since the term *budget effect* has often been used in indifference analysis to refer to the change in number of units of a good that are purchased, or to the change in number of real units of "all other goods" purchased, there is some advantage in not using the term *budget effect* to refer to dollar volume. Where physical quantities are the unit of measurement, the terms *transferred quantity effect* and *budgeted quantity effect* would be appropriate. These are not particularly useful in the analysis presented here, however, for price changes of one good may be used to affect sales of other goods that are physically dissimilar. In this case, the adding up of the total number of units sold before and after the price change took place can be quite meaningless. See Holdren, op. cit., p. 122.

known as *price leaders*; that is, their prices can be used to attract patronage to the retail store for both price-reduced and other goods. If products are used as price leaders by setting their price at a level that fails to cover unit variable cost, they are known as *loss leaders*.

The effect of price policy on sales is, however, less important than its effect on the total net contribution of sales to the firm's fixed costs. *Net revenue* is the contribution of sales to the firm's fixed costs and is the amount by which net sales exceed the firm's variable costs. The net revenue of a particular item is the excess of its revenue over its variable costs. For many products net revenue equals gross margin, for often the only variable cost is the cost of merchandise sold. If, however, any of the firm's operating costs can be imputed directly to particular items of merchandise, they, too, become a part of the variable costs of such items and should be included in the calculation of net revenue. The *net revenue effect* of a change in price is the change in the firm's total net revenue associated with a change in price. Such an effect may arise from changes in the volume of sales of either leader or nonleader items.

THE RELATIONSHIP OF PRICE TO SALES AND NET REVENUE

Figure 14.1 indicates the relationships among the principal determinants of the firm's total sales and its net revenue and the role of price in these relationships. Consumers' total expenditures are specified by consumer budgets, and the sales of a given firm, S, are equal to consumption expenditures in the firm, E_a.

$$E_a \equiv S$$

Expenditures are a product of unit retail price and quantity purchased. We shall divide total sales into products that are used as price leaders, X, and all other products, Y. These "other" goods comprise two groups: (1) those that are most effective as followers because the volume sold is highly sensitive to the retail prices of leader items, and (2) those that are neither good leaders nor good followers and whose sales display a relatively neutral reaction to the prices of other items in the store. Sales of Y goods are the product of the unit price of Y, p_y, and the quantity of Y that is sold, q_y,

$$S_y = p_y \, q_y$$

and similarly for S_x. Total sales are the sum of the sales of X and of Y:

$$S_t = S_x + S_y$$

The net revenue of the Y group of items, R_y, equals its sales minus the total variable costs of the Y items, C_y:

$$R_y = S_y - C_y$$

A similar calculation would establish the net revenue of leader items. The total net revenue of all items, R_t, is the sum of the net contributions of the leader and nonleader items:

$$R_t = R_x + R_y$$

Since the firm's total variable costs, C_t, are the sum of the variable costs of leader and nonleader items,

$$C_t = C_x + C_y$$

The firm's total net revenue is also the difference between total sales and total variable costs:

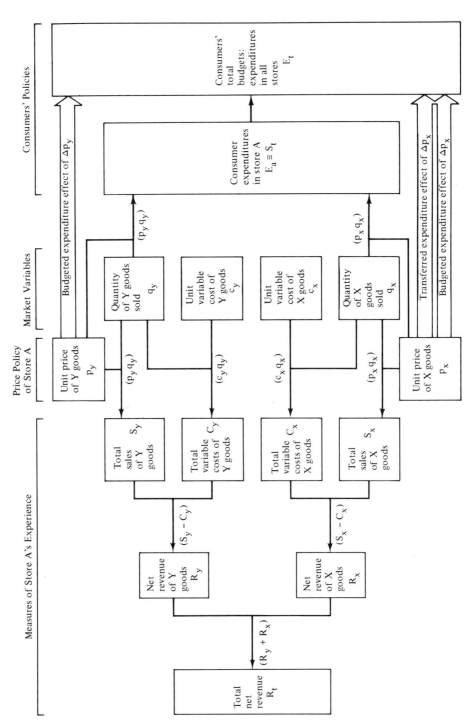

Figure 14.1. The relationship between pricing policies of a retail store and other internal and external variables related to the store's gross margin. (X goods are leader items; Y goods are all other items. Horizontal connections signify functional relations. Vertical connections signify addition; diagonal connections signify multiplication.)

$$R_t = S_t - C_t$$

Thus some of the relationships shown by arrows in Figure 14.1 are additive, while others are multiplicative.

Our principal concern in this discussion is with retail price. We have assumed in Figure 14.1 that store A had sufficient market power to have a retail price policy but that the wholesale prices of products it sells and the other costs that it has are market determined. Unless the firm is an extremely large buyer of goods in the wholesale market, it is unlikely that it will have much power to influence prices at that market level. Most firms do, however, have some ability to control unit variable costs, not through control of unit wholesale price but through efficient resource utilization. We shall, however, assume that all aspects of unit variable cost are determined externally.

The influence of price on consumer behavior is shown in Figure 14.1. The initial budgeted expenditure effect of a change in the price of leaders or of other types of goods is shown by the wide arrows as a change in price and, by implication, a change in consumers' budgets and, hence, in their total expenditure in all stores. Those products for which the demand is relatively elastic are ones for which retailers can induce consumers to spend more in total by reducing the price, but such price reductions do not necessarily result in a greater total expenditure by consumers for *all* products. Since the aggregate elasticity of consumption expenditures with respect to total disposable income is less than 1.00, it would appear that retail stores as a whole have rather limited opportunities in this direction, since aggregate price elasticity is related to income elasticity. Supermarkets in particular are likely to find little possibility for increased sales from the budgeted expenditure effect. We shall therefore simplify our analysis by assuming that the potential budgeted expenditure effect of price reductions in the supermarket is zero, thus concentrating our attention on the transferred expenditure effect.

The transferred expenditure effect is one of the keys to retail pricing in the supermarket. We have delineated the point of initial impact in Figure 14.1, where we show that a change in the price of leader items (Δp_x) can cause a change in the proportion of consumers' budgeted expenditures that are spent in store A. If the price of leader items is reduced, the proportion of their total expenditures that consumers make in store A are increased, quantities sold by the store are increased, and sales and net revenues may or may not be increased, depending on the elasticities and cross-elasticities of demand for X and Y types of goods. An example will help show some of these possible relationships and make clear how the sales and net revenue effects can sometimes be similar and sometimes quite different.

EXAMPLES OF SALES AND REVENUE EFFECTS

In Table 14.2 are hypothetical data that describe the sales and net revenue experience of a two-product store that experiments by (1) lowering the price of the product for which its own demand is relatively elastic and (2) both raising and lowering the price of the product for which its own demand is relatively inelastic.[10] Situation A describes the original status of the firm. Product A, for which the firm's own demand is relatively elastic, is priced at $4 per unit, and at this price 20 units are sold for a total sales volume of $80. The variable cost per unit, which we shall assume is the invoice cost less

---

[10]The importance of the distinction between elasticity of market demand and elasticity of the store's own demand, and the significance of both elasticities in the formulation of retail pricing policy, will be clarified in the following discussion. At this point, the elasticities under consideration refer only to the demand for the firm's own products and services.

Table 14.2 Some Possible Sales and Net Revenue Effects of a Decrease in the Price of One Product in a Two-Product Retail Firm[a]

Situation	Variable	Product A	Product B	Total
A. Original	Sales revenue	20 units @ $4	10 units @ $3	$110
	Variable cost	@ $2	@ $2	60
	Net revenue	$ 80	$30	$110
		40	20	60
		$ 40	$10	$ 50
B. After change in the price of product A				
1. Positive sales effect and negative net revenue effect	Sales revenue	30 units @ $3	15 units @ $3	$135
	Variable cost	@ $2	@ $2	90
	Net revenue	$ 90	$45	$135
		60	30	90
		$ 30	$15	$ 45
2. Positive sales effect and positive net revenue effect	Sales revenue	50 units @ $2.70	25 units @ $3	$210
	Variable cost	@ $2.00	@ $2	150
	Net revenue	$135	$75	$210
		100	50	150
		$ 35	$25	$ 60
C. After change in the price of product B				
1. Negative sales effect and positive net revenue effect	Sales revenue	19 units @ $4	8 units @ $4	$108
	Variable cost	@ $2	@ $2	54
	Net revenue	$ 76	$32	$108
		38	16	54
		$ 38	$16	$ 54
2. Negative sales effect and negative net revenue effect	Sales revenue	21 units @ $4	12 units @ $2	$108
	Variable cost	@ $2	@ $2	66
	Net revenue	$ 84	$24	$108
		42	24	66
		$ 42	$ 0	$ 42

[a]It is assumed that (1) product A has a microelasticity of demand with respect to price > 1 and product B has a microelasticity of demand < 1; (2) the cross-elasticity of demand for product B is < the cross elasticity of demand for product B with respect to the price of A.

discounts, is $2, and the firm's net revenue from this product is $40. Product B, for which the demand is relatively inelastic, is priced at $3 per unit for total sales of 10 units, yielding a sales volume of $30. With a variable cost of $2 per unit, net revenue from this product totals $10. Thus the firm's total sales volume is $110, total variable costs are $60, and net revenue (equal, in this case, to gross margin) is $50.

Situations B and C describe the firm's position after changes in the prices of products A and B. Situation B consists of two subcases. Both show the sales and net revenue effects of a reduction in the price of product A. In B1, product A has been reduced from $4 to $3, and sales volume increases from 20 to 30 units. Thus there has been a positive sales effect for product A. But there is also a sales effect on product B, for although the price of B has not been changed, apparently some of the new customers who came to the store to buy A also buy B. Sales of B rise from 10 to 15 units. Total store sales thus rise from $110 (situation A) to $135 (situation B1). To the retail firm, however, the sales effect is far less important than the net revenue effect. If we assume that the unit variable cost of products A and B has not altered from the original situation, we find that the total net revenue effect of the price change in product A has been negative, owing to the fact that while the net revenue of product B increased, it did not increase enough to offset the lower net revenue realized from product A.

Suppose, however, that the price of product A had been reduced still further, as in B2, to $2.70. Under our assumption of an elasticity of demand for the firm greater than unity, total revenue would rise. We assume that sales volume rose to 50 units and sales revenue to $135. If sales of B continue to show the same volume relationship to sales of A as previously (1 B unit for 2 A units), then sales of B would rise to 25 units, or $75, bringing total store sales to $210. With the same unit cost for A and B as previously, the net revenue would be $35 for product A and $25 for product B, or a total of $60 for the store—$10 more than in situation A. Although the total net revenue effect for product A was negative, the positive net revenue effect for product B was more than enough to result in a positive net revenue effect for the firm as a whole.

Both the cases shown for situation C involve a price change for product B, which is assumed to have an inelastic demand among the firm's customers. In case C1, the price of product B is raised from $3 to $4, causing a decline in the quantity sold of both products A and B, an increase in the dollar sales of B, a decrease in the dollar sales of A, and a decrease in the total dollar volume for the firm compared to situation A. But the pricing policy represented in C1 is better for the firm than that in the original situation, for the firm's net revenue is $4 greater in C1 than in A. On the other hand, situation C2 is the least desirable of the five possibilities in Table 14.2, for in this case both dollar volume of sales and net revenue effects of the decrease in price of product B are negative. It is, of course, the net revenue effect that would be determining in the firm's choice among the alternatives given.

While these examples are hypothetical and oversimplified by restriction to a two-product firm, the principle is the same in any multiproduct firm where there are differences in the response of consumers to the prices of various products in the firm's merchandise mixture and where cross-elasticities of demand cause price changes in one product to influence sales of another. While the retail firm is interested in the sales effects of both increases and decreases in prices of particular products, its primary interest is in the net revenue effects of such changes.

RECAPITULATION: THE CENTRAL PROBLEM OF SUPERMARKET PRICING

Table 14.2 demonstrates the central problem that confronts management of the typical supermarket. While the raising of the price of product B in Case C1 resulted in a higher net revenue than in the original situation, this effect could not be realized if other stores were, at the same time, following the policies illustrated by situations B1 or B2. Competition is likely, therefore, to force the retailer to increase his net revenue by cutting prices of strategic goods rather than raising prices of those goods for which the firm's demand is inelastic. The problem therefore is to determine on which goods prices should be cut in order to maximize the firm's *net revenue* in the market in which that firm operates. It is not enough to analyze buyers' responses to a given firm's price changes, assuming that the prices charged by all other firms remain constant. A firm must also take into account the possibility that competing firms will also be pursuing a dynamic pricing policy.

Which items are the best price leaders? If we assume that price cutting has no effect on consumers' total expenditures—that is, consumers budget no more nor less in total than they did before the price cut—then the desirability of a given price cut depends on two components: (1) its power to cause consumers to shift patronage from some other retail store to the price-cutting store, that is, its transferred expenditure effect, and (2) the relationship of the new sales-cost difference to the previous sales-cost difference, that is, the net revenue effect. A positive transferred expenditure effect that is combined with a positive net revenue effect is a *favorable transferred expenditure effect*.

The retailer's problem is to determine on which products price reductions will have the *most favorable* transferred expenditure effects and by how much prices must be reduced for those effects to be realized. Such products are those that make the best price leaders, and they do so because of the way consumers react to their prices. In the following discussion we shall consider the demand characteristics of products that are most likely to show favorable transferred expenditure effects from price reductions. We shall also examine evidence on pricing practices to determine whether empirical observations are consistent with expected pricing practices. Finally, we shall modify our analysis to take into account the impact of competitive structure on pricing.

DEMAND CONDITIONS RELATED TO FAVORABLE TRANSFERRED EXPENDITURE EFFECTS

Since changes in the prices of certain products will result in positive sales and net revenue effects, the supermarket will wish to determine for which products these two conditions are most likely to occur. Both of these phenomena are reflected in the demand attributes of the products. One can therefore most easily identify products with potentially high and favorable transferred expenditure effects through price reductions by examining the characteristics of product demand. We shall consider demand characteristics in two groups: (1) those related to positive transferred expenditure effects of price changes and (2) those related to positive net revenue effects resulting from transferred patronage. These are, in combination, the demand conditions that underlie effective use of price policy to maximize the supermarket's short-run profits.

Conditions Conducive to the Transfer of Expenditures

THE CONSUMER'S PERSPECTIVE

For the consumer to be attracted by selective price reductions in the retail firm, items on which prices are reduced must be established components of his level of consumption. If he regards them as "necessary," he is more likely to go out of his way—that is, to incur the necessary costs of transferring patronage—to take advantage of price reductions than if they are dispensable. This does not mean that patronage cannot be attracted by price reductions on "luxuries" that are purchased only (or in greater amounts) if the price is lowered—that is, those for which the market demand is highly elastic with respect to price—but, rather, that products that are regarded as indispensable are *more* effective in achieving patronage transfer.

From the consumer's point of view, a second condition related to a positive transferred expenditure effect is that his expenditure on the price-reduced item must represent a relatively high proportion of his budget. If it does not, the price reduction is less effective in attracting his patronage. The amount spent for a particular item is a function of its unit price and the quantity purchased. This means, therefore, that either variable can be important in determining whether an item is a significant one in the family budget. If the unit price is relatively high, this alone might be sufficient to make it effective as a price leader. On the other hand, if the unit price is relatively low but the amount purchased per week or month is considerable, the item may be an effective vehicle for achieving patronage transfer through a price reduction. Baking powder is not a good leader. No one buys enough of it for its price to make much difference in the family budget. But purchases of evaporated milk are sufficiently large in many families to make price reductions effective in attracting patronage.[11]

From the retailer's point of view, however, transferred patronage that results from price reductions on goods whose purchases represent a large proportion of the family budget do not result in as favorable net margin effects as price reductions on goods whose proportionate volume of sales per customer is less. We shall consider this offsetting factor in our discussion of conditions that affect the store's gross margin.

There are additional conditions necessary for margin differentials to be effective in attracting patronage. The consumer must be aware of how much he buys and must know that his purchases are enough for price differentials to make a difference to him, and he must be informed about prices in different stores. Moreover, he should not regard price as an indication of quality. If the customer believes that there is a positive correlation between quality and price, price leaders will not be effective.

THE RETAILER'S PERSPECTIVE

From the retailer's point of view, the greatest effect on patronage from the use of price leaders is realized if the price-reduced item is purchased by most consumers and purchased frequently. Unless it is a part of the pattern of consumption of most consumers, reduction of its price will not result in extensive transfer of patronage. Also, the more frequently it is purchased, the larger the proportion of the firm's potential customers who will wish to purchase it at any given time and, therefore, the greater the impact on patronage transfer. This does not mean that price reductions on other items may not also attract patronage but, rather, that high incidence of purchase is *more* effective in this respect.

---

[11] Data from Progressive Grocer's study of six Colonial Stores during the eight weeks November 4-December 29, 1963, show weekly sales per supermarket of 2,247 units of evaporated and condensed milk compared with 45 units of baking powder. Weekly sales of evaporated milk averaged $292.57 per store versus $8.23 for baking powder. Progressive Grocer, *Colonial Study* (New York: Progressive Grocer, [1964]), pp. C-26, C-34.

The essence of our observations to this point is (1) that the price reduction must make a difference to the consumer that is great enough to cause him to shift his patronage and (2) that the more consumers there are to whom it makes a difference, the greater the effect on the retailer's total sales. We shall turn now to a consideration of the conditions that will have the most favorable effects on the retail firm's net revenue from the transfer of expenditures resulting from the use of price leaders. It is important to observe that some of the conditions that have a favorable effect on the transfer of patronage do not have a favorable effect on the net revenue of the retail firm.

Conditions Conducive to Favorable Net Revenue Effects from Transferred Expenditures

PROPORTION OF EXPENDITURES

If a retailer reduces the price of certain items in order to attract customers, he will prefer that purchases of the items whose prices are reduced represent a relatively small proportion of consumer's total purchases. A price reduction causes the gross margin on that item to be less. If, as we have assumed, the consumer's total budget is fixed, and if the expenditure on the price-reduced item represents a large percentage of his total expenditure, any reduction in the margin of that item will have an effect on the margin of his market basket in proportion to the item's importance to the total basket. The store's total gross margin will therefore be affected adversely if such an item is used as a price leader. This is one reason why meat is not a good price leader. Expenditures by most consumers are sufficient to cause a drop in the store's total gross margin if the price of meat is reduced markedly. This does not mean, of course, that competition may not force the retailer to reduce margins on meat, and to do so for purposes of attracting patronage. Rather, it means that other items that are less important in the consumer's total expenditures are *better* leaders in terms of their effect on net revenue.

Note, however, that this attribute of a good price leader from the retailer's point of view is contrary to the attractiveness of price reductions from the consumer's viewpoint. The consumer prefers price reductions on those items that *are* important in his total expenditures, while the retailer prefers price cuts on those that are *not* important, provided, of course, that the price reduction is effective in attracting patronage. The retailer's problem is therefore one of balance between the effectiveness of the price reduction in attracting customers and its effectiveness in increasing the store's gross margin.

AVAILABILITY OF SUBSTITUTES

The retailer will realize the greatest benefits of his storewide gross margin if those items whose price is cut have the fewest good substitutes. If substitutes are available, purchases of the price-reduced item will rise at the expense of the substitutes. If the price-reduced item can be substituted for many other items—for example, if peaches can be substituted for all other fruits—then the low price means a loss of total margin on all fruits if customers concentrate their purchases on the leader item. If, on the other hand, customers regard peaches as unique and not a good substitute for other fruits, the reduction of the price of peaches will have a favorable effect on the store's gross margin.

This is one of the several reasons why coffee is such a good price leader. There are no close substitutes for it. Any one meat product, however, does not serve the retailer well as a price leader, for a reduction in the price of beef, let us say, will merely shift meat purchases from poultry, pork, and other meats to beef.

In this connection, it is appropriate to note that the retailer may choose one brand within a product cluster to use as a price leader. To the extent that customers regard different brands as reasonable substitutes for one another, the sales of the cluster will be concentrated on the price-reduced brand. This is often the case when there are price reductions on coffee. If Maxwell House coffee is used as a leader, sales of other brands may suffer. But fans of Maxwell House coffee to whom the differentiation is significant will be attracted to that store, and the net revenue effects from their other purchases may justify the price reduction. If no other firm used coffee as a price leader, then the nondifferentiating coffee user who does not care what brand he buys would also be attracted. This tends not to happen in practice, however, for coffee is widely used as a price leader. So long as each store does not reduce the price on the same brand, then the price reductions tend to distribute discriminating purchasers among different stores according to buyers' brand preferences and according to the aggregate price appeal the store offers nondiscriminating coffee purchasers through its total spectrum of price reductions. If a store's regular customers concentrate their purchases on the price-reduced brand without increasing their total expenditure, this tends to reduce the store's gross margin. These problems for the retailer are evident for a number of commodities that have many of the attributes of good price leaders but in which there are a number of brands that are good substitutes for each other, for example, mayonnaise and salad dressing, baby food, soaps and detergents, and canned milk. For such items to be good price leaders, price reductions must attract patronage from outside the store's regular clientele. The fewer the substitutes, therefore, the more effective the item will be as a price leader.

ELASTICITY OF DEMAND

It has often been stated that retailers will prefer to use as leaders items that have a fairly elastic market demand. Since consumers are responsive to price changes on such items, it would appear offhand that these would be ideal leaders. Such items do not, however, make the *best* price leaders. Let us determine why they do not.

We shall find it helpful to distinguish among three kinds of elasticity of demand with respect to price: macroelasticity, microelasticity, and cross-elasticity. *Macroelasticity* describes the effect of a change in *market* price on the total quantity sold in the market. Market price is either the price to which all retailers in the market adhere or a weighted average of the various prices in a given market. *Microelasticity* of demand refers to the effect of a change in the price charged by a given retailer on the quantity that he sells. Since this will be in part a function of the prices charged by other retailers, it is a meaningful concept only if the prevailing price of other retailers is given. Finally, *cross-elasticity* of demand is the effect of a change in the price of one item on the quantity sold of one or more other items. Each of these three elasticities has a bearing on supermarket pricing policies.

1. *MACROELASTICITY OF DEMAND.* If the market elasticity of demand for a product is quite high, a relatively small decrease in its price will result in a relatively large increase in the number of units purchased in the market. If a retailer cuts the price on such an item below the market average, his sales will increase. Where does this increase in sales come

from? Partly it comes from the retail firm's present customers who bought either less or none of the item when its price was higher. These additional sales do not generate any transfer effect. But some of the increased sales will come from "new" customers who would otherwise not have patronized this particular retail store. Sales to these customers of both price-reduced and other items will increase the firm's aggregate gross margin. However, some of this transfer effect is lost, because the customers who transfer patronage will have to do so at a cost, and this obliterates some of the retailer's potential gain from the price reduction. An item with an elastic demand is one on which the customer is mindful of price, and cost of patronage transfer, if it exists, will not elude him. This is not to say that all will refuse to incur the costs of patronage transfer. Rather, it is to say that an item for which demand is inelastic induces patronage transfer *more readily*, since the decision about whether to purchase or not is less closely tied to price.

There is still another limitation to the use of such items as leaders. If the price is reduced on a good with a high price elasticity of demand, total revenue from the sale of that item will increase. Unless consumers' total expenditures for all items in the retail store also increase, the increased sales of the price-reduced item will come at the expense of some other item. If, for example, all meats were reduced in price, much consumer spending would shift from other foods, such as dairy products, to meat. Certainly, too, with the availability of a wide range of substitutes within meats, a price reduction on any *one* meat would merely shift purchases from meats not reduced to the price-cut item. If, on the other hand, there is a negative budgeted expenditure effect (price down, total expenditures up), and consumers increase total spending at the expense of saving, or if they increase spending for the types of goods sold by this particular retail store at the expense of "noncompeting" stores, the price-cutting retailer gains.

Ignoring the probable size of variable costs other than that of merchandise, a food retailer might find it worthwhile, for example, to sell appliances at very low prices, since the transfer of patronage would be from appliance dealers to the food store, with a probable increase in total sales of the food store. But this would be a one-shot deal if the appliance store were able to retaliate. Also, the cost and promotional problems for the food retailer under these circumstances would probably be prohibitive. Only with such items as cigarettes, which, interestingly enough, do *not* have an elastic demand, has the food retailer found opportunities for benefiting from using as a leader an item that historically was within the merchandise spectrum of noncompeting retail firms. Yet competition has dispelled this element of assortment differentiation. So long as the increased sales that the retailer enjoys from a low-margin item come at the expense of sales of other items, the transfer effect of the price reduction is nil.

Suppose, however, that many consumers are willing to incur the costs of patronage transfer and do not reduce their expenditures on other items handled by the retail store to compensate for their increased purchases of the price-reduced item. Under these circumstances, is the price reduction on an item with a relatively elastic demand not justified? The answer is no, because a price reduction on an item that has an inelastic market demand would have an even *greater* effect on the firm's gross margin, assuming that the two items are equal with respect to the other factors that affect net revenue. The reasons should be clear from what we have said about the relationship between high demand elasticity and the effects of price cuts on the retail firm's total gross margin. If the demand is inelastic, consumers will tend to buy the product more or less irrespective of price. Such consumers are therefore more likely to undergo the costs of transferring patronage, if such costs are a fact, than consumers of a product for which the demand is elastic, for the latter product bears the burden of high consumer sensitivity to its price and the greater willingness of many consumers to do without it (or more of it) as an alternative decision.[12]

Another reason why retailers prefer to use as leaders items for which the market demand is inelastic is that the cut in price results in a reduced total expenditure on that item by consumers as a group. This opens the possibility for an increase in the retailer's total revenue. While at one time coffee may have had an elastic demand with respect to price, competition has driven its price down to the point where few people probably increase or decrease the amount of coffee they consume very much on the basis of its price.[13] The market demand is relatively inelastic with respect to price. A price reduction on coffee means, therefore, that consumers as a whole will probably not consume increased quantities of coffee but will, if they shift patronage to take advantage of the price reduction, be in a position to spend more on other goods than would have been possible without the price reduction. Thus the impact of the price cut is far greater than it would have been had consumers transferred *both* their patronage to the price-cutting store and their choice of market basket components to the price-cut item. This is equally important insofar as it applies to the store's regular patrons, for if those patrons do not buy greatly increased quantities of the price-reduced item in lieu of the store's other items, the store's aggregate gross margin will be increased.

A third reason why a decrease in the price of a good with a relatively inelastic demand is often more attractive to the retailer than that of one with an elastic demand is the possibility that the elasticity of market demand has stimulated competitive action among sellers to the point that the margins have been driven down to a level where further price cutting will push selling price below variable cost. If there is not much margin to play with, margin reductions are not so attractive to the retail merchant. In this case, the elasticity of demand can be said to have had a secondary effect on use of the product as a price leader. This would be true where the high elasticity stimulated competitive action, which, in turn, resulted in low margins that offered little opportunity for further price reductions.

We have explained why retailers will prefer to use as price leaders items for which the *market demand* is relatively inelastic. It is not because price reductions on items with an elastic demand might not, under certain circumstances, have a favorable effect on the firm's gross margin but, rather, that price reductions on items with an inelastic demand will, *other things being equal*, have a *more favorable effect* on aggregate gross margin.

2. *MICROELASTICITY OF DEMAND.* While the retailer will prefer to reduce margins on those items for which the market demand is relatively inelastic, he will prefer items for which the micro demand—that is, the demand for his own output—is elastic. In a purely competitive market the demand for the output of any retail firm will be perfectly elastic. Thus the retailer will accept the prevailing market price. A price greater than this will result in no sales. A price lower than this will reduce his margin but not increase his sales at all and will therefore be unattractive to him.

---

[12] This is true only, of course, if the other prerequisites to high transfer effects are also realized. We are assuming for the moment that these are equal for the items with elastic and inelastic demand. In our final synthesis we shall show that these often are not equal but may even have counteracting influences on the elasticity factor under discussion. It is necessary, however, to consider these one at a time before attempting a synthesis.

[13] They may, however, increase their purchases temporarily to take advantage of the price reduction. Compensation will occur in subsequent periods, when purchases are reduced because of the consumer stocks built up during the previous period of price reduction.

Competition in retailing is not perfect, however, and the elasticity of demand for the output of a single retailer, measured in terms of individual items or market baskets, is probably less than perfectly elastic. On which items will the retailer wish to cut margins the most—those for which *his* demand is elastic or those for which it is inelastic? In this case, the greater the elasticity of the demand, the greater will be the effect of a price cut.

The relationship of the retailer's markup and selling price to the elasticity of demand with respect to price *for his store* can be described in the following equations, in which p is retail price, e is the elasticity of demand with respect to price with the negative sign ignored, c_m is marginal cost, m is markup in dollars, m_c is markup as a percentage of cost, and m_r is markup as a percentage of retail price.[14]

1. The optimum price is

$$p = c_m \; \frac{|e_p|}{|e_p| - 1}$$

2. The optimum markup is

$$m = \frac{c_m}{|e_p| - 1}$$

3. The optimum markup as a percentage of cost is

$$m_c = \frac{1}{|e_p| \; 1}$$

4. The optimum markup as a percentage of retail is

$$m_r = \frac{1}{|e_p|}$$

Assume that the cost of an item is $10 and its assumed elasticity of demand with respect to price is -3. According to equation 1, the retail price will be $15:

$$p = \$10 \; \frac{3}{3 - 1} = \frac{\$30}{2} = \$15$$

According to equation 2, the markup is $5:

$$m = \frac{\$10}{3 - 1} = \$5$$

Markup will be 50 percent of cost (equation 3):

$$m_c = \frac{1}{3 - 1} = .50, \text{ or } 50\%$$

Markup will be 33 percent of retail (equation 4):

$$m_r = \frac{1}{3} = .33, \text{ or } 33\%$$

---

[14] The proof for each of these four formulas is developed in Appendix B of this chapter. Appendix A develops a proposition about elasticity of demand basic to the proof in Appendix B. The reader should note that in each of the equations given here the value of the elasticity of demand with respect to price is the value without respect to its negative sign. This is merely for ease of statement and calculation.

Had the elasticity of demand been -4, the markup would have been 33 percent of cost, or 25 percent of retail, resulting in a selling price of $13.33. Thus the higher the elasticity of demand for the individual firm, the lower the markup tends to be.

Another way of viewing the microelasticity of demand is the effect of a price reduction on the store's total revenue. An elastic demand for *that* store's output means that its total revenue increases with a reduction in price. This it does at the expense of other stores. It is for this reason that the size of margins is sometimes used as one measure of the degree of competition in the retail markets for various goods. Items carried widely by many stores will tend to have lower percentage margins than those carried by only a few firms, provided that other influences are equal.[15] Note that items for which the micro demand tends to be elastic are items that the retailer will *normally* sell at lower markups. Thus their usual margins may be so low that they can be used only as loss leaders.

3. *CROSS-ELASTICITY OF DEMAND*. The transfer effect of a price change is the change in the firm's gross margin resulting from a change in the price of one or more items sold by the firm. In our discussion of the relationship of elasticity to the transfer effect of price reductions, we have, up to this point, considered only the elasticity of demand for the item on which the price reduction is made. We have concluded that the firm will prefer to use as price leaders items for which the market demand is inelastic and for which the demand by the firm's clientele is elastic. We have, however, touched lightly on another aspect of elasticity that is of basic importance to the retailer in making his final decision—the cross-elasticity of demand.

Cross-elasticity measures the relationship between the relative change in sales of a given item and the relative change in the price of another item. If the cross-elasticity is positive, it means that consumers purchase more of item B as a result of an increase in the price of A. This is most likely to occur if B is a good substitute for A. A negative cross-elasticity means that consumers purchase more of item B as a result of a decrease in the price of A. It is negative elasticities in which the retailer will be most interested, for it is these that will make it possible for him to select certain items for price reduction, thereby realizing increased sales of other items on which he has not reduced price. Such sales will contribute to an increased aggregate gross margin. Therefore one of the conditions necessary for transfer effects to be realized from price reductions is that the store carry in stock, along with the price leaders, items that have high negative cross-elasticities to those that make good price leaders. It is even possible that consumers desire this condition, that is, that they will not be attracted by price leaders unless they can, on the same shopping trip, purchase goods that do not have high transfer effects.[16]

What are the characteristics of items that are likely to show the highest negative cross-elasticities to those that make good price leaders and are, *by this criterion*, the *best* followers? The most important characteristics of these items are (1) that they are complementary in marketing, that is, they are bought at the same time and place that other things are bought, and (2) that the choice of where and when they are to be

---

[15] An exception would be where the market demand is highly elastic and the retail store is a monopolist, in which case the macro demand is the micro demand. Thus the monopolist will trim his margin in order to benefit from the demand elasticity.

[16] One case does not prove this proposition but is highly suggestive. In the 1940s Macy's opened a small shop in Syracuse, New York, in which it stocked only low-margin, high-turnover items based on experience in its New York store. The store was closed after a year because the stock diversity was not sufficient to attract patronage. See Oswald Knauth, "Considerations in the Setting of Retail Prices," *Journal of Marketing* 14 (July 1949): 10.

purchased is based on the availability, quality, and terms of sale of the other goods to which they are complementary in marketing, that is, their purchase "rides" on the purchase of other goods. Items that fit these two characteristics include those for which there is little deliberation preceding the decision to purchase because the need for them is a short-term need that will not survive beyond a brief period, because their price is too low to warrant much deliberation, or because the product and its terms of sale are highly standardized. While few things are probably bought on "impulse" in its strictest meaning, those bought with little or no planning would fall into this category, as would the much larger number of staples purchased on a recurrent basis by most households—flour, sugar, cereals, thread, underwear. In these cases, some kind of long-run budget underlies specific purchases made at any one time. Likewise, things about which the consumer knows little and desires to know little will be bought with no comparison shopping.

Items that are *complementary in use* may or may not show high negative cross-elasticities of demand. Items that are complementary in use are sometimes also complementary in marketing, and this is particularly likely if one item is purchased *only* if the other is purchased. If the more expensive of the pair is cut in price, it may attract patronage and cause an increase in the sale of the complementary item. A reduction in the price of meat, for example, may increase the retailer's volume of meat sales and also his unit sales of meat sauce, a complementary item in use. But choice of such an item for price reduction because of its probable transfer effect and the increased sales of the complementary item might be ill-advised in light of the greater elasticity of demand for the high-priced item of a complementary pair. For the reasons already stated the item with the more inelastic demand might be the better choice if the cross-elasticity is significantly greater than 1.00.

Cross-elasticity is not always the same in both directions. For example, one does not buy a battery-operated transistor radio without also buying batteries, and he is likely to buy the batteries at the time and place at which he buys the radio. However, he is not likely to buy the radio *because* the batteries are reduced in price. In this case, the only way to attract patronage that will result in sales of another item is to cut the price of radios. If the price of batteries is reduced, it may, however, increase replacement sales of batteries to those now using transistor radios. But there is not likely to be any effect on sales of radios except that which is incidentally possible through promotional efforts exerted when the battery purchaser is in the store. On the other hand, from a long-run point of view the reduction in battery prices may have a considerable effect on radio sales if it results in habitual purchases at this place of business, which will give rise to radio purchases at the less frequent intervals when those purchases occur.

There are some extremely interesting cross-elasticities between merchandise and services where services are needed continually following purchase of a good. For example, an automobile dealer may find that most of his customers subsequently purchase his maintenance and repair services. Although the demand for the cars is more elastic than the demand for any one of the service transactions, it would pay the firm to cut its margin on the cars if its loss in aggregate gross margin on them is more than offset by an increase in the gross margin from its service business. This is a case where complementarity in use need not necessarily lead to complementarity in purchase but will sometimes tend to do so, either because the consumer's experience with one retail outlet is greater than with others or because there is a real or assumed monopoly element associated with the servicing of a given make of car.

In general, it would appear that the attributes of items with a high negative cross-elasticity of demand to items with a high negative transfer effect from price are the opposite of the characteristics of items with high transfer effect. Negative cross-elasticity is greatest for items that are small in volume of purchases, low in price, and standardized in quality and price in various outlets, for which there are no good substitutes, and about which the consumer desires no additional information.

A SYNTHESIS

A retailer will attempt to establish a markup on individual items in his store in such a way that the aggregate gross margin of the store is maximized. The critical factor is the relationship between the margin on a particular item and its contribution to the total margin of the retail firm. The influence of price is felt via its impact on sales of both the item itself and all other items in the store and the contributions of these sales to the store's total gross margin. The retailer's concern will be to adjust downward one or more prices so that he attracts new customers into his store and so that purchases by both old and new customers maximize storewide gross margin.

Those items that are most attractive to him as price leaders are ones that represent an established component of consumption and whose price is of sufficient importance for the consumer to be both aware and concerned. Ideally such items are purchased frequently and by most consumers. Also, they should be items on which the reduction in price is greater than the added cost consumers would incur by transferring their patronage in order to take advantage of the price reduction.

But the most effective price leaders must do more than merely result in the transfer of patronage. They must also result in an increased storewide gross margin. To fulfill this additional function, they must represent a small proportion of the consumer's total expenditure, be items for which there are few good substitutes, and have a negative, low macroelasticity of demand with respect to price (although a negative, high microelasticity of demand with respect to price) and a negative, high cross-elasticity of demand with other items in the store, particularly with those that make the best price followers, that is, those that, in combination with price leaders, contribute the most to the store's gross margin.

Seldom, however, will all of the characteristics of a good leader obtain for a particular good. For example, while the ideal leader is one for which the market demand is inelastic, other desired characteristics—such as high price, large volume of purchases, and consumer awareness of price—are more likely to occur where the demand is elastic. Therefore it is the total net effect of a number of market attributes that determines whether a product does or does not make a good price leader. The greater the number of relevant attributes it has, or the greater their influence, the more likely these will determine the optimum choice.

One other aspect of price leaders is the possible conflict of interest between consumers and retailers. Retailers prefer to use as leaders items for which the market demand is inelastic, while consumers prefer price cuts on items for which the demand is elastic. Similarly, retailers will prefer to use as leaders items on which consumer purchases are not too large, while consumers will prefer items on which their purchases are considerable. In the case of relative price, both consumers and retailers prefer price cuts on high-priced items. But consumer preference is based on the effect of the price cut on their expenditures, while the retailer's preference is based on the fact that price cuts on high-priced items are less likely to move margins down to cost of merchandise in order to be discernible to consumers. Where there are differences between consumers and retailers in price preferences, the retailer's preference will prevail so long as he is setting the price policy. It will not prevail if competition is so keen that he cannot have his own policy but must adhere to the total market's response to consumer preferences.

This brings us to the role of competition in pricing policies of the multiproduct retail firm. In the absence of monopoly, or of open or tacit collusion among stores in a given market, each store will follow the pattern of pricing described earlier but will, at the same time, attempt to differentiate itself with respect to the cluster of items it selects for price reductions. Empirical studies do not indicate the presence of much leadership-follower pricing in food retailing.[17] The reason would appear to be that more is to be gained from universal application of a selective pricing policy among stores of similar character, with differentiation between stores in their choice of the items on which these selective pricing policies will be utilized. The range of possibilities is sufficient to permit the policy to be effective in directing (or redirecting) patronage without its having to apply to all possibilities, or without its having to be an imitation of the choices of a competing firm. Out of this arise, of course, the dynamic aspects of the pricing situation. No store can afford to allow the application of its pricing policy to be static, for its effectiveness depends in part on differentiation in the choice of items to be used as price leaders. Differentiation is most likely if random choices were to be made by all competing retailers among the spectrum of items that serve best as leaders, or if each firm successfully predicted the choices of its competitors and deliberately avoided similar choices. It appears that prices are not random but that there is week-to-week diversification that reflects a tendency toward differentiation between stores within the constraints established by other operating policies. Advertising is often a tool, though not a prerequisite, for leader pricing; therefore the larger the store, the greater the opportunities it may have for employment of leader pricing to the extent that advertising increases the effectiveness of such a policy.[18]

AN ALTERNATIVE APPROACH TO RETAIL PRICING

We have pointed out that the aggregate gross margin of the retail firm is increased if price reductions are made on certain items sold by the store, provided that the store also carries

[17]See, for example, Paul E. Nelson and Lee E. Preston, *Price Merchandising in Food Retailing: A Case Study*, Institute of Business and Economic Research, Special Publications (Berkeley: University of California, Graduate School of Business Administration, 1966), pp. 73-84; Wroe Alderson, *Dynamic Marketing Behavior* (Homewood, Ill.: Irwin, 1965), pp. 211-238; Wroe Alderson and Stanley J. Shapiro, "Towards a Theory of Retail Competition," in Reavis Cox and Wroe Alderson, eds., *Theory in Marketing*, 2d ser. (Homewood, Ill. Irwin, 1964), pp. 190-212; William J. Baumol, Richard E. Quandt, and Harold T. Shapiro, "Oligopoly Theory and Retail Food Pricing," *Journal of Business* 37 (October 1964): 346-363.

Two of the three hypotheses tested in the latter study concerned price interaction among competing firms. One was that retail firms operating in the same market differ in their price behavior; some are imitators and some are leaders. This was not supported by the evidence. Rather, there appeared to be some support for the Bertrand-Edgeworth hypothesis that the price of one firm is a function of the prices of all other firms. A second hypothesis—that leaders seldom follow and followers seldom lead—was tested by three measures, all of which failed to support it. It was concluded that a better oligopolistic model needed to be evolved to explain supermarket pricing.

[18]Two valuable empirical studies of retailing pricing are Lee E. Preston and Reed Hertford, "The Anatomy of Retail Price Competition: A Study of Advertised Food Prices," *California Management Review* 6 (Spring 1962): 13-30, and George Fisk, Lawrence Nein, and Stanley J. Shapiro, "Price Rivalry among Philadelphia Food Chains," *Journal of Advertising Research* 4 (June 1964): 12-20.

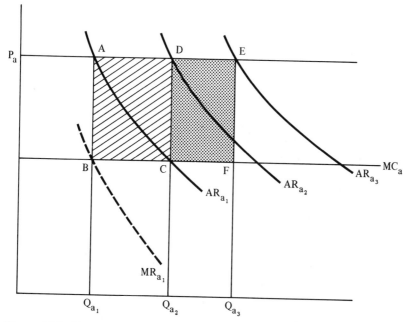

Figure 14.2. Revenue and cost of product A with and without a reduction in the price of complementary product B.

items for which there is a high negative cross-elasticity of demand between them and the price-reduced items. Richard Coase has explained this relationship using a somewhat different approach. We shall draw upon his analysis, and modifications made in it by Richard Holton, to describe the way in which cross-elasticity of demand can be employed to determine pricing policy for a potential price leader.[19]

Let us assume that we have two products, A and B. Product A has a high negative cross-elasticity of demand with respect to product B. Product B is an effective price leader. Average and marginal revenue of product A are shown in Figure 14.2 as AR_{a_1} and MR_{a_1}, and marginal cost, which we assume to be constant within the volume range under consideration, is represented by MC_a. Under these circumstances, Q_{a_1} will be sold at price P_a if the price of product B is P_{b_1}. If, however, the price of product B is reduced, it increases the amount of product A that can be sold. If the price of A is retained at P_a, quantity Q_{a_2} can be sold, because the price of B is now P_{b_2}. Thus the reduction in the price of B increases the contribution of A to the total gross margin of the store, and this increase is represented by the rectangle ABCD in Figure 14.2. If B is further reduced in price, we shall assume that the new demand curve, AR_{a_3}, becomes effective for product A, and sales, if the price of A is held constant, will become Q_{a_3}. The additional contribution to gross margin of the store is *CDEF*.

Corrected Costs

Coase suggests that these successive increases in contribution to the store's gross margin—first *ABCD* and then *CDEF*—can be viewed as a decrease in the cost of product B

[19] Richard H. Coase, "Monopoly Pricing with Interrelated Costs and Demands." *Economica*, n.s., 13, no. 52 (November 1946): 278, and Richard H. Holton, "Price Discrimination at Retail: The Supermarket Case," *Journal of Industrial Economics* 6 (October 1957): 13-32.

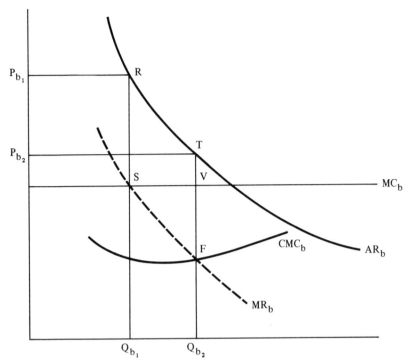

Figure 14.3. Revenue and cost of product B corrected for the effect of changes in the price of B on sales of product A.

to the store, since the acquisition of the additional margin results from a policy change with respect to product B. Figure 14.3 shows the change in product B's position. Under the original circumstances product B was priced at P_{b_1}, where the marginal cost of merchandise, MC_b, was equal to marginal revenue, MR_b. But B's price was then reduced to P_{b_2}, and sales of B increased to Q_{b_2}. When sales of B rose from Q_{b_1} to Q_{b_2} because of the lower price of B, sales of A also increased, to Q_{a_2} (Figure 14.2), since A is complementary to B. So the increased net return obtained from A, represented by area $ABCD$ in Figure 14.2, can be viewed as having reduced the marginal cost of B. Line CMC_b in Figure 14.3 represents the new marginal cost corrected for the impact of changes in the gross margin received by the firm as a result of A's contribution to that margin, which was derived from the reduction in the price of B. Thus, at sales volume Q_{b_2}, associated with a selling price for B of P_{b_2} (or TQ_{b_2}), the uncorrected marginal cost was MC_b (or VQ_{b_2}). But if we take into account the fact that the low price of product B increased sales of product A so that A's contribution to the store's total gross margin is increased by the amount represented by $ABCD$ in Figure 14.2, then the corrected marginal cost for the Q_{b_2} units sold is FQ_{b_2} instead of VQ_{b_2}.

An Example

Before examining the shape of the corrected marginal cost curve for B, let us introduce an arithmetic example. In Table 14.3 are outlined the revenue, cost, and sales positions of two products sold by a single store. We are assuming that there is negative cross-elasticity of demand for the purchase of tennis balls and tennis rackets in a given store, and that a reduction in the price of rackets increases sales of tennis balls because of the new

Table 14.3 An Example of Revenue and Costs of Products A and B Before and After Price Reduction of Leader Product B, with Which Product A has a High Negative Cross Elasticity of Demand

Situation and Item	Product A, Tennis Balls	Product B, Tennis Rackets
Position I	**Number**	
Unit sales	400	20
	Dollars	
Selling price	$ .50	$ 18.00
Average cost = marginal cost	.30	9.00
Average gross margin	.20	9.00
Contribution to total gross margin	80.00	180.00
Position II		
A. Before imputation	**Number**	
Unit sales	1,000	50
Δ unit sales from position I	+600	+30
	Dollars	
Selling price	$ .50	$ 12.00
Average cost = marginal cost	.30	9.00
Average gross margin	.20	3.00
Contribution to total gross margin	200.00	150.00
Δ contribution to total gross margin from position I	+120.00	−30.00
B. After imputation		
Marginal cost for		
A: same as position I	.30	
B: first 20 units same as position I		
		9.00
next 30 units imputed[a]		5.00
Imputed contribution to total gross margin by		
A same as position I	80.00	
B [(20 × $3.00 + (30 × $7.00)]		270.00

[a] Imputed marginal cost of the additional units of B sold after price reduction =

$$\left[\begin{array}{c}\text{Uncorrected marginal} \\ \text{cost of B}\end{array}\right] - \left[\frac{\Delta \text{contribution to total gross margin by A}}{\Delta \text{ unit sales of B}}\right]$$

customers who come to purchase the rackets and who also purchase balls while in the store, and because of the advertising value of the special sale on rackets to the store's regular customers as well as to others. The store becomes known as a place where "good buys" are to be found.

The store usually sells 400 tennis balls and 20 tennis rackets during the month. With a 40 percent markup on retail on balls and a 50 percent markup on retail on rackets, balls contribute $80 to the store's gross margin while rackets contribute $180.

The management decides to reduce the price of rackets from $18 to $12. The result is that sales of rackets increase to 50, and sales of tennis balls to 1,000. Balls continue to contribute $.20 each to the firm's gross margin if we assume that the cost of each ball to the retail store is the same whether it buys 400 or 1,000.[20] Thus the total contribution of the tennis balls to the store's total gross margin is $200, which is $120 greater than it was before tennis rackets were reduced in price. Since the cause of the increased contribution to gross margin by product A is the reduction in the price of product B, it is not illogical to impute this increased contribution to product B rather than to product A. This is done by correcting the marginal cost of B. Because A is complementary to B—that is, a reduction in the price of B increases the sales of A—the uncorrected, or original, marginal cost of B is reduced by the change in contribution of A to gross margin. Had we calculated each change in the contribution of A to gross margin resulting from each minute change in the price of B, we would have had a relatively smooth series of correction factors to subtract from the uncorrected marginal cost of B. Since our example is a "lumpy" one, however, involving a large change in the price of B and a large change in sales of A, we have prorated the change in A's contribution to gross margin over all of the change in sales of B and thereby estimated the average corrected marginal cost within the range of tennis racket sales of 20 to 50. In Figure 14.3, however, we have used a smooth curve, CMC_b, to describe the corrected marginal cost of B.

Note, however, that CMC_b in Figure 14.3 shows a decreasing and then increasing value, while the uncorrected marginal cost, MC_b, is constant at all volumes. The curvature of CMC_b is related to the effect of price reductions of B *at different price levels of B* on sales of A. For example, a small cut in the price of B may have some effect on sales of B but not much effect on sales of A. Then, as B is cut more and more in price, the relative effect on A of each dollar reduction becomes greater. In Figure 14.2, for example, AR_{a_2} shows the demand that results, let us say, from a $3 cut in the price of B. The increased contribution to gross margin is $ABCD$. Then if B is cut an additional $3, AR_{a_3} is the new demand curve for A, and the increased contribution now becomes $CDEF$, which is less than $ABCD$. Thus additional cuts in the price of B cause sales of A to increase so little that the increased contribution of A to the store's gross margin becomes less and less.

Profit for the firm will be maximized when the marginal revenue of B equals the corrected marginal cost of B. This occurs in Figure 14.3 at price P_{b_2} and sales of Q_{b_2}. Obviously the declining average revenue and marginal revenue in Figure 14.3 reflect the assumption that the firm does not operate in a perfectly competitive market and has, therefore, some discretion in setting prices, thereby affecting quantities sold.

The Loss Leader Case

Figure 14.4 represents the case of a loss leader, that is, an item sold at a price less than its cost to the store. The corrected marginal cost calculation is particularly useful in clarifying why retailers may logically choose to sell one or more items at less than the cost of goods. If there is no cross-elasticity of demand between product B and product A, the price of B will be P_{b_1}, and sales volume will be Q_{b_1}. At this price, marginal revenue equals marginal cost. If, however, the cross-elasticity of demand between product A and

---

[20] Dropping this assumption would not change the argument. We use a perfectly elastic marginal cost curve not only to simplify the presentation but also for consistency with the more common retail experience.

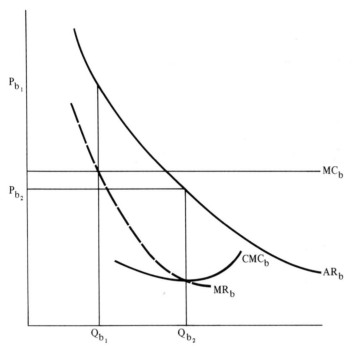

Figure 14.4. Revenue and cost of product B corrected for the effect of changes in the price of B on sales of product A when B was used as a loss leader.

product B is high and negative, cutting the price of B will have considerable effect on the unit sales of A without any change necessary in the price of A. As B is cut in price, A's contribution to the store's gross margin increases, and this is reflected in the declining segment of the CMC_b curve in Figure 14.4. It will pay the store to continue cutting the price of B until sales reach quantity Q_{b_2} and price is P_{b_2}, for at this point the corrected marginal cost, CMB_b, equals the marginal revenue of B. But note that price P_{b_2} is below the uncorrected marginal cost of product B, represented by MC_b. This is by definition, therefore, a loss leader. The loss, however, is spurious, resulting from the tying of the product's own cost to its own selling price rather than from relating the product's own selling price to the entire store's gross margin, as is done when CMC_b is used in lieu of MC_b.

Suppose, for example, that a retailer of TV sets also services sets and that he manages to retain about 80 percent of the service business on the sets he sells. If his margin on servicing is substantial, it might pay him to sell his sets at less than their wholesale cost to him if he then compensates for the loss in margin on the sets by the gain in margin on the servicing.

Does this kind of consumer behavior imply that the consumer is not very bright or, to use the more common designation, irrational? It does not. There are certain things that the consumer buys for which it pays him to shop or to shift patronage when the terms of purchase are more advantageous in one store. These are items for which his total expenditure is large relative to that for other items and ones for which the gains from patronage shifts are greater than the costs of those shifts. There are other items for which such shifts are not economical. These are the ones he tends to buy along with those for which he does make comparisons of quality and terms of sale. The cautious consumer who places a low value on his own time and energy because of low opportunity costs will move from store to store, selecting from each the various items that enter into his complete market basket, but most consumers will not regard such an extensive search as worth its cost. One condition that must prevail for these cross-elasticities *not* to reflect suboptimal behavior on the part of consumers is that the consumers must be informed as to market conditions. The extent of such information will be limited by the cost of obtaining it.

SOME OBSERVATIONS ON MULTIPRODUCT PRICING IN OTHER MARKETING INSTITUTIONS

In a number of marketing institutions, we can observe the presence of multiple lines of merchandise, joint costs, considerable cross-elasticity of demand, and a competitive structure that makes possible and induces a mix of marketing policies in which price plays a critical role. One may therefore ask whether the multiproduct pricing policy used by supermarkets is also appropriate as a pricing policy of other marketing institutions. We shall consider this question very briefly in terms of two important and quite different types of marketing firms—the department store and the wholesale firm.

Department Store Pricing

The department store shares many of the characteristics of the supermarket. Many of its costs are joint costs not allocable to a particular item or transaction, though this is less true than in the supermarket.[21] Its customers often buy more than one item on a given shopping trip and are likely to demand a cluster of services in connection with any one purchase. Its competition comes from large stores like itself and from smaller, specialized stores handling some portion of its merchandise lines. However, the internal and external environment within which department store management makes its pricing decisions differs from that of the supermarket in certain fundamental ways.

It would appear that department stores, in contrast to supermarkets, carry a larger percentage of goods for which seasonal and cyclical variability in demand gives rise to price variations. Although the supermarket has some seasonal and cyclical variability, cyclical variability is much less severe, and seasonal variability is created as much (sometimes more) by supply as by demand.

The department store is characterized by diversity in its output, arising out of the range of possibilities for product-service-promotion mix, and with these are related possibilities for diversity in pricing practices. There is some cross-elasticity of demand for items carried by the department store, but there is, at the same time, a greater tendency for consumers to show sensitivity to the price of a particular item than is true of the supermarket. The market basket concept is less applicable to the department store than

---

[21] See Malcolm P. McNair and Eleanor G. May, "Pricing for Profit," *Harvard Business Review* 35 (May-June 1957): 105-122. The approach of McNair and May is carried still further and utilized to determine contribution in relation to investment in Richard H. Holton, "A Simplified Capital Budgeting Approach to Merchandise Management," *California Management Review* 3 (Spring 1961): 82-104.

to the supermarket. To the degree that it does exist, the department store market basket is more elastic with respect to price than the supermarket basket.[22]

Finally, the competitive structure of the market in which the department store operates reflects the diversity that characterizes the department store itself. In a case study of department store pricing, Richard M. Alt has shown that the internal structure of the store has a significant bearing on the store's pricing policies. Its size, administrative organization, and budgetary procedure, and the relations of owners to management and interrelationships of units within the corporate group, were all found to have been conducive to the use of one-price policies, full-cost pricing, price lining, and leader pricing.[23] There is considerable opportunity for department store management to fit price into its total policy structure in a unique way and to retain its unique position by a dynamic policy in which it differentiates itself from its competitors. There would appear to be far less advantage in trying to meet competition identically than in differentiation.[24]

Thus while leader pricing plays a role in the department store's marketing mix, it is a less prominent, and certainly a less continuous, role than in the supermarket field, where the competition is between stores that are more like each other and where frequency of patronage and one-stop shopping make the appeal of price leaders stronger.

Pricing in the Wholesale Firm

It would appear that the multiproduct wholesale firm has many of the same opportunities to employ leader pricing as the retail firm. However, customers of the wholesale firm may have more information about market alternatives than customers of many retail firms. If their customers are in fact able to split their purchases among many suppliers, the problem of wholesale pricing becomes that of getting a cluster of "normal" prices that will result in optimum total sales. Where purchase segmentation does not occur, cross-elasticity of demand is important in determining how much of his clients' total patronage a single wholesaler receives. However, wholesale margins are narrower than those in retailing, and pricing must be finely drawn in a market that is characterized by

---

[22] In 1964, for example, sales of apparel and home furnishings by department stores reporting to the Controllers' Congress of the National Retail Merchants Association accounted for about 75 percent of total sales. These are goods for which substitutes are available from among the items that make up each group, of sufficiently high price to warrant consumer attention to price, and consumed in sufficient quantities and of sufficient durability to make it possible for the consumer to forgo replacement or additions to his stock if prices are high. As a group they are dispensable in a way not true of food. National Retail Merchants Association, Controllers' Congress, *Departmental Merchandising and Operating Results of 1964* (New York, 1965), pp. 14-32.

[23] Richard M. Alt, "The Internal Organization of the Firm and Price Formation: An Illustrative Case," *Quarterly Journal of Economics* 63 (February 1949): 92-110.

[24] Discussions of rules of thumb and some conventional practices in the setting of prices in department stores may be found in Oswald Knauth, op. cit., pp. 1-12; Q. Forrest Walker, "Some Principles of Department Store Pricing," *Journal of Marketing* 14 (January 1950): 529-537; W. G. McClelland, "Pricing for Profit in Retailing," *Journal of Industrial Economics* 7 (July 1959): 159-174. After discussing various procedures and practices, McClelland concludes that the only rule for retail pricing is that there is no rule. See also Richard M. Alt, "Department Store Price Policies," (Ph.D. Dissertation, Harvard University, 1946).

greater price variability between individual customers and between points of time than is found in retail markets.

On the other hand, the marketing or industrial firm that is a buyer in wholesale markets is likely to be confronted with a more limited range of alternative sources of supply than the consumer buyer. Purchases are typically made less frequently and involve a much larger dollar volume than those of the consumer buyer. If purchase contracts are used, buyer-seller relationships are established for a period of time and are altered only at intervals. Buyer-seller relationships may be even more firmly established through a voluntary chain or franchising operation, which sharply curtails the buyer's freedom. Where contracts are made to cover many transactions, leader pricing, if it is used, must be operative for the period of the contract. If contracts with all customers are not made at the same time, leader pricing is likely to result in problems under the Robinson-Patman Act. Thus while sellers in wholesale markets will be just as inclined to seek ways of "sweetening" their offerings in order to attract sales, the use of short-term leader pricing is likely not to be the most efficacious means of doing this. Discounts and advertising allowances that constitute across-the-board price concessions are more likely to prevail than selective price cutting, which the multiproduct retail firm finds so attractive.

APPENDIX A

THE RELATIONSHIP BETWEEN ACTUAL PRICE, MAXIMUM POSSIBLE PRICE, AND ELASTICITY OF DEMAND WITH RESPECT TO PRICE

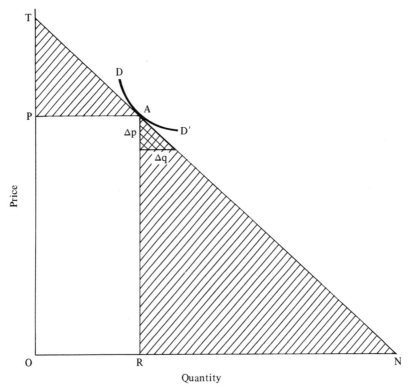

Figure 14A.1. Price-quantity relationships relevant to the determination of price elasticity.

The demand is described by DD' in Figure 14A.1. TN is tangent to the demand curve at point A. The elasticity of demand with respect to price, e_p, at point A is OP/PT.

Proof:

$$OT \parallel AR$$

Therefore TPA, ARN, TON and the small triangle whose two sides are Δp and Δq are similar triangles. Since corresponding sides of similar triangles are proportional,

$$\frac{AP}{PT} = \frac{RN}{AR} = \frac{ON}{OT} = \frac{\Delta q}{\Delta p}$$

By definition

$$e_p = \frac{\Delta q}{\Delta p} \frac{p}{q}$$

Since

$$p = AR = OP, \quad \text{and} \quad q = OR = AP$$

then

$$e_p = \frac{RN}{AR} \frac{AR}{OR} = \frac{RN}{OR} = \frac{OP}{PT} = \frac{AN}{AT}$$

Thus

$$e_p = \frac{OP}{PT}$$

APPENDIX B

THE RELATIONSHIP OF MARKUP AND ELASTICITY OF DEMAND WITH RESPECT TO PRICE

DD' in Figure 14B.1 represents the demand curve of the *retailer* (not of the industry). TN is tangent to the demand curve at point A. At this point selling price is OP or AR; marginal revenue, dd'', is MR or OS; and sales are OR or SM. Marginal cost, MC, equals marginal revenue, MR, at sales of OR. If average cost, AC, is perfectly elastic, then

$$MC = MR = AC$$

Markup on cost is then AM/MR, and markup on retail is AM/AR.

We assume that the retailer knows his MC. How can he determine his markup? To do so he must estimate what the elasticity of demand for his firm is. We have described his assumed demand curve as DD' in Figure 14B.1. The elasticity of demand with respect to price at point A is OP/PT. The retailer's price, p, will be

$$p = \frac{|e_p|(MC)}{|e_p| - 1}$$

We shall present our proof in two steps.

1. We shall first prove that the markup is p/e_p. The markup in Figure 14B.1 is represented by AM or PC. The selling price, p, is OP or AR. Since

$$TO \parallel AR$$
$$TPB = BMA \quad \text{and} \quad TP = AM$$

But

$$AM = AR - MR$$

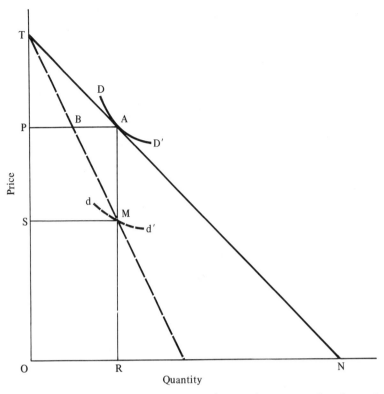

Figure 14B.1. Price-quantity relationships relevant to the determination of price elasticity and markup.

According to the proof presented in Appendix A, and ignoring the sign of e_p, we know that

$$e_p = \frac{OP}{PT}$$

Since $p = OP = AR$, $AM = PT = (AR - MR)$, and $e_p = OP/PT$, then

$$e_p = \frac{OP}{AR - MR} = \frac{p}{p - MR}$$

Taking the reciprocal of each side, we have

$$\frac{1}{e_p} = \frac{p - MR}{p} \qquad \text{or} \qquad \frac{1}{e_p} = 1 - \frac{MR}{p}$$

Subtracting $1/e_p$ from both sides and adding MR/p to both sides, we have

$$\frac{1}{e_p} - \frac{1}{e_p} + \frac{MR}{p} = 1 - \frac{MR}{p} - \frac{1}{e_p} + \frac{MR}{p} \qquad \text{or} \qquad \frac{MR}{p} = 1 - \frac{1}{e_p}$$

Multiplying both sides by p,

$$MR = p - \frac{p}{e_p}$$

Thus the price exceeds the MR by p/e_p.

But this is not very helpful in arriving at markup, for it describes the markup in terms of the price, and the price is the value that the retailer is seeking. A more useful approach would be to describe the markup in terms of the cost and elasticity, since cost is known and elasticity can be estimated. We shall therefore use these two as our known variables, with price as the unknown variable.

2. We shall now prove that the desired markup as a percentage of cost is $1/(e_p-1)$ and that the desired percentage markup on retail is $1/e_p$, with the negative sign of e_p ignored. Since we do not know MR, we shall assume that $MC = MR$ and use MC in lieu of MR.

We have shown in the preceding proof that the price exceeds the MR by p/e_p. Therefore

$$p = MR + \frac{p}{e_p}$$

If we substitute MC for MR,

$$p = MC + \frac{p}{e_p} \quad \text{and} \quad p - \frac{p}{e_p} = MC$$

Factoring out p, we find that

$$p\left(1 - \frac{1}{e_p}\right) = MC$$

so that

$$p = \frac{MC}{1 - \frac{1}{e_p}} = \frac{MC}{\frac{e_p - 1}{e_p}} = MC\left(\frac{e_p}{e_p - 1}\right)$$

Adding and subtracting 1 to the numerator, we have

$$p = MC\left(\frac{e_p + 1 - 1}{e_p - 1}\right) = MC\left(\frac{e_p - 1}{e_p - 1} + \frac{1}{e_p - 1}\right) = MC\left(1 + \frac{1}{e_p - 1}\right) = MC + \frac{MC}{e_p - 1}$$

Since the markup, m, equals $p - MC$, then

$$m = \frac{MC}{e_p - 1}$$

If p is the optimum price, the optimum markup as a percentage of MC is $1/(e_p - 1)$.

If $1/(e_p-1)$ is markup as a percentage of cost, markup as a percentage of retail can be easily determined. The relationship of markup on retail, m_r, to markup on cost, m_c, is

$$m_r = \frac{m_c}{c + m_c}$$

in which c is cost and is equal to 100 percent, or 1.00. If $m_c = 1/(e_p-1)$, then

$$m_r = \frac{\dfrac{1}{e_p - 1}}{1 + \left(\dfrac{1}{e_p - 1}\right)}$$

$$= \frac{\dfrac{1}{e_p - 1}}{\dfrac{e_p - 1 + 1}{e_p - 1}} = \frac{\dfrac{1}{e_p - 1}}{\dfrac{e_p}{e_p - 1}} = \frac{e_p - 1}{e_p(e_p - 1)} = \frac{1}{e_p}$$

For example, if $e_p = 3$, markup as a percentage of cost would be

$$m_c = \frac{1}{e_p - 1}$$

Therefore,

$$m_c = \frac{1}{3 - 1} = .50$$

or 50 percent of c.

Markup as a percentage of retail would be

$$m_r = \frac{1}{e_p} = \frac{1}{3} = .33$$

or 33 percent of retail. Using the marginal cost as a basis, therefore, we find that the selling price of a product whose MC is $10 and whose elasticity of demand with respect to price is -3 would be

$$p = MC \left(\frac{e_p}{e_p - 1} \right) = \frac{MC(e_p)}{e_p - 1}$$

$$p = \frac{\$10\,(3)}{3 - 1} = \frac{\$30}{2} = \$15$$

Were the elasticity-4, the desired selling price would be $13.33. Thus the higher the elasticity of demand with respect to price, the lower the markup tends to be.

The elasticity of demand to which we refer is that of the individual retail firm—not that of the market. Because the firm's elasticity is greatly influenced by the degree of competition, the size of margins is sometimes used as one measure of the degree of competition in a retail market. Inference of degree of competition from the size of margins will, however, yield a false conclusion if the demand is highly elastic in a market in which the retailer is a monopolist. In this case, the retailer's demand, which is also the market demand, is elastic, and his margin policy would reflect this even though market competition is nil.

15

Vertical Price Policy

I wonder often what the Vintners buy
One half so precious as the stuff they sell.

—Omar Khayyam

A vertical market structure consists of a set of firms and consumers whose functions are complementary and whose relationships are cooperative.[1] At various levels within a structure may be subsets of firms or consumers whose functions and relationships are competing. Each firm within a vertical system makes production and marketing decisions within the constraints created by its complementary and competing relationships. The totality of these decisions will determine the economic character of the vertical market structure.

In their excellent treatment of the vertical market system and the decisions that shape the system, Helmy H. Baligh and Leon E. Richartz have analyzed vertical price determination within the framework of the triangular cluster of price, output, and form.[2] A product is defined in terms of particular inputs, while form is the values that are functionally related to these inputs. Decisions of firms concerning price, form, and output in vertically related markets determine, in the short run, the allocation of productive and marketing activities among the participants in the various levels of the system, and in the intermediate and long-run periods, the number of firms and market levels as well. Thus price is viewed as a crucial variable in the allocation of functions in the vertical market structure. Baligh and Richartz then establish the basic decision rules for determining price-output-form under purely competitive conditions in each of three periods. These periods differ only with respect to the extent to which the number of decision-making units is fixed.

In our discussion of vertical market structure,[3] we have treated price and quantity relationships in fairly elementary terms as they would evolve under conditions of pure competition but, more specifically, under conditions of imperfect competition and

---

[1] This is not to deny the existence of *competing* relationships within the vertical structure. Clearly manufacturers will wish to sell a given quantity at as high a price as possible, wholesalers will wish to buy at as low a price as possible, and so on throughout the trade channel. Similarly, sellers may become dissatisfied with the abolition of functions by their customers, and buying firms may become dissatisfied with the reduced services they obtain from sellers. Evidence of the importance of these competing relationships lies in the ebb and flow of functions vertically and in the considerable degree of vertical integration during recent decades. But we adhere to our definition of a market as consisting of buyer-seller relationships. If there is not agreement by buyers and suppliers concerning the amount of product-services-price (or, to use Baligh's and Richartz's terminology, price, output, and form), there will be no market. Vertical market antagonists who do not consummate a transaction have an impact on transactions that are completed, but they themselves are not direct participants in vertical market relationships. Our focus will be on what happens in trade channels and why, rather than on what does not happen.

[2] Helmy H. Baligh and Leon E. Richartz, *Vertical Market Stuctures* (Boston: Allyn & Bacon, 1967), pp. 205-230.

[3] See Chapter 12.

varying cost structures. In that discussion we demonstrated that in imperfect markets the effect of retailer or wholesaler domination in vertical relationships will depend on the relative elasticity of demand and cost in all of the vertically related markets in the channel. We concluded that, in general, whether the quantity determined in a retailer-dominated market structure will be greater or less than that in a wholesaler-dominated structure will depend on the relative elasticities of the aggregate of the retailers' average net revenue (ANR) and the wholesaler's average cost (AC). The more elastic the aggregate ANR_r is relative to AC_w, the more likely it is that wholesaler domination will result in greater output. The more elastic AC_w is relative to ANR_r, the more likely it is that retailer domination will result in greater output.

It is the purpose of this chapter to pursue price relationships as a short-run problem under conditions of vertical price control. In keeping with the basic character of this section, which is concerned with marketing policies, we shall consider in this chapter only those aspects of vertical price relationships that are associated with policies of participants in the trade channel. We shall further restrict ourselves to policies that either are designed to achieve vertical price control or are the result of vertical price control. Thus we shall focus on what we may properly call vertical price policy. While control over such a policy may be vested in varying degrees in any one participant in the trade channel, we shall simplify our treatment by focusing on control vested in the manufacturer.[4]

We shall address ourselves to three questions: (1) Under what conditions will a manufacturer find it advantageous to control the resale price of his product? (2) Given one or more of those conditions, what will be the optimum price structure from his point of view? (3) What is the economic impact of vertical price control, particularly its effect on social welfare? As a background for the examination of these questions, we shall comment briefly on the various mechanisms for achieving vertical price control.

THE INSTITUTIONAL FRAMEWORK FOR A VERTICAL PRICE POLICY

In order for there to be a vertical price policy, one or more firms in a trade channel must have some degree of control over prices at levels in the trade channel other than those in the markets in which the firm's principal market activities occur. This might be a manufacturer who is able to control to some degree the resale price of his product at subsequent levels in the trade channel. The form of the product he has sold is changed by the rendering of additional marketing services at subsequent levels, but the physical product continues to be identifiable. Another possibility would be wholesaler control of prices at levels "behind" the wholesaler—that is, closer to the primary production level—or "beyond" the wholesaler, closer to the market in which consumers participate. Retailer control might be extended "back" toward wholesaling and manufacturing market levels.

By what mechanisms are these controls effected? The institutional structure through which vertical control is achieved in marketing channels may be described in terms of a continuum that ranges from a loosely defined, almost tacit, type of nonmarket coordination to the tightly controlled integration of vertically related functions. The

---

[4] Some of the modifications that would be necessary in our analysis were we to focus on the wholesaler or retailer as the locus of power in vertical price control are suggested by the discussion of vertical relationships under varying types of market dominance. See Chapter 12.

following are examples of degrees of control through which policy may exert its influence vertically:

1. Control through voluntary compliance (e.g., adherence to suggested prices)
2. Control by the use of market power (e.g., fear of retaliation for noncompliance)
3. Control by contract through
    a. a voluntary chain,
    b. a franchise, or
    c. resale price maintenance
4. Control through ownership, resulting in
    a. partial removal from market participation of one or more vertically related units, or
    b. full removal from market participation of one or more vertically related units

Analysis of the economic causes, processes, and consequences of vertical price control shows the effects of the method of implementation only to the extent that one method offers possibilities or constraints different from those of another method. We shall utilize resale price maintenance as the framework for our discussion of vertical price control, primarily because it is so clearly price oriented, minimizing the influence of nonprice variables on the vertical control. This does not mean that nonprice factors do not enter into and result from its use but, rather, that the contamination that such factors inject into the analysis is minimized. Resale price maintenance is the process by which sellers of an identifiable good may control the resale price of that good as it moves through one or more levels of the trade channel. While such control could result from voluntary contracts between seller and buyer, the more common, and more interesting, situation is one in which the control is compulsory.

While most discussions of resale price maintenance have assumed that its use, and hence enforcement, were predicated on special legislation, it is not impossible for enforcement to be based on a franchise that gives the seller the right to require compliance with specified resale prices. The following discussion will be concerned with resale price maintenance enforceable by the seller regardless of the presence of special legislation. We shall, however, conclude our discussion with a consideration of the welfare implications of resale price maintenance and, hence, the social implications of special legislation that encourages use of such a policy.

CONDITIONS FOR RESALE PRICE MAINTENANCE

The conditions under which resale price maintenance occurs may be grouped into those that are prerequisite to resale price maintenance and those that make resale price maintenance desirable.

Prerequisite Conditions

A first condition necessary to an effective resale price maintenance (RPM) policy is the existence of a product that is identifiable as it moves through the trade channel. The form (utility or value) of the marketable unit may change as it moves through the channel owing to the additional marketing functions that are performed and become a part of the object of negotiation, but the product itself must be physically identifiable. Resale prices cannot be specified under conditions of pure competition owing to the standardization of product and the inability of a single seller to distinguish his output. The output of a monopolist is unique, however, and amenable to the specification of resale prices. Differentiated products are also amenable to the specification of resale prices, and particularly so if there is no change in the physical attributes of the products as they move through the trade channel. Physical identity is a necessary but not sufficient condition for resale price maintenance.

A second prerequisite for an effective RPM policy is that services incorporated into the transaction at the point of resale must be sufficiently standardized to make the unit of the resale transaction—that is, the form of the product—the same for all resellers. Lack of standardization opens opportunities for resellers to change the form, and hence the nature, of the transaction and thereby the "quantity" received for a given price. Such a change could be made equivalent to a change in the price. If, for example, warranties, credit, guaranteed repairs and maintenance, and user instruction were offered by some sellers and not by others, this differentiation would make RPM ineffective.

Closely related to the standardization of services necessary for an effective RPM policy is the requirement that the quoted price under RPM be the fully negotiated price. If there are discounts of any sort, arising from such practices as trade-ins, an RPM policy can be negated.

A fourth condition necessary for an RPM policy to be effective is the existence of some degree of market control by a party that enforces the policy.[5] This can derive from the seller's monopoly position, collusion among buyers (having the effect of a monopsony), the seller's brand ownership and power to discipline a franchise system, and/or legislation that gives the owner of an identifiable product the legal right to establish and enforce RPM.

Each of the four conditions just cited is necessary for an effective RPM policy. Existence of all four conditions is sufficient to provide a market environment hospitable to an enforceable RPM policy.

Conducive Conditions

The second set of conditions to be considered are those that make RPM a desirable policy. Specifically, under what circumstances will a manufacturer (or wholesaler) find it to his interest to place his product under RPM? What is in his interest will depend, of course, on the firm's objectives. We shall assume that the principal objective is profit maximization and that a significant subsidiary objective is either maximization or stabilization of market share. The latter two might be perceived as means to achieve a long-run profit objective.

RETAILER COERCION

If retailers are able, through effective organization, to exert pressure on the manufacturer, they may choose to force upon him a system of RPM. Such collusion among the resellers of a product would most likely be generated by small firms that are losing sales to large

---

[5] This is discussed quite fully by Ward S. Bowman, Jr., in "Resale Price Maintenance—A Monopoly Problem," *Journal of Business* 25 (July 1952): 141-155.

firms, high-cost firms that are losing customers to low-cost firms, or retailers operating under conditions of excess retail capacity. The larger the retail firm, the greater the opportunities it has for benefiting, through cross-elasticity of demand, from the use of selective price leaders. Also, the larger the firm, the greater the opportunities, up to a certain point, for economies to scale to permit a general reduction in margins. Therefore small firms are more likely than large ones to want vertical price control if the effect of such control is to increase prevailing prices and partially destroy the strengths of the larger competitor. Similarly, retail stores with high cost ratios are likely to desire RPM more than stores with low cost ratios if the effect of RPM is to equalize margins, thereby eliminating the competitive advantage of the low-margin retail firms. If, in addition, there is excess capacity in retailing, the pressure on margins and profits may be sufficient to cause retailers to seek higher margins through RPM.

INDUCED SERVICES

There may, on the other hand, be reasons why the manufacturer will, of his own volition, choose to place his product under RPM. One argument advanced to defend such a decision is the effect of the retailer's margin on the amount and quality of services that he renders in retailing the manufacturer's product. If those services are important in the sale of the product, the manufacturer may seek ways to ensure that they are rendered. Giving the customer sufficient information, devoting adequate resources to personal selling and promotion at the retail level, maintaining adequate stocks for optimal consumer selection, and servicing the product after its sale are examples of services that may be of crucial importance to the sale of the manufacturer's product. If the willingness of retailers to render these services for particular items is related to the size of the margin received on the product, the manufacturer may be willing to incur the "cost" of RPM in order to induce the retailer to perform the requisite services. The "cost" of RPM to the manufacturer will be (1) the explicit costs of enforcement plus (2) any opportunity cost associated with a reduction in the number of outlets willing to handle the product due to the discrepancy between the vertically regulated margin and the margin deemed necessary by such outlets plus (3) any loss of margin to the manufacturer arising from the necessity of "giving" a part of his margin to the retailer in order to induce the services desired. These costs must be evaluted against the increase in revenue resulting from the services induced by RPM.

NUMBER OF OUTLETS

A second logical basis for a manufacturer's decision to employ RPM is the impact of guaranteed margins on the number of retail outlets handling the product. In the marketing of convenience goods, the number of outlets handling a branded product may be crucial to the product's competitive advantage. The size of the retailer's margin, and the degree to which that margin is assured, may be important in determining the number of retailers willing to stock the merchandise. Since wide dispersion will involve a large number of small retailers, it is possible that RPM will be one of the most effective devices for achieving this objective. The problem that arises, however, is the uniformity of margins vis-á-vis lack of uniformity in the operating-cost ratios of retail stores. If the margin established through RPM is to be attractive to marginal stores, it is likely that it will be much higher than that needed by low-cost stores, thereby encouraging the low-cost stores to seek alternatives that will enable them to benefit competitively from

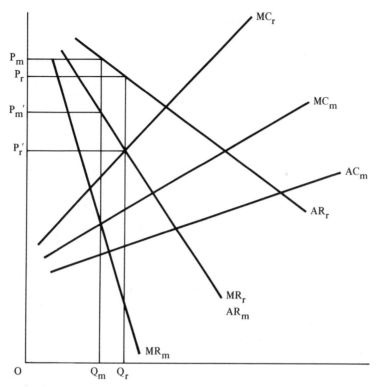

Figure 15.1. Price determination for a manufacturer selling to retailers operating in collusion to induce resale price maintenance.

their efficiency. Thus the large-volume, low-cost retailer may continue to handle the branded item being sold under RPM, but be encouraged to also handle other brands whose margins reflect more clearly the store's cost ratio. RPM on selected brands will, in fact, make prices of those brands stand in sharper contrast to those other brands not sold under RPM. To some extent this would therefore offset the effectiveness of the manufacturer's wide-dispersion policy.

PRICE DETERMINATION UNDER RESALE PRICE MAINTENANCE

Let us assume that a manufacturer (or wholesaler) is operating under conditions that make it possible for his product to be placed under resale price maintenance. We shall attempt, with greater precision than in the preceding discussion, to establish the conditions under which he will find RPM a desirable policy and, where RPM is desirable, the optimum output and price schedule. Our analysis will be made within the framework of the three conducive conditions identified earlier: retailer coercion, service inducement, and number of outlets.

Retailer Coercion: Bilateral Monopoly

The case in which retailers engage in collusive action to force manufacturers to undertake resale price maintenance is one of bilateral monopoly. The manufacturer is a monopolist of his brand, with the elasticity of aggregate demand for his brand greatly affected by the number and closeness of substitute brands. Retailers acting in collusion will behave as a monopsonist would. Therefore we shall examine price and output determination, using a bilateral monopoly model.

Figure 15.1 shows the relevant revenue and cost relationships. The symbols are as follows:

AR_r = average revenue of all retailers

MR_r = marginal revenue of all retailers

AR_m = average revenue of manufacturer

MR_m = marginal revenue of manufacturer

AC_m = average cost of manufacturer

MC_m = marginal cost of manufacturer

MC_r = marginal cost of merchandise to retailer

P = retail price

P' = manufacturer's selling price

Q = quantity offered or sold

Retailers, acting in collusion, will have a negatively sloping AR_r curve, since price will determine quantity sold. If they were able to specify the optimum retail price, they would desire the price P_r, with a manufacturer's price of P_r', at which sales would be Q_r. Were the manufacturer able to control the price, he would prefer P_m at retail and a selling price from the factory of P_m', with sales of Q_m resulting.[6]

It will be the relative bargaining power of the manufacturer and the retailers that will determine whether the retail price under RPM is set at P_r or P_m. The stronger the retailers' collusion, the more likely it is that the retailers will be able to drive the price to the level P_r. It is not possible to generalize about the strength of retail collusions. It seems reasonable to expect, however, that retail trade associations that have a strong professional orientation or strong leadership would be stronger than associations that have a more limited service function.[7] The National Association of Retail Druggists is a good example of the professionally oriented association, and the history of resale price maintenance in the United States is strongly colored by the aggressive action of this group, through both its lobbying activities in behalf of RPM legislation and its pressure on manufacturers to place their products under RPM and to grant retail margins of 33⅓ percent of retail.

The effect of retail coercion illustrated in Figure 15.1 would be to cause a lower retail price to prevail than would be true were the manufacturer-monopolist to determine the optimum price from his own point of view. This is not always the case, however. It is the elasticities of cost and revenue that determine whether retailer or manufacturer dominance would result in a lower retail price. The more elastic AR_r is relative to AC_m, the more likely it is that retailer coercion will result in lower volume and higher retail prices than would manufacturer control. Increasing costs in manufacturing are likely to cause greater restrictions of output and higher prices under retailer domination than if manufacturers determined RPM of their own volition.

---

[6] See Chapter 12 for a more complete treatment of these relationships.

[7] See Mancur L. Olson, *The Logic of Collective Action: Public Goods and the Theory of Groups* (Cambridge, Mass.: Harvard University Press, 1965), for an interesting hypothesis concerning the importance of nonlobbying functions in the creation of an institutional structure that makes it possible for the organization to become an effective pressure group.

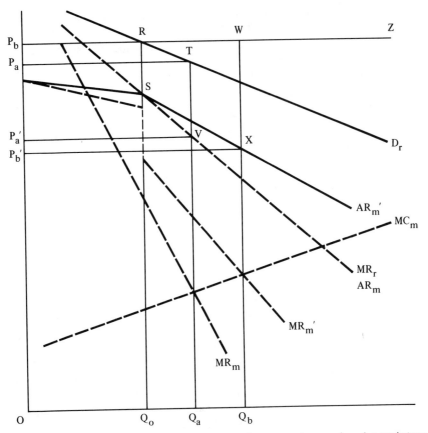

Figure 15.2. Price determination for a manufacturer using resale price maintenance as an inducement to expanded retailer services: two price alternatives.

Service Inducement

The second case that we shall consider is that in which a manufacturer places his product under RPM in order to guarantee retailers a margin sufficient to induce them to render services that will stimulate purchases of the product.[8] These services may result in changes in the form of the product—that is, the consumer gets "more" than he would without the services—or they may constitute promotional efforts that induce consumers to buy the product because they perceive the product's utility to them as greater than before.

We shall now consider how the manufacturer determines the resale price of his product

---

[8] The service argument for resale price maintenance is developed most fully by Lester G. Telser, "Why Should Manufacturers Want Fair Trade?" *The Journal of Law and Economics* 3 (October 1960): 86-105, especially pp. 89-96; E. R. Hawkins, "Further Theoretical Considerations Regarding Fair Trade Laws," *Journal of Marketing* 4 (October 1939): 126-134; E. R. Hawkins, "Vertical Price Relationships," in Reavis Cox and Wroe Alderson, eds., *Theory in Marketing: Selected Essays*, 1st ser. (Chicago: Irwin, 1950), pp. 185-189. It is also discussed by J. R. Gould and L. E. Preston, "Resale Price Maintenance and Retail Outlets," *Economica*, n.s., 32 (August 1965): 302-312, especially pp. 311-312.

and the margin he should grant his retail customers. These decisions must be made in the light of their effects on sales revenue and its relation to costs. Figure 15.2 illustrates the significant variables that enter into these decisions. The basic symbols are the same as those used in Figure 15.1.

PRICE WITHOUT RPM

We shall first examine price determination without RPM. Aggregate consumer demand is represented by D_r.[9] MR_r is the marginal return to all retailers taken together, and this represents the average revenue of the manufacturer of the branded product, AR_m. The manufacturer's marginal return is therefore MR_m. With marginal costs of MC_m his point of maximum profits will be at output level Q_a, a retail price of P_a, and a manufacturer's price of P_a', resulting in a retail margin of TV.

PRICE WITH RPM

Suppose that the manufacturer considers the desirability of placing his product under RPM. One reason he may choose to do so is the possibility that a resale price higher than P_a would induce the retailer to render more services to the consumer or to push the product more heavily. This would have the effect of moving the D_r curve to the right. For the moment let us assume that he considers setting a resale price of P_b on the product. What will the effect be on his volume of sales, and how much margin will he find it desirable to give to retailers? Clearly he could sell quantity Q_o at that price without any added or unusual effort on the part of retailers. But this is not an optimum position for the manufacturer, and he will surely elect to employ such a price only if sales are greater than Q_o as a result of increased sales effort by retailers.

He would like to have a new consumer demand curve represented by the horizontal line P_b, which is, of course, a perfectly elastic demand at the resale price. But to make D_r shift upward to line P_b from point R to Z, retailers will have to work harder to sell these greater quantities at this high price. Let us assume that they can be induced to do this if their margins are large enough. They would accept a margin of RS, for which they would buy and sell Q_o. But they will not work hard enough to sell quantity Q_b unless their margin is at least WX. Line AR_m' is therefore the new average revenue curve for the manufacturer. It represents the amount of revenue he can expect per unit if he allows retailers increasing margins to encourage them to hold sales to the level indicated by the horizontal line P_b. If the manufacturer cuts the margin below RS, he will find that some retailers will not handle the product, and others will push substitutes more aggressively. If he succeeds in selling quantities larger than Q_o, the margin he grants retailers must

---

[9] An additional refinement would be to subtract from the retail selling price the average variable cost of retailers to arrive at average net revenue (ANR_r) at different retail prices. If this were done, the crucial question would be whether AVC is increasing, decreasing, or constant at various sales levels. These differences would affect the slope of the ANR_r curve in relation to the D_r curve. We shall not include this refinement in our analysis, since we have observed generally that the principal variable cost in retailing is the cost of merchandise, with other costs of operation not easily allocated to specific items of merchandise. (See Chapter 14.) Where this is not the case, the situation is modified, although the analysis would proceed as we present it here. See expecially Neil T. Houston, "Methods of Efficiency Analysis in Marketing," Ph.D. dissertation, Harvard University, 1948, Chap. IX, where the effects of different variable cost structures on RPM are discussed.

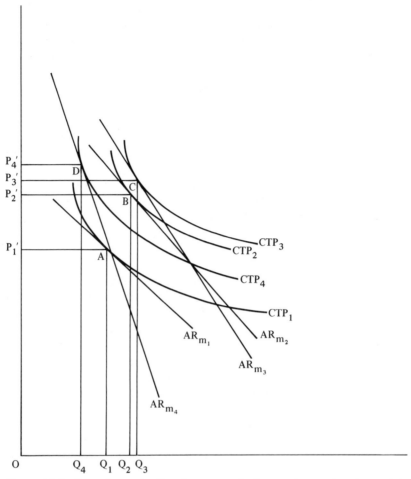

Figure 15.3. Price determination for a manufacturer using resale price maintenance as an inducement to expanded retailer services: four price alternatives.

increase as the quantity to be sold increases. Otherwise retailers will not put forth the sales effort necessary to sell the even larger amounts at this price. These larger margins are shown by the more steeply downward-sloping AR_m' curve beyong point S. The manufacturer's new MR_m' curve is now determined, and the optimum output is with the manufacturer's selling price P_b' and the retailer's margin WX.

In the preceding analysis AR_m' is what we call a neutral average revenue curve for the manufacturer.[10] It shows the highest price at which the manufacturer can sell his product to retailers and induce retailers, through the margin granted, to undertake the selling effort necessary to sell the quantities indicated at the maintained resale price. Every possible resale price has its relevant neutral average revenue curve based on the neutral markup. The manufacturer must decide, then, which set of possible relationships is optimal. In Figure 15.2 RPM at the level of P_b is better for the manufacturer than optimum pricing without RPM at price P_a. This is demonstrated by the fact that MR_m is

---

[10] This is the terminology employed by E. R. Hawkins, "Vertical Price Relationships," in Cox and Alderson, op. cit. pp. 185-189.

lower than MR_m'. If, on the other hand, margins necessary to induce retailers to render services necessary to sell volumes greater than Q_o were much larger, then AR_m' would be lower and MR_m' correspondingly lower. If MR_m' is lower than MR_m, the manufacturer would be better off not placing his product under RPM. In effect, the cost to him of the wider margins would more than offset the advantages of the higher resale price.

A manufacturer can manipulate the retailer's margin in either of two ways. He can raise the resale price of the product, or he can lower the manufacturer's price. But the more he raises the resale price, the larger the margin will have to be to induce the retailer to push sales in the light of the higher retail price. So there are limits on how far he can push this possibility. On the other hand, if he attempts to induce more sales effort by cutting the manufacturer's selling price, granting larger margins, this reduces his own margins and, if he is operating beyond the point of lowest marginal cost, can push sales into volume levels at which costs are rising.

Figure 15.3 illustrates the turnaround point for establishing the manufacturer's selling price. AR_m is the manufacturer's average revenue. This is the same as AR_m in Figure 15.2 and is shown in Figure 15.3 for four different manufacturer's prices. The four manufacturer's prices have corresponding retail prices not shown in Figure 15.3. Each AR_m is a function of one of those maintained retail prices and the margin that the retailers must obtain in order to sell the quantities indicated. P_1' is the manufacturer's optimum selling price given P_1 and the resulting AR_{m_1} curve. Thus P_1' is the manufacturer's price and Q_1 is the quantity sold.

CTP_1 is a constant total profit curve. It shows all the combinations of prices and quantities at which the firm can obtain the same total profit as it does with price P_1' and Q_1.

P_2' is his optimum price given P_2 and the resulting AR_{m_2} curve, with quantity Q_2. CTP_2 shows other combinations of price and quantity that would yield profits to the manufacturer equal to those that he obtains with P_2, P_2', and Q_2. But none of these other combinations is possible with AR_{m_2}. So he chooses to operate at the point of tangency, point B. The optimum price for the manufacturer is that which yields an AR_m curve tangent to the highest possible CTP curve. Of the four possibilities we consider in Figure 15.3, the best from the manufacturer's point of view will be price P_3' (and its corresponding P_3 for the retailer, which results in AR_{m_3}) and a sales volume of Q_3. A price lower than that will yield a lower total profit. A price higher than that will also yield a lower total profit, since price P_4' is tangent to CTP_4 at point D, and this is on a lower CTP curve.[11]

Number of Outlets Hypothesis

A third argument advanced to support a manufacturer's decision to place his product under RPM is the impact that price maintenance has on the willingness of retailers to handle the product.[12] If the successful marketing of a branded product requires wide

---

[11] The constant total profit curve is employed by E. R. Hawkins in "Further Theoretical Considerations Regarding Fair Trade Laws," *Journal of Marketing*, 4 (October 1939): 128. This is similar to Marshall's constant revenue curve. See Alfred Marshall, *Principles of Economics*, 8th ed. (London: Macmillan, 1920), p. 479.

[12] The development in this section owes a great deal to the excellent treatment by Gould and Preston, op. cit.

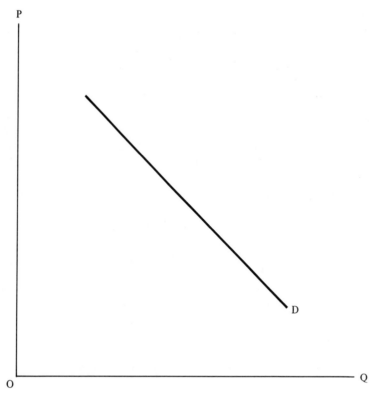

Figure 15.4. Aggregate demand at retail for a manufacturer's product when stocked by N_0 retailers.

dispersion of stocks among large numbers of retailers, guaranteed margins of adequate size may induce more retailers to handle the product. Smaller retailers in particular may find the guaranteed margin an added inducement to stock the goods. If minimum retail prices are specified, customers have no inducement to shop for lower prices so long as the minimum becomes, in effect, the actual price.[13] Thus marginal retailers may be induced to handle the merchandise.

It is possible to treat this problem in substantially the same way as the service inducement argument discussed in the preceding section. That is, larger margins are necessary to induce more retailers to handle the manufacturer's product rather than to render more promotional and other services. The following discussion is not, therefore, different in essence from that developed in the discussion of service inducement. A more explicit development of some of the relationships among the variables will, however, help crystalize the crucial factors in the decision-making process.

NUMBER OF RETAILERS

We shall develop our analysis with the aid of Figures 15.4–15.8. A manufacturer is confronted with a consumer demand for his product at the retail level, as illustrated by curve D in Figure 15.4. If we assume that the quantity demanded by consumers is in part

---

[13] If, on the other hand, not all retailers adhere to the minimum but some sell at higher prices, retail customers may still find shopping worthwhile.

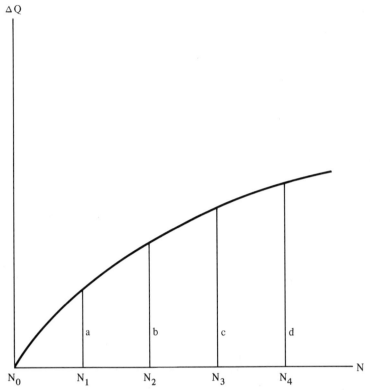

Figure 15.5. Changes in the quantity demanded at retail at any price as a result of an increase in the number of retail outlets stocking the manufacturer's product from N_0 to N_4.

a function of the number of retailers that handle the product, then curve D is related to a given number of retailers, which we shall designate as N_0. If a larger number of retailers handle the product, sales will increase. This relationship is demonstrated in Figure 15.5, where the increase in the quantity sold is a function of the number of retailers. We shall assume, therefore, that curve D will represent the demand when N_0 retailers handle the product. If N_1 retailers handle the product, line D will move to the right by the amount a. If N_2 retailers handle the product, D will move to the right by the amount b. Thus N_4 retailers would cause D to move to the right by the amount d.

RETAIL MARGIN

Let us assume that the manufacturer finds that he must increase the margin that he grants the retailer if he is to induce more retailers to handle the product. Figure 15.6 describes the assumed relationship between the retailer's dollar margin per unit and the number of retailers willing to stock the product. N_0 retailers are willing to handle the product if their margin is O dollars per unit. N_2 retailers will handle the product if their margin is b dollars per unit.[14]

---

[14] Note that Figure 15.5 shows the change in quantity sold in relation to number of retailers, while Figure 15.6 shows the absolute dollar margin required in relation to number of retailers. This differential treatment of these two sets of relationships simplifies the transition from Figure 15.4 to Figure 15.7.

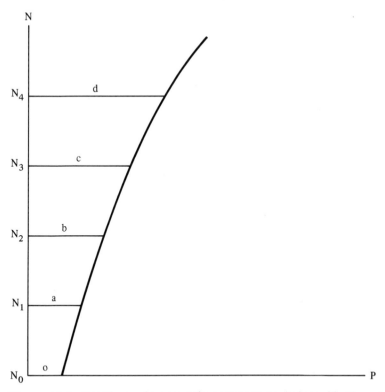

Figure 15.6. Retail margin per unit necessary to induce N_0-N_4 retailers to stock a manufacturer's product.

NET DEMAND EFFECTS

In Figure 15.7 we show the combined effects of number of retailers (from Figure 15.5) and margin concessions necessary to attract retailers (from Figure 15.6) on the price-quantity relationships with which we started (Figure 15.4). Figure 15.4 is moved to the right by the amounts shown in Figure 15.5 to yield $D_{N_0}, D_{N_1}, \ldots, D_{N_4}$. But each of these new demands can be realized only if retailers are given greater inducements to handle the product. We shall regard these increasing margins as deductions from the retailers' aggregate average gross revenue curve, shown in Figure 15.4 as the demand. Thus D_{N_0} moves downward to D_{N_0}' by the amount O in Figure 15.6. D_{N_1} moves down by the amount a in Figure 15.6 to become D_{N_1}' in Figure 15.7. The four demand curves without prime numbers become the four demand curves with prime numbers after adjustment has been made for the increasing margins necessary to induce retailers to stock the manufacturer's product.

Notice that the net effect of these two variables—one of which increases sales and the other of which decreases the retailer's net revenue—is positive up to N_3. Thereafter the net effect is negative, with D_{N_4}' lower than either D_{N_2}', or D_{N_3}'. This possibility was built into our problem by the curvilinear relationship we assumed to exist between numbers of stores and quantity sold and between numbers of retailers and required margins. This is an assumption of diminishing returns from the two policies. It is clear from Figure 15.7 that D_{N_4}' is inferior to D_{N_3}' and D_{N_2}'.

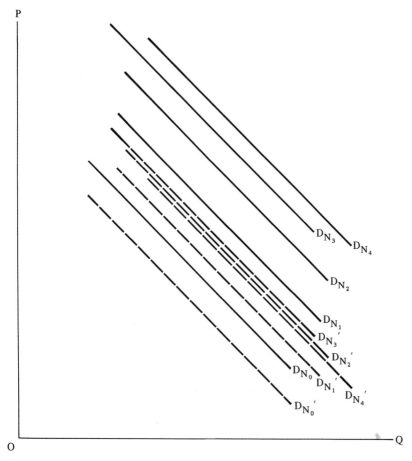

Figure 15.7. Manufacturer's unadjusted average revenue (D_N) based on number of retail outlets and adjusted average revenue (D_N') after required margin concessions are deducted from unadjusted average revenue.

DEMAND AND COSTS

But Figure 15.7 does not indicate how price and volume would be determined. Figure 15.8 adds the necessary information to show the relationship of costs and revenue. The D_N' curves in Figure 15.8 are the same as those in Figure 15.7. Each of these curves is the manufacturer's average revenue for different numbers of retail outlets, with the induced number a function of the margins received by them through an equal reduction in the manufacturer's revenue. We may regard these as the manufacturer's average net revenue curve after necessary margin guarantees. The manufacturer's relevant marginal revenue curves are, therefore, the MR' curves in Figure 15.8. He will choose a combination of price and quantity that will maximize profits, and this will occur where the difference between total cost and total revenue is greatest, that is, where the marginal return from various combinations of P and $Q-P_0Q_0$, P_1Q_1, P_2Q_2, P_3Q_3, P_4Q_4 —equals marginal cost at these respective quantities.

If the addition of additional outlets reduces sales per outlet so much that outlets

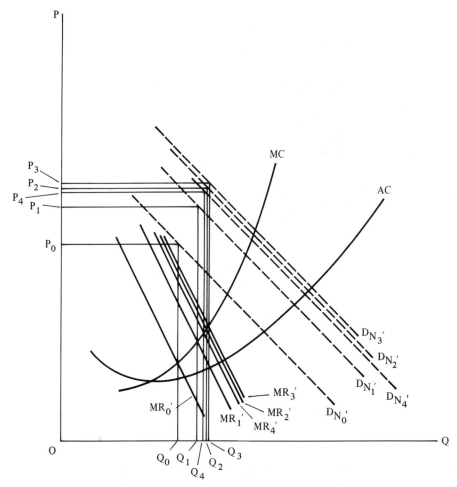

Figure 15.8. Manufacturer's adjusted average revenue (D_N') and marginal revenue (MR') for varying numbers of retail outlets.

become too small for efficient operation, then margins will have to rise very markedly to make it worthwhile for them to continue to handle the product. One of the conditions favorable to successful RPM is, therefore, that the average costs of retailing be relatively stable over quite a range of volume so that the increased numbers of stores will not force the manufacturer into greatly increased retail margins. It is unlikely, of course, that a single manufacturer can affect a retailer's volume to any great extent. The more critical aspect of the problem is to get the retailer to handle *his* brand in preference to alternative brands. Hence, retailer costs may be less crucial and competititve alternatives of much more importance.

In the example we have shown in Figure 15.8, both the manufacturer's and the retailer's prices are higher with RPM than they would be without RPM. Under what circumstances would RPM result in lower prices? One situation in which lower prices might result is where the manufacturer is operating on a falling marginal cost curve without RPM and finds a more profitable equilibrium point with increased revenue and lower prices if he attracts retail clients by RPM. This situation is not impossible, but is certainly not a likely one, particularly over any period of time. A more probable case in which lower prices would result from RPM is where the new demand associated with an increased number of dealers handling the product is more elastic than the old demand. The more elastic the demand becomes, the more likely it is that prices will be lowered. If RPM were to have this effect, it could result in lower prices.[15]

THE ECONOMIC EFFECTS OF RESALE PRICE MAINTENANCE

In the preceding analysis we have indicated several possible effects of RPM on prices at both retail and manufacturer levels and on volume of sales. We have also discussed the relationship of RPM to retailer coercion, service stimulus, and number of retail outlets handling the price-maintained item. In order to arrive at an overall view of RPM as a pricing policy, we shall, in the following discussion, examine systematically the conclusions we have reached concerning the impact of RPM on economic choices and add to those conclusions some additional hypotheses and observations concerning RPM.

Impact of RPM on Retailers' Margins and Prices

Where a manufacturer places his product under RPM, with exact resale prices specified, there will be greater price uniformity than without RPM. If the minimum resale price is specified, the uniformity may be less than where the exact resale price is specified, but it is still likely to result in more price uniformity than there would be if there were no RPM.

With the exceptions to be noted, it is also likely that RPM will result in higher retail prices on price-maintained goods than would occur without it. Costs of operation and retail margins are not the same for all retailers. Nor do all consumers demand the same retailing functions. Without RPM, therefore, margins on a given branded item of merchandise are likely to differ from one retailer to another to reflect differences in costs and in consumer demand. RPM standardizes margins, and is likely to do so at a level higher than would occur without RPM.

Quite apart from interstore differences in costs and consumer demand, there is still another reason why RPM is likely to lead to higher average prices on the price-maintained item. Those items where the pressure to place them under RPM is highest often have attributes that make them good price leaders. RPM eliminates this possibility. Branded merchandise that might otherwise be employed from time to time as a price leader will, if prevented from being so used, bear a higher average price than it would otherwise. As a result those items that have the attributes of good price leaders but are *not* placed under RPM become candidates for price leaders and will bear an increased share of the "burden" of that particular strategy.

There are, however, two cases in which margins and retail prices will be lower under RPM. One is the case where the manufacturer is operating on a downward-sloping MC curve before the introduction of RPM. Under these circumstances, his optimum output will be greater under RPM than without it, and the retail selling price will be lower. The second case in which retail prices might be reduced by RPM would be where the retailer is a monopsonist and finds it advantageous to restrict sales and charge higher prices than the manufacturer would prefer. If the retailer-monopsonists's average net revenue is more

---

[15] See Chapter 12, where this relationship is discussed in the context of retailer and wholesaler domination in markets with differences in relative revenue and cost elasticities.

elastic than the manufacturer's average cost, control of the retail price by the manufacturer would result in a lower price to the consumer and a larger volume of sales. But neither of these two cases is likely to occur very often. Many means exist by which manufacturers can expand output beyond the range of diminishing marginal cost. They would certainly try to do so, and not necessarily by the use of RPM. Also, our observation of market structure gives little evidence of the second case, that is, a retailer who is a monopsonist. Only where retailers combine and coerce the manufacturer into RPM do we find a situation that approximates that of bilateral monopoly. In this case, the effect on resale prices depends on the relative elasticities of retailers' aggregated net revenue vis-à-vis the elasticity of the manufacturer's average cost.

Impact of RPM on the Structure of Retailing

RPM is likely to provide short-term protection to the small retailer. The large retail store benefits from certain economies of scale, and most large stores probably have a relatively wide range within which average costs of operation are nearly constant. The large retailer has more to gain from flexibility in the determination of prices on particular items than from rigidity in margins. He also has more alternatives in terms of brands and product substitutes. In the long run, therefore, the large firm is not necessarily damaged by RPM unless the product is unique, the demand is large, and close substitutes do not exist. Even in this case, the large retailer will obtain the higher margin under RPM and benefit from other demand-generating powers that the store may have by virtue of its size. But in the short run the small retailer is likely to benefit most from RPM, particularly if the margin granted is more closely related to the cost ratio of small stores than that of large stores.

In the United States few grocery products have been placed under RPM. Where they have been, the margin granted by the manufacturer to the retailer has more closely approximated that of the large retail distributor. In drugs and cosmetics, however, the retail margins under RPM have tended to be closer to those of the small retailer. In these lines, institution of RPM generally caused chain stores and large retailers to raise their prices and small stores to decrease theirs slightly.[16]

RETAIL SERVICES

It is almost impossible to establish empirically the validity of the "service incentive" argument for RPM, which we used as the basis for one part of the analysis in the preceding section. What RPM does in this respect is to remove a disincentive to the rendering of related retailing services; that is, it makes it impossible for competitive forces to cut the margins on the price-maintained item. Whether the removal of this disincentive is sufficient to accomplish the desired objective is questionable.

B. S. Yamey discusses two types of services.[17] He argues that services such as credit, delivery, installation, and maintenance provide no support for RPM, since retailers are free to provide such services for consumers by charging those customers who want such services. Other types of services cannot be separated and charged for in the same way, he argues. These would include availability of selections, demonstrations, stocks of goods,

[16] Federal Trade Commission, *Resale Price Maintenance* (Washington, D.C.: GPO, 1945).

[17] B. S. Yamey, ed., *Resale Price Maintenance* (Chicago: Aldine, 1966), p.14.

and consumer information. Consumers may use these services without buying goods at the store where they obtained the service. Without RPM consumers might shop in stores with considerable stock depth, stock width, and knowledgeable salespeople, gather there the information necessary to make a purchase decision, but actually buy the merchandise in a low-price store that does not provide such services. It is the latter type of service that Yamey believes might justify RPM.

But this would seem to be a questionable basis for RPM. Can, in fact, one expect RPM on even a relatively small percentage of the retailer's merchandise to result in sufficient increase in his gross margin to induce the desired service policy? As Yamey points out, there is no assurance that the margins granted will be used for the particular services of the second type. They might just as well be used by the retailer to get a better location, add to consumer conveniences, and so forth. Also, services of the second type may not be desired by all consumers. If RPM stimulates the rendering of such services, services offered will be shifted away from those customers who do not want the services toward those who do.

From the manufacturer's point of view, the distinction between the two types of services seems overdrawn. Whether or not the service can be charged for separately is less significant in this context than the importance of the service to the sale of the *particular* product, and whether or not competition has forced the retailer's margin to the point where the service is not rendered. If RPM can be used to induce retailers to render one type of service, it could presumably be used to induce them to render the other. Even if controlled margins do induce the rendering of the second type of service, will the benefits accrue to the seller of a single brand? Might not the services rendered benefit sellers of other brands?

It would seem, therefore, that the probability of service inducement via RPM would be limited to those services that can be rendered exclusively for the price-maintained good. For these services, assured margins may provide an effective stimulus. But these are often the services that can be separately priced. If so, their inducement via RPM merely reduces the range of consumer choice by making it impossible for the consumer to choose whether he will or will not buy the service. Good examples of such services would be information, installation, and maintenance. The problem of services rendered by one store that benefit another store is also not solved by RPM. One store gives extensive information to customers, who then go, let us say, to another store to buy the merchandise at a low price but without the accompanying information from salespeople. RPM puts both stores on the same footing. But does it result in any increase in social welfare? It will do so only if the information is *necessary* to the realization of optimum utility from the product and is not likely to be made available through other means. In this case, social welfare is increased if we can assume that RPM is the most effective method of stimulating provision of the service required. But those consumers who do not want the information, or who obtain it from other sources, pay for the benefit of those who would use the service.

NUMBER OF RETAIL OUTLETS

Can RPM increase the number of stores handling a product? It is likely that it can. If the small store receives short-run benefits from RPM, it would appear that attractive protected margins will enhance the dispersion of products among possible outlets. This assumes that the margins are sufficiently wide to induce high-cost retailers in small market areas to stock the product. Under these circumstances, greater institutional and geographic dispersion of the product's distribution will probably occur. If the margins are so high that the product cannot compete with private brands, however, larger retailers may prefer not to handle it. It seems more reasonable to believe, though, that they will continue to handle it, benefiting from its higher price side by side with their lower-priced private brand as well as from the higher margins obtained on the RPM item from sales to those customers who prefer it. Margin stability may reduce risks and, thereby, increase institutional and geographic dispersion of a good.

From a social point of view, dispersion per se may or may not be desirable. If margin differentials, and retail price differentials, reflect differences in demand and supply conditions in different markets, obliteration of those differentials by price maintenance can only result in a less economic allocation of resources among alternative market centers. Only if there are nonmarketable social benefits derived from increased dispersion can RPM be justified on this basis. For example, if small towns have social benefits not manifested in the market place, policies that support the survival of small towns may be justified because their utility to society is recognized but not measured in the market place.

COMPETITION

Does RPM destroy competition in retailing? In a sense it does, for it injects rigidity into the pricing mechanism and substitutes authoritarian control over prices for market–determined prices. Walter Adams has argued, however, that "if resale price maintenance is practiced in a healthy competitive atmosphere no significant restraint on competition results."[18] He cites the low incidence of fair trade pricing among manufacturers in a large number of commodity lines in the United States and concludes that "so long as it is practiced in an atmosphere of genuinely free and open competition [fair trade] tends to safeguard the consumer against exploitation, protect the retailer against loss leader selling, and permit the manufacturer to defend his trademark and distributive system."[19] Pointing to the numerous alternatives by which sellers can control behavior of the firms to which they sell, he argues that maintenance of free and open competition, rather than prohibition of resale price maintenance, is the critical issue. His defense of fair trade is pragmatic, for he believes that without it manufacturers will use alternative means of price control that do not leave their branded products in as "free and open competition" as will a system of RPM. Other means that the manufacturer might use for achieving control over the marketing and pricing of his product are selective selling, exclusive dealing, consignment selling, franchises, and vertical integration.

Empirical data on the effects of RPM are far from conclusive.[20] The weight of existing

---

[18] Walter Adams, "Resale Price Maintenance: Fact and Fancy," *Yale Law Journal*, 64 (June 1955): 969. His position is attacked by Edward S. Herman, "A Note on Fair Trade," ibid., 65 (November 1955): 23-32. See also Adams, "Fair Trade and the Art of Prestidigitation," ibid., 65 (December 1955): 196-207.

[19] Adams, "Fair Trade and the Art of Prestidigitation," op. cit., p. 207.

[20] See Federal Trade Commission, op. cit., Ward S. Bowman, "Prerequisites and Effects of Resale Price Maintenance," *University of Chicago Law Review*, 22 (Summer 1955): 825-873; Sören Gammelgaard, *Resale Price Maintenance* (Paris: European Productivity Agency of the Organization for European Economic Cooperation, 1958); B. S. Yamey, op. cit.; J. F. Pickering, *Resale Price Maintenance in Practice* (London: Allen & Unwin, 1966); E. Raymond Corey, "Fair Trade Pricing: A Reappraisal," *Harvard Business Review* 30 (September-October 1952): 47-62; L. A. Skeoch, "The Abolition of Resale Price Maintenance: Some Notes on Canadian Experience," *Economica*, n.s., 31 (August 1964): 260-269

evidence, however, supports the contention that competition is, on balance, reduced by RPM. This would indeed be the logical effect. This is not to deny the possibility of some benefits from the practice. Even though a beneficial monopolist *may* contribute more to consumer welfare than a large number of small, avaricious sellers, the typical monopolist cannot be defended on these grounds. RPM would appear to be in opposition to the social interest in light of the constraints that it imposes on the marketing system.

RPM cannot, however, destroy competition, and its use will certainly stimulate competition to emerge in other ways. Abolition of RPM will not destroy vertical price control so long as there are conditions that make vertical price control attractive to either sellers or buyers and so long as there are ways of implementing that control. It has been estimated that about 25 percent of the consumer goods sold in the United States are marketed under a franchise system. This is a more powerful means of controlling resale practices than RPM. What we have observed about the impact of RPM on prices, output, competition, and consumer welfare is relevant to other forms of vertical control. Such forms of control may have still greater effects on retail policy, since they may embrace the entire gamut of the retail operation—not just price alone.

Finally, we should make some observations on the effect of RPM on the market relationships of competing manufacturers. A constructive consequence of RPM could result from its use by a manufacturer to mitigate the effect of the strength of the large retailer. If one or more large retail firms is able, *by virtue of market power*, to restrict output or to drive out efficient small retailers by temporary price cutting, use of RPM by a manufacturer could work to the long-run benefit of consumers. It is doubtful, however, that this result could spring from RPM alone, for one manufacturer's brand or family of brands may not be sufficient to affect the total competitive situation. But widespread use of RPM by several manufacturers of substitute products would, in effect, create a situation approximating bilateral monopoly. This would be beneficial for consumers if it resulted in reduced prices, increased volume, and the retention of a larger number of retail outlets than would occur in a purely monopolistic market situation. One cannot realistically believe that this consequence is likely to be a common one, even though a few examples can be found in the history of price maintenance. Sellers of certain perishable products have at times been greatly frustrated by the practice among some large chain firms of using the perishable product as a loss leader during its prime season. The effect of this was that other retailers were unwilling even to stock the product.[21]

RPM can also be a device by which manufacturers are able to achieve control in a cartel.[22] A cartel may easily be destroyed as a result of price cutting by any one member. RPM makes the collusion among manufacturers effective. The conditions necessary for RPM to be used as an effective means of achieving collusion among manufacturers are (1) exclusive dealerships (so that no one manufacturer participating in the cartel will be tempted to offer special price concessions) and (2) agreement among all manufacturers on the retail price schedule and margins. Thus RPM can become an instrument for effecting collusive action among manufacturers. This basis for RPM would clearly be contrary to consumer welfare.

---

[21] This has occurred, for example, in the fresh-apricot market. Sellers were faced with a marked decline in retailer demand for fresh apricots during the relatively short period that they are available. The perishability of the product forced sellers to sell in the canned (or other processing) market, thus depressing prices there. In this case, relief was sought through the so-called unfair practices act, which prohibits sales below cost, or sales below cost plus a specified or calculable percentage.

[22] A good treatment of this case, along with an illustration from the light bulb market, is presented in Lester Telser, "Why Should Manufacturers Want Fair Trade?" op. cit.

Finally, we should observe again the possibility that RPM will stimulate the proliferation of brands with its attendant costs. If RPM is used for a given product, however, brand proliferation is desirable to the extent that it counteracts the effects of RPM and constrains manufacturers in determining the resale price to be placed on their brands.

16

Product and Service Differentiation

Fashion wears out more apparel than the man.

—William Shakespeare

It has been traditional in economic analyses of consumer demand to incorporate into the demand function a variable for "tastes." When included in a four-variable function of the type

$$Q = f(Y, P, T)$$

Q is the quantity purchased, Y is purchasing power, P is the own-good price relative to the price of all other goods, and T is consumer taste. "Taste" in this sense embraces all of the factors that influence consumer demand except purchasing power and relative price. It is a summation of those elements known as preference. As such its parameter measures the impact of consumer needs, wants, attitudes, dispositions, and expectations on demand as these arise out of the sociopsychological milieu within which demand is generated and manifested.

In an attempt to respond to, or to control, this variable, sellers have altered their offerings in many different ways, thus modifying the nonprice component of the fully negotiated transaction. The competitive structure that results when such policies dominate is known as *nonprice competition*, although a seller will seldom choose to ignore the role of price in establishing his policy mix. In this chapter and the one that follows, we shall focus on some of the facets of nonprice competition that are important in the formulation of marketing policy. We shall examine first the nature of nonprice competition and the ways in which it is similar to and different from price competition.

FORMS OF NONPRICE COMPETITION

Economic analysis focuses on price as the equalizer of competitive and complementary market forces. The exchange transaction involves an exchange of purchasing power for title to a specified good or service. There are many ways in which these elementary components can be modified. A number of these are identified in Figure 16.1, which shows price as the central condition of exchange, surrounded by a variety of forms of nonprice variation.

These various forms of nonprice competition could be arrayed on a continuum, with one group somewhat amenable to the conventional demand-supply analysis and the other group not amenable to such an analysis. For example, the demand for advertising and personal selling is primarily a demand of sellers, who also determine the supply of these two promotional factors. These are therefore more nearly pure forms of nonprice competition. On the other hand, the demand for credit and warranties and product quality on the part of consumers can to some extent manifest itself independently, without supplier intrusion. These could therefore be classified as forms of quasi-price (or quasi-nonprice) competition, for the consumer can sometimes place a valuation on these components of market offerings. While all of the forms of competition in Figure 16.1 can

419

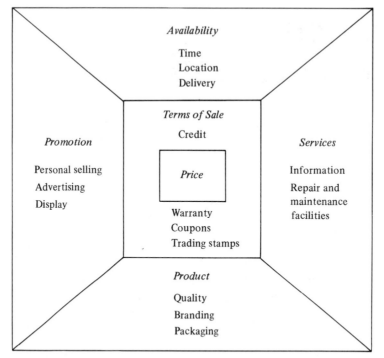

Figure 16.1. Price and forms of nonprice competition.

be quantified in a cost sense, all except price cannot be evaluated so easily from the viewpoint of consumer demand. Those whose values to consumers can be established with some difficulty are the ones we consider as forms of quasi-price competition. These include all except those listed under "Promotion," and perhaps also branding and packaging to the extent that these are promotional devices rather than utility-creating instruments of marketing policy. All others are what we shall regard as ordinary nonprice competition.

SOME IMPORTANT DIFFERENCES BETWEEN PRICE AND NONPRICE COMPETITION

The most obvious difference between these two broad categories of competition is the fact that while price differences are clear and commensurable, differences in nonprice offerings are either not comparable at all or only imperfectly so. Anyone can compare prices of two identical products, but most may find it impossible to arrive at even an approximate quantitative comparison between two clusters of nonprice variables.

A second difference is the possibility for diversification, which is, of course, much greater with nonprice competition. Once price differences are eliminated, quality and other nonprice variables can be altered in myriad ways. Therefore the area for competitive action is greatly widened and deepened by the use of nonprice competition.

A third difference is the relative importance of price and nonprice competition at various levels in the production process and in the channels of distribution. Gösta Mickwitz has pointed out the considerable importance of price competition in factor markets and its declining importance in markets dealing with semi- and fully processed goods. Nonprice competition becomes increasingly important as products move through trade channels toward the ultimate consumer.[1]

COMPLETE COMPETITION

This brings us to a consideration of the concept of complete competition. Complete competition exists when sellers have access to and are able to use all forms of price and nonprice variations.[2] This concept of competition is the product of the analyses of numerous writers, with Joan Robinson, Edward H. Chamberlain, John M. Clark, Arthur R. Burns, Arne Rasmussen, and Lawrence Abbott among the important contributors.[3] Only through a consideration of complete competition, including nonprice variables, can the most meaningful facets of competitive analysis be found as they relate to the formulation and evaluation of marketing policy. Yet it is interesting that most of the theoretical work in this field has been done by economists rather than by marketing anaylsts, with the exception of the outstanding work of the Copenhagen school.[4] On the other hand, much of the empirical work on aspects of nonprice competition appears in the marketing literature.

One of the most important attributes of competition as an aspect of market relationships is its dynamic character. Whether viewed from the vantage point of the firm or that of the society that it serves, *competition is a process of becoming rather than a state of being.* It is a process of accommodation, adjustment, and change. What that process is determines the effect of the behavior of market participants on one another and the overall effect of all market participation on the welfare of all the participants. The process of pursuit rather than the structure of possession is therefore the focus of competitive policy. This is particularly true of nonprice competition, for it is this area of

---

[1] Gösta Mickwitz, "The Means of Competition at Various Stages of Production and Distribution," *Kyklos* 11 (fasc. 4, 1958): 509-520

[2] The label "complete competition" has been borrowed from Lawrence Abbot, and we define it substantially the same way he does. Abbott's definition states: "When both price and quality are variables, competition is neither 'pure price' nor 'pure quality' competition, but a compound of both. It may then be called *complete competition.*" Lawrence Abbot, *Quality and Competition* (New York: Columbia University Press, 1955), p. 119. Abbott uses "quality" to embrace all of the elements in the competitive exchange process except advertising and sales promotion, although he does consider the relevance of these excluded variables in his analysis, particularly as they affect firm policy and equilibrium position.

[3] Edward H. Chamberlin, *The Theory of Monopolistic Competition*, Harvard Economic Studies, vol. XXXVIII, 5th ed. (Cambridge, Mass.: Harvard Univeristy Press, 1946), and *Towards a More General Theory of Value* (New York: Oxford University Press, 1957); Joan Robinson, *The Economics of Imperfect Competition* (London: Macmillan, 1933), and "Imperfect Competition Revisited," *Economic Journal* 63 (September 1953): 579-593; John M. Clark, "Towards a Concept of Workable Competition," *Amercian Economic Review* 30 (June 1940): 241-256, and *Competition as a Dynamic Process* (Washington, D.C.: Brookings, 1961); Arthur R. Burns, *The Decline of Competition* (New York: McGraw-Hill, 1936); Arne Rasmussen, *Pristeori eller Parameterteori*, Skrifter fra Instituttet for Salgsorganisation og Reklame, Handelshøjskolen i København (Copenhagen: Einar Harcks Forlag, 1955); Abbott, op. cit.

[4] A review of monopolistic competition theory in marketing can be found in E. T. Grether, "Chamberlin's Theory of Monopolistic Competition and the Literature of Marketing," in Robert E. Kuenne, ed., *Monopolistic Competition Theory: Studies in Impact* (New York: Wiley, 1967), pp. 307-328.

competitive activity that offers the richest opportunities for new and dynamic policies. While we shall concern ourselves with some questions about equilibrium conditions, this will be done to make clear the directions of accommodation and adjustment that characterize the competitive process.

OBJECTIVES AND LIMITS OF THIS DISCUSSION

Having assigned ourselves the task of analyzing policy determination where there is a wide range of policy alternatives arising out of the diverse possibilities for modification of numerous nonprice variables, we shall find it expedient to retreat to a more manageable type of analytical problem. Specifically, we shall use the term *quality competition* to embrace, not all possible changes in the nonprice aspects of a transaction, but only those associated with product differences. We shall, moreover, reduce the number and kinds of differences to a few that we can handle systematically in words and geometry. Through a few examples we shall attempt to gain some insight into the process of competitive reaction and change where competition is based on quality variations.

QUALITY COMPETITION

We shall limit ourselves to a consideration of product differences, and shall view these in terms of three major aspects: (1) why product differences exist and why product changes are made, (2) the kinds of quality differences that are possible and the varieties of quality competition that result from these differences, and (3) the conditions of and processes for achieving equilibrium under quality competition.[5]

Reasons for Product Differences and Product Changes

Because products are designed to serve the needs of users, the principal reasons why they differ lie in the nature of demand. This would apply to product differences for both consumer and industrial goods. Because product differences are greater, on an average, in consumer goods than in industrial goods,[6] we shall concentrate our discussion on the characteristics of demand in consumer goods markets that are a stimulus to the making of product differences. The second determinant of product differences that we shall examine consists of the responses of suppliers of products to the market demand in relation to their production potentials.

DEMAND AND PRODUCT DIFFERENCES

Human beings have basic wants arising out of their needs or desires—for nourishment, for bodily protection, for physical and psychological security, for the maintenance of

---

[5] Although the presentation in this section differs in minor ways from that of Abbott in his *Quality and Competition*, it has drawn so heavily on that source that it owes more than a small acknowledgment to Abbott's ideas and analysis.

[6] This is generally the case, but not always. For example, varieties of consumer apparel exceed by far the varieties of apparel designed especially for productive activity—uniforms, coveralls, safety shoes, etc. On the other hand, the varieties of such things as woodworking knives, sandpaper, and screws for industrial use would be far greater than where these are found in consumer use. Where a given good with specific physical attributes serves the needs of both producers and consumers, product differences are likely to be more numerous in that use which is more specialized.

communication and interaction with other humans, for the satisfaction of intellectual curiosity, for self-realization through a variety of experiences, and so forth. Products are merely means of satisfying these basic wants and are therefore evaluated by consumers in part in terms of their effectiveness in fulfilling these want-satisfying roles. One of the important reasons for product differences is the fact that there are many different basic wants, each of which can be satisfied in a unique way. But the much finer degree of differentiation that we find in similar products arises out of the fact that there are often many ways of satisfying a single basic want. The more personal and subjective the source of the want, the greater the diversity is likely to be in the ways in which want satisfaction can be achieved.

Another aspect of the want-satisfying ability of products is that one product alone seldom satisfies a want in its totality. Because of this, demands for products come in clusters. There is an overlapping of clusters due to the fact that one product may meet more than one want. Automobiles, for example, are demanded jointly with tires, batteries, gasoline, oil, repair parts, maintenance and repair service, and insurance. But automobiles may be enjoyed for far more than the transportation they provide; they may also be symbols of economic or social status, or yield aesthetic satisfaction. This clustering of demands means that changes in one of the products of the cluster may lead to changes in the position of other components of the cluster.

Another important set of variables that influence the extent of product differences derives from individual differences in both basic wants and the wants derived from those basic wants that manifest themselves in a desire for specific goods and services. The impact of culture and social structure will lead to some degree of focus in these individual demands, but individual preferences are never completely eliminated. Moreover, basic wants and the desire for goods that will meet those basic wants change over time, and this, in turn, induces producers to change the characteristics of the products that they offer.

A final point is well stated by Frank Knight:

Man's chief interest in life is after all to find life interesting, which is a very different thing from merely consuming a maximum amount of wealth. Change, novelty, and surprise must be given a large consideration as values *per se*.[7]

The stimulus and pleasure of the new experience are of no small consequence in human behavior, and they are manifest in the consumer's desire for, and response to, innovations and product changes.

SUPPLY AND PRODUCT DIFFERENCES

In their attempt to maximize profits or sales, to achieve stability in market shares, or to survive in the face of competitive forces, producers have two choices in their product decisions—adapt the product to the demand as given, or attempt to "bend" the demand to the production possibilities of the firm. Given the observations made in the preceding section about the nature of demand for products, it is clear that adaptation by firms to "the demand" is in essence adaptation to the many demands that evolve from consumers' perceptions of product utilities. In most cases it is probably less costly for producers to segment their markets and to adapt products to these diverse demands than to try to alter

---

[7]Frank H. Knight, *Risk, Uncertainty, and Profit* (Boston: Houghton Mifflin, 1921), p. 369.

demands to fit the products as they are. The latter can possibly be achieved by advertising, or perhaps by packaging and general promotion, to persuade consumers that the product does in fact possess those attributes necessary to satisfy their wants. This approach to market adjustment is likely to be used when consumers are easily persuaded or when the limits of production possibilities have been met, given the technological capabilities of production at that point in time. But the first policy—adaptation of products to the spectrum of consumer demands—is the more likely choice in most cases. This will clearly lead to product or service differences, except to the extent that increased differentiation becomes unprofitable (or detracts from achievement of other goals the firm may have).

In the supplying of goods and services, producers are extremely sensitive to competitors' policies. Each will try to produce a product that will be regarded as superior by *all* consumers, one that will be regarded as superior by *most* consumers, or one that will be regarded as superior by *some* consumers. The first of these will sweep the market. The second will increase market share. The third will increase one's market power over a certain segment of demand. Thus a firm's ability to affect its market position depends in large measure on the actions of its competitors.

One other facet of competitive interaction in suppliers' decisions is that product changes made by one producer in an industry will affect the product equilibrium position for the entire industry. If, therefore, product changes are occurring continually among competing firms in an industry, the equilibrium position among those firms will probably shift with each change, resulting in a floating equilibrium position if new changes occur before the old equilibrium has been reached. This is a reason for viewing nonprice competition as a process rather than a state of affairs.

This brings us to a third aspect of supply and the process of product innovation, adaptation, and differentiation. Here we are concerned primarily with the difference between short- and long-run adjustment processes. It is useful to view short-run product changes as a series of successive changes that are "small" (relative to those that occur in the long run) and occur through the product life cycle. Such changes tend to be continuous (or continual, with small time gaps between changes) and to reflect the effects of the diffusion of demand, the increased experience of consumers as they gain additional exposure to product use, and the response of competitive sellers as demand grows, ownership and experience become more widely diffused, and production knowledge and experience become more widely diffused among members of the industry. These are the changes that occur within the span of one product life cycle. Major innovations, on the other hand, are long-run phenomena. They occur discontinuously, with "long" intervals between, and they do not occur with regularity. They are associated with a new product life cycle.

A fourth supply variable that enters into product changes fulfills a constructive role for the seller but not for the product buyer. This is the use of product changes by the seller for the purpose of making it more difficult for consumers to compare products. If, for example, differentiation is employed as a means of making it more difficult for consumers to compare competing products or as a means of fooling the consumer, making him believe the product has attributes that it does not, it may have short-run profit-creating possibilities for the seller. It is unlikely that it will have long-run profit possibilities unless there is a continuous use of additional features of differentiation that appear to enhance the usefulness of a product but in fact do not. Repeated use of product differentiation for these purposes will be detected by consumers over a period of time, but irregular use by individual sellers and continual use by some sellers in a given

Table 16.1 Characteristics of Vertical, Horizontal, and Mixed Quality Competition[a]

Direction	None	Vertical	Horizontal	Mixed	
Type	I	II	III	IV	V
Cost	$C_n \leqslant C_o$	$C_n > C_o$	$C_n = C_o$	$C_n > C_o$	$C_n < C_o$
Consumer response	prefer / buy	prefer / buy	prefer / buy	prefer / buy	prefer / buy
Consumer group A	N / N	N / N	N / N	N / N	N / N
B	N / N	N / N	N / N	N / N	O / N
C	N / N	N / O	O / O	O / O	O / O

[a] N = new product; O = old product; C = unit cost.

industry may make it difficult for the consumer to detect such use and to protect himself. Effective consumer protection will depend on the existence of a systematic pattern of deceptive differentiation or a systematic procedure for detecting deception where it occurs randomly or irregularly.

Quality Differences and Competition

It is helpful in the analysis of quality competition to differentiate between two principal kinds of quality variations: vertical and horizontal. The characteristics of each are indicated in Table 16.1.

VERTICAL QUALITY COMPETITION

Vertical quality competition arises when an improvement is introduced that results in a product that all buyers regard as superior in performing the functions originally performed by an "old" product. If the cost of this new product is equal to or less than that of the old product (type I in Table 16.1), the new product will replace the old one, since all buyers prefer it, and the old product ceases to exist. In this case, there is no competition between the vertically related qualities, since the new product drives the old one out. But consider the case where the new product is regarded as superior by all buyers, but it costs more to produce (type II in Table 16.1). Buyers must now decide whether the value of the increased utility of the new product is equal to or exceeds the increased price of the product that results from higher costs of production. We have assumed in Table 16.1 that buyers in groups A and B do buy the superior product, while buyers in group C buy the old product because of its lower price. Vertical quality differences would, in this case, result in vertical comptition. The case of vertical competition that we shall examine will have the characteristics of type II, that is, it will involve changes in product attributes that all buyers regard as an improvement accompanied by higher costs of production. For such competition to persist, some buyers must be willing to pay the higher price for the higher-quality product, while other buyers stick with the old product although they regard the new product as superior. Unless both products remain on the market, the competition can only be potential competition.

HORIZONTAL QUALITY COMPETITION

Horizontal quality competition is illustrated by type III. This occurs where changes in an old product make it in essence a new product that some buyers regard as superior. Both products are made available. In the type III case the cost of the new (modified) product is the same as that of the old product. Consumers in groups A and B prefer the new product and buy it; however, consumers in group C prefer the old product and continue to buy it.

MIXED QUALITY COMPETITION

Thus we have vertical competition when some consumers prefer one product to another and will buy it even though its price is higher. We have horizontal competition when two substitute products are sold at the same price but some consumers prefer one and some prefer the other. Often, however, we have both vertical and horizontal competition. Two possibilities are illustrated by types IV and V. In both of these cases, some consumers prefer the new product to the old, while the others prefer the old product. This is indicative of horizontal competition. In type IV, group A consumers not only prefer the new product but are willing to pay the higher price to get it. In type V, group C consumers prefer the old product and are willing to pay the additional price necessary to buy it. Thus in type IV groups A and B illustrate vertical quality competition, while A and C illustrate horizontal competition. In type V groups B and C illustrate vertical competition, while groups A and C illustrate horizontal competition.

Equilibrium Under Quality Competition

We shall concentrate our analysis on quality competition types II and III, since these are more clear-cut with respect to preference patterns and cost relationships. In our analysis we shall assume that quality differences are possible for a given product type, that sellers can imitate differences, and that buyers and sellers are informed of what the possibilities are. Realistically one would expect buyers to take into consideration vertical quality relationships that are relatively close together; that is, they will consider the quality level immediately above or immediately below that which they have been using rather than some level greatly removed from their normal experience. On the other hand, it is possible for horizontal differences to cover a considerable range, since these cannot be ordered in the same way as those that are regarded as "superior" or "inferior." Any one buyer may, of course, place in ordinal positions the various horizontal alternatives according to his own set of preferences, but this order would not be the same for all buyers, since the distinguishing characteristic of horizontal differentiation is that individual preferences differ regardless of price.

In our discussion of competition in general, and quality competition in particular, we have emphasized the point that competition should be viewed as a process rather than a state of being. If may seem strange, therefore, to begin our analysis by seeking an

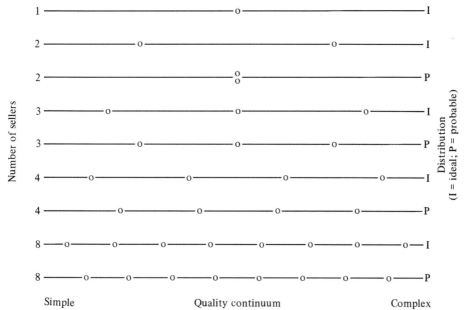

Figure 16.2. The ideal and probable positions of varying numbers of sellers along a quality continuum in which demand is distributed equally along the continuum.

equilibrium solution. Our purpose in this procedure is to provide a logical framework for viewing the adjustments made by firms as they move in some directed fashion. What constitutes equilibrium will change as costs and demand and quality are altered. A dynamic approach is conceptually difficult to achieve except in terms of a sequence of static states *toward* which the firm is moving at each successive moment.

To simplify our approach even more, we shall assume that there are no interfirm differences in the costs of producing a product of equal quality. We shall now turn to a consideration of the conditions of equilibrium under horizontal quality competition, vertical quality competition, and a combination of horizontal and vertical quality competition.

CASE I: HORIZONTAL QUALITY COMPETITION

Let us assume that there is a scalable horizontal variability of product quality and of buyer preferences.[8] In the first case we shall consider, Case IA, we shall assume that the demand is distributed evenly along the quality continuum. Each buyer will buy that quality, or brand that is nearest his preferred option, deviating from his preference to the extent necessary to obtain the product. This case is illustrated in Figure 16.2.

---

[8] This runs counter to the observation we have made concerning the possibility of ordering the individual's preferences and the probability of considerable interpersonal differences in individual scales so derived. We use this simplification here in order to make the problem analytically manageable. One of the objectives of marketing research has been to try to determine the extent to which *patterns* of preferences exist among consumers. If consumers can be clustered according to consistency in their preference patterns, then our simplifying assumption is not so unrealistic. See, for example, F. G. Pyatt, *Priority Patterns and the Demand for Household Durable Goods*, University of Cambridge, Department of Applied Economics, Monograph no. 11 (Cambridge: Cambridge University Press, 1964), and numerous studies of purchases and asset ownership within the life cycle.

1. *CASE IA*. If there is only one seller, he may locate any place on the quality spectrum, since buyers will be willing to sacrifice their preferences in order to obtain his output. However, he will minimize consumer dissatisfaction if he locates in the middle of the quality continuum, as indicated in the first line of Figure 16.2. In this case, buyers at the extremes will not obtain the exact quality they prefer, but the total deviation is minimized by the seller's offering a middle-quality product. Let us assume that the single seller assumes this ideal position.

Suppose now that a second seller enters the market. He could locate to the right or to the left of the first seller. If he locates to the first seller's right, he will be able to meet all the demand still further to the right plus half the demand between himself and the centrally positioned first seller. But if he gets half of the sales between himself and the producer of the middle quality, he will be inclined to snuggle up even closer to the first seller in order to get a still larger portion of the sales "between" them. If he moves to the left of the middle quality—let us say, to a point halfway between the original seller and the lower limits of consumer preferences—the new seller will have complete control over the one-fourth of customers between himself and the lower end of the spectrum and will dominate one-half of those between himself and the competitive firm. He has good reason therefore to move closer and closer to the original firm. In the end he will find it most advantageous to locate as close to the first firm as possible.

Suppose that a third firm enters the market. Consumer dissatisfaction would be minimized if each firm controlled exactly one-third of the total market, as indicated by the ideal distribution for three firms in Figure 16.2. But this is not likely to happen, for each of the firms at the extreme ends of the quality spectrum would adjust the quality of their products so that they move closer to the middle firm. So long as the gap between the firm producing the lowest quality and lowest quality level demanded is equal to, but no more than equal to, the gap between itself and its nearest competitor, or the gap between any other competitors, there will be no incentive for one of the competing firms to try to squeeze into that segment of the quality spectrum. It is true, of course, that the probable distribution of three firms illustrated in Figure 16.2 may be somewhat unstable as each firm tries to push its quality level closer to that of its next competitor. But this is the only distribution that can survive without inviting a successful invasion by existing competitors. If, however, these three firms are making abnormal profits, new competitors may be induced to enter the market with a differential quality level.[9]

We also show in Figure 16.2 the ideal and probable distributions of four and eight firms, each producing a different quality level. Note that as the number of firms increases, the portion of demand that is most strongly discriminated against—that at the two ends

---

[9] William J. Baumol has suggested that if two firms are producing at two points on the quality continuum, or within the quality space, the optimum strategy for a firm introducing a new item is to combine in that item characteristics of the products already available on the market. Thus the innovator would try to imitate both rather than to differentiate. However, by dropping Baumol's assumptions that (1) there will be no countermoves by other firms, (2) that there is a constant rate of substitution among the various characteristics of the product on the part of the consumer, and (3) that there is a constant total demand for the entire line of products produced by all competing firms making that type of product, Helmut Schuster shows that Baumol's conclusion is not correct but that the firm should differentiate itself from its rivals, as we have indicated in our discussion. See William J. Baumol, "Calculation of Optimal Product and Retailer Characteristics: The Abstract Product Approach," *Journal of Political Economy* 15 (October 1967): 674-685, and Helmut Schuster, "Further Remarks on the Theory of Product Differentiation," *Journal of Political Economy* 77 (September-October 1969): 827-833.

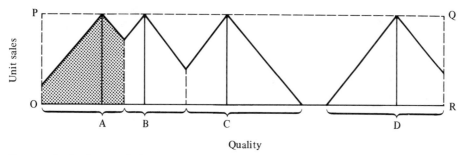

Figure 16.3. Sales of four unequally distributed quality levels to buyers who by preference are distributed equally along a quality continuum.

of the continuum—is a decreasing portion of the total demand.[10]

It is possible, of course, that firms may choose to cluster, so that two or three firms sell similar quality levels and divide a total quality segment among them. Under these circumstances, however, it is likely that one or more will decide that they could appropriate for themselves a portion of that total quality segment by merely adapting their product more closely to the quality demanded by that portion. This leads us therefore to conclude that the probable distribution will be that indicated in Figure 16.2.[11]

2. *CASE IB*. In the second case we shall assume that buyers are distributed evenly along a quality spectrum and that each buyer will buy that quality, or brand, which is nearest his preferred option *provided that it is not too far away*. As distance from his preference increases, his reluctance to accept this deviation increases. All buyers do not have the same reluctance, however, and so distribute themselves along another continuum reflecting their reluctance to adapt to a quality different from their first preference.

Let us assume that the quality spectrum is *OR*, as shown in Figure 16.3. If every possible quality possibility were offered on the market, every consumer would buy something and total sales would be represented by the area *OPQR*. Let us now assume that there are only four producers, and these have elected to produce quality levels A, B, C, and D, respectively. A's sales are represented by the shaded tent in Figure 16.3, and sales of B, C, and D are similarly determined. The downward-sloping sales line as distance from the quality level increases reflects the fact that *some* potential buyers refuse to buy if the quality deviates from that which they desire, and the number of buyers who react

---

[10] It is interesting to observe the similarity between these choices of sellers, producing differentiated products, and the choices of political parties, who are selling differentiated political creeds or platforms. If the voting population is evenly distributed over the political spectrum from conservative to liberal, in a two-party system the two parties will choose political positions near each other in the middle of the road. If one were to take a staunch liberal position and the other a conservative position, each could pick up votes by moving closer to the center. In a multiparty system, it is difficult for one party to get a majority for the reasons illustrated in Figure 16.2. If voters are not distributed equally along the spectrum, however, there will be reasons for a different distribution.

[11] The approach we have used in this discussion is adapted from location theory. We are using the concept of product space instead of geographic space, but the analysis is essentially the same. See Edward H. Chamberlin, *The Theory of Monopolistic Competition*, op. cit., pp. 236-241; Harold Hotelling, "Stability in Competition," *Economic Journal 39 (March 1929): 41-57; H. W. Singer, "A Note on Spatial Price Discrimination,"* Review of Economic Studies 5 (October 1937): 75-77.

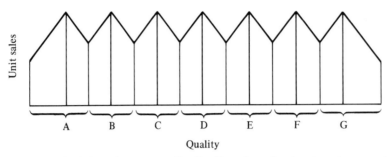

Figure 16.4. Sales of seven equally distributed quality levels to buyers who by preference are distributed equally along a quality continuum.

this way increases as the quality deviation becomes greater. In fact some consumers, whose preferences lie midway between quality levels C and D, do not buy at all because the offerings in either direction are too far from their preferences. We are assuming that the prices of these various qualities are the same.

Some producers will, of course, take advantage of the unmet demand between C and D and start producing a quality level to meet the needs of these customers, provided, of course, that the selling price is sufficient to make the venture profitable. If the quantity demanded by these consumers at this price is sufficient to attract seven producers into the industry, the conditions of final equilibrium will be as shown in Figure 16.4, with the producers of quality levels A and G each having a slightly larger share of the total market than each of the other firms because of the fact that it is not worthwhile for a producer to squeeze in on the "outer" side of either.

3. *CASE IC*. It is unlikely, of course, that buyers will be positioned at equal intervals along a quality spectrum. In spite of individual differences, human wants tend to bunch, particularly as the result of sociopsychological influences. Therefore the distribution of specialized firms producing different quality levels will tend to concentrate in a ratio consistent with the concentration of consumer preferences. If preference patterns are skewed, the location of firms along the quality continuum will be similarly skewed.

CASE II: VERTICAL QUALITY COMPETITION

It is now necessary to drop our assumption that quality differences are not associated with price differences. It is likely that quality differentials will involve price differentials. In the quality continuum that we have been considering, or the quality continua in a multidimensional product space, there is implied a "more" or "less" relationship between various quality levels. Such differences are likely also to involve price differentials implying vertical relationships. We turn therefore to a consideration of the competitive situation in which both quality and price differentials exist, with higher prices assoicated with more highly preferred quality.

We have defined vertical quality competition as that which arises when one or more superior products exist that are sold at higher prices and that some consumers prefer and are willing to buy at the higher price. We shall assume that the higher the quality, the higher the cost. Also, the higher the quality, the more willing people are to buy that quality. Before we try to look at quality variations *and* price variations together, it will be helpful to hold price constant and look only at quality changes. The simple model that we shall consider is that in which there are a given number of firms in the industry, each has the same average cost of production, each shares equally in the sales of the industry,

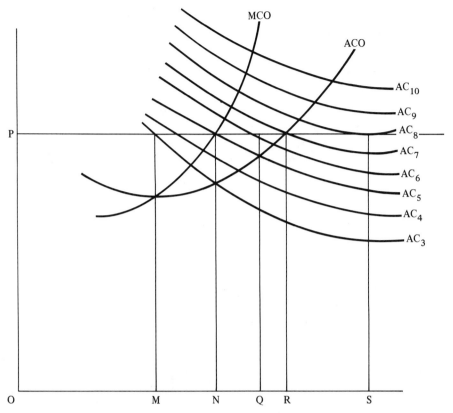

Figure 16.5. Average cost of producing various quality levels in a firm and average and marginal cost of buyer options.

selling price is given, and the average cost curve rises as the quality level of output increases.

The average cost curves are shown in Figure 16.5, which is taken from Abbott's exposition, with rising *AC* curves as quality level increases from quality 3 to quality 10.[12] Since the price is given, the firms will have to make a decision about the quality level at which they will produce. We shall assume that if one firm changes its policy so that it is operating more profitably, all other firms will do the same thing. Therefore the problem is to figure out which quality level is the most profitable under these conditions.

We need to know something about consumer demand. We are assuming that the price is set by the interaction of *total* demand and *total* supply so that the one attribute of demand in which we shall be interested is the effect of an increase in quality on consumers' willingness to buy the product. Since we are going to examine this from the point of view of sellers of the product, we shall utilize Abbott's *average cost of options* curve. This curve, *ACO* in Figure 16.5, shows the average cost of producing that quantity which will be demanded at price *OP* as quality is increased. It is a peculiar kind of demand curve, for it holds price constant and relates quantity purchased to quality of product. Quality of product is identified on the vertical axis by average cost of production of that particular quality level. This is the cost that the firm must incur in

---

[12] Abbott, op. cit., p. 156.

order to produce the quality that will result in the volume demanded by consumers at price *OP*. Instead of holding quality constant and varying cost, as is done in the conventional analysis of a firm's output decision, we are holding selling price constant and varying quality and, hence, cost of production of the quantities of each quality demanded at that selling price. For example, in Figure 16.5, if quality level 3 is produced, buyers will be willing to pay price *OP* for *ON* units. If quality level 5 is produced, buyers will be willing to pay price *OP* for *OQ* units. For quality level 7, they will pay price *OP* for *OR* units. We do not vary price, as in the usual demand curve, but consider instead the effect of change in quality on the number of units demanded and show the quality by *the cost of producing that quality in the quantity demanded*. Every possible selling price has its own *ACO* curve.

Notice the relationships between selling price and cost of production of the quantities demanded and produced at various quality levels in Figure 16.5. If quality level 3 is produced, we said that buyers would be willing to buy *ON* units at price *OP*. Average cost of production for this number of units is less than *OP*, however. If quality level 5 is produced, *OQ* units will be demanded at price *OP*. Cost of production per unit will be less than *OP*, but not as much less as was the case when *ON* units of quality 3 were sold. Now if the producer decides to produce quality 8, he will have to sell *OS* units merely to cover his cost of production. But buyers will not absorb that much of quality level 8 at price *OP*. They are willing to buy only *OR* units at price *OP*. Production of any quality level above 7 will mean that the cost of production will exceed the selling price *OP*. Therefore the firm will be restricted to the production of quality 7 or less, since qualities higher than that will entail costs that exceed the selling price, *OP*.

The average cost of options curve shows two important attributes of the market situation we are describing. First, it shows that as quality level rises, the cost of production also rises. Second, it shows that as quality level rises, the amount that consumers are willing to buy also rises. So we have an increase in cost of production *and* an increase in consumers' willingness to purchase as we move up the quality scale. We may also assume that when the firm is producing small amounts—that is, when it is operating to the left of OM—it will find that the increase in cost associated with an increase in quality is more than offset by the decrease in cost resulting from economies of scale. To show this, we have indicated that the *ACO* curve decreases up to the output level *OM*. Thereafter we have the two phenomena that characterize these types of markets—increasing quality and increasing willingness on the part of the consumer to purchase the higher qualities at a constant price. If we went to very high quality levels, we might find that the *ACO* curve becomes vertical if buyers cease to respond to additional quality improvements even though price remains constant.

Under the circumstances that we have described, what *can* a firm do, and what *will* a firm do? If the selling price is *OP*, the firm can produce quality level 7 and sell output *OR*. At this selling price and at this quantity and quality of output, it will cover costs, including, we shall assume, a normal profit. But the firm's most profitable level will be an output of *ON* of quality level 3. This we can determine by drawing a *marginal cost of options* curve that will indicate the *increase* in the cost of producing that quantity which will be demanded as quality is increased. Since we are assuming that price is fixed at level *OP*, the most profitable level of output will be *ON* of quality 3, for at this point the added cost of producing the quality that is salable is just met by the added revenue that will be received.

We have assumed throughout that the firm that we are looking at in Figure 16.5 is one of *n* firms in the industry. This number remains constant, and each firm has the same cost

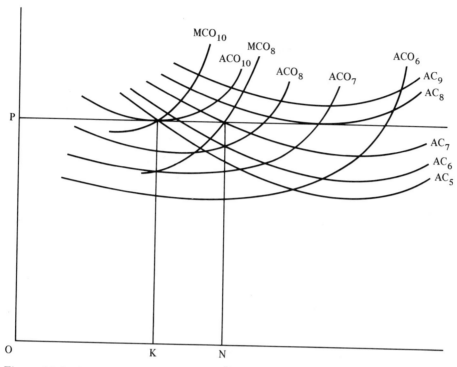

Figure 16.6. Average cost of producing various quality levels and average and marginal cost of buyer options where there are varying numbers of firms in the industry.

and demand structure. This is not a realistic assumption where there is freedom of entry, however, for if the short-run equilibrium situation we have described in which all of these firms produce ON output prevails, new entrants will view the large profits possible in this industry and will attempt to invade the market. This new possibility complicates our analysis, because in Figure 16.5 we assumed that the total market demand was being divided equally among the n firms in the industry. If there are more firms, the ACO curve will shift to the left. This means, therefore, that while the AC curves will vary purely on the basis of the quality of output, the ACO curve has to be redrawn to reflect the division of potential sales among differing numbers of firms in the industry.

In Figure 16.6 we show average costs for quality levels, 5,6,7,8, and 9. We also show the average cost of options (ACO) curves for a 6-firm industry, a 7-firm industry, an 8-firm industry, and a 10-firm industry. Suppose that we have 8 firms to begin with. The selling price is OP, and sales are divided equally among the 8 firms. Under these circumstances, each firm will produce ON of quality level 6, since the marginal cost of options at this point equals the selling price, or marginal revenue. By restricting output to this level, though, the firms in the industry are making profits that attract new entrants. Let us say that two new firms come into the industry, raising the total to 10. The ACO curve for 10 firms is farther to the left, for the sales are now divided among 10 firms instead of 8. Under these circumstances, a selling price of OP will permit each firm to produce output OK of quality level 5. At this output, selling price per unit exactly equals cost of production per unit and there is no inducement for more firms to come into the industry. If costs are assumed to include "normal" profit—that which is necessary to induce firms to remain in the industry—there is also no inducement for firms to leave, and the industry may be said to be in equilibrium.

CASE III: PRICE AND QUALITY COMPETITION

In our analysis of the output decisions of the firm under quality competition, we assumed that (1) the price was given and was the same for all firms, (2) each firm received an equal share of total sales, and (3) each firm produced the same quality, since the actions of any firm that realized a profit advantage through the production of a different quality level were imitated by all other sellers. These assumptions were introduced to simplify the analysis, but they must be removed if we are to come close to describing the real world in which differentiated products are produced and sold. Most firms producing a differentiated product are usually able to build up a certain degree of loyalty among some of their customers, and few customers will regard one firm's output as exactly the same as that of any other firm in the "industry." Even though several firms may produce products that are substitutes for one another in general, differences between the products are often discernible and meaningful to at least some consumers. Moreover, our analysis, in which we held price constant and allowed only quality to vary, is highly sterile. While it is not possible to handle the complete spectrum of market variables that exist under monopolistic competion using a two-dimensional geometric approach, we shall examine some of the implications of a combination of price and quality competition as they bear upon the decisions of the firm.

Let us assume that we have a firm that is producing a product that is differentiated either vertically or horizontally. Costs of production may be the same or different from those of competing substitutes. Some consumers regard this brand of quality as superior to others, but even some of those consumers who prefer this variety will buy an alternative item if the price of the alternative is sufficiently attractive relative to that of this brand. Although not essential for the analysis we shall present, it will simplify our treatment if we assume that there is only one substitute product.

Assume that consumers know the price of the substitute and its quality. With this information, their demand for the brand we are studying is shown as D_0 in Figure 16.7. We show this as a fairly inelastic demand. On the basis of costs and revenue, the firm would select a price of P_0 and an output of Q_0. This would bring MR_0 and MC into equality and would therefore maximize profits. Suppose, however, that the price of the substitute product is lowered. This alters the top part of the D_0 curve, shifting it to D_1. The new demand curve then becomes $D_1 S_1 D_0'$. As a result the new marginal revenue curve becomes MR_1, with a kink at the output level appropriate to S_1. The new profit maximizing position is at output Q_1, and the price is P_1. If the competing firm reduces its price further, the effect, let us assume, is to make the new demand curve for this firm $D_2 S_2 D_0'$. The new price becomes P_2 and the new output Q_2. A further reduction in the price of the competing product would lead to a still lower price for this product and a change in quantity, as illustrated by D_3, P_3, and Q_3. As has been shown by the traditional Chamberlinian analysis, equilibrium is achieved where the demand curve for the firm (i.e., its AR curve) becomes tangent to the AC curve, and this would be to the left of the point of lowest unit cost.

Now let us suppose that this firm is confronted, not with price cutting by producers of rival products, but by quality improvements. What would then be the effect? One possibility is that the entire demand curve, $D_0 D_0'$, would shift to the left. Still another is precisely what we have shown in Figure 16.7; that is, the demand for this firm's product will shift to the left in that vicinity within which there is competition. Let us say, for example, that the product in Figure 16.7 has been selling for around $10, and a new, highly superior brand is introduced at a price of $15. This might affect the demand for

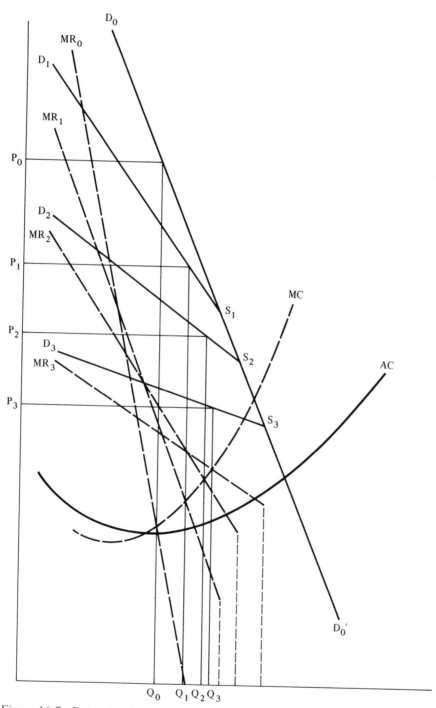

Figure 16.7. Determination of output and price in a firm responding to changes in price and quality in a competing firm.

the original, unimproved product in the range of $8 to $15, but it might not alter it at all below about $8. We could therefore regard D_1, D_2, and D_3 as representing new demands for the original product that result when product improvements are made and/or prices of those improved products are placed at successively lower levels. In this case, the new product is counterreacting by changing its price, its quality, or both. Which will it choose? Retaliation through quality changes may take time. This is why some firms make it a policy to work continuously on product improvement in order that they need not suffer from lags in adjustment but instead lead the pack in quality changes, or at least meet them almost instantaneously. Price adjustment may have long-run effects that will make the firm reluctant to take this route unless it has to. If the product is a durable good, a price reduction may result in disgruntled buyers who have recently purchased it at a higher price.[13] Or it may be difficult to get the price back up later, when quality adjustments have been made. Dealers may become reluctant to stock it owing to unstable prices. Even the "image" of the product may be damaged to the extent that price is a proxy for quality. The more inelastic the demand, the greater the pressure on the firm to avoid price cuts. Also, the more inelastic the demand, the greater the degree of customer loyalty the firm will start out with. Retention of loyalty may be more easily achieved via the quality route if the original demand is inelastic with respect to price than if it is quite elastic.

The basic process of adjustment is simply that the possibility of holding one's market (and profit) position by quality will depend on consumer responsiveness to quality vis-à-vis consumer responsiveness to price, and both of these have to be weighed in the light of the competitive environment and the actions that competitors have taken and are likely to take.

In Figure 16.8 we have attempted to show by use of a three-dimensional diagram the alternatives before the firm that is producing a differentiated product. We have used the term *perceived utility* to represent quality, thus restricting our concern to those attributes of quality recognized by consumers, whether they are real or imagined. We could extend the dimensions of this three-variable function by considering "relative price" rather than absolute price and "relative perceived utility" rather than absolute perceived utility. The surface has been drawn to suggest that if price is high and quality low, purchases are zero.

---

[13] The following example was reported by Consumers Union in 1971:

The buyer of a Polaroid camera must live with the sneaking suspicion that he might have bought a significantly improved camera if only he'd waited a while. Polaroid, after all, has a lock on the instant-picture market. If any company can plan obsolescence with confidence, Polaroid can.

In 1965, CU reported on the low-priced Swinger, not a bad camera for the price. But anyone who bought the Swinger found it was soon followed by the Big Swinger, which CU judged "a substantial improvement." Buyers who bought a Big Swinger might have ruefully noticed that the Colorpack II (an even bigger improvement, we thought) succeeded it almost immediately.

This year CU purchased a number of more-expensive Polaroid cameras, the 300 series, expecting to report on them this spring . . . But just as our tests were getting under way, we noticed a report . . . [that] Polaroid will introduce four new cameras this month and gradually phase out most of the cameras in the 300 series. . . .

Also, according to that report, "Polaroid is making available . . . 300-series advertising support and promotional funds to assist retailers in moving existing inventories of pack cameras before the new camera merchandising begins."

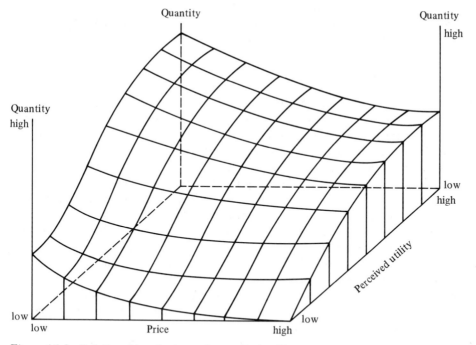

Figure 16.8. Relationship of price and perceived utility to quantity purchased.

If utility (quality) increases to its maximum and prices remain high, purchases will be moderate. Purchases are also moderate if utility is low but price is at its minimum. Purchases are highest if utility is high and price is low. Under dynamic competitive conditions this surface never remains stable. The firm can change it by its actions, and competitors can change it by altering the quality or price of competing products, thus changing the willingness of consumers to buy this particular one.

Some Observations on Quality Competition

By isolating quality as one variable in the competitive process, we have attempted to show some of the ways in which it can be viewed in relation to production and sales possibilities of the business firm. Our analysis is, however, far from exhaustive. Before we turn to some examples of quality differentiation in marketing, it seems appropriate to make some general observations about the nature of the quality competition process and its significance as an aspect of the marketing transaction.

ATTRIBUTES RATHER THAN GOODS

Competition should not be viewed as occurring between goods but between attributes of goods. Goods that are similar physically are competing goods if the *qualities* that they have give rise to substitution possibilities from the viewpoint of users of the products. Seldom do dissimilar products have the same set of attributes; therefore competition is generally nonperfect. Occasionally products with highly dissimilar attributes involve substitution possibilities. For example, mountains and beaches may both provide a type of aesthetic satisfaction. Competition arises, therefore, out of want-satisfying attributes of products and should be related to the wants satisfied rather than to the attributes or to the products themselves.[14]

COMPETITIVE SPACE

If one views competition as occurring in space, the contour of that space will vary depending on the closeness of substitutes within it.[15] In general, competition is greatest for next-door items. This is certainly the way in which the individual buyer or seller will view it, for the principal interest of a seller or consumer will lie in that which is next best or possible, whether "next" is in quality or price. But quality competition can extend beyond next-door items, for a series of quality-related items lying on a continuum or within a given space are likely to involve so much overlapping of relationship that it may be impossible to draw discrete lines to demarcate isolated quality types. If A affects B, and B affects C, and C affects D, and D affects E, then A can be said to have some remote effect on E. Even though the effect becomes less and less, the concept of a "total market" for goods that fulfill certain needs of buyers is not meaningless. Nor is the relationship of units widely separated in space merely that of Dulles' dominoes. Sometimes the need for variety may cause a big leap to a distant point in space rather than an evolutionary progression from an original preference. While the pattern of preference development is more likely to be evolutionary than revolutionary, latent or cumulative dissatisfactions, arising from the discrepancy between that which is desired and that which is realized, may on occasion incite reactions against the status quo through a "big leap" to a more remote point in space.

Much of our microeconomic theory has evolved analytical models that tend to support the position that society is best served by conditions of pure competition. Yet we know that such models do not take into account some of the attributes of transactions that are most meaningful and valuable to consumers. Quality constitutes an additional dimension of competition that must be taken into account if market behavior is to be understood. Products that are capable of fulfilling a specific human need are not necessarily physically identical, and competition between nonidentical goods is a reality confronting both sellers and users of goods.

DIVERSITY

This brings us to another observation about quality competition. Diversity is a service that has value to users of products. But diversity is the opposite of standardization, and standardization is one of the prerequisites to large-scale production. Hence, there may be a conflict between the realization of economies of scale and the meeting of diverse human needs. One consequence of economic growth and maturity is in fact two-pronged.

---

[14] This aspect of consumer demand and substitutability has been explored extensively in the various discussions of the "utility tree" by William M. Gorman, "Separate Utility and Aggregation," *Econometrica* vol. 27 (July 1959): 469-481; Robert H. Strotz, "The Empirical Implications of a Utility Correction and Further Appraisal," *Econometrica* 27 (July 1959): 482-489. It is also discussed in Abbott, op. cit. pp. 39-47. See particularly the excellent exposition by Kelvin J. Lancaster, "A New Approach to Consumer Theory," *Journal of Political Economy* 74 (April 1966): 132-157; and his more recent *Consumer Demand: A New Approach* (New York: Columbia University Press, 1971).

[15] See Robert E. Kuenne, "Quality Space, Interproduct Competition, and General Equilibrium Theory," in Kuenne, op. cit., pp. 219-250

Specialization leads to economies of scale, which lead to lower unit costs of production and, hence, increases in gross national product. But an increase in GNP, which makes possible higher levels of consumption, makes it possible for consumers to demand the diversity in consumption that is one of the hallmarks of affluence. This, in turn, leads to less specialization in production and, hence, to higher unit costs. The importance of marketing in a high-income economy is greatly increased by these contrasting facets of specialization and diversification.

INTRAFIRM QUALITY COMPETITION

Underlying much of our analysis of quality differentiation up to this point is the assumption that quality differences arise out of product differentiation *between* firms; that is, each firm produces one specific quality. We know, in fact, that this is not the case. Typically a single multiproduct firm is likely to produce a range of qualities. This opens the possibility of intrafirm quality competition and of interfirm quality competition of much larger proportions among fewer and larger producers. Thus economies of scale may still be realized in such firms to the extent that certain fixed costs are spread over a larger output that may be highly diversified.[16]

OPTIMUM NUMBER OF FIRMS

This brings us to one of the most interesting aspects of quality competition. Effective quality competition requires fewer firms than effective price competition. Too many firms producing differentiated products could, in fact, confuse the consumer if the number of quality differences exceeds the consumer's ability to discriminate. Under price competition, two firms are scarcely better than one firm. But under quality competition, two are greatly better than one. To use a political analogy, two parties are far better than one party. In consumer goods markets two qualities of automobiles are far better than one. Three are far better than two. Forty could conceivably be far worse than twenty. As John M. Clark has said,

> On the basis of observation, it appears clear that small numbers—say even three or four dominant firms in an industry—are enough to generate extremely vigorous competition in adapting the product to bid for the purchaser's favor.[17]

He also notes the limitations of small numbers:

> But if product competition is vigorous, even where numbers are small, this does not settle all questions about it. There are reasons for thinking that a considerably larger

---

[16] In his analysis of imperfect competition, Donald Dewey argues that fewer and larger firms may result in lower unit costs than the traditional tangency solution of Robinson and Chamberlin would suggest. The latter is unstable, and freedom to merge or to form a cartel would, he argues, lead to greater efficiencies. These advantages are then protected by policies that deter entry. He extends his argument to embrace differentiation. There is some optimum amount and degree of differentiation. "How closely this optimum is approached is a function of the demand for the set of differentiated products and the size of production and marketing units needed to manufacture and differentiate them in the most efficient way." Donald Dewey, *The Theory of Imperfect Competition: A Radical Reconstruction* (New York: Columbia University Press, 1969). See especially pp. 87-103. The quotation is from p. 102.

[17] John M. Clark, *Competition as a Dynamic Process*, © 1961 by the Brookings Institution, Washington, D. C.

number is called for in order that competition may be directed into the healthiest combination of rivalry in quality and price, well-balanced as between luxury and economy models, with an incentive to promote durability where the consumer's interest calls for it, and with an adequate readiness to serve the demands of minority groups of consumers.[18]

OPTIMAL DIFFERENTIATION

The process of quality determination is that of searching for the optimum amount and degree of differentiation. Just as there can be too little differentiation to achieve maximum consumer welfare, there may also be excessive differentiation. This occurs when the number of varieties results in marginal costs greater than the value of the increased utility derived from the number of varieties offered. Optimality pivots around increased utility versus the increased cost of differentiation. Perhaps the greatest limitation on increasing utility lies in the consumer's ability to discriminate. There is diminishing marginal utility from increased variety. In addition, differentiation is likely to result in increased costs unless it occurs in a firm with proportionately high fixed costs that is able to expand its output only through the production of differentiated products.

MARKET INFORMATION

Quality competition places an added value on product and market information on the part of both consumers and producers. For production decisions to achieve sellers' goals, they must be based on information about consumer wants and demand. This comes from either unsystematic market surveillance or systematic market research. From the consumer's point of view, the problem is even more serious. This is owing to the fact that the wide variety of wants that consumers have involve so many product type and quality alternatives that he has little chance of becoming expert in any one. Moreover, quality differences that are visible versus those that are invisible make an enormous difference in his ability to make objective decisions. One manifestation of the consumer's information deficiency is the evidence that price is often used as an indicator of product quality.[19]

ADVERTISING

Product differentiation and quality variations are closely allied to advertising. Products of superior quality may give rise to advertising as a means of informing consumers of their superiority. Products of equal but different quality may also give rise to advertising for purposes of informing buyers of differences and of persuading buyers that the differences have greater utility than buyers would assume without the exposure to advertising. Advertising may also be used in an effort to compensate for inferior quality. The latter possibility is particularly important where quality characteristics are not easily discernible. It is then that the persuasive effects of advertising can be most effective in achieving

---

[18] Ibid.

[19] Arthur G. Bedeian, "Consumer Perception of Price as an Indicator of Product Quality," *MSU Business Topics* 19 (Summer 1971): 59-65, and Folke Ölander, "The Influence of Price on the Consumer's Evaluation of Products and Purchases," mimeographed (Stockholm: Economic Research Institute, Stockholm School of Economics, 1967). An abridged version of the latter study appears in Bernard Taylor and Gordon Willis, eds., *Pricing Strategy* (London: Staples Press, 1969), pp. 50-69.

the goals of the advertiser. We shall pursue advertising's alliance to product differentiation further after we have examined the nature and potentiality of advertising as an instrument of marketing policy.[20]

SOME SPECIAL MARKETING PROBLEMS
RELATED TO PRODUCT QUALITY

We have sketched some of the elements of a theory of quality competition, with special attention to those aspects that bear upon marketing policy. In view of the pervasive influence of quality and product differentiation on marketing policy, it seems worthwhile to examine in some detail a few of the problems that arise in incorporating quality differentiation into the total marketing mix. We shall consider four aspects of quality variation: (1) the life cycle of a product or style, (2) product differentiation and price discrimination, (3) quality and size of firm, and (4) merchandise mix in retailing and wholesaling.

Life Cycle of Products and the Fashion Cycle

In spite of the fact that we have emphasized the importance of the dynamic aspects of quality competition, we have said little about the dynamic aspects of changes that take place in the cluster of attributes that demarcate what is commonly referred to as a product's life cycle. In a sense, of course, we are violating our concept of a product when we discuss its life cycle, for the attributes that a product has in its period of maturity may differ substantially from those that characterize its period of introduction and in this sense it could be reagarded as a separate product. But it is more useful to consider this evolving set of attributes as a single product rather than several in order to observe the historical and functional relationship of its characteristics through time.

What the product life cycle does is to delineate the phases of market development associated with (1) changes in the amount and rate of consumer acceptance, which determine the diffusion of purchases and ownership among potential consumers, and (2) modifications in the quality, price, distribution channels, and promotion of the product, which result from the response of sellers to changing market potentials. Life cycles are usually described in terms of either sales or ownership. The latter measure is especially important for durable goods.

The product life cycle is particularly helpful in the study of fashion merchandise, which is subject to a systematic sequence of consumer and producer responses. In fact, a good definition of fashion merchandise would be goods for which the demand moves in a cycle that approximates a biological growth cycle, including both expansion and expiration.[21] A staple, on the other hand, is an item for which the demand is relatively stable over

---

[20] See Chapters 17 and 18.

[21] See Raymond Pearl, *Studies in Human Biology* (Baltimore: Williams and Wilkens, 1924), chap. 24, and *The Biology of Population Growth* (New York: Knopf, 1925), chap. 1, and D'Arcy Thompson, *On Growth and Form*, 2d ed. (Cambridge: Cambridge University Press, 1952). A discussion of the mathematical theory of population growth curves can be found in Pearl, *Studies in Human Biology*, pp. 567-583. See also E. R. Hilgard. *Theories of Learning*. 2d ed. (New York: Appleton, 1956).

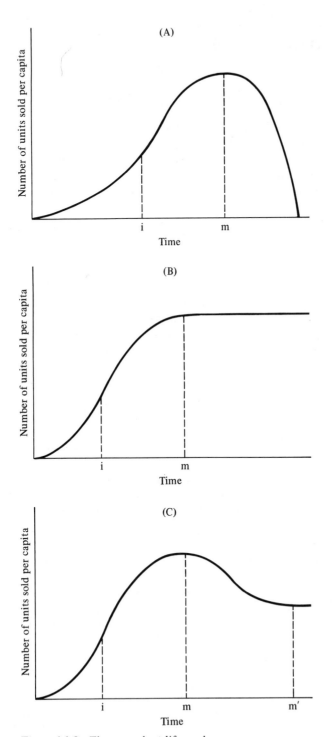

Figure 16.9. Three product life cycles.

time. Such a demand may have undergone a period of expansion when the item was first introduced, but the demand subsequently settled at some relatively stable level.[22]

LIFE CYCLE PATTERNS

In Figure 16.9 we show three life cycle patterns. In order to remove the influence of population growth on number of units sold, we have deflated sales volume by population, using number of units sold per capita. Cycle A is the typical fashion cycle, in which the number of units sold increases slowly at first, then quite rapidly up to point i, the point of inflection, after which there is a decline in the rate of increase but with sales growth continuing up to the point of maximum sales, m, after which sales decline very rapidly. The period of expansion is much longer than the period of contraction. Cycle B describes a situation in which a new nondurable product is introduced, its sales become diffused among consumers, and it becomes a staple that everyone buys at a constant replacement rate. A good example of this would be the sales of fresh oranges in the United States. Cycle C describes a similar situation for a durable good. The product is introduced, accepted by an increasing number of consumers, reaches a peak in sales per capita, and then, because of its durability, depends increasingly on replacement demand if saturation has been reached. How long it takes for the sales to reach a point of stability depends on the saturation level, the rate of diffusion, and the durability of the product and, hence, the occurrence of the first and subsequent replacement sales. It is possible for replacement sales to occur in successive waves. Sales of washing machines, refrigerators, and ranges have experienced this kind of expansion, saturation, and stabilization.[23]

STACKED CYCLES

Marketing policies must, of course, be geared to the attributes of the market situation in each of these periods. Policies with respect to price, promotion, product quality, and

---

[22]One objective basis for identifying "fashion" and "staple" items is their markdown rates. For example, in 1968 a markdown rate of 7.0 percent of sales was used in one study to differentiate between fashion and staple merchandise groups in department stores. Merchandise groups with a markdown rate of 7.0 or more percent of sales included nearly all departments handling apparel (women's, misses', juniors', girls', infants' and toddlers', and men's) plus certain accessories—millinery, female and girls' and boys' footwear, sleepwear and robes, and two types of hard goods—toys and wheel goods, and sporting goods and equipment. All other merchandise groups had a markdown rate of less than 7.0 percent of sales. Included in the latter group were a number of women's clothing accessories—handbags, lingerie, hosiery, gloves—all men's accessories and shoes, boys' clothing, all types of appliances and home furnishings, radios and TV, notions, baked goods and confections, smoking supplies, and alcoholic beverages. Since markdown rates vary from year to year, the 7.0 percent rate is not necessarily the appropriate value for every year.

Markdown rates are not, of course, a perfect measuring device for differentiating between fashion merchandise and staples, but these examples suggest that they do a fairly good job of separation. The logic of their use for this purpose lies in the fact that markdowns reflect (1) errors of buying judgment, which are likely to be greater for fashion merchandise than for staples owing to the greater risk and uncertainty associated with sales forecasting for fashion goods, and (2) the variability of demand and prices as products move through the product life cycle.

The data for 1968 are from the National Retail Merchants Association and were taken from R. Thomas Mitchell, "Computer Data Processing: Its Applications and Use in Retailing," (MBA Paper, Washington State University, 1970), pp. 27-31.

[23]See above Figure 6.2.

Table 16.2 Parameters and Selected Characteristics of Logistic Functions[a] That Describe the Number of Passenger Cars on December 31 of Each Year per 100 Households in the United States for Various Periods, 1910-1962

Equation Number	Original			Calculated					
	Years	N	Maximum Y	Parameters			Extremes for Which $Y_c \leq (Y \pm 2.00)$		.50k
				c	k	a − bx	Years	N	Year(s)
1	1911-29	19	77.41	0	83.08	2.9204-0.3081x	1910-30	21	1921-22
2	1912-20	9	32.80	0	43.56	1.8714-0.4092x	1910-21	12	1917-18
3	1919-27	9	69.75	30	39.96	2.5856-0.8362x	1920-27	8	1923
4	1933-61[b]	21	115.75	60	60.63	1.8767-0.2283x	1933-61[b]	21	1950
5	1932-42	11	76.06	65	13.79	1.5421-0.5821x	1932-40	9	1936
6	1938-52[c]	7	94.64	72	24.03	2.0139-0.9881x	1938-52[c]	7	1949
7	1950-58	9	110.81	92	18.96	2.8784-1.0276x	1950-57	8	1954

[a] $Y_c = c + \dfrac{k}{1 + e^{(a-bx)}}$

[b] 1942-1949 omitted.

[c] 1941-1948 omitted.

in which Y_c is the calculated number of passenger cars per 100 households, k is the asymptote, x is the year, a and b are calculated constants, and c is a constant selected by inspection of the data. The function was fitted to values for three years selected with the first and third equidistant from the second. Each value was an arithmetic mean of the observed values for that year, the year before, and the year following. The original years indicated in the table embrace exactly the extremes included in these three means.

Source: Edna Douglas, "The Growth of Ownership of Consumer Durables," 1964 *Proceedings of the Business and Economic Statistics Section* (Washington, D.C.: American Statistical Association, 1964), p. 27 Original data from Automobile Manufacturers Association, *Automobile Facts and Figures*, 1964 ed. (Detroit: Automobile Manufacturers Association, 1964).

distribution channels vary at different levels of the channel. Such policies may *reflect* the stage in the product life cycle, and they may *influence* the movement of the product through the life cycle by accelerating the sales expansion or slowing down the sales contraction.

There are two aspects of this "control" that are of special interest. Some studies of historical data indicate that there are, in fact, cycles on cycles, each of which is associated with a fundamental change in the attributes of the product. This has been observed in airline travel, in which each cycle was associated with a basic type of aircraft, moving from the Ford Tri-Motor, through the DC-3, the DC-6, and the DC-8, to the jet.[24] The jet itself has expanded from the Boeing 707 to the Lockheed L-1011 and McDonnell Douglas DC-10 and then to the Boeing 747.[25] The supersonic jet has been held in abeyance by public choice in the United States but has been produced in France as the Concorde. The traffic volume following the introduction of each major change in equipment reached a level approximately 50 percent above its level just before the innovation was made.

A study of passenger car stocks and of laundry equipment in households was made to determine whether this growth pattern also existed for these products.[26] Logistic curves were fitted to data on household stocks of these durables spanning five decades. The findings for passenger cars are shown in Table 16.2. Note that the two long spans, one for the pre-Depression years before 1930 and one for the period 1933-1961, showed that the maximum inventory level in the second wave—116 cars per 100 households—was about 50 percent greater than that of the first wave, 77 cars per 100 households. Each long cycle embraced two or three shorter cycles. Both short and long cycles were associated with substantive changes in the physical attributes of the products.

In one study of household laundry appliances, the product cluster was divided into the following components:

1. A new product: total washers (after World War I)
2. A mature product: total washers (after World War II), comprised of
    a. a successful innovation: automatic washers;
    b. a declining product: wringer washers; and
    c. an abortive innovation: combination washer-dryers
3. A new product with joint demand: dryers[27]

Sales per 1,000 households for most of these are shown in Figure 16.10 for the years 1921–1962. Demand functions based on both time series and cross-sectional data showed that income was the most important determining variable in the sales of these products but that its importance declined as the product experienced increased market maturity. The decline in income elasticities is shown in Figure 16.11. Price was important only during the 1920s. Such changing functional relationships have important implications for marketing policy and consumer welfare.

One of the probable effects of the declining imporatance of purchasing power and price upon consumer purchases as market maturity is reached is the pressure which this puts

[24] William M. Wallace, "An Analysis of Air Traffic Growth," *Review of Economics and Statistics* 45 (February 1963): 89-100.

[25] "Airlines Get Set for Jumbos," *Business Week*, October 5, 1968, pp. 151-152.

[26] Edna Douglas, "The Growth of Ownership of Consumer Durables," 1964 *Proceedings of the Business Statistics Section, American Statistical Association*, (Washington, 1964), pp. 26-35.

[27] Edna Douglas, "Secular and Cyclical Changes in the Demand for Components of a Product Cluster," *Review of Economics and Statistics* 49 (February 1967): 63-76.

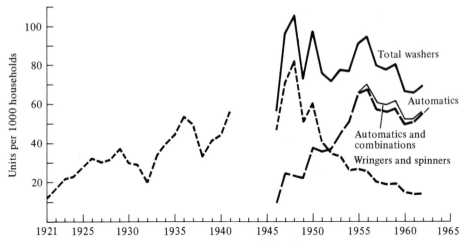

Figure 16.10. Manufacturers' sales of wringers and spinners, 1921-1941 and 1946-1962, and of automatic washers, combination washer-dryers, and total washers, 1946-1962, per 1000 households in the United States. Sources: Based on data from *Merchandising Week* (formerly *Electrical Merchandising*), Annual Statistical and Marketing Issue, 1922-1963; U.S. Bureau of the Census, *Current Population Reports, Population Characteristics*, Series P-20, No. 92, p. 4; No. 40, p. 6 (Washington, D.C.: GPO, 1959 and 1965).

upon sellers in a monopolistically competitive market situation to try to attract sales by other means. The consumer's stake in these "other means" is considerable. Advertising and sales promotion may be one tool employed. . . .

On the other hand, product improvement or accelerated obsolescence may be avenues by which producers seek to carve out a larger share of a demand which is tending toward greater stability. The quality of new appliances and of innovations was not included as a variable in this study but may be relevant to some of the sales movements observed. Perhaps the major, and particularly the minor, cycles bear some relationship to product changes. Most of the technical improvements in laundry appliances have affected the cleaning (or drying) ability of the machine, the variety of tasks it would perform, the degree of automation, and the durability or cost of operating the machine. There have also been marked changes in the qualities of fabrics. If these could be quantified in some meaningful way, it is possible that they would throw new light on sales experience.[28]

MULTIPLE CYCLES

A second aspect of product life cycles has been observed in the food industry in terms of market share achieved by an innovator as a result of interactions among the policies of the innovator and his competitors. This has been described by A. C. Nielsen in terms of primary cycles for brands of supermarket products and their subsequent recycles.[29] On the basis of data of 275 brands of health and beauty aids, household products, and food products for the period 1961-1966, A. C. Nielsen isolated primary cycles, associated with the introduction of a new brand, and recycles—smaller and shorter cycles occurring after sales had dipped to 80 percent of the primary cycle's peak. Figure 16.12 illustrates the

[28] Ibid., p. 74

[29] "The 'Life Cycle' of Grocery Brands," *The Nielsen Researcher*, no. 1 (1968).

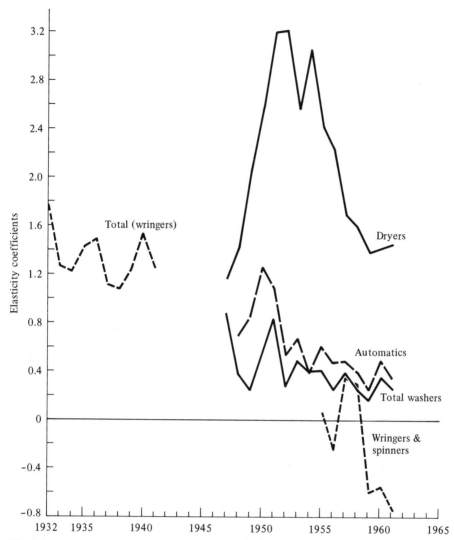

Figure 16.11. Elasticity of manufacturers' shipments of total washers, automatic washers, wringers and spinners, and dryers per 1000 households with respect to disposable personal income per household based on state data for each year, 1932-1941 and 1947-1961. Source: Edna Douglas, "Secular and Cyclical Changes in the Demand for Components of a Product Cluster," *Review of Economics and Statistics* 49 (February 1967): 73.

pattern showing an average brand's percentage of total sales of the product type. The primary cycle, A, was found to span a period of 10-60 months, with the average about 2-2.5 years for the three product groups studied. The decline in sales for this cycle was most often associated with the introduction of a competitive brand. Each recycle spanned a period of 4-40 months, with the average about 15 months. Food products had slightly longer recycles than household products or health and beauty aids. These were most often generated by some kind of promotional program, such as a change in size, coupon promotion, advertising, product improvement, a cents-off deal, a new package design, and the like. The most common method of generating a recycle was through a combination of more advertising dollars, copy change, and product innovations. Product

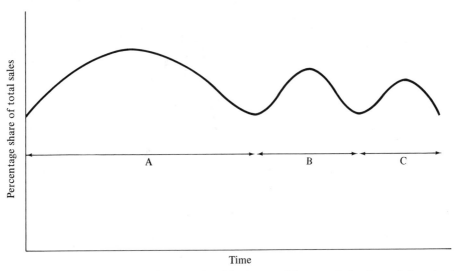

Figure 16.12. Life cycle of a nondurable item subject to imitation of its physical properties and marketing policies.

innovations ranged from basic changes to new packaging, new flavors or types, new sizes, or new premiums. New packaging was the most popular innovation in this period. The turning point of the recycle was most often due to some form of competitive action, including a new-brand introduction or matching action by competitors. The secular trend of the product can be downward, horizontal, or upward. Competitive forces will allow a horizontal or upward trend for any brand only if aggressive efforts are made to generate the recycle for that brand.

WELFARE IMPLICATIONS

Before we leave the matter of the product life cycle, we should comment on the welfare implications of this aspect of marketing. The fundamental question is whether quality competition of this sort is desirable from a social point of view. While we must recognize that there can be "too much" or "too little" of it, nevertheless it seems necessary to conclude that society is better off with it than without it for the reasons that quality competition through product innovations (1) creates opportunities for more fully meeting consumer wants and demand, (2) encourages experimentation and innovations in the identification and fulfillment of demand, and (3) generates strong competitive forces where the number of substitutes is limited and possibilities for effective price competition are few.

But we would be ignoring the realities of the marketplace were we not to recognize some possible disadvantages of product innovation from the consumer's point of view. One is that producers can generate product obsolescence by creating new products that accelerate the rate at which old products are replaced. Consumers may become unhappy with old products once they are aware of the availability of new products. While producers cannot force consumers to buy innovations or newly differentiated goods, of course, they have considerable control over the rate of product introduction and over the decision as to whether old products will continue to be available on the market. They have, therefore, a great deal of power to affect the range of alternatives from which the consumer can choose and can be expected to use that power to their own benefit unless forced to do otherwise by competitive forces or consumer resistance.

A closely related question concerns the matter of durability and obsolescence. The consumer's welfare is, or course, enhanced by greater product durability. It would be most economical if we had houses that never deteriorated, clothes that never wore out, cars that lasted a lifetime, and TV sets whose transistors lasted forever. If consumers were insensitive to the sameness of their possessions over time, their welfare would be enhanced by this interesting but unlikely condition. In the world of less-than-durable consumer goods, what we must seek is not infinite durability but optimum durability. But the producer of goods may prefer quality changes that increase obsolescence rather than durability. The greater the durability of the product he sells, the fewer sales he will make in the long run, for replacement sales will occur less frequently. It will take a long time, therefore, for the grateful consumer of a highly durable product to return to the seller for a replacement. The greater the lag, the greater the probability that a competitor will have introduced the greater durability into his product. At the same time, built-in obsolescence may not hurt the seller of a durable good in the same way inferior quality in nondurables would. It takes time for consumers to acquire experience with durables, and they seldom acquire the same range of experience with alternative brands as they can with nondurables. Only if the built-in obsolescence results in early and/or frequent repair problems does the consumer learn quickly. So the seller has more insulation than is likely where a product is bought frequently. There are special considerations that enter into the determination of the quality of durable products, and competition may function more sluggishly in these markets in encouraging producers to increase product durability. Market information, such as that provided by Consumers Union, can be highly effective in correcting this market imperfection that is likely to occur given the circumstances under which such goods would otherwise be acquired.

Another problem from the consumer's viewpoint is the possibility of a proliferation of brands and product differentials on the market. The frustration of any consumer who tries to select among the myriad varieties of sizes and brands of detergents, packaged cereals, toothpaste, shampoo, and countless other items on the shelves of supermarkets, drugstores, and general merchandise retailers should be taken into account in calculating the social cost of an economic system that rewards the creator of trivial differentiation.

For example, the A. C. Nielsen Company has calculated that in 1948 there were 25-30 different items in the powdered detergent and soap flake group. These "items" included choices among brands, sizes, and types. In 1965, it is estimated that there were 110-115 items in powdered detergents and soap flakes, 9-10 tablet detergents, and 72-75 liquid detergent items.[30] On the other hand, the 15-18 items of bar laundry soap in 1948 had decreased to 4-6 in 1965. Dry starch had 12-15 items in 1948, while there were 45-50 starches and fabric finishers in 1965. Liquid bleaches had increased from 15-20 in 1948 to 95-100 in 1965, with the latter including liquid, powdered, and tablet forms. Also, in 1965 there were 22-24 liquid and dry fabric softeners compared to none in 1948.

This is not to argue for standardization but for something less prolific than what we have. It almost seems as though the dilemma of the world's population growth has spread to brands of consumer goods that are trying to outbreed mankind. It would be helpful if we could devise a way of measuring this social cost of differentiation in order that we might incorporate it into our analysis in some objective and meaningful way.

---

[30]"This Matter of Selection, *The Nielsen Researcher*, no. 1 (1967), p. 13

In summary, we would have to say that quality competition through product innovation opens possibilities for excessive and frivolous differentiation, for confusing and deceitful variation, and for the exploitation of market power derived from initial market penetrations. But the possible virtues of quality competition should not be completely subordinated to the social costs that may result. Clark believes that the latter has been emphasized at the expense of the former:

> It seems . . . that the prevalent forms of theoretical analysis [of competition through product differentiation] concentrate on the defects to the neglect of the virtues and judge the defects by a standard of comparison (what *would supposedly* happen under pure or perfect competition) which is not only not feasible, but is, in terms of a present-day economy, meaningless.[31]

Product Differentiation and Price Discrimination

We have pointed out the conditions under which price discrimination is possible and desirable.[32] Product differentiation can be an important tool by which the producer segments his market, producing slightly different products for each and pricing them in accordance with the demand in each market. Segmentation of customers by income could be accomplished, for example, by producing a high, medium, and low quality, with each priced to equate the firm's marginal cost with that market segment's marginal revenue.

Writing in 1849, Jules Dupuit described the combining of product differentiation and price discrimination as practiced by the French railways:

> It is not because of the few thousand francs which would have to be spent to put a roof over the third-class carriages or to upholster the third-class seats that some company or other has open carriages with wooden benches. . . . What the company is trying to do is to prevent the passengers who can pay the second-class fare from traveling third class; it hits the poor, not because again for the same reason that the companies, having proved almost cruel to third-class passengers and mean to second-class ones, becomes lavish in dealing with first-class passengers. Having refused the poor what is necessary, they give the rich what is superfluous.[33]

In our present-day markets Sears Roebuck's and Montgomery Ward's good, better, and best are examples of a practice long known to enterprising sellers.

The use of product differentiation is not, however, a foolproof means of realizing price discrimination. If the markets to which the differentiated products are directed are not discrete—that is, if consumers can switch from one to the other—price discrimination will not be possible. Clark, for example, has pointed out the danger that a seller incurs in producing an economy model that might take sales away from the standard model.[34] This has certainly been evident in the automobile industry in the United States. During the

---

[31] Clark, *Competition as a Dynamic Process*, p. 214, © 1961 by the Brookings Institution, Washington, D. C.

[32] See pp. 351-360.

[33] Jules Dupuit, "On Tolls and Transport Charges," translated by Elizabeth Henderson from the *Annales des Ponts et Chaussees*, 2d ser., XVII (1849), quoted in Robert B. Ekelund, Jr., "Price Discrimination and Product Differentiation in Economic Theory: An Early Analysis," *Quarterly Journal of Economics* 84 (May 1970): 275.

[34] Clark, *Competition as a Dynamic Process*, op. cit., pp. 252-257.

1950s only American Motors made any attempt to market a low-priced economy car in the form of the Rambler. The dominant firms did not make one, probably because they knew it would take sales from the luxury and standards models. It was the impact of imports of economy models that finally forced firms of the industry to introduce similar low-priced models. There is therefore no assurance that the complete spectrum of possible differentiation alternatives will be exploited unless the appropriate competitive forces prevail in the market.

Quality Variations and Size of the Firm

The size of a firm can have an important bearing on its ability to introduce and benefit from innovations. Its innovative capacity is highly dependent upon the resources at its disposal for research and product development. The larger the financial resources, the greater the innovative potential. But the quality of resources is equally important. Sometimes quality can be controlled by the size of expenditures. Creativity, however, is not always responsive to market forces in the same way as other forms of output. The importance of creativity in the innovative process, and even the role of chance, can sometimes make possible opportunities for innovation by firms that lack extensive financial resources. In general, however, the larger the firm, the more resources it can allocate to research and development and the more opportunities it has for realizing economies of scale in the development process.

The quantity and quality of the firm's marketing resources are the important variables in determining the extent to which it can benefit from innovations. The large firm clearly has advantages in this respect. Not only are the resources available to it for advertising and promotion larger, but the effectiveness per dollar spent is likely to be greater. Moreover, the scope of its established marketing organization and the power inherent in its entrenched market position provide the framework for the rapid and wide dissemination of newly developed products. The small firm does not have either a comparable marketing budget or extensive distribution system for launching its innovations. The market power of the large firm is unquestionably one of its greatest advantages in the introduction of new products.[35]

The risks of innovation and differentiation are high for both large and small firms. In some respects they may be borne more economically in the large firm because no single innovation need represent a large percentage of its total output. Hence the pooling of uncertainties associated with the marketing of new or differentiated products can convert them into calculable risks—a possibility not open to the small firm. The high failure rate among new products is testimony to the importance of risk reduction in product innovation. This is sometimes possible through market research, and the scale economies of this activity are likely to benefit the large producer far more than the small one. On the other hand, the large firm whose innovation fails may find that the failure contaminates sales of its other products. The small firm, with less investment in its market reputation, has less goodwill to lose by the failure of a single innovation.

Even new products that succeed entail risks, however, for the probability of imitation by competitors is high. Some small firms may, in fact, avoid many of the risks of possible failure by specializing in the imitation of successful products developed by larger

---

[35] This has been particularly important for cigarettes, soft drinks, detergents, household cleaning products, and packaged food such as ready-to-eat cereals and prepared food mixes.

competitors. The ease and speed with which imitations can appear on the market has an important effect on the long-run profitability of an innovation. In this respect, the larger producer who is able to introduce innovations continually substitutes a series of successive short-term profitable ventures from its successful innovations for the long-run profits of fewer innovations. The small successful innovator will find this more difficult to do and may easily suffer from competitors' imitation of his product.

We know, however, that small firms do introduce new and different products and in many cases market them successfully and profitably. Why does this happen in view of the considerable advantages of large firms? There would appear to be two important strengths of the small firm in these cases. One is their flexibility in terms of both internal operations and market position. Innovation requires change, and the rigidities of the large firm can often stand in the way of these necessary changes. Creativity often thrives best in a smaller, less highly structured environment. In addition a small firm has more mobility with respect to its market position and may find it easier than does the larger firm to move, through product innovation, within the market's quality "space." It can look for opportunities to produce the unique product, and particularly one for which the market demand is not big enough for it to be attractive to a larger firm. The small firm's scale of manufacturing and marketing lends itself to the efficient production of specialty products and certain types of services. Also, the small firm has less commitment to a family brand and can be freer to experiment, moving into new product areas and tapping a new clientele.

The second advantage that the small producer has lies in his market share. A large firm that has garnered a substantial proportion of total market sales often finds it more difficult to increase its share than does a firm with a relatively small share. Brand loyalty is never complete. The larger a firm's clientele, the greater the number who are likely to be marginally loyal. A small firm that introduces a usefully differentiated product may find it easier to increase its market share from, let us say, 3 percent to 5 percent than would the large firm in attempting to increase its share from 53 percent to 55 percent. Moreover, a firm with a large market share may have to differentiate one product from another of its own products and, in so doing, take customers from itself. An example of this was the competition between freeze-dried and instant coffee when the former was introduced on the market. The smaller firm that produces a unique or distinctive product does not have this problem to the same degree.

In general, however, we have to conclude that the weight of advantage in quality innovation and product differentiation probably lies with the large firm, although there is an important place for the small innovator. From a social point of view we might be better served with more opportunities for the small innovator. While society benefits from the resources that the large firm can direct toward innovation and product development, and from interfirm competition between large innovators, the basic question is whether this results in the optimum rate of product development and differentiation in terms of total social costs and benefits.

Quality Variations and Merchandise Mix in Retailing and Wholesaling

There are many ways in which the "quality" of retailing can vary from one store to another and from wholesaler to wholesaler. The number, variety, and quality of services rendered is unique to each seller, although certain standardized procedures and practices have developed under a number of institutional arrangements in retail and wholesale trade. One aspect of policy that distinguishes individual retail and wholesale firms is the merchandise mix. Before we leave the question of quality variability and its impact on marketing policy, we should examine briefly the relevance of mix to the merchandising policy of retail and wholesale firms. The approach we shall use is that of William J. Baumol and Edward A. Ide, whose analysis of the demand for variety in retailing sheds light on some of the facets of this problem in the matter of deciding on the width of merchandise lines.[36]

THE DEMAND FOR VARIETY

One of the costs of marketing from the consumer's point of view is that of finding out what goods are available in the market place. If the shopper has in mind a specific item or product cluster that he wishes to purchase, he will prefer that situation which involves the least cost and/or effort on his part. Therefore we have two elements that make up the consumer's demand for variety. One is the probability that he will find a given item or, as most shopping is done, a variety of items from which he may either make a choice to meet a particular want or select a mixture that will meet a number of wants. The other is the cost of undertaking this search process. The net benefit that he expects to get from shopping in a particular store can be expressed as follows:

$$f(N, D) = wp(N) - v \left(c_d D + c_n \sqrt{N} + c_i \right)$$

in which $f(N, D)$ is a measure of the consumer's expected net benefit from entering the store, which is a function of $p(N)$, the probability that he will find in that store the item(s) that he wishes to purchase; D, the distance that he must travel to get there; N, the cost to him of searching within the store to find what he wants; and c_i, the opportunity cost of shopping there.

A comment or two about each of these variables is in order before we look at the kind of function this is likely to become when it is quantified. The variable $p(N)$ is the probability of finding an item that is desired in a particular store. The larger the stock of items there and/or the more closely the store's stock is known to fit the shopper's purchase preference, the greater the probability of success. Therefore the constant w is assigned by the shopper on the basis of past experience with stores of this type and size. The constants c_d, c_n, and c_i are also assigned by the individual shopper to reflect the cost per mile (or possibly per minute of traveling time) to get to the store, the cost of searching through a store of this size for the desired merchandise, and the opportunity cost of shopping. The greater the distance, the less appealing a particular outlet will be. The internal cost of search within a store is assumed to be directly related to the number of square feet in a one-story store. Hence, the square root of N is used to reflect the linear distance that the customer must cover to find the desired item. The opportunity cost of shopping is the value of time spent for this purpose that might be spent in other pursuits. It is worth noting that a consumer who enjoys traveling to a store or shopping center, looking for the right goods in the store, or shopping in general might assign negative values to one or all of these three "cost" variable, thereby reflecting their positive utility to him. In general, though, both logical and empirical observation would support the position that these would normally have disutility to the consumer and should therefore

---

[36] William J. Baumol and Edward A. Ide, "Variety in Retailing," *Management Science* 3 (October 1956): 93-101. We are taking from this analysis that portion which deals with the demand for variety and shall reserve for latter consideration the problem of costs and profit maximization. The reason for this segmentation in our approach is that the cost variables relevant to the profit-maximization solution are related to the costs of acquiring, holding, and replacing inventory. These specialized costs are related to the performance of stock-holding functions and will be discussed in Chapter 19. We shall consider at this point only those costs of variety which are incurred by the consumer.

be deducted from the probability of a successful "find" in order to arrive at an expected net benefit value.

The important question to ask is how $f(N, D)$ varies according to the value of N. When N is small, $f(N, D)$ will be negative, the value assigned to w will be small (or zero if N is zero), and any positive values assigned to distance, in-store search, and opportunity costs of shopping are likely to exceed the very low value of the store's extremely small stock. But if the stock is extremely large, the value of $c_n\sqrt{N}$ can become very large, while that of $wp(N)$ can never be greater than w (since p can never exceed 1.00). Therefore infinitely large stores cause the cost of in-store shopping to become infinitely large without causing the probability of shopping success to increase proportionately. Some intermediate size of store is to be preferred. The size that will be preferred between the extremes will depend on how the consumer balances the probability of finding there what he wants against the cost to him of getting there and searching that possibility out. Presumably there will be some optimum $f(N, D)$ possible. After that point has been reached, $c_n\sqrt{N}$ will continue to grow and thereby reduce the benefits of shopping there.

OPTIMUM VARIETY: DENSITY CONSIDERATIONS

There is an optimum variety for each customer. There can be too little, or there can be too much. Whether he will go where he can have access to this optimum variety will depend on the cost to him of doing so. The greater the distance he has to travel, the greater the variety has to be to make it worth his while. As students of retail trading areas have long observed, consumers who travel a considerable distance to shop will do so in response to greater variety of merchandise and will be particularly responsive to varieties of shopping goods whose selection depends on a comparison of quality and price. The limits of a trading area are reached when the value of the added variety offered is just equal to the added cost of reaching and shopping that center. As Baumol and Ide show, this is where $f(N, D)$ is equal to zero. The distance of this point from the store, or shopping center, will be

$$D_m = \frac{w}{vc_d}p(N) - \frac{1}{c_d}(c_n\sqrt{N} + c_i)$$

The retailer has to decide how many items of merchandise to stock in terms of the effect of merchandise stocks on sales and on net profits. The retailer's problem is more than a mere summing of individual responses, for he has to consider not only the response of individuals who reside close to his store but also the matter of how many added individuals he can attract from greater distances through the variety of merchandise he has to offer. Thus the critical factor becomes the effect of N on D_m and the density of potential customers within the limits of that distance from which he can attract customers. It will be found that the sales volume to be expected will vary directly with the cube of the distance if the area that spreads out in all directions from the retailer's place of business is of equal density. It will vary directly with the square of the distance if the population density varies inversely with distance from the store, that is, population density declines linearly as distance from the store increases.[37]

---

[37] The basis for these relationships is developed in the discussion of retail trading area determination in Chapter 20.

It would appear that a store that carries an increasing number of items will first experience increasing sales, then decreasing, average and marginal sales. Therefore no store should increase its stocks indefinitely. If average sales per item carried increase up to some point as the store increases its variety of merchandise, this can come about only through increased numbers of customers, if one assumes that each customer buys what he planned to buy. But increased sales per item can also come about through the effect of increased merchandise stocks on a store's ability to attract customers who, once they are in the store to search for specific items, also make impulse purchases. This latter possibility offsets to some degree the disutility of the store's large stocks to the customer who dislikes having to search through so much merchandise in order to find what he planned to buy when he came into the store.

We should consider the possibilities that this approach opens up for marketing policy. There is an optimum stock for a given area with a specified population density and consumer distaste for shopping and travel. The size of the area from which customers will be drawn will depend on the merchandise mix that the retailer maintains and the cost of traveling to his place of business. By increasing or altering his merchandise selection, the retailer may affect the number of customers he attracts and, hence, the sales volume he can have. If he can devise ways of reducing the cost of shopping for the customer, he can extend that area and his appeal. This he might do through skillful arrangement of the merchandise in the store, making it easy for the customer to find what he wants. In this respect, note the advantages that newly designed stores, and particularly those whose space allocations can be planned from the beginning, have over older stores in structures designed for other types of retailing arrangements.[38] Easy and accessible parking facilities, elevators, and delivery of packages may reduce customer discomfort associated with getting from one place to another while shopping. The pleasantness of shopping in a store can increase the store's ability to attract customers from a considerable distance. These methods of sales appeal have been employed extensively by downtown department stores characterized by considerable stock depth and width and large retail trading areas. Similarly, supermarkets and planned shopping centers have been placed strategically with respect to customer location and movement and have attempted to minimize some of the cost of shopping by designing convenient layouts.

OPTIMUM VARIETY: PROFIT CONSIDERATIONS

We have discussed merchandise variety in terms of sales maximization. The retailer must consider not only sales effects of his merchandise variety but also profit effects. The calculation of profits will depend on the sales effect minus the cost effect. The larger the stock, the greater the investment in inventory and the greater the cost of maintaining inventories. On the other hand, the larger the sales per item of merchandise stocked, the lower the unit cost of maintaining stocks for that item. The optimum reorder quantity will also have to be determined and related to the cost of inventory maintenance. Since all of these cost elements are related to inventories, we shall reserve until later a consideration of their effects on the retailer's decisions with respect to inventory size.[39]

---

[38] Have you ever tried to find something in Boston's downtown Jordan Marsh when you were in a hurry?

[39] See Chapter 19.

17

Advertising Expenditure Models

Synchronized miracles,
revealed truths,
tell the much and not-at-all
with every rise and fall of bow,
each toss of self
(collective selfhood;
reaper of tones to sow).

—Ruth Slonim

Few subjects in marketing can arouse more emotional argument than advertising. Most people have judgments about the goodness or badness of advertising and its role in contemporary society. Businessmen who use it often do so without knowing what, in fact, its effects are, yet "believing" that it benefits both themselves and society as a whole. Others deplore its materialistic orientation, its bias, its appeal to emotions, its flamboyance and bad taste. Economists as a whole have been far more critical of advertising than has any other identifiable professional group, with the possible exception of Consumers Union.

It is the purpose of this and the next chapter to examine advertising within the framework of economics. This is not an easy task, for there is serious question about the appropriateness of economics to the understanding of many aspects of advertising that do not fit the ends-means schema that underlie economic analysis.[1] But this is not true for all aspects of advertising analysis. Advertising budget decisions can be viewed within an economic framework with results useful to the firm in making decisions. We shall examine ways of viewing this type of decision. Some broader questions concerning social effects of advertising, however, can less readily be analyzed within a purely economic framework. In these cases, we shall push the analysis to the limits of economics and, we hope, be able to ask some of the important questions that remain to be answered. This we shall do in the next chapter.

Before we focus on this highly specialized and controversial area of marketing activity, it would be helpful to view its place within the context of the total cluster of marketing activities. We shall then view it from the perspective of the decision-making firm and, finally, from that of society as a whole.

THE NATURE OF SELLING COSTS

A useful classification of business costs can be made in terms of three categories:[2]

---

[1] See, for example, Alfred Sherrard, "Advertising, Product Variation, and the Limits of Economics," *Journal of Political Economy* 59 (April 1951): 126-142.

[2] This classification is based in part on the imaginative discussion of costs by Børge Barfod. The following outline is adapted from his *Reklamen i Teoretisk-Økonomisk Belysning*, Skrifter fra

1. Transformation costs: costs incurred for the purpose of effecting changes in the physical attributes of the product or service. These are what we have referred to as form production costs, resulting in changes in the form of the product. Most costs of agriculture, forestry, fishing, mining, and manufacturing would fall into this category.
2. Physical distribution costs: costs incurred in (a) moving goods from the point of their physical transformation to the point of sale to users, and (b) holding goods for sale. These are the costs of physical aspects of marketing—transportation and storage—and are essential to the completion of the production process, broadly defined.
3. Selling costs: costs incurred (a) to achieve a larger share of an existing generic demand and/or (b) to enlarge the generic demand. These may result in the alteration of consumer preference patterns or in the broadening of market areas, physically or economically. They may be *expansionary*, resulting in increased demand either generically or specifically, or they may be *retentative*, resulting in less decrease in demand. Costs associated with the widening of geographic areas might arise from the addition of salesmen or selling outlets. Those associated with economic expansion might arise from consumer demand analysis or channel restructuring to achieve increased market segmentation, or from advertising to untapped market segments. Advertising is a common selling cost that can be directed toward an expansion of either generic or specific demand or toward the retention of demand. Through its impact on consumer preferences, it may enlarge market share or increase the generic demand over what that demand would have been without the advertising. It seeks to alter consumer behavior by presenting information, logical argument, or subjective persuasion.

In Table 17.1 are identified some of the variables over which sellers have some degree of control and that can be altered to influence the pattern of consumer preferences. These are differentiated into transformation possibilities and communication possibilities, that is, into those concerned with the product and/or service provided and those concerned with the consumer's perception of the product and/or service provided. A manufacturer could, for example, alter the "thing" the consumer is offered in the market place by changing the product's characteristics in a fundamental or trivial way, by altering the services that are a part of the transaction—credit, guarantees, delivery, return goods privilege, installation, maintenance, and so forth—or by changing the product's availability through the quantity manufactured and the distribution channels and outlets through which the product is distributed. He may also pursue policies that will result in changing the consumer's mind. This line of attack could either complement or substitute for changes in the product and services available. Most often, it would complement the transformation possibilities. Changes in the product, in the services surrounding the product, or in product availability give the seller something to talk about. Hence, advertising, packaging and displays, and personal selling will be geared to projecting the virtues of the product. If packaging and display are used for more than merely getting a message across or making the product more appealing, then this might become a transformation possibility. For example, if the container is useful for some other purpose, the product itself becomes different. But we shall not quibble at this point over the shading that may lie between the two levels of variables identified in Table 17.1.

Institutter og Studiekredse, Udgivet af Den Handelsvidenskabelige Laereanstalt, II (Copenhagen: O. C. Olsen, 1937), p. 45. See Figure 17.A.1, where we have outlined in more detail the differentiations suggested by Barfod.

Table 17.1 Variables that Sellers Can Manipulate to Influence Consumer Choice.

Determinants of Consumer Preference	Variables That Sellers Can Manipulate to Influence (Alter) Consumer Choice		
	Transformation Possibilities		
UTILITY SOURCE (object of the exchange transaction)	Functional attributes of the product	Services accompanying the product	Product availability
	Communication Possibilities		
PERCEPTION OF UTILITY (potential consumer's evaluation of the object vis-à-vis his needs)	Advertising through mass media	Packaging and display	Personal selling

THE ROLES OF ADVERTISING

Advertising is the use of mass communication media to attempt to increase the demand for the seller's product and/or services or to prevent a decrease in demand. How can advertising do this? We shall regard these "ways of doing" as the roles of advertising used as an instrument of marketing policy and shall employ the threefold classification of roles developed by Børge Barfod.[3] Advertising has a manipulative role; that is, it seeks to persuade consumers to buy the product or to lay the groundwork for a subsequent buying decision.[4] It has an informational role; that is, it informs consumers of the availability of goods and services, their prices and terms of sale, and their particular attributes. Its catalytic role is to reduce frictions in the marketing system, that is, to effect equilibrium in markets more readily and more nearly completely than would occur without advertising.

The line between advertising's manipulative role and its informative role is not clearly defined. It is perhaps better to think of these two as on a continuum, with one end representing objective information about a potential transaction, such as price, and the other end representing highly subjective feelings, attitudes, or dispositions toward a transaction, such as a conviction that a purchase will enhance one's sense of self-esteem. An advertiser who attempts to use logic or facts to "persuade" or "manipulate" a

---

[3] Barfod, op. cit. See also Figure 17A.1.

[4] In this discussion, we are assuming that advertising is an instrument of the seller rather than of the buyer. This is most often the case in marketing transactions, but it need not always be true. If consumer tastes have been developed on the basis of experience with plentiful supplies and subsequent shortages of supply occur, competition among buyers may become far keener than among sellers. Buyers may then advertise to obtain scarce supplies. In this case, the advertising will be directed toward the seller rather than the buyer.

potential buyer is operating in the gray area between these two extremes. In its catalytic role advertising alters the potential buyer's preferences *or* informs him of the attributes of the product or service in order to correct allocative errors on the part of the seller, the buyer, or other segments of the market. An overstock that arose out of the producer's forecasting error may be sold through persuasive or informative advertising, thus clearing the market by advertising rather than by a price reduction. The overstock may be due to the seller's misinformation, or it may be due to changes in buyers' behavior that were not anticipated by the sellers.

In the performance of its informational function, advertising reduces market imperfections, thereby fulfilling a constructive function in the economy. Its catalytic role is equally constructive, for rigidities are lessened, contamination of the marketing system is reduced, and the optimum accommodation is more nearly realized more quickly. The manipulative function of advertising is the role that has caused most of the controversy over this area of business policy.

ADVERTISING VERSUS PRICE COMPETITION

Of the various ways by which a firm might promote its marketing objectives, advertising is a peculiarly attractive alternative to price competition. Its appeal as a means of sales stimulus pivots upon three advantages that it offers over price competition. First, advertising permits experimentation on the part of the seller by offering him a policy alternative from which he can retreat if he finds it unsuccessful. While he can retreat from a price change that he finds ineffective, fluctuating prices are *more likely* to damage the firm's market position than fluctuating advertising expenditures. Moreover, the opportunities for changes in advertising policy embrace changes in *how* the advertising dollar is spent as well as in how much is spent. Price changes do not have this dual character. This is not to say that poor use of advertising cannot harm a firm. Rather, it is to say that the firm is *less likely* to be damaged by a change in advertising policy than by a change in price policy. A firm may often retreat from advertising with fewer damaging effects than from a given price policy.

The second advantage of advertising over a price reduction as a means of increasing sales is that imitation is more difficult. A price reduction is likely to evoke identical or similar behavior on the part of the firm's competitors. An advertising program may do likewise, but a firm's competitors are not likely to imitate the advertising precisely. Thus differentiation is preserved. But price cuts of equal amounts on two competing brands are identical, and nonequal price cuts can be compared precisely.

Finally, the imperfection of consumer knowledge makes advertising a particularly attractive promotional medium, and this is especially so where the utility of a product lies in its covert qualities. Any consumer can compare two prices on two identical items. But the most astute consumer may find it difficult to compare the qualities of two products, particularly where these qualities are hidden. Advertising is designed to change demand; price manipulation can change only the quantity demanded.

ADVERTISING EXPENDITURES: STATIC SALES RESPONSE MODELS

How does a firm determine the size of its advertising budget? The most common practice among both manufacturing and marketing firms is to allocate a percentage of budgeted sales to advertising, based on the firm's historical experience with advertising, actions of competitors, and the role of advertising in the firm's overall marketing program. In this section, we shall consider some simplified models for determining the size of the advertising expenditure under static conditions. We can then show how additional variables can convert these into more dynamic, and hence more realistic, decision-making models.

The Dorfman-Steiner Model

Robert Dorfman and Peter O. Steiner have presented a set of decision models structured within the classical tradition.[5] They consider joint optimization of the advertising budget, price, and quality; optimization of various combinations of these three variables; and optimization of each, holding the others constant. Their basic conclusion is that price adjustments, advertising budgets, and quality changes should be undertaken up to that point where the elaticities of demand with respect to each variable have been brought into equality, as indicated by the following relationships:

$$e_p = e_a' = \frac{p}{c} e_k$$

in which e_p is the elasticity of demand with respect to price, e_a' is the elasticity of net revenue with respect to advertising expenditure (which is assumed to be > 0), e_k is the elasticity of demand with respect to a quality index, p is selling price per unit, and c is unit cost, including the cost of the quality change.[6] In the following discussion we shall concentrate on the optimization of advertising and price.

ELASTICITY OF DEMAND WITH RESPECT TO PRICE AND ADVERTISING

The elasticity of demand with respect to price (we shall hereafter refer to this as price elasticity) is defined as

$$e_p = \frac{-p \, \delta q}{q \, \delta p}$$

in which p is price and q is the quantity sold.

Dorfman and Steiner define the elasticity of demand with respect to advertising in a specialized way. They call it "marginal value product of advertising" and define it as

$$e_a' = \frac{p \, \delta q}{\delta a}$$

in which p is the price, δq is the change in the quantity sold as a result of advertising, δa is the change in the dollars spent for advertising, and e_a' is the elasticity of expenditure

---

[5] Robert Dorfman and Peter O. Steiner, "Optimal Advertising and Optimal Quality," *American Economic Review* 44 (December 1954): 826-836. An excellent exposition of and commentary on the Dorfman-Steiner models can be found in Frank M. Bass et al., *Mathematical Models and Methods in Marketing* (Homewood, Ill. Irwin, 1961), pp. 195-202, 214-219. Another very good summary is in Kristian S. Palda, *Economic Analysis for Marketing Decisions* (Englewood Cliffs, N.J.: Prentice-Hall, 1969), pp. 9-11.

[6] We are changing the symbols to be consistent with those we shall employ in this and other expositions.

from advertising defined as the marginal value product of advertising.[7] This elasticity is the rate of increase in gross receipts as advertising expenditure increases while price remains constant.

If we ignore all costs except that of advertising, price changes and changes in the advertising expenditures will be made so long as they increase profits. When their contribution to profits is zero, equilibrium will have been achieved. Thus

$$q\delta\rho - \delta a = 0$$

It follows from this that

$$q\delta p = \delta a$$

at the point of equilibrium.

Since

$$e_p = \frac{-p\,\delta q}{q\,\delta p}$$

then

$$q\,\delta p = \frac{-p\,\delta q}{e_p}$$

Similarly,

$$e_a' = \frac{p\,\delta q}{\delta a}$$

Therefore

$$\delta a = \frac{p\,\delta q}{e_a'}$$

Substituting these equivalents for $q\delta p$ and δa, with which we first started, we find that

$$\frac{-p\,\delta q}{e_p} = \frac{p\,\delta q}{e_a'}$$

Dropping the negative sign, $e_p = e_a'$ at the point of optimum utilization of advertising and price adjustments. This is valid if advertising is a positive sum. If advertising is zero, then the advertising elasticity may equal or be less than the price elasticity, since a negative advertising expenditure is generally not considered to be realistic.[8] If advertising elasticity is greater than price elasticity, it pays to increase advertising. As advertising is increased, it is assumed that its elasticity will tend to rise and then decline. Thus increased advertising expenditures by a firm whose elasticity with respect to advertising is greater than with respect to price will push its advertising appropriations to the point where the advertising elasticity falls to the level of its price elasticity.

Three possible situations are shown graphically by Dorfman and Steiner. These are illustrated in Figure 17.1, in which the advertising expenditure is shown on the horizontal axis and the elasticity coefficients on the vertical axis. It is assumed that the advertising

---

[7] We shall use the symbol e' for the elasticity of advertising defined in terms of marginal value product of advertising, and the symbol e for the elasticity of advertising as defined in the conventional sense.

[8] The possibility of a negative advertising expenditure is not without practical and theoretical interest, however.

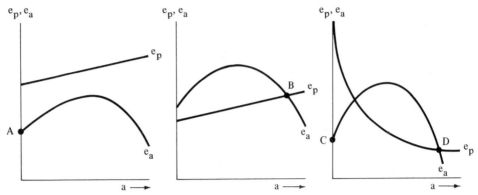

Figure 17.1. Advertising and price elasticities.

elasticity rises and then falls as advertising expenditures increase. The points of profit maximization shown on the graph are *A, B,* and *C* or *D.*

If a firm wishes to hold price constant and vary its advertising, its optimum position will be where

$$\delta a = p(1 - \frac{1}{e_a})$$

in which δa is the marginal cost of advertising.

If price p is constant, advertising changes δa, quantity sold changes δq, and nonadvertising costs change δc, then profit changes δR. These are related as follows

$$\delta R = p\delta q - \delta c - \delta a$$

In equilibrium, $\delta R = 0$. Therefore

$$p\delta q - \delta a = \delta c$$

Dividing by δq, we find that

$$p - \frac{-\delta a}{\delta q} = \frac{\delta c}{\delta q}$$

Since

$$e_a' = \frac{p \, \delta q}{\delta a}$$

then

$$\frac{\delta a}{\delta q} = \frac{p}{e_a'}$$

and

$$p - \frac{p}{e_a'} = \frac{\delta c}{\delta q}$$

in which $\delta c/\delta q$ is marginal cost of production exclusive of advertising cost. This can be written as

$$\frac{\delta c}{\delta q} = p(1 - \frac{1}{e_a})$$

The Dorfman-Steiner model is in essence a marginal cost/marginal revenue approach. Its usefulness lies in clarifying, within the neoclassical tradition, the conditions under which advertising expenditures should be modified, and in showing the interrelationships among advertising, price, and quality policies. It is, unfortunately, static in character, thereby failing to incorporate into its structure some of the more significant dynamic elements that determine the effectiveness of advertising as a marketing policy.

The Zeuthen-Barfod Model

Two major contributions to the analysis of advertising expenditures under static conditions are those of Frederik Zeuthen and Børge Barfod.[9] While their analyses are static, they provide a useful initial view of advertising and price policies and their joint impact on the sales and profit position of the firm.

We shall employ the following symbols in our restatement of their approach:

C_m	=	unit variable cost of manufacturing (assumed in our examples to be constant)
$C_m{'}$	=	marginal cost of manufacturing
D_o	=	original consumer demand (assumed in our example to be linear)
A'	=	marginal cost of advertising
$C_{(m+a)'}$	=	marginal cost of manufacturing and advertising combined $(C_m{'} + A')$
E	=	optimum profit point associated with constant amounts of increase in demand resulting from advertising, and constant variable manufacturing costs without reference to advertising costs
R'	=	marginal income from advertising (i.e., marginal revenue from the successively higher pq values that define line E)
p	=	unit price
q	=	quantity

The original demand is D_o in Figure 17.2. Variable costs of production per unit are C_m. The optimum price is p_o, the optimum quantity q_o, and the profit per unit $e_o c_o$. There is no advertising at this point.

Advertising is introduced beginning at output level q_o. With a marginal expenditure for advertising of $a_1{'}$, demand rises to D_1, and the point of optimum sales, *excluding advertising costs*, becomes q_1 with a price of p_1.[10] Increased marginal advertising expenditures, described by A', will cause the demand curve to shift to the right, and the point of maximum profits, independent of advertising costs, to be a function of rising unit price and quantity. These successive points of maximum profits are described by the expansion curve, E_1.

But the optimum advertising expenditure and the optimum price must be determined by taking into account *both* manufacturing costs and advertising costs. Marginal total

[9]Frederik Zeuthen, "Effect and Cost of Advertisement from a Theoretic Standpoint," *Nordisk Tidskrift for Teknisk Økonomi*, 1, no. 1 (1935): 62-72; Børge Barfod, op. cit., and "The Theory of Advertising," *Econometrica*, 8 (July 1940): 279-281. See also Børge Barfod, "Elements of a Demand Theory for Promotional Factors," in Max Kjær-Hansen, ed., *Readings in Danish Theory of Marketing*, (Copenhagen: Einar Harcks Forlag, 1966), pp. 195-221.

[10]The line E_1 is at the midpoint of each demand curve generated by the expenditure for advertising that lies above the production costs, C_m, per unit. This would yield the maximum revenue above total production costs for linear demand functions.

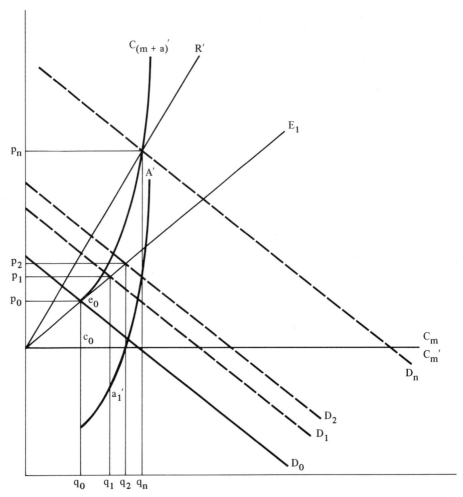

Figure 17.2. Determination of optimal advertising expenditures: increasing demand and constant elasticity of demand.

costs are described by line $C_{(m+a)}'$, which is simply a summation of constant marginal costs of manufacturing (C_m') and marginal costs of advertising (A'). R' describes the marginal return that would result from the increased demands generated by advertising. At price p_n and output level q_n, the firm reaches its optimum position, taking into account the marginal revenue generated by advertising and the marginal costs of production. At this point, these two are equal. Beyond this price and output level, the marginal cost of production, including advertising, exceeds the marginal revenue generated by the advertising expenditure.

Restrictive assumptions underlie the situation described in Figure 17.2. We assume constant variable costs of manufacturing and a linear demand function. We further assume that advertising expenditures result in a constant increase in demand so that the new demand curve parallels the old. It is also assumed that the marginal costs of advertising rise sharply as they increase the demand and that the firm's optimum position as a result of the advertising is achieved with both higher prices and greater sales volume.

Suppose we relax the assumption that the demand is increased parallel to itself. Often advertising is directed toward lower-income consumers who begin to show an increasing

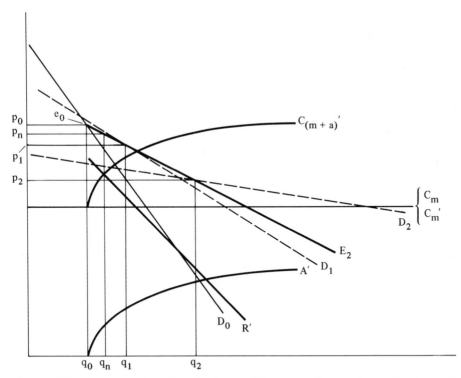

Figure 17.3. Determination of optimal advertising expenditures: increasing demand and increasing elasticity of demand.

willingness to buy the advertised product at a higher price than they would have without the influence of advertising, or to buy larger quantities at any specific price. This is illustrated in Figure 17.3. Demand increases at lower price levels, and the elasticity of demand also increases with increased advertising expenditures. Here we assume that the marginal cost of advertising to achieve these results, A', increases at a decreasing rate. Increasing demands at lower levels cause the optimum price to fall and the optimum quantity to increase so that the expansion line, E_2, moves downward to the right. The marginal revenue is described by R'. The combined marginal costs are $C_{(m+a)}'$, and the point of optimum profits when advertising costs are taken into account will be reached with an output of q_n and a price of p_n, since this is where marginal costs, including advertising, equal marginal revenue from the demands generated by advertising. While in the case of Figure 17.2 p_n was greater than p_o, in the case of Figure 17.3 p_n is lower than p_o.

Figure 17.4 shows a third possibility. In this case, advertising has the effect of increasing the demand at higher price levels so that the expansion curve rises upward to the left from point e. The marginal income resulting from increased advertising expenditures *and* increased prices will be R'. If we assume that the advertising cost must rise precipitately as higher and higher prices must be exacted, A' will slope up sharply to the left, and $C_{(m+a)}'$ will similarly reflect this fact. The equilibrium position for the firm will be at price p_n and volume q_n.

The relationship of R' in Figure 17.4 to E_3 warrants special comment. In Figures 17.2 and 17.3 R' was related to E_1 and E_2 in a manner much like that of a marginal revenue curve to an average revenue curve. R' is the marginal revenue resulting to the firm from the total revenue associated with each new equilibrium position arrived at on the basis of a new demand curve associated with an increased advertising expenditure. In Figure 17.2, increasing advertising expenditures resulted in increasing quantity and increasing unit price. Thus the E_1 curve was positively sloped, and the related marginal revenue curve was also positively sloped, rising much more rapidly than the curve that described the price-quantity equilibrium points. In Figure 17.3, increasing advertising expenditures resulted in increasing quantity and decreasing unit price. The E_2 curve was negatively sloped, and the related marginal revenue curve was also negatively sloped, falling much more rapidly than the curve that described the price-quantity equilibrium points. In Figure 17.4, however, increasing advertising expenditures resulted in decreasing quantities and increasing unit price. Thus the E_3 curve was negatively sloped, rising from point e_0 upward to the northwest. The resulting marginal revenue with each increase in advertising expenditure, R', was associated with a rising price *and* a declining quantity sold. As we move west from point e_0, marginal revenue declines, moving from positive values to zero and then to greater and greater negative values.[11]

In Figures 17.2, 17.3, and 17.4, we have described only three possible choices among an infinite number of theoretical possibilities and a large finite number of realistic possibilities. Ignoring for the moment the complex question of the effect of advertising expenditures, which depends on *how* the money is spent, and considering only the effect of *different amounts spent in a given way*, we can recognize that any alteration in our A'

---

[11] This can be illustrated by a simple linear function. Assume that in Figure 17.3 the E_2 curve is described by the following values for price, quantity, total revenue, and marginal revenue, with marginal revenue calculated as we move from e_0 to lower prices and greater quantities:

		p	q	R	R'
e_0	=	$8	1	$8	
					$6
		7	2	14	
					4
		6	3	18	
					2
		5	4	20	
					0
		4	5	20	
					-2
		3	6	18	

Assume that in Figure 17.4, the E_3 curve describes the following values, with marginal revenue calculated as we move from e_0 to higher prices and smaller quantities.

		p	q	R	R'
		$8	1	$8	
					-$6
		7	2	14	
					-4
		6	3	18	
					-2
		5	4	20	
					0
		4	5	20	
					2
e_0	=	3	6	18	

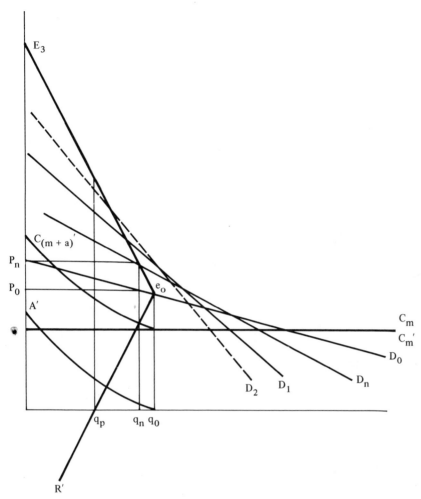

Figure 17.4. Determination of optimal advertising expenditures: increasing demand and increasing inelasticity of demand.

curves not only would alter the total marginal cost curve, $C_{(m+a)}'$, but would also alter the expansion curve, E. We must therefore resort to contour curves if we are to view the alternatives we describe with any perspective. Figure 17.5 shows one approach to this problem. There is a linear demand when there is no advertising. This is indicated by the straight-line curve labeled $A_0 = 0$. These are the quantities that can be sold at various prices without any advertising. The largest total revenue that can be obtained from such a demand is $225 at point O. However, a total revenue of $225 could have been achieved by other combinations of price and quantity, and these are shown by the curve $R_0 = 225, which is convex to the origin. Total costs of manufacturing are shown on the vertical lines. If the firm produces 100 units, its total cost of manufacture is $200. If 200 units are produced, costs of manufacture total $300. Since the production of 150 units, which produces the maximum revenue of $225 when there is no advertising, would entail manufacturing costs between $200 and $300, it would appear that this is an unprofitable level of operation for the firm.

If the firm spends $100 for advertising, it can, through different advertising appeals, increase the demand to the level described by $A_1 = 100$. The maximum total revenue received from this curve will be $600. This occurs at point P. The curve $R_1 = 600$ de-

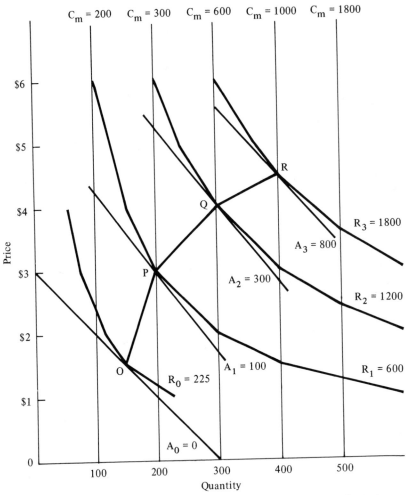

Figure 17.5. Determination of optimal advertising expenditures from iso-revenue curves and costs.

scribes the various combinations of p and q that will yield a total revenue of $600. At point P, manufacturing costs are $300 and advertising costs are $100: total profit will be $200. At point Q, advertising expenditures are $300, manufacturing costs are $600, revenue is $1,200, and total profit is $300. At point R, advertising costs are $800, manufacturing costs are $1,000, and total revenue is $1,800. Thus total profit is zero. Q is therefore the optimum of the possibilities described in Figure 17.5.

The line OPQR will rise to a peak and then is likely to turn down. Probably advertising expenditures will have varying impacts, depending on their level. Figure 17.6 shows six possibilities that have been considered in various studies of the impact of advertising. The evidence that exists, skimpy though it be, probably supports patterns A and B somewhat more than the others, and C and D somewhat more than E and F.

The Rasmussen Static Model

Beginning with a static model, Rasmussen utilizes the concept of elasticity of demand with respect to advertising to shed new light on the common practice of business firms of

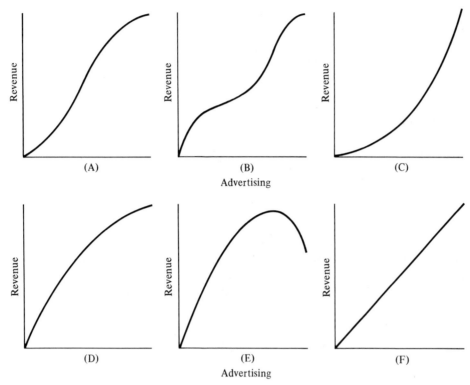

Figure 17.6. Some possible relationships between advertising expenditures and revenue.

setting advertising budgets as a percentage of sales. We shall reveiw his static model and then show how he introduces some dynamic factors into it.[1][2]

THE STATIC MODEL

Rasmussen's concept of elasticity of demand with respect to advertising differs from the "marginal value product of advertising" as defined by Dorfman-Steiner. The latter is the change in the firm's revenue relative to the change in the dollars spent for advertising. Rasmussen's definition of elasticity of demand with respect to advertising more closely parallels that of elasticity of demand with respect to price. He defines advertising elasticity of demand as the *relative* change in units sold associated with a *relative* change in advertising expenditure. Thus

$$e_a = \frac{dq/q}{dA/A} = \frac{dqA}{dAq}$$

where dq is a small change in quantity sold, q is quantity sold, dA is a small change in the advertising expenditure, A is the advertising expenditure, and e_a is elasticity of demand with respect to advertising in the conventional sense.

Selling price must, however, be taken into account if one is to determine the optimum

---

[1][2] Based on Arne Rasmussen, "The Determination of Advertising Expenditures," *Journal of Marketing* 16 (April 1952): 439-446; *Pristeori eller Parameterteori*, Handelshojskolen i København, Skriftrække F, nr. 16 (Copenhagen: Einar Harcks Forlag, 1955), especially pp. 194-202; "Theoretical Determination of Optimal Price and Optimal Advertising," in Kjær-Hansen, op. cit., pp. 139-148.

advertising budget, for the advertising expenditure must be related to the revenue it generates. The term r is introduced to symbolize gross revenue per unit, that is, price per unit minus variable cost per unit, excluding advertising. Advertising expenditures should be increased up to the point where the change in advertising expenditure equals the change in net revenue associated with the change in advertising. Thus advertising budgets will be expanded up to the point where $dqr = dA$

Dividing by rdA, we have

$$\frac{dq}{dA} = \frac{1}{r}$$

and multiplying by A/q, we have

$$\frac{dqA}{dAq} = \frac{A}{rq}$$

The left-hand side of the equation is the elasticity of demand with respect to advertising, and the right-hand side is advertising expenditure as a percentage of gross revenue from sales (i.e., sales minus variable costs other than advertising). The optimum is, therefore, where the advertising elasticity of demand equals the ratio of advertising to total gross revenue.

One other relationship is apparent from this equilibrium condition:

$$A = \frac{dqA}{dAq} rq$$

that is, the optimum advertising budget is that which equals the product of the advertising elasticity of demand and the total gross revenue, or

$$A = e_a rq$$

If, for example, the advertising elasticity of demand is estimated at 0.10, and expected gross revenue is $100,000, the advertising budget can be increased up to $10,000. The advertising budget would be 10 percent of sales, which is equal to the advertising elasticity.

Rasmussen has carried his analysis one step further to embrace the multiproduct firm and the problem that arises when the advertising of one product affects the sales of others. Suppose that product A is being advertised and that sales of product B are thereby affected.

The elasticity of demand for products A and B with respect to the advertising of product A will be as follows:

$$e_{a(A_a)} = \frac{dq_a/q_a}{dA_a/A_a} = \frac{dq_a A_a}{dA_a q_a} \quad \text{and} \quad e_{b(A_a)} = \frac{dq_b/q_b}{dA_a/A_a} = \frac{dq_b A_a}{dA_a q_b}$$

in which the subscript a refers to product A, and b to product B. The optimum condition will be

$$dA_a = dq_a r_a + dq_b r_b$$

If A and B are substitute products, $dq_b r_b$ will be negative. If they are complementary, the value of $dq_b r_b$ will be positive.

We shall divide the equation, which describes the conditions of optimality, by dA_a and $r_a r_b$, which yields

$$\frac{1}{r_a r_b} = \frac{dq_a}{dA_a r_b} + \frac{dq_b}{dA_a r_a}$$

Multiplying by $A_a/(q_a q_b)$, we get

$$\frac{A_a}{(q_a r_a)(q_b r_b)} = \frac{dq_a A_a}{dA_a q_a (q_b r_b)} + \frac{dq_b A_a}{dA_a q_b (q_a r_a)}$$

or

$$\frac{A_a}{(q_a r_a)(q_b r_b)} = \frac{e_{a(A_a)}}{q_b r_b} + \frac{e_{b(A_a)}}{q_a r_a}$$

This is the familiar "advertising as a percentage of sales" relationship. The left-hand side of this equation is advertising expenditures as a percentage of total gross revenue (of both products A and B), which, under optimum partial conditions, equals the sum of the ratio of advertising elasticity for product A relative to gross revenue of product B and the advertising elasticity for product B relative to gross revenue of product A. The absolute amount to be spent for the advertising of product A can be derived by multiplying the last equation by $(q_a r_a)(q_b r_b)$:

$$A_a = e_{a(A_a)}(q_a r_a) + e_{b(A_a)} q_b r_b$$

The optimum amount to spend for advertising of product A will equal the advertising elasticity of product A times the expected gross revenue from product A plus the elasticity of product B with respect to the advertising of A times the gross revenue expected from sales of product B. This can be further transposed to become

$$e_{a(A_a)}(q_a r_a) = A_a - [e_{b(A_a)}q_b r_b]$$

or

$$e_{a(A_a)} = \frac{A_a}{q_a r_a} - e_{b(A_a)}\frac{q_b r_b}{q_a r_a}$$

This last expression says, in effect, that the advertising elasticity of product A should equal the advertising expenditure for product A as a percentage of gross revenue of product A corrected by the elasticity of product B with respect to the advertising of product A times the ratio of the sales of B to the sales of A.

The sign of $e_{b(A_a)}$ is critical in determining the amount of the advertising budget and the necessity for $e_{a(A_a)}$ to be of a certain size. If products A and B are substitutes, the sign of $e_{b(A_a)}$ will be negative; that is, effective advertising of product A will probably take sales away from product B. If they are complementary, the sign of $e_{b(A_a)}$ will be positive. If $e_b(A_a)$ is negative, this has the effect of making the last term in the equation positive, thus necessitating a higher advertising elasticity for product A to justify a given advertising expenditure. If gross revenue from product B is not very high relative to that of product A (i.e., $q_b r_b$ is quite small in relation to $q_a r_a$), then the effect of $e_{b(A_a)}$ when the two products are substitutes is not so great.

But if products A and B are complementary, $e_{b(A_a)}$ will be positive, and thus its effect is subtracted, making it less necessary for $e_{a(A_a)}$ to be high in order to justify a given advertising expenditure.

THE PERCENTAGE-OF-SALES METHOD OF BUDGETING ADVERTISING

Rasmussen's partial short-run static analysis has established equilibrium for the firm's advertising at that point where advertising as a percentage of sales equals the elasticity of demand with respect to advertising:

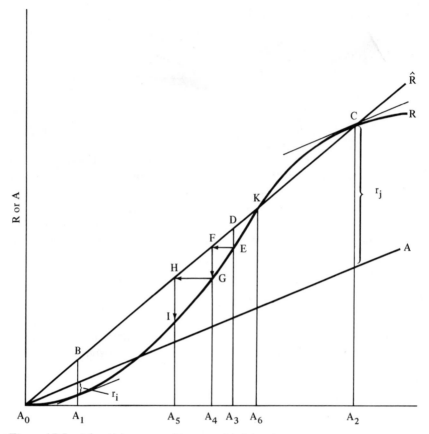

Figure 17.7. Advertising expenditures and total net revenue.

$$\frac{dqA}{dAq} = \frac{A}{rq}$$

This suggests, therefore, that when the firm uses a percentage-of-sales method in determining its advertising expenditure, it may be approaching the equilibrium condition described by the equation given earlier. For this to be true, however, the ratio of advertising expenditure to sales revenue must equal the advertising elasticity. Use of the percentage-of-sales method for establishing advertising budgets in no sense ensures that this will be the case.

In Figure 17.7 we show the relationship between advertising expenditures, A, and total net revenue, R, of a hypothetical firm. Total net revenue is the difference between total gross revenue and total variable costs, except advertising costs. The difference between total net revenue and advertising costs is the contribution to fixed costs and profit. The objective of the firm will be to maximize this contribution. Maximization is accomplished with an advertising budget of A_2, net sales revenue of C, and contribution of r_j. At this level of expenditure, the elasticity of advertising expenditure is equal to the elasticity of net revenue, as indicated by the equal slopes of A and R at this point.

But note that R has been described in Figure 17.7 as an S-shaped curve. Under these circumstances, there is another value for A at which the elasticity of advertising expenditure equals the net revenue elasticity. This occurs at an advertising expenditure level of A_1, with sales revenue of B and a negative contribution of r_i. In this case, however, net revenue is less than the advertising budget. Thus there are two points at which advertising and revenue elasticities are equal, but only one at which positive profits are maximized.

Suppose that the firm budgets its advertising as a percentage of expected sales and selects an amount between B and K in Figure 17.7. where $\hat{R}$ is expected net revenue. If the firm expects sales of D, it will budget advertising at A_3. Actual net revenue will be not D but E. Therefore the firm will adjust its advertising budget downward, spending A_4 in the subsequent period if it expects sales once again to equal E. But again actual revenue is less than expected revenue, and a further downward adjustment is made in advertising expenditures. By these successive moves the firm will eventually arrive at an advertising budget of A_O at which actual sales equal expected sales. But an advertising budget of A_O zero, yielding no net revenue. It is highly unlikely that a firm will reach the optimum if it is guided by a percentage-of-sales criterion. Expected and actual sales revenues will be brought into equality at K and C. Only point C is optimal, and only by chance will the expected-revenue line $\hat{R}$ intersect R at point C. If the firm reaches this point—and it will do so if it moves beyond point K and makes successive adjustments in its advertising expenditures to bring them into line with actual sales—it will have reached the optimum level of advertising but for the wrong reasons!

If the effect of increasing amounts of advertising expenditures is in fact the S-shaped sales response curve we indicate in Figure 17.7, the percentage-of-sales method of determining the advertising budget is at best a crude basis for allocating resources to the advertising function and one that is not likely to result in an optimal decision. If, on the other hand, the revenue curve is linear, rather than curvilinear as we have shown it, a percentage-of-sales method for advertising budgeting would yield correct results *if the correct percentage were determined*. There is, however, little evidence to support the linear revenue function. In our later consideration of dynamic models, we shall again encounter the proposition that advertising should remain a constant percentage of sales, but only under conditions of stability in other determining variables

The Johnsen Nomograph

Erik Johnsen has employed nomographs to show some of the relations among alternative and complementary marketing policies.[13] This is a graphic approach to the problem of dealing with advertising, as well as other marketing variables in the marketing mix, which offers some insights not so clearly apparent in the models we have described. Johnsen focuses on the effects of alternative policies on consumer preferences and, hence, on demand. This emphasis is justified, for the primary distinction between the analysis of costs in processing and in marketing is the fact that marketing costs can influence demand

---

[13] Johnsen's approach is particularly well developed in Erik Johnsen, "En Note om Handlingspara-metrenes Samspil," *Det Danske Marked* 18 (November 1959): 205-216, which has been reformulated in English under the title "On Combination and Interaction of Parameters of Action," Kjær-Hansen, op. cit., pp. 182-194. See also his earlier "Spilteori og Salgspolitik," *Det Danske Marked* 17 (June 1958): 73-84, which is translated into English as "Theory of Games and Marketing Policy," in ibid., pp. 60-72, and "Control of Indirect Costs," in Max Kjær-Hansen, ed. *Cost Problems in Modern Marketing*, Skrifter fra Instituttet for Salgsorganisation og Reklame, Handelshøjskolen i København, Skriftraekke F, nr. 35 (Copenhagen: Einar Harcks Forlag, 1965), pp. 66-84. Johnsen has extended his consideration of multipolicy alternatives in terms of certain operations research models in "Analytiske Operationsanalysemodeller i Virksomhedens Marketingfunktion," *Det Danske Marked* 21 (May 1962): 228-244, and "Operationel Værditheori," *Det Danske Marked* 23 (June 1964): 74-89.

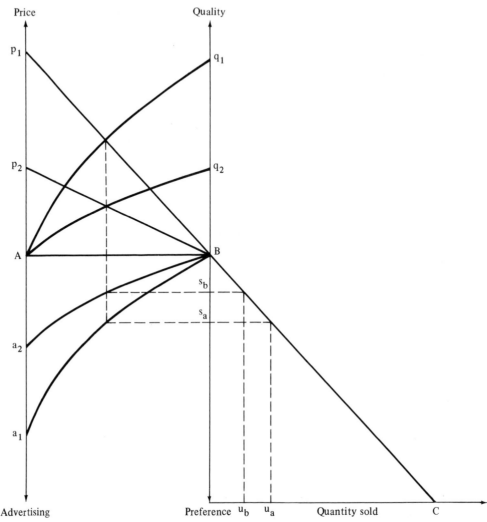

Figure 17.8. The Johnsen price-quality-advertising-preference nomograph. Source: Based on Erik Johnsen, "En Note om Handlingsparametrenes Sampsil," *Det Danske Marked* 18 (November 1959): 210-211.

and are often selected on the basis of that influence. The resulting demands must, of course, be judged in relation to the associated costs.

THE FUNCTIONAL RELATIONSHIPS

We have adapted Figure 17.8 from Johnsen's nomographs. Assume that a firm has three alternatives with respect to its marketing policies: price, quality of product, and advertising. Modifications of these variables, separately or in combination, will affect consumer preferences for the seller's offerings on the market. Consumer preferences are a function of product quality, volume of advertising, and price, and it is assumed that preferences bear a positive relationship to product quality and amount of advertising and a negative relationship to unit price. Preferences can then be transformed into quantities that will be purchased. Quantities purchased become a measure of the strength of preferences. The functional relationship between quantities purchased and preferences is analogous to the conventional (narrow) demand function, but is different in that quantities purchased are related not only to price, as is true of the conventional demand function, but also to quality and advertising.[14]

In Figure 17.8 we show unit price on the northwestern vertical axis, quality on the northeastern vertical axis, advertising on the southwestern vertical axis, and consumers' preferences on the southeastern vertical axis. Points A and B on the vertical axes are zero if the scale is arithmetic or 1 if the scale is logarithmic, and the scalar direction is indicated by the fact that $p_1 > p_2, q_1 > q_2, a_1 > a_2$, and $s_a > s_b$. AB is equal to 1.[15]

We show two choices with respect to each of three product attributes. If p_1 is chosen in combination with q_1 and a_1, consumer preferences will be s_a and the quantity sold will be u_a. If quality and price are q_2 and p_2, respectively, and a_1 is the advertising expenditure, preferences will again be s_a and sales of u_a will result. This case would reflect the fact that a lower quality, which would presumably affect preferences and sales, is offset by a lower price so that preferences and sales are the same. If, however, p_2 and q_2 are adopted and advertising is a_2, preferences will be s_b and sales u_b. Eight possible combinations are shown in Figure 17.8.

In Figure 17.9 we show a single state in which the combined effects of a given price, quality, and promotional policy result in consumer preference s, which in turn leads to unit sales of u. Variations in the policy parameters can be made by changing the angles x, y, or z. Johnsen shows[16] that these angles are related to the level of consumer preference in the following way:

$$s = \frac{(\tan x)(\tan z)}{\tan x + \tan y}$$

---

[14] We have short-circuited Johnsen's approach somewhat by considering only the relationship of price, quality, and advertising to preferences and, hence, to purchases, While Johnsen's refinements are not necessary for the exposition we wish to present at this point, they are important for a class of problems that need to be explored more fully in demand analysis. We can view consumer preferences as a function of the product's price, quality and promotion, or we can view preferences as a function of the consumer's perception of a product's price, quality, and promotion. In the latter case we distinguish between *actual* product attributes and those *perceived* by potential buyers. These two sets of data are not necessarily the same. Both the buyer and the seller may use resources to change the consumer's perception of product attributes without necessarily altering the attributes. The distinction between actual and perceived product, price, and promotion attributes is very useful in the analysis of the differential effects of informational and persuasive advertising.

Johnsen extends his statement of functional relationships still further to include also competitors' product attributes, as perceived by consumers, and the "normal level" of sales, a concept introduced by Max Kjær-Hansen and Arne Rasmussen to refer to the minimum price-quality-promotion combination that results in the sale of one unit.

See Johnsen, "On Combination and Interaction of Parameters of Action," op. cit., pp. 182-185, 188-193.

[15] This is based on the assumption that the probability of using one marketing policy only, the other marketing policy only, or some combination of the two is equal to 1.00. See R. Duncan Luce and Howard Raiffa, *Games and Decisions* (New York: Wiley, 1957), pp. 394-399, 424-432, where a similar graphic technique is employed to describe the evaluation of choices in a two-person zero sum game.

[16] This can be proved as follows:
In Figure 17.9 let
$$AB = 1$$
Then
$$p = \tan y$$
$$q = \tan x$$
$$a = \tan z$$

Thus we could conceive of a total system of alternative prices, qualities, and advertising expenditures that would result in varying levels of preference and, hence, in varying amounts purchased. (See Figure 17.10.)

OTHER CONSIDERATIONS

Johnsen's nomographs describe a fixed set of relationships that affect the outcome, but they do not indicate what an optimum solution would be. For this to be determined one would also need to know the firm's objectives and the relationship of sales volume to those objectives and to the other variables, such as costs, that bear upon the firm's achievements. As Johnsen has indicated, there are a number of additional considerations that would affect the preference level and sales outcome that the nomographs describe. One if the fact that the effect of a change in any one policy on buyer preferences will depend on the level from which one starts at the time the change is instituted. In other words, there may be increasing and decreasing returns from incrasing use of a single policy variable. Another consideration is whether the lines in the nomographs are straight or curvilinear, for this affects the point of intersection and must therefore properly reflect the impact of a given policy on the preference level. In Figures 17.8, 17.9, and

---

Since
$$\tan z = \frac{d}{e}$$

then
$$d = \tan z(e) \quad \text{and} \quad e = \frac{d}{\tan z}$$

But
$$\frac{e}{1} = \frac{q}{p}$$

so
$$e = \frac{g}{\tan y}$$

Substituting for e, we see that
$$d = \frac{\tan z(g)}{\tan y}$$

Also,
$$\tan x = \frac{g}{f} \quad \text{and} \quad g = \tan x(f)$$

Since
$$f = 1 - e$$

then
$$g = \tan x(1 - e)$$

Substituting for e, we see that
$$g = \tan x(1 - \frac{d}{\tan z})$$

Substituting for g, we see that
$$d = \frac{(\tan z)(\tan x)(1 - \frac{d}{\tan z})}{\tan y}$$

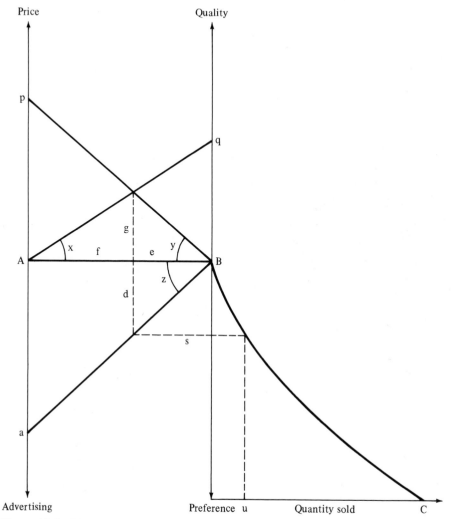

Figure 17.9. The relationship of marketing policies to consumer preferences.

This reduces to

$$d(\tan y) = (\tan z)(\tan x)(1 - \frac{d}{\tan q})$$

$$d(\tan y) = (\tan z)(\tan x)(\frac{\tan z - d}{\tan z})$$

$$d(\tan y) = (\tan x)(\tan z) - d(\tan x)$$

$$d(\tan y) + d(\tan x) = (\tan z)(\tan x)$$

$$d(\tan y + \tan x) = (\tan z)(\tan x)$$

Therefore

$$d = \frac{(\tan x)(\tan z)}{(\tan x) + (\tan y)}$$

and

$$d = s$$

See Johnsen, "En Note om Handlingsparametrenes Samspil," op. cit., p. 211.

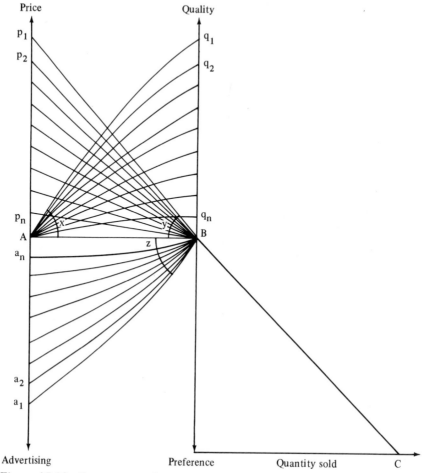

Figure 17.10. Consumer preferences as trigonometric functions of price, quality, and advertising.

17.10, we have shown both linear and curvilinear lines, but the reality of these must be established empirically.

A more serious problem exists with respect to policy interaction. In Figure 17.9, for example, we show one form of "interaction" in the sense that a specified price, quality level, and amount of advertising *together* determine what the level of buyer preferences will be. But there may be still another interaction effect in the sense, for example, that a large advertising expenditure has one effect on preferences when it is incurred in combination with a high price and a high quality, but a different effect when it occurs in combination with a low price and low quality. In Figure 17.8 we assume that low price, low quality, and low advertising result in the same preference level as high price, high quality, and low advertising, but this may not be so because of the possibility of interaction between price and quality, on the one hand, and advertising, on the other.

Johnsen poses a different kind of interaction problem that may be of importance in certain markets. If buyers use prices as proxies for quality, or if there is a snob appeal related to high prices, then the quality level, *as perceived by the buyer*, may go up when price is increased. In Figure 17.8, for example, if price is raised from p_2 to p_1, but quality *in fact* remains at q_2, it is possible that buyers may alter their perception of quality so that they now view the product as having q_1 quality and behave accordingly.

One final problem concerns the interpretation of the nomograph in terms of policy changes. If we describe relations that exist among several variables in a given state and compare them with the relations that would exist in another state, we are not necessarily describing what would happen if we moved from one state to another. This problem is shared by all static models. Johnsen proposes an imperfect solution by suggesting that the relationships described by the nomograph be viewed as a part of a system "in which one changes the change mechanism in the course of a sequential process."[17] This would mean not only that the interaction of parameters would be taken into account but also that the sequence of decisions through which policy evolves would become a part of the model. The nomograph does not lend itself to dynamic analysis, and the inclusion of decision changes, as well as changes in the decision process, would require a much more elaborate formulation.

ADVERTISING EXPENDITURES: DYNAMIC MODELS

In all of the models that we have discussed, the effect of advertising on sales is described in terms of the elasticity of demand with respect to advertising, and the value of this elasticity coefficient is assumed to be known and to be stable. The sales response models described earlier are essentially static. But perhaps more than most marketing policies, advertising is dynamic in nature. In order to fulfill its role of differentiation in markets where differences, once created, can be obliterated by imitation, advertising will itself change in reflection of changes in the market situation. In so doing it creates change, becoming itself a dynamic force that alters market structure and policy. It is appropriate therefore to consider those factors that influence the advertising eleasticity, and particularly those influences that cause the sales response to advertising to change over time. If these dynamic influences on the advertising elasticity of demand can be identified, they can then be incorporated into expenditure models that are more dynamic and, hence, more realistic representations of the environment within which advertising budgets are established over varying periods of time.

Determinants of Advertising Elasticity

We have established the identity of price elasticity and advertising elasticity under equilibrium conditions. From this, we might conclude that advertising elasticity is likely to be high where price elasticity is also high. High price elasticity of demand is likely to be associated with dispensability of the product to the consumer when the tariff is burdensome, and with a strong willingness on the part of consumers to buy when the tariff is lowered. This would typically be a more fertile situation into which advertising might be injected than would a situation where sensitivity to price is low. If inelasticity of demand with respect to price occurs in a market where potential consumers are few in number, well informed, and no longer easily persuaded, the potential impact of advertising on sales is likely to be low. If, however, price inelasticity occurs in a market where potential consumers are numerous, uninformed, and unpersuaded, advertising could be highly effective. Thus a discrepancy between price elasticity and advertising elasticity would induce action with respect to either price or advertising that would bring

---

[17] Johnsen, "On Combination and Interaction of Parameters of Action," op. cit., p. 193.

these elasticities into equality. There is, moreover, evidence that price elasticity of demand changes over time. This may be associated with the achievement of market maturity and/or with the impact of advertising itself on elasticity.[18]

In general, one would also expect advertising elasticity to be high where income elasticity is high. High income elasticity suggests a strong consumer desire for the product, with abstention from consumption when the income constraint is sufficient. Again, this is likely to be a more fertile environment for an advertising program than a situation where desire is less strong or where desires have been satisfied among low-income groups. If a consumer will buy something only if his income reaches a certain level, his favorable disposition toward the product may be sufficient to permit himself to be persuaded that he should lower his income constraint, that is, buy the product at an income level lower than he would otherwise have thought minimal. There is evidence, in fact, that advertisers have played a significant role in apprising low-income consumers of the characteristics and virtues of products consumed primarily by high-income con-sumers—products that are subsequently made appealing to low-income consumers through the advertising message.

A third factor that will affect the elasticity of demand with respect to advertising is the consumer's perception of the product and his ability and willingness to allow the advertiser's presentation to alter that perception. Neil Borden has observed that products with hidden characteristics and emotional—versus functional—appeals are those whose demand can be most easily altered through advertising.[19] It has also been recognized that the social climate within which advertising occurs has a significant bearing on the effects of that advertising on consumer behavior. Specifically, if there are fundamental needs that can be met by the advertised good, and if the sociopsychological climate generates favorable attitudes on the part of consumers toward the advertised good, a given dollar expenditure will have a much more favorable effect on demand than it would in a less favorable social environment.[20]

A fourth factor that enters into the sales response to advertising at any given moment is the cumulative effects of advertising. The impact of advertising can be compounded over time. If so, the effect of a dollar spent for advertising at any one moment is a function of the dollars spent in earlier periods. Kristian S. Palda has made the most comprehensive attempt to measure the cumulative effects of advertising in an analysis of the relationship between advertising and sales of Lydia Pinkham's Vegetable Compound over the period 1907-1960.[21]

A fifth variable that has a bearing on the advertising elasticity of demand, and particularly that associated with any given point in time, is in essence a set of two delayed effects from advertising. The first of these—"natural decay"—is closely related to the cumulative effect of advertising. This effect derives from the fact that while an advertising

---

[18] A declining price elasticity has been observed in the market for certain household appliances as those appliances achieved maturity. See Edna Douglas, "Secular and Cyclical Changes in the Demand for Components of a Product Cluster," *Review of Economics and Statistics* 49 (February 1967): 63-76.

[19] Neil H. Borden, *Economic Effects of Advertising* (Chicago: Irwin, 1942), pp. 425-426.

[20] Borden observed this in terms of the relationship between a growing primary demand and the effectiveness of advertising in stimulating selective demand for such products as cigarettes, dentrifrices, oranges, and refrigerators. Ibid., pp. 207-438.

[21] Kristian S. Palda, *The Measurement of Cumulative Advertising Effects* (Englewood Cliffs, N.J.: Prentice-Hall, 1964).

expenditure at one point in time can have an effect on sales at a subsequent point, this effect declines as the time span lengthens. We refer to this as "natural decay" to indicate that it is related to the decline of consumer recall as memory weakens. The second form of delayed effect we shall label "forced decay." This reaction arises from competitors' retaliation. Advertising, unlike price competition, makes it more difficult for competitors to react with identical policies. Nevertheless, given time, they will respond to successful advertising by competitors with policies designed to retain or recover sales.

A sixth factor bearing upon advertising elasticity at a given point in time is related to the stage at which the advertised product is in its life cycle. The life cycle for a primary demand will embrace life cycles for selective demands within the primary group. In marketing a new primary product, a seller will direct his advertising toward building a primary demand, but he may quickly move into the building of selective demand as product differentiation and branding progress and the number of substitutes increases. A dollar expenditure for advertising will not have the same impact on sales at all stages in the product's life cycle. Some possible patterns of reaction are illustrated in Figure 17.6. The rate of sales growth resulting from advertising expenditures will be highest where the slope of the response curve is greatest. It is not reasonable, therefore, to expect the advertising elasticity to remain stable through time. Only in the unusual case in which, for example, market maturity has been achieved, the number of producers is relatively small and stabilized, and advertising costs have been built into equilibrium costs of the industry would one expect the advertising elasticity of demand to approach a constant.

A seventh variable that will have a bearing on sales response to advertising is the share of market held by the advertiser. There are two contrasting influences to be reckoned with. On the one hand, the larger one's share of market, the greater the impact of advertising expenditure to the extent that the good will accumulated from past advertising exceeds that of competitive firms. Also, the larger the firm, the larger the resources that may be allocated to advertising. If the sales effect of a given advertising expenditure at one point in time bears a curvilinear relationship to the advertising budget, there will be some range within which larger funds will yield greater benefits than smaller funds.[22] These two facets will combine to give certain advertising advantages to a dominant firm in the industry.

On the other hand, a firm with a small market share may find it easier to nibble away the marginal customers of larger firms in the industry. This would be true if as a firm acquires more and more customers its marginal customers are more weakly tied to the advertiser. It might also result from the fact that the dominant firm adheres to the middle of the road in product and promotion policies, while the small firm may stake out its claim at the fringes of the product-promotion spectrum. In the automobile industry, for example, widespread advertising within the industry has contributed to the growth of total demand for automobiles, while the small-scale unique advertising of one brand—for example, Volkswagen—can conceivably capture a disproportionate share of the total demand that has been generated, in part, by the advertising of all firms.[23] This, however, injects the element of quality as well as quantity of advertising into our discussion, and at

---

[22] For example, Borden concluded that the effectiveness of advertising for cigarettes, dentifrices, and refrigerators was related to the presence of adequate unit margins and/or a large volume of sales out of which advertising budgets could be financed. Borden, op. cit., pp. 426-427.

[23] Note the similarity between this proposition concerning size of firm and advertising effectiveness and that which we developed in our discussion of quality variations and size of firm. See Chapter 16 pp. 451-452.

the moment we are considering basically quantitative relationships between advertising expenditure and sales.

We have now spelled out some of the principal determinants of the elasticity of demand with respect to advertising, or the sales response to advertising. Most of these determining conditions are dynamic in character, necessitating the incorporation of time into an advertising function if such a function is to reflect realistically the environment within which advertising budget decisions must be made. In the section that follows we shall consider some of the attempts that have been made to include one or more of these dynamic factors in the advertising expenditure function.

The Palda Model: Cumulative Advertising Effects

Palda has presented the most comprehensive analysis of the cumulative effects of advertising.[24] Using data on advertising and sales of Lydia Pinkham Vegetable Compound for the period 1907-1960, he experimented with a number of variables in an attempt to derive a sales function. His contribution lies in the incorporation of a variable to reflect the cumulative effects of advertising. After experimentation with L. M. Koyck's method of calculating geometrically weighted lags,[25] he adopted the simple Koyck model using one lagged and one unlagged exogenous variable. He found that the variable S_{t-1} (sales during the preceding period) was a satisfactory proxy for past advertising outlays. This can be regarded as a weighted moving average of all past advertising outlays or, perhaps with greater precision, as a measure of all the factors that have influenced consumer purchases.[26] Those models that yielded the best results included sales lagged one year as a proxy for the cumulative advertising effects, the log of the current year's advertising expenditure, one or more dummy variables to demarcate periods when a basic change in advertising policy has occured, a time variable, and in one equation, disposable income. He found that the distributed lag models resulted in a better fit for the Pinkham data and a better forecast than models without lags. He calculated the average of marginal rates of return on the invested advertising dollar. For the period 1908-1934, when advertising was high, the return was 15.6 percent; for 1926-1960, it was 33.0 percent; and for 1908-1960, it was 53.0 percent.

The essence of this approach to the analysis of advertising expenditures is to view advertising not as a current expense but as a capital expenditure.[27] In such an approach advertising is perceived as a component of the investment mix that must be evaluated in terms of its impact on future earnings as reflected in discounted costs and cash flows. If advertising is viewed within such a framework, current advertising budgets can be

---

[24] Palda, op. cit.

[25] L. M. Koyck, *Distributed Lags and Investment Analysis* (Amsterdam: North-Holland, 1954).

[26] Note the similarity of this interpretation of Palda's lagged sales variable to that of the stock variable employed by Houthakker and Taylor in the analysis of demand for consumer nondurables. In the latter case lagged purchases were interpreted as representing a "psychological stock"–i.e., a set of consumption habits that are reflected in previous sales. See H. S. Houthakker and Lester D. Taylor, *Consumer Demand in the United States: Analyses and Projections*, Harvard Economic Studies, vol. CXXVI, 2d enl. ed. (Cambridge, Mass.: Harvard University Press, 1970), pp. 9-13.

[27] This view of advertising and its implication are discussed by Joel Dean, "Does Advertising Belong in the Capital Budget?" *Journal of Marketing* 30 (October 1966): 15-21. See also Martin R. Gainsbrugh, "Advertising as Investment, Not Cost," in C. H. Sandage and Vernon Fryburger, eds. *The Role of Advertising* (Homewood, Ill.: Irwin, 1960). pp. 74-80.

evaluated in terms of their incremental effects on future cash flows. In this approach it is the long-run effects of advertising that are crucial.

In a study in which advertising expenditures are viewed as creating an intangible asset, Yoram Peles has attempted to measure the annual rate of depreciation of this asset in three industries in the United States from about the mid-1950s to the mid-1960s, using models in which distributed lags were employed for both the firm's advertising and that of its competitors.[28] For the largest six firms in the cigarette industry, he found the annual rate of amortization of advertising expenditures to be about 35-45 percent. For the four largest firms in the beer industry, it was about 40-50 percent. In the automobile industry, however, he found that the rate of amortization was 100 percent owing to the fact that while current advertising has a positive effect on future sales, this is offset by the fact that current sales, by increasing stocks, lead to decreases in future sales.

The long-run effects of advertising may be greater for some firms and some products than for others. It is probably wise to consider both short- and long-term effects and to attempt, as Palda did in his study of Lydia Pinkham Vegetable Compound, to incorporate both current and cumulative advertising variables into the demand function.

The Vidale-Wolfe Model and the Rasmussen Dynamic Model: Delayed Effects

It is generally recognized that the effect of advertising over time declines as the time period is extended. This rate of decline is similar to that which occurs in individuals' retention over time of that which they have learned or information to which they have been exposed. This wearing off of advertising effectiveness we have labeled natural decay. This phenomenon has been examined empirically by M. L. Vidale and H. B. Wolfe.[29]

The second delayed effect that we shall consider we have labeled forced decay. This is associated with the fact that a successful advertiser will find that competitors react to his success by using promotional or production policies designed to retain or recover clientele lost to the successful competitor. This phenomenon has been explored by Rasmussen.[30]

THE NATURAL SALES DECAY MODEL

The Vidale-Wolfe model of sales decay assumes a constant rate of decline over time in sales of a product that is *not* advertised. The data that they examined yielded the following model:

$$R_t = R_o e^{-\lambda t}$$

in which

R_t = sales at some point in time after the advertising has ceased

R_o = sales at the point of time at which advertising is ceased (an original point of time)

λ = the sales decay constant

t = time

---

[28] Yoram Peles, "Rates of Amortization of Advertising Expenditures," *Journal of Political Economy* 79 (September-October 1971): 1032-1058.

[29] M. L. Vidale and H. B. Wolfe, "An Operations Research Study of Sales Response to Advertising," *Operations Research* 5 (June 1957): 370-381.

[30] Arne Rasmussen, "Theoretical Determination of Optimal Price and Optimal Advertising," op. cit., pp. 139-148. See especially pp. 145-148.

In this perspective, the effect of advertising undertaken after t_o is to offset the sales decay.

It is not unreasonable to extend the Vidale-Wolfe model to embrace still another aspect of advertising's effect. If we know the short-term sales response to advertising, we may assume that this response declines as time passes. Thus as the effect of advertising wears off, the sales response will be less. In this case, we would assume that λ would represent the sales decay effect that occurs *after* a given advertising expenditure. This is looking at the other side of the sales decay coin, but this complementary interpretation of the decay process would appear reasonable.[31]

THE FORCED SALES DECAY MODEL

A second view of sales decay pivots around the assumption that competitors will react to successful advertising in such a way that the effects of advertising are reduced in time. The question in this case then concerns (1) the sales response up to the time that competitors react and (2) the sales response of the original advertiser after competitors have reacted.

Rasmussen has treated this phenomenon by introducing a multiperiod analysis of future sales and future costs and by discounting revenue and costs.[32] He assumes that there is a basic change in advertising policy and that a new advertising program is evaluated as a long-term policy. Use of a long-term approach is more likely to occur in a large firm than in a small firm, of course. The immediate effect of an increase in advertising, or a change in advertising policy, is an increase in sales resulting from the effect of the advertising on primary demand (total demand for the product regardless of brands) and also on selective demand (demand for the particular advertised brand that comes from customers who switch from competing brands). After competitors react by imitating the new advertising policy, additional sales for the original advertiser can come from the response of primary demand to the advertising.

According to Rasmussen's analysis, an advertiser will increase his advertising expenditures so long as the following condition obtains:

$$\frac{A - (1 + i)^{-n}}{qr - (1 + i)^{-x}} - \frac{dq_2\, A - (1 + i)^{-(n-x)}}{dAq - (1 + i)^{-x}} < e_a$$

The notation is similar to that which we have employed.

A = advertising expenditure

q = quantity sold (with subscript 2 for the period $n - x$)

r = net revenue per unit (selling price - marginal cost)

i = rate of interest per time unit

n = planning period of the firm

x = time at which competitors respond

e_a = advertising elasticity

---

[31] This is the interpretation placed upon the model by Wentz and Eyrich. Walter B. Wentz and Gerald I. Eyrich, *Marketing: Theory and Applications* (New York: Harcourt Brace Jovanovich, 1970), pp. 422-423.

[32] Rassmussen, "Theoretical Determination of Optimal Price and Optimal Advertising," op. cit.

If advertising is to be profitable, the advertising elasticity, e_a, must be greater than: (1) advertising expenditures as a percentage of sales, A/qr, adjusted for the rapidity with which competitors respond to the advertising by imitation or other reactions, with a greater impact on the "required" value of e_a when competitors react quickly (i.e., when x, the time it takes competitors to react, is low relative to n, the planning horizon for the firm), and (2) the advertising elasticity in the second period, after competitors react, relative to that in the first period, adjusted for the relative lengths of the two periods. This second term shows the comparative impact of advertising on "old" customers (after competitors have taken away the advertiser's initial advantage) relative to its impact on "new" customers (those attracted by the initiating advertiser), corrected for the relative time spans of the two periods. The greater the long-run sales effect from advertising relative to its short-run effect, the less an advertiser need fear competitors' reactions.

It seems reasonable to believe that much of any positive effect of advertising on the sales of a single producer of a differentiated product after his competitors have reacted to his advertising will come through the effect of the total industry's advertising on the primary demand, in contrast to the selective demand for a single seller's advertised product. The Rasmussen model assumes that competitors can successfully react to a promotional innovation. If, however, the advertising innovator cannot be imitated, or retains a differential advantage in his competitive relationship to other advertisers because he was the originator of the competitive sequence, he may continue to reap increased benefits from his differentiated position.

The Rasmussen model focuses on the span of time within which advertising budget decisions are made and the relationship of that time span to the length of time it takes for competitors to react. It discounts future revenue and costs, converting these into present values, and takes into account the contribution of a competitive lead to profits and the detraction of rapid competitive imitation from profits of the original advertising firm. Rasmussen has pointed out the similarity between his model and the theory of the kinked oligopoly demand curve. Because his model is couched in dynamic terms, embracing two time periods and the effects of competitive response, it injects dynamic considerations into the static model of the kinked demand curve.[33]

The Benjamin-Jolly-Maitland Model:
Dispersion and Saturation

Benjamin, Jolly, and Maitland proposed an advertising model built on an epidemiological analogy. The spreading of ideas or information from advertising was viewed as analogous to the spreading of an infection among a population and the eventual decline in the incidence of disease.[34] The three important ideas that they included were the curvilinear dispersion of advertising effects, market saturation, and declining effects. William King

---

[33] Still another treatment of delayed effects, viewed as carry-over effects and habitual brand choice behavior by consumers, may be found in Alfred E. Kuehn, "A Model for Budgeting Advertising," in Bass. op. cit., pp. 302-353, and Alfred E. Kuehn, "How Advertising Performance Depends on Other Marketing Factors," *Journal of Advertising Research* 2 (March 1962): 2-10.

[34] B. Benjamin, W. P. Jolly, and I. Maitland, "Operational Research and Advertising: Theories of Response," *Operational Research Quarterly* 11 (December 1960): 205-218.

incorporated these into a dynamic budgeting model in which sales response, market saturation, and sales decay are variables.[35]

The sales response ratio (the ratio of change in sales to a $1 change in advertising expenditure) is not likely to remain constant throughout the life cycle of a product. When a product is introduced the sales response ratio may be very low. Once it has been purchased by some users and knowledge about it has spread, the sales response ratio is likely to increase. As sales become dispersed over a wide spectrum of the population, possibilities for further sales expansion become more limited. Market saturation may therefore impose an upper constraint upon sales growth.

The sales response constant, s, is the effect of a first dollar expenditure for advertising on sales. The coefficient of advertising efficiency at any revenue level, R, is s_R. The relationship of $^S R$ to s is determined by the difference between the saturation level, M, and the current revenue level, R, as a ratio of M. Thus s_R is the effect of advertising on sales to potential customers:

$$s_R = s \left(\frac{M-R}{M} \right)$$

indicating that the impact of a given dollar expenditure for advertising decreases as sales come closer to the maximum. ΔR is the change in revenue that will result from a change in advertising expenditure, ΔA. Therefore

$$\Delta R = s_R \ \Delta A \qquad \text{and} \qquad \Delta R = s \left(\frac{M-R}{M} \right) \Delta A$$

If we introduce a sales decay factor to show that the effectiveness of advertising declines as time passes, the model would then become

$$\frac{dR_t}{dt} = s \left(\frac{M-R}{M} \right) A_t - \lambda R_t$$

in which R_t is the sales revenue at a given point in time, λ is the sales decay factor, A_t is the advertising expenditure at time t, and dR_t/dt is the rate of change of R_t.

If the firm desires to maintain sales at a constant level, then

$$\frac{dR_t}{dt} = 0$$

and

$$A = \left(\frac{\lambda}{s} \right) \left(\frac{RM}{M-R} \right)$$

The closer sales are to the saturation level, the more difficult it is to affect them by advertising. The farther removed the sales period is from the period in which the advertising expenditure was made, the less effect the advertising will have on sales revenue.

This model fails, of course, to take into account the importance of repeat sales to existing customers. Where replacement or repeat sales represent a relatively large percentage of total sales, this model does not provide sufficient information for advertising budgeting. However, its usefulness derives from the fact that it focuses on market potential as a factor in advertising effectiveness, a matter of considerable

---

[35] William King, *Quantitative Analysis for Marketing Management* (New York: McGraw-Hill, 1967), pp. 370-373. See also Wentz and Eyrich, op. cit., pp. 423-430.

Table 17.2 Hypothetical Examples of Exposure to Advertising and Buying Behavior

Exposure to Advertising	Number of Households		
	Buy	Do Not Buy	Total
Market A			
Exposed	350	150	500
Not exposed	100	400	500
Total	450	550	1,000
Market B			
Exposed	200	50	250
Not exposed	250	500	750
Total	450	550	1,000
Market C			
Exposed	250	250	500
Not exposed	200	300	500
Total	450	550	1,000

importance for products that are moving toward market maturity.

A simplified, arithmetical approach can be used to determine M (market potential). Assume that a manufacturer is comparing his sales experience in three different markets, in each of which he has been advertising by varying amounts. He finds the relationships between exposure to his advertising and sales of his product in the three markets to be as indicated in Table 17.2. We shall assume that each customer contributes as much net revenue to the seller as any other customer and shall ignore the question of the amount of revenue obtained and the amount of advertising cost. The question on which we shall focus is: In which market would increased advertising expenditure, resulting in increased exposure, be most profitable?

This is essentially a problem in estimating market potential. If we assume that those people who were not exposed to the seller's advertising in each of these markets would have behaved, had they been exposed, as did those who were exposed, then we have a basis for reaching a conclusion to the question we have posed. In market A, for example, 70 percent of those exposed to the advertising bought the product (350/500). Only 20 percent of those not exposed bought the product (100/500). If all were exposed to the advertising, we can hope for a 70 percent sales ratio at the best, but no more. If we multiply this differential—70 percent minus 20 percent, or 50 percent—by the percentage of the total population who were not exposed—50 percent—we have a potential of 25 percent of the total population of households in this market that we might hope to place in the "buy" column by exposing them to the firm's advertising.

In market B, however, 80 percent of those exposed to the advertising bought the product, while 33 percent of those who were not exposed bought it. The difference—47 percent—multiplied by the percentage in the "not exposed" group—75 percent—equals a 35 percent potential. In market C, 50 percent of those exposed bought the good, while 40 percent of those not exposed bought it. The differential of 10 percentage points, multiplied by the 50 percent in the "not exposed" group—the "potentials"—yields only a 5 percent untapped potential. What we are saying is that (1) if advertising converts nonexposed consumers to the buying patterns of exposed consumers, (2) if we know the buying patterns of exposed consumers, and (3) if we know the number of consumers who were not exposed, then we can estimate what we can expect by advertising to these nonexposed individuals in the population.[36] To complete our analysis we would need to know what the advertising would cost and what the revenue effect would be.

The Nerlove-Arrow Model: A Multivariate Approach

No model of advertising expenditures has been evolved that embraces all of the variables that have been considered by students of advertising analysis. That which comes closest to including a large number of determining variables is the dynamic model of Marc Nerlove and Kenneth Arrow.[37] We shall summarize their advertising budget function in order to show the variables that were incorporated and their functional relationship to the long- and short-run advertising budget. The following symbols are used:

A = good will at any one moment (a cumulative function of past advertising)

r_A = natural and forced sales decay in good will over time

a = current advertising expenditure

q = unit sales

p = unit price

z = other variables not controlled by the firm (income, consumer tastes independent of advertising, population, prices of other goods, etc.)

i = rate of interest

e_A = elasticity of demand with respect to good will

e_p = elasticity of demand with respect to price

c' = marginal cost of production

r_z = proportional rate of change in z

e_y = elasticity of demand with respect to income (or other z variable)

It is assumed that the change in good will per unit of time is equal to the advertising expenditure during that period less the decay associated with good will.

$$\frac{dA}{dt} = a - r_A A$$

The demand function is

$$q = k p^{-e} p A^{e_A} z^{e_y}$$

If we assume that the marginal cost, c', is a constant, the optimal amount of good will (i.e., cumulative advertising effect) will be

$$A = \left[\frac{k e_A c'^{(1-e_p)}}{(e_p-1)(i+r_A)} \right]^{1/(1-e_A)} \left[\frac{e_p}{e_p-1} \right]^{-e_p/(1-e_a)} z^{e_y/(1-e_A)}$$

---

[36] Some of the aspects of this type of approach are considered by Fred T. Schreier, *Modern Marketing Research: A Behavioral Science Approach* (Belmont, Calif.: Wadsworth, 1963), pp. 324-341. Special problems associated with joint relations and interaction effects are further considered in pp. 341-353.

[37] Marc Nerlove and Kenneth J. Arrow, "Optimal Advertising Policy Under Dynamic Conditions," *Economica*, 22 (May 1962): 129-142. A good summary of the assumptions of, and conclusions from, this approach may be found in Palda, op. cit., pp. 178-180.

In essence the optimal level of good will is a function of the discounted value of the revenue produced by the advertising elasticity, the price elasticity, and the elasticity of other variables.

The optimum advertising expenditure at any point in time is

$$a_t = \left[r_A + \frac{e_y}{1-e_A} \right] r_z A^*$$

in which A^* is the optimum level of good will. Expressed as a percentage of sales, the optimal amount of current advertising, a, is

$$\frac{a}{pq} = \frac{e_A}{e_p(i+r_A)} \left[r_A + \frac{e_y r_z}{1-e_A} \right]$$

This assumes a constant ratio of advertising to sales. For this to be a desirable policy, however, the advertising elasticity, price elasticity, rate of sales decay, income elasticity, and rate of interest must remain constant. Only constant rates of change are assumed for each variable. Alteration of any one of these rates would alter the desired advertising-sales ratio. In this sense, therefore, the Nerlove-Arrow model is less dynamic than that of Rasmussen. The latter crudely but clearly demarcates two periods in which there may be differential impacts from the advertising variable.

A Concluding Note on Advertising Budgeting by the Firm

What we have attempted to do in this discussion is to set forth in a systematic fashion some of the principal approaches that have been developed for determining the optimum expenditure for advertising. These various approaches have differed with respect to the variables to be included and to the hypothesized relationship of the variables to one another and, particularly, to the sales response. It is appropriate at this point to make some observations on the viability of the models that we have reviewed and on their relevance to the practical problem of budgeting expenditures for advertising.

Advertising is a part of the marketing mix, and its impact on sales depends in part on its interaction with the other policy variables that are within the control of the firm. When used as a promotional device, it beomes a part of the total environment within which buyers' purchase decisions are made. As such it interacts with variables that lie outside the control of the individual firm, such as purchasing power and consumer taste resulting from nonadvertising influences. Advertising expenditures must therefore be examined within the context of a multivariate demand function, probably one of considerable complexity.

We have said little about the differential effects of advertising on the industry and the firm. Some advertising may be industry-oriented, that is, directed toward the expansion of primary demand rather than the demand for specific differentiated products. Sales of differentiated products or brands may be affected by industry advertising, and advertising to stimulate selective demand may affect industry sales. These different aspects of advertising may be particularly crucial at particular stages in the product life cycle.

One of the most aggravating problems in advertising expenditure analysis is the impossibility of establishing with precision the relationship of sales to advertising expenditures. Part of the problem is empirical, deriving from the complexity of the interaction effects among a wide range of environmental and policy variables that bear upon consumer response.[38] But equally important is the fact that there is no precise quantitative relationship between a dollar expenditure for advertising and sales because the effect on sales depends to no small extent on what the dollar is spent for. Often a premium in sales response results from uniqueness of the advertising message or the method by which it is conveyed. Not only does the expenditure-sales relationship vary through time and in response to environmental and competitive forces, but it can vary purely as a consequence of the character of the advertising itself. While this is handled in economic models by indicating that the advertising expenditure will be used "in the most effective way possible," this does not resolve the problem of the firm or the advertising agency that must decide what that "most effective way" actually is.

Göran Albinsson, Sten Tengelin, and Karl-Erik Wärneryd have observed that empirical studies of advertising budgeting indicate that firms make little use of marginal analysis in arriving at their expenditure decisions. Rather, they use a variety of methods arising out of the special circumstances surrounding the firm's competitive situation, and marginal analysis may not be found to be the most expedient basis for arriving at a budgeted amount.[39]

It seems fairly clear, however, that for all of their pitfalls, models of advertising expenditure can be useful adjuncts to the budgeting process. They force the analyst to specify the relevant variables and to hypothesize about the relationship of the independent variables to sales and profits. By providing a framework for examining empirical data, they reveal the pitfalls of both the data and the model. One of the things made most clearly apparent by the analyses that have thus far been made is the need for better models—models that will make it possible to isolate the impact of advertising on sales and profits under various conditions with respect to the other variables that bear upon the firm's operating results. Such models will have to include more variables and take account of the dynamic and interaction effects among decision-making and environmental variables.

But the problem is more than one of adequate models. The accuracy and refinement of data are essential to successful measurement of advertising effectiveness. Data that most firms have available are neither sufficiently free of contamination nor sufficiently detailed to make possible valid statements about the relationship of advertising to the firm's sales or profit experience. The usefulness of better models can be greatly enhanced if the quantity and quality of relevant data are improved.

APPENDIX A

BARFOD'S CLASSIFICATION OF PRODUCTION AND EXPANSION COSTS

The classification scheme developed by Børge Barfod for the various components of production and promotional costs is reproduced in Figure 17A.1.

---

[38] See, for example, Richard E. Quandt, "Estimating the Effectiveness of Advertising: Some Pitfalls in Econometric Methods," *Journal of Marketing Research* 1 (May 1964): 51-60.

[39] Göran Albinsson, Sten Tengelin, and Karl-Erik Wärneryd, *Reklamens ekonomiska roll*, Industriens Utredningsinstitut (Stockholm: Almqvist and Wiksell, 1964), pp. 72-91.

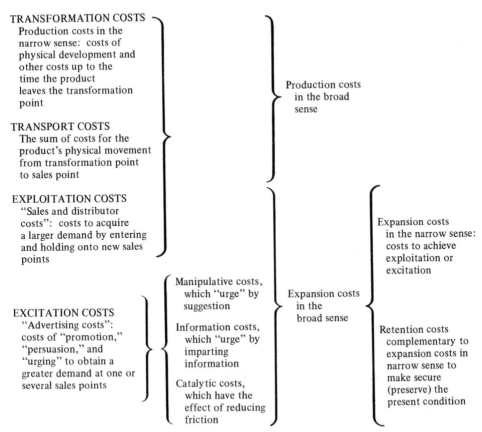

Figure 17A.1. Barfod's classification of production and expansion costs. Source: Børge Barfod, *Reklamen i Teoretisk-Økonomisk Belysning*, Skrifter from Institutter og Studiekredse, Udgivet af Den Handelsvidenskabelige Laereanstalt, II (Copenhagen: O.C. Olsen, 1937), p. 45.

18

Economic Effects
of Advertising

I've seen so many painted wooden spoons
when we lacked buckwheat for the soup . . .
and I reflected on the true and false,
the passage of the true into the false.

—Yevgeny Yevtushenko

In our discussion thus far we have viewed advertising from the vantage point of the firm, focusing on the decisions that management makes in determining the expenditures for this component of the market mix. We shall turn now to a consideration of some of the broader aspects of the market for advertising in the economy as a whole.

By 1972 firms in the United States were spending more than $23 billion per year for advertising, or $109 per capita, compared to $66 per capita in 1960. About three-fourths of the increase in per capita expenditure could be accounted for by the rise in the Consumer Price Index. The $66 expenditure per person in the United States in 1960 was about two and one-half times that in Switzerland, Sweden, and the United Kingdom, and more than three times that in Denmark, Norway, West Germany, and Finland in that year. It was, in fact, five times the expenditure in all of Western Europe in 1960 (see Table 18.1) and was about two-thirds of the total for the noncommunist world (see Table 18.2). Advertising expenditures in the United States have for many years ranged between 2.0 and 2.4 percent of gross national product, and were 2.0 percent in 1972. They have ranged between about 2.5 and 3.0 percent of the national income.[1]

The purpose of this large expenditure by advertisers is to increase profits (or prevent a decrease in profits) by increasing demand (or preventing a decrease in demand) through information and/or persuasion. Is the allocation of this portion of the gross national product to this function desirable from a social point of view? We shall examine this question from four viewpoints: (1) the demand for and supply of advertising, (2) advertising and the level of national output, (3) advertising and the prices of goods and services, and (4) advertising and the allocation of resources.

THE DEMAND FOR AND SUPPLY OF ADVERTISING

It is reasonable to believe that consumers would be willing to pay explicitly for a certain amount of advertising. Let us assume that the relationship between the demand for and supply of advertising of various amounts is illustrated by Figure 18.1.[2] D_c represents the demand for advertising by consumers; D_s is the demand by sellers. Consumers will be

---

[1] Data on advertising expenditures in the United States are from U.S., Bureau of the Census, *Statistical Abstract of the United States*, 1973, 94th ed. (Washington, D.C.: GPO, 1972), p. 757. Annual estimates reported there are from McCann-Erickson, Inc., 1935-66, compiled for Decker Communications, Inc., New York, N.Y., in *Printers' Ink* (copyright); 1967-69, in *Marketing/Communications* (copyright). Beginning in 1970, estimates were compiled for Crain

Table 18.1 Advertising Expenditures in Western Europe, 1960[a]

Area According to		Advertising Expenditure (Millions of U.S. Dollars)	Total Population (Millions)	Total Advertising Per Person (U.S. Dollars)
Language(s)	Country			
Total German, Dutch and Flemish		1,455	83.6	17
German	West Germany	1,100	55.6	20
	Austria	75	7.1	11
	Switzerland (70%)	105	3.8	28
	Luxembourg (75%)	(b)	0.2	n.a.
Dutch	Netherlands	125	11.5	11
Flemish	Belgium (60%)	50	5.4	9
Total English		1,295	55.3	23
English	United Kingdom	1,275	52.5	24
	Ireland	20	2.8	7
Total French		555	50.4	11
French	France	490	45.5	11
	Belgium (40%)	35	3.8	9
	Switzerland (20%)	30	1.0	28
	Luxembourg (25%)	(b)	0.1	n.a.
Total Nordic		410	20.4	20
Scandinavian				
Swedish	Sweden	190	7.5	25
Danish	Denmark	85	4.6	18
Norwegian	Norway	65	3.6	18
Icelandic	Iceland	(b)	0.2	n.a.
Swedish	Finland (10%))	70	4.5	16
Finnish	Finland (90%)			
Total Italian		165	50.0	3
Italian	Italy	150	49.4	3
	Switzerland (10%)	15	0.6	28
Total Spanish and Portuguese		120	39.2	3
Spanish	Spain	80	30.1	3
Portuguese	Portugal	40	9.9	4
Total Greek		10	8.9	1
Greek	Greece	10	8.3	1
	Cyprus	(b)	0.6	n.a.
Grand Total		4,010	307.8	13

[a]*Western Europe* is used as a political rather than a geographic term.

[b]Negligible.

Source: Ilmar Roostal, "Common and Uncommon Advertising in Western Europe," in *Studying the Enlarged European Market with Emphasis on the Future*, Selected Papers from the Second International Seminar on Marketing Management, Stresa, Italy, July 1-14, 1962, Indiana Readings in Business no. 38 (Bloomington: Indiana University, Graduate School of Business, 1963), pp. 235-236.

Communications, Inc., in *Advertising Age* (copyright). Gross national product and national income data are from *Economic Report of the President,* (Washington, D.C.: GPO, 1973), p. 193.

[2] This figure and analysis are from Peter O. Steiner, "Discussion" [of "Supply and Demand for Advertising Messages" by Lester G. Telser], *American Economic Review* 56 (May 1966): 472-475.

Table 18.2   Advertising Expenditures by Continent, 1960[a]

Continent	Total Advertising Expenditure (Billions of U.S. Dollars)	Likely Margin of Error (Billions of U.S. Dollars)	Percentage of Total World Advertising	Percentage of Total World Population
North America	12.5	+1.0 to −1.0	66.0	7.0
Western Europe	4.0	+1.0 to −0.5	21.0	10.0
Latin America	0.7	+0.6 to −0.3	4.0	7.0
Free Asia (mainly Japan)	0.6	+0.1 to −0.1	3.0	32.0
Eastern Bloc	0.5(?)	(?)	3.0	35.0
Australasia	0.4	+0.1 to −0.1	2.0	1.0
Africa	0.3	+0.3 to −0.1	1.0	8.0
Total World	19.0	n.a.	100.0	100.0

[a]Estimates for Western Europe and Eastern Bloc by Ilmar Roostal, IMARCO AG, Zurich; all other estimates by J. Fayerweather on the basis of International Advertising Association data and local data. Population estimates based on United Nations data for 1959.

Source: Ilmar Roostal, "Common and Uncommon Advertising in Western Europe," in *Studying the Enlarged European Market with Emphasis on the Future,* Selected Papers from the Second International Seminar on Marketing Management, Stresa, Italy, July 1-14, 1962, Indiana Readings in Business no. 38 (Bloomington: Indiana University, Graduate School of Business, 1963), p. 231.

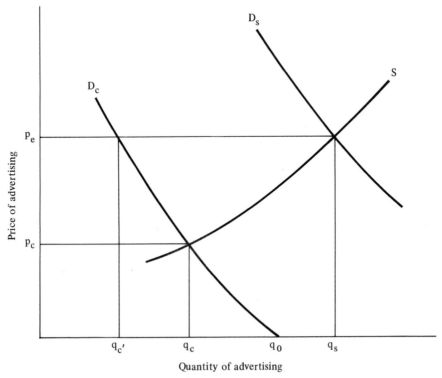

Figure 18.1. The demand for advertising by sellers and by consumers and the supply of advertising. Source: Based on Peter O. Steiner, "Discussion" [of "Supply and Demand for Advertising Messages" by Lester G. Telser], *American Economic Review,* 56 (May 1966): 473.

willing to buy increasing amounts of advertising only if the price per unit declines. Even at zero price, however, they would want no more than q_o advertising. If sellers wanted exactly the same amounts as consumers would at various prices, there would be no reason for sellers to interfere with the quantitative decision that would be arrived at without their intervention. But sellers would presumably demand more advertising than would consumers, as indicated by D_s. S is the amount of advertising that will be supplied at various prices. The equilibrium price will be p_e and the equilibrium quantity q_s, since sellers, rather than consumers, actually buy the advertising. At this price, sellers can sell $q_{c'}$ to consumers at the equilibrium price, but they will have to pick up the tab for the balance (or, if they can arrange to do so, sell amounts up to q_o at the prices consumers are willing to pay, with the differential between the declining D_c line and the horizontal p_e line paid for by the sellers). If consumers alone made the advertising decision, they would buy q_c advertising at price p_c. Thus the amount of advertising provided by sellers will in this case greatly exceed the amount consumers would buy, and it would even ex-ceed the amount they would want at no cost at all. The size of the differential between what consumers want and what sellers provide will depend on how much the demands of these two groups differ. Since there are good reasons for believing that sellers desire more advertising than consumers, and since the amount of advertising is determined by sellers, it is clear that the amount provided will be greater than it would be were buyers the sole purchasers.

Lester Telser's analysis of the advertising market focuses on the supply of advertising.[3] Advertising is provided as a joint product with the good that is advertised. Because of this, the advertiser avoids the costly transactions that would be necessary to collect the price of advertising from each consumer were advertising sold to consumers in the market. He argues that there are two supply curves for advertising—one when the seller pays for the advertising and one when consumers pay for the advertising.

This is illustrated in Figure 18.2, in which D_c is the demand for advertising by consumers, D_s is the demand by sellers, S_s is the supply of advertising to sellers, and S_c is the supply of advertising to consumers. The latter represents higher unit costs to reflect the transaction costs involved in peddling advertising in small units to large numbers of consumers. We have drawn S_c in relation to S_s in such a way as to suggest that the unit cost of these transactions would probably decline as more and more advertising is sold; that is, S_c is more elastic than S_s.

Under these assumed conditions, were the advertising decision made by consumers and were advertising explicitly paid for by them, q_c would be provided at a unit price of p_c. If sellers make the decision and buy the advertising, quantity q_s will be provided at price p_s. In Figure 18.2 quantity q_s again happens to exceed q_o, though it need not do so if D_s is closer to D_c than we have indicated. However, it seems reasonable to believe that there is a considerable gap between these two demand functions.

Consumers' Demand for Advertising

The market in which advertising is bought and sold is different from most markets because there are two levels of demand. Business firms demand advertising and potential buyers also demand it. The demand by business firms will be a function of the anticipated

---

[3] Lester G. Telser, "Supply and Demand for Advertising Messages," *American Economic Review* 56 (May 1966): 457-466.

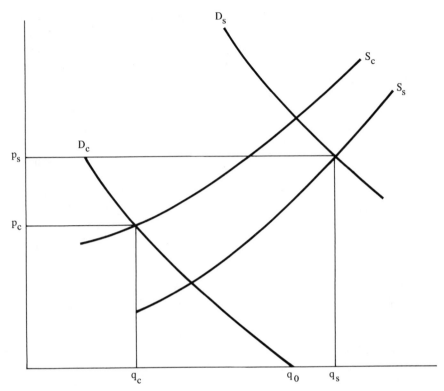

Figure 18.2. The demand for advertising by sellers and by consumers and the supply of advertising to sellers and to consumers.

revenue effect of advertising, which was the subject of the preceding chapter. We shall now examine the demand for advertising by potential buyers of the advertiser's product. We shall focus primarily on the consumer buyer, although buyers of industrial goods manifest many of the same attributes as consumer buyers with a probable difference in emphasis.

INFORMATION

The demand on the part of potential buyers for advertising is in part a demand for information about the availability of goods and services, attributes of goods offered, and prices and terms of sale. Information can range all the way from hard data about tensile strength, size, price, and the like to evaluations and assessments based on scientific or socially established standards. Information about market alternatives can be obtained through many means—experience with the good, shopping to observe market offerings and prices, talking with salespeople, consulting authorities, reading periodicals and books, watching TV, reading manufacturers' and sellers' information bulletins, and so forth. Advertising is only one source of information for most consumers. Use of advertising may be preferred by the consumer, however, if it entails less cost to him than, for example, shopping in the market.

In order for advertising to fulfill the information function for potential buyers, it must provide the information that they wish to have. Not all potential buyers want the same information, nor do all buyers want the same amount. Most buyers may not know what information is relevant and may not, therefore, know what they want. But it is likely that even the latter group would be willing to pay for information about market alternatives. Most buyers will want information that is accurate and complete. And probably most, but not all, would want information that includes both positive and negative facts and viewpoints.[4] Some may want only partial information, to be supplemented by information obtained from other sources. There is probably a demand for much of existing advertising as it is; that is, consumers would be willing to pay something for some of the advertising to which they are now exposed. What we do not know, of course, is in what ways advertising might be altered and result in an increased demand for it on the part of consumers. For example, we do not know how much consumers would be willing to pay for varying amounts of advertising that is accurate and complete and contains both favorable and unfavorable information about the product. The consumer's demand for advertising is so intimately related to the quality of the advertising that we cannot consider the quantities demanded without making some assumption about the qualities of the advertising.

PERSUASION

It has also been suggested that there may be a demand on the part of consumers not merely for the information contained in advertising but for the persuasion of advertising. A good portion of advertising effort is directed toward creating an atmosphere or aura around a product—a favorable image of the product. The advertiser tries to lead the potential customer into believing that if he uses the product he will experience success, security, love, joy, or some other desired end. This may or may not be true. Let us assume that it is not true or only partially true. Does such an image have utility to the consumer? No human lives without illusions. Just as humor may keep one sane in the midst of insanity, so illusions may fulfill a constructive role in the midst of life's frustrations and disappointments. They may be fun in their own right. Many consumers will pay a magician to fool them, and many would be willing to pay a seller to create an illusion of happiness or pleasure.

It is not our purpose to explore this in terms of mental hygiene but merely to point out that even the most ephemeral aspects of advertising, whether true or false, may not be devoid of utility to some consumers. As Harry Johnson has pointed out, it is possible that psychiatric treatment, long a superior good among the affluent, may be provided the less affluent through the "hidden persuaders," whose services can be bought with the groceries.[5] In this sense, advertising can be viewed as the poor man's psychiatrist.

DISUTILITY OF ADVERTISING

If we are to know the net utility of advertising to consumers, we must substract from the gross utility of advertising, resulting from the information it provides for consumers and perhaps on occasion from the pleasures that derive from the illusions it creates, the

---

[4] This would not be true for a recent buyer who seeks from advertising information that will eliminate his postpurchase anxiety. See Bruce Straits, "The Pursuit of the Dissonant Consumer," *Journal of Marketing* 28 (July 1964): 662-666, which is based on Leon Festinger, *A Theory of Cognitive Dissonance*, (Stanford, Calif.: Stanford University Press, 1958).

[5] Harry G. Johnson, "The Consumer and Madison Avenue," *Current Economic Comment* 22, no. 3 (August 1960): 3ff., reproduced in S. George Walters, Max D. Snider, and Morris L. Sweet, eds., *Readings in Marketing* (Cincinnati, Ohio: South-Western, 1962), pp. 49-57.

disutility of advertising. Disutilities may be due to false advertising, which misdirects consumer choice. Misleading advertising may be the result of untrue statements or, more often, of incomplete information. What is "truth" is never easy to establish, but we can say that when advertising creates an expectation on the part of the buyer that cannot be realized after the purchase has been made, it is untrue. A still more common problem in advertising is the absence of complete information, and this is likely to be a consequence of control over the advertising message by the seller of goods. It occurs when the seller withholds from the potential buyer information that would discourage purchase. Both errors of commission and omission in advertising may detract from the consumer's satisfaction to the extent that the consumer believes the misleading advertising and uses this "information" in making his decision. False and incomplete information is most costly to the consumer when it is believed *and* deters him from seeking better information.

Still another source of disutility is advertising that the consumer finds offensive or distasteful. Finally, there is the disutility that arises because consumers who have been exposed to advertising become dissatisfied with the stocks of goods they now own but are unable to replace, given prices and their budget constraints. An example is the advertising of new automobiles, in which their new features and virtues are extolled. Car owners who were satisfied with their old models now become dissatisfied, deriving less utility from their present stock than they would have had they not seen and believed the advertising. It could be argued therefore that consumer ignorance of new models would have left them better off. But this is really not an economic question. By such a view we might say that the economic problem of scarcity can be dealt with not merely by increased production but also by increased asceticism. The point, however, is not whether it is "good" or "bad" to want more or less but, rather, that in a "real goods" sense obsolescence can be "created" by persuading buyers that what they have is not so desirable as it could be.

In this connection, it is of interest to observe that the study of consumers' reactions to advertising conducted by Raymond Bauer and Stephen Greyser in the mid-1960s indicated that consumers appeared not to be grossly dissatisfied with advertising.

> While a considerable portion of the American population are mixed (34%) or indifferent (8%) in their overall attitudes toward advertising as an institution and activity of our society, of those who take a definite stand on one side or the other, the people classified as unfavorable toward advertising (14%) are far outnumbered by those classified as favorable (41%).[6]

But whether favorable or unfavorable on the whole, consumers drew clear-cut distinctions between what they liked and did not like about advertising. The reason they most often gave for approving of advertising was its informational role.

> The necessity for an informational function is recognized, and ads and advertising are approved of for filling this role. Disapproval comes in part for deficiencies in this

---

[6] Raymond A. Bauer and Stephen A. Greyser, *Advertising in America: The Consumer View*, A Report and Interpretation of the American Association of Advertising Agencies' Study on the Consumer Judgment of Advertising (Boston: Harvard University, Graduate School of Business Administration, Division of Research, 1968), p. 331.

information role, but more from the fact that ads themselves are unpleasant and intrusive.[7]

However, this disapproval was based on a minority of experiences; most people thought most advertisements were pleasant rather than unpleasant.

The disutility of this kind of advertising arises through the opportunity cost to the consumer by diverting him from more fundamental information that could result in still greater utility or, even more sadly, through the disillusion that comes when the illusion is proven to be false. On balance we would opt for truth without illusion.

The Supply of Advertising

JOINT SUPPLY

We have said little about the supply of advertising except to point out that it is provided in joint supply with the goods and services advertised. The seller of goods, not the consumer, makes the decision concerning both the quantity and quality of advertising produced.

There is one additional aspect of advertising's joint supply that should be noted. This is the joint supply of the services of certain communications media—television, radio, newspapers, and other periodicals. A substantial portion of the costs of publication and broadcasting are met by advertising.[8]

This places upon the producers of periodicals and newspapers the problem of arriving at a subscription price that will achieve the circulation necessary to attract that amount of advertising revenue which, in combination with the subscription income, will maximize profits in the long run or, in the short run, yield an adequate cash flow to cover variable costs and ensure survival. Separate pricing of the two services would give the consumer greater freedom of choice, possibly with some loss of economies of scale that result from the joint supply. From the consumer's point of view, part of the problem with joint supply is the probability that there will be more advertising than he would demand, as we have indicated in Figure 18.2. With newspapers and periodicals the consumer has greater freedom to ignore advertising, if he wishes to do so, than with television or radio broadcasting. The consumer's discretion in consuming advertising space is probably greater than in consuming advertising time, although some consumers have devised means of accomplishing the latter.[9]

There is yet another facet to the media's control over advertising. The medium has the power to decide who can use its services and what the "position" of the advertiser will be in that medium. For example, it is very difficult for small companies to obtain

---

[7] Ibid., p. 334.

[8] Data from the U.S. *Census of Manufactures* for 1967 indicate that advertising revenues were 70.2 percent of total receipts for newspapers in that year and 58.0 percent for periodicals. For the television and radio broadcasting industry, data reported by the U.S. Federal Communications Commission for 1970 show that advertising contributed 97.2 percent of television broadcasting revenues and 98.8 percent of radio broadcasting revenues. U.S., Bureau of the Census, *Statistical Abstract of the United States, 1972* (Washington: GPO), pp. 498, 500.

[9] Some cities find that the water pressure declines markedly during those minutes of the hour when commercials are being presented on particularly popular television programs.

commercial time on TV during prime time. In March 1966 there were 1,697 commercial announcements on the three TV networks during prime time. Twenty percent of these were placed by five companies—Bristol-Myers, Procter and Gamble, General Foods, American Home Products, and Colgate-Palmolive.[10] Prime time is generally preempted by network programs for firms that make large total advertising expenditures, with the result that small firms do not have equal access.

ADVERTISING BY SPECIFIC FIRMS AND INDUSTRIES

We have discussed advertising in general without much reference to the differential rates of advertising among various products and services. For what products is advertising most important, and what are the reasons for differentials in the use of advertising by different firms and industries?

There are several ways of measuring advertising expenditures: (1) total dollar expenditures for advertising, (2) advertising expenditures as a percentage of sales, (3) advertising as a percentage of gross margin, and (4) advertising expenditures as a percentage of total marketing expenditures. The last two—advertising as a percentage of gross margin or of total marketing expenditures—are considerably more refined than the first two. However, not much data are reported that way, and we shall use the other two measures—absolute dollar expenditures and advertising as a percentage of sales—even though those indexes lack some of the refinement of the other two.

In Table 18.3 are listed the 40 firms (plus the U.S. government) that spent $50 million or more for advertising in 1972. Advertising expenditures as a percentage of sales are also noted. Table 18.4 shows advertising expenditures as a percentage of sales for selected firms in 1972, ranked by advertising-sales ratios, and Table 18.5 shows similar data for a number of industrial subgroups for 1969-1970. In all of these tabulations we have identified only the largest advertisers as indicated by these two measures. From these and other data, it is possible to identify the characteristics of products, demand, or markets that characterize the larger users of advertising.

Advertising tends to be greatest at two points in the product life cycle—during the period when the rate of sales expansion is accelerating, and after the point of sales inflection, when the rate of growth slows and sales are more difficult to make. The number of competitors and the nature of the competitive weapons employed will also be important determining factors. Advertising is particularly important in industries characterized by a few relatively large producers selling highly differentiated products. Manufacturers of cigarettes, drugs, cosmetics, liquor, packaged foods, soaps and detergents, soft drinks, and automobiles fall into this category, and all of these are prominent in Tables 18.3, 18.4, and 18.5.

Subjective human needs are better candidates for an advertising expenditure than objective needs. Advertising is particularly effective where there are few facts and where persuasion is the chief line of selling appeal. If this is combined with a product whose attributes are hidden, these two conditions are reinforcing in their impact on the seller's preference for advertising rather than other methods of promotion.

Other factors that have an important bearing on whether or not manufacturers and

---

[10] John M. Blair, *Economic Concentration* (New York: Harcourt Brace Jovanovich, 1972), p. 314, based on U.S., Senate, Committee on the Judiciary, Subcommittee on Antitrust and Monopoly, *Hearings on Possible Anticompetitive Effects of Sale of Network TV Advertising*, 89th Cong., 2d sess., 1966, pt. 1, p. 119.

marketing firms devote more or less of their resources to advertising rather than other marketing activities are purchasers' buying habits such as the frequency of purchase, the extent to which buyers shop, the importance of convenience in accessibility of the product to the buyer, and the relative importance of branding. While in some cases the promotional objective of advertising is dominant, in all cases the informational aspect is present, and in some it exceeds the promotional in importance. Motion picture theaters, insurance offices, subdividers and developers, and book publishers are examples of industries in Table 18.5 that make considerable use of advertising as a means of giving information about market alternatives.

Table 18.3 Firms Whose Expenditures for Advertising Exceeded $50 Million in 1972

Rank	Firm	Advertising	
		Amount	Percentage of Sales
1	Procter & Gamble	$275,000,000	7.0
2	Sears, Roebuck & Co.	215,000,000	2.2
3	General Foods Corp.	170,000,000	8.6
4	General Motors Corp.	146,000,000	10.5
5	Warner-Lambert Pharmaceutical	134,000,000	14.6
6	Ford Motor Co.	132,500,000	0.7
7	American Home Products	116,000,000	9.4
8	Bristol-Myers Co.	115,000,000	12.0
9	Colgate-Palmolive Co.	105,000,000	12.1
10	Chrysler Corp.	95,415,400	1.3
11	American Tel. & Tel. Co.	86,700,000	0.4
12	International Tel. & Tel.	85,055,000	1.8
13	Sterling Drug Inc.	83,933,600	17.1
14	RCA Corp.	78,750,000	2.0
15	R. J. Reynolds Tobacco Co.	78,200,000	2.6
16	General Electric Co.	77,500,000	0.9
17	Gillette Co.	72,000,000	8.3
18	Coca-Cola Co.	69,000,000	3.7
19[a]	Distillers Corp.-Seagrams Ltd.	69,000,000	4.4
20	General Mills	67,100,000	4.2
21	Goodyear Tire & Rubber Co.	66,000,000	1.6
22	U.S. Government	65,828,000	—
23	Richardson-Merrell Inc.	65,576,000	25.8
24	Lever Brothers	65,000,000	12.3
25[b]	Nabisco	65,000,000	7.5
26	Kraftco	64,500,000	2.4
27	Alberto-Culver Co.	62,000,000	33.9
28	Philip Morris Co.	61,000,000	2.9
29	Westinghouse Electric Corp.	59,000,000	1.5
30	Rapid-American Corp.	57,500,000	2.4
31	American Brands	57,000,000	1.9
32	American Cyanamid Co.	56,000,000	5.8
33	Heublein Inc.	55,000,000	5.5

Table 18.3 Continued

Rank	Firm	Advertising	
		Amount	Percentage of Sales
34	Firestone Tire & Rubber Co.	55,000,000	2.0
35	Standard Brands Inc.	54,000,000	5.6
36	J. C. Penney Co. Inc.	53,000,000	1.0
37	Eastman-Kodak Co.	52,800,000	2.5
38	DuPont	52,752,000	1.2
39	Norton Simon Inc.	52,250,000	3.5
40	Brown & Williamson Tobacco	52,200,000	6.0
41	PepsiCo	51,500,000	19.4

[a] Also ranks as number 18.

[b] Also ranks as number 24.

Source: Reprinted with permission from the August 27, 1973 issue of *Advertising Age*, p. 28. Copyright by Crain Communications, Inc.

Table 18.4 Advertising Expenditures as a Percentage of Sales of Selected Firms, 1972[a]

Firm	Percentage of Sales
Alberto-Culver Co.	33.9
Carter-Wallace Inc.	30.7
Noxell Corp.	29.6
Block Drug Co.	27.5
Richardson-Merrell Inc.	25.8
Mennen Corp.	21.4
Miles Laboratories	20.7
PepsiCo	19.4
S. C. Johnson & Son	17.9
Sterling Drug Inc.	17.1
Chesebrough-Pond's Inc.	16.8
Warner-Lambert Pharmaceutical	14.6
Schering-Plough Inc.	14.2
Wm. Wrigley Jr. Co.	13.5
Smith Kline Corp.	12.5
Lever Brothers	12.3
Colgate-Palmolive Co.	12.1
Bristol-Meyers Co.	12.0
Clorox Corp.	11.2
Mars Inc.	10.0
American Home Products	9.4
General Foods Corp.	8.6
Gillette Co.	8.3
Norton-Norwich Products	7.9
Nabisco	7.5

Table 18.4 Continued

Firm	Percentage of Sales
Procter & Gamble	7.0
Time Inc.	6.8
Revlon Inc.	6.8
Thomas J. Lipton	6.6
Kellogg Co.	6.5
Pfizer Inc.	6.1
Brown & Williamson Tobacco	6.0
American Cyanamid Co.	5.8
Standard Brands Inc.	5.6
Merck & Co.	5.6
Heublein Inc.	5.5
Polaroid Corp.	5.5
Mattel Inc.	5.5
Nestle Co.	5.2
Loews Corp.	5.2
Johnson & Johnson	5.1

[a]Included are only firms that were among the 100 that had the largest total dollar expenditure for advertising in that year and whose advertising expenditures were 5 or more percent of sales.

Source: Reprinted with permission from the August 27, 1973 issue of *Advertising Age,* p. 28. Copyright by Crain Publications, Inc.

Table 18.5 Expenditures for Advertising as a Percentage of Sales of Selected Industrial Subgroups, 1969-70

Industrial Subgroup[a]	Percentage of Sales
All industrial groups	1.13
Soap, related products (M)[b]	10.09
Drugs (M)	9.10
Educational services	6.51
Motion pictures	5.51
Tobacco manufacturers (M)	5.36
Malt liquors and malt (M)	5.33
Bottled soft drinks and flavorings (M)	5.01
Watches and clocks (M)	4.26
Insurance, loan, and law offices and other real estate	4.00
Cutlery, hard tools, and hardware (M)	3.90
Grain mill products (M)	3.84
Books and greeting cards (M)	3.60
Motion picture production, distribution and related services	3.37
Optical, medical, and ophthalmic goods (M)	3.18
Furniture, home furnishings, and equipment stores	3.13
Alcoholic beverages, except malt liquors and malt (M)	3.10

Table 18.5 (Continued)

Industrial Subgroup[a]	Percentage of Sales
Subdividers, developers, and operative builders	3.06
General merchandise stores	2.60
Air transportation	2.45
Canned and frozen foods (M)	2.38
Personal credit agencies	2.35
Radio, television, and communication equipment	2.24
Scientific instruments, watches and clocks (M)	2.13
Apparel and accessory stores	2.12
Photographic equipment and supplies (M)	2.12
Hotels and other lodging places	2.02

[a]Data were available for 217 subgroups. Only industrial subgroups in which the expenditure was 2 percent or more are listed in this table. Excluded are some whose expenditure was 2 percent or more that were identified as "miscellaneous" or "not allocable" to a particular subgroup.

[b](M) = manufacturing. Others not so labeled are retailing or service businesses.

Source: Reprinted with permission from the July 16, 1973 issue of *Advertising Age*, p. 34. Copyright by Crain Publications, Inc. These data are based on 1,658,820 corporate tax returns for 1969 or 1969-1970. Approximately half of the corporations reported on a fiscal year basis. The detailed breakdowns in this table were obtained by *Advertising Age* from the original data, which were summarized on a 65 industrial group basis in U.S., Department of the Treasury Internal Revenue Service, *Statistics of Income 1969, Corporation Income Tax Returns*, Preliminary (Washington, D.C.: GPO, 1973).

ADVERTISING AND ECONOMIC WELFARE

Throughout our discussion of advertising we have indicated a number of situations in which there are favorable and unfavorable effects from advertising on the economy as a whole, and particularly on the welfare of consumers. It is appropriate therefore that we conclude our discussion by pulling together some of these observations and looking more carefully at advertising as a phenomenon of the economy and of the society to which it renders service, as some would claim, or disservice, as others would contend.[11] We shall consider advertising as a source of information for buyers of products and its relationship to the level of productivity in the economy, the prices of goods and services, and the allocation of resources.

Advertising as a Source of Information

To what extent does advertising provide information to consumers about the availability of products, the attributes of products relevant to the meeting of consumer needs, and

[11]Several authors have surveyed some of the broader economic issues in advertising. We have found four particularly helpful: Nicholas Kaldor, "The Economic Aspects of Advertising," *Review of Economic Studies* 18, no. 45 (1949-1950): 1-27; Peter Doyle, "Economic Aspects of Advertising: A Survey," *The Economic Journal* 78 (September 1968): 570-602; Julian L. Simon, *Issues in the Economics of Advertising* (Urbana: University of Illinois Press, 1970); Neil H. Borden, *The Economic Effects of Advertising* (Chicago: Irwin, 1944).

the price and terms of sale? Although this question cannot be answered categorically, we can make some general observations.

First, the advertiser is the seller of the product or service. As such he may have more information about the product or service than anyone else. This is particularly true where the advertiser manufactures the product and has detailed information about the materials that go into it, the results of laboratory tests, or the experience of previous users. It is less likely to be the case if the product is new and experience has been limited. A marketing firm may have more knowledge of buyer use and response, while a manufacturing firm may have more knowledge of the product's technical attributes. Sometimes, of course, this kind of information is not detailed or complete.

Whether the seller's knowledge of his product is actually used extensively in the design of advertising programs would have to be established by a careful study of the procedures employed in planning advertising copy. If advertising agencies, for example, are found to be the ones that select from the cluster of product characteristics those that are to be stressed in a particular promotional program, it would suggest that the seller's intimate knowledge of his product is less important in determining what information gets to the consumer than other facets of that choice, such as the probable impact of a given piece of information on consumer response in light of the product's historical image and competitors' policies.

On the other hand, much advertising is highly informative. This is particularly true of want ads, of manufacturers' advertising that informs potential buyers of the availability of products and of their attributes, and of retailers' advertising of product availability, characteristics, and prices. Wholesalers use less advertising than manufacturers or retailers, but where it is employed, as in the marketing of industrial supplies, it is likely to contain considerable information or be restricted to information about the availability of goods.

Much of the information conveyed in advertising is accurate, and this is most likely to occur where the potential buyer is well informed and where the information itself is of a nature that it is likely to be conducive to purchase. Advertising of industrial goods and supplies, for example, is often heavily laden with information about product attributes because of the interests and knowledge of potential customers. In the advertising of all goods—consumer or industrial—products that have useful attributes can be sold more effectively on the basis of information about those attributes than on the basis of false information.

Although much advertising is truly informative, the greatest risk and uncertainty from the potential buyer's point of view is the absence of any objective control over the advertiser's decisions as to what information he will convey. Seldom will an advertiser choose to convey information that would be damaging to his profit or sales objective; yet such information may be essential if the buyer is to make an optimum choice. When information about a product is obtained from a party whose welfare can be (and usually is) affected by the quantity and quality of that information, there is good reason to question the validity of the information likely to come from that source. There are so many subtle ways by which an advertiser can distort information without overstepping the bounds of truth as defined legally and pragmatically in human affairs. Everything he says may be literally true, but the omission of pertinent facts or knowledge can result in a perception of the product and its potential on the part of the buyer that deviates from what his perception will be once he has actually used the product. Such distortions may be willful, mischievious, accidental, or unintended, but their effect can be the same regardless of motivation. One important question therefore is whether advertising is a source of accurate and complete information about goods and services for potential buyers of goods and services. We must conclude that not all information conveyed by advertising is likely to be accurate or complete for the very simple reason that the criteria by which the advertiser judges advertising's effectiveness are not the same as those by which the potential buyer judges its desirability. Only if the means by which those criteria are realized overlap for buyer and seller does advertising fulfill the needs of both parties. Thus the critical factor is the possible conflict between the advertiser's objectives and those of the buyer.

This brings us to a final point. Granted that advertising may be informative in varying degrees, is this the *best* source of information for consumers? If we could sort out from the $23 billion that we spend in the United States for advertising in a year that portion which could properly be labeled "informational," the question becomes: Is this the most effective way to spend that much for buyer information?[1][2] We would have to conclude that it is not, primarily because the advertiser's decisions about how much and what kinds of information to give would be guided by his own interests, which are not necessarily realized by fulfilling the buyer's need for information.

Advertising and the Price of Goods

ECONOMIES OF SCALE

Advertisers are prone to argue that advertising increases the demand for goods, thereby enabling firms to become larger and to achieve economies of scale associated with their greater size. This results in lower costs and, hence, lower prices. The argument is not groundless to the extent that (1) advertising does increase the demand for goods *and* (2) lower unit costs of production are realized *and* (3) these lower costs result in lower unit prices to buyers. We shall assume that (1) is a fact. Lower unit costs may or may not be realized, depending on the possibilities for economies of scale that exist after the effect of the advertising has been felt. It is not impossible that advertising could lead a firm to larger and larger shares of the market to the point that increasing costs are experienced. The third necessary condition is that lower costs result in lower prices. This will depend on the effectiveness of competition in an industry where advertising is an important variable in marketing policy. If advertising is an important influence on demand, the amounts spent may be critical in determining the extent of its effect, thereby giving special advantages to those firms with large resources for advertising. This combination of factors by no means gives assurance that there will be effective competition; the contrary may be the more likely case. One of the goals of advertising is to build customer loyalty, which will insulate the firm from price competition. This may be difficult to achieve, but to the extent that it is achieved it is likely to work in the direction of increased profits rather than in the direction of reduced selling prices.

OLIGOPOLY AND EQUILIBRIUM COSTS

Let us pursue this line of reasoning one step further. Assume that advertising does increase demand and that it is most effective in increasing the demand for specific brands within a line of goods. Let us further assume that the advertising elasticity of demand is quite high and that at this stage in the product's life cycle large expenditures have a

---

[1][2] See Kaldor, op. cit.

higher advertising elasticity than smaller amounts of expenditure. In the industry, then, all firms can benefit from advertising, but the larger firms will benefit disproportionately because of their greater resources. Therefore the effect of the advertising is to give large firms an ever larger share of the market. Let us assume that we end up with an oligopolistic market in which a relatively few large firms dominate. Each will have a large advertising budget, though differences may exist between firms, depending on the marketing mix that each establishes as its basic policy. Under these circumstances, it seems reasonable to believe that advertising expenditures will become a part of the equilibrium costs of the industry. No one firm wishes to give the others an opportunity to pick off some of its customers through negligence of its advertising appropriation. The total advertising by the industry, then, settles into a more or less stable volume in relation to sales. Witness, for example, the patterns prevalent in the soap, drugs, and cosmetics industries in 1972. (See Table 18.5.) In fact, every firm listed in Table 18.3 is in an industry charcterized by oligopoly. It is hard to believe that any one of the large advertisers in any of these industries would be willing to risk any substantial reduction in its advertising expenditure in relation to sales so long as it is convinced that the firms with which it competes will keep their advertising budget within the vicinity of its present level.[13] If our reasoning is correct, it would seem that one of the consequences of advertising in certain industries is to facilitate the development of oligopolistic market conditions in which advertising costs become a part of the equilibrium costs of the industry. This is not to imply that advertising alone *causes* the oligopoly to evolve, nor does it mean that in the absence of advertising there will not be alternative costs that would arise as firms attempt to secure their position in the industry. Rather, it is to say that advertising can be *one* tool that facilitates the development of a market structure in which advertising costs then become a part of the equilibrium costs of the industry.

CONCENTRATION

A number of studies have been made to test whether concentration is in fact related to advertising expenditures. Telser, using data for 1947, 1954, and 1958, found a positive but low relationship between concentration ratio and percentage of sales allocated for advertising.[14] In a later study by H. Michael Mann, J. A. Henning, and J. W. Meehan, Jr., it was found that a more detailed breakdown of industries resulted in slightly higher relationships on the basis of data for 1954, 1958, and 1963.[15] F. N. Scherer concluded that the available empirical evidence suggests that advertising expenditure ratios are

---

[13] John Kenneth Galbraith discusses this phenomenon in markets of oligopoly in terms of two advertising effects. One is the effect on the firm's sales and the other is an industry effect. The latter results from the fact that each firm's advertising contributes to an increased demand for the output of the industry so that all firms benefit. In addition, he argues, advertising by oligopolists proclaims the virtues of "the planning system," in which such firms are participants, and of the system's commitment to growth. Thus the power of the system itself is enhanced. For these reasons, he believes that advertising by oligopolists is not wasteful from their viewpoint but contributes positively to the goals of the system. John Kenneth Galbraith, *Economics and the Public Purpose* (Boston: Houghton Mifflin, 1973), pp. 139-141.

[14] Lester G. Telser, "Advertising and Competition," *Journal of Political Economy* 72 (December 1964): 537-562.

[15] H. Michael Mann, J. A. Henning, and J. W. Meehan, Jr., "Advertising and Concentration: An Empirical Investigation," *Journal of Industrial Economics* 16 (November 1967): 34-45.

slightly higher in markets of oligopoly but not greatly higher than those in less concentrated markets.[16]

PROFITS

Perhaps of more significance in our consideration of the relationships of oligopoly and/or market concentration to the use of advertising are the findings of William Comanor and Thomas Wilson.[17] They analyzed the relationship between advertising expenditures and the average 1954-1957 after-tax return on stockholders' equity in 41 consumer goods industries. In contrast to Telser's findings, they observed

> that the inter-industry variation in profit rates can be explained quite well by a model incorporating the rate of growth of demand, some measure of advertising intensity, and variables reflecting the importance of concentration and technical barriers to entry.[18]

Specifically with respect to advertising:

> The primary finding is that advertising has a statistically significant and quantitatively important impact upon profit rates which provide a measure of market performance as well as indicate the existence of market power.[19]

While they began their study assuming that the independent variables, including advertising, were causally related to profit rates, they concluded that there was *also* the possibility of a reverse direction of causality:

> A plausible case can be made that a significant feedback exists from profits to advertising expenditures, since advertising reflects the discretionary behavior of firms as well as the extent of product differentiation.[20]

They conclude:

> On the basis of these empirical findings, it is evident that for industries where products are differentiable, investment in advertising is a highly profitable activity. Industries with high advertising outlays earn, on average, at a profit rate which exceeds that of other industries by nearly four percentage points. This differential represents a 50 percent increase in profit rates [12 percent versus 8 percent]. It is likely, moreover, that much of this profit rate differential is accounted for by the entry barriers created by advertising expenditures and by the resulting achievement of market power.[21]

Dealing with the same question of relationship between advertising and concentration but using a different method of anlysis, Louis Guth also found evidence that advertising appeared to be related to increased concentration and to serve as a barrier to entry.[22]

---

[16] F. N. Scherer, *Industrial Market Structure and Economic Performance* (Chicago: Rand McNally, 1970), pp. 341-343.

[17] William S. Comanor and Thomas A. Wilson, "Advertising Market Structure and Performance," *The Review of Economics and Statistics* 49 (November 1967): 423-440.

[18] Ibid., p. 436.

[19] Ibid., p. 423.

[20] Ibid.

[21] Ibid., p. 437. Data in brackets have been inserted.

[22] Using Lorenz coefficients as a measure of concentration, he found that an industry with a

These findings have been followed by an interesting discussion of appropriate analytical procedures. In a more recent study Roger Sherman and Robert Tollison took a different tack in their analysis of the relationship of advertising and concentration.[23] They argued that cost variability is more closely related to Lerner's measure of monopoly power and is a better index of monopoly power than concentration ratios.[24] When cost variability (or its inverse, cost fixity) was incorporated into a function along with both advertising expenditures and profits, they found that cost variability, rather than advertising, was a "determinant" of profit rates in both consumer goods and other industries.

> Cost variability was shown able to predict advertising-sales ratios and to reduce the advertising-sales measure to an insignificant role in explaining profit-rates. . . . This is not to say that advertising is irrelevant; an industry that has a very high level of advertising expense surely will be more difficult to enter, and our tests were biased against detection of such a role for advertising. However, we have shown that plausible, largely technological conditions can invite firms to engage in heavy advertising, and we argue that these conditions, *not advertising itself*, should be examined for their effect on profitability and market performance.[25]

Comanor and Wilson, however, point out that Sherman and Tollison measured cost fixity, which they had employed as the inverse of cost variability, in such a way that it was bound to be related to both profit rates and advertising-sales ratios.[26] Using a different measure of fixed costs, Comanor and Wilson found no such significant relationship as that observed by Sherman and Tollison. They further indicate that in their yet unpublished analyses they have found evidence "that although advertising is influenced by profitability, there is no reason to believe that our original estimates of the impact of advertising are biased *upwards*."[27] In fact they believe that the effect of advertising on profitability is even greater than they originally estimated it to be.

ADVERTISING AS A SUBSTITUTE FOR OTHER COSTS

There is one other cost-reducing possibility inherent in the use of advertising that we should mention. This is the possibility that it may be used as a substitute for more costly methods of market communication. If, for example, advertising can be substituted for personal selling, it may be that the unit selling costs are lower. This might arise from the fact that use of mass communication media reduces the cost per message to a very low

---

concentration ratio of 34.7 could increase its level of concentration by more than 30 percent from an increase of 5 percent in its advertising-to-sales ratio. He concluded that advertising appeared to increase concentration and acted as a barrier to entry. However, firms could sometimes exist on the fringes. Louis A. Guth, "Advertising and Market Structure Revisited," *Journal of Industrial Economics* 19 (April 1971): 179-198.

[23] Roger Sherman and Robert Tollison, "Advertising and Profitability," *Review of Economics and Statistics* 53 (November 1971): 397-413.

[24] Lerner proposed that monopoly power could be measured by $(p\text{-}m)/p$, in which p is unit price and m is marginal cost. Abba P. Lerner, "The Concept of Monopoly and the Measurement of Monopoly Power," *Review of Economic Studies* 1 (June 1934): 157-175.

[25] Sherman and Tollison, op. cit., p. 404.

[26] William S. Comanor and Thomas A. Wilson, "On Advertising and Profitability," *Review of Economics and Statistics* 53 (Novermber 1971): 408-410.

[27] Ibid., p. 410.

level compared with the cost of one message transmitted person to person, as it would be in personal selling.

If advertising were abolished, what costs would be incurred to take its place? Other promotional methods would doubtless be devised, and we have no way of knowing exactly what they would be or what costs they would entail. We can assume that if business firms are now making the most effective use of their expenditures, they would derive fewer benefits from an equal amount of dollars spent for other promotional methods.

Advertising and the Level of Output

One of the arguments often presented for advertising is that it stimulates demand, thereby stimulating production, which, in turn, stimulates income. This suggests that there is a multiplier effect from advertising, and this might follow logically from the perception of advertising as a capital expenditure. Another defense of advertising is that it is one of the competitive tools in a mature economy in which product differentiation and innovations are important attributes. It is particularly important, so it is argued, as a means by which innovators can gain a foothold in the market. We shall assume that the continuous growth of GNP is desirable.[28] Because the rate of innovation is critical to economic growth, this marketing support also becomes critical in encouraging new products, product changes, and growth. Both of these defenses of advertising—a stimulus to demand and a means by which innovations are encouraged—have to be viewed in terms of (1) whether or not they are true, (2) whether they are desirable ends, and (3) if so, to what extent advertising is the best way of achieving those ends. We shall focus on questions (1) and (3).

GNP AND INNOVATION

We have already indicated that it is not possible to measure the effects of advertising for a particular firm with a high degree of accuracy, and this holds even more for advertising in the economy as a whole. That is, we do not know the extent to which advertising has served as a stimulus to demand in either the short run or the long run. The secular trend in advertising expenditures has been upward at a rate that just about equals that of the gross national product. It is clear that advertisers *believe* that advertising is a stimulus to sales, and there are many cases to convince us that it is an effective stimulus to sales of particular brands. Whether it has increased the demand for goods as a whole over a span of time is less clear and will have to remain a moot question until meaningful measurements can be evolved. To the extent that advertising is a part of the total economic climate within which GNP has grown secularly over the decades, and particularly a part of the dynamic elements of the climate, it may have had a role in the growth of national productivity.

On the basis of case studies rather than aggregative data, it appears that advertising has played a critical role in product and service innovations. To this extent, it is reasonable to impute to advertising some (but an unknown amount) of the growth in national income that has occurred over the years. There are many cases in which advertising has been a

---

[28] This is a debatable assumption, but we shall not debate it at this point.

critical factor in the introduction of new products and product changes, and there is fairly convincing evidence that it has been an effective means of establishing market communication between innovators and consumers.

Let us examine this role of advertising in a slightly different light. Assume (1) that the encouragement of innovations and product improvements is desirable in the economy, (2) that information about the nature and availability of innovations must reach potential buyers if innovators are to be stimulated to introduce improved products, and (3) that advertising is an effective means of conveying this information, thereby playing a role in the innovation process. A very important two-part question still remains to be asked: Is advertising the only way of dispensing that information, and if not, is it the best way? Certainly it is not the only way, for there are other procedures for accomplishing this informational function through, for example, a formalized public or private information-dispensing agency. From the consumer's point of view, the latter is more likely to report information impartially than the advertiser. But from the innovator's point of view, the advertising is probably a more appealing avenue because the advertiser can control the information disseminated and employ whatever persuasive techniques he believes will enhance his profit-making opportunities. Advertising enables the innovator to present his product in the best possible light; therefore the possibility that he can do this enhances his profit-making opportunities. To compete in the more rigorous market in which alternatives are viewed with as much objectivity as possible may not be so appealing to him. This is a situation where buyers' and sellers' interests are not the same.

CYCLICAL ADVERTISING EXPENDITURES

There are some other factors that we have to consider in examining the relation of advertising expenditures to the gross national product. Secularly we find that advertising expenditures have remained a fairly stable portion of gross national product, fluctuating during the years 1935-1971 between about 2.1 and 2.4 percent of the GNP in the United States. This stability may be in part a result of the fact that most business firms budget a fairly stable percentage of expected sales for advertising, and sales would tend to follow the level of GNP. One consequence of this is that through the business cycle advertising expenditures tend to move with the cycle rather than against it. Thus there is little evidence, except in the case of particular products, that advertising is employed for countercyclical purposes. Advertisers as a whole apparently do not believe that it can be an effective countercyclical device. During the depression of the 1930s, for example, advertising volume declined more than either industrial production or department store sales.[29] During the 1950s, the pattern was somewhat mixed. Between 1953 and 1954, for example, GNP remained almost constant in current dollars while advertising expenditures increased 5 percent. But between 1957 and 1958, GNP grew by $6 billion while advertising expenditures decreased by $9 million. Thus it appears that advertising has not been employed to counteract declining demand during periods of depression.

COMPETITION

There is one final point we should make about advertising and GNP. The nature of competition can be affected by advertising. While the demand-creating potential of

---

[29] Borden, op. cit., pp. 714-736, esp. pp. 716-722.

advertising may encourage new firms to enter an industry and existing firms to expand their product lines, we have observed that one of the factors that appears to be associated with the successful use of advertising is the availability of large amounts of funds for this purpose. Large advertising appropriations make it possible to realize economies of scale in the use of such funds due not merely to lower unit costs but to a greater potential impact on revenue, and they also make it more difficult for new firms to enter the industry. Thus the availability of funds for extensive advertising serves, not to stimulate innovations and sales promotion by many firms, but, rather, to restrict these possibilities to the larger firms of the industry, which can support large promotional budgets. Greater concentration of production is more likely to result in rigidities in market structure and behavior. Such markets may not be without social benefits, but they lack the vitality that characterizes competition between a larger number of smaller firms.

Advertising and the Allocation of Resourses

One other question that we should answer in our overall appraisal of advertising is its impact on resource allocation. Let us assume that advertising can in fact increase the demand for specific products and specific brands within a product group. To the extent that this diverts consumer expenditures from other goods and services whose demand is less responsive to the persuasive effects of advertising, there is a reallocation of resources. If consumers experience the increased satisfactions that they anticipate as a result of this, welfare is enhanced by this reallocation. To the extent, however, that consumers are disappointed with the consequences of the decisions that they make based on advertising, there is a resulting misallocation of resources and reduced total welfare.

Some people deplore this aspect of advertising on the basis of value judgments. Specifically, they believ that the "things" that much of our advertising glorifies are undesirable because they are inconsistent with what these individuals believe are "good" for human beings. We have observed that advertising expenditures are greatest, and the potential effects on demand greatest, where products have hidden qualities and where the wants that are satisfied by those products are of a high order and subjective. Some of the critics of advertising believe that these high-order, subjective wants are frivolous and that advertising, through its influence, diverts more of our resources to fulfilling these wants than is desirable. They expand their criticism to include the fact that hidden qualities can be more easily falsified or exploited through advertising and that advertisers can and do take advantage of human ignorance and lack of experience in meeting these more marginal wants, which emerge to become important demand determinants only after more basic biological and sociopsychological needs have been satisfied.

ADVERTISING AND WANT FORMATION

Advertisers cannot *make* consumers behave in a specific way. They can persuade them, and their skills of persuasion often exceed the consumer's skills of self-protection. Consumer wants are a part of human wants and as such are the product of the culture in which the individual evolves. The nature of culture and the processes of cultural change are therefore more fundamental to an understanding of consumer demand than is any one element of that culture, such as advertising. Germane to the structuring of consumer demand is the whole process by which human beings learn to want most of the things that they desire and demand in the market place. Advertising is one of the ways by which people learn, but it is by no means the only way and is certainly not the most important way.

John Kenneth Galbraith has viewed the process of want creation in affluent economies within the context of what he has labeled the "dependence effect," involving, first, the satisfying of less urgent wants as affluence increases, and second, the increasing necessity for production to create the wants that it satisfies in an affluent society. It is the second of these two aspects of the dependence effect that concerns advertising's role in the economy. Galbraith describes this relationship as follows:

> As a society becomes increasingly affluent, wants are increasingly created by the process by which they are satisfied. This may operate passively. Increases in consumption, the counterpart of increases in production, act by suggestion or emulation to create wants. Or producers may proceed actively to create wants through advertising and salesmanship. Wants thus come to depend on output. In technical terms it can no longer be assumed that welfare is greater at an all-round higher level of production than at a lower one. It may be the same. The higher level of production has, merely, a higher level of want creation necessitating a higher level of want satisfaction.[30]

He elaborates further:

> If production is to increase, the wants must be effectively contrived. In the absence of the contrivance the increase would not occur. This is not true of all goods, but that it is true of a substantial part is sufficient. It means that since the demand for this part would not exist, were it not contrived, its utility or urgency, *ex* contrivance, is zero. If we regard this production as marginal, we may say that the marginal utility of present aggregate output, *ex* advertising and salesmanship, is zero.[31]

This is a very strong indictment of the character of demand in a high-income economy, such as that of the United States, and specifically of advertising and other promotional efforts.

One of the most compelling arguments against Galbraith's judgment and concern has been articulated by Johnson.[32] He points out that Galbraith's view that wants satisfied in a high-income economy are less urgent is a tautology, since less urgent wants are always satisfied after more urgent wants or, as he believes is true in Galbraith's case, that the notion of urgency is a value judgment. Johnson's analysis of the second aspect of Galbraith's concept of the dependence effect is of more direct importance in the analysis of advertising's role. He points out that the aim of economic activity is, as both Alfred Marshall and Frank Knight have indicated, not merely the fuller satisfaction of given wants but the further evolution of wants for increased satisfaction to consumers. Thus progress is viewed not only as increasing the production function but also as improving the consumption function in order "to derive more and better satisfaction from production."[33]

---

[30] John Kenneth Galbraith, *The Affluent Society*, 2d ed. (Boston: Houghton Mifflin, 1969), p. 152.

[31] Ibid., pp. 153-154.

[32] Harry G. Johnson, op. cit.

[33] Ibid., p. 54.

He further argues that wants are not necessarily less valuable because they are acquired through emulation or advertising. Since most wants are learned, there is no logical basis for saying that one way of learning—for example, through one's family or one's formal education—is superior to another—for example, through advertising. Concluding, then, that want creation does not invalidate the assumption that a rise in national income carries with it an increase in welfare, he argues that if the evolution of wants is guided by standards that society regards as reflecting an improvement in the quality of wants, then want-creating activity such as advertising will evolve a rational set of guidelines that will direct demand toward goods that can meet wants most cheaply and profitably. Within this context, advertising becomes a logical tool of a high-income, mass consumption society.

Johnson's analysis leaves unanswered two critical questions. One is a matter of value judgment and the other a matter of economics. It is on the basis of value judgment that we must assess the role of advertising in the expansion and direction of human wants. The question is basically this: Are advertisers, motivated by their own economic interests, those *best* qualified to play a role in the direction and expansion of want patterns? This is particularly critical where advertising is directed toward children, that most sensitive and vulnerable segment of our society, whose lifetime values are being shaped by their exposure and experiences. We must be concerned both with what advertisers are attempting to do and with what they succeed in doing.

The economic question that must be answered does not avoid value judgments any more than any economic choice made in the market place, but it casts the question into a different framework: Are the nearly $25 billion spent for advertising each year the *best* use of those resources?

CONCLUSION

Since advertising is such an endogenous part of the market economy, on which we still depend for the largest percentage of our output in the United States, and is accepted, although not without considerable annoyance and concern, by most people in the United States, it is not likely that its abolition will be sought or would be tolerated. Were it abolished, alternative methods of promotion would be devised. The problem is essentially that of (1) learning to measure both its micro and macro effects so that it can be employed most efficiently from the viewpoint of both firm and society, and (2) imposing strong social controls that will eliminate or minimize the deleterious effects of advertising on social welfare.[34]

---

[34] See, for example, John A. Howard and James Hulbert, "Advertising and the Public Interest," A Staff Report to the United States Federal Trade Commission, February 1973, esp. chaps. VIII and IX.

19

Marketing Logistics: Merchandise Stocks

Time present and time past
Are both perhaps in time future,
And time future contained in time past.

—T. S. Eliot

The term *logistics* is borrowed from military science, where it refers to the details of transporting, quartering, and supplying troops. It includes the classification, movement, and evacuation of personnel; the production, distribution, and maintenance of matériel; and the construction, operation, and distribution of facilities. Thus it is concerned with the control of the physical resources employed in the conduct of military operations.

By definition marketing includes productive activities that result in transactions between buyers and sellers of goods and services. In this volume, we have focused on those activities associated with the transfer of title to goods, touching also on the transfer of services when these accompany the exchange of goods. We shall therefore restrict our use of the term *logistics* in marketing to those activities related (1) to the provision and maintenance of stocks of goods for potential buyers or users, (2) to the location of marketing enterprises and their stocks, and (3) to the movement of goods between buyers and sellers.

While increased specialization in the study of marketing has led to a sharpening of the dichotomy between the promotion-pricing-negotiatory functions of marketing, on the one hand, and the physical supply functions, on the other, students of marketing are increasingly recognizing the importance of the interrelationships between the interpersonal (and interinstitutional) and the physical aspects of marketing activity. The physical availability of goods to buyers is generally essential to the realization of their utility and, hence, to the completion of the marketing process. Marketing cannot be viewed as a coordinated system unless the functions of physical supply are incorporated into the model. For this reason, we do not share the view of some marketing scholars who have failed to give any consideration to physical functions in their discussion of the marketing system.

In a study of the management of physical supply and distribution, J. L. Heskett, Robert Ivie, and Nicholas Glaskowsky have estimated that the movement of goods in the U.S. economy accounted for about 9 percent of the gross national product in 1960 and the maintenance of inventories for about 6 percent.[1] Less than 0.5 percent should be added to this to cover managerial costs, bringing the total to slightly more than 15 percent of gross national product. Probably about half the costs of those firms that we identify as marketing firms are for the performance of these two functions of physical

---

[1] J. L. Heskett, Robert M. Ivie, and Nicolas A. Glaskowsky, Jr., *Business Logistics–Management of Physical Supply and Distribution* (New York: Ronald, 1964), pp. 10-17.

515

supply—the maintenance and movement of inventories.[2] These estimates suggest that logistical costs are a substantial portion of the total cost of marketing. In our discussion of marketing logistics, we shall first consider policies concerning the maintenance and replenishment of merchandise inventories. In the next chapter we shall explore policies concerning the location of marketing establishments and merchandise stocks and the movement of goods between buyers and sellers.

INVENTORY FUNCTIONS AND DECISIONS

In making decisions concerning the size and composition of inventories, marketing management will be seeking an optimum relationship among three important determinants of their inventory policy: the cost of getting goods to buyers, the convenience to buyers of having goods available at the time wanted (or the inconvenience of delay), and the value to buyers of a variety of stock as a source of market information. The objective will be to achieve an optimum combination of cost, convenience, and variety. We shall examine the nature of these objectives in terms of the functions of inventories. Our focus will be on the specialized marketing firm, although many of our generalizations would also be applicable to inventory policies in the manufacturing firm.

Functions of Inventories

Inventories are maintained because they are utility creating, cost reducing, and/or a medium for speculation.

UTILITY-CREATING FUNCTIONS

An inventory may serve as a buffer to compensate for (i.e., prevent the negative utility that would be associated with) discontinuities in production or in sales or consumption. Discontinuities may be due to predictable fluctuations that are related, for example, to seasonality of production or consumption or to uncertainties in which safety stocks are used to take care of unanticipated variations in production or consumption. Fluctuations in sales may arise from fluctuations in consumption or from variations in the rate of stock accumulation among the firm's customers.

A second utility-creating function of inventories is to serve as a source of market information for consumers by having available to them for inspection a variety of merchandise alternatives. Only samples need be held for this purpose, unless the information provided by the stocks available generates instant demand. Although the concept of "impulse buying" among ultimate consumers is fuzzy, studies of consumer behavior in such places as supermarkets suggests that consumers do in fact utilize merchandise stocks extensively as a source of market information.

---

[2] This is a very crude estimate based on (1) the Heskett-Ivie-Glaskowsky estimate of 15 percent of gross national product, less 4 percent, which is the cost of maintaining inventories by manufacturers and agricultural enterprises, and (2) the estimate by Cox for 1947, in which "distribution industries" are reported to account for 20.7 percent of the total contribution of all industries to the net national product, based on the input-output study for that year. Since this is an institutional approach to the calculation of the relative importance of physical costs in marketing, it does not necessarily yield the same results as would a functional cost calculation for the total economy. See Reavis Cox, *Distribution in a High-Level Economy* (Englewood Cliffs, N.J.: Prentice-Hall, 1965), pp. 123-130.

COST-REDUCING FUNCTIONS

Inventory costs can be used economically as compensating costs when they make possible lower costs in complementary functions. For example, it is sometimes desirable to incur the costs of holding inventories if they make it possible to place large orders and thereby achieve lower buying costs. In manufacturing it is sometimes possible to achieve lower processing costs as a result of holding goods in stock, which will make possible an even flow of materials through the production process. In these cases, the increase in costs resulting from the carrying of stocks must be less than the reduction in the complementary costs if the cost-reducing function of inventories is to be realized.

SPECULATIVE FUNCTIONS

The use of inventories for speculative purposes is related to buyers' or sellers' expectations of changes in costs and/or demand. If the holder of inventories is correct in his expectations, he will realize greater profits, if he is a firm, or a more favorable utility-cost ratio, if he is a consumer. This function is essentially one of arbitrage through time. If the effect of inventory speculation is a reduction in price variability over time, it reduces the degree of risk in market participation. If, on the other hand, it accentuates price fluctuations, it increases risk and may even inject added uncertainties. Some marketing firms prefer not to engage in speculative accumulation or decumulation of inventories but to specialize in the performance of other marketing functions as their source of profits. In our discussion we shall deal primarily with the utility-creating and cost-reducing functions of inventories rather than with their speculative possibilities.

Inventory Decisions

The two decisions that have to be made with respect to inventory are, (1) When should the inventory be replenished? and (2) How much should be added? Most firms establish some kind of policy that is related to one or both of two variables—when the inventory is equal to or less than some given quantity that is an optimum safety factor, or when a certain period has elapsed. The decisions concerning how much to add are also based on one or both of two variables—a specified lot size is ordered when the time to order has been reached, or the lot size to be ordered is that necessary to bring the inventory to some desired level. We shall show some examples of inventory control systems in which these variables are employed in making inventory replenishment decisions. Before describing these systems, however, we shall examine some of the factors that have a bearing on the choice of a firm's inventory policy.

FACTORS THAT INFLUENCE INVENTORY POLICIES

The characteristics of demand, costs, and replenishment are the important factors that bear upon the firm's inventory policies.[3] The symbols for the variables that we shall use in this discussion are as follows:

---

[3] This section and the one that follows have drawn extensively on Eliezer Naddor, *Inventory Systems* (New York: Wiley, 1966), pp. 21-44.

c_1 = unit carrying cost per unit of time

c_2 = unit shortage cost per unit of time

c_3 = unit replenishing cost per unit of time

C_1 = total carrying cost per unit of time

C_2 = total shortage cost per unit of time

C_3 = total replenishing cost per unit of time

L = lead time between the placing of an order and receipt of goods in stock

q = quantity ordered (replenishment quantity)

Q = inventory in stock at a given point in time

r = quantity demanded per unit of time (demand rate) ($r = x/t$)

t = period for which inventory is required

t' = replenishment period (period over which replenishment order is received)

T = a given point in time

x = quantity demand (total units sold) in a period

Demand Variability

The principal factors of importance in viewing the demand for goods as a determinant of inventories are the variability and predictability of demand over time. If the size of demand is the same from period to period, demand is constant and problems of inventory control are greatly simplified. Even if the demand is not constant, however, a deterministic inventory system is possible if the size and rate of change of demand are known. For example, if the amount or rate of growth is constant, or if accurate forecasts can be made of changes in demand, the system will be deterministic. If, however, the size of demand cannot be known in advance, management will probably have to work with a probabilistic system, provided that probabilities can be estimated. If necessary, subjective probabilities can be used based on the firm's historical experience.

Since the rate at which inventory disappears is a function of the rate at which customers demand goods, the demand rate (or sales rate) is a critical variable in a firm's inventory policy. We shall define the demand rate as the sales per unit of time:

$$r = x/t$$

in which r is the demand rate, x is sales (quantity demanded), and t is the period of time in which x sales occur. If t is one year, r would be sales per year. The amount of inventory on hand at any one point can be represented by

$$Q_{T_1} = Q_{T_0} - x$$

in which Q_{T_1} is the amount of inventory at time 1, Q_{T_0} is the amount of inventory at time 0, and x is the volume of sales during period t (T_0 to T_1). Figure 19.1 shows some of the ways in which these x sales might have reduced inventory during the course of period t. If the rate of depletion were uniform, stocks would decline as in (a). If sales all occurred at the beginning of the period, stocks would immediately drop from Q_{T_0} to $Q_{T_0} - x$, as in (b).

The opposite of (b), of course, would be a case in which all sales occur at the end of the period. If sales accelerated as time passed, the pattern might be as in (c). If the rate of sales decelerated as time passed, stocks would fall quickly at first and then less rapidly, as

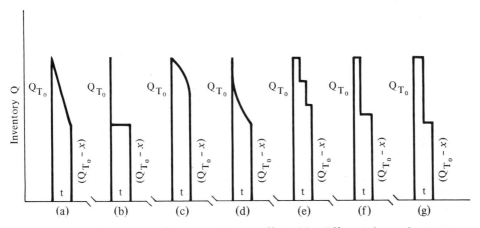

Figure 19.1. Some patterns of inventory size as affected by different demand rates.

in (d). Other patterns could also occur, as shown in (e), (f), and (g). The importance of these patterns lies in the fact that they have an important bearing on the amount of goods in stock at any one point in time and, hence, on the total cost of holding the stock for the period in question.

If the patterns of demand are deterministic, the costs of being out of stock need not occur. If the demand is probabilistic, such risks may be quite important. The total cost of being out of stock depends on whether or not shortages can be made up when inventories are replenished. If, for example, customers will wait for replenishment, then the marketing firm can recoup what would otherwise have been lost sales. If not, the sale is lost forever. Occasionally demand in one period will depend on stocks in the previous period. In this case, x then becomes a function of prior stocks. In order to simplify our presentation, we are not including price as a determining variable, but it is important to recognize that this will be an important influence on both past and present stocks. One other qualifying factor is the return-goods privilege. To the extent that this is possible, it would affect stocks in a given period independently of the firm's own system of inventory control.

Inventory Costs

There are three cost components for inventories—carrying cost, shortage cost, and replenishment cost—which together make up total inventory costs.[4] The carrying cost includes cost of the investment in inventories, storage, taxes on inventories, noninsurable physical depreciation, market obsolescence, and insurance of inventories. Carrying costs are usually expressed as a fraction of the total value of the inventory. Most studies show that these vary between 5 and 25 percent of inventory value, depending on both the volume of inventory and its nature.

---

[4] There is one extremely important cost that has to be incorporated into an inventory decision model that is not included in this discussion. This is the cost of merchandise, which is, of course, a function of unit price and number of units purchased. In the absence of monopsonistic or oligopsonistic market power, the buyer cannot control unit price but can affect total purchase cost by the number of units purchased at one time. This element of cost is not an "inventory cost" as we use the term in this section. We shall therefore reserve consideration of purchase cost of merchandise ordered for inventory to the following section, in which we discuss systems of inventory control.

Shortages can be viewed as cost creating or revenue decreasing. There is some advantage in viewing them as cost creating, for their impact on the firm's profitability can then be viewed in combination with other cost-creating aspects of inventory maintenance and acquisition. Inventory deficiencies can cause a loss of specific sales, of good will, and of customers. Their impact on present and future sales revenue will depend on both the degree and duration of the shortage.

It is not always easy to calculate the cost of inventory shortages. Most easily calculated is the short-term loss of gross margin associated with being out of stock. It is more difficult to know with precision what the long-run effects of an out-of-stock condition are on the firm's sales. One qualifying variable that may enter into the calculation of shortage costs is the possibility of recovering sales lost through inventory shortages by means of rapid inventory replacement. Even in this case, however, the temporary shortage may affect future sales.

Inventory Replenishment

Costs of replenishing inventories for the marketing firm are the ordering costs, including expenditures for clerical services, administration, transportation, unloading, and placing goods in stock. There are several variables that have to be taken into account in making replenishment decisions. One concerns the size of the order to be placed, while others relate to the scheduling of replenishment and the lead time that must be allowed between the placing of an order and receipt of the goods into stock. In the section that follows we shall consider in some detail the determination of economic purchase quantities under different inventory systems and the effects of lead time on the timing of replenishment orders.

SYSTEMS OF INVENTORY CONTROL

Inventory control systems are designed to enable the firm to control the placement of orders at the time and in amounts that will result in optimum inventories given the various costs that are subject to the firm's control, the variability in customer demand, and the conditions under which inventory replenishment must occur. While the firm can, through its product, pricing, and promotion policies, influence total sales and the demand rate, it is more reasonable to assume that the variables under its control are the costs associated with maintaining and replenishing its inventory stocks. If it is possible to do so, the firm will attempt to control all its inventory costs—carrying cost, shortage cost, and replenishing cost—in order to achieve optimal costs in relation to demand variability. Sometimes, however, one or two costs are controllable—such as carrying cost and shortage costs, or carrying cost and replenishing cost—while the third cost is not controllable. The more variables the firm includes in its inventory decision model, the more complex its inventory control system will become.

We introduce a few new concepts that we shall employ in decribing some types of inventory policies that firms have evolved for achieving desired results within the possibilities of cost control open to it. The following symbols will be used, in combination with those we have already introduced, in discussing systems of inventory control:

s = minimum stock (safety level) at which reordering occurs

S = maximum desired inventory level after replenishment

z = minimum stock on hand *and* on order at which reordering occurs when there is a time interval between placing an order and receiving goods in stock

Z = maximum desired inventory level after replenishment when there is a time interval between placing an order and receiving goods in stock (= stock on hand + stock on order + amount ordered)

Most policies of inventory control involve the designation of key values that will serve as trigger points to activate purchasing action which will achieve the desired inventory goals. For example, one key value is the stock level below which the firm is unwilling to see its actual inventory fall. This is the minimum stock, or safety level, which we shall designate s. One policy would be to place an order of a given size whenever the stock on hand declines to a prescribed safety level. This is known as an (s, q) inventory policy. Since the purpose of a safety stock is to take care of unexpected demand, under an (s, q) policy stock on hand may in fact fall below s if a review period is required to organize the ordering of replenishment stocks efficiently.[5] If there is a lead time involved in getting goods into stock after an order has been placed, this affects the s level that is used as the stock-ordering trigger point. Thus s becomes z, and the inventory policy becomes a (z,q) policy.

Another policy arrangement is to place an order at the end of a given period for whatever quantity is necessary to bring the inventory to a desired level. This is known as a (t, S) system. If there is a lead time, it becomes a (t, Z) system.

A third type of policy allows the period between orders to be variable, and the trigger point is the safety stock level, or s. When the amount of goods in stock reaches the s level, an order is placed for the quantity necessary to bring the inventory up to the desired stock level, S. This is known as an (s, S) policy. Again, where a lead time is involved the system is subject to a (z, Z) policy.

Still another policy requires the placing of orders for a given quantity at regular intervals. This simplistic approach is known as a (t, q) policy. Although not realistic for conditions under which demand is highly variable, the simplicity of the (t, q) policy makes it useful to illustrate some of the considerations that enter into the determination of an optimum t and q, and we shall employ the (t, q) policy for such purposes. In the following section we shall give some examples of inventory systems, indicating their characteristics and, in the case of the simpler systems, conditions of optimality.[6]

---

[5] Some years ago a young man was allowed to take the family boat for a Saturday fishing expedition with one of his friends. Late in the evening he had not returned, and his family became quite concerned. After much agitation, they were finally relieved to see the boat towed into dock by another boat. Their first question: "What in the world happened?" The boys said they had run out of gas and had to wait for another boat to come along and tow them in. "But didn't you know there was an extra can of gas stored in the back of the boat?" "Oh, yes, we knew that. But we thought that was for emergencies!"

[6] As a subject evolves, terminology and symbols employed tend to standardize. Some of this has occured in the field of inventory management and control. However, students of inventory management have come to the problem from many different backgrounds—engineering, economics, business management, operations research, etc.—with the result that terminology and symbols have not been standardized. While in this discussion we shall draw extensively on the presentation of Eliezer Naddor, a specialist in operations research, we have chosen to alter the labels that he has attached to various inventory systems in order to focus more sharply on terms that we believe would be more meaningful to the economist and marketing student. We have weighed carefully the probable utility of what we believe is more meaningful language for the clientele for whom we write against the probable disutility of imposing *our* preferred labels in a field that needs more, rather than less, consistency. We hope that our estimate of a net positive utility resulting from our decision is correct.

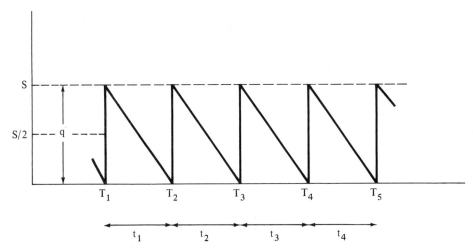

Figure 19.2. The classical order size (s, q) system in which $s = 0$.

Examples of Inventory Systems

DETERMINISTIC SYSTEMS

A deterministic system is one in which the quantity demanded and flow of demand through any given period (i.e., the demand rate) is known. A probabilistic system is one in which the amount demanded and its rate through time are not certain but can be described in terms of probabilities derived from either historical experience or subjective expectations. We shall first describe some deterministic systems.

1. *THE CLASSICAL ORDER-SIZE SYSTEM.* This is an (s,q) system in which $s = 0$. It could also be labeled a (q) system, since the problem is basically one of determining the optimum quantity to be ordered. This system was first analyzed by F. W. Harris in 1915.[7] Following the disturbing inventory experiences of 1921, several authors developed similar approaches to the determination of economical purchase quantities in the mid-1920s.[8]

The following assumptions are made in the classical order size system: (1) Demand is deterministic at a constant rate of r quantity units per unit of time. (2) Whenever inventory reaches zero, replenishments are made in a constant amount, q. (3) Lead time is zero. (4) The only costs to be consider are carrying costs (C_1) and ordering costs (C_3). (There is no C_2 cost because there is no need to be out of stock when demand is at a constant rate.) Figure 19.2 illustrates the pattern of inventory movement. When the amount of goods in stock equals zero, an order is placed for q units, which are instantaneously placed in stock, bringing the inventory level to the desired maximum, S. The demand for period t is known, and quantity q equals the amount that will be demanded

[7] Naddor, op. cit., p. 16.

[8] These include Benjamin Cooper, Ralph C. Davis, George F. Mellen, H. S. Owen, Gordon Pennington, R. H. Wilson, and W. A. Mueller, all of whom are cited in Thomas M. Whitin, *The Theory of Inventory Management* (Princeton, N.J.: Princeton University Press, 1953), p. 32.

during that period. Since the demand rate is constant, the inventory declines by a constant amount in each unit of time within period t. The average inventory in each time period is therefore $S/2$, which is also equal to $q/2$.

The problem is to determine the economic order size. This will be the quantity that will result in the lowest total inventory cost for the system. The two costs to be considered are the carrying cost and the ordering cost. The total cost that we shall consider is the total variable cost associated with the acquisition and maintenance of inventory, and we shall designate this as ΣVC, which is the sum of C_1 and C_3. C_1 is usually expressed as a percentage of the amount of goods in stock.

It will simplify our exposition, however, if we think of both unit carrying cost, c_1, and unit ordering cost, c_3, in terms of monetary units. Total carrying cost will be

$$C_1 = c_1(q/2)$$

or unit carrying cost times the average inventory. Total ordering cost will be

$$C_3 = c_3\left(\frac{x}{q}\right)$$

or the unit ordering cost times the number of orders placed.

The number of orders placed will, of course, be reflected in the total sales during the period in relation to the amount ordered each time an order is placed. Thus the total variable cost in this model will be

$$\Sigma VC = c_1\left(\frac{q}{2}\right) + c_3\left(\frac{x}{q}\right)$$

Differentiating total variable cost with respect to the amount ordered each time, we have

$$\frac{d(\Sigma VC)}{dq} = \left(\frac{c_1}{2}\right) - \left(\frac{c_3 x}{q^2}\right)$$

Setting this equal to zero in order to find the optimum quantity per order, we have

$$\left(\frac{c_1}{2}\right) - \left(\frac{c_3 x}{q^2}\right) = 0$$

Solving for q yields

$$q^* = \frac{\sqrt{2xc_3}}{c_1}$$

Thus the economic order volume varies directly with the square root of the cost of ordering merchandise and inversely with the square root of the carrying charges. Under these conditions, the minimum cost of the system can then be determined by substituting in the equation for the total cost of the system the economic order volume. Since

$$\Sigma VC = c_1\left(\frac{q}{2}\right) + c_3\left(\frac{x}{q}\right)$$

then

$$\Sigma VC = \frac{c_1\sqrt{2xc_3/c_1}}{2} + \frac{xc_3}{\sqrt{2xc_3/c_1}}$$

$$= \sqrt{2xc_3 c_1}$$

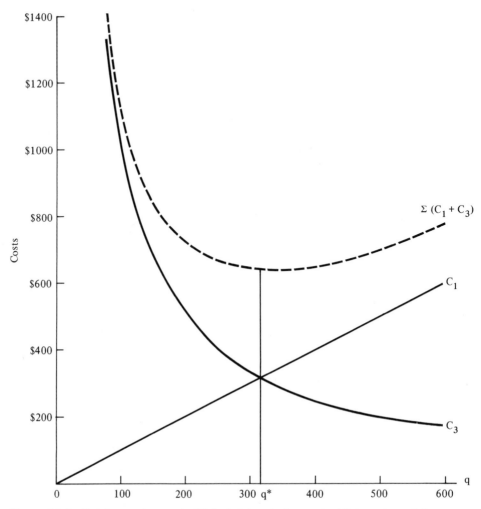

Figure 19.3. Total carrying costs (C_1), total ordering costs (C_3), and total inventory costs $[\Sigma(C_1 + C_3)]$ in a system in which $\Sigma VC = \$2(q/2) + \$100(x/q)$.

The relationship between these two components of inventory cost and quantity ordered is illustrated graphically in Figure 19.3. In this example, we have assumed that the total carrying costs per unit are $2. Since the average inventory during a period is $(q/2)$, orders of 100 units will result in total carrying costs of $c_1 (q/2)$, or $100. Orders of 200 will result in carrying costs of $200. We have assumed that the ordering cost is $100 per order and that sales during the period are 1,000 units. If 100 units are ordered per order, total ordering cost will be $c_3 (x/q)$, or $1,000. If 200 units are ordered each time, only 5 orders will need to be placed and total ordering costs will drop to $500. Total costs are the sum of ordering costs and carrying costs and are illustrated by $\Sigma(C_1 + C_3)$ in Figure 19.3. Quantity $q*$ is that order volume at which total inventory costs will be minimized. Whether or not the lowest cost point occurs where $C_1 = C_3$ will depend on the slopes of C_1 and C_3.

If a quantity discount is involved in the price paid for merchandise ordered, this must also be taken into account in determining the optimum order size. In Figure 19.4 we show the total inventory cost curve in section (A), in which orders above level q_1 are subject to a quantity discount. Without such a discount, q_0 would be the optimum order

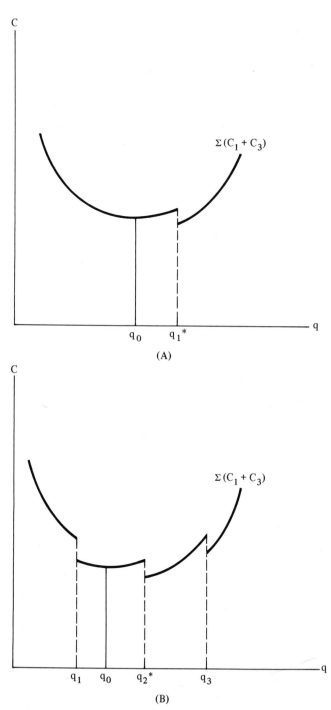

Figure 19.4. Total inventory cost curve, $\Sigma(C_1 + C_3)$, in a classical order size system where there is a single-quantity discount level (A) and a multiple-quantity discount level (B).

size. Since, however, the total cost at order size level q_1 is lower than at q_0, q_1 is the preferred order size. In section (B) of Figure 19.4, we show a situation in which quantity discounts are offered for orders of q_1, q_2, and q_3. Without quantity discounts, q_0 would be the optimum order size. With the quantiy discounts, however, q_2 becomes the

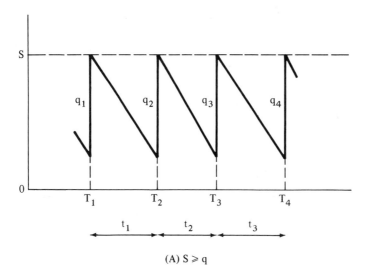

(A) $S \geqslant q$

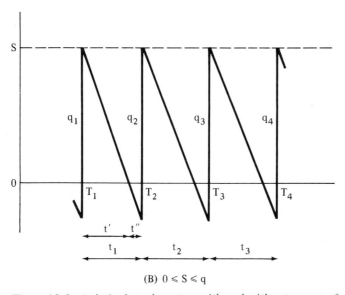

(B) $0 \leqslant S \leqslant q$

Figure 19.5. A desired-stock system with and without an out-of-stock condition.

lowest-cost order size with respect to the two variable costs we assume in the system we describe.

Although the assumptions of this highly simplified classical inventory model are seldom realized in practice, the generalization that it yields—that the optimum order quantity varies directly in relation to the square root of ordering cost and inversly with the square root of carrying charges—is often cited as "the" solution to the determination of order volume. In the following sections we comment briefly on some of the additional variables that can be incorporated into inventory control systems.

2. *THE DESIRED-STOCK SYSTEM.* This is a (t, S) system in which t is a constant. In Figure 19.5 we illustrate the operation of such a system. Orders are placed at regular intervals, T_1, T_2, T_3, and so on. If we assume a deterministic demand in which the quantity demanded is known and the rate of demand is constant, a given quantity will be ordered each time, and this is sufficient to bring the inventory to the desired level, S. In section (A) of Figure 19.5, we assume that the firm never runs out of stock. In section (B), however, we assume that during the period t_1 the firm will be in stock during subperiod t' but out of stock during subperiod t''. The problem, then, is to determine the optimum S level. We shall consider the case illustrated in section (B) of Figure 19.5, since this involves the cost of being out of stock.

The two costs in this situation are the cost of holding inventories, C_1, and the cost of being out of stock, C_2. Since the order size is constant and the ordering interval is contant, there is no variability in total costs associated with cost of ordering. We shall again employ the total variable cost of inventory formula, for which we shall need to determine the average inventory and the average shortage. Average inventory for period t_1 in section (B) of Figure 19.5 is the average inventory in subperiod t', weighted by the relative importance of t' to t_1, plus the average inventory in period t'', weighted by the relative importance of t'' to t_1. The average inventory in period t' is $S/2$. The average inventory in period t'' is zero. Therefore the average inventory in the two subperiods combined is $S/2$ weighted by the relative duration of t' in period t_1. Since $t'/t_1 = S/q$, we can substitute S/q for t'/t_1, and the average inventory in period t_1 is

$$\left(\frac{S}{2}\right) \left(\frac{t'}{t_1}\right) = \left(\frac{S}{2}\right) \left(\frac{S}{q}\right) = \frac{S^2}{2q}$$

Similarly, the average shortage during time t' is zero, while during t'' it is $(q - S)/q$, weighted by the relative importance of t'' to t_1. We find that $t''/t_1 = (q - S)/q$. Therefore the average shortage during period t_1 is

$$\left[\frac{q - S}{q}\right]\left[\frac{q - S}{q}\right] = \frac{(q - S)^2}{2q}$$

Total cost of the system then becomes

$$\Sigma VC = c_1 \left[\frac{S^2}{2q}\right] + c_2 \left[\frac{(q - S)^2}{2q}\right]$$

Differentiating with respect to S, we find that

$$\frac{\delta(\Sigma VC)}{\delta S} = c_1\left(\frac{S}{q}\right) - c_2 \left(\frac{q - S}{q}\right)$$

To find S^*, the optimum S level, we set the first differential equal to zero and solve for S:

$$c_1\left(\frac{S}{q}\right) - c_2\left(\frac{q - S}{q}\right) = 0$$

Therefore

$$S^* = q \frac{c_2}{c_1 + c_2}$$

Thus the optimum desired-stock level, S^*, is a function of the ratio of out-of-stock unit costs to total costs, weighted by the quantity ordered. The essence of this optimum quantity lies in the balancing of out-of-stock costs against carrying costs.[9]

3. *THE DESIRED-STOCK–ORDER-SIZE SYSTEM.* We have discussed the order-size system, that is, the (s, q) system in which $s = 0$. In this system, carrying costs, C_1, and ordering costs, C_3, are the controlling variables. We have also discussed the desired-stock system, that is, the (t, S) system in which t is a constant. In this case, the carrying costs and out-of-stock costs are relevant. We now combine these two into a desired-stock-order size system. This involves a (t, S) policy, an (s, q) policy, and an (s, S) policy. These three policies will not necessarily result in the same inventory decision. We shall simplify our consideration of these three alternative policy sets into a single set, which will be an extension of the (s, q) system, in which $s = 0$, and of the (t, S) system. We shall call this an (S, q) system, since the problem is to determine the optimum desired-inventory level, S^*, and the optimum order quantity, q^*.

The difference between this and the two simpler systems discussed earlier is that we now have three costs to consider—carrying costs, out-of-stock costs, and ordering costs.[10] Total costs for the situation described in section (B) of Figure 19.5 will be

$$\Sigma VC = \frac{c_1 S^2}{2q} + \frac{c_2 (q - S)^2}{2q} + \frac{c_3 s}{q}$$

Differentiating with respect to S and with respect to q, and setting these simultaneous equations equal to zero, the optimum quantity to be ordered and the optimum desired-inventory level become

$$q^* = \sqrt{2xc_3} \sqrt{\frac{c_1 + c_2}{c_1 c_2}}$$

$$S^* = \frac{q^* c_2}{c_1 + c_2} = \sqrt{\frac{2xc_3}{c_1}} \sqrt{c_2 (c_1 + c_2)}$$

---

[9] This may also be viewed in the following manner:

$$S^* = q\left(\frac{c_2}{c_1 + c_2}\right)$$

From this we can calculate the following equality:

$$S(c_1 + c_2) = q c_2.$$

Simplifying, we have:

$$c_1 S + c_2 S = q c_2,$$
$$c_1 S = c_2 q - c_2 S,$$
$$c_1 S = c_2 (q - S), \quad \text{and}$$
$$\frac{S}{q - s} = \frac{c_2}{c_1}$$

But we know that

$$\frac{t'}{t''} = \frac{S}{q - s}$$

Therefore,

$$\frac{t'}{t''} = \frac{c_2}{c_1}$$

[10] This is from Naddor, op. cit., pp. 80-81.

The minimum total cost is

$$C* = \sqrt{2xc_3} \sqrt{\frac{c_1 c_2}{c_1 + c_2}}$$

PROBABILISTIC SYSTEMS

In the systems that we have discussed, we have assumed that the sales volumes in the period for which inventory is planned were known and that the rate at which sales occur is constant. Most firms must formulate inventory plans without perfect knowledge of future demand. Additional variables may also enter into the inventory plan, depending on whether depleted inventories can be replenished continuously (e.g., gasoline) or must be replenished in discrete units (e.g., case lots of food), and on whether replenishments occur instantaneously or involve a lead time between the placement of orders and the receipt of goods in stock.

In Figure 19.6 we describe graphically and with brief comments how variations in demand and in lead time could affect the structuring of inventory control systems. This is not an exhaustive listing of possible variations, nor do we present the solution to problems posed by these alternative systems. An analysis of these and other systems can be found in Naddor[11] and in the classic study by Kenneth Arrow, Theodore Harris, and Jacob Marschak.[12]

A Comment on the Economics of Inventory Systems

These examples of systems of inventory control have been presented for two purposes. One is to demonstrate the extent to which inventory systems are amenable to analysis within the framework of mechanistic systems of the type that have been developed in operations research. A second purpose is to show the relevance of economic cost analysis to the inventory problem. In the classical order size system, for example, declining costs of ordering must be evaluated against increasing costs of carrying inventories as order size increases. Similarly, in the determination of optimum S levels in a (t, S) system in which reordering intervals are held constant, we can observe the balancing of rising carrying costs, as inventories increase, against the lower out-of-stock costs. In all of these cases, the marginal costs govern the optimum, and these are a function of a combination of rising and falling costs as the total system responds to varying quantities ordered or varying frequency of orders to achieve the objectives of desired or minimum stocks.

HOUSEHOLD INVENTORIES

Up to this point, our discussion has focused on the inventory policies of business firms. This, however, neglects a significant area of inventory decisions—those concerning goods to be owned and/or held by households. The importance of these stocks of goods, the

---

[11] Ibid.

[12] Kenneth J. Arrow, Theodore Harris, and Jacob Marschak, "Optimal Inventory Policy," *Econometrica* 19 (July 1951): 250-272.

conditions that determine their size and composition, and their implications for marketing are important aspects of the role of inventories in the marketing system.[13]

Dimensions of the Household Stock Problem

The goods owned and/or held by households are generally called consumer goods. Although we shall follow this custom, it is worthwhile to point out that not all household

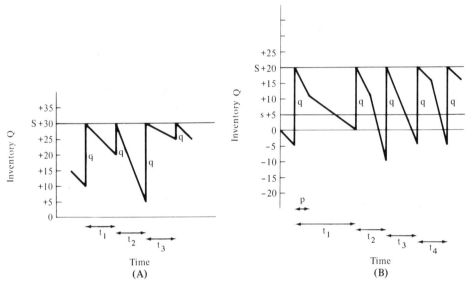

Figure 19.6. Four probabilistic inventory systems. Source: Based on Eliezer Naddor, *Inventory Systems* (New York: Wiley, 1966).

(A) Probabilistic Desired-Stock and Scheduling-Period System Without Lead time. This is a (t, S) system designed never to be out of stock. An order is placed at regular intervals in amounts sufficient to bring goods in stock to the desired inventory level, S. Thus, q will vary. The problem is to determine the optimum time interval that will avoid an out-of-stock condition and result in minimum costs based on carrying costs and ordering costs. The system described in this graph assumes instantaneous movement of goods ordered into stock. The system could be extended to take into account the lead time necessary to get orders into stock.

(B) Probabilistic Minimum-Stock and Desired-Stock System Without Lead Time. This is an (s, S) system. The example given here assumes no leadtime. In this example, the desired stock is 20 units and the safety level 5 units. Sales are in units of 5. Thus, $S = 20$, $s = 5$, $u = 5$. At the end of each review period, p, an order is placed if the stock is at or below the s level. The amount ordered, q, is variable and is enough to bring the stock level to the desired S level. Both q and t will vary, depending on the actual stock level. The problem will be to determine the optimum S and/or the optimum s. Conversion of the system to a (z, Z) system, which would take into account lead time, would introduce an additional dimension.

---

[13]For some reason the term *stocks* has come to be used for "inventories" held by households or consumers. Since we view the economic attributes of business inventories and of household stocks in the same light, we shall use the terms *inventories* and *stocks* interchangeably for all market participants.

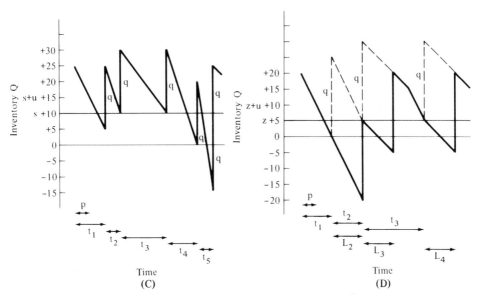

Time
(C)

Time
(D)

(C) Probabilistic Minimum-Stock and Order-Size System Without Lead Time.
This is an (s, q) system in which the minimum stock is established on the assumption that an order that is placed will enter the stockpile instantaneously. In the example given here, the safety level is 10, all sales are in units of 5, and all orders are in units of 20 ($s = 10$; $u = 5$; $q = 20$). The review period is p. At the end of each review period, the inventory is examined to determine whether an order should be placed. An order will be placed if the inventory level is at or below the safety level, s. The order is placed for each t period. The number of q's ordered is that necessary to bring the inventory up to or above the safety level. The problems to be solved are the determination of the optimal order size and/or the optimal safety level.

(D) Probabilistic Minimum-Stock and Order-Size System with Lead Time.
This is a (z, q) system in which the minimum stock is established in consideration of the lead time necessary between the placement of an order and its receipt in stock. This lead time safety level is designated as z. In the example given here, $z = 5$, $u = 5$, and $q = 25$. The planning period is p, and $L = 2p$. An order will be placed if the goods in stock plus the goods on order are equal to or less than the safety level, z. The number of q's ordered is that necessary to bring the inventory plus the goods on order up to or above the safety level. The problems to be solved are the determination of the optimal order size and/or the optimal safety level.

goods are "consumer goods" in the strictest sense. There is a significant difference, for example, in the purposes for which members of a household own clothing and those for which they own a clothes washer. Although for the moment we shall not distinguish between these components of household inventories, in a later section we shall make some observations about the implications of this differentiation for marketing.

The volume of assets held by consumers in the form of stocks of goods has been estimated from time to time.[14] Most estimates have concentrated on the net value of

---

[14] Durable goods and housing are the components most frequently estimated, although attempts have been made at various times to include also estimates of semi- and nondurable assets. See, for example, the studies by Raymond W. Goldsmith: *The National Wealth of the United States in the Postwar Period*, Studies in Capital Formation and Financing no. 10, National Bureau of Economic Research

housing and durable goods owned by consumers, or on fianancial assets, including both liquid assets and equities in corporate enterprises.[15] One estimate placed financial assets, durable goods, and housing owned by consumers at $3.0 trillion on December 31, 1971, and the net worth of consumers at $2.6 trillion.[16] This excludes the value of semi- and nondurable goods owned by households.

The second dimension of consumer stocks is their composition. What kinds of goods do consumers own and hold in their inventories? We shall explore this aspect of consumer stock holdings—not in terms of quantities but, rather, in terms of the factors that influence the patterns of asset diversification.

Determinants of the Size and Composition of Consumer Stocks

In our discussion of business inventories, we identified the functions of inventories as utility creating, cost reducing, and speculative. The same functions are fulfilled by consumer stocks. Consumers hold stocks because the presence of such stocks is necessary for their services to be obtained, because ownership or possession may make it possible to obtain the services of goods at lower unit cost, or because stocks provide a speculative medium for either maximization of the utility-cost ratio of goods or an increase in the consuming unit's flow of real income over time. We shall now consider the factors in the consumer's milieu that affect the way in which these functions become operative and, hence, the way in which consumers arrive at their stock decisions.

CONSUMER PREFERENCES FOR HOUSEHOLD STOCKS

Households hold stocks of goods primarily for the services that such stocks can render as a source of satisfaction for consumer members of the household or for their usefulness in household operation. Stocks of both durables and nondurables assure the availability of such services at the time wanted. The usefulness of stocks of nondurables to consumers rests primarily on the convenience of having such stocks available. With durables, however, a stock is not merely convenient. Its existence is a necessity if any utility is to be realized by the user at one point in time. Durables whose services are consumed

---

(Princeton, N.J.: Princeton University Press, 1962); *A Study of Saving in the United States*, 3 vols. (Princeton, N.J.: Princeton University Press, 1955-1956); and (with Robert E. Lipsey) *Studies in the National Balance Sheet of the United States*, Vol. 1, Studies in Capital Formation and Financing no. 11, National Bureau of Economic Research (Princeton, N.J.: Princeton University Press, 1963). Some of these data have been extended in Edna Douglas, "The Structure of Consumer Assets: An Exploratory Study," *Journal of Marketing Research* 3 (August 1966): 293-310. This article also contains a detailed bibliography of studies of consumer assets.

[15] Financial assets have been examined in such studies as Dorothy S. Projector and Gertrude S. Weiss, *Survey of Financial Characteristics of Consumers* (Washington, D.C.: Board of Governors of the Federal Reserve System, 1966); Robin Barlow, Harvey E. Brazer, and James N. Morgan, *Economic Behavior of the Affluent* (Washington, D.C.: Brookings, 1966); and the annual *Survey of Consumer Finances* of the Survey Research Center, University of Michigan (Ann Arbor: University of Michigan, Institute for Social Research, Survey Research Center, annual through 1970, biennial 1971-1972).

[16] The National Consumer Finance Association based its estimates on the financial assets reported by the Board of Governors of the Federal Reserve System in its flow-of-funds accounts. To this estimate it adds its own estimates of the value of homes and durable goods owned by households. National Consumer Finance Association, "Consumer Balance Sheet," *Finance Facts*, April 1, 1972, p. 1, and S. Lees Booth to Edna Douglas, February 4, 1971.

continually are often most economically owned by the consumer, although increasingly these are made available through rental markets.[17]

A second source of utility to consumers from holding stocks of goods is their symbolic value as measures of status. There is too much evidence from sociological studies of consumer preference structures to ignore this additional aspect of consumer stock accumulation. Goods held in consumer stocks are particularly useful for these ostentatious purposes, for not only can they be made conspicuous, but the cost of conspicuousness per "showing" can be minimized by a stock that is reusable for many such showings.

There are two additional aspects of the household's demand for goods to be held in stock that are of considerable importance to sellers of such goods. One is the differentiation between new demand, in which households that never before held such stocks buy goods to be placed in inventory, and replacement demand, in which households buy goods to replace expiring stocks. These two types of demand pose quite different problems for marketers of storable goods.

Another aspect of consumer preferences is associated with the historical development of stock preferences. As either a household or an economy matures, consumer preference patterns unfold in a way that reflects the consumer's desire for increasing diversity in the services he obtains from goods. The evidence of this desire for diversity manifests itself in both the total size of inventories as affluence increases and the increasing diversity within inventories. Not only is diversity sought, but a balance is desired among the assets held. These patterns have been explored as they relate to the balance between liquid and nonliquid assets, and between the components of asset clusters.[18]

In Table 19.1 we show the estimated consumption expenditures for durable goods as a percentage of total consumption expenditures in 1965 for the United States and 12 OECD countries. Some of the differences noted are probably related to differences in the national accounts of the various countries. There would, however, appear to be a positive relationship between level of per capita income and percentage spent for durables, but there is by no means a perfect relationship. One could argue that the percentage should be highest at the point(s) in an economy's development where consumers are able to add significantly to their stocks, and this would occur prior to the time at which economic maturity is achieved. Also, one would need to consider the kinds of durables being purchased. Expenditures in a mature economy could be quite high for "new" durables (e.g., TV, second cars), while they might be equally high as a proportion of total expenditures in a developing economy that is accumulating "old" durables (ranges, refrigerators, washing machines). The cyclical variability in durable goods sales would, of course, make data for a single year less than adequate to show the average relationship

---

[17] For example, household appliances are often made available to household tenants on a rental basis. Laundromats are a means of providing washer and dryer services on an ad hoc rental basis. Automobile rentals, while still predominately for business use, are being used increasingly by ultimate consumers.

[18] See, for example, Douglas, op. cit.; Gregory C. Chow, *Demand for Automobiles in the United States: A Study in Consumer Durables*, Contributions to Economic Analysis, vol. XIII (Amsterdam: North-Holland, 1957); Jan S. Cramer, "Ownership Elasticities of Demand," *Review of Economic Studies* 25 (February 1958): 87-96; Jan S. Cramer, *The Ownership of Major Consumer Durables*, University of Cambridge, Department of Applied Economics, Monograph no. 7 (Cambridge: Cambridge University Press, 1962); Harold W. Watts and James Tobin, "Consumer Expenditures and the Capital Account," in Irwin Friend and Robert Jones, eds., *Study of Consumer Expenditures, Incomes and Savings*, vol. II (Philadelphia: University of Pennsylvania, Wharton School of Commerce and Finance, 1960), pp. 1-48.

Table 19.1 Estimated Consumption Expenditures for Durable Goods in the United States and 12 OECD Countries as a Percentage of Total Consumption Expenditures, 1965

Country[a]	Percentage
Denmark	17.2[b]
Netherlands	14.1
United States	12.4
Sweden	12.3
Belgium	11.8
Canada	10.9
Norway	10.9
Spain (1964)	10.4
Ireland	9.8
France	9.1
United Kingdom	9.0
Greece (1962)	5.9
Italy	5.4

[a]OECD countries excluded are those whose national income accounts did not include data on durable goods expenditures.

[b]Includes maintenance of private vehicles.

Source: Calculated from *National Accounts Statistics,* 1956-1965 (Paris: Organisation for Economic Cooperation and Development, 1967).

over a longer span of years. It is interesting to note, however, that the high expenditure ratios were two or more times the low ratios.

INCOME-PRICE RELATIONSHIP

One of the most important influences on the size and compostion of consumer stocks is income flow, and particularly flow of income over a period in relation to the price of the product. Serving both to make possible and to constrain purchases of goods, income can be related to size of stocks through measures of stock elasticity of demand with respect to income. Durables that have become an accepted part of the level of consumption of most people tend to show relatively low ownership elasticities, while those in which rate of ownership in the standard of consumption greatly exceeds that in the level of consumption (i.e., aspiration level exceeds achievement level) are those that will tend to show high income elasticities and can appropriately be classified as luxuries. Since purchasing power may be derived from sources other than income—for example, liquid assets or credit—these too may be significant variables explaining the size of stocks.

INVENTORY COSTS

Households, no less than business firms, are faced with a variety of inventory costs when they maintain stocks of goods for future consumption. We grouped business inventory costs into three categories—carrying cost, out-of-stock costs, and ordering costs. Consumer costs that parallel these are carrying costs—insurance, taxes if any, interest on "investment" for future consumption, depreciation of goods while being held in stock, and management of stocks; the real cost of an out-of-stock condition through lost utility;

and ordering costs—the cost of placing an order, receiving or obtaining goods, and placing the goods in the household stock.

We exclude from household inventory costs any expenditure that is in the nature of a "capital" expenditure—for example, a proportionate share of original cost imputed to a given period—and current operating costs—those expenditures essential to obtain current services from a durable good that renders services over both current and future periods. Often, however, durables held in consumer inventories require expenditures for maintenance merely to keep them in operating condition. As a colleague once observed after a year's leave of absence, "washing machines just don't like to sit around unused." Maintenance costs incurred to preserve the utility-generating ability of goods in stock are appropriately identified as inventory costs, since their purpose is to offset what would otherwise be depreciation.

One of the most neglected costs of consumer inventories is the cost of management. Part of the management function concerns control over the physical aspects of keeping goods on hand; part concerns the decision-making activities associated with acquiring, maintaining, and using stocks of goods. Sometimes the management function can be purchased, but generally members of households perform the management functions themselves and the cost becomes, therefore, a real cost. While there may be some economies of scale in household inventory management as stocks grow up to some point, beyond that point diseconomies are likely to arise as the amount, and hence the variety, of goods in stock becomes greater. We know too little about the conditions under which household management occurs and the economies and diseconomies associated with this aspect of stock ownership.

SPECULATION

A fourth factor that underlies consumer decision making with respect to stocks of household goods is the speculative potential of such stocks. Stocks may be accumulated in anticipation of rising prices, increasing needs, or both. If secular increases in prices are anticipated, this may encourage stock accumulation. Also, cyclical fluctuations in purchases of consumer durables are sometimes based in part on cyclical price expectations. Equally important is seasonal variability in prices and the opportunities that this gives for speculative stock accumulation of both nondurables and durables during periods of low seasonal price levels. When possibilities for speculative buying opportunities are combined with anticipated increases in consumer demand in the future, as, for example, during various stages in the family life cycle, the ratio between present cost and anticipated future utility, compared with anticipated future cost and future utility, may stimulate speculative investment in inventories.

Implications for Marketing Policies

The factors underlying consumer stock accumulations and the resulting patterns of diffusion and ownership have important implications for marketing policy. The diffusion of stock ownership among households requires response and adaptation of marketing policies to a new and growing clientele. When market maturity has been achieved, sales then depend largely on replacement rates and multiple ownership, which are governed by quite different forces. The introduction of new and different products or the increased differentation of existing products is likely to reflect sellers' response to greater sales stabilization, as will also the firm's pricing and promotion policies. The discrepancy between current consumer sales and current consumption of a durable good forces sellers to be unusually sensitive to the longer-run implications of a particular sales trend. Cyclical fluctuations in durable goods sales are quite marked, reflecting the accelerator effect of changes in the number in use and the consumer's ability to determine the time at which replacement purchases will be made. Consumers' stock decisions also affect the location of the storage function in the trade channel. Hand-to-mouth buying of nondurables shifts the storage function to the retailer, while this may not be feasible for durables, which are discrete "capital" units capable of rendering service for many years. But in this case, access to and ownership of a durable can be separated through a leasing policy. If the holding of inventories carries considerable risk for the retailer when, for example, the probability of style obsolescence is high, he can shift the storage function forward to consumers through the pricing of his merchandise.

Marketing policy will be based in part on consumers' decisions with respect to their ability to hold and desire to have consumer stocks that make it possible for them to get a unique service when that service can be obtained only from such a stock, and to have optimum convenience, flexibility, and variety in arriving at future consumption decisions. The other important cluster of influences will be the revenue, cost, and profit accruing to the marketing firm in maintaining a stock relationship that is complementary to that of households.

SOME SOCIAL ISSUES IN INVENTORY BEHAVIOR

Inventories and the Product Life Cycle

The optimum inventory size and rate of investment in inventory varies through the product life cycle. During the early stage of product introduction, inventories are likely to be accumulated in anticipation of sales. During the expansion phase of the cycle, stocks are increased but need not be increased in proportion to the increase in sales. Stocks needed to avoid an out-of-stock condition are the crucial variable during the period of expansion. When a product has achieved market maturity, however, the risk of overstock becomes dominant. At that point, replacement sales become a larger percentage of total sales. If the good is durable, the exercise of consumer discretion concerning the point in time when replacements will be made injects an additional element of uncertainty into the situation so that short-term stock surpluses and shortages may occur. If demand for a product declines, inventories rise and price reductions are likely to take place.

In this cycle, inventories are a signal that triggers adaptive or corrective action. Accurate information on purchases for use or sale versus purchases for stock is essential for market experience to be properly interpreted. The greater the length of the trade channel, the more critical this information is for planning at those levels most removed from the consumer. As the rate of product innovation increases, sales uncertainties associated with such innovations increase the difficulty of determining and achieving optimum inventories. Failure to achieve inventory optimality through the product life cycle is one of the costs of innovation.

Inventory control of fashion merchandise is particularly affected by high risks of overstock and understock. Effective sales forecasting techniques are critical to the achievement of optimum inventories for this type of good. In their absence the greatest need is for rapid inventory data to permit rapid corrective action. As is the case with

Table 19.2 Book Value of Manufacturing and Trade Inventories, December 31, 1969, and Ratio of Average End-of-Month Inventory (I) to Monthly Sales (S), 1969

Type of Firm or Establishment	Inventories		I/S Ratio
	Amount in Billions	Percentage	
Total, all firms and establishments	$164.9	100	1.53
Manufacturing, total	$ 95.9	58	1.69
Durable goods firms	$ 63.5	38	1.99
Nondurable goods firms	32.4	20	1.31
Retail trade, total	$ 44.6	27	1.47
Durable goods stores	$ 20.0	12	2.05
Nondurable goods stores	24.6	15	1.19
Merchant wholesalers, total	$ 24.4	15	1.19
Durable goods establishments	$ 14.6	9	1.53
Nondurable goods establishments	9.8	6	.89

Source: *Survey of Current Business* 51 (January 1971): S-5.

innovation in general, inventory losses associated with the fashion cycle are a cost of style innovations.

One of the most effective techniques for achieving corrective action in fashion merchandise is through changes in prices. Widespread use of high margins during the period of introduction and early expansion, selective price reductions as the peak is approached, and extensive and intensive cuts in price as the rate of stockturn declines mean that the seller of such goods must calculate total margin vis-à-vis total inventory costs within the span of the complete fashion cycle in order to assess short-term policies properly. Over the longer term this calculation could be cast into a probabilistic mold if experience permits generalization with respect to the distribution of consumer acceptances versus rejections of large numbers of style innovations.

PRODUCT PROLIFERATION

From a social point of view, one of the most serious problems that has resulted from product innovation is related to the increase in product diversification and the proliferation of product lines. This has led to the spreading of sales volume over a greater variety of items. The larger the sales of a particular item, the lower the inventory can be without risk of lost sales due to an out-of-stock condition. If, however, sales are spread over several items, each with a small proportion of the total, the stock of each must be larger, relative to sales, then would be true were sales concentrated on a single item.

Suppose that we have a product whose expected sales per period are 100 units. The desired stock at the beginning of the period is 115 units in order to protect against an out-of-stock condition, which was the approximate ratio for nondurable goods retail stores in 1969. (See Table 19.2.) Suppose that substitute items are placed on the market and that these substitutes absorb and divide among themselves the total demand of 100 units that was formerly met by the original product. We shall call these new items A, B, and C. Unit sales are as follows: A, 50; B, 30; C, 20. How much stock will sellers have to carry in order to reduce to zero, or some desired percentage, the risk of an out-of-stock condition? The answer will depend, of course, on the variability of sales and the degreee of accuracy with which management is able to forecast that variability. In general, the

Table 19.3 An Example of the Relationship Between Sales Volume and Inventories Where the Objective Is to Reduce the Risk of Becoming Out of Stock to a Predetermined Level

Item	Sales	Inventory	I/S Ratio
Original	100	115	1.15
New			
A	50	60	1.20
B	30	40	1.33
C	20	30	1.50
Total	100	130	1.30

ratio of stock to sales that is required to avoid loss of sales due to stock deficiency increases as the volume of sales decreases.

This is illustrated with hypothetical data in Table 19.3, where we show higher stock/sales ratios as volume of sales declines.[19] While the original item could sustain sales of 100 units with a beginning stock of 115, the substitution of new items A, B, and C for the original caused the stock requirements to rise to 130 units. The risk of being out of stock in the new competitive situation is enhanced if A, B, and C are substitutes for one another, as they are if each is an alternative to the original item. Were we to assume that we place a single order for the desired stock for each period prior to the beginning of the sales period for which we are budgeting inventory, we would then be introducing the additional question of the optimum order quantity into our problem. If this is also taken into account, the required order quantity, and hence inventory, would increase still more as we move from the larger concentrated demand to smaller and smaller segments of demand, for there is a direct relationship between the optimum order quantity and the square root of sales.

The implications of the trend toward product differentiation and brand proliferation for the inventory problem cannot be overemphasized. Its effects are particularly apparent in the supermarket field, where store size, measured by both stocks and sales, has increased tremendously. Not only do more items and more brands mean that more stocks must be carried, but stock-sales ratios of particular items must increase. This pressure for high stock-sales ratios may be compensated for by larger stores, which find themselves out of stock of particular items but in a position to offer some alternatives. Also, a large store has greater sales of each of the particular items it sells, thus reducing the required inventory for each of those items compared with what would have been necessary in a smaller store. Thus large stores have found that their size offsets some of the disadvantages of increased width of total offerings. Improvements in inventory control systems have also helped offset the effects of product proliferation on inventory requirements. Stock-sales ratios tended to decline secularly up to the mid-1950s, and after the mid-1950s they did so in manufacturing. Improved inventory control systems in retailing and wholesaling and increasing size of marketing firms following the mid-1950s apparently held the line against the pressure for larger inventories associated with a wider range of product types and varieties. It is reasonable to conjecture that in the absence of product and brand proliferation stock-sales ratios would have declined.

---

[19] See the discussion by John F. Magee, "The Logistics of Distribution," *Harvard Business Review* 38 (July-August 1960): 89-101.

THE PROMOTIONAL IMPACT OF INVENTORIES

In our discussion of the firm's inventory policies, we have concentrated on the determination of optimum order quantities and inventory size, given the structure of demand and of costs of acquiring and maintaining inventories. In the inventory models we have used, the structure of demand is given, and it is assumed to be known precisely or as a probability distribution. But we know that the goods carried in stock can affect demand. This is true for both business demand and consumer demand, and particularly the latter. We shall consider two facets of this from the viewpoint of both industrial and consumer buyers and then show how these, in combination with other factors, have an effect on the size of marketing firms and market areas.

Stock width has two advantages for the buyer: (1) It increases the probability that he will be able to find items of merchandise with characteristics and terms of sale that will match his predetermined demand. (2) It increases the amount of information that he can obtain from shopping. By inspecting a wide variety of goods, a shopper obtains a tremendous amount of information about product quality and market alternatives, and is more likely to find the cluster of product attributes and the price that he desires. The wider the stock, the greater the information and the greater the probability of success in finding the desired item. But the larger the stock, the greater the cost the consumer will incur in assessing it, although it may be possible for the buyer to arrange his stock review in such a way that he achieves economies of scale, as, for example, in reviewing stocks for many types of items on a single market trip. Beyond some point of lowest unit cost, however, the more stock there is to survey, the more each additional discovery will cost.

How much utility the buyer gets from further searches among stocks depends in part on the distribution of stock characteristics among the total stock in the market. If the distribution is normal—for example, if most brands cluster around the mean and fewer and fewer are found as the extremes are approached—continuing inspection of a probability sample of stocks would, after a certain point, yield information with rapidly diminishing marginal utility to the buyer unless uniqueness is of great value. The higher the premium the buyer places on uniqueness, the greater the cost he is willing to incur to find it.[20]

But stocks are rarely distributed randomly in a market area. Most consumers have some prior information about where the desired stock, or the desired stock information, is most likely to be found. If, therefore, buyers organize their stock inspections in such a way that they inspect first those stocks that are most likely to provide the information desired, or to have the predetermined merchandise characteristics, then successive inspections are even more likely to yield information with rapidly declining marginal utility. Certainly if too much merchandise is inspected, it can contribute confusion rather than enlightment to the buyer's decision making.

It is important to recognize, however, that the informational function of merchandise stocks can be met by other means. Branding and advertising, for example, are alternatives. Nevertheless, there is a good deal of evidence that buyers do use merchandise displays as a means of getting market information. This is apparent in industrial and consumer trade shows as well as in the extensive consumer involvement in merchandise inspection in retail stores.

---

[20] A Swedish economist reported orally on a study of buying practices of Swedish retail buyers in which it was found that many buyers were willing to see and talk to every single salesman who came to their place of business. The reason was they were afraid to miss out on a possibly unique item that one of the salesmen might have.

An important question is how much stock width is needed for the optimum matching and informational function of inventories to be realized. Surprisingly enough, not very much stock is probably required for these two functions to be performed. The reason is that samples would suffice. But samples do not suffice in other respects. Stock depth is also desired. Stock depth—the carrying of similar items within a given merchandise line—has the advantage to the customer of ensuring immediate delivery, or at least of reducing the probability of an out-of-stock condition.

We have already introduced the information-generating aspects of stocks in our inventory models by including the cost of being out of stock in some of our models. We have noted that an out-of-stock condition affects sales, not only at the time the out-of-stock condition occurs but also in future periods. If, for example, customers believe that a store will always have goods in stock, this can be a very strong factor in its ability to attract shoppers. In this way, stock depth, through its effect on customer expectations, can affect sales volume. Stock depth may, however, affect sales in still another way. Mass displays of merchandise have a promotional impact. Twenty cases of Campbell's soups on the shelf may result in far more sales than ten cases, even though forward and reserve stocks total the same in both instances. How much impact mass displays of many goods have on *total* store sales is not well established by empirical studies. But sales of *particular* brands have been found to be strongly influenced by the amount and location of shelf space allocated to them, and this is one basis for competition among sellers of branded products—competition for shelf space and for optimum location of that space. It also seems reasonable to believe that the store with a reputation for having both wide and deep inventories will be able to attract customers more readily than stores without these larger inventories.

The impact of stock width and depth on sales, in retailing particularly, has probably contributed to the increasing size of stores. Up to a point, larger stores can display larger varieties of goods and maintain greater stock depth, and these are likely to have a favorable effect on the store's ability to attract customers and promote sales. Beyond some optimum point, however, mass displays serve to confuse customers, or to entail search costs that customers will find prohibitive. Only if economies of stock acquisition and holding are sufficient to result in lower prices that more than offset the higher customer buying costs will consumers be willing to incur the increasing inconvenience of making their selections from an ever widening and deepening stock of goods. From the buyer's point of view, optimum width and depth is essentially a question of the trade-off between the value to him of the functions performed by width and depth—information and matching, and rapidity of physical possession-and the cost of fulfilling those functions—the net cost to marketing firms of maintaining width and depth and to consumers of assessing such stocks. But from the seller's point of view, stock width and depth is also a means of differentiating the firm. If buyers desire greater stock selection, sellers who provide it have a competitive advantage. This aspect of inventory policy, in which inventories are used as a form of nonprice competition, should be analyzed as a nonprice decision concerning quality of services offered. The promotional aspects of inventories should not be evaluated in lieu of their inventory considerations but, rather, in addition to other factors that enter into the determination of optimum inventory policy.

Much of what we have said about marketing firms or establishments applies also to trading centers. One of the variables that will attract buyers to a trading center is the range of its merchandise offerings and the timing of product availability. In this sense, the total of all inventory policies of all sellers in the trading center determines the inventory pattern for the center and affects the ability of the center to attract customers.

Inventories and Business Cycles

One of the most important effects of variations in business inventories is their role in cyclical fluctuations in the economy. This is true in spite of the fact that inventories account for a very small percentage of total assets. Their impact is felt through *changes* in the volume of inventories held rather than through their absolute level. Accumulation of (investment in) inventories and reduction of (disinvestment in) inventories are important components of variations in the demand for total output. These variations affect the level of production and, through feedbacks in the economy, the level of spending. We shall examine the basis for these interactions and the empirical evidence that has been obtained on inventory investment movements and their relationship to business cycles.

The model that we shall describe is essentially that of L. A. Metzler, in which actual inventory investment in any period is the sum of planned inventory investment plus unplanned change due to the difference between actual sales and anticipated sales.[21]

PRODUCTION-SALES-INVENTORY RELATIONSHIPS

In Figure 19.7, which is taken from Paul G. Darling, the relationships among production, sales, and inventory investment are illustrated. The model has been structured in terms of the aggregate output of the entire economy.[22] Similar relationships can be observed within a single firm. In order to present some of the feedback relationships, we shall view the problem in terms of the total economy. The output of goods and services flows through the production valve and enters the vat within which inventories of goods are stored. The greater the demand for goods and services, the wider the demand valve will be opened, and the greater the volume of sales. When production exceeds final sales, inventories increase; when final sales exceed production, inventories decrease.

In the model presented here the desired level of inventories depends on final sales. Thus if sales increase, the splashboard moves to the right, the cord on the pulley is extended to the right, and the index card that indicates the desired level of inventories rises, indicating that the desired level of inventories has increased because of higher sales. In this case, decision makers in the economy will try to increase the flow of goods into the inventory vat by opening the production valve wider. If, on the other hand, sales fall off, the splashboard moves to the left, the index card is lowered into the inventory vat, and the desired level of inventory falls below the actual level. Production will be curtailed by closing the production valve to some degree or by opening the demand valve if sellers are in a position to stimulate demand.

Up to this point, we have ignored an important interrelationship. Whenever production is increased, this leads to an increase in income and in demand. Inventories can stimulate an increase in production by being deficient. A deficiency in inventories is a result of final sales greater than production. What we have is, therefore, the possibility of forces that are reinforcing—sales greater than demand that lead to an inventory deficiency, which

---

[21] L. A. Metzler, "The Nature and Stability of Inventory Cycles," *Review of Economics and Statistics* 23 (August 1941): 113-129.

[22] Paul G. Darling, "Inventory Fluctuations and Economic Instability: An Analysis Based on the Postwar Economy," in *Inventory Fluctuations and Economic Stabilization, pt. III, Inventory Fluctuations and Economic Instability*, Materials Prepared for U.S., Congress, Joint Economic Committee, 87th Cong., 1st sess. (Washington, D.C.:GPO, 1961), pp. 3-68.

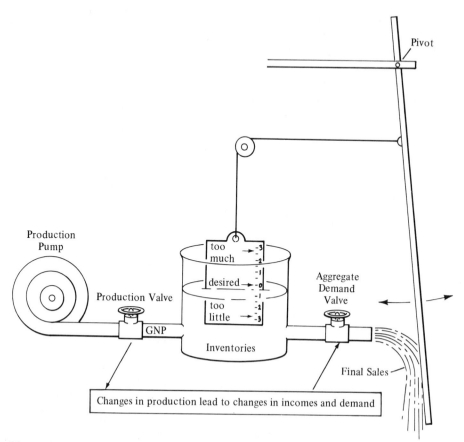

Figure 19.7. Schematic presentation of relationships among production, final sales, and inventory investment. Source: Paul G. Darling, "Inventory Fluctuations and Economic Instability: An Analysis Based on the Postwar Economy," in *Inventory Fluctuations and Economic Stabilization*, Materials Prepared for the Joint Economic Committee, U.S. Congress, 87th Cong., 1st sess., pt. III, *Inventory Fluctuations and Economic Instability* (Washington, D.C.: GPO, 1961), p. 12.

stimulates production, which, in turn, further stimulates demand by resulting in increased income. The total consequence of the responses we have traced out is an increase in the discrepancy between actual and desired inventories in the direction of increased disequilibrium. But this will not happen if the increase in income that arises from increased production does not have as much effect on demand as the increased production has on inventories. It is not likely that the relationship between desired inventories and sales will be linear or constant. Nor is it likely that the change in production, and hence in income, will lead to a linear or constant change in demand. For this reason, what appears to be a tendency toward increasing disequilibrium in inventories may in fact not occur over a period sufficiently long for the braking influence of less-than-proportionate changes to be felt.

There is a further possibility that we should consider in viewing the relationships among the parts of Figure 19.7. Lags in sellers' responses to changes in demand can mean that changes in the desired level of inventory are made only after a lapse of time after changes have occurred in final sales. Thus a temporary surplus or deficit in stocks may appear. But once this is recognized as more than a temporary condition, producers adjust output and, through feedback in the system, cause income to change in the same direction. Thus a slowness to adjust means that producers allow the size of the needed adjustment to become greater than would otherwise have been the case, and this, in turn, causes the feedback effect on income and demand to be proportionately greater. By this process, the effects of the delay become compounded. But again, the net effects depend on the degree of producer response to changes in sales and inventories, and the degree of consumer response to changes in income as producers alter their level of output. It is likely that excess inventories eventually get worked off and that deficiencies in inventories are made up. But it is possible for this adjustment process, involving positive changes that lead other changes, in combination with lags in the responses of decision makers, to set in operation a cyclical movement of production, income, demand, and stocks in which the size and interpretation of inventories play critical roles.

The picture that we have presented of movements in aggregate stocks is much too simple to explain the inventory policy of a particular firm, or the impact of a given policy on sales volume and production policy. There are many different kinds of stocks. Manufacturers hold raw materials, goods in process, and finished goods. Inventory decisions will vary depending on the fabrication level involved. Similarly, decisions will vary depending on the nature of production and the patterns of demand. Durable goods stocks are not controlled in the same way as nondurable goods stocks. Changes in technology, in transportation, in the size of firms, in the trends in sales of various firms, and in a myriad of other factors that bear upon production and sales possibilities will cause the inventory policies, and hence the level of inventories, to fluctuate differently in different firms and in different periods.

Another variable that has to be taken into account in examining inventory movements is the extent to which responses of management are a result of information obtained from the market or a result of intrafirm information. The flow of information vertically through the channels in which goods move will not be the same where the market is the medium of information flow rather than the firm. In some cases, markets may result in faster transmittal; in other cases, intrafirm transmittal may be faster. In addition, we could incorporate parameters to take account of expectations, as well as realizations, of output, sales, and prices, and also to take account of errors in such expectations. One of the major refinements of this model has involved the use of unfilled orders in lieu of, or in addition to, existing stocks in analyzing inventory status and decisions.

Empirical studies of inventory cycles and estimates of the parameters of various inventory models have occupied the attention of a large number of investigators, particularly during the decades following World War II.[23] In the sections that follow we shall describe the different kinds of inventories held by businesses, examine some of the findings from empirical studies in which inventory models were tested, and draw some conclusions about the effects of inventory cycles on marketing.

TYPES OF BUSINESS INVENTORIES

The relative importance of inventories in manufacturing and trade firms will change in different phases of the business cycle. Also, the nature of inventories will vary cyclically

---

[23] Examples of a number of inventory models, some with estimates of the value of parameters from empirical data, are found in *Inventory Fluctuations and Economic Stabilization*, op. cit., I, II, III, and IV. Included are studies by Thomas M. Stanback, Jr.; Mabel A. Smith; Lawrence Bridge and Clement Winston; Charles C. Holt and Franco Midigliani; Ruth P. Mack; Paul F. McGouldrick; Michael C.

Table 19.4 Distribution of Inventories of Manufacturers of Durable and Nondurable Goods According to Level of Fabrication, December 31, 1969

Fabrication Level	Durable Goods Firms	Nondurable Goods Firms
Materials and supplies	28%	37%
Work in process	47	16
Finished goods	25	47
Total inventories	100%	100%

Source: *Survey of Current Business* 51 (January 1971): *S-5*.

according to product durability and stage in the production process. It is instructive, nevertheless, to observe the relative importance of types of inventories at one point in time. Such data are presented in Tables 19.2 and 19.4 for December 31, 1969. Manufacturing firms accounted for about three-fifhs of all business inventories at that time, with retail trade establishments holding about two-thirds of the stocks of goods in trade firms. The average firm or establishment had an inventory at the end of each month that year that was about 50 percent larger than average monthly sales. Durable goods firms in retailing and manufacturing had end-of-month stocks about twice the size of their monthly sales, while nondurable goods establishments in retailing and manufacturing had stocks about 20-30 percent more than monthly sales. Wholesalers clearly had the highest stockturn, as reflected in the low inventory-sales ratio in Table 19.4.

In Table 19.4 we show that about half of the stocks held by durable goods manufacturers were goods in process, while about half of those held by nondurable goods manufacturers were finished goods. From the viewpoint of marketing policy, work in process is not the same as materials and supplies or finished goods. The former may be held because they result in buying or storage economies, or because they contribute to efficiency in the use of the other resources involved in the manufacturing of goods. If we eliminate goods that were in stock merely because they were tied up in the manufacturing process and regard the remaining stock of goods as "marketing stock," we had about 60 percent of the total stock in Table 19.2 in this category.[24] Of this 60 percent of total stocks that we identify as "marketing stocks," about 25 percent was held by retailers, about 20 percent by manufacturers, and about 15 percent by wholesalers.

INVENTORY MOVEMENTS THROUGH BUSINESS CYCLES

1. *MANUFACTURERS' INVENTORIES.* Most of the empirical studies of inventory movements through the business cycle have been concerned with manufacturers' inventories.[25] These studies show that inventories appear to have played a more important role in business contractions than in business expansions, and a more important role in contractions before World War II than since the war. They played a

---

Lovell; Nestor E. Terleckyj; Paul G. Darling; Lawrence R. Klein and Joel Popkin; and Elmer C. Bratt. Also included is a selected bibliography by Julius W. Allen and Richard H. Gentry.

[24] This consisted of the approximately 40 percent of total inventories held by retail and wholesale establishments, plus the finished-goods stocks of durable goods manufacturers—approximately 10 percent—and those of nondurable goods manufacturers—approximately 10 percent. See Tables 19.2 and 19.4.

[25] Many of the generalizations in this section are based on *Inventory Fluctuations and Economic Stabilization*, op. cit., pts. I, II, III, and IV. See also *International Encyclopedia of the Social Sciences*, s.v. "Inventory Behavior."

major role in the mild recessions of the 1920s, the late 1930s, and the 1950s. Other influences, however, appear to have been far more important in the major depression of the early 1930s. Inventories have increased during periods of business expansion, but their effect appears to have been greatest early in the expansion, peaking out at a point in time before the general level of business reached its peak.

In the postwar years purchased materials held by manufacturers turned downward at about the same time that the business cycles turned at its highest point, but they lagged about 4 to 8 months at the trough. Finished goods lagged 6 to 8 months at the peak of the cycles and 1 to 11 months at the troughs. Goods in process appear to have led or to have been coincident at the peak of the cycle, and to have been coincident or lagging at the trough. As a whole, manufacturers' inventories lagged behind business cycle peaks following World War II by 2-4 months and behind business cycle troughs by 1-8 months.

2. *VERTICAL RELATIONSHIPS.* The analysis of the cyclical movement of marketing stocks, and particularly those of retail establishments, has been less extensive, and the relationship of these movements to the business cycle are less clearly defined.[26] In her study of cycles in the shoe, leather, and hide business, Ruth Mack found that investment in inventories of shoes and leather (the change in inventory from one month to another) increased or decreased when shoe or leather output increased or decreased, while investment in stocks of hides moved inversely with output. Thus, investment in finished goods stocks moved inversely to investment in raw material stocks or goods-in-process. In the short cycle, spanning about 18 months, about half the fluctuation in receipts of shoes by retailers was accounted for by fluctuations in their inventory investment. Similarly, about half the changes in leather stocks of shoe manufacturers were for stocks, with the remaining related to changes in output. In the industry's major cycles, inventory investment was found to play a less important role in fluctuations that occurred in early stages of production than in later stages of production and sale. Although the timing of inventory cycles tended to coincide at various production levels, the amplitude was greater, especially for minor movements, toward the center of the vertical sequence. Fluctuations in sales and stocks at the retail level were magnified at the manufacturer level, and fluctuations at the manufacturer level were demagnified at the tanner level.

The key variables that emerged in Mack's exploration of the determinants of these movements were (1) the existence of a desired inventory level on the part of retailers in terms of an absolute amount rather than an amount specified in relation to sales; (2) orders placed ahead of time in anticipation of sales; (3) sales anticipations based on past sales experience; and (4) subsequent correction of errors in the amount ordered on the basis of actual sales experience. Corrective orders tended to lead sales. The purchase order was found to be the agent by which changes at one level in the trade were transmitted to other levels, and the direction of transmission was from consumer purchases to purchases of hides. Orders tended to reach peaks and troughs before sales. Part of this was due to

---

[26] See Lawrence Bridge and Clement Winston, "Inventory Investment in Trade," in *Inventory Fluctuations and Economic Shabilization*, op. cit., pt. I, pp. 165-180. Ruth Mack has also made a careful analysis of pre-world War II inventory movements in both manufacturers' and trading firms' stocks of shoes, leather, and hide in *Consumption and Business Fluctuations: A Case Study of the Shoe, Leather, Hide Sequence* (New York: National Bureau of Economic Research, 1956). Terleckyj includes trade inventories along with manufacturing inventories in his analysis. See Nestor E. Terleckyj, *Measures of Inventory Conditions*, Technical Paper no. 8 (New York: National Industrial Conference Board, 1960), reproduced in *Inventory Fluctuations and Economic Stabilization*, op. cit., pt. II, pp. 159-193.

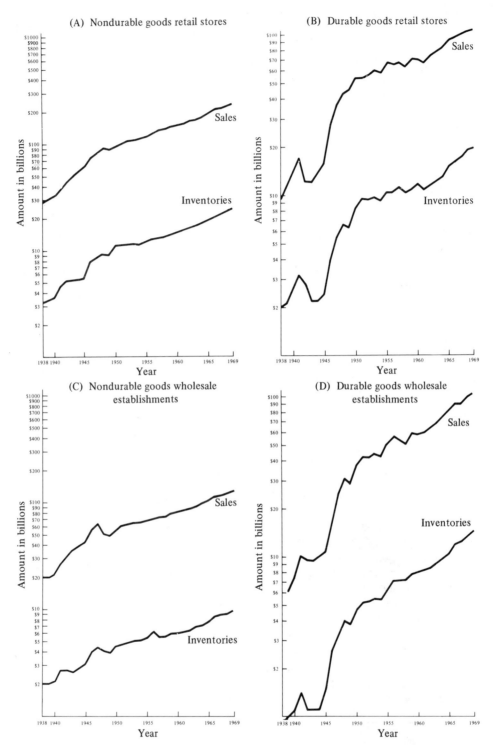

Figure 19.8. Annual sales and book value of end-of-year inventories of nondurable and durable goods retail stores and wholesale establishments, 1938-1969. Data for both sales and inventories for 1938-1947 are slightly understated relative to data for 1948 and later years. Sources: U.S. Bureau of the Census, *Historical Statistics of the United States: Colonial Times to 1957* (Washington, D.C.: GPO, 1960); U.S. Department of Commerce, *1967 Business Statistics* (Washington, D.C.: GPO, 1968); *Survey of Current Business*, various issues, 1968-1970.

the fact that retailers were anticipating consumer demand. But there were market conditions that affected the timing of orders, since retailers anticipated longer delivery periods and possible shortages when sales were rising, and also considered the possibility of rising prices. This was a case study of only one industrial sequence, and it contained many of the elements of the Clark, Metzler, and Abramovitz models that preceded it.

3. *EMPIRICAL DATA.* Figure 19.8, parts A, B, C, and D, show the annual sales and end-of-year inventories of retail and wholesale firms handling nondurable and durable goods for the years 1938-1969. Annual data suppress information about monthly or quarterly movement of stocks and conceal, therefore, most of the short-term cycles observed by Mack. Longer cycles are indicated, however, although the span of leads and lags between stocks and sales is not shown precisely. In general, inventory investment in nondurable goods retail establishments followed sales trends closely, exhibiting little cyclical movement after 1954. Stocks of durable goods stores showed deeper cyclical movements, with troughs coinciding with those of general business activity and of durable goods retail sales and peaks of stocks tending to precede sales declines. Wholesale stocks of nondurables showed more distinctive cycles than wholesale sales. Wholesale stocks of durables, while exhibiting cyclical movements, showed less distinct cycles than wholesale sales of durables. In fact the rate of growth of wholesale stocks of durables was remarkably stable in the 1950s and 1960s.

Inventory cycles show greater amplitude than sales cycles, and this is particularly apparent among firms stocking durable goods. To the extent that these deeper fluctuations are due to errors of anticipation, better forecasting would avoid the errors; more effective stock control would hasten the correction and shorten the span of time during which the stock-sales ratio is maladjusted. To the extent that deeper fluctuations are due to the accelerator effect of movements in desired stock-sales ratios, damping of the cycle can probably be achieved only by price adjustments. However, the cost of the latter in terms of lower revenue to sellers when prices are cut in order to move surplus stock, or in terms of higher prices to buyers (and possible market disruptions) when prices are raised to conserve surplus stock, must be weighed against the gains resulting from greater stability in inventories.

From a social point of view, we do not yet know precisely the extent to which inventory investment and disinvestment—adding to stocks or depleting stocks—contributes to business cycles and particularly to business cycle turning points. Although the volatility of manufacturers' inventories appears to be greater then that of retailing and wholesaling stocks, "marketing stocks" as we have defined them account for about 60 percent of total inventories. Marketing policy with respect to inventories is not, therefore, an unimportant part of this bigger question. Stocks today are lower in relation to sales than was true before World War II. This appears to be related to better management techniques, and specifically to the use of electronic data processing in the implementation of newly developed inventory control systems.

Some Unanswered Questions

OPTIMUM STOCKHOLDING LOCI IN THE TRADE CHANNEL

One question that has not been explored in depth is where stock holding *actually* occurs in the trade channel and where such stockholding *should* occur. Although this could be examined under static conditions, its importance is particularly apparent in the dynamics of market adjustments over time. As changes occur in the structure of demand or costs, institutions accommodate to these changes. One of the common forms of adaptation within the marketing channel is the shifting of functions forward or backward to minimize losses that occur at one level of the trade channel or to increase the profitability at another level. One marketing function that has shown some mobility from time to time is the holding of inventories. If the gross margin of a retail firm is declining, one way to reduce operating expenses is to buy on a hand-to-mouth basis, reducing investment in inventories and the costs associated with holding stocks physically. If this does not result in a proportional reduction in sales revenue, it will increase the profitability of retailing. But this forces onto the wholesaler, or manufacturer, the stockholding function. If this increases the costs of wholesalers or manufacturers with no effect on their revenue, they will find it necessary to raise prices if they are to maintain the same gross margin. Whether or not they do raise prices will depend on (1) the elasticity of retailers' demand with respect to price and (2) the nature of the competitive pattern in the wholesale markets in which they operate.

From a social point of view, the question is whether the locus of a given function is optimal. This has to be viewed in terms of the effect of its locus on the utility-cost relationship in the *total channel*. The ability of the market to achieve optimality depends to a large extent on competitive structure. If there is inequality in bargaining power between vertically related firms, this may result in an uneconomic allocation of storage (as well as other) functions. Exploration of this issue, theoretically and empirically, would call for an analysis of inventory policies and practices as one part of all marketing policies and practices, and for a consideration of aggregate stock distribution throughout the economy as well as within a single distribution channel.

OPTIMUM ASSET CLUSTERS

A second approach to the analysis of inventory accumulation has been utilized by some economists who have viewed the problem as one of achieving some kind of optimum cluster of assets. In this approach, the question for the business firm is the revenue-cost relationship for aggregate asset holdings of various amounts, and the revenue-cost relationship of alternative asset holdings within the aggregate.[27] For the consumer the problem is essentially that of effecting the desired balance between, for example, durable goods and other forms of assets, and among durable goods, the allocation of consumer "investment" in some desired proportions among specific product alternatives. The extent of use of this approach has not begun to match the use of the income-expenditure approach in the analysis of market behavior, but it promises rich rewards as a complement to the traditional flow analysis in the study of investment in both business capital and what we can appropriately term "consumer capital."

---

[27] Kenneth E. Boulding has built an analysis of the firm's behavior and of macroeconomic behavior on the balance sheet in which he relates the dynamics of behavior to the changing "states" or "frames" reflected in the asset and liability structure of the firm, the household, and the economy. Kenneth E. Boulding, *A Reconstruction of Economics* (New York: Wiley, 1950).

20

Marketing Logistics: Space Relationships

Who wields the power to originate motion
must control the main accesses to time;
for the concept of motion *requires*
the Siamese-twinning of space-time.

—Ann Douglas

In the preceding chapter we considered the problem of maintaining stocks of merchandise, taking into account the costs of acquisition and maintenance and the demand for merchandise availability at specified times. We turn now to another facet of marketing logistics—space relationships. Our discussion will be directed toward two basic questions. The first concerns where an establishment should be located. While the basic principles that govern establishment location are the same whether the establishment is engaged primarily in processing or in marketing, the specific factors that enter into the determination of location decisions will differ in nature and relative importance between these two kinds of business firms. We shall concentrate on the location of the specialized marketing establishment—the retail store and the wholesaling establishment—rather than on the location of manufacturing or other form production enterprises. The second question we shall consider is what determines the geographic area serviced by the marketing establishment. This is not, of course, unrelated to the first question, for the size of market area—or the market area potential—is a significant element in the determination of optimal location. In this discussion, we shall be concerned with the locus of that marketing establishment which provides a full range of marketing services, including not only activities associated with the buying and selling of goods but also those related to the maintenance of physical supplies.

The concept of a region as used in economic analysis is helpful in our study of marketing location because it is the broad concept that embraces the more specialized notion of a market area. In empirical studies of regions two approaches have been used to arrive at a meaningful clustering of spatially dispersed economic units and functions.[1] The first is the *functional integration principle*, which is the delineation of a region on the basis of those spatial units that are tied to a central node. For example, all the loci where consumers live who buy merchandise from the retail stores located in a given "center" would make up a region by this principle of delineation. A second basis for delineation is the *homogeneity principle*, in which a region is defined to include all units within a given space that are alike, or nearly alike, with respect to a variety of attributes *and* therefore different in these ways from the units that are in another space. Similarities within an area may be structural, with the focus on organization or environment, or they may be largely behavioral, with the emphasis on activities. For example, by the homogeneity

---

[1] See Hugh O. Nourse, *Regional Economics: A Study of the Economic Structure, Stability, and Growth of Regions* (New York: McGraw-Hill, 1968), pp. 130-131.

approach a retail market area could be delineated on the basis of consistency among the households of a given area with respect to household size and income level (structural criteria) or with respect to the patterns of buying behavior that they exhibit (behavioral criteria). A market area delineated by either approach would be distinguished from other areas within which the structure of households or buying behavior differed significantly from that of other areas.

From the viewpoint of marketing these two approaches *could* be integrated into a single approach by viewing the market transaction as the basis for delineating both the functionally integrated region and the region characterized by the commonality of market participation by consumers and firms residing within that area. But this stretches the two concepts more than is desirable. The functional integration principle focuses so sharply on the essence of a market—the exchange relationship between buyers and sellers—that it is a logical basis for examining geographic structure in the marketing of goods and services. Within any given space one often finds some degree of heterogeneity in the economic attributes of the units that are tied to a given market center. For example, a retail center may draw customers from a wide geographic area that contains a considerable range of income levels and cultural patterns. Or a wholesale center may serve a geographic area that embraces a variety of industrial users whose demands are influenced by quite different factors. The functional integration principle of defining the market area in each of these cases permits a layer-cake approach to the analysis, with the boundaries of the area defined in terms of the cake's diameter and its internal differentiations in terms of the differences between each layer. Strict application of the homogeneity principle would, on the other hand, either necessitate the separate delineation of each layer, gaining accuracy in the specification of the layer's diameter (in contrast to the averaging process inherent in the total-cake approach) by isolating each layer for purposes of analysis, or require the delineation of a series of cupcakes from the total, each with sufficient homogeneity to warrant its identification as a separate market area. Since the focus of marketing is on the transaction, the functional integration approach to market area delineation would seem far more useful for the analysis of market relationships on a geographic basis. Which buyers (or sellers) are tied to one center and why they are tied there are the questions that can be explored through this approach.

This brings us to a final dimension of the market area concept. A market area may be viewed as a buying area or a selling area. It is traditional in economic and marketing analysis to use the term *market area* to identify selling areas and the term *supply area* to identify buying areas.[2] The dichotomy is useful—in fact essential for adequate analysis of geographic trading patterns—but the terms are unfortunate, since "market" becomes identified with selling to the exclusion of buying. We shall use the term *market areas* in our discussion to refer to both buying and selling areas and shall try to make clear whether we are referring to selling areas or to buying areas at the time the term is used.

In the sections that follow we shall consider, first, the general economic factors that determine the location of marketing establishments, the areas that those establishments serve, and the areas from which buyers obtain the goods and services that they purchase. Before we examine some of the patterns of location of retail and wholesale establishments, we shall trace briefly the essential elements of central place theory, which provides a useful framework for viewing the geographic distribution of trading centers

---

[2] See for example, his discussion, "Market Areas and Supply Areas," in Edgar M. Hoover, *The Location of Economic Activity* (New York: McGraw-Hill, 1948), pp. 48-50.

and areas. We shall then consider the structure of retail market areas, drawing upon empirical studies as a means of demonstrating the usefulness of central place theory and of showing some of the refinements necessary in order to explain the geography of retailing. We shall then turn to wholesale location and market areas, focusing on those problems most directly related to the location of reserve stocks.

GENERAL DETERMINANTS OF LOCATION AND AREAS

Some years ago the author was engaged in a study of selling areas of industrial goods wholesalers and manufacturers' branches in an important wholesaling center in the Southeast. In the course of the field investigation, a machine tool distributor was asked why he had chosen to locate his firm in that particular city. With considerable indignation he replied, "Because I was born here."

There are many reasons why marketing establishments are located where they are and service the areas they do. In this discussion, we shall focus almost exclusively on the economic factors underlying the location of market centers and the structure of market areas. The analysis is essentially a revenue-cost approach, involving the demand for delivered goods, on the one hand, and the internal and external costs of supplying goods, on the other.

The Demand for and Costs of Delivered
Goods and Services

The demand for goods and services is a demand for delivered goods and services. However, buyers may find it possible, sometimes necessary, and sometimes advantageous to separate their demand for delivered goods into two parts, consisting of the demand for the undelivered component and the demand for the delivery. We shall have occasion to make such a separation, since there are many cases in which buyers can and do purchase delivery service in a separate market from that in which they acquire title to goods. The buyer (1) may "produce" the delivery service (by driving himself to the seller's place of business, for example), (2) may incur the explicit cost of delivery directly and separately from the cost of the merchandise at the seller's place of business (by paying delivery charges, for example, on mail order purchases), or (3) may incur an implicit delivery cost when the price quoted is a delivered price.[3] The cost to the buyer of obtaining goods from a distance will therefore affect his willingness to buy.

One other facet of the demand for transportation in marketing is evident particularly in retail markets. One of the services that consumers demand in the marketing process is information. There is a great deal of market information that is made available to

---

[3] In situations (1) and (2), the delivery cost borne by the buyer will equal the market value of that cost, since the buyer buys the service in the market. In situation (3), however, the seller may quote a delivered price that includes FOB price plus delivery costs that are greater than, equal to, or less than the actual cost of transportation to that particular buyer. Charges greater or less than actual costs would not be possible in the long run under pure and perfect competition, but in markets characterized by oligopoly, and sometimes monopolistic competition, systems of freight absorption and freight overcharges may develop to alter the competitive position of firms in different market areas.

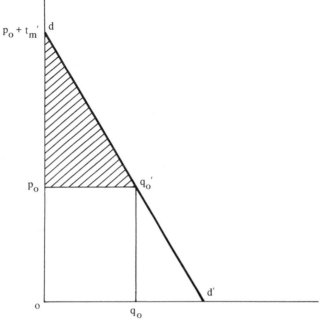

Figure 20.1. Transport costs and the quantity demanded by a single buyer.

individuals who are present in the market place. For this reason, consumer buyers often find it advantageous to go to a market center themselves in order to shop, and this is one of the locational costs in marketing that is different from the movement of goods themselves. Industrial buyers may be confronted with similar conditions where inspection of merchandise is an important means of acquiring market information necessary for making optimal decisions. In these cases, centralized market facilities are likely to develop—as in apparel and furniture markets—and the costs of contact are thereby affected.

An additional aspect of demand for delivery is its relationship to time. Transport service can be differentiated with respect to speed and risk. There are therefore several demands that are manifest when we speak of "the demand" for transportation.

The costs that are relevant to our analysis include both external and internal costs. External costs are comprised of incoming costs—FOB price and inward transportation—and outgoing costs—outward transportation. We shall note some of the opportunities for substituting one of these costs for another. One cluster of locational costs that are internal to the firm are site-related processing and handling costs. For marketing firms one of the most important of these is rent, although geographic differences in wage rates may also be critical. The other cost variable that we shall consider is the functional relationship between size of firm (or establishment) and volume of sales. Where there are economies of scale in the marketing establishment, these economies may be critical in determining the size of the establishment's marketing area and, hence, the relative importance of transport and other locational costs in the total cost of the establishment or in the total price that consumers pay for goods and services.

While transport costs will be found to play a key role in the determination of location and area limits, such costs have to be considered in combination with all other costs, since transport costs are not necessarily independent of other production costs. Similarly, the demand for delivered goods is not independent of the demand for the utility components

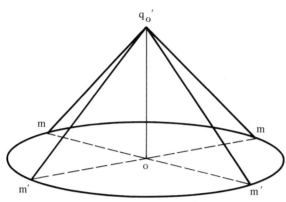

Figure 20.2. Quantity demanded, q', at price p_o plus transport costs to varying distances, m, from point o.

of those goods that exclude delivery. We shall examine the demand for delivered goods vis-à-vis total costs, including incoming and outgoing transport costs and all other costs of processing and marketing.

THE LÖSCH APPROACH

In Figure 20.1 we show a conventional linear demand curve for an individual buyer.[4] We shall consider the case of a consumer buyer for purposes of illustration. The seller offers the product at his place of business for price p_o. If the buyer resides so close to the seller's place of business that he incurs no cost in getting there, he will purchase q_o quantity of the good. If, however, the buyer lives elsewhere and must bear the cost of transportation and loss of time in order to buy from this seller, the effective price is the p_o price plus the explicit and implicit costs of getting possession of the good. We shall simplify by assuming that the transportation cost is the only added cost involved and that this is a linear function of distance. The quantities that the consumer will buy if he must pay different transport costs are indicated by that portion of his demand curve, dd', in which transport costs, t_m, are added to the store price, p_o, and this is the shaded area beneath dq_o' in Figure 20.1. Therefore $p_o + t_m$ is a function of distance. We show that t_m' is the cost of transport that, when added to p_o, causes the buyer's willingness to buy to fall to zero. If the transport cost is less than t_m', he will be willing to buy but will buy less than he would have had the transport cost been zero—as it would be if he lived right at the seller's place of business and purchased q_o.

Figure 20.2 extends the problem to cover all buyers and sellers, who, we shall assume, are scattered at equal distances over a circular surface extending outward from the seller's place of business. The plane oq_om is comparable to the shaded area of Figure 20.1, p_oq_o' $(p_o + t_m')$. The vertical line oq_o' in Figure 20.2 is comparable to p_oq_o' in Figure 20.1. If all buyers have a preference pattern similar to that displayed in Figure 20.1, then the

---

[4] In this and the sections that follow, we have drawn extensively on the approach of August Lösch, *The Economics of Location*, 2d rev. ed., trans. W. H. Woglom and W. F. Stopler (New Haven, Conn.: Yale University Press, 1954), pp. 105-108. Lösch's first edition was *Die räumliche Ordnung der Wirtschaft* (Jena: Fischer, 1940); the second edition was published in 1944. See also Brian J. L. Berry, *Geography of Market Centers and Retail Distribution* (Englewood Cliffs, N.J.: Prentice-Hall, 1967), pp. 59-62.

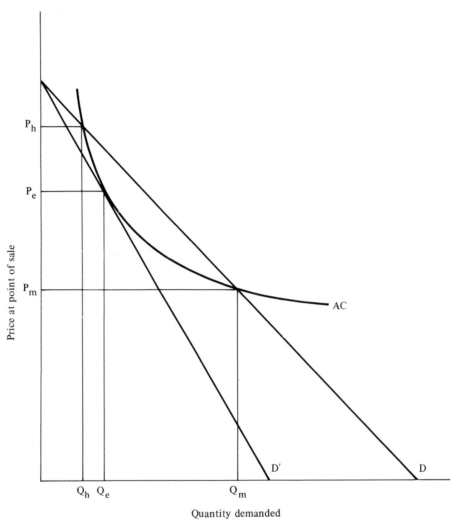

Figure 20.3. Aggregate demand for goods and services of a trading firm at a given location and long-run average costs of the firm.

total demand for goods offered by the seller at point o at price p_o will be represented by the area of the cone described by $q_o'm$ as it pivots around $360°$. There will be similar cones for each price at the point of sale. The aggregate demand for goods of the seller at point o will be the aggregate areas of all possible cones for all possible prices. This aggregate demand is shown as a linear quantity in Figure 20.3.[5] The long-run average cost curve for the firm (i.e., the envelope of short-run average cost curves) is shown in Figure 20.3 as AC. At price P_m the firm can sell the largest possible volume and still cover its

---

[5] If the demand of individual buyers is curvilinear and/or if the cost of transportation is not a linear function of distance, the aggregate demand curve, D, will be curvilinear. Empirical studies suggest that the cost of travel, or the resistance to travel for purposes of shopping, increases in proportion to the square of distance for consumer-buyers, suggesting that the aggregate demand curve in Figure 20.3 would be concave to the origin as each added unit of distance results in progressively more resistance to customer movement. The opposite might be true in transport of goods at wholesale if there are economies of scale in long-haul transport.

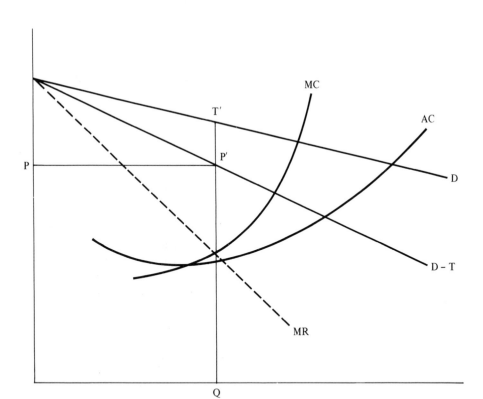

Figure 20.4. Short-run costs and revenue for a firm under conditions of imperfect competition with transport costs paid by buyers.

costs. At prices below P_h and above P_m, the firm will make a profit. If profit making attracts competing firms that cut into the demand for the products of this particular firm, reducing demand to D', long-run equilibrium for this firm will be at price P_e and Q_e.

This highly simplified approach assumes that all customers have the same individual demand, that potential customers are distributed at equal intervals over an area, and that selling areas are circular. We know that individual demands are not the same and that geographic distribution is more likely to be clustered than scattered evenly. Also, we shall show that selling areas are more likely to be hexagonal than circular in order that all the area is allocated to some one market center. The Lösch approach shows the effect of transport cost on the quantities buyers at various locations are willing to purchase, thereby introducing the proposition that depth of market penetration by a seller at a given market center is a function of distance of buyers from the market center. Thus market areas can be viewed as three-dimensional, with depth quite as significant as extent.

TRANSPORT COSTS AND SHORT-RUN PRICE AND QUANTITY

The demand curve in Figure 20.3 is that which results after buyers have taken into account the effects of distance, and the equilibrium price and quantity shown are based on long-run costs. The short-run solution is shown in Figure 20.4. Again we shall assume that the preferences of all customers are the same but that some customers live nearer the seller's place of business than do others. We shall also assume that this is a market of less than pure competition. The demand curve, D, shows the quantities that buyers would purchase from an individual seller located at a trading center if transportation costs were zero. Since buyers are located at various distances from the trading center, and since they will incur costs in order to get to and return from the center, the curve $D - T$ shows the demand when transportation costs are taken into account. The curve $D - T$ is more inelastic than D, since the seller will find it necessary to lower his price at his place of business a great deal if he is to attract the more distant consumer and thereby increase his sales. His most profitable volume will be Q, to be sold at price P at his place of business. Each customer pays his own transportation costs, each varying according to distance from the trading center. The most distant customer pays a transport cost of $T'P'$.

TRANSPORTATION AS A PRODUCTION COST

In the examples that we have considered thus far, transportation costs (which we are using as a proxy to cover all costs incurred to overcome the separation of buyers and sellers in space) have been analyzed as if they were incurred explicitly by buyers. Suppose, however, that the seller we have been considering in Figure 20.4 examines his situation and begins to wonder whether he could improve his position by paying for transportation costs himself. In this case, he would consider transportation charges as a part of his total cost of doing business. If he is a retailer, he could run a bus throughout his trading area or pay customers a mileage fee when they shop with him, and he could pay the delivery costs for merchandise purchased from him. If he is a wholesaler or manufacturer, he would quote delivered prices and pay the transport costs himself.

In Figure 20.5 we examine this possibility. The demand is the same as in Figure 20.4, but in this case we work with the demand that would prevail were transportation costs not taken into account. Thus the marginal revenue of the seller would be greater at each price than was true in Figure 20.4, where marginal revenue is related to $D - T$ rather than to D. AC in Figure 20.5 does not include transportation costs. Average costs with transportation costs included are shown by the $AC + T$ curve. The seller's optimum volume will be Q_n at a price of P_n per unit. How much has the transportation cost raised prices for consumers? One way to look at this is to ask what the price would have been had the transport costs been zero. The answer is that the average price would have been P_o and Q_o units would have been sold. It appears therefore that the price has risen only slightly as a result of the seller's bearing the burden of the transport cost. In this particular case, it has not even risen as much as the average transport cost. Where each consumer pays his own transport costs, and where such costs vary according to distance from the trading center, different consumers will, of course, pay different delivered prices for their goods, with the differences equal to differences in transportation costs. Where the seller pays the transport costs as a part of the total cost of doing business, all consumers pay an equal transport cost. In both cases the "burden" of the transportation costs is borne by consumers in the form of higher delivered prices and smaller quantities consumed than would prevail if transport costs were zero, and by sellers in the form of lower total profits than would prevail if transport costs were zero.

AGGREGATION OF DEMANDS IN DIFFERENT
SEGMENTS OF A SELLING AREA

In our analysis thus far it has been assumed that the demands of all potential buyers were the same. This is, of course, unlikely to be true. It has also been assumed that buyers were distributed equally over the market area, whereas we know that both consumer buyers and industrial buyers will cluster in such a way that all subareas within a total selling area

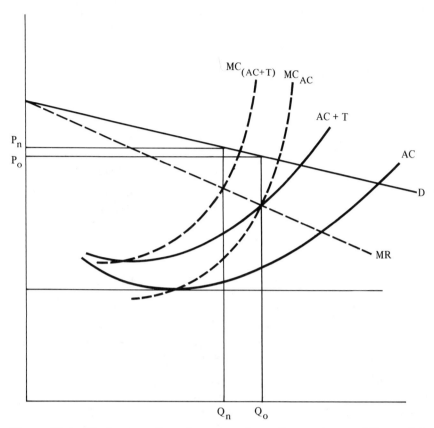

Figure 20.5. Short-run costs and revenue for a firm under conditions of imperfect competition with transport costs paid by the seller.

will not be equal in quantities demanded, quite independently of the preference patterns of individual buyers in those areas.

In Figure 20.6 the total demand for a good made available in a given center, DD', is the aggregate of the separate demands in three subareas of the trading area served by suppliers in the center.[6] We shall think of these demands as consumer demands, although the reasoning would be just as applicable to industrial goods demands. In subarea A_1, the demand is represented by d_1. In subareas A_2 and A_3, the demands are d_2 and d_3, respectively. However, the total demand at the market center is reduced by the amount of the transport costs for buyers to get to and return from the trading center with the merchandise. Subarea A_1 is the most distant from the trading center, and the effect of transport cost is shown by the transport gradient, indicated by a dotted line in Figure 20.6, which connects d_1 to d_1'. Thus d_1 is consumer demand in subarea A_1 unadjusted for transport costs, while d_1' is the same demand as it manifests itself in the market

---

[6] Figure 20.6 is the same kind of diagram developed by Hoover and extended by Isard to show the division of a market among several supply points, except that the figure that we present here shows the division of a market's total demand among buyers at several buying points. See Edgar M. Hoover, Jr., *Location Theory and the Shoe and Leather Industries* (Cambridge, Mass.: Harvard University Press, 1937), pp. 16-23, and Walter Isard, *Location and Space-Economy* (New York: MIT Press and Wiley, 1956), pp. 155-157.

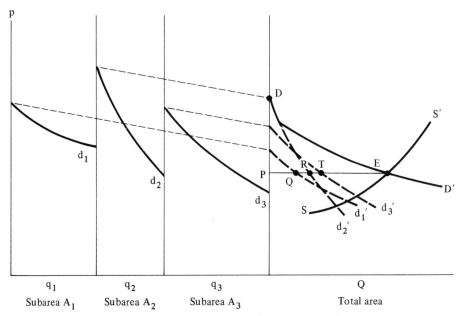

Figure 20.6. Demands in three subareas located at varying distances from the selling center, and total demand and supply. Source: Derived from Walter Isard, *Location and Space Economy* (New York: MIT Press and Wiley, 1956), pp. 155-157.

center after adjustment for transport costs. The demands in subareas A_2 and A_3 are similarly adjusted for the cost of transportation between these localities and the trading center. The summation of d_1', d_2', and d_3' is shown by DD', the aggregate demand at the trading center adjusted for the cost of transportation between the subareas and the center. The supply at the center, which will be the marginal cost if there is only a single seller, or the summation of marginal costs if there are several sellers, is shown by SS'. Thus the price at the center will be P, and total sales will be PE. Sales to customers from subarea A_1 will be PQ; sales to customers from subarea A_2 will be PR; sales to customers from subarea A_3 will be PT. Total sales, PE, will equal $PQ + PR + PT$. Increases in transport costs will lower DD and, hence, lower the quantity sold and the price. Similarly, changes in demand in one or more subareas will alter the total demand and the corresponding volume and price, as will changes in supply.

ECONOMIES OF SCALE

Internal economies of scale that may be realized by marketing establishments make possible greater centralization of such establishments and wider market areas. For the independent marketing establishment it is useful to classify the sources of economies in terms of their relationship to the performance of what are essentially physical functions, such as receiving goods, classifying and sorting goods, storing, mixing lots, and delivery; nonphysical functions, such as acquiring and dispensing market information, establishing and maintaining market contacts, negotiating and consummating transactions, and decision making with respect to external and internal policy; and strategy functions, such as promotion (in contrast to the dispensing of factual information), differentiation, and securing market position by achieving control. Up to a point, most establishments can realize significant economies in many of these functions as size increases. Beyond that

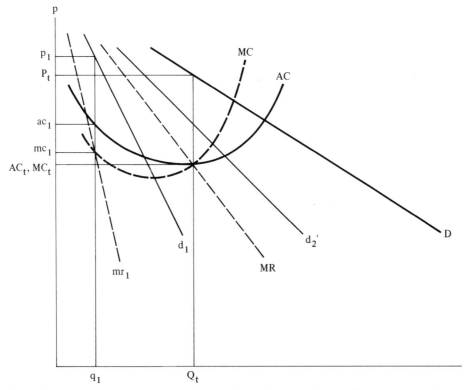

Figure 20.7. Determination of optimum price and output for a seller under conditions of imperfect competition with local and more distant market areas.

point, diseconomies associated with such problems as coordination and control result in rising costs.

The functions conducive to large *establishments* differ from those conducive to large *firms*. Because of this, multiunit wholesale and retail firms occupy an important place in marketing. The wholesale or retail establishment is concerned primarily with physical functions and with dispensing information, establishing and maintaining contacts with customers, and engaging in negotiation. Other nonphysical functions, particularly buying and policy making, are largely within the province of the firm, for they can be performed more economically there, resulting in economies of scale for the firm. Similarly, strategy functions are largely firm functions, again because of possibilities for economies of scale.

A simplified example of the economies of scale made possible by the extension of a firm's selling area is illustrated in Figure 20.7. Assume that a one-establishment wholesale firm is located in a given market center and that the market is one of monopolistic competition. Sales may be made by the wholesaler to retailers in the same center with transportation costs close to zero.[7] Assume that the demand by these retailers is represented by d_1 and the marginal revenue by mr_1 in Figure 20.7. AC and MC represent the firm's average and marginal costs, respectively. If the firm's sole clientele consists of

---

[7] There will, of course, be some transportation costs even within a trading center, but we shall consider these as negligible and focus instead on the much higher transportation costs associated with sales to customers who are some distance from the center.

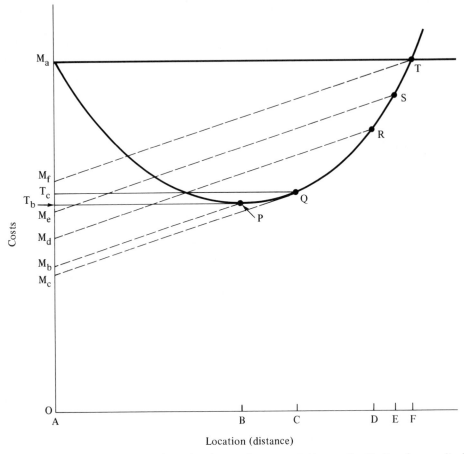

Figure 20.8. Marginal costs of production and transportation as the limits of one seller's market area are extended. Source: Adapted from Walter Isard, *Location and Space Economy* (New York: MIT Press and Wiley, 1956), pp. 148-150.

local customers, its most profitable point of operation will be to sell quantity q_1 at price p_1. Thus the firm would be operating at an output level considerably below that at which unit costs are lowest. It would, in fact, be operating at a level below the lowest possible marginal cost.

Suppose that potential customers also exist in another town some distance from this center. The demand of these customers is, let us assume, greater than the demand of the firm's local customers. This demand must, of course, be adjusted to take into account the cost of transportation between the wholesale center and the more distant town. The curve d_2' represents that adjusted demand, that is, the original demand lowered by the unit cost of transportation.[8]

---

[8] We are ignoring possibilities of economies of scale in transportation, which may, in fact, be of considerable importance. We are assuming that it costs twice as much to transport two units as it does to transport one unit. However, it may be possible in practice to derive considerable economies in transportation by buying in larger quantities and thereby reducing the unit cost of transportation. This refinement would not change the essential nature of what we show in Figure 20.7, but it could be important in affecting the nature of the demand function.

If the firm sells to customers in both towns, the total demand for goods from the wholesaler will be represented by the aggregate demand curve, D. This is the sum of d_1 and d_2'. The prices are the unit prices at the seller's place of business. To these prices, buyers in the more distant city will add transportation costs. The marginal revenue the seller will receive if he sells to both groups of customers will be MR. His most profitable point of operation will be to sell quantity Q_t to the two groups of customers at a point-of-purchase price of P_t, to which buyers in the second market area will add transport costs. In this particular case, this volume of business happens to result in the lowest possible unit cost.

If we considered demands of customers in additional cities to which the wholesale firm could make shipments, the resulting output and price level is likely to differ from that shown in Figure 20.7. The point demonstrated in Figure 20.7 is simply that local customers alone may sometimes not permit a firm to take advantage of opportunities that it has for achieving greater efficiency in the short run. We could also extend the analysis to take into account economies of scale in the long run as a firm of still larger capacity is established in the process of the market area's growth.[9]

As a firm's selling area grows, transportation costs increase. But if a firm's growth makes possible lower costs of operation, the question then concerns the net effect of higher transport costs, lower operating costs, and the responsiveness of buyers to changes in the seller's offering price. This combination will establish the limits of the seller's trading area. In examining this problem we shall employ Hoover's approach in determining the margin line, or limits, of a selling area.[10]

In Figure 20.8 we show how decreasing costs can be achieved by a centrally located marketing establishment that increases the size of its selling area up to a certain point, and how that selling area is limited as increasing costs are incurred. In keeping with Isard's interpretation of Hoover's analysis, we shall consider only marginal costs and shall assume that the firm's selling price is equal to the marginal cost of the product at its door, as would be true under pure competition.[11]

Assume that a one-establishment wholesale firm is located at point A. The wholesaler prices his goods FOB his place of business, and the customer pays the transportation charges. Consider first the firm's sales to customers who are located at point A and who would not, of course, have to pay any transportation costs. The marginal cost to the seller of meeting this local demand would be represented by OM_a in Figure 20.8. His selling price is OM_a, and at this price marginal revenue equals marginal cost. If, however, he extends his sales to customers located at point B, some miles from A, his marginal costs will fall to OM_b. But these goods have to be transported to B so that buyers at B whose FOB price is OM_b will have the cost of transportation added. If the cost of transportation is so much per unit per mile, then the average cost of transportation will equal the marginal cost of transportation. Let us assume that this transport cost per mile

---

[9] See the brief treatment of economies of scale in the long run in Lösch, op. cit., pp. 175-176.

[10] See Hoover, op. cit., pp. 15-17. See also Isard, op. cit., pp. 148-150.

[11] If we wished to consider a market of monopolistic competition, we would also expect the firm to price its product at a price that would maximize profits, and this would occur, as in pure competition, where marginal cost equals marginal revenue. The difference is that in monopolistic competition the marginal cost will be less than the selling price. Since in Figure 20.8 we are examining only marginal costs, it makes it simpler to consider the pure competition case, although the diagram is just as relevant to the case of monopolistic competition.

from A to B is represented by $M_b T_b$. The marginal cost of a unit sold to a customer at point B will be $OM_b + M_b T_b$, or OT_b, which also equals BP. The dotted line, $M_b P$, is the transportation cost gradient between A and B. Any buyer between A and B could pay the FOB marginal cost, OM_b, plus the transport cost to the buyer's place of business, and this would be represented by the height of the $M_b P$ line at the appropriate distance from point A. By extending its selling area to point B, therefore, the firm will have brought its marginal cost of operation and transportation to the lowest point, and all buyers would benefit because all would enjoy the lower FOB price made possible by the increased volume of business.

Let us assume that by extending his area still further to point C, the wholesaler located at A will then reach the lowest FOB marginal cost, OM_c. But in order to transport the product to customers at C, the cost of transportation is $M_c T_c$, bringing the marginal cost of the delivered good to OT_c, or CQ. If sales are extended to point D, the marginal FOB cost rises to OM_d, and the transport gradient necessary to serve all the customers between A and D is shown by the sloped line $M_d R$, with marginal cost of the delivered product at point D equal to OM_d plus the relevant transport cost, or DR. If he extends his sales to point F, serving all customers between A and F, marginal FOB cost is OM_f, with transport cost added in proportion to the distance from A. The marginal cost of meeting demand at point F will be OM_f plus the appropriate transport cost, with the marginal cost of delivered goods at point F being equal to OM_a, or FT. Beyond point F, buyers will find it more advantageous to buy from local sellers so long as the marginal FOB cost of such sellers is no greater than OM_a.

The line $M_a PQRST$ is called by Hoover a "margin line" that shows how the marginal cost of the delivered good varies at the limits of seller A's market area. As that market area expands outward, this marginal cost falls and then rises. Where the limits of the wholesaler's area are will depend on the corresponding FOB and transport costs for sellers located in other trading centers who are extending their areas toward point A. We shall consider that relationship in a later section. Before we examine in detail the determinants of market areas, we shall look briefly at the inverse problem—how quantities purchased and prices are determined where buyers in a given center are obtaining goods from several sellers located at varying distances from the buying center.

AGGREGATION OF SUPPLY FROM DIFFERENT
SEGMENTS OF A BUYING AREA

Just as sellers find it advantageous under certain circumstances to service buyers in an area surrounding their place of business, so buyers often find it advantageous to patronize sellers located at varying distances from the buyer's point of purchase. Industrial buyers may purchase raw materials or operating supplies from several suppliers located at different distances from the buyer's place of business.[12] Wholesalers may assemble goods

---

[12] Most of the work on this subject has used as an example the mnufacturer who is obtaining raw materials from a variety of sources located at various distances from the point of manufacture. In this case, the focus is on the accumulation of the required quantities of raw materials, for example, at optimum cost. We shall limit our discussion at this point to the problem of accumulating required quantities of goods from several sources of supply, but shall include in our consideration the needs of wholesaler, retailers, and consumers, as well as manufacturers. It is appropriate to point out, however, that buyers may patronize sellers from varying distances not only to obtain requisite quantities at optimum cost but also to obtain differentiated qualities. We shall have more to say about the importance of quality differences in determining the limits of buying areas when we discuss consumer buying practices and their effects on retail trading areas.

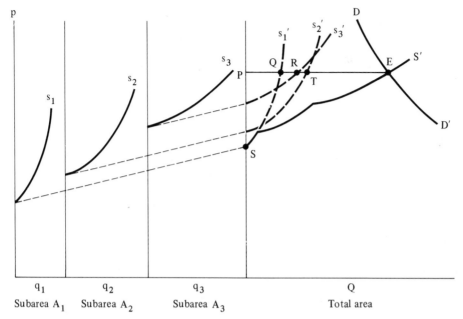

Figure 20.9. Supplies in three subareas located at varying distances from the buying center, and total demand and supply. Source: Based on Walter Isard, *Location and Space Economy* (New York: MIT Press and Wiley, 1956), pp. 155-157.

of many manufacturers located at varying distances from the wholesaler's warehouse, and consumers may buy certain goods from two or more sources of supply away from their place of residence. The analysis of the aggregation of these supplies parallels our consideration of centralized selling to dispersed buyers. We shall now consider the case in which buying is centralized and sellers are dispersed.[13]

In Figure 20.9 we show three sources of supply. The supply made available by each subarea for buyers in the centralized location is represented by s_1, s_2, and s_3. This may be thought of as a supply curve from several producers or the marginal cost curve for a single producer. Subarea A_1 is the most distant from the buying center, and the cost of transportation to the center is reflected in the transport cost gradient shown as a dotted line connecting s_1, as it exists in subarea A_1, to s_1', which is the supply from subarea A_1 when prices have been adjusted upward to take account of the cost of transportation to the center. Similarly, s_2 is adjusted upward by transport costs per unit times distance to become s_2' in the central market. The supply from subarea A_3 is also adjusted upward, but less so than that of subareas A_1 or A_2 because of its closeness to the center. These adjusted supply curves are then aggregated in the central market to form SS'. Given the demand in the central market, DD', the equilibrium price is P and the equilibrium quantity PE, of which PQ is supplied by subarea A_1, PR by subarea A_2, and PT by subarea A_3.

The effect of aggregation after transportation costs have been added is to make the supply more elastic than it was at the point of production in the subareas. This is in contrast to what happens when buyers consider their own cost of transportation in deciding how much they will buy at a given selling center. In the case of cumulative

---

[13] We again follow the analysis first developed by Hoover and extended by Isard. Hoover, op. cit., pp. 15-17; Isard, op. cit., pp. 148-150.

demand, adjusted downward for cost of transportation, the adjusted demand is more inelastic with respect to price than is the unadjusted demand.[14] From Figure 20.9 one can visualize the direction of change that would result from rising or falling costs at the point of supply, rising or falling costs of transportation, and rising or falling demand at the buying center.

Determinants of Area Limits

In the preceding section, in which we considered the determinants of the demand for and cost of delivered goods, we focused on the interaction of FOB costs, transportation costs, and demand for delivered goods to show how as distance from the point of supply or demand increases, transportation costs become increasingly important in limiting the ability of buyers or sellers at one point in space to undertake exchange relationships with their counterparts at more distant locations. At the same time, if economies of scale at a given location more than offset the higher transportation costs necessary to widen the market area sufficiently to make these economies possible, then economies of scale become a dominant factor in determining the extent of the market. We have not said very much, however, about how the precise limits of a market area are established. In order to explore this question, we shall have to consider not only one center in which there are sellers (or buyers), but also competing centers whose market areas have a limiting effect on other market areas with which they are in competition, particularly where the limits of different centers' areas are contiguous or overlapping. We shall confine our discussion to selling areas, since the impact of competition between alternative centers is so sharply defined in these cases.[15]

THE GENERAL CASE

Where two trading centers are competing for customers at an intermediate point between those centers, the boundary between the selling areas will be established at the point where

$$p_1 + r_1 m_1 = p_2 + r_2 m_2$$

---

[14] This can easily be demonstrated by arc elasticities. If sellers adjust their prices upward to take care of transportation costs, this means that a given quantity will be offered only at a higher price. Assume that without adjustment for cost of transportation, sellers would have offered 3 units at $10 each or 2 units at $8 each. The elasticity of supply is 1.8. But when transportation costs of $2 per unit are added, 3 units are offered at $12 and 2 units at $10. Now the arc elasticity becomes 2.2.

Let us say that buyers will purchase 2 units at $10 and 3 units at $8, assuming that they have no transportation costs to pay. The elasticity of demand is −1.8. But if they have to pay transportation costs of $8 per unit, they will be willing to pay only $8 for 2 units and $6 for 3 units. Now their elasticity of demand is −1.4.

[15] An early analysis of this problem was that of Frank Fetter, "The Economic Law of Market Areas," *Quarterly Journal of Economics* 38 (May 1924): 520-529, in which he allowed prices to vary at two different supply centers but had the same shipping costs per ton mile for both sellers. From this he delineated that area within which each seller would be able to sell at a lower price than the competing seller. With equal prices at the two centers (and equal shipping costs), the division between the two would be a straight line midway between them. As the selling price at A, let us say, became lower and lower, A's territory would begin to extend toward B, and B's area would become smaller and smaller.

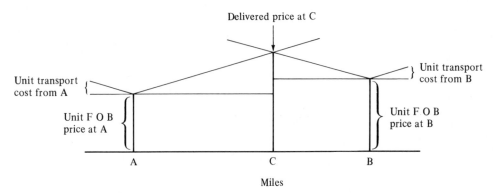

Figure 20.10. Breaking point between market areas of sellers located at sites A and B. Source: Adapted from Tord Palander, *Beiträge zur Standortstheorie* (Uppsala: Almqvist & Wiksells Boktryckeri, 1935), p. 380.

in which p_1 is the FOB price at market center 1, r_1 is the transportation cost per mile within market area 1, m_1 is the number of miles from market center 1 to the locus of the buyer, and p_2, r_2, and m_2 are the same, respectively, for market area 2. Buyers who live on the boundary of the two trading areas will be indifferent as to whether they buy in market center 1 or market center 2, since the delivered cost of goods to them will be the same from either center. If FOB prices and unit shipping costs are the same for both centers, m_1 will equal m_2, and the boundary of the trading areas will be halfway between the two centers.

Often, however, prices at two different centers will not be the same. In this case, the boundary line is moved toward the center with the higher FOB price, since buyers at the midway point will prefer to patronize the sellers at the low-cost center, substituting transportation costs for other production costs up to the point where the total delivered prices from the two centers are equalized. This is illustrated in Figure 20.10, where because of a lower FOB price a seller located at site A enjoys a much larger selling area than a similar seller located at site B.

The breaking point between two trading centers will occur where

$$r_1 m_1 - r_2 m_2 = p_2 - p_1$$

that is, where the difference in the transportation costs from the center to the point of delivery (rate per unit per mile times number of miles) for the two centers equals the difference in the FOB prices for the two centers. If the breaking point is midway between the two centers, then the difference in prices at the two centers will equal one-half of the total distance between the two centers times the difference in the unit transportation cost per mile for the two centers.

This follows from the following relationships. The breaking point occurs where

$$p_1 + r_1 m_1 = p_2 + r_2 m_2$$

The limits of the area would be a parabola around that market with the higher base price and away from that market with the lower base price.

Later, C. D. and W. P. Hyson, in "The Economic Law of Market Areas," *Quarterly Journal of Economics* 54 (May 1950): 319-327, analyzed the same problem in terms not merely of varying base prices but also of varying freight rates. They showed that there would be *hypercircles*, rather than *parabolas*, surrounding the center in which the base price plus transport costs was highest.

If the breaking point is midway between the two centers, then

$$m_1 = m_2$$

Therefore

$$p_1 + r_1 m_1 = p_2 + r_2 m_1 \quad \text{and} \quad r_1 m_1 - r_2 m_1 = p_2 - p_1$$

This means that

$$m_1 (r_1 - r_2) = p_2 - p_1$$

Also,

$$m_1 = \frac{p_2 - p_1}{r_1 - r_2}$$

which means that the distance from the breaking point to each center is equal to the ratio of the difference in prices at the two centers relative to the difference in transportation rates.

Suppose, however, that the breaking point is not equidistant from the two centers. How can it be determined? In order to state this in miles, we must know what the total distance is between the two centers. We shall designate this as d, and it will be the sum of m_1 and m_2:

From this,

$$m_1 + m_2 = d$$

$$m_2 = d - m_1$$

Substituting $d - m_1$ for m_2; we have

$$p_1 + r_1 m_1 = p_2 + r_2 (d - m_1)$$

It can then be shown[16] that the value of m_1 is

$$m_1 = \frac{p_2 - p_1}{r_1 + r_2} + \frac{r_2 d}{r_1 + r_2}$$

The value of m_1 is measured in miles from trading center 1, assuming that r_1 and r_2 are rates per mile. The breaking point, measured in miles from trading center 2, will be

$$m_2 = \frac{p_1 - p_2}{r_1 + r_2} + \frac{r_1 d}{r_1 + r_2}$$

C. D. and W. P. Hyson have delineated areas of competing centers in terms of hypercircles and have shown how a family of indifference curves can be described from the following relationships:

Let

$$h = \frac{r_2}{r_1} \quad \text{and} \quad k = \frac{p_2 - p_1}{r_1}$$

Then

$$m_1 - h m_2 = \pm k$$

---

[16] This is derived as follows:

$$r_1 m_1 - r_2 (d - m_1) = p_2 - p_1$$
$$r_1 m_1 - r_2 d + r_2 m_1 = p_2 - p_1$$
$$r_1 m_1 + r_2 m_1 = p_2 - p_1 + r_2 d$$
$$m_1 = \frac{p_2 - p_1}{r_1 + r_2} + \frac{r_2 d}{r_1 + r_2}$$

in which k describes a family of indifference curves.[17] When $(p_2 - p_1)/r_1$ is greater than zero, k will be positive; when $(p_2 - p_1)/r_1$ is less than zero, k will be negative.

INCREASING COSTS AND SELLING AREAS

In Figure 20.8 we considered the case of a seller at a given center who, by expanding sales to customers outside the trading center itself, can realize decreasing total unit costs, including costs of delivery along with other costs, up to a certain volume level. Beyond that point, marginal costs rise. We observed in Figure 20.8 that when the firm located at point A expanded its selling area to include customers at point F, such customers would find that the marginal costs of the seller from A had risen to the point where a local firm would be just as economical if such a firm had the same cost experience as the one at A. By the time the firm at A delivered the goods to point F, its marginal costs of operation and delivery would have risen to OM_a (or FT), which was exactly the same as its marginal costs when the firm sold only to customers located at the trading center.

In Figure 20.11 we show not only the marginal delivered-cost curve for the seller at A but also a similar curve for the seller at location Z, who is, let us assume, A's nearest potential competitor. The curve M_aPSTM_x is the "margin line" for the firm located at A. The curve $M_z'VSWM_y'$ is the "margin line" for the firm located at Z. On the right side of the graph, as one moves from right to left, it shows the marginal cost for sales made to

---

[17]This can be derived as follows:

If

$$p_1 + r_1 m_1 = p_2 + r_2 m_2$$

then

$$p_2 + r_2 m_2 - p_1 - r_1 m_1 = 0$$

and

$$(p_2 - p_1) + (r_2 m_2 - r_1 m_1) = 0$$

Dividing by r_1, we have

$$\frac{p_2 - p_1}{r_1} + [\ \frac{r_2}{r_1}\ m_2 - m_1] = 0$$

and

$$\frac{p_2 - p_1}{r_1} = m_1 - \frac{r_2}{r_1}\ m_2$$

This says that the line of demarcation between the trading areas of two selling centers will occur where the difference between the two prices in the two trading centers as a ratio of the transportation cost per mile from market center 1 equals the distance in miles to market center 1 less the transportation rate from center 2 relative to that from center 1 times the distance from market center 2. If we let

$$\frac{p_2 - p_1}{r_1} = k \quad \text{and} \quad \frac{r_2}{r_1} = h$$

then

$$k = m_1 - hm_2$$

Hyson, op. cit.

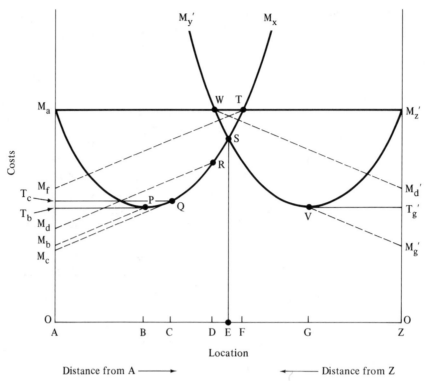

Figure 20.11. Marginal costs of production and transportation as the limits of two sellers' market areas are extended. Source: Adapted from Walter Isard, *Location and Space Economy* (New York: MIT Press and Wiley, 1956), pp. 148-150.

customers at point Z, where no delivery cost is entailed, OM_z'; the marginal cost of the seller when his sales are extended to include customers at point G, OM_g'; the cost of delivery from Z to V, shown by the transportation cost gradient, $M_g'V$; the resulting marginal cost, including transportation, of OT_g' (=GV); the marginal cost of extending service to include customers at E (the transportation gradient is not shown, but transportation costs are included in the cost ES); and the marginal cost of selling to still more customers at point D, OM_z' (= DW), which is the point at which marginal costs, including transport costs, have risen to equal the marginal cost when local customers at point Z are the only ones serviced by the firm. The curve $M_z'VSWM_y'$ is the same as $M_aPQRSTM_x$, except that the former is shown from right (nearest location) to left (farthest location), while the latter is shown from left (nearest) to right (farthest). B is closer to A than it is to Z, while G is closer to Z than it is to A. E is halfway between A and Z. Buyers at E will be indifferent as to whether they buy from sellers at A or Z. This is the breaking point at which the delivered price from the seller(s) located at Z equals the delivered price from the seller(s) located at A. Buyers at D will prefer to buy from A, because marginal costs of selling to D are DR when buying from A, instead of DW, as when buying from Z. Buyers at F will prefer to buy from Z rather than to pay a price of FT to the seller at A.

We have assumed in this example that transport costs per unit per mile are the same for both sellers. The determining factor then becomes the selling price. Were the cost curves of the two firms different, that firm with the lowest marginal cost would be able to expand its selling area at the expense of the higher-cost firm.

CENTRAL-PLACE THEORY

Classical central-place theory was formally developed by Walter Christaller, geographer, and August Lösch, economist, although some of its elements were anticipated by other writers.[18] There is basic agreement between Christaller and Lösch on the spatial arrangements in the distribution of a single good, but they differ in their treatment of multigood markets. Lösch's analysis is oriented toward primary and secondary production, while Christaller's is more useful in viewing the geographic market structure for specialized marketing institutions.[19]

The Nature of Central Places and Regions

The concept of centrality in the geographic structure of markets is similar to that of a nucleus around which mass is crystallized. A central place is the nucleus of a region and is characterized by the performance there of one or more functions, not only for the benefit of the inhabitants of the central place but also for those of the region complementary to the center. We are, of course, interested primarily in *market centers* and *market areas* for both buying and selling. Such centers are places where one or more marketing functions are performed for the benefit of buyers or sellers in the region served by that center. Subject to the modifications we shall introduce shortly, the area serviced by a given center can be thought of as circular around the center, assuming that users of the center's services are distributed equally in space and that there are no artificial barriers to trade movements in any direction. Because of the cost involved in maintaining market contacts and moving goods between sellers and buyers separated in space, the ability of a market center to serve the area that surrounds it declines as the distance from the center increases. We have characterized this declining demand for the services of a center as a demand cone covering the entire market area but greatest in height at the center itself.

A market center is both a buying and a selling center. A wholesaler buys a range of goods from numerous suppliers who are located at various selling centers that supply goods to wholesale buyers in other centers. But wholesalers are not only the center of their own buying area but also sellers in their selling area, servicing retail or industrial customers located at varying distances from the center. The wholesaler's buying and selling areas will not be identical, but they are interdependent, for buying and selling costs both enter into the wholesaler's total costs of doing business and, hence, into his decisions with respect to the location of his operations and the movement of goods into and out of the warehouse.

A retail center is similarly both a buying and a selling center. Purchases are made from manufacturers, wholesalers, and other sellers in some specified geographic area, and sales are made to households within the center's selling area. Households are, in turn, the

---

[18] Lösch, op. cit., esp. pt. I, "Location," and pt. II, "Economic Regions." Walter Christaller, *Central Places in Southern Germany*, trans. E. W. Baskin (Englewood Cliffs, N.J.: Prentice-Hall, 1966). Christaller's original was *Die zentralen Orte in Süddeutschland* (Jena: Fischer, 1933). A concise summary of classical central-place theory and of later refinements can be found in Berry, op. cit.

[19] Berry, op. cit., pp. 59-60.

center of buying and selling areas. The principal selling area in which members of a household operate is that in which their services—or labor—are sold. While other factor markets may be important to particular households, the labor market is the one through which most households obtain their purchasing power. The household is also the center of the area in which its buying takes place. This may be a small area, consisting principally of the city in which the household members live, or a much broader area, consisting of other cities to which members of the household go for shopping or from which they obtain goods and services.

Since this volume is concerned primarily with commodity markets, and with only those services that directly accompany the purchase and sale of commodities, in our discussion we shall consider central places as they affect labor markets only incidentally, concentrating instead on the relevance of central-place structure to the understanding of commodity marketing. We shall now describe how the system of market centers evolves as a part of the economic landscape.

Reasons for Agglomeration

A market center is a place where buyers and sellers meet, communicate, negotiate, and/or consummate transactions. Buyers and sellers attract each other, and they must communicate in order to effect a transaction. It is not necessary that they do so face to face, but face-to-face contacts are characteristic of many market relationships. This mutual economic attraction is, therefore, one reason for a market center. But this is not an adequate explanation of why more than one buyer and one seller meet in one place. A market center is characterized by the existence of several buyers and sellers, and large market centers by many buyers and sellers. What are the forces that lead to this clustering of buyers and sellers, commonly referred to as *agglomeration?*

NUMBER OF OPTIONS

While buyers and sellers attract each other, buyers may be repulsed by the presence of other buyers and sellers by the presence of other sellers. However, buyers are more attracted to many sellers (of identical items) than to one or a few, for the larger number of alternatives enhances the buyer's confidence that he will find the most favorable price and terms. Similarly, sellers are not attracted to competing sellers but are attracted to competing buyers, for again this assures the seller that he will obtain the most favorable price. If we extend the options of buyers and sellers still further to include not only price-quantity alternatives but also qualitative alternatives, the same reasoning would hold: Buyers will prefer a market situation in which there are many sellers with many options, and sellers will prefer a market situation in which there are many buyers with many options. We should qualify our statements in one significant respect, however. Neither sellers nor buyers will want an unlimited number of their market counterparts to choose among, for the cost of assessing the alternatives may be greater than the value of the benefits. Thus buyers may conceive of an optimum number of options among sellers, and sellers of an optimum number of options among buyers' offerings. The first reason, therefore, for the clustering of sellers and buyers in a central place is the fact that this gives both buyers and sellers information about, and opportunities to obtain, a broader range of market alternatives.

ECONOMIES OF SCALE

The second major reason for agglomeration in the location of buyers and sellers is the possibility that it opens up for economies of scale. Individual sellers will be able to realize economies associated with larger-scale buying of merchandise for resale, the maintenance of smaller inventories per dollar of sales and more rapid stockturn, more efficient use of capital equipment, greater returns from expenditures for promotional purposes—advertising, stock displays, store size and image—and more intensive utilization of managerial skills and greater ability to acquire managerial competence with its accompanying technology.

But centrally located sellers may also enjoy external economies of scale associated with the size of the center as well as economies associated with the size of the individual selling unit within the center. The development of a network of transportation and financial institutions that service the center may result from the clustering of firms (or establishments) there, but once established, such facilitating institutions may, in turn, serve to attract still more sellers because of the services available and their relative cost to users. From the viewpoint of seller promotion, a market center has greater attractions to customers because of the variety of choices it offers to buyers in merchandise, services, and prices.

In anticipation of our discussion of the hierarchy of market centers, we should also mention an economy of scale that affects both the individual seller *and* the market center as a whole. There are some types of specialized marketing institutions that could not exist unless the demand reaches a certain total level. That is, the demand necessary to support such an institution may be so large that it requires a large market area for that volume of demand to be realized. For example, a store that specializes in millinery could not even exist in a village. The more centralized the market, however, the broader the market area will be and the greater the probability that a specialty store of this type will be able to cover its costs. As centralization increases and the market area widens, the degree of specialization that can be supported will increase. We are likely, therefore, to find a millinery store specializing in high-fashion items only in a highly centralized trading center with a large regional or national market area. In one sense this is a problem of economies of scale for the store, for the store has to be quite large to operate economically. But it involves more than that. It is a matter not merely of reaching an optimum size but of reaching a size sufficient so that it can even exist. In the absence of centralization not only does such a store fail to reach its optimum size, but it fails to reach any size at all! One could also say that the ability of a more highly centralized center to support such a specialty store results in external economies of scale, for all the sellers in the center, and all the buyers who patronize that center, benefit from the presence there of this highly specialized service that would otherwise not be available as an attraction to customers (from the other retailers' point of view) or as a service to customers (from the customers' point of view).

SUMMARY

In summary, a large supply center offers the possibility to buyers of lower prices due to economies of scale and intensity of competition; a greater variety from which choices can be made, including variety with respect to both quality and price options; and flexibility (variety through time) in meeting the changing demands of buyers. It is these attractions to buyers that give rise to profit potentials for sellers who locate in market centers. Offsetting those agglomerating influences that give rise to market centers are the costs of concentration. These include the costs of maintaining contacts between buyers and sellers when both are not located in the center, costs of moving merchandise physically from the center to buyers located in the area, and costs of congestion. The latter may, in fact, become so onerous in extremely large centers as to cause marked geographic reallocation of subsidiary market centers within the boundaries of politically defined centers.

Competing Centers and the Shape of Market Areas

Having established that a market center exists for reasons of efficiency or promotional strategy (with its implied profit potential), we turn now to the location of competing centers and the contour of the market areas they serve. A single center serving an area in which buyers are distributed evenly over the surface and in which there are no artificial or natural barriers would tend to have a circular trading area. If FOB costs or the costs of transportation are reduced, this will tend to widen the market area. If, however, the demand is sufficient to support more than one center, how will the area be divided among these centers?

Assume that we have a flat landscape and that buyers are evenly dispersed over the total area. Under these circumstances, it is tempting to say that each center will have a circular area contiguous to but not overlapping the areas of competing centers. But section (A) of Figure 20.12 shows that if this is the case, the total area is not covered. Buyers who reside in the spaces not contained within a circular area would not be serviced. Suppose therefore that we cover the entire area by permitting the overlapping of circles, as in section (B). This will mean, of course, that each center shares a part of its area with each of the six areas with which it overlaps.[20] If we assume that buyers in these areas of overlap will prefer the closest trading center, then the areas of overlap will be divided by a straight line, resulting in the hexagons shown in section (C) of Figure 20.12. It is on this basis that Lösch concluded that competing market ares will tend to be hexagonal in shape.[21]

If the demand density is constant throughout a trading surface, if FOB prices and transport costs per unit per mile are the same for all competing centers, if sellers are free to enter the market and locate in such a way that they will maximize their profits, and if no part of the trading surface is excluded from the area of one trading center, then sellers will enter the market and locate on the surface in such a way that their selling areas are

---

[20] Only the central area in Figure 20.12, section (B), shows the six overlaps. Not shown in this diagram are the other areas that could compete with the five outside trade centers.

[21] See Lösch, op. cit., pp. 105-114. Lösch's position on this has been challenged by Mills and Lav, however. They have demonstrated that if there is free entry of firms, it will not result in the filling of all space with hexagon-shaped market areas. Rather, they find (1) that a "firm will choose a circular market area unless competitors constrain it to some other market-area form," (2) that free entry need not result in space-filling market areas but can instead result in areas so structured that some segments of the total space are not serviced by any trading center, and (3) that free entry can result in market areas that are either circular or *s*-sided polygons in which values of *s* are integer multiples of six. They say they cannot prove that *s*-sided polygons that result from free entry cannot be integers of something other than six, but their analysis leads them to believe that this is the case. Edwin S. Mills and Michael R. Lav, "A Model of Market Areas with Free Entry," *Journal of Political Economy* 72 (June 1964): 278-288. The quotation is from p. 282.

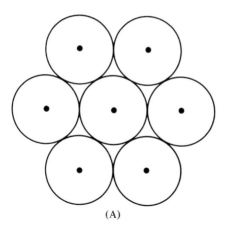

(A)

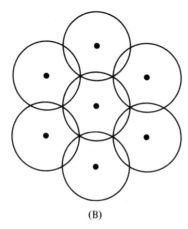

(B)

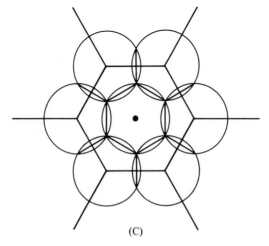

(C)

Figure 20.12. How circular market areas become hexagonal. (A) Nonoverlapping circles. (B) Overlapping circles. (C) Nonoverlapping hexagons.

equal and hexagonal.[22] If the sellers cluster, thereby forming a market center, then each center will likewise tend to be hexagonal so that the entire surface is covered by continuous hexagonal areas of comparable centers.[23]

Market Hierarchies

Our discussion up to this point has concerned trading centers that are essentially alike. If, however, we consider the reaction of consumers to their market alternatives, we know that they look to different centers for different goods and services. Similarly, wholesalers and industrial buyers obtain different types of goods, and particularly different services, from different supply centers. One of Christaller's major contributions to central-place theory was his detailed delineation of the hierarchy of market centers and the utilization of this classification in both describing and explaining the relationships of market centers and areas of different sizes to each other. For purposes of illustration we shall describe this hierarchy as it appears in retail trade.[24]

Consider first a large regional retail trading center that provides an extremely wide range of goods and services for consumers. Such a center will draw its clientele from a very wide market area, and in it can be found highly specialized goods and services not available in centers of a lower order. The size of the center's market area will be that necessary to provide the requisite demand to support the degree of specialization found in the commodity and institutional structure of the center. The goods and services provided are those of the highest order in the sense that their specialization and limited demand make them economical parts of the merchandising mix only where the market area is extremely great.

Goods of the next order are somewhat less specialized and can be sold economically in trading centers whose market areas are somewhat smaller. Goods of a still lower order will be the highest-order goods found in still smaller centers, each with a smaller trading area. Fourth-order goods are the highest-order goods found in still smaller centers serving still smaller market areas, and so on through the spectrum of goods and services arrayed from highest to lowest in terms of their degree of specialization, and/or the importance of range of choice to consumers in exercising their buying function.

The highest order of goods carried in a market center is highly correlated with the

---

[22] It is important to note that the conditions of long-run equilibrium described by Lösch indicate that the delivered price exceeds marginal costs, including cost of transportation. This is demonstrated in Figure 20.4 See Lösch, op. cit., pp. 105-108.

Mills and Lav point out, however, that a welfare model that requires long-run equality of marginal cost and delivered price would not be satisfied by Lösch's conditions, in which output is less than would be necessary to achieve social optimality. Therefore the division of the total surface into hexagonal markets, resulting in maximization of profits by freely entering sellers (or centers), would lead to higher prices than would be realized were there fewer and larger sellers (or centers). See Mills and Lav, op. cit., pp. 286-288.

[23] We are assuming, of course, that the trading centers are alike. Just as two different sellers are seldom homogeneous with respect to costs and services and, hence, the size and shape of their respective selling areas, so trading centers, in which many sellers cluster, are still more likely not to be homogeneous with respect to their offerings and costs. We shall consider later some of the important ways in which heterogeneity affects area limits and contours.

[24] A hierarchy also exists for wholesale trade. The underlying principles would be the same as for retail market centers, but the determining variables would be those peculiar to the demand for and supply of

population of that center (or metropolitan area) and with the population of the trading area served by that center. New York and Chicago are certainly outstanding regional centers and, in many respects, national centers. Other regional centers would include Los Angeles, Denver, Atlanta, and Boston. Large cities are within the area dominated by a regional center but are themselves the centers of substantial trading areas. Surrounding Chicago, for example, are Detroit, Milwaukee-Racine, Minneapolis-St. Paul, and St. Louis. Centers of still lower order in this same vicinity include Grand Rapids, Davenport-Rock Island, and Indianapolis. At the next level are such places as St. Joseph, Madison, Winnebago, Rockford, Peoria, and Fort Wayne.

The position that any market center holds in the hierarchy of centers depends on the highest order of goods that it carries. The higher the order of the center, the greater the variety of demands that it is prepared to meet. In New York and Chicago, for example, highly specialized goods and services can be found. But along with these are large quantities of shopping goods as well as convenience goods. Buyers may come to Chicago from extremely great distances in order to purchase a violin. While there for that purpose, they may also purchase shopping goods. Other buyers will come to Chicago to acquire shopping goods, either because they are seeking something unique within shopping-goods lines, or because they wish to inspect the stocks of goods available in the Chicago market center as a source of market information before making a purchase decision. It is unlikely that the limits of the area from which Chicago draws shopping-goods customers will be as great as that from which it draws buyers of highly specialized goods, such as violins, and particularly rare violins. Chicago will also sell convenience goods, but the bulk of these sales will be made to customers residing in Chicago itself. Customers from out of town who purchase convenience goods in Chicago probably buy them there because it is less costly to buy all goods on a single shopping trip.

The principle underlying this ordering of goods and, hence, of market centers is that of minimizing the costs associated with satisfying a particular demand. The more specialized the demand or the supply, the greater the size of the market area necessary for the aggregate demand to be sufficient to support the supply of that good or service economically. The other facet is consumer willingness to go to a larger and more distant market center for higher-order goods. The higher the order of a good or service, the higher the price consumers are willing to pay per unit. Possibly, also, the demand for such goods will be more inelastic than for less specialized items. These are goods for which consumers are most willing to incur the costs of traveling to a more distant market and of having goods transported from a distant market center to them.

Arrangement of the Hierarchy of Market Centers and Areas

How will markets, classified according to the highest order of goods they carry, arrange themselves on the economic landscape? Christaller has described three possible arrangements appropriate for the hierarchy of urban centers, one of which is particularly appropriate in viewing the marketing functions of urban centers. He calls this a system of central places according to the marketing principle.[25] Figure 20.13 illustrates this

---

goods at wholesale and would therefore be less directly affected by the characteristics of consumer buying behavior.

[25] Christaller, op. cit., pp. 58-72.

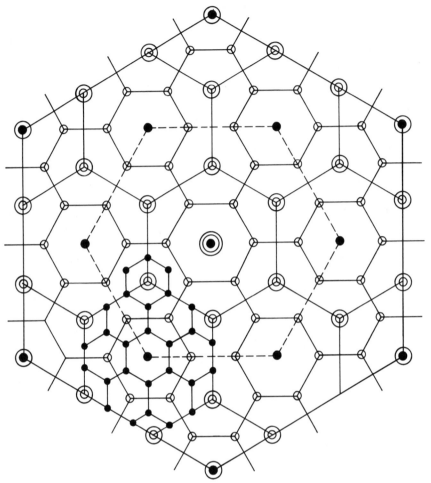

( ) Level VI   Regional center

( ) Level V   Large cities

• Level IV   Small cities

( ) Level III Large towns

○ Level II   Small towns

• Level I   Villages

Figure 20.13. Marketing areas in a six-level system of central places.

arrangement. There is an urban center that is an important market center for the entire region. This is the market center indicated as level VI in Figure 20.13.[26] At that center can be found the widest range of goods of any center in the area. Goods of the highest

---

[26]We have changed Christaller's terminology to labels more appropriate to the United States. In our discussion we shall refer to the smallest central place as level I, with places of higher order ranging upward: level II, level III, etc. Our level I is the equivalent of Christaller's M places.

order—highly specialized goods in short supply or demanded by only a few consumers—are sold in this center and will draw customers from the hexagonal area delineated by lines connecting level V centers.

Although virtually all goods and services may be purchased in the level VI center, market centers of lower order will develop as enterprisers see opportunities to provide lower-order goods, that is, goods for which the demand is sufficient to support economic distribution outlets nearer to consumers, who will thereby be able to meet their demands at point-of-sale prices plus transport costs that are more favorable than those possible by traveling to the level VI center. Thus a series of six level V centers develop, located at the points of a hexagon surrounding the level VI center. Therefore the level VI center dominates sales of these level V goods to customers who are closer to center VI than they are to center V. This smaller area of dominance is shown by the hexagon that connects the level IV centers. The level IV centers spring up in order to provide customers within their areas with level IV goods, plus goods of lower orders that customers who live close to these centers will buy there.

A set of lower-level centers will develop around each higher-level center so long as the lower-level center finds that the amount of goods it can sell is sufficient to enable it to survive. These goods will tend to be goods of a lower order than those sold by the next-higher-level center. In the hexagon in the southwestern part of the area that we show in Figure 20.13, we have indicated the areas of the level II centers but have not indicated market areas for the level I centers, which would tend to be quite small.

THE MARKETING PRINCIPLE

We turn now to the question of why centers of a lower order are located where they are. One basis of explanation is the *marketing principle*. We have already shown that complete coverage of a surface and minimization of transport costs will be achieved through hexagonal market areas surrounding a center. Each center is surrounded by six centers of the next-lower order. Centers of equal order are an equal distance from each other. In keeping with the principle of minimizing transport costs, centers of lower order will be located at a point midway between three centers of the next-higher order. This system of market areas has been called the $k=3$ system.[27] Each market area includes k areas of the next-lower order. In Figure 20.13, for example, there are six level IV centers. Each of these includes one-third of the market area of each of six level III centers, plus its own level III area. There is a total of three level III areas within its own level IV area. If the level I area is 1 square mile, the level II area will be 3 square miles, level III will be 9 square miles, level IV will be 27 square miles, and so on. Thus as the number of centers increases from the highest order center to the lowest order, the number of *market areas* of successively lower orders will be in the ratio of 1, 3, 9, 27, 81, ... The number of *centers* will grow as we move from the highest order to the lowest order at the ratio of 1, 2, 6, 18, 54, 162, ...[28]

---

[27] Lösch, op. cit., pp. 130-132.

[28] The reason why the number of centers moves from 1 to 2 rather than from 1 to 6 can be explained by reference to Figure 20.13. After center VI has been created, the six V centers will develop. However, these are also functionally related to other VI centers. Only one-third of the market area of each of these level V centers lies within the area of the level VI center. Therefore instead of there being 6 level V centers for each level VI center, there are ⅓ (6), or 2, level V centers for each level VI center. When still lower level centers are developed, however, their entire area falls within the level VI

THE TRANSPORTATION PRINCIPLE

Suppose, however, sudsidiary centers grow up, not at midpoints between *three* centers of the next-higher order, but at midpoints between *two* centers of the next-higher order. This would result in an arrangement of centers and areas according to the *transportation principle*.[29] In this system, new subsidiary centers grow up along transport routes that have developed between centers of a higher order. Although centers of equal order will be an equal distance from one another in this system, traffic routes will include centers of both higher and lower orders. Each center will be an equal distance from two centers of the next-higher order.

COMPARISON OF THE MARKETING AND TRANSPORTATION PRINCIPLES

Differences between the locational system according to the marketing principle and the locational system according to the transportation principle can be seen by comparing parts A and B in Figure 20.14. Part A illustrates the marketing principle, which minimizes distance between a center and all parts of the center's area. Part B illustrates the transportation principle, which minimizes distance between a center and all centers of the next-lower order. Principal transportation routes in each are shown by the dashed lines.

While the marketing principle results in a $k = 3$ system, the transportation principle results in a $k = 4$ system. In a $k = 4$ system the number of centers necessary to support a given population is greater than in a $k = 3$ system. In a $k = 3$ system, the number of *centers* progresses at the rate of 1, 2, 6, 18, 54, ... In a $k = 4$ system, the rate of progression is 1, 3, 12, 48, 172, ... Since the number of subsidiary areas within a given center's area of dominance is 4 in the $k = 4$ system, in contrast to 3 in the $k = 3$ system, the number of market *areas* in the entire system will progress more rapidly in the $k = 4$ system than in the $k = 3$ system. The total number of market areas in the system will be 1, 4, 16, 64, 236, ... In essence, then, location of centers according to the transportation principle results in more centers and more market areas. The smaller centers that locate along main transport routes are likely to have areas that are "wider" than they are "long"; that is, the limits of the area along the route will be affected by the location of the next center on the route, while the absence of centers to the "left" and "right" of the transport route will mean that the small center's area extends outward in both those directions in order to serve customers who are not on the main transport route.

The marketing principle results in the most economical arrangement of centers except where there are extenuating circumstances such as the following:

1. A situation in which a particular area draws large quantities of the goods it consumes from distant points and develops, therefore, important long-distance through routes along which centers of lower order develop, in contrast to a more self-sufficient area where traffic is short-distance traffic and market centers are located as close as is economical to consumers

---

area. Therefore the six level IV centers and their respective areas are totally "imputed" to the level VI center.

[29] Christaller, op. cit., pp. 72-77. Christaller's translator calls this the "traffic principle," but we believe the term *transportation principle* is better.

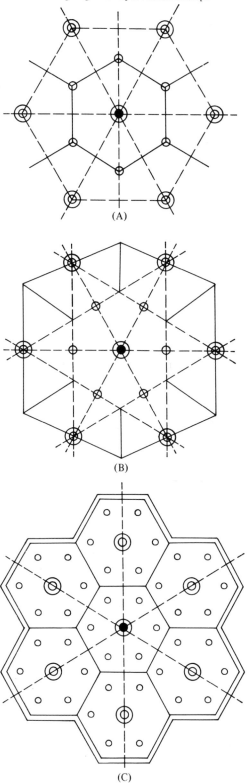

Figure 20.14. Marketing areas in a system of central places structured according to the marketing principle (A), the transportation principle (B), and the separation principle (C).

2. A high-income economy in which the luxury of the "surplus" centers that develop under the transport principle can be indulged in
3. Natural barriers that make it necessary for market centers to be built in a line, for example, where a road moves through a valley and trading centers develop along it because this is the only place where towns and cities can be built

If consumers are distributed evenly over a given surface, the marketing principle will provide market facilities more economically than the transportation principle.

THE SEPARATION PRINCIPLE

The third principle governing the location of urban centers and the area they serve is the *separation principle.*[30] This is sociopolitical in origin and can also be labeled the *administration principle.* The governing system developed in an area may result in discrete units of area in which the governing unit located at a centralized point services a given area—a city, a county, a district, a state, a nation. It has long been recognized that in areas that are predominately agricultural the county seat occupies a particularly important place as a focal point for legal and political activities of the surrounding area. Because of its political importance, it may also become a market center.

In part (C) of Figure 20.14, the relationships of levels of centers organized according to the separation principle are shown. The dotted lines show principal transportation routes. Level III might be regional centers where branch offices of state government are located, while level II centers would be county seats. Level I centers are small towns within the county. Level I centers are tied to level II centers by legal relationships, as level II centers are tied to the level III center. Thus the boundaries of areas are politically determined, and the ties between centers are legally established. In keeping with the hexagonal structure of areas assumed in all the location systems stemming from central-place theory, the administrative principle assumes that each central place will service six centers of lower order. This is a $k = 7$ system. Since political rather than economic conditions determine the relations of centers to each other and the contour of their areas, hexagonal areas will be accidental except where the efficiency of intergovernmental relationships is affected by distance and becomes a factor in determining centers and related areas.

Social factors could lead to similar areas where social groupings result in boundaries across which group members will not move. For example, this could show up in marketing if there are areas within a city or metropolitan area that become self-contained, such as the ghetto areas of minorities. There is considerable evidence that blacks who reside in ghettos do not move out of the ghetto to purchase merchandise, even though buying opportunities are more extensive outside.

MARKET CENTERS AND AREAS

The marketing principle provides the most useful framework for describing and analyzing *market* areas, for it is based on a cost-revenue approach to the analysis of the location and areas of marketing establishments. But there are many examples of locational patterns that have followed the transportation principle or the separation principle, and market areas have frequently conformed to these alternate patterns. Sometimes the three types of area organization have intermingled to yield a mixed area pattern.

---

[30] Ibid., pp. 77-80.

Most of the time we have been assuming that population is distributed over a given surface equally. This is not, of course, what generally occurs, and it is particularly unlikely as an economy obtains an increasing proportion of its output through secondary and tertiary industries. People will bunch into an urban center, both because of the opportunity afforded them for employment there and for the advantages it offers as a center in which they can buy goods and services.

A system of market centers and areas is not static. Over time there will be changes in consumer demand, in technology and production potential, in costs of production and marketing, and in institutional arrangements and processes by which marketing functions can be performed. In addition, consumers themselves may show more or less mobility and respond to geographic conditions by altering their own location. Once a geographic pattern has been established, the pattern itself becomes a determinant of subsequent patterns, for the cost of change may not be inconsequential. An old and well-established trading center may perpetuate itself for many years long after the original reasons for its existence have disappeared, doing so primarily by the ease (i.e., low cost) with which it can maintain a strong competitive position vis-à-vis alternative centers that may evolve to threaten it. But cities can and do die, and market centers can and do expire, or at least change their relative importance. Such changes reflect alterations in the underlying demand and supply conditions that shape the geographic structure of marketing. Central-place theory provides a framework for viewing and analyzing this structure and suggests some of the criteria by which that structure can be appraised.

RETAIL MARKET AREAS

In our discussion of the general determinants of location and market areas and of central-place theory, we have drawn a number of examples from retailing. It is appropriate to review briefly some of the empirical work on retail trading areas and to show in what particular ways central-place theory should be modified in order for it to be useful in retail market area analysis.

Some Empirical Studies

REILLY'S "LAW" OF RETAIL GRAVITATION

William J. Reilly's "law" of retail gravitation was formally stated in 1931.[31] On the basis of evidence obtained through a national study (which he does not describe), Reilly concluded that the two important variables that determine the amount of retail trade in a city are its population and its distance from a comparable city, and that these two variables are a reliable index of other variables that might bear upon a city's retail volume. His generalizations are relevant to retail trade in shopping goods.

His basic proposition is that

two cities attract retail trade from any intermediate city or town in the vicinity of the breaking point approximately in direct proportion to the population of the two cities

---

[31] William J. Reilly, *The Law of Retail Gravitation* (New York: William J. Reilly, 1931).

and in inverse proportion to the square of the distances from these two cities to the intermediate town.[32]

This can be stated as follows:

$$R_a = \left(\frac{P_a}{P_b}\right)\left(\frac{D_b}{D_a}\right)^2$$

in which R_a is the amount of trade drawn to city A from the intermediate point relative to the amount drawn to city B; P_a and P_b are the populations of cities A and B, respectively; and D_a and D_b are the distances of the intermediate point from cities A and B, respectively.[33] Reilly established the exponent for P_a/P_b as 1.0 from "personal investigation."[34] The exponent of 2.0 for D_b/D_a was established on the basis of information obtained about the breaking point between cities as reflected in retail credit records of cities in 20 states and the District of Columbia that he visited during the period 1927-1930.[35] Data from studies of 255 cities and towns in Texas yielded a distance exponent of about 1.51-2.50, with computed values ranging from approximately 1 through 12.[36]

From the basic formula another formula can be derived that indicates the breaking point of the selling areas between two competing cities, since this would be the point where $R_a = 1$:

$$M_b = \frac{D_a + D_b}{1 + \sqrt{\dfrac{P_a}{P_b}}}$$

in which M_b is the breaking point in miles from B.[37]

---

[32] Ibid., p. 9.

[33] We have substituted R_a for B_a/B_b in Reilly's original formula. B_a is generally defined as the proportion of retail trade from the intermediate point attracted by city A, and B_b as the proportion of retail trade from the intermediate point attracted by city B, but this is not accurate. It is not the proportion of total retail trade accounted for by residents of the intermediate point. Nor is it the proportion of total retail trade accounted for by residents of the intermediate point that goes to A and B. The exact values of B_a and B_b will vary depending on the population and on the distance, and whether distance is measured in miles, kilometers, feet, yards, or whatever. B_a/B_b is meaningful only as a ratio of the (unspecified) amount of trade that goes to A relative to the (unspecified) amount that goes to B. If one wished to calculate that proportion of trade which goes to A from the intermediate point's total trade with both A and B, this could be done by converting B_a/B_b into $B_a/(1.00 - B_a)$. In the equation we use here, we have adhered to Reilly's original formula except that we have substituted the term R_a for B_a/B_b. If R_a is found, for example, to equal 1.2 for point X, which is between A and B, this means that of the total trade that customers at X do with both A and B, the amount that goes to A is 20 percent greater than the amount that goes to B. Therefore A obtains 54.5 percent of X's out-of-town trade. ($R_a = B_a/B_b = 1.2$. If $B_a + B_b = 1.00$, then $B_a = 1.2/2.2 = .545$, or 54.5 percent.)

[34] Ibid., pp. 71-72.

[35] Ibid., p. 64.

[36] William J. Reilly, *Methods for the Study of Retail Relationships*, University of Texas, Bureau of Business Research, Studies in Marketing, no. 4 (Austin: University of Texas Press, 1929), pp. 49-50.

[37] This can be derived as follows:

$$R_a = \left(\frac{P_a}{P_b}\right)\left(\frac{D_b}{D_a}\right)^2$$

The breaking point is where

$$R_a = 1$$

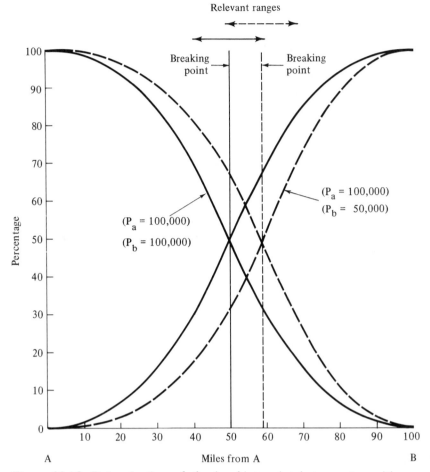

Figure 20.15. Determination of the breaking point between two cities according to Reilly's law of retail gravitation.

In Figure 20.15 we show the values of $[B_a/(B_a + B_b)]$ and $[B_b/(B_a + B_b)]$ for different sites between cities A and B on the basis of Reilly's formula. The two cities are 100 miles apart. In one case, we assume that each city has 100,000 population. In the other case, we assume that city A has 100,000 and city B has 50,000 population. The relevant range, as Reilly pointed out, is that near the breaking point between the two cities. When the population of the two cities is equal, the breaking point is midway between the two—50 miles from A and 50 miles from B. If B's population is half of A's, the breaking point moves to a point 59 miles from A and only 41 miles from B.

Therefore, at the breaking point

$$1 = \left(\frac{P_a}{P_b}\right)\left(\frac{D_b}{D_a}\right)^2$$

Taking the square root of both sides, we find that

$$1 = \sqrt{\frac{P_a}{P_b}}\left(\frac{D_b}{D_a}\right)$$

One of the reasons we have included Figure 20.15 is to show very clearly that Reilly's equation is appropriate only for the calculation of share of trade near the breaking point and not for other points closer to the competing cities. For example, if the cities are of equal size, is there any reason to believe that, at a point 30 miles from city A, 16 percent of the out-of-town shopping done by people who live there will be done in city B? If B is no bigger than A and is no better as a shopping center, why would buyers travel 70 miles when they could accomplish the same thing by traveling 30? If, of course, B is a better shopping center than A, then this differentiation would have to be taken into account in the formula; but it is not. It would be helpful to have a formula that is sufficiently general to indicate share-of-trade information for all points between two competing centers.

CONVERSE'S REFINEMENTS

On the basis of his extensive empirical testing of Reilly's formula, Paul D. Converse has contributed two additional findings to Reilly's generalizations.[38] Where the population of one of two competing towns is more than 20 times the population of the other, the appropriate exponent to use for the distance ratios is 3 rather than 2.[39] In these cases, the breaking point becomes

---

Multiplying both sides by D_a/D_b, we have

$$\frac{D_a}{D_b} = \sqrt{\frac{P_a}{P_b}}$$

and multiplying both sides by D_b, we get

$$D_a = D_b \sqrt{\frac{P_a}{P_b}}$$

We then add D_b to both sides:

$$D_a + D_b = D_b + D_b \sqrt{\frac{P_a}{P_b}} \quad \text{and} \quad D_a + D_b = D_b \left(1 + \sqrt{\frac{P_a}{P_b}}\right)$$

Dividing both sides by $1 + \sqrt{\frac{P_a}{P_b}}$, we have

$$\frac{D_a + D_b}{1 + \sqrt{\frac{P_a}{P_b}}} = D_b$$

Therefore the breaking point is where

$$D_b = \frac{D_a + D_b}{1 + \sqrt{\frac{P_a}{P_b}}}$$

---

[38] Among the studies by Paul D. Converse are *A Study of Retail Trade Areas in East Central Illinois*, University of Illinois, Bureau of Economic and Business Research, Business Studies no. 2 (Urbana: University of Illinois, 1943); "Analysis of Retail Trade Areas," *National Marketing Review* 1 (Spring 1936): 316-325; "Is There a Law of Retail Gravitation?" *Printers' Ink*, September 10, 1943, p. 36; (with R. V. Mitchell), "The Movement of Retail Trade Within a Metropolitan Area," *Journal of Marketing* 2 (July 1937): 61-67; "A Retail Trading Area," *Journal of Marketing* 7 (October 1942): 160; *Retail Trade Areas in Illinois*, University of Illinois, Bureau of Economic and Business Research, Business Studies no. 6 (Urbana: University of Illinois, 1948); *Survey of the Kankakee Retail Trade Area* (Urbana: University of Illinois, Bureau of Economic and Business Research, 1949); and "New Laws of Retail Gravitation," *Journal of Marketing* 14 (October 1949): 379-384.

[39] Converse, "New Laws of Retail Gravitation," op. cit., pp. 383-384.

$$\text{Breaking point in miles from B} = \frac{D_a + D_b}{1 + \sqrt[3]{\dfrac{P_a}{P_b}}}$$

Where there is a satellite town within the trade area of a larger trading center, the total trade of that satellite town is divided between local stores and those in the larger trading center in direct proportion to the populations of the two towns and inversely as the squares of the distance, using 4 as the distance factor for the home town.[40] The appropriate formula is

$$R_a = \left(\frac{P_a}{P_h}\right)\left(\frac{4}{D_a}\right)^2$$

in which R_a is the portion of trade attracted by central city A relative to that retained by the home town, P_a and P_h are the populations of central city A and the home town, respectively, and D_a is the distance between the home town and central city A. Converse calls 4 an inertia factor. Another way of regarding it is to consider this the normal distance traveled by consumers who shop in the home town, compared to D_a, which is the distance they would have to travel to shop in the central city.

HUFF'S PROBABILISTIC MODEL

A more recent refinement of Reilly's population-distance formula has been developed by David L. Huff in terms of a probabilistic model:

$$P_{ij} = \frac{S_j/T_{ij}^{\lambda}}{\sum\limits_{j=1}^{n} S_j/T_{ij}^{\lambda}}$$

in which P_{ij} is the probability P of a consumer originating at a given point i shopping at a particular retail location j; S_j is the size of a retail location j measured in square feet of selling or building area; T_{ij} is the distance, T, expressed in terms of physical distance, time, or cost, separating i and j; λ is a parameter that reflects the sensitivity of various kinds of shopping trips to distance; and n is the number of retail locations.[41] λ is determined from empirical observation. For any given retail site probability isocurves can be established that show equal probabilities of shopping at the specified retail site.

Huff's model is not basically different from Reilly's, but it focuses more sharply on meaningful determinants or their proxies. It permits more flexibility by incorporating all possible market center alternatives and leaving the value of λ unspecified. But λ has to be determined empirically, as was the case with the exponents in Reilly's formula. Huff substitutes selling area or building area for population size of a center and broadens the acceptable measures of travel cost, both of which are improvements over the Reilly formula. By recasting the drawing power into a shopping probability, he makes it possible

---

[40] Ibid., pp. 380-383.

[41] David L. Huff, *Determination of Intraurban Retail Trade Areas* (Los Angeles: University of California, Real Estate Research Program, 1962), and "A Probability Analysis of Shopping Center Trading Areas," *Land Economics* 53 (February 1963): 81-90; David L. Huff and Larry Blue, *A Programmed Solution for Estimating Retail Sales Potentials* (Lawrence: The University of Kansas, Center for Regional Studies, n.d.); David L. Huff, "A Programmed Solution for Approximating an Optimum Retail Location," *Land Economics* 42 (August 1966): 293-303.

to view more clearly interpersonal differences in shopping behavior and intertemporal differences for one person.

INTRACITY TRADING AREAS

Reilly's basic approach to trading area analysis, involving the use of population as a proxy for a center's attracting power and distance as a factor generating resistance or inertia, has also been used in studying the internal trading-area structure of urban centers. Extending this approach to the study of area overlap as well as area limits, Louis P. Bucklin has utilized a *contour profile* to show the probability that a consumer who is located at a given point will shop in a given center.[42] From this profile, the probability of overlap between two competing centers can be measured. Bucklin reasoned that this overlap would be a function of buyers' sensitivity to market alternatives (his term is *sensitivity to product*)—the importance attached to finding the right price, quality, and service, and buyers' perception of the extent of variability for these among various outlets—and a function of their sensitivity to travel—out-of-pocket and opportunity costs of reaching a certain store. He hypothesized that (1) the greater the distance between sellers, the less the extent of area overlap, and (2) the more sensitive buyers are to product differences and market alternatives, the greater area overlap would be. An examination of buying behavior patterns for supermarkets, automobiles, and household goods in selected segments of the Berkeley-Oakland areas of California tended to substantiate his hypotheses, suggesting that area overlap may be quite important for alternative outlets located close to one another and that the distance exponent of the traditional (e.g., Reilly) models is not fixed but varies as distance increases. Most empirical studies of retail trading areas have demonstrated the importance of area overlap resulting from the fact that customers in some locations will prefer one shopping center while others in the same location will prefer another.

EMPIRICAL STUDIES OF HIERARCHIAL SYSTEMS

In the second part of his study of central-place theory, Christaller reports the results of his study of the number, sizes, and distribution of the central places in southern Germany. In the English translation of his work, only the L system of Munich is described in detail.[43] He found that centers in southern Germany were amenable to classification according to the hierarchy principle and that their arrangement most often followed the marketing principle, although some evidence of the operation of the transportation and separation principles was also found. He regarded the transportation and separation principles as secondary, accounting for deviations from the marketing principle. Deviations from the theoretical central-place system structured according to the marketing principle were due to (1) a raising of the center's level above that which was expected because of unusual wealth or population density, (2) a narrowing or widening of distances associated with unusual strength or weakness of the central place and competing places, (3) a greater or smaller number of central places in relation to the theoretical number, related to deviations in the level of wealth or population density. Local

---

[42] Louis P. Bucklin, "Trade Area Boundaries: Some Issues in Theory and Methodology," *Journal of Marketing Research* 8 (February 1971): 30-37.

[43] Christaller, op. cit., pp. 137-226.

deviations were found to be related to specialized local resources, such as spas or mines, and to the effect of barriers on local prices. Deviations from the expected pattern that were due to noneconomic factors included those related to historical development, physiological factors such as the terrain, and social influences such as the desire for centralization or federalism, plus those caused by military needs, such as fortresses.[44]

One of the best examples of a hierarchy of central places in a spatial system is found in Iowa. A relatively flat land surface that is threaded by a system of vertical and horizontal transport routes, and the combination of agricultural and industrial development and of rural and urban centers, have resulted in a spatial system that shows remarkable consistency with central-place theory. The characteristics of this particular market system, as established by numerous studies, are well summarized by Berry.[45] Combining data from the Iowa studies and similar studies in South Dakota, Berry has introduced some refinements into the analysis of a system of trading centers that make it possible to establish upper and lower limits to the size and functions of trading centers and, correspondingly, the size of the areas they serve.

Figure 20.16 shows the relationship between different kinds of trading centers and the population and geographic areas they serve. Villages are indicated by 1, towns by 2, small cities by 3, large cities or regional centers by 4. Rural areas lie in trapezoids A and B, indicating low population density. Urban areas are in the D and E trapezoids. Occasionally an urban center will serve an extremely large trading area with a relatively low average population density throughout the area in spite of the population concentration at the center. This is symbolized in Figure 20.16 by the 4 that appears in the population density trapezoid B. Other urban centers may have a much higher average population density in the areas they serve, and this is indicated by the 4 that appears in population density trapezoid D.

As we move from villages (1), to towns (2), to small cities (3), to large cities (4), the maximum reach of each in square miles increases. In Iowa, for example, it was found that the maximum reach of villages was about 90 square miles, of towns about 300 square miles, and of small cities about 1,000 square miles. Regional centers in Iowa and South Dakota were found to have an area limit of more than 10,000 square miles. These limits are shown by the horizontal lines above the villages, towns, small cities, and large cities, which represent the maximum reach of these centers in these two states at the time they were studied.

The threshold level is measured by the population served (horizontal axis) and shows that population level at which functions of increasing order occur. For example, in Iowa village-level functions (e.g., groceries) appeared at a population level of about 400; town-level functions (e.g., dry cleaning) appeared at about 2,500 population, and small-city functions (e.g., clothing) appeared at about 20,000 population. This is shown by the position of the lower left-hand corner of the trapezoid that embraces each set of centers in relation to the horizontal axis and is known as the *threshold level*. This does not mean, of course, that village functions are not also performed in towns and cities. Rather, we are demarcating the population level at which the next-higher order of function first appears.

---

[44] Ibid., pp. 190-197.

[45] Berry, op cit., pp. 1-25. Other studies of selected hierarchial systems in Great Britain, Europe, Africa, Asia, and the United States are described by Peter Scott, *Geography and Retailing* (Chicago: Aldine, 1970), pp. 112-154.

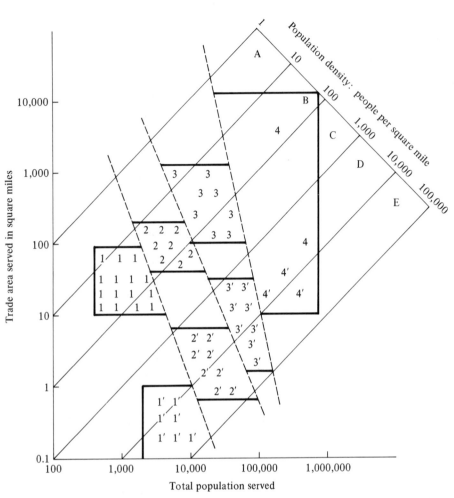

Figure 20.16. Distribution of marketing centers serving urban and rural populations according to trade area served in the logarithm of square miles and the logarithm of total population. Source: Adapted from Brian J. L. Berry, *Geography of Market Centers and Retail Distribution* (Englewood Cliffs, N.J.: Prentice-Hall, 1967), pp. 33-34.

The maximum distance traveled by consumers to obtain successively higher-order functions increases as the number of central functions increases. This is shown in Figure 20.16 by the increasing size of the trade area served as the level of the trading center increases. Closely related is the fact that inbound and outbound trips for a given center bear a systematic relationship to the number of central functions performed. For example, in Iowa the number of trips to and from villages was at a rate of 24×2^0, the number of trips to towns was 24×2^1, and the number of trips to small cities (mostly county seats) was 24×2^2, resulting in a progression of 24, 48, and 96, reflecting the progression in number of functions as well as in the number of trips to those centers.

We shall now extend our description to include not only villages, towns, and small cities but large cities and regional centers, indicated by 4 in Figure 20.16. If the regional centers are very large cities or metropolitan centers, they develop an internal geographic structure of retail trade, which we show at the bottom of Figure 20.16 as $1'$, $2'$, $3'$, and $4'$ intracity trading centers. Of these, $1'$ represents a store rather than a center. These are convenience goods stores that are isolated units located close to residential areas. Their goods and services are similar to those of village stores. Neighborhood shopping centers are indicated by 2'. Such stores are likely to concentrate on convenience goods, with some shopping goods also available. They have greater stock depth than the isolated convenience store.

Shopping centers are indicated by 3'. These serve a substantial segment of the city's population. They may be planned or unplanned shopping centers that handle a variety of goods, including both convenience and shopping goods but concentrating on the latter, with more stock depth than is found in neighborhood centers but much less than in the downtown shopping centers. The downtown shopping center is indicated by 4'. In these centers, stock depth and width are maximized.[46]

The upper limits for the population served by villages, towns, and small cities in Figure 20.16 are linked by straight lines to the upper limits of convenience stores, neighborhood centers, and shopping centers. Note, however, that these straight lines are not vertical but slope back to the left. This means that as population density drops, a trading center of a given level will serve a larger geographic area, but the increase in size of that area is not commensurate with the decrease in population density. Therefore the total population served by centers in low-density areas will be lower than that of similar centers in high-density areas.

The process of adaptation that follows from this fact is important in understanding how rural centers are related to urban centers. As towns, for example, provide the same functions as neighborhood centers in cities, they do so with much lower population density and much bigger areas. Their population base (as seen on the horizontal axis) is less than that for neighborhood centers in cities. Therefore the threshold level for third-level functions is lowered for the simple reason that towns become smaller and smaller and are not able to support as many functions. People in sparsely populated areas appear to be more willing to drive to larger cities for goods and services, so the population base for the large city increases and that for the small town decreases. Retail stores of a given type (or level) in cities serve more customers than do their rural counterparts. For this reason, a small-town retail trading center of type 3 is far less complex than a 3' urban shopping center.

In keeping with these observed relationships with respect to population density, Berry found that the spatial structure of retail trading centers in Iowa followed a rectilinear or rhomboidal pattern along transport routes, most of which were essentially straight and latticed, with small cities, villages, and towns alternating in the pattern indicated in Figure 20.17. The number of establishments in centers of successively higher order in Iowa was 24, 48, 96: 24×2^0; 24×2^1; 24×2^2. The general expression for the progression of business types at different levels of the hierarchy is dk^{w-1}, in which w is the order of the hierarchy, k is the number of lower-order centers for each center of higher order, and d is population density. In Iowa the bifurcation ratio, k, was found to be 2, since for each center of a given level in Figure 20.17 there were 2 centers at the next-lower level.

A comment should be made concerning the relatively blank density band labeled C in Figure 20.16. This is what Berry identifies as the "phase shift." As population density

---

[46] In certain sections of the United States, such as parts of California, where relatively high population density is spread over broad geographic areas integrated by horizontal transportation more than by vertical transportation (i.e., by automobiles more than by elevators), regional shopping centers have developed that have, in some cases, replaced downtown areas in the hierarchy of market centers. Where this has occurred, the regional shopping center rather than the downtown center would be considered type 4'. Downtown centers would then be subordinate to the regional center and would be classified as 3' Generally, however, downtown centers continue to be the centers of highest order.

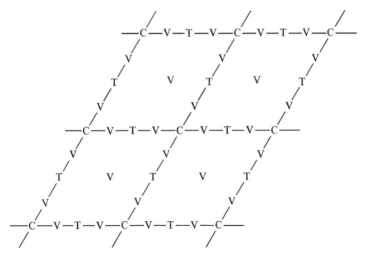

Figure 20.17. The rhomboidal spatial pattern of villages, towns, and small cities in Iowa. Source: Brian J. L. Berry, *Geography of Market Centers and Retail Distribution* (Englewood Cliffs, N.J.: Prentice-Hall, 1967), p. 39.

increases up to that point, market centers tend to be villages, towns, or small cities serving rural areas. When population density reaches approximately 1,000 or more per square mile, cities begin to emerge. Density E is the urban center, while density D is suburban in character. Density C is that in which dispersed cities develop in such a way that consumers often have equally attractive options in going to one or the other, and in which varying specialties may emerge, with each city becoming best known for and most competent in providing a particular service. As these cities grow, however, they become urban centers and provide the full spectrum of urban services.

ZIPF, BOGUE, AND STEWART STUDIES

G. K. Zipf, Don J. Bogue, and John Q. Stewart have each observed and analyzed regularities in the geographic location of population and of certain types of market activities. Zipf utilized the rank-size rule to describe the empirical regularities in population distribution among cities.[47] The rank-size rule is

$$\log R = a - b \log P$$

in which P is the population of a city, R is its rank in population, and a and b are constants. There is a tendency for b to equal -1.00. If the logarithm of population is plotted against the logarithm of population rank, the slope tends to be -1.00, meaning that a 1 percent change in rank is associated with a 1 percent change in population size. While empirical data tend to substantiate the relationship described by the rank-size rule, the fit is not perfect.

Don J. Bogue has also found some regularities in retail, wholesale, and service sales, as

---

[47] G. K. Zipf, *National Unity and Disunity* (Bloomington, Ind.: Principia Press, 1941), *Human Behavior and the Principle of Least Effort* (Cambridge, Mass.: Addison-Wesley, 1949).

well as population, per unit of land area and distance from the nearest metropolis.[48] The relationships tended to be linear when logarithmic values were used.

Stewart employed the same notions as Reilly in establishing population contours that would reflect what he called "population potential" at various distances from metropolitan centers.[49] This potential is an aggregate of the individual potentials at that one point. The potential of a given population, N_1, at a distance, d_1, is N_1/d_1, or the population divided by distance, yielding potential per mile (or per unit of distance).[50]

Stewart's definition of the potential of population at point 1 for individuals located at point 2 is

$$V_2 = \frac{GN_1}{r}$$

in which V_2 is the influence of population at point 1 on the population at point 2, G is a constant, N_1 is the population at point 1, and r is the distance from point 1 to point 2. The total population potential for any given point is therefore the total impact from all other points whose population could influence the population at a specific point, or

$$V = \int \frac{1}{r} D dS$$

in which D is the density of population over the infinitesimal element of area dS. The potential thus becomes the reciprocal of the proximity of that point to all people.[51]

By calculating potentials for various localities in the United States, Stewart was able to establish contours of equal population potential that show a systematic decline in potential as distance from New York City increases in the direction of the Rocky Mountains. The equal potential lines decline in the opposite direction—that is, toward the east—as one moves away from West Coast cities. Stewart's potential of population, based on distance and population, is easily translatable into Reilly's trading-area equation.[52]

We have mentioned these few studies of population distribution and the geographic patterns in population interaction because marketing is one of the most important ways in which humans interact through space. If there are regularities in the distribution of

---

[48] Don J. Bogue, *The Structure of the Metropolitan Community* (Ann Arbor: University of Michigan, Horace H. Rackham School of Graduate Studies, 1950).

[49] John Q. Stewart, "Potential of Population and Its Relationship to Marketing," in Reavis Cox and Wroe Alderson, eds., *Theory in Marketing,*, 1st ed. (Chicago: Irwin, 1950), pp. 19-40, "An Inverse Distance Variation for Certain Social Influences," *Science* 93, no. 2404 (January 24, 1941): 89-90, "Empirical Mathematical Rules Concerning the Distribution and Equilibrium of Population," *Geographical Review* 27, (July 1947): 461-485, and "The Development of Social Physics," *American Journal of Physics*, 18, (May 1950): 239-253.

[50] This potential of population is analogous to gravitational influence in physics, m/d, in which m is mass and d is distance.

[51] Stewart presents another measure, which he calls *energy of interchange* or *demographic energy*. He regards this as quite as important as the concept of *potential of population*. It is $N_1 N_2/d$. This is identical to Zipf's PQ/d and his PQ/d hypothesis—i.e., that PQ/d is linear—which Zipf used to try to explain many forms of interchange between populations (railway express shipments, telephone messages, bus passengers, railway passengers, air passengers, obituaries in the *New York Times*, daily circulation of the *New York Times*, charge accounts of a department store, truck and passenger car trips, and marriage licenses).

[52] A good summary of these and some other studies of this type appears in Isard, op. cit., pp. 55-76.

people over space, market relationships are critical to that distribution and interaction. Central-place theory, and particularly more recent refinements that are reaching toward the integration of central-place theory into a systems theory, provide a framework within which these observed regularities can be explored.

Geographic Concentration and Dispersion in Retailing: A Summary

It would be helpful at this point to pull together the various threads of our discussion in the form of a summary of the important forces that shape the geographic structure of retailing. We shall do this in terms of those conditions that are conducive to agglomeration and those that are conducive to dispersion. In each case we shall consider three important clusters of variables—demand, transportation—communication, and supply.

AGGLOMERATING INFLUENCES

One reason consumer buyers tend to reside in cities, or in localities accessible to cities, is that this is where employment opportunities are greatest. In addition, consumers often prefer shopping in a large shopping center rather than a small one because of choices and the amount of market information available in such markets.

Retail agglomeration is also induced by supply factors. The larger the market area, the greater the possibilities for retailers to become specialized and to benefit from profit opportunities associated with product and service differentiation. There are also economies of scale that are possible for large establishments supported by a large demand base in a sizable trading area. Such economies may be internal or external to the retail establishment, resulting from the development of transportation facilities, financial institutions, warehousing facilities, specialized advertising and promotional services, and similar facilitating services and facilities whose costs can be shared by all retailers in a given retail center. Other forms of external economies are those that result from the enhanced drawing power that a large trading center has owing to the presence of resources not directly related to retailing such as medical facilities, governmental services, industrial and wholesaling facilities, educational institutions, theaters and entertainment, and nonmarketing professional resources, any of which might attract out-of-town visitors for purposes other than retail buying but whose attracting power spills over to the benefit of retail sellers located there.

DISPERSING INFLUENCES

One of the most powerful influences that deters unlimited growth of the centralized retail agglomerate is the cost of transportation and communication. The larger the center, the greater the area it will tend to serve if it is to operate economically. The greater the area, the greater the direct cost to the consumer for transportation of himself and of the goods he purchases and the greater the indirect opportunity cost in the form of time forgone in order to visit and shop in the larger center. The other transportation cost that larger retail agglomerates entail is that of congestion, in terms of both intrastore traffic and street traffic of the center. Many people prefer suburban or small-town living—more outdoor activities, participation in community affairs, single-family dwellings, and so forth versus urban congestion, high crime rates, and distances.

Among the important supply variables that operate in favor of smaller stores in smaller centers are the diseconomies of scale that set in after an establishment or center has reached a certain size. Rising costs associated with larger stores are related to the difficulties of internal coordination and control of the store's operations and the petering out of the store's appeal to customers as its merchandise lines get wider and wider and its stock depth greater.

One more cost variable that plagues the retail store in the large urban shopping center is rent. The supply of centrally located sites in centralized markets is so inelastic that rents are largely demand determined. In the long run competition among retailers, and other competing tenants, will bring the rental value to a market-determined relationship to net sales revenue. But real estate markets are imperfect. They are greatly affected by past and expected real estate taxes, which become a part of the capitalized value of the land. In many cases they are also affected by imperfect competition among relatively large retail firms, which may be the only active competitors for particular sites. Long-term capital commitments to particular sites and long-term leases are also conducive to slower adjustments in the rental values of retail sites than occur in some of the markets in which retail firms are buyers of goods and services. Rent differentials may encourage the movement of some stores from high-rent to low-rent locations.

To the extent that wage rates in urban centers are higher than comparable wages in smaller centers, this difference is particularly important to retail stores. Wages represent the largest element of operating cost in retailing, and opportunities for increased productivity in retail stores in large cities may not be equal to the higher wage rates that must be paid there.

CONCLUDING NOTE

Two of the growing demands of consumers are for choice and convenience. The adaptation of retailing to this by means of geography has been dramatic. It has resulted in new buying centers, including many in which the structure of the entire center is planned rather than the result of many independent decisions made over a period of time. This has, of course, led to problems of adaptation in older centers where sunk costs deterred mobility. Many new centers, planned in anticipation of a growing demand, have involved aggregate commitments far greater than those of many older centers. Future work on the geographic structure of retailing needs to focus on these dynamic aspects in order to increase our understanding of how these processes work themselves out in time and how better locational decisions can be made.

WHOLESALE LOCATION AND MARKET AREAS

Among the distinguishing features of wholesaling are the facts that sales are made to industrial or retail firms rather than to ultimate consumers and that the physical and dollar volume of the typical transaction is much greater than that in retailing. For these reasons, a large percentage of the costs of wholsaling are associated with the handling of goods physically—moving them between the point of original production and the wholesaler's warehouse and between the warehouse and the place of business of the industrial or retail buyer, and handling them within the warehouse by sorting, holding them in stock, and mixing lots. While nonphysical functions are also important, it is the efficiency with which physical functions are performed that are usually critical in determining the success of the wholesale enterprise.

If we assume that the FOB price for all wholesale buyers is the same, regardless of where they are located, some of the important costs that would enter into a decision concerning the optimum location for the wholesale firm's system of warehouses would be (1) the transportation costs from the source of supply to the warehouse, (2) the transportation costs from the warehouse to the wholesaler's customers, (3) variable warehousing costs (space, insurance, physical depreciation, taxes, losses from pilferage, interest on investment), and (4) warehouse administration and other fixed costs. These costs have to be viewed in relation to the demand in order to arrive at an optimum number and location of warehouses.

The Baumol-Wolfe Example

William J. Baumol and Philip Wolfe have presented a simplified problem dealing with this type of location problem.[53] They assume that public warehouses are used for the storage functions so that only variable costs of warehousing have to be considered. They also make assumptions about the number of factories from which the wholesaler can buy, the capacity of each factory, the number of retail customers that the wholesaler has, and the demand on the part of each customer. Transportation costs from each factory to each warehouse are known, as are transportation costs from each warehouse to each retail customer.

The problem then becomes one of determining from which factories the merchandise should be purchased and in which warehouses it should be stored. The objective is to minimize the total delivery cost:

$$\Sigma_{i,j,k} \; C_{ijk}(X_{ijk})$$

subject to three constraints:

1. All goods must be shipped out of the factory:

$$\Sigma_{j,k} \; X_{ijk} = Q_i$$

2. No warehouse capacity can be exceeded:

$$\Sigma_{i,k} \; A_{ijk}(X_{ijk}) \leqslant R_j$$

3. All customer demands must be met:

$$\Sigma_{i,j} \; X_{ijk} = S_k$$

In the preceding equations

X_{ijk}	=	the quantity shipped from factory i via warehouse j to the retailer at location k
$C_{ijk}(X_{ijk})$	=	the cost of this shipment, including the relevant inventory cost
Q_i	=	the quantity shipped from plant i
R_j	=	the capacity of warehouse j
S_k	=	the quantity required at destination k
$A_{ijk}(X_{ijk})$	=	the amount of inventory that will be held as a result of the flow X_{ijk}

---

[53] William J. Baumol and Philip Wolfe, "A Warehouse-Location Problem," *Operations Research* 6 (March-April 1958): 252-263.

They then describe an iterative process by which the optimum distribution can be selected, involving, first, the determination of the lowest possible transport cost for servicing each retailer. Warehousing costs for each such channel are then determined. These are added to the transport cost, and the best channel is chosen for each retailer, using the sum of these two costs. Since marginal warehousing costs are assumed to be curvilinear (a function of the square root of the number of units handled), marginal warehousing costs are then calculated based on the new channel decisions that were made when transport costs were added to the warehousing costs. Total costs of the system can then be determined on the basis of this first iteration. If the channels arrived at by this first iteration are no different from those that were arrived at when transport costs and warehousing costs were first added together, there is no improvement and the first solution is accepted. If, however, there was an improvement over the first calculation, then an additional iteration can be undertaken, using revised warehousing costs, to see if still further improvement in total costs would result from shifts in the channels. When successive iterations produce no cost improvement, the calculation is stopped and the last solution is accepted.

An Alternative Approach

Alfred A. Kuehn and Michael J. Hamburger believe that the Baumol-Wolfe procedure is defective because it fails to take into account fixed warehousing costs and because it has a bias in the direction of locating more warehouses than the optimum number.[54] They propose instead the use of a heuristic program in which the best possible site is selected for the first warehouse, with additional warehouses added one at a time. Each addition is one that will produce the greatest cost savings for the entire system. When new warehouses are added, those warehouses that have become uneconomical as a result of the placement of subsequent warehouses are eliminated. Also, the possibility of shifting existing warehouses is considered.

Other Factors Affecting Wholesale Location and Market Areas

There are, of course, a number of additional factors that a wholesale firm would wish to consider in arriving at a decision concerning optimum location of stocks. These would include the utility of speed of delivery to buyers, the variability of quantity demanded as price is raised or lowered, the variability of demand through time, elasticity of the supply available from the wholesale firm's resources, the stability of supply through time, and the short- and long-run behavior of competitors. A wholesale firm's promotional efforts do not have the same character as those in retailing, but these may also be important in locational decisions. The ability of the firm to initiate and maintain contacts with customers may be important in their competitive position. The most economical areas for salesmen to cover may not coincide with that for warehousing. This cost variable may have to be combined with that of physical movement of goods to arrive at a locational decision for the *totality* of the firm's functions.

---

[54] Alfred A. Kuehn and Michael J. Hamburger, "A Heuristic Program for Locating Warehouses," *Management Science* 9 (July 1963): 643-666.

V

Appraisal of Market Structure and Behavior

21

Marketing and Economic Development

There are no laws regarding the *content*
of economic behavior, but there are laws
universally valid as to its *form*.

—Frank H. Knight

We have defined marketing as the activities of business firms and consumers directly related to achieving exchange relationships. Buying and selling are the principal activities through which the market nexus is created, but the movement of goods through time and space are also necessary for market relationships to be viable. In this volume, we have attempted to delineate, describe, and explain the behavior of the social entities that participate in these transactions and to show the patterns of relationship and the principles that govern what we call "the marketing system."

In Part I, we introduced some basic concepts and showed how personal, natural, and social inequalities create situations in which the equilibrating effects of marketing increase the welfare of buyers and sellers, thereby unifying the segments of an economy into an economic system. In Part II, we examined the important characteristics of consumer demand and some of the economic, social, and psychological factors related to demand, and showed how demand filters through the marketing channel to become one of the directors of primary production decisions.

In Parts III and IV, we were concerned with the supply of marketing services, viewing these, first, in terms of the institutional structure of the marketing industry—the kinds of firms that have developed to provide specialized marketing services and their relationships to one another and to the producers and consumers whom they serve—and second, in terms of the policies that are the framework within which decisions concerning marketing activities are formulated. In this treatment of the marketing industry and policies, we have attempted not only to describe what businessmen actually do but also to indicate what they should do in order to achieve various objectives. We have also considered many characteristics of institutional structure and marketing policies in terms of their effects on the welfare of consumers.

What we shall try to do in Part V is to pull the threads of our description and analysis together and view the marketing system as a whole. Our perspective will be not that of consumers *or* producers, but of the whole society. We shall concern ourselves with two basic questions: (1) How much of society's resources are devoted to marketing and what governs the size of that allocation? (2) What conclusions can we draw about the effectiveness with which the marketing system functions in both developing and mature economies?

Our discussion up to this point has focused primarily on markets in relatively mature economies. It is appropriate therefore that we also consider the role of markets in underdeveloped and developing economies and determine the extent to which they do or do not contribute to the processes of economic development.[1] This will comprise the subject matter of this chapter.

STAGES OF ECONOMIC GROWTH

Although no two economies follow exactly the same path in economic development, there are similarities in the development experience of different economies and certain dominant forces in various growth situations. In Figure 21.1 we show four stages in the development process. These are similar to the five stages identified by Walter W. Rostow in his discussion of economic growth.[2] We are using real output per capita, rather than gross output, as the measurement of the level of development. Population growth is often associated with initial increases in output and may, for a considerable time, exceed the increase in total product.

The different "stages" of development indicated in Figure 21.1 are for convenience in specifying (1) the level of real per capita income achieved, that is, low, medium, and high; (2) the level of development relative to the maximum income in the most highly developed economy, that is, underdeveloped, partially developed, and mature; and (3) the rate of change in per capita income from year to year—static, growing slowly, growing rapidly, or again growing slowly. We have not included in Figure 21.1 a period of declining income, since it is assumed that some growth will continue. Although the curve in Figure 21.1 is not the usual production function, the similarity between the curve we show and that used in the analysis of the first three stages of increasing and decreasing physical returns is readily noted. The curve is also similar to the product life cycle curve. All of these types of growth reflect a pattern similar to those of biological growth.

One assumption underlying our discussion in this chapter is the desirability of the movement from a state of underdevelopment to one of intermediate development. This assumption is not unequivocal, for some might, and do, defend the virtues of the way of life that characterizes a society in which incomes are low. It is our view that poverty is not conducive to the achievement of the optimum well-being of human beings. We do not argue that affluence is essential or conducive to optimum social welfare, but we do take the position that human welfare is generally enhanced by the movement away from extremely low incomes and that economic development is a desirable goal of low-income economies.

---

[1] In his excellent study of consumer goods marketing in Greece, Lee Preston suggests that developing countries be broken into two groups for purposes of analysis—"those just emerging from a primitive state, in which virtually all aspects of higher civilization, including commercial market activities, are essentially foreign," and those "which are well advanced in the development process, yet still relatively poor and characterized by sharp differences between traditional and modern sectors." Examples of the former can be found in Africa and in certain parts of Latin America and Asia. The latter is illustrated by most of the Latin American countries, southern Italy, the countries of the Eastern Mediterranean, India, the Philippines, and Puerto Rico. Lee E. Preston, *Consumer Goods Marketing in a Developing Economy*, Center of Planning and Economic Research, Research Monograph Series no. 19 (Athens, 1968), pp. 23-24.

In this chapter, we shall draw examples from marketing in countries representing both of these stages of development. Because the forces operative in these two situations are quite different, we should keep in mind the level of development associated with each of the situations we present as we sample this smørgåsbord of markets in underdeveloped and developing countries.

[2] Walter W. Rostow, *The Stages of Economic Growth* (Cambridge: Cambridge University Press, 1960), esp. pp. 1-92.

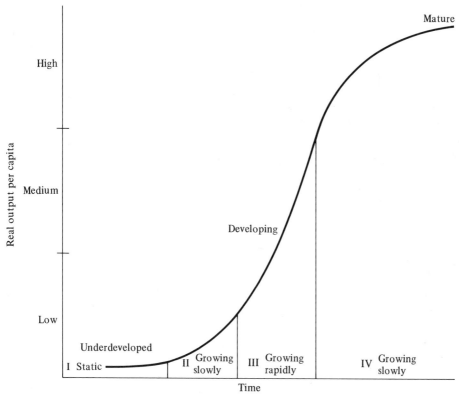

Figure 21.1. Periods of economic growth.

CRITERIA FOR EVALUATING MARKETING IN ECONOMIC DEVELOPMENT

Before we examine marketing institutions and market behavior in relation to economic development, we shall indicate the four criteria by which we shall judge the contribution of marketing to the development process.

First, does the market effect changes in the economy that will bring resource utilization and allocation closer to the optimum? Second, are the desired changes effected precisely; that is, are the goals neither overshot nor undershot? Our first criterion concerns the direction of change, while the second concerns the amount of change.

Our third question concerns whether changes are effected at an optimum rate. This criterion warrants special comment. Development processes involve reconciliation of short- and long-term objectives and potentials. The market is peculiarly involved in this reconciliation, for it must bring short-run cost-revenue relationships, which are often known, into proper relationship to long-run cost-revenue relationships, which are often not known or known only probabilistically. In one sense, of course, this is related to our second criterion—the effecting of changes precisely, for we shall wish to avoid over- or under-investment in particular industries due to errors of information or analysis or to institutional or legal barriers to effective performance by market participants. Sometimes, however, several different amounts of change could be absorbed without short-term loss, but one of those alternatives would result in an optimum rate of long-run development. For example, consumption demands expand in the process of economic growth. Expansion of certain demands out of proportion to others may cause long-run optimum welfare to be realized later than would have been the case had the growth of specific demands been programed in such a way as to achieve the optimum mix at the optimal time. Marketing firms are greatly involved in the melding of short- and long-run needs and potentials, and the effectiveness with which they function in this capacity is one measure of their contribution to economic development.

A fourth criterion is also important in evaluating marketing performance. Part of the cost of growth is adjustment. It is therefore appropriate to ask whether the adjustments in the economy that are made by marketing processes are made not only correctly but at minimum cost. This is not to say that marketing costs should be minimized but, rather, that the use of resources in marketing should be properly related to the functions that the market is to perform. This is an efficiency criterion. For example, the role of marketing in accentuating or mitigating cyclical fluctuations may bear significantly on both short- and long-run development levels.

SOME CHARACTERISTICS OF MARKETS
IN UNDERDEVELOPED ECONOMIES

An underdeveloped economy is one in which per capita income is quite low compared with the real per capita income in the United States, Canada, Australia, New Zealand, and countries of Western Europe. Benjamin Higgins has suggested that such economies be identified by per capita incomes equal to or less than one-fifth to one-quarter those in the United States.[3] Numerous studies have been made of various underdeveloped economies. Most of these studies have focused on the structure and performance of the economy as a whole, although some have been concerned primarily with the marketing system.[4] These studies have revealed great diversity in the importance of markets, in their organization,

---

[3] Benjamin Higgins, *Economic Development*, rev. ed. (New York: W. Norton, 1968), pp. 8-11.

[4] Three volumes in which attributes of markets in a number of underdeveloped or developing countries are explored are Montrose S. Sommers and Jerome B. Kernan, eds., *Comparative Marketing Systems* (New York: Appleton, 1968); Reed Moyer and Stanley C. Hollander, eds., *Markets and Marketing in Developing Economies* (Homewood, Ill.: Irwin, 1968); Robert Bartels, ed., *Comparative Marketing: Wholesaling in Fifteen Countries* (Homewood, Ill.: Irwin, 1963). The role of marketing in economic development was explored in a substantial portion of the program of the American Marketing Association's Fall Conference, 1965. See Peter D. Bennett, ed., *Marketing and Economic Development, Proceedings of the American Marketing Association,* Fall Conference, 1965 (Chicago, 1965), pts. II, III, and IV, pp. 11-201. Part III contains case studies of European, socialist state, Latin American, African, and multinational markets.

Among the studies of markets in Caribbean economies are Sidney W. Mintz, "The Role of the Middleman in the Internal Distribution System of a Caribbean Peasant Economy," *Human Organization* 15 (Summer 1956): 18-23, "Peasant Markets," *Scientific American* 203 (August 1960): 112-122; and "The Jamaican Internal Marketing Pattern: Some Notes and Hypotheses," *Social and Economic Studies* 4 (March 1955): 95-103. See also John K. Galbraith and Richard H. Holton et al., *Marketing Efficiency in Puerto Rico* (Cambridge, Mass.: Harvard University Press, 1955).

Two studies of Latin American markets are Rolf J. Luders and Allen F. Jung, "Retail Competition in Chile," *Journal of Marketing* 28 (April 1964): 22-24, and Donald G. Halper, "The Environment for Marketing in Peru," *Journal of Marketing* 30 (July 1966): 42-46.

Studies of African marketing include those of P. T. Bauer, *West African Trade* (Cambridge: Cambridge University Press, 1954); Raymond W. Baker, "Marketing in Nigeria," *Journal of Marketing* 24 (July 1965): 40-48; Lee E. Preston, "Marketing Organization in Arab Socialism," *Journal of Marketing* 31 (October 1967): 1-7. Certain countries of both Africa and Europe are considered in S.

and in the performance patterns of various market participants. These diversities led Reavis Cox to say, concerning the emerging interest in comparative marketing studies, "How justified are we in supposing that there is anything to compare?"[5]

It is reasonable to hypothesize that markets will differ at various levels of economic development, and that markets at the same stage of economic development, while differing from one another with respect to some characteristics, will have certain characteristics in common. What we seek in comparative marketing studies, therefore, are similarities and differences between different marketing systems with the hope that these will provide a basis for classifying markets into groups that display common characteristics and common differences between themselves and other groups.

In order to suggest the extent of similarities and differences among markets of less highly developed economies, and between such markets and those of more highly developed economies, we shall review very briefly in this section some of the market attributes that have been found in the various studies. We have selected only a few attributes of markets to discuss and have examined data from only a few countries.

The Market as a Means of Resource Allocation

Many underdeveloped economies are ones in which there is a high degree of self-sufficiency among individuals in the population. Production is largely agricultural, and output is generally for oneself or one's family. In these cases, domestic markets are means of distributing surpluses, and trade is a peripheral and not an integral part of the system of resource allocation. In some cases, however, as in Malaysia, there is a much

---

Agapitidis et al., *Markets and Marketing as Factors of Development in the Mediterranean Basin*, papers presented at the Second Assembly of the Mediterranean Social Sciences Research Council at Cairo, December 1-4, 1962 (The Hague: Mouton, 1963). See also A. Coskun Samli, "Wholesaling in an Economy of Scarcity: Turkey," *Journal of Marketing* 28 (July 1964): 55-58.

Marketing in Asian countries has been analyzed in Leon V. Hirsch, *Marketing in an Underdeveloped Economy* (New York: Free Press, 1959), and Dole A. Anderson, *Marketing and Development–The Thailand Experience* (East Lansing: Michigan State University, 1970).

Dealing with both domestic and international trade, Ian Little, Tibor Scitovsky, and Maurice Scott, *Industry and Trade in Some Developing Countries: A Comparative Study,* Published for the Development Centre of the Organization for Economic Cooperation and Development (London: Oxford University Press, 1970), includes studies of Argentina, Brazil, Mexico, India, Pakistan, the Philippines, and Taiwan.

Studies of marketing in more highly developed economies include Hugh G. Wales, F. F. Winklé, and C. Bak, "Marketing in South Africa," *Journal of Marketing* 27 (October 1963): 42-47; Hans B. Thorelli, "South Africa: Its Multi-Cultural Marketing System," *Journal of Marketing* 32 (April 1968): 40-48; David Carson, "Marketing in Italy Today," *Journal of Marketing* 30 (January 1966): 10-16; Edwin H. Lewis, "Marketing in Spain," *Journal of Marketing* 28 (October 1964): 17-21; A. J. Alton, "Marketing in Finland," *Journal of Marketing* 27 (July 1963): 47-51; Yoram Wind, "The Role of Marketing in Israel," *Journal of Marketing* 31 (April 1967): 53-57.

Marketing in socialist economies is discussed in Marshall I. Goldman, *Soviet Marketing: Distribution in a Controlled Economy* (New York: Free Press, 1963); Berend H. Feddersen, "Marketing Behind the Iron Curtain," *Journal of Marketing* 21 (July 1967): 1-5; G. Peter Lauter, "The Changing Role of Marketing in the Eastern European Socialist Economies," *Journal of Marketing* 35 (October 1971): 16-20.

[5] Reavis Cox, "The Search for Universals in Comparative Studies of Domestic Marketing Systems," Bennett, op. cit., p. 147.

higher degree of specialization in production, and in these economies markets perform an indispensible exchange function.[6]

Where markets exist in underdeveloped economies, they can be an important medium for capital investment. Because fixed capital is limited, much of the capital investment in an underdeveloped economy is in working capital, often in the form of stocks of goods and goods in transit. Investment in the goods in marketing channels often represents a high percentage of the total capital investment in an underdeveloped economy.[7] But the overall low level of capital investment, including such facilities as storage, tends to narrow the market and restrict specialization in trading operations.[8]

Pricing in markets of these economies often reflects values that derive less often from a revenue-maximizing calculus than from a psychic-income-maximizing calculus. Although many economies, both developed and underdeveloped, appear to have negatively sloping supply curves for labor, particularly at low levels of wages, these are particularly conspicuous in underdeveloped countries because of the low level of income and the relatively high value placed on leisure. When income rises to a certain point, people may prefer to withdraw from the labor market. J. H. Boeke cites several examples in Indonesia of a similar reaction to prices of commodities where the income from labor is directly related to the price of the commodity product. For example, if the price of coconuts rises, there may be a decrease in the number offered for sale, or if the price of rubber falls, the number of trees tapped may increase.[9] Because of the direct relationship between the employment of labor and the production of products, which is characteristic of a less highly developed economy, the supply curve for labor is directly related to the supply curve for commodities.

In some less developed economies it appears that there is not much price competition. For example, in Indonesia before independence, prices were quite rigid, every customer knew them, and there were no deviations.[10] Yet in other underdeveloped countries considerable price competition has been observed. Hirsch states, "India is a price-oriented market; almost all merchants and the large majority of consumers are sensitive to even slight price differences."[11] Bauer indicates that African consumers are very sensitive to price differences because of low incomes and the low value of time spent in finding price differences.[12]

Institutional and Competitive Structure

Most underdeveloped economies are characterized by markets in which there are a large number of traders, with most doing a very small volume of business.[13] Bauer points to

---

[6] See, for example, Alice G. Dewey, *Peasant Marketing in Java* (New York: Free Press, 1962), pp. 4-13, in which Malayan marketing is contrasted with marketing in Java.

[7] Bauer, op. cit., p. 14.

[8] Ibid., p. 57.

[9] J. H. Boeke, *Economics and Economic Policy of Dual Societies* (New York: Institute of Pacific Relations, 1953), p. 40.

[10] Ibid., p. 48.

[11] Hirsch, op. cit., p. 293.

[12] Bauer, op. cit., p. 62.

[13] See, for example, William H. Nicholls, "Domestic Trade in an Underdeveloped Country—Turkey," *Journal of Political Economy* 59 (December 1951): 463-480.

the large number of traders selling imported merchandise in West Africa, and to the slightly smaller number (but still a large number) handling produce.[14] The reason for the larger number is the substitution of an abundant resource for which there is little demand (labor) for a scarce resource (capital). In discussing this attribute of West African markets, Bauer distinguishes between "technical efficiency" in marketing, which is lacking there partly because of the abundant labor resources allocated to marketing, and "economic efficiency," which may actually be quite high in view of the limited alternatives that large numbers of traders have.[15]

In many cases it appears that retailing is a form of unemployment relief for people whose marginal productivity in other occupations is either low or zero. Galbraith and Holton indicate that some retailers in Puerto Rico went into business in order to avoid either idleness or working in the cane fields.[16] While the shortage of capital restricts the size of both retail and wholesale trading firms and increases their number, wholesaling firms in underdeveloped economies are generally larger than retailing firms.

Often traders in less highly developed economies regard marketing as a peripheral part of their work. Bauer suggests, for example, that they often do not regard trading as an occupation but as a part of existence.[17] In many such markets women are important traders.[18] In some cases there just is not much housework for women to do, and they turn to trading as a part-time occupation. In West Africa there is, in addition, a bride price (a type of dowry in reverse), which a husband can regard as an investment in a trading concern. Or the wife may wish to "repay" the bride price, thereby earning her right to divorce.[19] Often husbands and wives trade with each other, and they may even sue one another for debts. Trading is not a sideline occupation in India, however, where traders are all drawn from trading castes.[20]

There appears to be considerable product diversification among marketing firms in certain underdeveloped countries.[21] Where the market is narrow, expansion may be possible only through product diversity. Risks are spread and managerial talent can be used more fully.

Galbraith and Holton characterize the Puerto Rican retail market as one of monopolistic competition based on the large number and small size of firms in combination with a live-and-let-live attitude among retailers and wholesalers, on the important role of personal relationships, and on customer loyalty tied to the availability of consumer credit.[22] Although a number of underdeveloped countries appear to have markets in which market knowledge on the part of ultimate consumers is meager, Bauer

---

[14] Bauer, op. cit., p. 22.

[15] Ibid., p. 27.

[16] Galbraith and Holton, op. cit., p. 3. See also Harper W. Boyd, Jr., Abdel Aziz El Sherbini, and Ahmed Fouad Sherif, "Channels of Distribution for Consumer Goods in Egypt," *Journal of Marketing* 5 (October 1961): pp. 26-33, where it is pointed out that retailing is an important form of unemployment relief, since investment requirements are low and entry is easy.

[17] Bauer, op. cit., p. 11.

[18] Ibid., pp. 11-13. Boeke indicates that occasional trade in certain village communities is almost wholly in the hands of women. Op. cit., p. 48.

[19] Bauer, op. cit., pp. 11-12.

[20] Hirsch, op. cit., pp. 282-283.

[21] Ibid., pp. 288-291.

[22] Galbraith and Holton, op. cit., pp. 72-73.

indicates that this is not true in West Africa. He believes that consumer knowledge there is considerable, being based on consumption experience, and that consumers do shop carefully and make rational choices. He cites examples in which consumers showed a preference for bicycles that would withstand poor roads and paths, for corned beef with high fat content (which they like), for sardines packed with four large ones in a can instead of many small ones, since they eat them as a fish instead of in sandwiches, and for salt that is light and fluffy and, hence, more easily transported.[23]

In summary, most descriptions of marketing in underdeveloped economies indicate that there is an abundance of resources, particularly labor, in marketing, that the number of firms is large and the sales volume per firm quite low, and that competition is sometimes quite sluggish, with, however, conspicuous exceptions as noted.

Wholesalers are more important in terms of their marketing power than retailers in many underdeveloped countries, particularly where imported goods are an important part of the total volume of goods traded. Although wholesalers are numerous and their volume of sales in most underdeveloped countries is small, in some cases they have come to occupy a dominant position in the trade channel because of their extension of credit to retailers.[24] However, wholesale markets are generally ones of monopolistic competition, even though the size and efficiency of firms is larger than in retailing.[25] In West Africa Bauer has found that market risks and uncertainties have encouraged wholesalers to stock a range of goods that increases their size and makes entry more difficult.[26]

Although in some underdeveloped markets there is not a great deal of vertical integration among wholesaling and retailing firms, Bauer found considerable vertical integration in West Africa, particularly for imported goods. His explanation is that West Africa did not have a substantial local "capitalist class" and that European enterprisers who controlled the importing business integrated vertically toward the consumers. Also, there were strategic advantages that prompted such a move.[27] The extension of credit often achieves some of the effects of integration without the occurrence of actual ownership. Hirsch observed a considerable lack of vertical differentiation in marketing functions among sugar traders in India.[28] This phenomenon, observed in India as well as in Puerto Rico and West Africa, reflects the lack of specialization in a less tightly knit marketing system.

Import Markets

Because of their limited resources some underdeveloped economies import substantial quantities of goods. Where this has occurred it has resulted in two important developments in marketing. One is the important role of the importing firm in the total

---

[23] Bauer, op. cit., p. 62.

[24] Boyd, Sherbini, and Sherif, op. cit., pp. 26-33.

[25] See, for example, Willard F. Mueller, "Some Market Structure Considerations in Economic Development," *Journal of Farm Economics* 44 (May 1959): 414-425.

[26] Bauer, op. cit., p. 57.

[27] Ibid., p. 56.

[28] Hirsch, op. cit., pp. 285-288.

marketing system, and the other is the frequent control of such firms by foreigners.[29] Paralleling this tendency for wholesaling to become the province of exogenous entrepreneurs is the historical tendency in most developing countries for trading functions to fall into the hands of minority ethnic groups.[30]

Margins and Output

More often than not retail and wholesale margins in underdeveloped economies are lower than in highly developed economies. Ralph Westfall and Harper Boyd found retail margins of perhaps 10 percent of sales in India and wholesale margins less than half that.[31] Hirsch's detailed study of sugar marketing in India reveals a total marketing margin during 1955-1956 of 11.5-12.5 percent of the retail price, compared to wholesale and retail margins in the United States during the years 1900-1952 of about 19 percent.[32]

But this pattern does not always prevail. Galbraith and Holton found in Puerto Rico that the average gross margin for food retailers was 23 percent of sales, ranging between 16 and 34 percent. Food wholesalers' margins averaged 14 percent of sales. In their model distribution system for food, the authors estimated that they could reduce retail margins to about 14 percent over cost (12 percent of sales) if services were retained at the same level, but to do so firms would have to be increased substantially in size. They estimated that they could reduce wholesale margins to about 8 percent of cost (7 percent of sales) if larger size were achieved.[33] It appears that these high margins in Puerto Rico were a reflection of structural and operating inefficiencies.

On the other hand, where low margins are found in underdeveloped countries, are they evidence of efficiency? Comparable international input-output data would be necessary to answer this question. Incomplete but relevant information about these marketing systems indicates, however, that these low margins result from differences in the role of markets and marketing in less highly developed economies compared to their role in more

---

[29] Several of the studies in Moyer and Hollander, op. cit., deal with the comparative effects of domestic versus foreign control of marketing in developing economies. See specifically Elliot J. Berg, "Socialist Ideology and Marketing Policy in Africa," pp. 24-47; P. T. Bauer, "Some Aspects and Problems of Trade in Africa," pp. 48-69; J. C. Abbott, "Marketing Issues in Agricultural Development Planning," pp. 87-116; William Y. Adams, "The Role of the Navajo Trader in a Changing Economy," pp. 133-152, all of whom find considerable benefits from marketing activities controlled by foreign interests, at least up to a certain level of economic development. On the other hand, William Glade and Jon G. Udell, "The Marketing Behavior of Peruvian Firms: Obstacles and Contributions to Economic Development," pp. 153-169, Sidney W. Mintz, "Peasant Market Places and Economic Development in Latin America," pp. 170-189, and Marvin P. Miracle, "Market Structure in Commodity Trade and Capital Accumulation in West Africa," pp. 209-227, discuss both pros and cons on the matter of domestic versus foreign marketing control.

[30] See, for example, William P. Glade, "Approaches to a Theory of Entrepreneurial Formation," *Explorations in Entrepreneurial History*, 2d ser., 4 (Spring-Summer 1967): 245-259, and Lloyd A. Fallers, "Comments on 'The Lebanese in West Africa,' " *Comparative Studies in Society and History* 4 (April 1962): 334-336.

[31] Ralph Westfall and Harper W. Boyd, Jr., "Marketing in India," *Journal of Marketing* 25 (October 1960): 11-17.

[32] Hirsch, op. cit., pp. 300-305.

[33] Galbraith and Holton, op. cit., pp. 29, 54, 74-124.

highly developed economies. The proportionate share of the burden of economic production that is borne by the marketing system in less highly developed economies is far lower than that of the marketing system in mature economies. Low margins are often the result of using low-cost resources, particularly labor, whose marginal productivity is low and whose productive alternatives are either limited or zero. Even though margins may be low, the absence in underdeveloped economies of many services associated with the marketing of goods in highly developed economies may mean that marketing costs are in fact relatively high. The range of services offered by the marketing system in high-income economies, the possibilities for a more vigorous and effective competitive system, the existence of greater opportunities for the realization of economies of scale in marketing, and the greater range of opportunities for substituting marketing for nonmarketing costs suggest that low margins are not in themselves a sufficient basis for comparing the efficiency of marketing in two countries at two different levels of economic development.[34]

MARKETING AND ECONOMIC DEVELOPMENT

In what ways can the structure and functioning of markets contribute to economic growth? Are markets necessary and/or sufficient for economic development to occur? If they are capable of contributing to development, or if they are necessary to development, what characteristics should they have to function optimally? In what ways can markets restrict economic growth?

These are the kinds of questions to which we now turn. Neither our theory nor our data will permit us to answer these categorically. Answers must depend in part on the specific situation, particularly upon the level of economic development already achieved, as well as upon the total technological and social environment within which the economy functions. But even though we cannot answer these questions unequivocally, we raise them because of their importance and because our exploration of their meaning and implications can shed some light on marketing's role in the important process of economic development.

The Role of Marketing in Economic Expansion

The widening of markets, the development of increased specialization between marketing and nonmarketing firms, the growth of specialization among marketing firms, and the improvement in techniques of moving, storing, and exchanging goods have focused increased attention upon the marketing process in the functioning of highly developed economies. Economic historians have been mindful of the role of marketing in the world's economic development, and certain periods have been identified as ones in which marketing activities played a particularly critical role. The "Commercial Revolution," extending from the late fifteenth century through the seventeenth, was characterized by an enormous expansion in European commerce both domestically and internationally. The economic structure of the medieval period was overturned, and new trade routes were established that reduced the dominance of Italian and Hanseatic League traders.

---

[34] See Chapter 23.

These developments of this era are recognized as part of the forces that contributed to the rise of capitalism over time.[35] In other periods there were other developments in trade that were less dramatic but whose cumulative effects on the level of economic growth have been as great. Let us examine some of the specific ways in which the development of a marketing system and of increasing efficiency in marketing can contribute constructively to economic growth.[36]

COSTS OF PRODUCTION

Assume that there is an economy with a relatively low per captia income. Improvements in the techniques of marketing are introduced that lower transport and storage costs, which encourages marketing firms to expand their scale of operation, thereby achieving efficiency, which makes possible lower marketing margins and retail prices. The greater volume of sales makes possible large-scale production and the efficiencies associated with increased specialization, increased accumulation and use of capital equipment, and the development and use of greater managerial skills. Thus the widening of markets results in greater economies in both marketing and form production activities. A facet of this well-known principle was stated by Adam Smith as the title to one of his chapters in *The Wealth of Nations:* "That the Division of Labour Is Limited by the Extent of the Market."[37]

It is not necessary, however, for the widening of markets to come only through lower marketing costs. A reduction in the cost of capital could lead to lower production costs, making possible lower prices, wider market areas, and increased marketing activity. Economies of scale in manufacturing through more efficient use of one or more productive factors will often lead to a need for wider markets as a means of achieving the volume necessary for such economies to be realized.

However, the optimum size of a manufacturing plant is not necessarily the same as the optimum size of the market area which that plant serves. Therefore it is the combination of the two costs components that determines the optimum size of the total operation, with the total operation defined to include both the manufacturing and marketing aspects of the enterprise. Often the unit cost of marketing will rise as large-scale production techniques are employed in processing. This is economic so long as the increase in the cost of marketing is more than offset by the decrease in the cost of processing.

---

[35] Higgins, op. cit., pp. 169-170.

[36] Of the classical economists, Malthus more than any other recognized and stated formally many of the roles of marketing in the process of economic development. These he discussed in his Book II, "On the Progress of Wealth," under the following section titles, which are indicative of the nature of his interest: Section VI, "Of the Necessity of a Union of the Powers of Production with the Means of Distribution in Order to Ensure a Continued Increase of Wealth"; Section VII, "Of the Distribution Occasioned by the Division of Landed Property Considered as the Means of Increasing the Exchangeable Value of the Whole Produce"; Section VIII, "Of the Distribution Occasioned by Commerce, Internal and External, Considered as the Means of Increasing the Exchangeable Value of Produce"; and Section IX, "Of the Distribution Occasioned by Personal Services and Unproductive Consumers, Considered as the Means of Increasing the Exchangeable Value of the Whole Produce." T. R. Malthus, *Principles of Political Economy* (1819; reprint ed., New York: Augustus M. Kelley, 1951), pp. 361-413.

[37] Adam Smith, *The Wealth of Nations* (1776; reprint ed., New York: Modern Library, 1939), pp. 17-22.

DEMAND AND CONSUMPTION

Not only do markets contribute to a lowering of costs of production, but they also contribute to economic expansion through their effects upon demand and consumption. One of the most obvious roles of the market in influencing consumer demand is in making known to potential consumers the alternatives that producers are able to offer. In addition, aggressive traders may attempt to persuade consumers of the desirability of their wares and bring still more influence to bear upon their choices.

There are two other ways in which markets can be indirectly instrumental in shaping consumption. The supply curve of labor appears to be negatively sloping in many economies, and this is particularly apparent in underdeveloped areas. If the market becomes a medium through which economic education takes place, resulting in a rise in the standard of consumption, it could serve to reduce the negative slope of the supply curve for labor, or even to shift it to a positive slope. It is doubtful, of course, that the market can accomplish this alone. Rather, it would appear that it is *one* means by which standards of consumption are stimulated through greater familiarity with what is possible.

Finally, modification of the standard of consumption via the influence of market forces can affect the birthrate. If market forces are important in influencing the standard of consumption, and if members of society come to regard children as competitive with consumer goods and services, it is possible that the rising standard of consumption will be conducive to smaller families. This then will make possible higher per capita consumption levels, which, in turn, may be a stimulus to increased production. However, the *initial* impact of a rise in per capita income in low-income countries is to *increase* the demand for children. Therefore it takes time, and apparently considerable time, before rising incomes will be conducive to a lower birthrate.

The thrust of this discussion of the interrelationship of markets and the expansion of consumption in low-income societies centers on the role of markets as media for the transmission of goods to consumers, as media for the transmission to consumers of information about goods, and as the generators of forces that stimulate demand. The expansion of wants can occur without markets, but markets provide a structured medium through which at least some of the forces that influence consumer wants are transmitted.

It seems doubtful, however, that a low-income producing economy will "take off" on the basis of want expansion alone, that is, that consumers' desires increase to the point where consumers are converted from leisure-seeking individuals to goods-seeking individuals and demonstrate this conversion by increased work effort. It is much more logical to believe that production is increased first by whatever means possible, and that the availability of increased amounts of goods to at least some members of society demonstrates the value of productive activity and results in restructured and expanded preferences on the part of consumers.

The following statement by Schumpeter describes the probable direction in which the producer-consumer relationship tends to be established in the process of economic change:

> The spontaneity of wants is in general small. To be sure, we must always start from the satisfaction of wants, since they are the end of all production, and the given economic situation at any time must be understood from this aspect. Yet innovations in the economic system do not as a rule take place in such a way that first new wants arise spontaneously in consumers and then the productive apparatus swings round through their pressure. We do not deny the presence of this nexus. It is, however, the producer who as a rule initiates economic change, and consumers are educated by him if necessary; they are, as it were, taught to want new things, or things which differ in

some respect or other from those which they have been in the habit of using. Therefore, while it is permissible and even necessary to consider consumers' wants as an independent and indeed the fundamental force in a theory of the circular flow, we must take a different attitude as soon as we analyze change.[38]

Once consumers become aware of what the consumption potential is and learn to desire that potential, then they are likely to behave in both the commodity and labor markets in such a way as to make that potential possible. This so-called "demonstration effect" is more likely than anything else to shape the growth of consumer demand.

DIRECTION AND RATE OF GROWTH

Among the most important factors in economic development are the rate at which capital and consumer goods are acquired, the rate of consumption, and the rate and nature of stock accumulation. The rate of capital formation is probably the most critical of these.

The organization through which investment and production decisions are arrived at can range all the way from a highly centralized decision-making structure, such as a bureaucratic agency, to a highly decentralized system of capital and consumer goods markets in which individuals participate as buyers, sellers, entrepreneurs, or investors. In any economy, even one that has chosen to depend primarily upon decision making coordinated by authoritarian means, markets have played at least some role in the determination of the quantity and quality of output, especially where consumer goods are concerned.[39]

For markets to perform this allocation function adequately, there must be surpluses from which investment funds can come, there must be investors willing to risk those surpluses for probable returns on capital investment, and there must be entrepreneurs who will bring the resources together for the production process to get under way. All of these are likely to be in very short supply in underdeveloped and developing economies. Therefore it is quite likely that some type of social intervention, and possibly external intervention, will be necessary for capital investment to occur.[40]

ENTREPRENEURSHIP

A number of writers have discussed the role of entrepreneurship in the economic development process and have given consideration to those conditions under which it can be most effectively stimulated to achieve development. Our interest in this aspect of development concerns the relationship of entrepreneurship to the structure and

---

[38] Joseph A. Schumpeter, *The Theory of Economic Development* trans. Redvers Opie, Harvard Economic Studies, vol. XLVI (Cambridge: Harvard University Press, 1934), p. 65.

[39] See, for example, Marshall I. Goldman, op. cit., esp. pp. 51-81, 188-200.

[40] There are some interesting theories about the qualitative character of the investment that is necessary for development to occur. Ragnar Nurkse has argued that in order for economic development to take place there must be what he calls "balanced growth," by which he means a "synchronized application of capital to a wide range of different industries." Hans Singer and Albert Hirschman, on the other hand, have argued against a concept of "balanced growth" and in favor of what is essentially a "big push," consisting of large investments in strategically selected industries or sectors of the economy in order to get a stagnant underdeveloped economy off dead center. Each investment may temporarily create an imbalance, but each successive investment reduces that imbalance by expansion in some other direction. Thus growth takes place by a series of upward surges toward an increase in output. See Higgins, op. cit., pp. 327-342.

functioning of markets. We shall examine briefly this problem as it has been treated by three individuals—Joseph Schumpeter, Peter Bauer, and William Baumol.

In the Schumpeterian system a critical role is assigned to entrepreneurial functions in the economic development process.[41] He defines development as the "carrying out" of new combinations in the production process. This could result from introducing a new good with which consumers are not familiar or a new quality of good, from introducing a new method of production or marketing, from opening a new market, from obtaining a new source of supply, or from creating a new organizational structure in an industry.[42] The carrying out of these new combinations he calls "enterprise," and the individuals whose function it is to carry them out he calls "entrepreneurs." Thus entrepreneurs are not managers or owners or risk bearers, although they may be one or more of these in addition to being entrepreneurs. The role of the entrepreneur is leadership in the sense that he leads "the means of production into new channels,"[43] for which he receives entrepreneurial profit, not as a return on the capital he owns, nor for the risk he assumes, but for his putting into effect new combinations in the production process. It is Schumpeter's contention that the emergence of entrepreneurs depends upon the existence of entrepreneurial profits and on the social climate. The latter is the social, political, and psychological environment within which economic activity occurs. Although the type of economic leadership that characterizes Schumpeter's entrepreneur can emerge in a nonmarket economy, the economic and social climate of a free market economy is particularly conducive to this form of activity because of the opportunities it provides for the individual to effect change and to profit from change. Much of Schumpeter's analysis was, however, devoted to a consideration of the instability of the system that he described.[44]

In a somewhat related vein Bauer states that the widening of markets brings into prominence a trader-entrepreneur who is accustomed to the ways of an exchange economy that involves regular and systematic use of money.[45] Bauer's concept of an entrepreneur is quite different from that of Schumpeter, who excluded managerial and other functions of a routine nature from those of the entrepreneur. Bauer's trader-entrepreneur does perform routine functions, although he may also perform other functions. Trader-entrepreneurs are in his judgment more likely than others to accumulate savings and place them into productive employment. He believes that in underdeveloped economies alien traders are especially useful because they bring to the developing economy managerial and technical skills.

Baumol's analysis of the conditions of growth pivots upon the pattern of entrepreneurial behavior resulting from the oligopolist's perception of his market position and potential. He argues that an oligopolist not only desires profit maximization, in the sense of a static optimum, but is also preoccupied with the amount of growth (which entails the concept of a moving optimum), with the rate of growth, and with market share.[46] In

---

[41] See, for example, Schumpeter, op. cit., pp. 57-94, 128-156.

[42] Ibid., p. 66.

[43] Ibid., p. 89.

[44] See, for example, ibid., pp. 212-255, and Joseph A. Schumpeter, *Business Cycles*, vols. I and II (New York: McGraw-Hill, 1939).

[45] Bauer, op. cit., p. 29.

[46] William J. Baumol, *Business Behavior, Value and Growth*, rev. ed. (New York: Harcourt Brace Jovanovich, 1967), pp. 86-104.

the growth model that he sets up, the role of *expansion effort* is critical. The expansion effort is a function of the skills and willingness of the population to work and involves the effort of labor as well as of management and the entrepreneur. The problem of development then becomes one of determining the best way to encourage this expansion effort. The market could provide one mechanism for encouraging this expansion effort through wages, profits, and return on capital investment. In a mature economy, the market may be an effective means for sustaining growth by the rewards it offers to expansion efforts. In an immature economy, particularly one that has suffered from stagnation at a relatively low level of income for a long period, private market participation alone is not likely to induce the effort necessary to cause growth to take place. In these cases, Baumol suggests some alternatives. One is education through which people learn to work and to desire the products of work. But he questions whether we know how to teach people to want to do the things that make for economic growth. Another alternative is through coercion, as used, for example, in totalitarian economies. Baumol suggests still another alternative as more palatable—the use of pecuniary rewards (subsidies) and penalties (taxes) to induce behavior consistent with society's growth objectives. On balance, he believes that the last of these is probably the most appealing of the policy alternatives implied by his theory of growth. Thus the unregulated market would not be relied upon. Rather, the directive role of market rewards would be sweetened by social intervention in order to induce expansionary efforts.

What is the unifying thread in these three approaches to the role of markets in stimulating entrepreneurship as a factor in economic development? Each of the authors cited recognizes that the market mechanism can provide both a means and an incentive for effective entrepreneurial activity. On the basis of his study of marketing in West Africa, Bauer is inclined to place considerable reliance upon the market mechanism, with a minimum of government intervention, for bringing forth activity conducive to growth.[47] Schumpeter and Baumol, on the other hand, recognize the importance of other means of inducing entrepreneurial activity. Baumol in particular believes that under most circumstances these other means may be superior to the free market as a mechanism for achieving the entrepreneurial stimulus essential to growth. Thus there is not consensus that a relatively free market is the best way to achieve the full benefits of entrepreneurial decision making and action in underdeveloped economies. Rather, it is recognized that markets *can* perform this function but that supplementary means may be more effective under certain circumstances. This brings us to a consideration of the specific limitations of markets in the economic development process.

LIMITATIONS OF MARKETS IN ECONOMIC DEVELOPMENT

There is serious doubt on the part of many students concerning the ability of the market to serve as the sole, or even principal, instrument for achieving economic development. Some of the criticisms are directed toward market performance in underdeveloped countries; still others focus upon market performance in developing and mature economies. We shall examine some of these objections to the market as a growth-inducing vehicle.

---

[47] See, for example, his discussions of the West African marketing boards and of the various proposals that have been made for economic reform in marketing in this geographic area. Bauer, op. cit., pp. 316, 347-376.

Prerequisite Attitudes, Knowledge, and Skills

The market is not an effective instrument of resource allocation and output distribution if members of the society are either unwilling or unable to assume the responsibilities of production. This involves their willingness and ability to work as laborers and managers, to accumulate capital and assume the risks of its ownership, and to carry out the functions of entrepreneurship. In our discussion of entrepreneurship we have already alluded to some of the difficulties of depending upon the market to generate the conditions necessary to evoke the entrepreneurial activity that is essential for growth to take place.

Maximization of one's income through wages, profits, or other returns may not be desired by members of a society that has come to value cooperation more than competition. Boeke, for example, discusses the lack of competition in marketing in certain underdeveloped economies.[48] He refers to Alfred Rühl's analysis of this in his *Vom Wirtschaftsgeist im Orient (Economic Mentality in the East)* as lack of individualism. The individual feels that he is part of a group and sees his market fellows as companions rather than rivals. No one begrudges another a better wage or better price. "To feel comfortable is more important than high wages."[49] Similarly, attitudes toward saving and investing may not be the same in a less highly developed economy where experience has been limited. Such limitations are not comon to all underdeveloped economies, as Hirsch's description of sugar marketing in India shows.[50] Where they do exist, however, they will prevent marketing from functioning effectively as the principal means of implementing investment and production.

Low educational and skill levels are additional factors that lessen the effectiveness of markets in less highly developed economies. Eliminating this constraint on market effectiveness by formal education is a slow and arduous process.[51] A study by Irma Adelman and Cynthia Morris, however, indicates that markets themselves can play an important role in helping develop attitudes and behavior that are conducive to growth.[52] In their econometric analysis of data for underdeveloped countries in the nonsocialist world, they used a discriminant function in which four variables were found to be most reliable for classifying countries according to their potential for successful economic performance. Ranked in the order of their importance, these were identified as the degree of improvement in financial institutions, the degree of modernization of outlook, the extent of leadership commitment to economic development, and the degree of improvement in agricultural productivity.[53] The second of these, degree of modernization of outlook, was, in turn, a function of the extent of dualism in the economy, the level of adequacy of physical overhead capital, and the size of the traditional agricultural sector. The latter bore a negative relationship to modernization of outlook; the first two were positively related. Dualism was used to show the impact of the modern sector of the

---

[48] Boeke, op. cit., pp. 84-85.

[49] Ibid., p. 86.

[50] Hirsch, op. cit., esp. pp. 368-374.

[51] Baumol, op. cit., pp. 139-148.

[52] Irma Adelman and Cynthia Taft Morris, "An Econometric Model of SocioEconomic and Political Change in Underdeveloped Countries," *American Economic* Review, 58 (December 1968, Pt. 1): 1184-1218.

[53] Ibid., p. 1188.

economy and the concomitant expansion of the market economy. The development of transportation was present in the physical capital variable. The agricultural sector was the nonmonetized segment of the economy.

The authors' assessment of the role of markets in determining the degree of modernization is reflected in the following statement:

> Viewed broadly, the equation for attitudinal modernization suggests that the underlying influences most conducive to transforming ideas and attitudes in low-income countries are the geographic linking together of the population through the creation of transportation networks and the economic integration of the country by means of the spread of the market throughout the nation.[54]

Other Market Imperfections

At any stage of economic development, markets may exhibit imperfections that cause them to fail as a mechanism for directing resource utilization and allocation.

MARKET CONTROL

If market control is highly concentrated in private hands, there may be both underutilization of the economy's resources, resulting in a lower total output than possible, and misallocation of resources, resulting in the production of less of particular items than would occur in the absence of such control.

Fundamental to the effective functioning of any market system is the existence of incentives in the form of profits or comparable rewards. Willard Mueller has hypothesized that market structure is itself a determinant of entrepreneurial attitudes toward profits.[55] Employing Leibenstein's approach, he suggests that where monopoly or cartelized industries develop, market participants will tend to prefer zero-sum games, which merely redistribute income, rather than positive-sum games, which increase the economy's productivity and wealth. A firm that is able to obtain a fairly secure market position may prefer long-run security rather than large short-term profits. Its decision not to rock the boat is understandable, but this preference is not conducive to growth.

This is not necessarily an argument for trying to create in a developing economy a market structure that approximates pure and perfect competition. The volume of output in such an economy is not likely to be large enough to support economically a large number of small production and/or marketing units. Even where large numbers of small production units have been observed in developing economies, however, underemployment of resources is not uncommon.[56] If an economy can economically support large numbers of enterprises, and if the profits are a strong motive for entrepreneurs, then the self-regulating mechanism of the market can be relied upon to direct the economy's productive efforts. Otherwise some form of social intervention may be necessary to prevent enterprises with considerable market power from utilizing that power in ways contrary to the growth objectives of the economy.

---

[54] Ibid., p. 1191.

[55] Willard F. Mueller, "Some Market Structure Considerations in Economic Development," *Journal of Farm Economics* 41 (May 1959): 414-425.

[56] As indicated in retailing, for example, by Galbraith and Holton, op. cit., p. 3.

CYCLICAL FLUCTUATIONS

A second way in which market imperfection can affect the level of economic development is through cyclical fluctuations. While it would be inaccurate to say that market structure alone causes recessions and depressions, it is correct to say that market structure can be a contributing factor to fluctuations in output. We shall examine three types of situations in which markets may provide an imperfect medium for the transmission of information necessary for correct production decisions.

1. *LONG GESTATION PERIOD.* In industries where there is a long gestation period between initial investment and ultimate output, over- and underinvestment may easily occur. Under these circumstances, errors of judgment can easily occur because future demand has to be anticipated so far in advance.

2. *NUMBER OF DECISION MAKERS.* Suppose, in addition to a long gestation period, that the number of producers making investment decisions in a particular industry is quite high. Under these circumstances, it is easy for current market information to provide an inadequate basis for a large number of independent decisions. Let us explore this in more detail.

Assume that the market is purely and perfectly competitive, containing a large number of sellers, no one of whom can influence the market by his behavior. Assume further that the supply of the product becomes increasingly elastic over time, with the short-run supply very inelastic and the long-run supply more elastic. In Figure 21.2(A) we show two supply curves, S_1 representing the highly inelastic short-run supply and S_2 the long-run supply curve, which is still inelastic but less inelastic than S_1. Given the demand, D_1, and the short-run supply, S_1, the equilibrium quantity will be Q_1 and the equilibrium price P_1. If there is an increase in demand to D_2, the long-run equilibrium quantity will become Q_3 and the long-run equilibrium price will be P_3. Assume, however, that it takes a while for the long-run adjustment to be made and that this adjustment is the result of a large number of independent decisions on the part of all the small producers in the industry. In the short run the price will rise to P_2 and the quantity Q_2 will be bought and sold on the market. P_2 is a very attractive price to sellers, and it is one that will increase their profits. If the sellers then expand their output *on the assumption that this price will continue,* output would be expanded to an amount greater than Q_3, as indicated by the dotted line between S_1 and S_2 at price P_2. But buyers will not buy that much at this price. So the price falls to a level below P_3, as indicated by the vertical dotted line between S_2 and D_2. The firms in the industry have overproduced and suffer a decline in profits from falling prices. A recession occurs in the industry, and investment plans are cut back on the assumption that this new price, lower than P_3, will prevail. The vacillation of prices results in increases and decreases in profits. Marginal firms are driven out when prices fall, and long-run investment is contracted. But it may well be overcontracted. Then prices rise and long-run investment is expanded. In section (A) of Figure 21.2, we show a situation in which this process of overexpansion and overcontraction continues but leads eventually to the equilibrium price, P_3, and the equilibrium quantity, Q_3. In order to reach that point, however, firms in the industry experience considerable fluctuation in prices and outputs.

Section (B) shows a more disturbing situation in which the elasticity of long-run supply is greater than that of the new demand, D_2. Under these circumstances, the rise in price from P_1' to P_2' leads to an expansion in long-run output much greater than Q_3', which

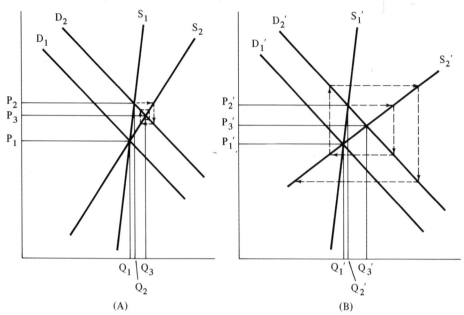

Figure 21.2. The cobweb effect.

would be the long-run equilibrium output. As successive adaptations are made by firms in the industry, increasing disequilibrium is experienced, with a movement away from the long-run equilibrium quantity of Q_3' and price of P_3'.

The classic example of this cobweb effect is the corn and hog cycle in American agriculture, in which changes in the price of meat affect the willingness of farmers to raise hogs. It is the combination of two factors that causes the cycle. One is the length of time between making a decision to raise more hogs and putting the hogs on the market. The other is the fact that independent decisions are made by large numbers of livestock producers. Since the demand for corn is derived from the demand for hogs, the price of corn and the level of output is also affected. But corn prices can vary because of changes in supply due, for example, to weather. So short-run changes in the output of corn can affect the price of corn and, hence, the profitability of hog production. This, then, is an additional variable that can affect the short- and long-run equilibrium positions.

This problem is likely to occur where there is a very inelastic short-run supply and where demand is shifting either upward or downward. Many American agricultural markets demonstrate this phenomenon and illustrate its role, not only in cyclical fluctuations but also in making long-run adjustments almost impossible to achieve by dependence upon the operation of unregulated markets. This is one of the reasons why public control has been injected into the functioning of these markets.

3. *VERTICAL DISPERSION OF MARKETING FUNCTIONS.* One additional market imperfection derives from the gaps injected into the production process by the separation of processers and consumers in both time and space. By breaking up the marketing effort among specialized marketing agencies, the effective transmission of information necessary for correct decisions to be made at the processing level becomes highly important. More independent decisions have to be integrated if the trade channel is lengthened. The longer

the movement through the channel takes, the longer the *ex ante* period for production decisions.

Specialization of function, and the lags that this injects into the communication process, are well illustrated in the effects of inventories on short-term fluctuations in demand and output. The two-year cycle in production that has been of historical importance in the textile industry appears to have been closely related to inventory accumulations and depletions and to the lag in the transmission of this information through the pipeline of the marketing system to the point of manufacturing. If, in addition to the extended filtration time and its cumulative effects, we add the impact of speculative inventory investment, we have two major avenues by which errors in calculation are compounded by the multiplicity of decisions that exaggerate changes in demand and/or supply.[57]

BALANCE WITHIN THE MARKETING SEGMENT

One of the findings of the various studies of marketing in developing economies edited by Moyer and Hollander[58] is the importance of ancillary marketing institutions and services in the developing countries. In addition to importers, wholesalers, and retailers, many other types of institutions are needed to provide what have often been identified as "facilitating functions" of marketing. These institutions can be private or public. They are needed to provide credit and financial instruments for trading purposes, facilities for transporting goods, storage facilities, advertising services, and market research and information. Standardization of weights and measures, standardization of products and grading, and censuses of business and population are market information services essential for markets to function with any degree of efficiency.

Provision of these ancillary institutions and services often awaits the evolution of the market system, but at the same time, the evolution of that system may await the appearance of these facilitating functions. If there appears to be some sluggishness in the provision of these services by individual entrepreneurs, public intervention may be desirable.

Still another possibility for imbalance to develop in the market structure arises where market rigidities become constraints upon the establishment of the marketing institutions necessary to permit consumers an opportunity to express a wide range of preferences and investors to respond through a variety of production alternatives. Sometimes a small, developing market center inherits customers and restraints that make it difficult for new firms to enter and new trading patterns to be established.

In their analysis of industry and trade in seven developing countries (Argentina, Brazil, Mexico, India, Pakistan, the Philippines, and Taiwan), Ian Little, Tibor Scitovsky, and Maurice Scott concluded that the following policies affecting the structure and functioning of markets would be desirable if markets were to be made more effective in encouraging development:

1. Channels were needed for directing personal savings into capital investment through attractive financial assets since institutions in the capital markets through which savings flowed into industry were found to be inadequate in most developing countries.

---

[57] See Chapter 19, where inventory cycles are discussed.

[58] Moyer and Hollander, op. cit., pp. 230-231.

2. Labor should not be overprotected so that the use of capital is encouraged at the expense of labor.
3. Exports should be encouraged through trade fairs, overseas market information, and merchant shippers.
4. Undue concentration of production should be prevented, not necessarily by promoting domestic competition where that is found to be uneconomical, but by encouraging imports which would compete with domestic products.[59]

The policies they propose are directed toward the encouragement of free markets where they can be made viable and effective, and toward changes in market structure and behavior where these are found to interfere with efficiency in resource utilization. They are policies designed to achieve balance in the marketing system in the sense that their purpose is to allow resources to move sensitiviely and freely in response to private and public demand. Other kinds of policies might be more appropriate in other kinds of situations.

It seems reasonable to hypothesize that markets will be most effective as media for stimulating economic development in those economies that have already begun to grow (although even among these countries selective social intervention may be desirable), but that an economy that has been stagnant for some time will require external stimulation in order to grow. This external stimulation could come through public intervention in the economic process, through an infusion of capital from external sources, or through newly developed market contacts with other economies. In other words, the domestic market is unlikely by itself suddenly to kindle economic growth in a stagnant economy without some kind of new stimulus. But the domestic market may be much more successful in encouraging further growth once an economy has begun the process of expansion. More studies of the role of markets in economic development will be needed, however, before we can be sure exactly what these interrelationships are.

Public Goods and Services

While few goods and services are completely nonmarketable, a society may decide that certain things are best provided by public action outside the marketing system or through some combination of public and market control. Such decisions entail cases in which markets are found to be incapable of doing the job of economic resource allocation at any price, are capable of doing it only imperfectly, or are capable of doing it adequately but at extremely high costs.[60]

In addition, there is the possibility of a discrepancy between the long- and short-run benefits to be derived from a particular policy decision. In the process of economic development, this shows up as particularly important in the acquisition of capital. Long-run capital investment is often essential for economic development to take place. Yet the acquisition of capital must be out of saving and, hence, at the expense of current consumption unless credit is available that makes it possible for future consumption to be assessed for capital accumulation. The individual's willingness to reduce present consumption for a higher discounted future income may be insufficient to ensure the capital accumulation necessary for that higher future income to be realized. Part of this is

---

[59] Ian Little, Tibor Scitovsky, and Maurice Scott, op. cit., pp. 334-337.

[60] These are discussed in detail in Chapter 24.

likely to be rooted in lack of awareness of these relationships, that is, in market imperfections due to imperfect knowledge. But part of it is due to the fact that the long run for the individual is different from the long run for society. If a society's economic calculus concerns variables that embrace a longer time span than those that enter into an individual's calculus, then society may choose to allow its decision-making processes to supersede those of the individual operating in the market.

Another situation in which public action will be undertaken to replace or regulate market action occurs where the goals not of society as a whole but of the government—those in society who have political power to make decisions—differ from those of individuals of that society. A dictator, for example, may wish to see his country become economically strong, and he proceeds to achieve this by a deliberate policy of large capital investment in selected industries that he believes will increase the long-run producitivity of the economy. He regulates imports and exports, controls wages and returns to other productive factors, regulates prices, and may even make output decisions with respect to specific goods and services. The kinds of decisions that he has to make are no different from those that would be made in the market place, but they are made by authoritarian control, perhaps with supplementary reliance on markets for some decisions.[61]

Among the arguments for using authoritarian means of achieving economic development is the speed with which development can occur when it does not have to wait for individuals to respond in the market to production incentives and when it can cut through the rigidities in the institutional framework through which productivity increases have to come when the market system is relied upon as the regulating mechanism. Arguments against it are the economic question of whether centralized decision making can in fact generate optimum economic decisions, and the political and social question of whether the impact of such a system on human welfare in terms of both economic and noneconomic effects is a net benefit or cost.

The Special Problem of Dualism

A number of writers have described and analyzed the problem that arises in underdeveloped areas when material or financial resources, management, entrepreneurship, technology, and economic and social organization of another culture come into the underdeveloped society and exist side by side with the culture endogenous to that society. Analyses of this phenomenon have usually focused upon either cultural or technological dualism.[62] The importance of dualism lies, first, in the effects that it has on

---

[61] See, for example, Goldman, op. cit., Reed Moyer, "Marketing in the Iron Curtain Countries," in Sommers and Kernan, op. cit., pp. 265-277, and J. Hart Walters, Jr., "Retailing In Poland: A First-Hand Report," in ibid., pp. 289-300.

[62] See, for example, J. H. Boeke, op. cit., where he discussed what is commonly identified as sociological, or cultural, dualism. Boeke's analysis was based on his observations in Indonesia, but he believed that the generalizations he derived from that situation were applicable elsewhere. For a summary and critique of Boeke's views, see Higgins, op. cit., pp. 227-241.

One treatment of technological dualism, which appears in the development of technologically advanced sectors separated functionally from agricultural sectors, is that of Hla Myint, "An Interpretation of Economic Backwardness," *Oxford Economic Papers*, n.s., 6 (June 1954): 132-163. See also Higgins, op. cit., pp. 296-326, where the interactions of traditional and technically advanced sectors are considered.

the development process, that is, whether it encourages or impedes adjustments essential to achieve increased productivity. It is also important for the effect that it has on the individuals of the society who feel personally the impact of its presence. We shall comment briefly on the relationship of the market system to dualism.

The market system in a mature, highly developed economy is far more complex and its functions more pervasive than is true of the market in a less highly developed economy. If, in the development process, marketing institutions and techniques appropriate to the developed economy are injected into the underdeveloped economy, problems may result if the attitudes, experiences, and rules of behavior necessary to the effective functioning of these newly imposed market structures are different from those of the endogenous markets. For example, the market system is more effective in encouraging development if supply curves are positively sloping. This may not, however, be the case, particularly with labor. Similarly, growth is more likely to be encouraged if increased output results in increased demand. But again, experience may not have provided a sufficient background for this demand expansion to take place as a result of increased earnings. An American salesman working in a low-income underdeveloped country once commented on the "damned wantlessness" of the people to whom he was trying to sell his wares. This is a matter of the difference between the lack of expansiveness of consumer demand in an economy that has not experienced a rapidly growing income and the continually expanding demand in the United States. The cultural bases of demand and supply, the structure of markets, and the rules of behavior of participants are so much the product of the culture in which they evolve that it is not productive to transfer marketing institutions and practices from developed to underdeveloped countries without careful consideration of their relevance to the needs of the developing economy.

Equally important is the role of marketing in creating dualism in a developing economy. Often the market is the avenue through which exogenous influences enter an economy. "Foreign" capital or management may come in through private investment. Often the entrepreneurship necessary to build the market system itself, which is essential for growth to occur, will come from outside, as it has, for example, in many of the West African, Southeast Asian, and East African countries.[63] These "outside" traders can play a very significant role in developing transportation and communication facilities and in stimulating demand.[64]

Consider, however, the problems that outside traders can create. Boeke cites an interesting example.[65] A railway line was built between Madras and Calcutta, bringing the fishing area along Chilka Bay in Orissa within reach of the Calcutta fish market. Prior to this, the fish market had been a local one and the fisherman an important and stable element in the village economy. With the opening of this new outlet, traders bought fish from the fishermen at prices higher than the villagers were paying and shipped them to the Calcutta market. The villagers turned against the fisherman who had participated in this new development, refusing to sell agricultural products or services to them. In time interest rates to the fisherman rose to the point where the higher prices received were fully discounted. While disruptions of this sort may be necessary to effect the changes required for economic development to occur, the impact of the disruption cannot be

---

[63] See Myint, op. cit., p. 146, and Bauer, op. cit., p. 55.

[64] Hla Myint, "The 'Classical Theory' of International Trade and the Underdeveloped Countries," *Economic Journal* 68 (June 1958): 321-322.

[65] Boeke, op. cit., pp. 81-82.

ignored. The critical question is whether the transition is made at optimum speed and cost. Imperfect markets and monopolistic control in markets may either hinder economic adjustment or enforce changes that are more costly than they need to be.

Our conclusion is paradoxical. Market development can be a significant instrument by which outside forces enter an economy and stimulate its development. In the process of performing this function, however, the market lays the society for which it forms this bridge open to the problems of dualism that arise from contact with divergent technical and cultural patterns of organization and behavior. These changes can be highly disruptive. The cost of this short-run disruption must be weighed against the possible long-run benefits from the new cultural contiguity or mix.

Another aspect of dualism is evident when a domestic market in an underdeveloped country becomes a part of the international market. This occurs when the local economy imports goods or resources that it needs and exports its output in payment. The smaller the developing economy's size and the more specialized its resources, the more important the development of foreign market relationships are likely to be in its development process. This opens the domestic market and the domestic economy to a vast range of influences that do not originate within its own boundaries.

Thus far we have considered the effect of the widening of markets upon the number and kinds of economic and cultural influences felt by a developing economy and the problem of absorbing these external influences without disruption or cleavage. There is still another problem that may be critical. Often marketing, particularly international marketing but also domestic marketing, is initiated and controlled by traders from the mature economy. These traders serve as a buffer between the underdeveloped and developed economies and can, with skill, perform a highly useful function in cultural as well as economic coordination. But they can also inhibit growth by delaying the development of a group of skilled traders in the underdeveloped economy. From the viewpoint of the developing economy's long-run welfare, this inhibition can be quite serious.

Myint points to the importance of these buffer middlemen in Southeast Asia, where they are often Indians and Chinese, in East Africa, where they are Indians, and in West Africa, where they are Syrians and "Coast Africans."[66] Higgins believes that the abundance of labor in Asia and Africa has caused middlemen in these areas to perpetuate their market position by discouraging greater use of technology and capital equipment. In America, foreign middlemen played an important role in agriculture in the South and in the Canadian prairies. They finally took over the land, foreclosed on debtors, and amalgamated small land holdings into larger units on which technological innovations became economic. This experience in America, he believes, was due to the shortage of labor, which forced small farmers to turn to technological innovations that they then found themselves unable to finance. The abundance of labor in Africa and Asia has not yet made technological innovations in agriculture equally attractive.[67]

The melding of influences of foreign and domestic markets creates a situation that calls for readjustment of resource allocation, not only domestically but also in other countries with which trading relations are maintained. The role of these market relationships is to reflect the different influences in the two economies and to fit the two economies into an

---

[66] Hla Myint, "An Interpretation of Economic Backwardness," op. cit., pp. 132-163.

[67] Higgins, op. cit., pp. 268-271.

effective complementary relationship. Lack of responsiveness on the part of traders inhibits the adjustment process.

Backwash Effects

We come finally to a fifth limitation on economic development via market interactions. Gunnar Myrdal has discussed this under the label "backwash effect."[68] It is his contention that trade between developed and underdeveloped areas, rather than tending toward equality of marginal productivity and incomes, moves the economies away from equilibrium. The superior area has a strong agglomerative pull, causing economic activity to shift from the poor region to the more productive region. This can be caused by such things as a change in terms of trade, high fertility in the underdeveloped area, or migration out of the poor area, affecting the age distribution of its population. Thus increased trade, rather than reducing inequalities, confers competitive advantages on the advanced area, thereby aggravating inequality between the two areas.

The "good" effects of increased trade between advanced and less highly developed areas are labeled by Myrdal "spread effects." He believes that when trade takes place between highly advanced and less advanced areas, the spread effects are less strong than the backwash effects. On the other hand, when trade occurs between two areas, both of which are highly developed economically, the spread effects are stronger.

There is considerable evidence to support this thesis. The inequality of income distribution among areas of the world has not been substantially reduced during periods when trade has increased between highly developed and underdeveloped areas. In fact inequality in the distribution of income among countries of the world is increasing rather than decreasing. Within the United States it has been quite recently, after achievement of a relatively high average income among all areas, that the inequality in the distribution of average income among states has been reduced substantially. This argument must therefore be given considerable weight in evaluating the probable effects of increased trade between developed and underdeveloped areas. The greater the disparity between the two in the level of income, the greater the probability that the advantages of trade will accrue in greater proportions to the more advanced economy owing to an inherent tendency for adjustment processes and policies to develop that tend to accentuate rather than mitigate international differences. This suggests that market forces alone will be ineffective as a means of reducing inequality between economies that display great differences in their levels of economic development.

THE CLARK-FISHER HYPOTHESIS AND MARKETING IN DEVELOPING ECONOMIES

We have described some of the attributes of markets in underdeveloped and newly developing economies and have considered the reasons why marketing can and cannot contribute to economic development. We turn now to some generalizations about markets and marketing in the process of economic development.

---

[68] Gunnar Myrdal, *Economic Theory and Under-developed Regions* (London: Duckworth, 1957), pp. 27-35.

The Clark-Fisher Hypothesis

In 1935 Allan G. B. Fisher, and in 1940 Colin Clark, stated what has become known as the Clark-Fisher hypothesis.[69] The hypothesis states that in the course of economic development an economy moves from a state in which primary industries are dominant to one in which secondary industries become increasingly important and then into one where *service* (Clark's preferred term) or *tertiary* (Fisher's term) industries account for an increasing share of employment and output.[70] Primary industries are agriculture, forestry, and fishing; secondary industries are manufacturing, defined by Clark as "continuous transformation on a large scale, of raw materials into transportable products";[71] and services are all other activities, including small-scale manufacturing and handicrafts, construction on site, wholesale and retail trade, finance, and all other personal and business services.[72] Clark is careful to distinguish between services that are associated with the increased output of goods and services that are rendered directly to consumers. He believes that the rising demand for services as an economy matures is the result of the former rather than the latter.

Reasons advanced for the rise in proportionate employment and output in service industries as per capita income rises are the increasing demands made on the distributive system as income rises due to increased specialization in production associated with a shift from a subsistence economy to a market economy; to the tendency for a larger proportion of income to be spent on services as per capita income increases; and to a tendency for service industries to experience a lower annual rate of increase in productivity than other segments of the economy.

Our principal interest in the Fisher-Clark hypothesis concerns employment and output in marketing enterprises. Clark's empirical data on employment and net product by industries for different countries during various years of the nineteenth and twentieth centuries show the employment in commerce and finance combined (which includes marketing) as a percentage of the total labor force was higher in high-income nations than in low income nations at any given point in time and tended to increase over time in any one nation.[73] The pattern of proportionate employment in transportation is somewhat different, showing a tendency for low-income nations to have a small percentage of the labor force in transportation and communications compared with high-income nations, for the percentage in transportation and communication to rise within a nation as its national output increases, and then, after reaching a level of about 6 percent of the labor

---

[69] Allan G. B. Fisher, *The Clash of Progress and Security* (1935; reprint ed., New York: Augustus M. Kelley, 1966), pp. 28-43, and "Production, Primary, Secondary and Tertiary," *Economic Record* 15 (June 1939): 24-38; Colin Clark, *The Conditions of Economic Progress*, 3d ed. (London: Macmillan, 1957), pp. 490-564.

[70] Clark has on occasion employed the term *tertiary* industries in lieu of *service* industries but indicates that he believes the term *tertiary* has "reached the end of its term of usefulness." Clark, op. cit., p. 491.

[71] Ibid., p. 326.

[72] Clark believes that mining falls between primary and secondary production without fitting neatly into either. Fisher defines tertiary industries to exclude agriculture and manufacturing and to include all other production, such as "facilities for travel, amusements of various kinds, governmental and other personal and intangible services, flowers, music, art, literature, education, science, philosophy and the like." Fisher, op. cit., p. 28.

[73] There are some exceptions that may be real or may be due to inconsistencies in data. See Clark, op. cit., Table III, pp. 510-520.

force, for the percentage in this industry to decline. There are differences between nations that are not related to level of income but, rather, to the area of the country (e.g., Canada) and to the role of transportation as a source of income through international shipping (e.g., Norway).

Clark's data on net income produced by commerce and finance and by transportation and communication are more limited than his data on employment. The time series are shorter, and data for some countries were not available at the time of his publication. There is some evidence that the proportion of income produced by commerce and finance tends to rise as national income rises but that the proportionate share of income from commerce and finance levels off for very high-income nations. The rise in share of income in this industrial segment is not as great as the rise in employment; therefore output per person tends to rise much less rapidly than in other industries. The share of income produced by transportation and communication tended to rise as income increased in relatively low-income nations, but eventually the percentage share declined. Clark's figures showed a secular decline in the United States from 1849 on, with some variation in particular years.

Criticisms of the Clark-Fisher Hypothesis

During the 1950s an extended debate developed around the Clark-Fisher hypothesis.[74] Criticisms of the hypothesis concerned both its logic and the nature of the empirical data available for testing it.

THE LOGIC

It was alleged that the hypothesis failed to take into account the fact that as economic growth takes place, there may be an increase in the quality of primary and secondary goods produced so that employment and value of output in these segments of the

---

[74] Arguments in defense of and in opposition to the Clark-Fisher proposition about the proportion of the labor force employed in service industries in countries at various stages of development appeared in the *Economic Journal*, the *Review of Economics and Statistics*, and the *Quarterly Journal of Economics*. The discussion in the *Economic Journal* included the following: P. T. Bauer, and B. S. Yamey, "Economic Progress and Occupational Distribution, *Economic Journal* 61 (December 1951): 741-755; Allan G. B. Fisher, "A Note on Tertiary Production," *Economic Journal* 62 (December 1952): 820-834; S. G. Triantis, "Economic Progress, Occupational Redistribution and International Terms of Trade," *Economic Journal* 58 (September 1953): 627-637; Allan G. B. Fisher, "Tertiary Production, A Postscript," *Economic Journal* 64 (September 1954): 619-621; P. T. Bauer and B. S. Yamey, "Further Notes on Economic Progress and Occupational Distribution," *Economic Journal* 64 (March 1954): 98-106. Articles in the *Review of Economics and Statistics* were the following: Simon Rottenberg, "Note on 'Economic Progress and Occupational Distribution,'" *Review of Economics and Statistics* 35 (May 1953): 168-170; P. T. Bauer and B. S. Yamey, "Economic Progress, Occupational Distribution and Institutional Wage Rigidities: A Comment," *Review of Economics and Statistics* 36 (November 1954): 461-462; Simon Rottenberg, "A Reply," *Review of Economics and Statistics* 36 (November 1954): 462. Another series in the *Quarterly Journal of Economics* included the following: Richard Holton, "Marketing Structure and Economic Development," *Quarterly Journal of Economics* 61 (August 1953): 344-361; Allan G. B. Fisher, "Marketing Structure and Economic Development: Comment," *Quarterly Journal of Economics* 68 (February 1954): 151-154; Richard Holton, "Reply," *Quarterly Journal of Economics* 68 (February 1954): 154. Within the same period another, more lonely article appeared on the subject: A. L. Minkes, "Statistical Evidence and the Concept of Tertiary Industry," *Economic Development and Cultural Change* 3 (July 1955): 366-373.

economy would not necessarily be expected to decline proportionately as aggregate output of the economy increased. The assumption that the demand for secondary goods would decline relative to the demand for services was also challenged on the ground that the income elasticity of demand for manufactured goods might in many cases be greater than that for services. The simplicity of Clark and Fisher's approach to their generalization about the proportionate employment in service industries was also attacked on the ground that it failed to take into account the role that price changes might play in determining the quantity of different goods and services that would be demanded and supplied and, hence, the labor employed in production. In view of the importance of international trade in the development process of many countries, changes in the terms of trade were also regarded by some critics as sufficiently significant to affect the structure of output and, hence, the occupational distribution of the labor force. One other price variable was also introduced in the critiques of the Clark-Fisher hypothesis— the wage rate, and particularly the extent to which differentials between wage rates in manufacturing and marketing did or did not accurately reflect differences in the marginal value product of labor in these two segments of the economy.

THE DATA

A number of criticisms of the Clark-Fisher hypothesis, however, concerned the nature of data on the occupational distribution of the labor force, and the particular problem of determining empirically occupational distribution in less highly developed economies. In underdeveloped countries many workers are engaged in both primary and service production, and it is almost impossible to separate occupations by classifying individuals. As an economy matures, increased specialization is likely to occur, and a laborer may more easily be designated as in one or the other industrial segment. But even in mature economies there is an amazing amount of overlap in the kinds of functions performed by certain individuals, and particularly a given firm. The problem of occupation counting is further confused in the underdeveloped country by a difference between the "entrepreneur," an individual who is designated as gainfully employed, and the members of his family, who may from time to time contribute to his productive activity but may not themselves be identified as "employed."

Statistical Evidence

Several individuals have attempted to test the Clark-Fisher hypothesis by examining empirical data on occupational distribution in countries at various levels of economic development to determine the extent and nature of the relationship between level of per capita income and the portion of the total labor force employed in marketing.[75] We are, of course, most interested in that segment of the labor force which is employed in

---

[75] In our statement of the Clark-Fisher hypothesis, we indicated that as economic growth occurs, both the proportion of total employed people engaged in service industries would rise and the proportion of total output generated by the service sector would rise. As we have indicated, Clark included in his study data on both of these measures of the relative importance of the service sector, although his data on comparative outputs are much more limited. We shall deal here only with the employment ratio measurement, reserving for later consideration the question of productivity and comparative output ratios as economic maturity occurs. See Chapters 22 and 23.

marketing. Generally this segment constitutes a relatively high portion of the labor force in services, particularly in less highly developed economies.

Clark's statistical findings, based on data from a number of countries, first appeared in 1935 and were updated in later editions of his book, which appeared in 1951 and 1957.[76] A. L. Minkes reported a study based on 1930 data for countries of eastern and southeastern Europe.[77] A study of European marketing by James Jefferys and Derek Knee used census data for 1930, 1950, and 1955 and data for about 1950 from the Twentieth Century Fund study of European economies.[78] Two later studies were by Walter Galenson and Lee E. Preston, both of whom used employment data from the International Labour Office.[79] We shall summarize the findings of Jefferys and Knee, Galenson, and Preston.

JEFFERYS AND KNEE: WESTERN EUROPE

Jefferys and Knee estimate that the percentage of the total estimated labor force who were in retail and wholesale trade in Western Europe increased from 8.9 percent in 1930 to 10.3 percent in 1950 and to 11.0 percent in 1955. Of the 17 countries of Europe for which they were able to obtain census data for one year around 1950, the percentage of the total labor force in retailing and wholesaling ranged from 7.6 percent in Spain to 22.8 percent in Great Britain. Ranking these countries according to their per capita consumption as estimated for 1955 by the Twentieth Century Fund study, there was clearly a positive and close relationship between consumption level and percentage of the labor force in marketing. Of the seven countries with a "high" per capita consumption (Great Britain, Sweden, Norway, Belgium, Switzerland, Denmark, France), all had a labor force ratio in marketing ranging between 15.4 and 22.8 percent. Five of the six countries ranked as having a "medium" per capita consumption (Ireland, Germany, Austria, Iceland, Finland) had a labor force ratio in marketing ranging between 9.7 and 15.1 percent. Of this "medium" group, only the Netherlands, with 19.8 percent of its labor force in marketing, fell beyond the 10-15 percent range of the other five. The four countries with a "low" consumption per capita (Italy, Portugal, Greece, Spain) had labor force ratios in marketing ranging from 7.6 to 9.4 percent.[80]

GALENSON: 25 COUNTRIES

Galenson's analysis of employment trends in 25 countries during the period of approximately 1952-1962[81] included 11 countries with per capita national income (1956-1958) of over $575 a year, 6 with per capita income between $200 and $575, and 8 with per capita income below $200. Relating the average annual percentage increase in

---

[76] Clark, op. cit.

[77] Minkes, op. cit.

[78] James B. Jefferys and Derek Knee, *Retailing in Europe: Present Structure and Future Trends* (London: Macmillan, 1962), pp. 1-23. Some of their data were from J. Frederick Dewhurst et al., *Europe's Needs and Resources* (New York: Twentieth Century Fund, 1961).

[79] Walter Galenson, "Economic Development and the Sectoral Expansion of Employment," *International Labour Review* 87 (June 1963): 505-519, and Lee E. Preston, "The Commercial Sector and Economic Development," in Moyer and Hollander, op. cit., pp. 9-23.

[80] Jefferys and Knee, op. cit., p. 13.

[81] For some of the countries data for slightly shorter periods were used.

manufacturing employment to that for employment in tertiary industries, he found the following:

$$E_t = 1.083 + 0.581\ E_m$$

in which E_t is the average annual rate of change in employment in tertiary occupations and E_m is the same for employment in manufacturing.

> Thus, over the period studied, employment in tertiary industry was increasing at slightly over 1 percent a year regardless of the increase of manufacturing employment. In addition, for every percentage increase in the number of manufacturing jobs there were almost 0.6 percent more jobs in the tertiary sector. Inspection of the data . . . indicates that for the developed countries, this relationship was nearer one to one, while for the less developed countries manufacturing employment tended to outrun tertiary employment.[82]

But Galenson's study suggests caution in the use of the Clark-Fisher hypothesis to predict what will happen in a given country with respect to the distribution of its employment, especially in a span of years shorter than a decade. He compared the ratio of manufacturing employment to tertiary employment in each of the 25 countries at the beginning and the end of a 3-10-year period. He found that manufacturing employment generally grew relative to tertiary employment in the underdeveloped countries, but this growth also occurred in most of the higher-income countries to a lesser degree.

He also found some interesting differences between countries. Manufacturing employment in Belgium was about 78.0 percent of tertiary employment at the beginning of the period, but this dropped to 65.2 percent by the end of the period. In Great Britain, however, it was 75.0 percent to begin with and remained at 75.1 percent at the end of the period. Canada's ratio dropped from 49.1 percent at the beginning to 40.8 percent at the end, while the ratio for Japan rose from 47.7 percent at the beginning to 49.3 percent at the end. The changes that took place were not the same for two countries that began the period with approximately the same distributional pattern. While the ratio of manufacturing employment to tertiary employment tended to be much lower for low-income countries than for high-income countries, there were numerous exceptions. At the end of the period, for example, the ratio in Canada was 40.8, in Ireland 39.6, and in the Philippines 46.0. These three countries were in the high-, medium-, and low-income groups, respectively. Among the 8 low-income nations studied, the ratio ranged from 9.1 percent in Nigeria to 46.0 percent in the Philippines. Among the high-income countries, it ranged from 40.2 percent for Israel to 78.6 percent in Luxembourg. Changes in this ratio within a country over a span of some 6 to 10 years were far less than differences between countries in the same income group at any one point in time.

In spite of these variations, however, Galenson concludes that the normal path of economic development involves an expansion of manufacturing. This, in turn, has a multiplier effect on tertiary employment, resulting in the increased demand generated by the higher productivity possible in manufacturing. At the same time, industrial expansion requires "a superstructure of commercial, governmental, and other services"[83] to support it. The latter involves a technological relationship beteen jobs in manufacturing and those in supporting services.

---

[82] Galenson, op. cit., p. 510.

[83] Ibid., p. 514.

Galenson also makes some observations about the breakdown of tertiary employment among commerce, transportation, and services in different countries and observes that the correlation between manufacturing and commerce is much weaker than that between manufacturing and tertiary industries as a whole. He believes that this is due to differences among nations in the way they classify occupations or in the way they actually distribute employment among tertiary industries. The high-income countries showed no consistent pattern in this respect, while low-income countries showed a greater tendency to utilize tertiary employees in service occupations than in commerce. Thus Galenson's data tend to support the Clark-Fisher hypothesis, but certain countries showed patterns inconsistent with those of other countries at similar levels of income.

PRESTON: 74 COUNTRIES

The most comprehensive study of employment ratios in marketing and tertiary industries relative to total employment in various countries was made by Lee Preston, using occupational data for about 1960 from the International Labour Office and gross domestic product data for about the same year from the United Nations. (See Table 21.1). The detailed data in Table 21.1 are summarized in Table 21.2. This shows that employment in commerce (wholesale and retail trade) increased as per capita gross domestic product (GDP) increased.

Fitting both linear and logarithmic functions to the data for 74 countries,[84] Preston found the following relationships:

$$\log Y_1 = -.17045 + .44 \log X \qquad r^2 = .50$$
$$(.05)$$

$$Y_1 = 6.1 + .008 X \qquad r^2 = .54$$
$$(.0008)$$

in which Y_1 is the ratio of employment in commerce relative to the total labor force and X is the GDP per capita in dollars. According to the arithmetic function just given, each $100 change in GDP per capita had associated with it a change in employment in marketing relative to total employment of 0.8 points. Thus if marketing employment were 8.6 percent of total employment to begin with, a $100 increase in GDP would have associated with it a rise in marketing employment to 9.4 percent of the total. According to the logarithmic function just given, each 1.00 percent change in GDP per capita had associated with it a 0.44 percent change in the marketing employment ratio. These equations indicate that about half of the variance in the employment ratio was explained by per capita GDP.

Omitting three cities from the data he analyzed (Hong Kong, West Berlin, and Luxembourg) and the four "new world" countries (Australia, New Zealand, Canada, and the United States), Preston then attempted to generalize about the relationship between GDP per capita and the marketing employment ratio. The basic pattern that he found was that in countries with GDP of less than $500 per capita, each $100 change in GDP had associated with it about a 1.75-point change in the ratio of marketing employment to total employment, with the a value ranging between 1 and 5 percent. Between $500 and $1000 GDP per capita, each $100 change in GDP had associated with it about a .75-point

---

[84] Five were omitted from the 79 listed in Table 21.1 because of gross inconsistencies in the data.

Table 21.1 Gross Domestic Product (GDP) per Capita and Percentage of Total Labor Force[a] in Commerce[b] and Tertiary Industries[c] in 79 Countries, ca. 1960

Country	Continent	GDP per Capita (US$)	Employment as Percentage of Labor Force	
			Commerce	Tertiary
Mozambique	Africa	45	1.40	9.27
Nepal	Asia	50	1.40	4.16
Tanganyika[d]	Africa	52	39.25	71.00
Pakistan	Asia	63	4.88	14.73
India	Asia	67	4.06	14.90
Indonesia	Asia	69	6.71	18.29
Thailand	Asia	78	5.64	11.57
Haiti	N. America	80	3.52	8.47
Congo	Africa	87	1.48	3.60
Bolivia	S. America	104	5.40	13.98
Korea	Asia	105	9.07	23.24
Paraguay	S. America	111	6.78	25.93
Taiwan	Asia	115	6.70	24.42
United Arab Republic	Africa	116	8.11	28.75
Ceylon	Asia	122	8.22	27.83
Rhodesia[d]	Africa	134	25.73	62.37
Northern Rhodesia[d]	Africa	134	18.06	58.20
Syria	Asia	138	11.33	30.01
Tunisia	Asia	147	4.72	13.12
Peru	S. America	148	4.52	10.18
Surinam	S. America	148	11.70	15.46
Iran	Asia	159	5.85	20.01
Morocco	Africa	159	14.37	16.74
Guatemala	N. America	164	5.43	16.94
Ecuador	S. America	179	6.18	22.32
Ryukyu[d]	Asia	180	18.76	38.60
Philippines	Asia	191	8.88	22.60
Honduras	N. America	192	4.58	5.69
El Salvador	N. America	198	6.24	21.80
Turkey	Europe	201	3.11	10.21
Fiji Islands	Oceania	212	6.66	23.65
Iraq	Asia	215	5.11	24.35
Federation of Malaya	Asia	216	9.01	27.22
Portugal	Europe	218	7.96	26.21
Algeria	Africa	220	4.96	11.35
Mauritius	Africa	221	10.03	35.29
Gabon[d]	Africa	240	37.10	81.86
Nicaragua	N. America	249	4.62	16.97
Brazil	S. America	250	6.27	26.11
British Guiana	S. America	250	11.33	34.16
Hong Kong	Asia	258	10.83	39.85
Japan	Asia	284	18.90	39.73
Mexico	N. America	288	9.48	26.10
Colombia	S. America	301	5.42	24.81

Table 21.1 (Continued)

Country	Continent	GDP per Capita (US$)	Employment as Percentage of Labor Force	
			Commerce	Tertiary
Greece	Europe	310	7.31	23.61
Spain	Europe	322	7.84	26.36
Martinique	N. America	330	8.82	25.27
Panama	N. America	348	9.12	32.04
Costa Rica	N. America	358	7.87	26.10
Jamaica	N. America	361	9.93	34.92
Cuba	N. America	370	11.83	37.12
South Africa	Africa	386	4.92	28.38
Cyprus	Europe	403	6.90	26.53
Chile	S. America	409	9.56	14.60
Argentina	S. America	474	11.90	38.17
Ireland	Europe	474	14.76	38.81
Italy	Europe	490	13.21	31.90
Trinidad	S. America	532	11.31	40.10
Israel	Asia	579	12.41	48.16
Puerto Rico	N. America	581	16.82	48.60
Austria	Europe	656	10.96	37.07
Finland	Europe	750	11.62	32.80
Netherlands	Europe	767	16.21	46.66
West Berlin	Europe	893	16.48	50.19
German Federal Republic	Europe	931	13.81	39.25
Iceland	Europe	937	9.12	31.50
Venezuela	S. America	975	12.64	40.84
Denmark	Europe	975	14.97	44.29
Belgium	Europe	1029	14.57	44.66
Norway	Europe	1035	13.28	43.67
United Kingdom	Europe	1078	13.97	45.37
France	Europe	1113	13.18	38.63
Australia	Oceania	1211	19.60	47.78
New Zealand	Oceania	1281	18.21	48.49
Sweden	Europe	1313	13.51	40.80
Switzerland	Europe	1316	13.78	38.26
Luxembourg	Europe	1333	18.75	34.01
Canada	N. America	1767	19.66	53.49
U. S. A.	N. America	2324	22.53	54.55

[a]Labor force is defined as the economically active population.

[b]Commerce = wholesale and retail trade, finance, insurance, and real estate.

[c]Tertiary = commerce, transportation, and services.

[d]Omitted from the statistical analysis.

Source: Lee E. Preston, "The Commercial Sector and Economic Development," in Reed Moyer and Stanley C. Hollander, eds., *Markets and Marketing in Developing Economies* (Homewood, Ill.: Irwin, 1968), pp. 22-23, copyrighted 1968 by the American Marketing Association. GDP data are from United Nations, *Yearbook of National Accounts Statistics*, 1963, Table 3A. Employment data are from International Labour Office, *Yearbook of Labour Statistics*, 1964, Table 4.

Table 21.2 Average Ratio of Employment in Commerce and in Tertiary Industries as a Percentage of Total Labor Force in 79 Countries Classified by Gross Domestic Product (GDP) per Capita, ca. 1960

GDP per Capita in U.S. $[a]	Number of Countries	Employment as Percentage of Total Labor Force	
		Commerce	Tertiary
Less than $200	29	8.93	22.56
200-499	28	9.80	29.71
500-799	6	13.22	42.23
800 and over	16	15.50	43.49
Total	79	10.90	30.80

[a] Average GDP, all countries = $450.

Source: Lee E. Preston, "The Commercial Sector and Economic Development," in ed. Reed Moyer and Stanley C. Hollander, eds., *Markets and Marketing in Developing Economies,* (Homewood, Ill.: Irwin, 1968), p. 14, copyrighted 1968 by the American Marketing Association. The detail on which this table is based is shown in Table 21.1.

change in the marketing employment ratio, with the *a* value ranging between about 5 and 10 percent. At a GDP per capita of about $1000, the market employment ratio leveled off at about 14-15 percent of total employment. There were marked deviations from this pattern, with about one-third of the underdeveloped countries (GDP per capita of less than $500) falling above the calculated ratio indicated. Also, of course, Australia, New Zealand, Canada, and the United States, with employment ratios greater than 20 percent, were not included.

CONCLUSIONS

Our principal interest in this review has been in the relationship between employment in marketing and total employment at various stages of economic development. The Clark-Fisher hypothesis was stated, however, in terms of the relationship between service (or tertiary) employment and total employment. As we have indicated, Galenson found that this relationship is more consistent than that between marketing employment and total employment. Preston's findings support this.[85] Therefore the use of marketing employment alone is not a completely fair test of the Clark-Fisher hypothesis as it was originally stated.

Nelson Foote and Paul Hatt have suggested that the service, or tertiary, sector should be broken down into tertiary, quaternary, and quinary industries for greater insight into the sequence of the development process.[86] They describe their proposed breakdown as follows:

---

[85] He found, for example, that when he related tertiary employment as a percentage of total employment to GDP per capita in a linear function, the r^2 value was .58, compared to an r^2 of .54 for a similar function with employment in commerce as a percentage of total employment. For the logarithmic function, the r^2 for tertiary employment was also .58, compared to .50 for commerce. Preston, "The Commercial Sector and Economic Development," op. cit., p. 15.

[86] Nelson N. Foote and Paul K. Hatt, "Social Mobility and Economic Advancement," *American Economic Review* 43 (May 1953): 364-378.

The first of these we shall again call tertiary industries, defined as domestic and quasi-domestic services: restaurants and hotels, barber and beauty shops, laundry and dry cleaning, repairing and maintenance, and a sprinkling of handcrafts, once performed at home, which Clark lumps with "small scale manufacturers." . . . if the principle of tracing them to the home is followed, they can be quite inclusively identified.

Next, under the caption of quaternary industries we shall group transport, commerce, communication, finance, and administration. The principle governing this grouping is that these are the industries which facilitate or effectuate the division of labor. Their office is to knit together in a working system the specialized producers of raw materials, manufactured goods, and other services. . . .

Logically and empirically, quinary industries as we shall define them are not once more a residual category. These industries comprise medical care, education, research, and recreation (including the arts). The principle which guides this grouping is that they all have to do with the refinement and extension of human capacities. They differ from the domestic and quasi-domestic tertiary industries in that they are not devoted simply to the maintenance of individuals in the style to which they are accustomed but to the cultivation of behavior to which they are not accustomed.[87]

Clearly marketing would be a part of the quaternary industry group according to the classification scheme of Foote and Hatt.

Can the Clark-Fisher hypothesis be used to describe the relationship between employment in marketing and total employment in countries at various levels of economic development? On the basis of the empirical studies that we have briefly surveyed, we can conclude that it is more often true than not that the percentage of the total labor force that will be employed in marketing will increase as a country's per capita income rises. However, there are numerous deviations from this pattern. We should not, therefore, make unqualified use of the Clark-Fisher hypothesis to predict marketing employment in a *particular* country, or changes in marketing employment in a *particular country over time*, without careful attention to the economic and social forces operative in that specific situation. Nevertheless, there is an empirically verified *tendency* for marketing employment ratios to be positively related to per capita income, and this suggests that there will also be a tendency for marketing costs as a percentage of total costs of production to increase as per capita income rises. We should therefore draw together the various reasons for these observable relationships.

Reasons for the Increasing Importance of Marketing in Expanding Economies

The expansion of marketing activities and the increasing relative importance of marketing in the total economy generally accompanies the expansion of national output. It is in the period of most rapid economic growth, usually characterized by greatly increased industrialization, that marketing absorbs an increasingly significant share of the total labor force and produces a much less rapidly increasing share of national output. Once economic maturity has been reached, the portion of the labor force in marketing tends to stabilize, and marketing's share of total output either stabilizes or declines slightly. Why is

---

[87] Ibid., p. 365.

the growth in the marketing employment ratio greatest during that period when the rate of growth in total output is greatest?

The reasons are not difficult to establish. Specialization of production, undertaken to benefit from differences in resources or demands, or to realize the benefits of economies of scale, increases the absolute level of income, throwing increased outputs upon whatever marketing system exists. Of even greater importance, however, is the fact that increased specialization makes exchange among specialized producers necessary if the surplus outputs of producers are to find their way into the possession of potential users. In addition, the scale of marketing expands to the point where it too can find economies through specialization. Specialized marketing institutions develop because the volume of goods to be marketed has increased sufficiently to make them economical units, and marketing becomes increasingly segregated from nonmarketing units. Part of the emergence of marketing as an increasingly important part of the economy during these expansion periods is due to the sheer fact of its identity, which was less clear when small-scale agricultural and manufacturing units performed their own marketing functions.

Associated with a rising level of output is still another change that makes marketing important. The higher per capita income is, the greater the diversity of goods and services a consuming unit will demand. The range of items demanded will make the assembly and dispersion function of the marketing institution more critical than ever. The more specialized production is in the face of an increasingly diversified demand, the more the marketing system will have to do in order to bring these into equilibrium.

The move toward economic maturity gives rise to still another phenomenon that manifests itself in the changing role of marketing. This is the tendency for the competitive structure of the economy to shift as a result of oligopolistic market relationships among large-scale producers and the increasing importance of nonprice competition, product diversity, and demand stimulation when consumption reaches a higher level. Under these circumstances, market control and the use of marketing's creative functions come into play as important elements of production policy.

If the marketing system could respond to these changes in the same way processing industries can, its relative importance in the total economy might not be altered at all. But marketing is not that kind of business. Its principal productive resource is labor; except in transportation industries, possibilities for increased capital investment are limited. Therefore in competition with processing industries that are amenable to marked increases in the amount and quality of capital resources, marketing institutions are likely to represent an increasing proportion of total human productive effort as the volume and variety of goods that move through the marketing system increase. We shall explore this in much more detail in the chapter that follows.

22

The Price of Marketing

I took one Draught of Life—
I'll tell you what I paid—
Precisely an existence—
The market price, they said.

—Emily Dickinson

In our discussion of marketing in developing economies, we used the proportion of the labor force engaged in marketing activities as an indication of the relative importance of marketing in the economy. Since labor is only one of the productive factors used in marketing, a better indication of marketing's relative importance would be the proportion of all resources devoted to marketing activities. This allocation, expenditure, or cost can be viewed as the aggregate price of marketing. In this chapter, we shall consider what the meaning of this aggregate value is, the demand and supply forces that determine its size, and some of the empirical evidence that we have on total expenditures for marketing.

THE MEANING OF THE PRICE OF MARKETING

It has been traditional in pricing theory to structure the analysis in terms of units and aggregates. We speak of average and marginal cost and of average and marginal revenue, each relating to a unit of output. A manufacturer of goods finds it convenient and useful to organize his cost-revenue analysis in this way, since each unit is basically identical to every other unit of that product type and quality.

But is this a logical way for the marketing firm, or the manufacturing firm that is selling mixed lots of goods and services, to view its "unit"? Consider, for example, the way a supermarket functions. The typical customer is likely to make his selection among items that will yield an overall "price" that he finds justified by the overall utility he expects from the mixture of goods and services that he acquires. In other words, in marketing the *transaction*, rather than the *physical unit* of goods, would seem to be the better "unit" for price analysis. This would also be true for a wholesale firm that mixes lots. If, on the other hand, there is a physical product that is typically sold one unit at a time, the number of transactions and the number of physical units will be the same. Even in this case, however, the transaction involves services that are not a part of the physical good.

If the transaction is the appropriate unit to consider in the analysis of the demand for and supply of marketing services, then we are dealing with units that are often differentiated, and sometimes highly differentiated, from one another. Each transaction involves a cluster of services, and the value placed on that cluster is what we call the price of marketing. If the range of choices in the market makes it possible for the buyer to select among goods with varying amounts of marketing services attached, price differentials should reflect the supply of and demand for differences in the package of services. To the extent that such choices are possible, the price of marketing will be a function of costs and of the willingness of buyers to incur expenditures for the services involved.

Similarly, aggregate marketing expenditures will be a function of aggregate supply and demand. By referring to this aggregate as "total marketing expenditures" rather than "total cost of marketing," we are reminded that *both* supply and demand enter into the determination of the amount involved and avoid any implication that this is a minimal or unavoidable cost, since it reflects buyer and seller interactions and may or may not involve abnormal profits to those who provide marketing services.

We shall now consider some of the important factors that underlie consumer demand for marketing services and the supply of those services by processors and specialized marketing firms, focusing not upon particular consumers or particular marketing firms but upon the marketing system as a whole.

THE DEMAND FOR MARKETING SERVICES

The demand for marketing services is derived from the demand by potential buyers for the rights of ownership of goods and services that are made physically accessible to them. Because these services necessary to complete the marketing task may be performed at various levels of the trade channel, the aggregate demand for such services by ultimate buyers is often segmented into a series of vertically related demands, each of which is manifest at an appropriate level.

There is, however, a demand for an aggregate of marketing services, and it is this aggregate on which we focus in this discussion. This can be thought of in a mini macro sense as the demand for all the marketing services associated with the transfer of ownership and physical possession of a *particular good*, such as automobiles. In a macro sense, it is the aggregate of all services associated with the transfer of ownership and physical possession of *all goods and services*. These services are what we call the *marketing transformation*, and they are comparable to the physical transformation that characterizes the processes by which the physical attributes of goods are altered to make those goods more useful.

We shall examine four attributes of the demand for marketing services: (1) complementary and competing demands for marketing services, (2) cross-elasticities of demand for marketing and nonmarketing services, (3) marketing's "own" price elasticity of demand, and (4) producer-created demands for goods and marketing services.

Complementary and Competing Demands for Marketing Services

COMPLEMENTARY (JOINT) DEMANDS

It is obvious that the demand for marketing services accompanies the demand for the processing of the goods that are being marketed. The services that make up the marketing mix are a cluster, and the demand for one element of the cluster may depend on there being also a demand for another element of that cluster. If we extend the notion of a cluster to the physical processing of goods, we can view that too as a cluster of services. The demand for the processing cluster and the demand for the marketing cluster are complementary.

COMPETING DEMANDS

But this conveys only a part of the picture so far as consumer choice is concerned, for each of these clusters offers opportunities for substitution. An example of the substitution possibilities would be that of an industrial buyer who finds that changes have occurred in the relative prices of goods of different qualities (processing costs) and the prices from sources of supply offering different locational advantages (marketing costs). If he finds that he now prefers to incur more marketing costs in order to get a lower-priced good of high quality from a more distant source than formerly, the optimum combination of processing and marketing costs will have shifted in the direction of more marketing and less processing. A closely related example of substitution possibilities between marketing and nonmarketing components of the final transactional "package" would be between locally produced goods at high cost (due to natural or structural diseconomies) and goods produced at more distant points at much lower cost (due to natural or structural economies). The former would entail proportionately lower marketing costs and higher nonmarketing costs, while the opposite would be true for the good that is processed at greater distance. What we are considering is the possibility that economies of scale in the performance of one function may sometimes offset the diseconomies of scale that result in a complementary function. When these offsets occur in the marketing and processing segments of the economy, and when changes occur in the comparative costs of activities in these two segments, it can result in a shifting of functions between the two.

Complementarity and competition between clusters of functions can best be analyzed within the context of cross-elasticity of demand. We turn now to this aspect of the demand for marketing and nonmarketing services in production.

Cross-Elasticity of Demand for Marketing and Processing Services

Because marketing and processing are both necessary to complete the production process where there are specialized production units, they are complementary and display a negative cross-elasticity coefficient. A rise in the price of manufacturing services, for example, would result in fewer units being demanded and cause a reduction in the quantity of marketing services necessary to effect the physical and ownership transfer of goods to consumer. But we have also pointed out that marketing services can be substituted for processing services to some extent, and this would be conducive to a positive cross-elasticity. Therefore the size and the sign of the net cross-elasticity coefficient will be a function of several variables.

MARKETING QUANTITY AND THE PROCESSING PRICE

The functional relationship can be indicated by

$$e_{qmpf} = f[(M/T),(e_{qt}),(u_m/u_f)^\beta]$$

in which (e_{qmpf}) is the elasticity of demand for marketing services with respect to the price of form production services, M/T is the cost of marketing relative to the total cost of the good (marketing + form production costs), e_{qt} is the elasticity of the demand for the fully produced good, and u_m/u_f is the ratio of the utility of one unit of marketing relative to one unit of processing, with β as the rate of substitution between the two.

We can make some observations about the relationships of these variables. The larger M is relative to T, the lower the cross-elasticity is likely to be, for this would mean that a sizable change in the price of the processing cost would have little effect on the amount of marketing services demanded. The higher the elasticity of demand for the final product, the higher the cross-elasticity is likely to be, other things being equal. If consumers are very sensitive to price changes for the final product, this will affect the demand for the marketing cluster much more than if buyers are very insenstive to changes in the price of the final product. Finally, the extent to which marketing and nonmarketing activities can be substituted for one another will affect the responsiveness of consumers to changes in the price of nonmarketing activities. The greater the substitution possibilities, the lower the cross-elasticity is likely to be, for sellers can then increase or decrease marketing expenditures, which will not have changed in price, for the nonmarketing costs, which will have changed in price. There can never be perfect substitution, however. Therefore it is unlikely that the substitution possibility will be sufficient to make the cross-elasticity positive. Partial substitutability is likely to reduce the absolute value of the negative cross-elasticity. If, on the other hand, marketing and processing were almost purely complementary, each necessary for the utility of the other to be realized, then substitution possibilities would be zero and the cross-elasticity unaffected.

PROCESSING QUANTITY AND MARKETING PRICE

What can we say about cross-elasticity of demand in the other direction, that is, the effect of a change in the price of marketing on the quantity of processing services demanded? The parameters of the relationships should be the same as those we have considered, with one exception. The exception concerns the parameter for M/T. In this case, if there is a change in the price of marketing (M), the larger M is relative to T, the higher the cross-elasticity is likely to be between the price of marketing and the quantity of processing services demanded. For the other variables the relationship will be the same as we have described—the higher the elasticity of demand for the final product, the greater the cross-elasticity is likely to be; the more possibility there is for substitution of marketing and processing for one another, the lower the cross-elasticity is likely to be.

Marketing's "Own" Price Elasticity

We have indicated that marketing services are both complementary to and competing with processing services. So many of the services in each of these clusters are unique to their own clusters, however, that it is more likely that marketing will be complementary rather than competing. In light of this, is it possible to conceive of the demand for marketing services as in any sense an independent demand? That is, if the price of marketing services were to vary without any change in the price of nonmarketing services, would there be any variation in the quantity of marketing services demanded?

QUANTITY OF MARKETING SERVICES PURCHASED

There is one way in which buyers can respond to changes in the price of marketing via the quantity of marketing services purchased without affecting the amount of proceeds (*not* the share) received by processing. Buyers may simply purchase fewer marketing services when their price increases without altering their purchases of processing services. Whether or not this is possible depends on the extent to which consumers can choose more services when their price falls, or forgo some of them when their price rises. This is possible if the retailer gives the consumer the option of taking (and paying for) certain services or not taking (and not paying for) certain services. The choice is more likely to be accomplished, however, by the consumer's choosing from among different retail outlets that offer different bundles of services and, hence, different prices on the marketing service cluster.

RELOCATION OF PRODUCTION

Another way in which buyers can adjust the quantity of marketing services bought in response to changes in the price of marketing is through increased production of those services for themselves when they are costly, or through increased purchases of them when they are cheaper. This is not really a change in the quantity of marketing services *acquired* but a change in the quantity *purchased* in the market.

An industrial buyer, for example, may avail himself of credit services when it is cheaper to acquire them from the seller than to provide them for himself. If, however, interest rates rise so that credit purchases become much more costly, the buyer may then look to see if the opportunity cost for his own capital is sufficiently low for it to be used for purposes of financing purchases. If financial markets were perfect, interest rates should be the same in both circumstances. But imperfections related to differences in risk or access to capital may give some buyers greater options in choosing among alternative sources of capital, and this may be a way of adjusting to changes in the marketing costs associated with the provision of capital for financing purchases. Unused capacity in a buying firm often gives the firm opportunities for producing certain services for itself that might otherwise be purchased in the market at higher cost. Similarly, production at full capacity may make it more attractive to purchase certain marketing services from sellers in order that the buyer may enjoy greater returns from alternative uses of his resources.

Some of the best examples of self-produced services in marketing are in consumer buying. Rising costs of retailing over the years that have been associated, for example, with increasing wage rates, have put great pressure on market participants, including both sellers and buyers, to search for ways of increasing output in retailing. One common resolution of the problem has been to increase the use of self-service in retail selling, under which the consumer performs for himself many of the functions formerly performed by retail personnel.

For a rational decision to be made in the shifting of functions, it is necessary that the cost of performance of newly acquired or discarded functions be assessed in their alternative locations. Where there is unused capacity in either the buying or selling unit, the short-run variable costs of shifted functions may be so low as to make the shift desirable. In the long run, however, excess capacity will tend to disappear and the assessment of optimal location of function to be altered accordingly.

DEMAND ELASTICITY RELATIONSHIPS IN THE MARKETING CHANNEL

We have shown that the elasticity of demand in the marketing channel is a function of demand derived from the demand for the final product.[1] We have also shown that the costs incurred at each successive channel level are an important variable in determining the willingness of buyers at that level to purchase goods from suppliers for further marketing transformation and transmission to their customers. At this point, we shall

---

[1] See Chapters 7 and 12

expand this discussion of a single channel to include the total marketing system to see what observations we can make about the relationships between demands for marketing services at various levels in the total marketing system.

We shall employ the concepts of unit price and quantity, but these will refer to the unit price of an average transaction—any old transaction—and the average quantity or bundle of goods and services in such a transaction. We shall not concern ourselves with aggregate marketing or processing costs, but merely with the elasticities of the vertically related demands in the aggregate trade channel. In this channel, there is a final total demand for goods and services that comprises a demand for processing (form production) services and a demand for marketing services. Let

r = unit retail price

p = unit processing price

m = unit marketing price

q = quantity sold

Δr = change in unit retail price

Δm = change in unit marketing price

Δp = change in unit processing price

e_r = elasticity of demand for final good (including marketing and processing) with respect to retail price of goods

e_m = elasticity of demand for marketing services with respect to price of marketing

e_p = elasticity of demand for processing services with respect to price of processing

We assume that each final transaction contains a combination of processing and marketing services. Since we are concerned with comparative elasticities at those points on the demand curves at which transactions actually take place, we shall assume that the number of final goods equals the number of marketing service bundles and the number of processing bundles. Thus $q = q_r = q_m = q_p$.

By definition the elasticities of demand for the final good, marketing, and processing are

$$e_r = \frac{\Delta q}{q} \frac{r}{\Delta r}$$

$$e_m = \frac{\Delta q}{q} \frac{m}{\Delta m}$$

$$e_p = \frac{\Delta q}{q} \frac{p}{\Delta p}$$

It would be useful to see these elasticities in relationship to one another. Since $\Delta q/q$ is the same for the final good, marketing, and processing,

$$\frac{\Delta q}{q} = e_r \left(\frac{\Delta r}{r}\right) = e_m \left(\frac{\Delta m}{m}\right) = e_p \left(\frac{\Delta p}{p}\right)$$

Substituting these values for $\Delta q/q$, we have

$$e_r = e_m \left(\frac{\Delta m}{m}\right) \left(\frac{r}{\Delta r}\right) = e_p \left(\frac{\Delta p}{p}\right) \left(\frac{r}{\Delta r}\right)$$

$$e_m = e_r \left(\frac{\Delta r}{r}\right) \left(\frac{m}{\Delta m}\right) = e_p \left(\frac{\Delta p}{p}\right) \left(\frac{m}{\Delta m}\right)$$

$$e_p = e_r \left(\frac{\Delta r}{r}\right) \left(\frac{p}{\Delta p}\right) = e_m \left(\frac{\Delta m}{m}\right) \left(\frac{p}{\Delta p}\right)$$

These three equations may be restructured to show more meaningful relationships:

$$e_r = \left(\frac{r}{m}\right) \left(\frac{\Delta m}{\Delta r}\right) e_m = \left(\frac{r}{p}\right) \left(\frac{\Delta p}{\Delta r}\right) e_p$$

$$e_m = \left(\frac{m}{r}\right) \left(\frac{\Delta r}{\Delta m}\right) e_r = \left(\frac{m}{p}\right) \left(\frac{\Delta p}{\Delta m}\right) e_p$$

$$e_p = \left(\frac{p}{r}\right) \left(\frac{\Delta r}{\Delta p}\right) e_r = \left(\frac{p}{m}\right) \left(\frac{\Delta m}{\Delta p}\right) e_m$$

One of the problems we are interested in is the elasticity of demand for marketing services. If we examine the equation for e_m carefully, we can see that the elasticity of demand for marketing services with respect to the price of those services is the product of the ratio of the cost of marketing to the retail price of good (m/r), the ratio of the change in the retail price of goods relative to the change in the price of marketing ($\Delta r/\Delta m$), and the elasticity of demand for the final product. From this, we can see the following relationships, other things being equal:

1. The higher the elasticity of demand for goods at retail, the higher the elasticity of demand for marketing services.
2. The higher the marketing cost as a percentage of the retail price, the higher the elasticity of demand for marketing services
3. The higher the change in retail price associated with a given change in the price of marketing, the higher the elasticity of demand for marketing will tend to be.

None of these is surprising. The equation merely shows these relationships in a compact model.

One can observe another possibility from the e_m equation. Even though marketing costs may be a very high percentage of the retail price, the effect of this on elasticity of demand for marketing services could be offset by a very low elasticity of demand for the good at retail. Also, even though a change in marketing costs has a disproportionately large effect on the change in retail prices, the volume of marketing services purchased will be affected much less if marketing is a relatively small percentage of the retail price and/or if the elasticity of demand at retail is quite low.

The second equality in the e_m equation shows that the elasticity of demand for marketing services is a product of the price of marketing as a percentage of the price of processing, the change in processing price as a percentage of the change in marketing price, and the elasticity of demand for processing.

It is important to remember that the equalities we have identified would be expected for vertically related functions (or clusters of functions) where the quantities that move through each level are equal.[2]

---

[2] It is easy to confuse questions of elasticity with questions of changes in demand. Since the demand for marketing and processing is a joint demand, we would expect a negative cross-elasticity of demand,

We shall now move one step further and show the effect of a change in marketing costs (the price of marketing) on the final retail price. We can modify the equation for e_m to yield the following:

$$\left(\frac{\Delta r}{\Delta m}\right)\left(\frac{m}{r}\right) = \left(\frac{e_m}{e_r}\right)$$

Therefore

$$\left(\frac{\Delta r}{\Delta m}\right) = \left(\frac{r}{m}\right)\left(\frac{e_m}{e_r}\right) \quad \text{and} \quad \Delta r = \Delta m \left(\frac{r}{m}\right)\left(\frac{e_m}{e_r}\right)$$

The effect of a change in marketing price on processing price can be shown in the same way:

$$\left(\frac{\Delta p}{\Delta m}\right)\left(\frac{m}{p}\right) = \left(\frac{e_m}{e_p}\right) \quad \text{and} \quad \Delta p = \Delta m \left(\frac{p}{m}\right)\left(\frac{e_m}{e_p}\right)$$

While our approach in this discussion has been to read the sequence of changes as a change in other prices resulting from a change in marketing prices (or costs), we could also consider the effects of a change in other prices—the price of processing, or the final sales price of the good—on the price of marketing. In a dynamic market situation it is most likely that changes in output and price will be initiated in primary production or in consumer goods markets and filter up or down to the intermediate wholesale markets. However, marketing firms in the middle of the channel may initiate price changes under two circumstances. One would be where they are anticipating changes in demand or supply and reflect their anticipations in the prices they ask or offer. The other case in which they would be pricesetters would be where the intermediate marketing firm has greater market power than those from which they buy or to which they sell.

Producer-Created Demand

We have blithely proceeded in our discussion of marketing services as though the demand for them exists and the responsibility of sellers is to try to meet that demand. The doctrine of consumer sovereignty is based upon the following assumption: People demand goods and a spectrum of services, including goods-related services that make products available for use, and the activities of sellers are in response to that demand, which is manifested in the market place.[3]

---

meaning that a rise in the price of one component—marketing, let us say—causes buyers to buy less of that cluster *and also* less of the processing cluster. Thus a rise in the price of marketing results in a decrease in the quantity of marketing services demanded and a *decrease in demand* for processing, with a resulting fall in its price. But this is not a matter of elasticity of demand so far as processing goes. It *is* a matter of elasticity of demand so far as marketing is concerned, for the elasticity of demand indicates how much decline there will be in the purchase of marketing services as a result of a rise in its price. But the effect of this is transferred to the processing services market via a *change in demand* in that market. Hence, the issue there is not what the elasticity of demand for processing services is but, rather, how much the change in marketing price affects the quantity of processing demanded.

[3] What we are dealing with in this section is producer-created demand for a specific output of a specific producer rather than aggregate demand for aggregate supply of the total economy. The nature of the

In recent years a number of writers have challenged this assumption and pointed out in detail the ways in which business firms can be shown to generate the demand necessary to absorb the goods and services that producers are capable of producing and, it is hoped, to do so under terms compatible with the short- and long-term goals of producers. John Kenneth Galbraith and Ezra J. Mishan are among those who have been most articulate in refuting the existence of self-created demands sufficient to explain the level of production achieved in affluent societies.[4] Galbraith argues that as a society becomes more affluent, wants are increasingly created by the process through which they are satisfied. This interaction between output and wants he calls the "dependence effect." Insofar as consumption leads to the generation of wants on the part of potential emulators, and to the extent that producers of goods create wants through advertising and sales promotion, we cannot say, he believes, that wants come first and production follows in order to satisfy the demand that exists. The sequence is, in his judgment, the reverse.

Mishan carries the argument still further, dealing with the question of the desirability or undesirability of extending the consumer's range of choice, and particularly with the fact that the range of choice is not specified by the consumer but offered to the consumer at the option of sellers. Moreover, new offerings on the market frequently entail the withdrawal of old ones, and there is no assurance that the net effect of this reallocation is to increase consumer welfare. He also raises the equally serious question of whether consumers are capable of making optimum choices for their own welfare.

In our discussion of the "demand" for marketing services, we have thus far ignored this problem, but we cannot leave the subject of demand without recognizing that a part of

---

relationship between aggregate demand and aggregate supply was first formally stated by J. B. Say in what has come to be known as Say's "law of markets." The essence of Say's proposition was that the total demand for all goods and services of an economy "is capable of being equal to its aggregate supply price for all volumes of total ouput." Thus equilibrium in total output is possible for all possible aggregate outputs, but equilibrium between the supply of and demand for a particular good is not possible for all possible outputs of that good. See Joseph A Schumpeter, *History of Economic Analysis* (New York: Oxford University Press, 1954), p. 624.

In his interpretation of Say's treatise, Schumpeter points out that demand and supply are concepts appropriate in the analysis of relations *within* the spectrum of outputs of a given economy but are not really appropriate when considering the system as a whole. If the terms *aggregate demand* and *aggregate supply* are used, it should be recognized that they are not independent of one another, since the demand "for the output of any industry (or firms or individuals) comes from the supplies of all the other industries (or firms or individuals)" and will therefore increase when these supplies increase and decrease when they decrease. See A. P. Lerner, "The Relation of Wage Policies and Price Policies," *American Economic Review*, suppl. 29 (March 1939): 158, as quoted in Schumpeter, op. cit., p. 617.

Numerous criticisms have been made of Say's "law," and Schumpeter attributes this in part to the lack of clarity in Say's exposition. He points out that in response to criticism of his first statement, which appeared in 1803, Say expanded his exposition in subsequent editions, "growing more wooly all the time," (Schumpeter, op. cit., p. 615.) The most important omission in his proposition is failure to include a role for the maintenance of cash balances. Underlying the "law" is the assumption that the value of each increment of production will result in *both* income and spending of equal value. If consumers and businessmen prefer increased liquidity to increased goods and services, actual purchases will fall short of potential purchases. See ibid., pp. 615-625 for a thorough analysis, and Gardner Ackley, *Macroeconomic Theory* (New York: Macmillan, 1961), pp. 109-123, for a more recent summary.

[4] See John Kenneth Galbraith, *The Affluent Society,* 2d ed. rev. (Boston: Houghton Mifflin, 1969), pp. 134-154, esp. pp. 149-154, and Ezra J. Mishan, *The Costs of Economic Growth* (New York: Praeger, 1967), pp. 109-133, esp. pp. 109-112.

the demand of which we are speaking is producer influenced or generated.[5] We shall return to this important question in the final chapter.

THE SUPPLY OF MARKETING SERVICES

The marketing services produced by the marketing industry result in the movement of goods through space, time, and channels of ownership. They are physical to the extent that the handling and movement of goods are a part of the exchange process, but they are also social in nature, involving communication, information, and negotiation between buyers and sellers. Through the activities of marketing, interactions between producers and consumers of goods occur, thereby coordinating those decision-making units of the economy that are directed by an exhange mechanism rather than by authoritarian control. In this section, we shall attempt to identify some of the important attributes of the supply of marketing services.

Joint Supply

Just as the demand for marketing is linked to the demand for the processing services, so the supply of marketing is a joint supply in two respects. Many marketing activities are carried on by firms whose primary function is processing rather than marketing. In many cases processing and marketing functions are performed by the same departments or individuals, and the distinction between them is conceptual and functional rather than organizational. Vertical integration in trade channels has also increased the degree of joint supply. A second type of joint supply in marketing arises from the fact that even a specialized marketing firm performs a variety of activities associated with the buying and selling of goods and services.

The significance of joint supply in marketing lies in the fact that it increases the range of options open to the integrated firm or consuming unit by placing under the control of that decision-making unit a broader spectrum of production possibilities. It may result in more or less efficiency, depending on the ability of the firm or consuming unit to coordinate its functions or to utilize integration as a means of achieving greater market control.

Specialized Supply

Although there are many places in our economy where we find that marketing and processing functions are combined, or where a fairly broad spectrum of marketing functions are performed by a single enterprise, there is a contrasting characteristic of the marketing system that affects its efficiency and its potential for effective competition. This is the tendency in expanding economies for marketing to be performed by an

---

[5] We are avoiding the phrase "producer-created" because it is doubtful that any demand can in fact be fully "created." Demand is a manifestation of human intent, and we believe that the organism exhibiting an intention to buy has at least some role of its own in arriving at that decision, even though that role may be minimal or, in many cases, highly circumscribed by social and psychological constraints and stimuli.

increasing number of specialized institutions. The larger the market, the greater the probability that specialization will take place owing to the possibility of economies of scale.

As economic maturity is reached, the increase in specialization among marketing institutions may cease, for specialization makes it necessary to have some kind of coordination of the outputs of specialized marketing enterprises. In the United States tendencies toward integration, both horizontal and vertical, have been stronger since World War II than the forces making for greater specialization. Part of this has been based on economies of scale and part on the advantages to the firm of greater market power. Thus Hotpoint ranges add Hotpoint refrigerators, Coldspot refrigerators add Coldspot ranges, and Frigidaire ranges bake the turkey that has been kept cool in a Frigidaire refrigerator.[6]

Specialization of any sort, whether in processing or marketing, increases the number of markets and the number of transactions involved in getting goods moved through the trade channel. Integration, on the other hand, shifts the decision-making process from the realm of market interactions to internal adminstrative control.

Elasticity of Supply

It is not possible to generalize about the supply of marketing services or the competitive structure of marketing in the United States in a few sentences.[7] We can, however, indicate some of the important factors that determine the sensitivity of suppliers of marketing services to changes in the prices of those services and, hence, in their offerings.

One of the important determinants of the elasticity of supply is the degree of specialization in the kinds of resources used. In general, resources utilized in marketing tend to be quite unspecialized. Capital equipment employed is limited in amount and has considerable versatility. Much of the labor is unskilled, and even skilled labor is often versatile across commodity lines, as, for example, in selling. Capital investment in inventories is short-term investment, which does not entail long-term commitments characteristic of fixed capital. In these respects, there are a minimum of barriers to expansion and contraction of industry resources over both the short and the long pull. This is reflected, for example, in the rather wide sales volume ranges within which average cost curves in retailing, and some wholesaling, firms appear to be quite flat. On the other hand, long-run investments in advertising, brand identification, and good will are less flexible and may entail rigidities that are not conducive to rapid investment response. These are most likely to be associated with manufacturers' marketing positions or those of vertically integrated firms.

A second variable affecting the short-run elasticity of supply of marketing services is the ability of existing firms and establishments to add to and subtract from their marketing mix on the basis of short-term changes in price. There appears to be considerable flexibility in this respect. Part of this flexibility in the short run stems from

---

[6] Howard H. Hines, "Effectiveness of 'Entry' by Already Established Firms," *Quarterly Journal of Economics* 71 (February 1957): 132-150.

[7] This is made especially clear in Richard H. Holton, "The Role of Competition and Monopoly in Distribution: The Experience in the United States," in J. P. Miller, ed., *Competition, Cartels and Their Regulation* (Amsterdam: North-Holland, 1962), pp. 263-307.

the large number and variety of institutions at various levels of the trade channel, and this is particularly evident at the retail level. Part of it stems from the flexibility of resources used, to which we have already referred. Part of it also stems from the multiproduct nature of most marketing firms, which permits variation in product lines and service mix without great trauma. In fact short-run sensitivity may be too great, resulting in firms' overshooting short-run increases and decreases in market demand.

The long-run sensitivity of suppliers of marketing services to changes in price depends on their ability to enter and to leave the industry. In this respect, retailing probably shows the greatest flexibility, with lack of specialization of resources and fewer constraints on entry and exit than in many industries. However, even in retailing this flexibility is becoming less as the power of the large firm, the large retail establishment, and the integrated distributor makes it more difficult for the small store to be established and to survive. Large firms and establishments in marketing that have arisen as a result of new and greater capital requirements, and particularly human capital in the form of managerial skill, are the result of forces that can, if used properly, make for greater efficiency. Large firms and establishments that have achieved their share of market through the exercise of market power associated with such things as branding, advertising, and promotion are more suspect from a social point of view. Constraints on competition are necessarily greatest where such power exists.

AGGREGATE MARKETING EXPENDITURES

In the preceding sections we have considered briefly some of the important factors that affect the demand for and supply of marketing services. It is the interaction of these demand and supply forces that determines the "price" of marketing. The value of marketing services reflects the utility of those services to buyers and the costs incurred by sellers in rendering them.[8] If we add up all of these "prices," we then have a "total price" of marketing in the economy, which is a portion of the total price of processing plus marketing. The marketing portion of this total price has been labeled "the total value of marketing," "the total value added by marketing," "the total cost of marketing," or "the total expenditure for marketing." Each of these is reflected in the price placed on marketing services by buyers and sellers of those services. We shall use these terms interchangeably in this discussion. If we interchange the terms *cost of marketing* and *expenditure for marketing,* however, this should not obscure the importance of *both* supply and demand in determining what that "cost" or "expenditure" is. We are describing the total outlay by buyers of goods and services for payments to the productive resources utilized in rendering marketing services, without any implication that such a cost is or is not optimum.

The first problem we shall consider is that of arriving at estimates of the total expenditure for marketing. We shall then review the empirical evidence on aggregate marketing expenditures, particularly the relationship of marketing costs to nonmarketing costs of production. Since a large proportion of marketing costs are for wages, we shall also look at employment ratios in marketing to determine their relative size and trends.

---

[8] We shall reserve for later consideration the question of whether all services rendered by the marketing system are useful to buyers or whether in fact some are useful only to sellers because they aid in achieving their market objectives.

Problems of Estimation

To arrive at an estimate of the overall cost of marketing for any one good is an onerous task; to arrive at such an estimate for all goods is an even more formidable task. If we were to include the cost of marketing services as well as goods, we are confronted with an almost impossible job. The problem of estimation has been dealt with at some length by several individuals who have attempted to make estimates, and we shall merely summarize some of the reasons why estimates are at best crude.

The first problem is clarification of the functions to be evaluated. We have defined marketing as those functions directly associated with effecting the exchange transaction, but some functions are more clearly those of marketing—such as buying and selling—than others—such as product planning and development. The final decision as to what activities to include is arbitrary to some degree and results in a classification based on whether the activity is concerned *primarily* with buying and selling or with physical processes of production. The second problem is to sort out functional costs from data made available on an institutional basis. Where the institution is almost totally engaged in marketing, there is little problem. Where the institution is partly in marketing and partly in processing, the mixture of expenditures makes the allocation difficult. If expenditures for *activities*—for example, advertising—or for *factors* allocated to marketing—for example, salespeople or delivery trucks—can be identified, separation is possible. Where there are fixed costs covering both areas of activity—such as management's salary or the profits in a manufacturing firm—allocations cannot be made on a meaningful basis.

Another problem concerns the comparison of marketing expenditures through time, particularly where the nature of products changes and where the services of marketing are not stable. This is a problem common to the particular type of time series we are interested in here and to the calculation of price indexes. The other problem inherent in marketing expenditure analysis is that of measuring the inputs and/or outputs of marketing. The general solution to this problem has been to find one or more proxies for the output of marketing. The three proxies that have been employed are (1) the cost of factors used in performing marketing functions; (2) the gross margin of specialized marketing institutions, or that portion of gross margin of nonspecialized institutions which can appropriately be imputed to marketing; and (3) the value added by the performance of marketing tasks. The latter technique is the most sophisticated and involves the calculation of expenditures for labor, capital, and rent employed in marketing activities.

Expenditure Estimates

In the tables of this chapter, including those in the Appendix, we have summarized some of the results of empirical studies of expenditures for and employment in marketing in the United States. We include the results of only those studies that represent major milestones in the empirical work in this field. Some of the results of studies of marketing costs in Denmark, Norway, Sweden, and Finland are included in the Appendix for comparison. All studies yield at best rough estimates of expenditures, which should be subjected to far more intensive technical appraisal than we shall attempt in this discussion. Our purpose here will be to summarize some of the principal findings.

Although we shall not detail or evaluate the procedures employed, we hope that other students will continue to pursue the nagging technical questions implicit in estimates of this sort. Only when such questions are resolved can we be assured of valid and reliable measures of the relative importance of marketing in the total economy.

TOTAL EXPENDITURES

In Table 22.1 is a summary of the estimated marketing costs in the United States relative to the total cost of goods and services, or total cost of goods, made in various studies during the period 1929-1958.[9] The studies by Converse and Cox are the most useful, both because they are comprehensive and because they offer the greatest possibility for comparative analysis over the span of two decades. Both used the "value added" approach in arriving at their estimates, but Cox had access to national input-output data that were not available to Converse. If we omit the Twentieth Century Fund study for 1929 by Steward, Dewhurst, and Field, in which Malenbaum found a serious technical error, and examine the data for the other studies, the similarity in findings is remarkable. Barger's estimates, ranging from 37 to 41 percent of the retail value of goods, are low because they are based primarily on retail and wholesale margins, which include some nonmarketing services but exclude a number of marketing services produced in other parts of the marketing system. The other estimates are of a magnitude ranging from about 42 to 51 percent of the value added in the processing and marketing of goods, and the more recent studies based on input-ouput data indicate that 42-45 percent of the value of all goods and/or consumer goods is accounted for by marketing activities.[10]

We can summarize Table 22.1 as follows:

1. Expenditures for marketing activities account for about 42-45 percent of the total value added to goods by industrial activities.
2. This percentage did not increase over the three decades after 1929 and probably decreased.
3. Expenditures for marketing represent a larger percentage of the value added for consumer goods than for industrial goods.

---

[9] Even where services are included in Table 22.1 as a basis for calculating the marketing cost percentage, it is important to recognize that the cost of *marketing services* is not included as a part of the marketing costs that go into the numerator of that fraction. The estimation of the cost of marketing services is an almost impossible task. So many services are produced in a "processing" sense by the same individual who is producing them in a "marketing" sense that it is almost impossible to say what parts of those activities are processing and what parts are marketing. The marketing of .services is not an unimportant part of their production, but we say little about costs for this phase of marketing. Mainly we concentrate on the marketing of goods, where processing and marketing can be more easily identified and measured.

[10] To illustrate the complexity of the estimation problem, we shall comment on Cox's 1958 estimate of marketing costs, which he arrived at by using Converse's methods. His estimate is that marketing costs represented 46 percent of total costs of production for 1958. Converse's method assumes that the values added by wholesaling and retailing are equal to the gross margin of wholesaling and retailing firms. Since retailing and wholesaling margins involve some costs that are not marketing costs, Cox estimates that a correction for this overstatement would reduce the value added by marketing for 1958 by about 4 percentage points. He also points out that the estimates that he made, using Converse's methods, are not comparable for 1954 and 1958, since the 1958 estimate is based on newer data, adjusted data, and a number of refinements in concept. It is Cox's judgment that a revision of 1954 data in terms of 1958 concepts would reduce the 1954 value added by marketing by roughly 2 percentage points. We do not explore in this discussion the details of estimating procedures, since these are highly technical problems that warrant careful and separate analysis. See Reavis Cox, Charles Goodman, and Thomas C. Fichandler, *Distribution in a High-Level Economy* (Englewood Cliffs, N.J.: Prentice-Hall, 1965), pp. 158-161, 307-313.

LOCUS OF EXPENDITURES

Cox's estimate of the breakdown of total marketing expenditures by the subsidiary industries that comprise marketing are shown in Tables 22.2 and 22.3. He estimates that a little more than 70 percent of goods-producing marketing activities are carried on in specialized marketing firms, nearly 25 percent in manufacturing firms, and the balance in other nondistribution industries. Retailing and wholesaling together account for over one-half of marketing costs. Thus the three top producers of marketing services are retailing (about one-third), manufacturing (about one-fourth), and wholesaling (about one-fifth), together producing about three-fourths of the total that is expended for marketing goods in the United States.

In a study of marketing costs in Denmark in 1963, Max Kjær-Hansen has estimated that marketing of goods and services to ultimate consumers accounted for about two-thirds of the total expenditure for marketing in that year, with the other one-third accounted for by industrial market transactions. (See Table 22A.2.) He also attempted to break the total expenditure for marketing down into two components, one representing "distribution" and the other "promotion." Expenditures for distribution are those necessary to get the good to the consumer and to complete the transaction, while those for promotion are incurred to change consumer demand. The former would include expenditures for rent, inventory maintenance, "normal" credit facilities, packing, transportation, administration of orders, and collection of payments. Promotional expenditures would be for salesmen's earnings, advertising, services, merchandising, and other sales promotion methods. To the extent that the data permitted a separation of expenditures into these two groups, he estimates that 70 percent of the marketing costs incurred in Denmark in 1963 were for distribution and 30 percent for promotion. This kind of dicrimination is not easy to make in empirical studies, but it would be useful to have such estimates for their utility in evaluating the aggregate marketing budget.

EXPENDITURES FOR SPECIFIC GOODS

In Table 22.4 we have summarized some of Cox's data on marketing costs for specific manufacturing industries. We have selected most of the goods-manufacturing sectors included in his analysis of input-output relationships of industries whose output is sold directly or through trade channels to households.[11] Our purpose is to show the diversity among industries in the relative importance of marketing activities and also the comparative importance of the five subsidiary marketing industries—retailing, whole-saling, transportation, warehousing and storage, and advertising—in the net output of various manufacturing industries.

Of the 40 industries from which households obtain manufactured goods directly or indirectly, distribution industries accounted for an average of 31 percent of the total value added. Excluded from this would be marketing activities carried on within the manufacturing and other nondistribution industries; the relative importance of this locus of marketing varied among the 40 industries detailed in Table 22.4. This 31 percent is *not* the total proportionate value of marketing in the output of each industry but, rather, the proportionate value of marketing that is provided by the indentifiable marketing

---

[11] See Cox, op. cit., pp. 282-306, for a discussion of the procedures followed in applying the household bill of goods to the inverse input-output matrix and in estimating the portion of value added accounted for by marketing costs of each industry.

Table 22.1 Comparison of Several Estimates of the Relative Cost of Marketing in the United States Based on Different Data, Periods, and Estimating Methods

Author	Reference	Measurement	Date	Percentage
Paul Stewart, J. Frederick Dewhurst, Louise Field	(1)	Commodity distribution costs as percentage of total sales to terminal buyers	1929	59
Wilfred Malenbaum	(2)	Correction of conceptual error in Stewart, Dewhurst, Field calculation to yield commodity distribution costs as percentage of total national commodity provided	1929	51.1
Paul D. Converse	(3)	Value added by marketing as percentage of total value added by marketing and "production"	1929 1939 1948	49.2[a] 50.5 48.1
Harold Barger	(4)	Value added by retailers' and wholesalers' margins plus freight as percentage of retail sales	1869 1929	37.7 41.7
		Value added by margins of retailers and wholesalers as percentage of retail sales	1929 1939 1948	36.6 37.3 37.4
Reavis Cox, Charles Goodman, Thomas C. Fichandler	(5)	Value added by distribution activities in supplying		
		all goods and services	1947	39.7
		all goods, excluding public utilities, services, miscellaneous	1947	41.7
		all consumer goods and services	1947	42.6
		all consumer goods, excluding public utilities, services, miscellanoues	1947	45.3

Value added by marketing as percentage of total value added by marketing and "production" (using Converse's method)

1954	45.3[b]
1958	46.3[b]

[a]Original estimate 52.2; revised estimate 49.2

[b]Cox indicates that the estimates for 1954 were prepared to obtain maximum comparability with Converse's estimates for 1948, and he believes that his estimate for 1954 is as close methodologically to Converse's estimate for 1948 as Converse's estimates for 1929, 1939, and 1948 were to each other. Cox's estimate for 1958, however, was based on newer data and several reinements and adjustments that make the values for that year not strictly comparable to those for 1954. He believes that a revision of 1954 data to be consistent with 1958 concepts would reduce the 1954 value added by marketing by approximately two percentage points.

Source: (1) Paul Stewart, J. Frederick Dewhurst, and Louise Field, *Does Distribution Cost Too Much?* (New York: Twentieth Century, 1939), esp. pp. 58-68, 116-244. (2) Wilfred Malenbaum, "The Cost of Distribution," *Quarterly Journal of Economices* 55 (February 1941): 263-265. (3) Paul D. Converse, Harvey W. Huegy, and Robert V. Mitchell, *The Elements of Marketing*, 5th ed. (Englewood Cliffs, N.J.: Prentice-Hall, 1952), pp. 789-792. See also 2d ed. (1935), pp. 983-985, 3d ed. (2d rev. ed.) (1940), pp. 817-819, and 4th ed. (1946), pp. 693-694. (4) Harold Barger, *Distribution's Place in the American Economy Since 1869*, National Bureau of Economic Research, General Series, no. 58 (Princeton, N.J.: Princeton University Press, 1955), pp. 55-64, 112-151. (5) Reavis Cox, Charles Goodman, and Thomas C. Fichandler, *Distribution in a High-Level Economy* (Englewood Cliffs, N.J.: Prentice-Hall, 1965), pp. 118-161, 282-313.

Table 22.2 Cox's Estimate of the Market Value in Billions of Dollars Added by Distribution and Nondistribution Activities in Supplying Goods to All Final Buyers in the United States, 1947

Industry	Total	Nondistribution Activities	Distribution Activities	Distribution as Percentage
		Billions of Dollars		
Nondistribution industries	106.5	89.2	17.3	16.3
Agriculture, forestry, fisheries	18.9	16.9	2.1	10.9
Mining	6.5	6.0	0.5	8.1
Manufacturing	71.6	57.8	13.8	19.3
Public utilities, services, miscellaneous	9.4	8.5	0.9	10.0
Distribution industries	41.4	–	41.4	100.0
Transportation	9.7	–	9.7	100.0
Warehousing and storage	0.2	–	0.2	100.0
Wholesale trade	11.0	–	11.0	100.0
Retail trade	18.6	–	18.6	100.0
Advertising	1.9	–	1.9	100.0
Total	147.9	89.2	58.7	39.7
Total excluding public utilities, services, miscellaneous	138.4	80.7	57.8	41.7

Source: Reavis Cox, *Distribution in a High-Level Economy*, © 1965, p. 148. Reprinted by permission of Prentice-Hall, Inc., Englewood Cliffs, New Jersey.

Table 22.3 Cox's Estimate of the Value Added Through Distribution Activities of Distribution and Nondistribution Industries in Supplying Goods to All Final Buyers in the United States, 1947

Industry	Market Value Added by Distribution Activities (Billions of Dollars)	Percentage of Total
Nondistribution industries[a]	16.4	28.4
Distribution industries	41.4	71.6
Transportation	9.7	16.7
Warehousing and storage	0.2	0.3
Wholesale trade	11.0	19.0
Retail trade	18.6	32.3
Advertising	1.9	3.3
Total[a]	57.8	100.0

[a]Excluding public utilities, services, miscellaneous.

Source: Reavis Cox, *Distribution in a High-Level Economy*, © 1965, p. 148. Reprinted by permission of Prentice-Hall, Inc., Englewood Cliffs, New Jersey.

industry to the output of each manufacturing industry. We know from Table 22.3 that nondistribution industries contributed 28 percent of the total value added by distribution activities. Our interest in Table 22.4 is in the 72 percent contributed by distribution industries per se, that is, by those business firms whose principal activity was retailing, wholesaling, transportaion, advertising, or warehousing and storage.

In Table 22.5 we have arrayed the 40 industries according to the percentage of their total value added that was contributed by the five distribution industries. The most striking fact apparent in these data is the wide range in the contribution of the total distribution industry to the output of various goods-manufacturing industries. At one extreme we have meat, meatpacking, bakeries, printing and publishing, soap and related products, sugar, and textiles, all with a distribution industry contribution of less than 25 percent of each industry's total value added. At the other extreme are optical and medical goods, alcoholic beverages, drugs and medicines, coal, musical instruments, and jewelry and silverware, with more than 40 percent from distribution industries.

Table 22.6 shows those manufacturing industries to which each of the five distribution industries made a contribution somewhat greater than the average for all goods-manufacturing industries. If we characterize the manufactured goods that have relatively high costs in these five marketing industries, we can get some insight into the factors that influence marketing costs for specific products.

Retailing costs tend to be high where the level of selling skill required is extremely high, where there is considerable time involved in a single transaction, where centralized retail location is important and site costs high, where dispersed retail outlets are important for consumer convenience, where the size of stock necessary for adequate consumer selection among varieties is high and stockturn consequently low, where installation services are a necessary or important part of the retailer's services, where retailer risk is high because of physical deterioration or social obsolescence, where special physical facilities are necessary for storage or selling of merchandise, and/or where arrangements for financing consumer purchases are important. Only one or two of these conditions need be significant in a given commodity market to cause a relatively large retailing-cost ratio.

Wholesaling is important where there is specialized production and unspecialized consumption, specialized consumption and unspecialized production, unspecialized consumption and unspecialized production, need for storage due to seasonal demand and/or seasonal supply, presence of reserve stocks that make service to smaller buyers or small suppliers economical, and/or storage and mixing of lots that occur together.

Note that for those industries in which transportation is particularly important there is often considerable product bulk, and particularly large unit bulk in relation to low unit value. Distance of the source of supply from buyers is also important, as are conditions in which production or consumption or both are widely dispersed. Where special facilities are required in the course of transportation—to protect fragile or perishable items, or to handle liquid or flammable goods—and where rapid transit is important owing to perishability, costs are likely to be high.

High advertising costs are associated with the extent of product differentiation, the size and market power of sellers, the importance of information to buyers of products, and the extent to which the product is "advertisable"—that is, it has hidden qualities, or personal and emotional appeals are effective in influencing demand.

Warehousing and storage are most likely to be important where items are bulky, where the demand or supply is seasonal, where specialized physical facilities are necessary for effective storage, and where the number of producers and users is quite large and collecting facilities between them are economical.

Table 22.4 Total Market Value Added by Distribution and Nondistribution Industries and Percentage of Total Value Added by Each of Five Distribution Industries to the Output of Selected Goods-Producing Industries from Which Household Purchases Were Made in the United States in 1947[a]

Industries from Which Household Purchases Were Made[b] (1)	Total Market Value Added by Distribution and Nondistribution Industries (2)	Percentage of Market Value Added by					
		Total Distribution Industries (3)	Wholesale Trade (4)	Retail Trade (5)	Transportation (6)	Warehousing and Storage (7)	Advertising[c] (8)
Meat, animals, products	$ 979	8.3	1.7	2.1	4.2	0.1	0.2
Meat packing, wholesale poultry	9,967	22.2	4.1	11.5	5.5	0.3	0.8
Poultry, eggs	3,023	26.4	7.7	11.0	6.4	0.2	1.1
Farm dariy products	4,074	33.0	14.0	13.8	4.1	0.1	1.0
Processed dairy products	2,645	26.3	6.6	13.8	4.6	0.2	1.1
Vegetables, fruits	4,432	35.5	11.0	14.1	9.3	0.2	0.9
Canning, preserving, freezing	3,025	30.7	8.7	13.9	5.8	0.4	1.9
Grain mill products	1,384	30.4	5.6	14.5	8.4	0.3	1.6
Bakery products	3,612	20.8	3.5	10.1	5.7	0.2	1.3
Sugar	636	24.5	3.2	8.9	11.5	0.3	0.6
Alcoholic beverages	2,380	44.0	14.6	21.3	5.1	0.1	2.9
Tobacco manufactures	2,315	34.9	9.8	18.5	3.2	0.1	3.3
Spinning, weaving, dyeing	1,325	24.6	7.0	13.5	2.9	0.2	1.0
Apparel	13,528	31.2	4.9	22.5	2.2	0.1	1.5
Household furnishings, nonapparel	1,322	37.9	8.7	24.7	2.9	0.1	1.5
Footwear	2,418	28.8	3.5	20.8	2.7	0.2	1.6

Lumber, wood products	296	32.8	5.0	16.8	10.2	0.1	0.7
Wood furniture	1,873	37.4	3.7	26.9	5.0	0.1	1.7
Paper, allied products	582	38.0	15.2	15.9	5.6	0.1	1.2
Printing, publishing	1,945	22.1	3.8	13.9	3.0	0.1	1.3
Coal	919	41.3	1.1	17.1	22.6	0.1	0.4
Crude petroleum, natural gas	56	31.4	0.5	20.1	9.8	0.1	0.9
Petroleum products	4,094	38.3	10.9	16.4	9.9	0.1	1.0
Drugs, medicines	994	43.5	10.0	24.7	3.9	0.1	4.8
Soap, related products	1,078	22.7	4.6	6.4	5.8	0.2	0.7
Paints, allied products	43	29.2	7.4	15.3	4.9	0.2	1.4
Tools, general hardware	114	35.7	8.6	22.8	2.9	0.1	1.3
Heating equipment	660	38.2	6.8	25.8	3.8	0.1	1.7
Radio, related products	1,091	37.6	10.7	21.9	3.0	0.1	1.9
Motor vehicles	4,573	30.6	5.4	18.5	5.2	0.1	1.4
Motorcycles, bicycles	165	31.6	8.1	18.1	4.3	(d)	1.1
Tires, inner tubes	694	35.3	8.2	21.2	4.0	0.2	1.7
Optical, ophthalmic, photo equipment	406	47.1	12.6	30.2	2.2	(d)	2.1
Medical and dental instruments, supplies							
Watches, clocks	259	46.9	15.6	24.4	2.9	0.1	3.9
Jewelry, silverware	547	39.8	7.7	27.4	2.3	(d)	2.4
Musical instruments, parts	1,347	40.6	7.2	28.7	2.3	(d)	2.4
Toys, sporting goods	160	41.0	6.6	29.5	2.3	(d)	2.6
	718	34.3	10.8	18.6	3.0	(d)	1.9

Table 22-4 (Cont.)

Industries from Which Household Purchases Were Made[b] (1)	Total Market Value Added by Distribution and Nondistribution Industries (2)	Percentage of Market Value Added by					
		Total Distribution Industries (3)	Wholesale Trade (4)	Retail Trade (5)	Transportation (6)	Warehousing and Storage (7)	Advertising[c] (8)
Office supplies	184	31.8	4.4	23.2	2.6	(d)	1.6
Plastic products	120	33.6	8.4	20.9	2.9	0.1	1.3
Total goods industries[e]	$95,582	31.1	7.1	17.3	4.9	0.2	1.6

[a]The value added by wholesale and retail trade, transportation and storage industries, and advertising that became a part of the final output of the industries listed in the left column from which consumers purchased goods are indicated in columns 3-8 in this table. Not included in this table, however, is the value added to household purchases by these distributive industries, public utilities, and service industries where their output was sold directly to consumers without association with the goods-producing industries listed in this table as sources of consumer purchases.

[b]Goods industries include agriculture, forestry, fisheries, mining, and manufacturing. Not all goods-producing industries are included in the detail. Those excluded have, however, been included in the total for all goods industries. The industries listed in the left column sold their output to consumers directly or through trade channels, generally without additional physical transformation.

[c]Advertising includes the contribution of the printing and publishing industry and other industries that devote a substantial part of their output to advertising services.

[d]Less than 0.05.

[e]Total includes the value added by some goods-producing industries that are not detailed above.

Source: Adapted from Reavis Cox, *Distribution in a High-Level Economy*, © 1965, pp. 284-289. Reprinted by permission of Prentice Hall, Inc., Englewood Cliffs, New Jersey. Based on U.S. Bureau of Labor Statistics, *1947 Interindustry Relations Study*.

Table 22.5   Importance of Marketing Industries to Manufacturing Industries

Forty Goods-Manufacturing Industries in the United States Arrayed According to the Percentage of the Industry's Total Market Value Added by Distribution Industries, 1947

Industry	Percentage of Value Added by Distribution Industries
Optical, ophthalmic, photo equipment	
Medical, dental instruments	
Alcoholic beverages	45%
Drugs, medicines	
Coal	
Musical instruments	
Jewelry, silverware	
Watches, clocks	40%
Petroleum products	
Paper	
Heating equipment	
Household furnishings	
Radio	
Wood furniture	
Tools, general hardware	
Vegetables, fruits	
Tires, inner tubes	
Tobacco manufactures	35%
Toys, sporting goods	
Plastic products	
Farm dairy products	
Lumber, wood products	
Office supplies	
Motorcycles, bicycles	
Crude petroleum, natural gas	
Apparel	
ALL GOODS INDUSTRIES	
Canning, preserving, freezing	
Motor vehicles	
Grain mill products	
Paints	30%
Footwear	
Poultry, eggs	
Processed dairy products	
Spinning, weaving, dyeing	25%
Sugar	
Soap, related products	
Meatpacking, wholesale poultry	
Printing, publishing	
Bakery products	
—	20%
—	
Meat, animals, products	10%

Source: Reavis Cox, *Distribution in a High-Level Economy,* © 1965, pp. 284-289. Reprinted by permission of Prentice-Hall, Inc., Englewood Cliffs, New Jersey.

Table 22.6 Manufacturing Industries in Which Specific Marketing Institutions Were Unusually Important

Goods-Manufacturing Industries in the United States to Which Retailing, Wholesaling, Transportation, Advertising, and Warehousing and Storage Industries Contributed a Higher-than-Average Percentage of Total Value Added, 1947

Percentage of Total Value Added by

Retailing

%	Products
30.0%	Optical, ophthalmic, photo equipment Musical instruments
27.5%	Jewelry, silverware Watches, clocks Wood furniture
25.0%	Heating equipment Drugs, medicines Household furnishings Medical, dental instruments
22.5%	Office supplies Tools, general hardware Apparel Radio
20.0%	Alcoholic beverages Tires, inner tubes Footwear Plastic products Crude petroleum, natural gas

Wholesaling

%	Products
15.0%	Medical, dental instruments Paper, allied products Alcoholic beverages Farm dairy products

Transportation

%	Products
22.5%	Coal
	—
12.5%	Sugar Lumber, wood products
10.0%	Petroleum products Crude petroleum, natural gas Vegetables, fruits Grain mill products
7.5%	Poultry, eggs Soap, related products Canning, preserving, freezing Bakery products Paper, allied products Meatpacking, wholesale poultry Motor vehicles Alcoholic beverages
5.0%	Wood products

Advertising

%	Products
5.0%	Soap, related products
4.0%	Drugs, medicines Medical, dental instruments
3.0%	Tobacco manufactures

Optical, ophthalmic, photo equipment ——— 12.5%
Vegetables, fruits
Petroleum products
Toys, sporting goods
Radio
Drugs, medicines ——— 10.0%

Alcoholic beverages
Musical instruments
Watches, clocks
Jewelry, silverware
Optical, ophthalmic, photo equipment ——— 2.0%

Warehousing and Storage

Canning, preserving, freezing ——— 0.4%
Meatpacking, wholesale poultry
Grain mill products
Sugar ——— 0.3%

Source: Reavis Cox, *Distribution in a High-Level Economy*, © 1965, pp. 284-289. Reprinted by permission of Prentice-Hall, Inc., Englewood Cliffs, New Jersey

Table 22.7 Barger's Estimate of the Value Added by Distribution as a Percentage of the Retail Value of Commodities in the United States, 1869-1929

Year	Percentage of Retail Value Added by			
	Wholesalers	Retailers	Wholesalers + Retailers	Wholesalers + Retailers + Freight Charges[a]
1869	9.5	23.2	32.7	37.7
1879	9.6	24.1	33.7	39.1
1889	9.6	25.1	34.7	38.8
1899	9.2	26.2	35.4	39.8
1909	8.9	27.6	36.5	40.1
1919	8.5	28.0	36.5	39.6
1929	8.1	28.9	37.0	41.7
1929[b]	8.0	28.6	36.6	—
1939[b]	7.6	29.7	37.3	—
1948[b]	7.7	29.7	37.4	—

[a]Between processor and initial distributor.

[b]Data for these years are based on *Census of Business* reports that were not available for earlier years. The second estimate for 1929 is based on *Census of Business* data, while the first one is based on the old method of estimation employed for years prior to 1929.

Source: Reprinted by permission of the National Bureau of Economic Research from *Distribution's Place in the American Economy Since 1869* by Harold Barger (1955), pp. 57, 60. See pp. 80-90, 112-115, for a discussion of methods of estimation.

Changes in Expenditures Over Time

The total amount spent for marketing in a given period of time depends on the price of marketing services per transaction and the number of transactions. If this aggregate increases or decreases over time relative to the amounts spent for processing or nonmarketing services, this could be due to a change in demand for marketing services, a change in the supply of marketing services, a change in the quantity demanded or supplied because of a change in price, or some combination of these. The demand for marketing is essentially a function of buyers' purchasing power and their preferences for the services of marketing in relation to other goods and services. The supply of marketing services is related to the price of factors used in the production process and to the productivity of those factors. Productivity can be affected by changes in the efficiency of one or more factors, or by changes in the combination of factors employed.

Omitting shifts in the price level over time and focusing only on real changes in expenditures for marketing, we can find still another variable underlying changes in demand for and supply of marketing services in the quality of marketing services. If the variety of services in the marketing mix is changed, or if the quality of any one service is changed—that is, its utility is altered—this is likely to be related to new patterns of demand and supply, since preferences will be modified and factor components or efficiency changed. Processes of economic change over the long run seldom involve changes in *either* demand or supply; changes in *both* tend to occur as sellers and buyers respond to changing needs of buyers and sellers and to new technical and economic opportunities.

The data that we examined from studies of marketing expenditures for various years between 1929 and 1958 from Table 22.1 indicate that in the United States marketing expenditures (or the contribution of marketing to the market value of goods produced) did not change very much and may in fact have declined slightly during the last decade of this 30 year period. The similarity of findings from these various studies is all the more remarkable when we consider the crudeness of the data and the imperfection of comparisons from one study to the other.

DIVERGENT MOVEMENTS

If we go back to earlier years, what changes are most clearly apparent? Unfortunately we do not have data for years prior to 1929 that embrace all that was included in the studies reported in Table 22.1. Barger's figures, however, are based on time series with some degree of comparability. In Table 22.7 we show his estimates of the value added by distribution as a percentage of the retail value of commodities in the United States for 10 year intervals spanning the period 1869-1929. The combined percentage for wholesaling and retailing increased somewhat over this 60 year period, and all of this was accounted for by retailing margins. The addition of freight charges to retail and wholesale margins results in a much smaller relative increase, and more irregularity in the direction of change. From Table 22.8, where we show figures for the contribution of retail trade, wholesale trade, and transportation to the national income for the period 1929-1970, it is clear that these three together showed a downward secular trend in their proportionate contribution to national income. This was also true for retailing and wholesaling (without transportation) after the late 1930s. Nor was the downward drift in marketing, as measured by these three relatively crude values, related to the rise in service industries until after World War II. Both services and marketing reached a low percentage during World War II. After the war, marketing declined from about 25 percent to about 19 percent of national income, while services rose from about 8 percent to about 13 percent by 1970.

For retailing and wholesaling the highest percentages occurred in the years 1929-1931, 1936-1940, and 1946-1949. The percentage of national income accounted for by these two marketing industries was unusually low during the early depression years of the 1930s and the years of World War II. This was not true for transportation, however, whose percentage dropped more in the late 1930s and then rose slightly during World War II. The lag during the 1930s was probably due to the fact that transportation rates are regulated and not as flexible as retail and wholesale margins. The increase in transportation during World War II was associated with the movement of war materials, troops, and the civilian population rather than marketing per se.

Some interesting and significant trends can be observed following World War II. The wholesaling ratio declined from the end of the war until 1954; then it rose again until 1959; then it declined until 1965-1966; thereafter it rose again. The retailing ratio, on the other hand, declined fairly steadily, from 13.0 percent following World War II to about 9.5 percent in 1968. Transportation tended to decline in relative importance throughout the postwar period all the way up to 1970. The three industries together declined from a high of nearly 25 percent in the late 1940s to a low of about 19 percent in the second half of the 1960s.

PATTERNS OF CHANGE

Putting all these observations together, what can we say about the trend in marketing costs in the United States during the 100 years following 1869? Barger's estimates

Table 22.8 Percentage of National Income Produced by Retail Trade, Wholesale Trade, Transportation, and Service Industries in the United States, 1929-1970[a]

			Percentage of National Income from			
Year	Retail Trade	Wholesale Trade	Retail + Wholesale Trade	Transportation	Retail + Wholesale Trade + Transportation	Services
1929	10.66	4.91	15.57	7.61	23.18	10.19
1930	10.97	5.42	16.39	7.42	23.81	11.10
1931	11.21	5.40	16.61	7.31	23.92	12.12
1932	10.12	5.14	15.27	7.52	22.78	13.23
1933	9.46	4.49	13.95	7.54	21.49	12.75
1934	11.64	5.14	16.78	6.90	23.69	11.68
1935	11.25	5.20	16.44	6.46	22.90	10.81
1936	11.51	5.06	16.56	6.56	23.12	10.53
1937	11.38	5.39	16.77	6.29	23.07	10.20
1938	12.25	5.71	17.95	6.02	23.97	10.72
1939	12.03	5.34	17.37	6.40	23.77	10.41
1940	12.28	5.55	17.82	6.21	24.04	9.89
1941	11.64	5.06	16.70	6.05	22.75	8.51
1942	10.36	4.54	14.90	6.28	21.18	7.49
1943	9.96	4.06	14.02	6.34	20.36	6.92
1944	9.92	4.19	14.11	6.16	20.27	7.21
1945	10.89	4.54	15.43	5.80	21.24	7.78
1946	13.28	5.74	19.02	5.68	24.71	9.16
1947	13.00	5.87	18.85	5.82	24.69	9.09
1948	12.04	5.74	17.78	5.71	23.49	8.93
1949	12.34	5.60	17.95	5.54	23.49	9.41
1950	11.46	5.52	16.98	5.54	22.53	9.03
1951	10.69	5.53	16.22	5.38	21.60	8.47
1952	10.67	5.35	16.02	5.31	21.33	8.60
1953	10.33	5.18	15.51	5.20	20.70	8.80
1954	10.70	5.04	15.92	4.82	20.74	9.16
1955	10.40	5.39	15.79	4.81	20.60	9.40
1956	10.11	5.51	15.62	4.84	20.46	9.66
1957	10.09	5.55	15.64	4.75	20.39	9.96
1958	10.19	5.64	15.84	4.50	20.34	10.44
1959	10.15	5.68	15.83	4.48	20.31	10.44
1960	9.96	5.58	15.54	4.38	19.92	10.73
1961	9.83	5.67	15.50	4.27	19.77	11.04
1962	9.79	5.57	15.36	4.16	19.53	11.07
1963	9.68	5.55	15.23	4.16	19.39	11.23
1964	9.78	5.53	15.31	4.10	19.41	11.40
1965	9.56	5.38	14.94	4.10	19.04	11.35
1966	9.35	5.38	14.73	4.00	18.73	11.45
1967	9.53	5.39	14.92	3.86	18.78	12.02
1968	9.52	5.40	14.92	3.78	18.70	12.05
1969	9.56	5.47	15.03	3.78	18.81	12.39

Table 22.8 (Continued)

Year	Retail Trade	Wholesale Trade	Retail + Wholesale Trade	Transportation	Retail + Wholesale Trade + Transportation	Services
			Percentage of National Income from			
1970	9.69	5.65	15.34	3.70	19.04	12.96

[a]The industrial classification for 1929-1947 was based on the 1942 Standard Industrial Classification; for the years following 1947 it was based on the 1957 Standard Industrial Classification.

Source: U.S., Department of Commerce, Office of Business Economics, *The National Income and Product Accounts of the United States,* 1929-1965 (Washington, D.C.: GPO, 1966), pp. 18-21; "U.S. National Income and Product Accounts, 1963-66," *Survey of Current Business* 47 (July 1967): 9-44; "U.S. National Income and Product Accounts, 1967-70," *Survey of Current Business* 51 (July 1971): 9-46.

indicate that during the first half of this 100-year span—up to 1929—retailers increased their share of the retail value of commodities by about 25 percent, while wholesalers' share declined about 15 percent, resulting in a net increase for the two combined of about 13 percent. If we include freight charges also, the increase in the proportion of total value added by distribution was about 11 percent. The biggest chunk of this increasing proportion came in the period 1869-1909. Thereafter, marketing's share continued to increase at a decreasing rate.

Shifting to the data we have computed from national income accounts, we find that after 1929 marketing's share of national income as measured by these three industries—retailing, wholesaling, and transportation—was fairly stable for about 20 years—until the end of World War II. From then until the middle 1960s, the share of these three industries in national income declined about 25 percent.

In summary, between 1869 and 1909 there was a noticeable increase in the relative importance of retailing in the production of goods in the economy, a smaller proportionate increase in the importance of transportation, and a decline in the importance of wholesaling. These trends continued from 1909 to 1929 but at slower rates, except for a continued marked decline in the importance of wholesaling. After 1929, these three industries maintained a fairly stable position in the total economy for 20 years. After 1950, they declined in relative importance, with transportation showing the largest relative decline and retailing the largest absolute decline. From the middle of the 1960s to 1970, the percentage of national income accounted for by each of these industries increased, but the period is too short and the change too little for this to be called a trend.

OMISSIONS

What is left out of this picture? According to Cox's data in Table 22.3, retailing, wholesaling, and transportation accounted for a little more than two-thirds of the cost of marketing in 1947. We are therefore omitting from consideration all marketing activities performed by specialized marketing firms other than retailing and wholesaling, of which advertising would be the most important, and also the marketing activities of nonmarketing firms. The latter accounted for more than one-fourth of the total cost of marketing in 1947.

Table 22.9 Some Estimates of the Importance of Distribution Activities of Nondistribution Industries

Value Added by Distribution Activities of Nondistribution Industries as a Percentage of the Total Value Added by Such Industries and of the Total Value of All Distribution Activities of All Industries

		Value Added by Distribution Activities as Percentage of	
Year	Source[a]	Total Value Added by Non-distribution Industries (Distribution + Nondistribution Activities)	Total Value Added by Distribution Activities of All Industries (Distribution + Nondistribution Industries)
1929	Stewart, Dewhurst	(b)	26.2
1929	Converse	26.1[c]	32.4[c]
1939	Converse	20.6	25.5
1947	Cox	16.3	28.4
1948	Converse	19.1	25.5
1954	Cox	21.7	33.4
1958	Cox	23.3	35.2

[a]Concepts, data, and methods are not comparable for all of these estimates. Comparability is probably highest for estimates for 1939, 1948, and 1954. In his estimates for 1954 and 1958, Cox attempted to follow Converse's procedure. His 1958 estimate, however, involves refinements not possible in the 1954 estimate.

[b]Comparable data for total value added not available.

[c]Based on unrevised data.

Source: Calculated from Paul W. Stewart and J. Frederic Dewhurst, *Does Distribution Cost Too Much?* (New York: Twentieth Century, 1939), p. 118; Paul D. Converse and Harvey W. Huegy, *The Elements of Marketing,* 2d rev. ed. Englewood Cliffs, N.J.: Prentice-Hall, 1940), p. 817, 5th ed. (Englewood Cliffs, N.J.: Prentice-Hall, 1952), p. 789; Paul D. Converse, "The Total Cost of Marketing," *Journal of Marketing* 10 (April 1946): 389; Reavis Cox, *Distribution in a High-Level Economy* (Englewood Cliffs, N.J.: Prentice-Hall, 1965), pp. 148, 159.

Is this a serious omission from Table 22.8 that would change the declining marketing percentage shown there to a stable or rising percentage? The problems of marketing value estimation are so complex that it is not possible to answer this question categorically. We have, however, tried to pull together some of the marketing valuation studies for the period 1929-1958 to see if there is an apparent trend in the relative importance of marketing activities of nonmarketing firms. The figures that we present in Table 22.9 are drawn from the studies by Stewart and Dewhurst, Converse, and Cox. Although these are not strictly comparable, there seems to be a suggestion in the data that nondistribution industries, of which manufacturing would be the most important, were performing a larger share of the marketing functions in the 1950s than they did in earlier years. With the exception of Converse's 1929 estimate, what we have shows that the share of the value added by marketing accounted for by nonmarketing firms increased from around one-fourth of the total during the 1930s and 1940s to about one-third of the total during the 1950s. While the evidence of a significant shift is skimpy, the hint is there. It is probably important to keep this in mind in looking at trends in the other more specialized parts of the marketing industry. If we combine all of the evidence that we have about marketing in the 1950s and 1960s compared with the 1930s, it seems

Table 22.10 Barger's Estimate of the Number of Persons Engaged in Distribution in the United States as a Percentage of the Total Labor Force in Goods and Service Production and of the Labor Force in Goods Production in the United States, 1870-1950

Year	Number of Persons Engaged in Distribution as Percentage of	
	Total Labor Force in Goods and Services Production	Total Labor Force in Goods Production
1870	6.1	8.1
1880	6.7	8.7
1890	7.7	10.6
1900	8.6	12.0
1910	9.3	13.9
1920	9.9	14.7
1930	12.9	21.3
1940	14.4	24.4
1950	16.4	28.9

Source: Reprinted by permission of the National Bureau of Economic Research from *Distribution's Place in the American Economy Since 1869* by Harold Barger (1955), p. 8. Based on data from Daniel Carson, "Changes in the Industrial Composition of Manpower Since the Civil War," *Studies in Income and Wealth*, XI (New York: National Bureau of Economic Research, 1949), p. 47, and U.S., Bureau of the Census, *Census of Population*, 1950, vol. II, pt. 1, Table 130. See Barger, pp. 4-5 and 101-111, for a description of the estimation procedures.

reasonable to conclude that marketing's share of the national output in the 1950s and 1960s was certainly no greater than in the 1930s and probably somewhat less.

Employment in Marketing

Before we leave the matter of secular trends in the importance of marketing, we should take a brief look at employment in this segment of the economy. Barger's data for the period 1870-1950 are shown in Table 22.10. These figures are from the population census and relate the number of individuals in occupations that are identifiable as marketing to total labor force and to the total labor force in goods production.

The figures in Table 22.11 cover the period 1919-1970 and include only those in retail and wholesale trade as a percentage of the total employment in nonagricultural industries. According to the latter table, 21 percent of those engaged in nonagricultural occupations in 1970 were in retail and wholesale trade. If we used those in goods-related occupations as our base (nonagricultural plus agricultural minus services minus government minus finance-insurance-real estate), the wholesale plus retail trade ratio would increase to 32 percent of the total employment in these occupations.

Thus between 1870 and 1930 employment in marketing doubled in relation to total employment, and more than doubled in relation to those engaged in goods production. It continued to increase during the 1930s and 1940s, but at a much slower rate. During the 1950s and 1960s the percentage in retailing and wholesaling remained remarkably stable, with a slight decrease in the percentage in wholesaling and a slight increase in retailing. The period of greatest expansion in employment in marketing for the years for which we have data occurred during the 50 years "surrounding" the turn of the century. By the

Table 22.11 Percentage of Total Labor Force in the United States Employed in Wholesale Trade, Retail Trade, and Transportation and Public Utilities, 1929-1970

	Percentage of Labor Force in				
Year	Wholesale Trade[a] (1)	Retail Trade[a] (2)	Wholesale + Retail Trade (3) = (1) + (2)	Transportation + Public Utilities (4)	Transportation + Public Utilities + Wholesale Trade + Retail Trade (5) = (3)+ (4)
1919			16.66	13.70	30.36
1920			16.33	14.62	30.95
1921			18.82	14.19	33.01
1922			18.98	13.57	32.55
1923			18.63	13.67	32.30
1924			19.28	13.57	32.85
1925			19.38	13.29	32.67
1926			19.40	13.22	32.62
1927			19.71	12.99	32.70
1928			19.58	12.76	32.34
1929			19.54	12.50	32.04
1930			19.70	12.52	32.22
1931			20.20	12.21	32.41
1932			19.82	11.92	31.74
1933			20.05	11.27	31.32
1934			17.63	9.18	26.81
1935			20.07	10.30	30.37
1936			19.97	10.22	30.19
1937			20.19	10.10	30.29
1938			21.15	9.80	30.95
1939	5.50	15.48	20.98	9.59	30.57
1940	5.42	15.43	20.85	9.38	30.23
1941	5.12	14.60	19.72	8.96	28.68
1942	4.54	13.20	17.74	8.62	26.36
1943	4.10	12.34	16.44	8.59	25.03
1944	4.21	12.64	16.85	9.14	25.99
1945	4.61	13.50	18.11	9.67	27.78
1946	5.26	14.84	20.10	9.74	29.84
1947	5.38	15.03	20.41	9.49	29.90
1948	5.54	15.11	20.65	9.33	29.98
1949	5.68	15.48	21.16	9.14	30.30
1950	5.57	15.19	20.76	8.92	29.68
1951	5.45	14.91	20.36	8.83	29.19
1952	5.50	14.99	20.49	8.70	29.19
1953	5.43	14.97	20.40	8.54	28.94
1954	5.59	15.29	20.88	8.33	29.21
1955	5.52	15.27	20.79	8.17	28.96
1956	5.50	15.22	20.72	8.10	28.82
1957	5.47	15.11	20.58	8.02	28.60

Table 22.11 (Continued)

Year	Wholesale Trade[a] (1)	Retail Trade[a] (2)	Wholesale + Retail Trade (3) = (1) + (2)	Transportation + Public Utilities (4)	Transportation + Public Utilities + Wholesale Trade + Retail Trade (5) = (3) + (4)
			Percentage of Labor Force in		
1958	5.54	15.38	20.92	7.74	28.66
1959	5.52	15.35	20.87	7.52	28.39
1960	5.54	15.47	21.01	7.38	28.39
1961	5.54	15.44	20.98	7.22	28.20
1962	5.50	15.31	20.81	7.02	27.83
1963	5.47	15.30	20.77	6.88	27.65
1964	5.47	15.38	20.85	6.77	27.62
1965	5.45	15.46	20.91	6.64	27.55
1966	5.37	15.34	20.71	6.49	27.20
1967	5.35	15.31	20.66	6.47	27.13
1968	5.32	15.42	20.74	6.35	27.09
1969	5.32	15.52	20.84	6.30	27.14
1970	5.45	15.71	21.16	6.36	27.52

[a]No detail before 1939.

Source: U.S., Bureau of Labor Statistics, *Employment and Earnings Statistics for the United States*, 1909-1970, Bulletin no. 1312-8 (Washington, D.C.: GPO, 1970), p. xvi, and *Monthly Labor Review* 94 (June 1971): 112.

middle of the 20th century, employment in retail and wholesale trade had stabilized at about 21 percent of the total labor force.[12]

FACTORS UNDERLYING TRENDS IN MARKETING EMPLOYMENT AND COSTS

One of the interesting facts that emerges from our data for the period since 1869 is that margins of retailers, wholesalers, and transportation agencies have not increased markedly in the course of this period. Even though this increase may be slightly understated in recent years because of the omission of nondistributors' marketing activities, it is important to consider the significance of this relatively small rise in light of the fact that (1) employment in marketing increased greatly compared to that in the total economy up to World War II, and (2) it is commonly believed that marketing expenditures rise sharply relative to other expenditures in a period of rapid industrial growth such as we experienced during the last quarter of the 19th century and the first quarter of the 20th

[12]Inclusion of employment in transportation and public utilities yields a higher ratio—about 30 percent in the middle of the century—with a decline to slightly more than 27 percent in the next 20 years.

century. We need to address ourselves to these two matters and examine the reasons why marketing output does or does not increase with changes in other segments of the economy.

If we examine data on the real output of goods in the United States over time, it is clear that the marketing system has increased the amount of goods that flow through its pipelines very greatly during the span of years that we have been studying but has been able to do so without a commensurate increase in its proportionate share of total national product. One of the reasons is that capital equipment has become increasingly important in nonmarketing production but has not made a comparable contribution to marketing productivity. This would therefore allow the nonmarketing portion of output to grow out of proportion to any growth experienced in the marketing portion.

Much of what we observe, however, is due to the nature of labor in marketing. Wages in marketing, and particularly in retailing, where marketing employment is greatest, have traditionally been low. This was partly due to the exclusion of retailing from minimum wage legislation for many years. But even with the extension of minimum wage legislation to retailing, output per worker is low and retailing is often the refuge of marginal workers. Part-time employment is important, and women comprise a larger-than-average proportion of the total number of employees. Unionization has been minimal until recent years. The low productivity and the limited opportunities for increasing productivity have forced employers to pay minimum wages, and marginal labor, unable to find employment elsewhere, has sought employment here because of the frequent absence of proficiency standards and because of the amenities associated with part-time employment possibilities and minimal sex discrimination. Another historical factor accounting for the increase in the proportionate number of workers employed in marketing has been explored by Barger at great length.[13] This is the decreased length of the workweek in marketing enterprises. We began the century we are describing (1869-1970) with a workweek in retailing far above that in other occupations. As the average workweek declined toward that prevalent in all industries, the relative number of marketing employees increased.

Combining measures of volume of goods handled, number of transactions, amount of capital investment, and number of employees, David Schwartzman has concluded that the quantity of service in retail trade per dollar of sales decreased over the period 1929-1963. This made it possible for marketing margins to remain fairly stable relative to total output in the face of rising productivity in nonmarketing segments of the economy.[14] Sales per manhour increased, but this was possible, he concludes, because of the decline in services. The average transaction size increased and the quantity of service per transaction decreased, resulting in lower service per dollar of sales. Rising wage levels in the economy as a whole contributed to the rising average transaction size. But rising wages also brought about an increase in retail wages and in the price of retailing services. As the price of services increased, consumers demanded fewer services.

There are many functions of marketing that the consumer is doing for himself today that he did not formerly do. He wheels his own cart in the supermarket and collects his

---

[13] Harold Barger, *Distribution's Place in the American Economy Since 1869*, National Bureau of Economic Research, General Series, no. 58 (Princeton, N.J.: Princeton University Press, 1955), pp. 10-14.

[14] David Schwartzman, *The Decline of Service in Retail Trade*, Washington State University, College of Economics and Business, Bureau of Economic and Business Research, Study no. 48 (Pullman: Washington State University, 1971). pp. 167-190.

own market basket of goods; he buys in large quantities per shopping trip and per week, transporting the goods himself and storing them for subsequent use. Retail stores have benefited from economies of scale made possible by carrying a wide variety of goods from which the consumer makes his selection, which he then carts to his residence. The amenities for customers per transaction and per dollar of sales are probably less than they were in the 1920s. Just as consumers have absorbed more marketing functions, so manufacturers have done likewise. There is more prepackaging, more dependence on manufacturer promotion, more use of manufacturer warranties, and even use of preticketing, manufacturers' inventory control systems, and other types of retailer aids.

As retail wages have risen in the face of competition from employment opportunities in nonmarketing lines, retail firms have been forced to seek ways of increasing output per salesperson. Capital equipment offers only limited possibilities, but it is utilized where possible. Self-service gives the retailer the "free" labor of the customer. Sales promotion through product diversification, leader pricing, improved store facilities and atmosphere, and advertising may be far more attractive as profit-increasing alternatives than increased efficiency through changes in a resource structure that is capable of responding only slightly to more rigid merchandise and employee control. Computers have offered important possibilities for better merchandise and financial control, and routinization of operations has sometimes facilitated greater employee control.

We cannot say that the era we have been talking about in American marketing, 1869-1970, is really one where marketing costs have risen drastically. They rose somewhat, but adjustments were made in the system that enabled it to absorb these increases without a great change in the overall cost ratio relative to the total output of all goods industries. It is likely that the increase in proportionate marketing expenditures is greatest in that era when an economy moves from what is predominately one of self-sufficiency of economic units to one of greatly increased concentration in, and specialization of, production. At this point, trade has to take place in order for specialized outputs to be exchanged. Specialization, growing out of differences in , resources or in demands, or arising from economies of scale made possible by concentrated production, in combination with an increased volume and diversity of output, generates a need for greatly expanded market activities.

It is reasonable to conjecture that the period of greatest increase in specialized production in the United States took place around the middle of the 19th century, when manufacturing was becoming increasingly important. While the growth of specialization continued during the period following the Civil War, economies of scale that occurred within marketing itself probably offset some of the increased marketing activity associated with further growth of specialized manufacturing units and urbanization of population; that is, marketing was becoming both a more important *and* a more efficient segment of the economy. If we examine the data on retail and wholesale margins in less highly developed countries, there is evidence that the most rapid growth of marketing coincides with the take-off phase of industrial expansion, as the economy moves from what is made up predominately of farmers and craftsmen to one made up of factory production by employed workers.

The relative importance of marketing in the total economy differs at various stages of economic development. Changing economic forces have an impact on the functioning of the market and, hence, on the structure of marketing institutions and the behavior of market participants. The market transmits these forces, and the rate of change in the economy is in part a function of the efficiency with which the marketing system serves as the economy's communication network. Also, through its creative role the marketing system is a generator of forces that affect the level of economic activity. In general, we find that the higher the level of economic development, the greater the proportion of total productive activity accounted for by marketing. This is apparent, for example, in a comparison of marketing costs in the United States with those in the Scandinavian countries. (See Tables 22A.2 and 22A.3) The complex interactions among marketing and nonmarketing productive efforts are so important that we shall devote the next chapter to consideration of the normative aspects of marketing costs, involving both reasons for the level of costs and questions of marketing efficiency.

APPENDIX A

Table 22A.1 Converse's Estimate of the Value Added by the Production and Marketing of Goods in the United States, 1948[a]

	Sales Receipts[b] (Add 000,000)	Values Added (Add 000,000)		
Industry		Total	By Production	By Marketing
Mining & quarrying	$ 7,900	$ 7,353	$ 6,760	$ 593
Agriculture	28,800	23,818	21,228	2,590
Manufacturing	210,900	83,500	64,519	18,981
Construction	9,900	4,900	4,208	742
Wholesaling	190,500	22,860	—	22,860
Retailing	130,500	35,235	—	35,235
Transportation and storage				
Railroad freight	7,976	5,105	—	5,105
Trucking & warehousing	2,497	2,097	—	2,097
Railway express[c]	443	266	—	266
Pipe lines	348	278	—	278
Water transportation	2,086	1,085	—	1,085
Totals		$186,547	$96,715	$89,832
Percentages		100.0	51.9	48.1

[a]See source for method of estimation.

[b]Sales receipts exceed value added, since the former involves double counting. Sales receipts for manufacturing, for example, cover not only value added by manufacturing but also cost of raw materials and fuel. Total value added by all industries listed in this table is less than national income, since services, amusements, hotels, financial organizations, and government are not included here.

[c]1947 data.

Source: Paul D. Converse, Harvey W. Huegy, and Robert V. Mitchell, *The Elements of Marketing,* 5th ed. (Englewood Cliffs, N.J.: Prentice-Hall, 1952), pp. 789-792.

Table 22A.2   Kjær-Hansen's Estimate of Marketing Costs in Denmark, 1963

Classification	Sales (Millions of D. Kr.)	Gross Margin or Marketing Cost as a Percentage of Sales	Marketing Costs (Millions of D. Kr.)
Industry			
Retail trade	28.6	21	6.0
Wholesale trade	38.0	12	4.6
Manufacturing	39.0	15	5.8
Other industries and trades	13.8		1.8
Retailing	7.1	15	1.1
Wholesaling	6.7	10	0.7
Total	119.4	15	18.2
Sector			
Consumer goods and services	36.0	33	12.0
Other goods and services	83.4[a]	7[a]	6.2
Total	119.4	15	18.2
Marketing Function			
Distribution[b]			12.6
Promotion[b]			5.6
Total	119.4	15	18.2

[a] Kjær-Hansen's percentage cost of marketing for other goods and services is given as 11 rather than the 7 percent we have indicated here. He does not state explicitly the sales base that he used to derive this; he may have excluded some items from the D. kr. 83.4 we have assigned, by imputation, as the sales of "other goods and services." Since his summary article does not clarify the basis for his 11 percent estimate, we shall not attempt to reconcile his calculation and the one we have arrived at by imputation.

[b] Distribution costs include "the expenditure at the minimum level required in order to place a good on the market, as well as the cost of transport and administration necessitated by the volume of sales at the time in question." (See source, p. 38.) Included are costs of rent, inventory maintenance, normal credit facilities, packing, transport, administration of orders received, and collection of payment for goods sold. Promotion costs are incurred to manipulate customer demand. These include costs of salesmen's earnings, advertising, services, merchandising, and other sales promotion methods.

Source: Max Kjær-Hansen, "An Analysis of Marketing Costs in a National Economy," in Max Kjær-Hansen, ed., *Cost Problems in Modern Marketing* Skrifter fra Instituttet for Salgsorganisation og Reklame, Handelshøjskolen i København, Skriftrække F, nr. 35 (Copenhagen: Einar Harcks Forlag. 1965), pp. 24-43.

Table 22A.3 Kjær-Hansen's Estimate of the Cost of Sales for Distribution and Selling of Goods in Denmark, Norway, Sweden, and Finland, 1953

Item[a]	Denmark		Norway		Sweden		Finland	
	Billions of D. Kr.	Percentage	Billions of N. Kr.	Percentage	Billions of S. Kr.	Percentage	Billions of F. Mk.	Percentage
All Goods								
Gross profit, retail trade	2.1	38	1.45	36	3.8	40	60	46
Gross profit, wholesale trade	1.5	26	1.30	32	2.8	29	40	31
Cost of sales, producers	2.0	36	1.25	32	3.0	31	30	23
Total cost of sales, all goods	5.6	100	4.00	100	9.6	100	130	100
Consumer Goods								
Gross profit, retail trade	2.1	55						
Gross profit, wholesale trade	0.9	24						
Cost of sales, producers	0.8	21						
Total cost of sales, consumer goods	3.8	100						
Producer Goods								
Gross profit, wholesalers	0.6	33						
Cost of sales, producers	1.2	67						
Total cost of sales, producer goods	1.8	100						
Selling costs, all goods	1.4		0.8		2.2		23	
Gross national product	28.6		23.1		40.0		805	
Total cost of sales, all goods, as percentage of GNP		19.5		17.5		24		16
Selling costs, all goods, as percentage of total cost of sales, all goods		25		20		22.5		18
of GNP		4.8		3.5		5.5		2.9
Total retail sales	10.7							
Total cost of sales, consumer goods, as percentage of total retail sales		36						

Total sales of producer goods	ca.	18.0
Total cost of sales, producer goods, as percentage of total sales of producer goods	ca.	10

[a]Total cost of sales is the estimated total cost of marketing (distribution plus selling costs). Distribution costs are for the technical distribution of goods and include transportation costs, packing expenses, interest on investment in inventory, rent, office salaries, and office expenses. Selling costs are for promotion and include agents' commissions, advertising, merchandising, and service costs. The allocation is admittedly subjective in many respects.

Source: Max Kjær-Hansen, *Salgs- og Reklameomkostningerne i Norden*, Nordisk Salgs- og Reklameforbunds Skriftserie nr. 1 (Copenhagen: Einar Harcks Forlag, 1956), pp. 20-33. (There is an English summary, pp. 109-44, with these data on pp. 115-117.)

23

Marketing Efficiency

For a salesman, there is no rock bottom to the life. He don't put a bolt
to a nut, he don't tell you the law or give you medicine. He's a man
way out there in the blue, riding on a smile and a shoeshine and when
they start not smiling back—that's an earthquake. And then you get
yourself a couple of spots on your hat, and you're finished. Nobody
dast blame this man. A salesman is got to dream, boy. It comes with the
territory.

—Arthur Miller

In this volume, we have considered facets of one of the most important of our social
systems and have tried to show how an ordered system of exchange relationships is one of
the means by which human and physical potentials are brought more nearly into unity
with individual and social needs. We have focused primarily on the individuals, groups,
and institutions whose behavior governs marketing processes. Our approach has been
positive to the extent that we have described and explained the organizational structure
within which marketing takes place, and the decision-making process through which
transactions are generated, showing how various policy decisions and practices should be
arrived at in light of the alternatives and objectives of the decision-making unit. We have
also employed a normative approach when we have considered the impact of specific
decisions on other market participants, particularly consumers, with the view that some
policies and practices have more desirable personal and social effects than others.

We shall now extend our horizon still further, attempting to put these various parts into
perspective in order to arrive at some judgment as to how effectively the marketing
system as a whole fulfills its role in the economy and society of which it is a part. We
cannot reach firm conclusions on so broad an issue. But if we can begin to sketch the
framework within which the analysis should proceed, perhaps we can ask some of the
important questions that will eventually lead to answers to the more fundamental
question of system effectiveness, continuing to seek, with imperfect perception. the clues
that may lie in imperfect data.

The approach we shall use is to consider in this chapter the nature of marketing
efficiency, the problems involved in its measurement, and some of the conditions
conducive to greater or less efficiency in specific markets and in the marketing system.

In the chapter that follows we shall examine some of the broader aspects of the market
system of economic control, its virtues and its weaknesses, and the conditions under
which alternative means of coordination and control may be superior. We shall conclude
with some observations on the relationship of the marketing system to the total social
system. The latter embraces the full range of individual and soical values, resources,
organization, and experiences.

THE CONCEPT OF MARKETING EFFICIENCY

Efficiency is a relative concept. It is the relationship between inputs and outputs, and is
most easily conceived of in terms of the productivity ratio, outputs/inputs. The higher the
ratio, the greater the efficiency level. Theoretically, one may conceive of an absolute level

of efficiency that represents the maximum possible, or of a condition of optimal efficiency, taking into account all possible alternatives. But practically, most individual and social choices are between two or more states that differ in comparative efficiency as reflected in their productivity ratios. We seldom know what all possible alternatives are.

Technical Efficiency

Efficiency in an engineering sense is technical efficiency and is measured in terms of physical units of output per physical unit of input or, in the case of noncomparability of units of input or output, the aggregate value of output per unit of input, or per unit value of input. The use of market values of inputs and outputs introduces an economic method of aggregation Transactions per manhour would represent measurement in physical units; dollar sales per manhour or transactions per dollar cost of labor would represent an economic measure of technical efficiency.

Managerial Efficiency

Another concept of efficiency, suggested by Margaret Hall and Christopher Winsten, is managerial efficiency, in which environmental constraints are taken into account.[1] This would be the output, measured in physcial or value units, relative to inputs, with environmental conditions held constant. For example, if the managerial efficiency of two retail stores is to be compared, such stores should be comparable in terms of location, type of merchandise and services sold, and method of operation. This is clearly a more restricted concept of efficiency in the nature of a short-run approach in which management is assumed not to have control over certain variables.

Social Efficiency

A third concept of efficiency is social efficiency. The economic system, of which marketing is a subsystem, is the social organization through which society's scarce resources are employed for human welfare. Those whom it serves are both individual and social entities. The definition of social optimality involves complications not inherent in the measurement of technical or managerial efficiency. These complications arise from the fact that output is valuable to society because of its value to the individuals of society, and the aggregation of utilities or value to individuals raises serious questions concerning interpersonal comparisons. Differences in individual perferences and inequality in the distribution of output among members of society make it necessary for certain assumptions to be made in order for the social value of total output to be determined.

The Approach of This Chapter

Appraisal of the efficiency of marketing institutions, markets, and marketing systems depends on meaningful definitions and measurements of outputs and inputs. We shall

---

[1] Margaret Hall and Christopher Winsten, "The Ambiguous Notion of Efficiency," *Economic Journal*, 69 (March 1959): 71-86.

consider these conceptual and measurement problems in the assessment of technical and managerial efficiency in marketing, an approach that is particularly appropriate for evaluating specific marketing institutions.[2] We shall then consider the special complications that arise in evaluating marketing from a social point of view.

TECHNICAL AND MANAGERIAL EFFICIENCY IN MARKETING

Marketing Outputs

Marketing institutions are engaged primarily in economic, social, and psychological transformations that are essential to ownership transformation. They are also engaged in physical transformation to the extent that time and space relationships are altered at their behest. Ownership transformation is accompained by the (1) collecting; (2) sorting, mixing, holding lots: and (3) dispersing of goods in a physical sense. Hence, output in marketing is a cluster of services that make goods and personal services physically and legally accessible to potential buyers.

Specification of these services is not, however, completely satisfactory as a basis for empirical work in marketing productivity analysis. There may be two sources of confusion. What is a "service" in one instance is not necessarily a "service" in another

---

[2] There is a great deal of literature dealing with productivity in marketing. Most of the works that we note here are concerned primarily with technical efficiency.

Three studies by Victor Fuchs for the National Bureau of Economic Research have analyzed productivity in service industries: *Productivity Trends in the Goods and Service Sectors, 1929-1961–A Preliminary Survey*, National Bureau of Economic Research, Occasional Paper 89 (New York: National Bureau of Economic Research, 1964), *Production and Productivity in the Service Industries*, Studies in Income and Wealth, vol. XXXIV (New York: Columbia University Press, 1969), and with Jean Alexander Wilburn, *Productivity Differences within the Service Sector*, National Bureau of Economic Research, Occasional Paper 102 (New York: National Bureau of Economic Research, 1966). Some of the general problems of productivity analysis are discussed in John W. Kendrick, ed., *Output, Input, and Productivity Measurement*, National Bureau of Economic Research, Studies in Income and Wealth, vol. XXV (Princeton, N.J.: Princeton University Press, 1961).

Two discussions by Reavis Cox survey the status of productivity analysis on the macro level: "Productivity in Marketing–Prospects for Improvements in the Sixties," in *Proceedings of the Business and Economic Statistics Section, American Statistical Association*, (Washington, D.C.: American Statistical Association, 1960), pp. 319-322, and "New Possibilities in the Measurement of Productivity in Marketing," in *Productivity in Marketing*, J. L. Heskett, ed. Papers of the Theodore N. Beckman Symposium on Marketing Productivity, April 22, 1965 (Columbus, Ohio: Ohio State University, College of Commerce and Administration, 1966), pp. 39-57. See also Theodore N. Beckman, "Measuring Productivity in Marketing," in *Proceedings of the Business and Economic Statistics Section, American Statistical Association*, (Washington, D.C.: American Statistical Association, 1960), pp. 308-318; Neil T. Houston, "Methods of Efficiency Analysis in Marketing," Ph.D. Dissertation, Harvard University, 1948; David Schwartzman, *The Decline of Service in Retail Trade*, Washington State University, College of Economics and Business, Bureau of Economic and Business Research, Study no. 48 (Pullman: Washington State University, 1971).

Three British studies have made substantive contributions to the methodology of productivity analysis in marketing: K. D. George, *Productivity in Distribution*, University of Cambridge, Department of Applied Economics Occasional Papers no. 8 (Cambridge: Cambridge University Press, 1966); K. D. George and P. V. Hills, *Productivity and Capital Expenditure in Retailing*, University of Cambridge, Department of Applied Economics, Occasional Papers no. 16 (Cambridge: Cambridge University Press, 1968): Margaret Hall, John Knapp, and Christopher Winsten, *Distribution in Great Britain and North America: A Study in Structure and Productivity* (Oxford University Press, 1961).

instance. Merchandise mixing or transportation that is useful to buyers can correctly be called a "service." Merchandise mixing that is not desired by buyers or confuses buyers as well as unnecessary transportation are not "services." If we sort out from among the things that marketing firms do those that result in increased utility to buyers and consider these alone as marketing services, we avoid the problem of including nonuseful activities. But this is difficult to do when using empirical data. Waste and disutility are not easy to identify and isolate.

The other problem in defining marketing output is that some of that output is beneficial to the seller rather than to the buyer. While advertising is not always valueless to buyers, it is likely to be desired far more by sellers than by buyers. The same can be said about certain aspects of product quality and differentiation. If policies and practices with respect to these areas of promotion are beneficial to sellers, perhaps because they are substitutes for alternative policies and practices, they should be regarded as inputs rather than outputs. But if *some* buyers benefit from them, their utility to buyers is greater than zero, and that portion which is beneficial should be counted as part of the output of marketing. But what part is utility producing for consumers and what part is not?

Measurement of Output

In one sense the problems we have just posed are those of measurement rather than of concept. Let us turn therefore to ways in which output has in fact been measured in the study of productivity in marketing establishments and firms.

VOLUME OF SALES

One approach has been to measure the volume of goods sold. This has been used in cross-sectional studies where the output of similar establishments and firms has been assumed to be indicated by the units of goods sold or by the total volume of sales in dollars. In each case services rendered are assumed to be a stable proportion of sales. Physical units sold can be used for comparison purposes only when the physical units are comparable. Since most marketing institutions sell a variety of goods, and since varieties are seldom identical physically from one institution to another, aggregation for comparison purposes has to be made most often in terms of dollar volume. This, however, injects the additional problem of price differences between goods and the probability that services rendered are not only not a constant proportion of number of physical units but also are not a constant proportion of the number of physical units sold weighted by the unit price. If there are economies of scale in the rendering of certain services, this would cause their supply price to alter as the institution's volume of sales changes, and alteration of the supply price would be expected to alter the market price used in weighting physical volume. In comparisons over time, changes in product and service mix are likely to force the use of dollar volume of sales, which should, of course, be adjusted for changes in price levels. In this case, the assumption that there is a constant percentage relationship between the volume of real sales and the quantity of marketing services is suspect owing to changes in the ratio of product value to service value over time.[3]

---

[3] See, for example, Schwartzman, op. cit., in which he has attempted to measure the decline in the amount of service rendered in retail trade over the period 1929-1963.

It appears therefore that volume of goods sold, measured in either physical units or dollar volume, is at best a very crude proxy for services rendered by marketing institutions either at one point in time or at different points in time. Its use in comparative studies of marketing productivity has been based on convenience more than logic.

GROSS MARGIN

In an attempt to isolate from the total value of retail sales that portion imputable to marketing institutions, some students of marketing productivity have used the gross margin as a measure of the marketing institution's contribution to the sales value of its transactions. Certain problems inhere in the use of this measure. One is the omission from such a calculation of the marketing output generated by industries whose functions are primarily nonmarketing but that in the course of production perform some of the marketing functions and thereby contribute to the marketing output. Other problems arise because of the imperfection of the markets in which firms in distributive trades operate. Two firms that are the same in their real output of services could differ in gross margins if one enjoys monopoly profits and the other does not. Still another aspect of market imperfection is the fact that firms in distributive trades often operate with conventional margins. Where margins are slow to respond to changing supply and demand conditions, they will tend to over- or understate the "value" of services rendered.

A more complicated factor arising out of market imperfections is related to the quality of productive factors employed in different institutions of the same type, and particularly in institutions of quite different types. Low-quality labor or low-quality management in one marketing firm or in marketing in general might cause margins to be high even though productivity is low if imperfect markets prevent wage rates from reflecting perfectly the differentials in productivity. Imperfection in knowledge and in the mobility of productive resources may lead to a differential between costs incurred and productivity of the factors purchased. In these cases, margins would not be an accurate indication of productivity.

There is yet another problem to be considered. Substitution is possible between costs of goods sold and operating costs. For example, one wholesale firm may buy in large quantities and employ the services of highly skilled buyers. Such a firm will show a low cost of goods sold relative to sales, a high gross margin, and a high operating cost compared with another firm that does the same volume of business but buys in small quantities and spends far less in operating expenses for its buying functions. There is no assurance that the firm with the large gross margin is more efficient than the one with the small margin. It is possible that they are equally efficient, with one spending more for merchandise and the other more for operating costs.

Still another problem with the use of gross margin is the fact that some of the operating costs incurred by marketing firms are to purchase goods and services produced by other firms. Such goods are logically the output of the firms that produce them, and their value should not be included as a part of the output of the marketing firm. Saleschecks and paper bags, for example, are the products of the paper and printing industries, not of the marketing firm that uses them. They are variable capital inputs for the marketing firm but are not a part of the firm's output.

A corollary problem arises in the interpretation of marketing margins where substitution of functions takes place over time between vertically related firms. If, for example, storage is performed by the manufacturer, this will tend to decrease the margin of the wholesaler. If later the wholesaler begins to do more storing, his margins will rise

Table 23.1 Hypothetical Employment, Output, and Marketing Margins in Two Areas

Item	Area A	Area B
Employed in manufacturing	10,000	7,500
Employed in marketing	5,000	7,500
Units produced	10,000	15,000
Units per marketing employee	2	2
Marketing margin[a]	33%	50%

[a]Assuming only wage costs, with wages of a marketing employee equal to wages of a manufacturing employee.

proportionately, but the *total* marketing output for the goods involved is not changed. This difficulty could be resolved if margins were reported on a functional basis rather than an institutional basis, but this is not the way margin data are assembled in practice. Institutional margins appear to be deficient in reflecting precisely what the output of the marketing effort is.

If we carry this problem still further, we can see the complication that arises when we are comparing productivity in marketing in two discrete markets.[4] Suppose that in one section of the country high productivity is possible in manufacturing owing to extensive use of capital and effective management, while marketing productivity depends largely on the use of labor. In another section of the country, manufacturing is less productive, but marketing productivity is essentially the same as in the other section. Assume the figures of Table 23.1, in which we eliminate capital and management and consider only output per worker. Each area has the same total labor force, but the two areas differ in the distribution of the labor force between manufacturing and marketing and in the portion of the total cost of production that goes for marketing (the marketing margin). Yet the output per marketing employee is the same in the two areas. This example, which we have already alluded to in our discussion of differences between marketing costs as a percentage of total costs in more or less highly developed economies, forces us to be very cautious about using marketing margins as a measure of productivity in marketing when comparing two institutions or two markets at different levels of economic development and market maturity.

The only situations in which margins should be compared in productivity analysis are those between two establishments, two firms, two areas, or two points of time in which *the same marketing functions* are being performed and the same inputs result in comparable productivity potentials. Even then differences in degree of market imperfection may cause the value of margins to differ in their relationship to real output. If market structure and inputs can be assumed to be identical, margin comparison can be meaningful.

VALUE ADDED

A measure that has been adapted for marketing from its use in the analysis of manufacturing is value added. This is the gross margin adjusted to reflect that portion of

---

[4] This point is taken from Hall, Knapp, and Winsten, op. cit., p. 42.

the market value of the marketed product which can be imputed to the marketing firm. From the sales revenue of the firm would be deducted the cost to the firm of the goods sold and the value of capital and operating supplies. The important difference between the value-added method and the gross margin method of estimating marketing output is that in the value-added method the value of goods and services purchased by marketing firms from firms in nonmarketing industries is excluded.

The marketing output of firms whose principal function is nonmarketing is not easily arrived at by either the value added or gross margin methods of output calculation. The reason is that either method tends to be institutional in its approach to the problem of measuring output. In the gross margin approach, it is assumed that the establishment's or firm's margin and output are equal. In the value added approach, gross margin is further adjusted to eliminate goods produced by other industries. This can rarely be done on a functional basis; it is usually calculated on an institutional basis. Therefore the marketing fuctions performed by firms whose principal activity is nonmarketing are not easily calculated. Yet such activities should be included in the tally of marketing output.

Another problem inherent in value added analysis is the same as that involved in the use of gross margins to reflect the value of marketing output. Efficiency in the buying of resources whose value is imputed to other industries may result in higher operating costs and, hence, in a higher value added than would be true in a firm that puts more of its total sales revenue into resources bought from other industries and less into its own operations. If these are trade-offs, value added data derived from operating statements can be misleading.

NUMBER OF TRANSACTIONS

Another measure of marketing output employed by some students is the number of transactions. The reasoning underlying this choice of proxy is that the transaction is the fulcrum of marketing activities, and the volume of transactions is a reflection of the value of marketing output. The problem, of course, is that the utility of all transactions is not equal. The more units involved in a given transaction, the more likely it is that utility is greater than for a transaction with fewer units. Substitution of units in each transaction for the number of transactions would not be an improvement, however, unless units were of equal amounts or value. What is needed is a measure of the utility of the transaction, and this comes close to the value added concept of output.[5]

CONCLUSIONS ON MEASUREMENT OF OUTPUT

Each of the measurements of output that we have considered bears some meaningful relationship to the utility of marketing services, but none is a completely satisfactory indicator of the utility created by marketing. Each is an imperfect proxy. Part of the

---

[5] Wroe Alderson introduced the concept of the *transvection* to marketing to include the complete sequence of exchanges (transactions) *and* transformations that occur as resources move from their natural state to a finished good that is useful to the consumer. This is, of course, the totality of production, which can be broken down into a series of steps, some of which involve sorting and some of which are physical production. He shows that these alternate in the production process. But transactions, which link two market participants, are not synonymous with "sorts," since sorting can be internalized within the firm. See his *Dynamic Marketing Behavior* (Homewood, Ill.: Irwin, 1965), chap. 3, "Transactions and Transvections," pp. 75-97.

imperfection arises from the fact that the utility of marketing is not consistently related to these objective market indexes. Most of the indexes are measures of the results of interaction of both supply and demand factors and do not isolate demand variables alone. Marketing activities are valueless in isolation from the goods and services marketed. Hence, marketing output has to be provided in combination with the output of processing. Opportunities for substituting marketing activity for processing activity without necessarily affecting the net utility of the final product give rise to the question of whether the output of one or the other of these two production segements has in fact been shifted.

The practical solution that seems best in light of the dilemmas posed is (1) to measure aggregate outputs of a marketing institution in terms of the real units of goods sold to buyers and (2) to compare outputs between markets or marketing institutions only when the services associated with each unit of goods sold to buyers appear to be nearly identical. The degree to which they are identical can be measured by such things as merchandise type or types (width), merchandise depth, market information, nonprice terms of sale ("fringe" benefits or costs of the transaction), the place and time of availability of merchandise stocks, and the conditions of negotiation (haggling versus a single price and set of sales terms, etc.). This is the basis on which Hall, Winsten, and John Knapp compared outputs in domestic marketing in their intracountry and international study of marketing productivity.[6]

Marketing Inputs

LABOR

The productive factor of greatest importance in marketing is labor. Number of employees and number of manhours have both been used extensively as measures of productive inputs for purposes of efficiency analysis. Sales per employee and per manhour are among the most frequently used measures. Wages paid can also be used as a means of aggregating labor input. This, however, divorces the productivity measurement from the real units of input and injects into the analysis problems inherent in using the price of labor, which is a product of *both* the demand for and the supply of labor in the labor markets within which marketing employees are obtained.

One problem that arises from the use of labor as a measure of marketing input is that numbers of employees and manhours fail to take into account quality of labor. Where the latter is deemed pertinent, age, sex, and educational level can be employed as indicators of comparative labor quality.

Part-time employment is common in many marketing occupations, particularly retailing, and makes number of manhours more meaningful than number of employees. Conversion of the employment data into full-time equivalents is possible but does not result in a perfect correction, since part-time and full-time employees may differ qualitatively. Variations in the length of workweek have made time series comparisons of output per employee less useful than output per manhour. Finally, the use of enterpreneurial labor and labor of entrepreneurial families in small-scale enterprises in retailing and wholesaling have made it desirable to include this variable where it was

---

[6] Hall, Knapp, and Winsten, op. cit., p. 45.

important and estimates of its quantity could be obtained. Enterpreneurial and family labor are particularly important in marketing in less highly developed economies.

The one labor input that is seldom taken into account in marketing studies is the input of consumer buyers. Labor employed in a purchasing department of a firm usually *is* counted, but labor of consumer buyers usually is *not* counted. Number of shopping hours is perhaps the most clear-cut measure to employ, but this is not easily calculated.

CAPITAL

Capital in marketing consists of fixed plant, which is generally measured in square feet or cubic feet of space; semifixed capital such as operating equipment for storing, handling, or moving merchandise stocks and for maintenance of general office operations; and variable capital such as operating supplies and inventories of merchandise for resale. Advertising and promotion expenditures could be regarded as either semifixed or fixed capital in the sense that they build good will, resulting in revenue in periods subsequent to that in which their cost is incurred.

MANAGEMENT

The input of management into the marketing firm is not easy to estimate. In his study of retailing productivity in Great Britain, K. D. George imputed a component that he called "technical and organizational knowledge" as a part of the retailing inputs.[7] This was a residual that was estimated by subtracting from the total change in *output* that portion due to labor (measured in wages in constant pounds) and that due to capital (measured in value of total assets = fixed capital + capitalized value of rental property + inventories), with the residual imputed to "technical and organizational knowledge." This is essentially a measure of managerial competence.

Another measure of managerial input could be profits. But this, as with George's residual imputed to "technical and organizational knowledge," raises the same question as when using gross margin or sales as a measure of output. If profits contain a monopoly return, they are not a good measure of input in real terms. On the other hand, if the environment within which the marketing firm functions is sufficiently close to pure and perfect competition to warrant the assumption that profits are a reflection of managerial competence, they may be used as a variable to reflect managerial input. Because they are a price for managerial talent, however, they are a result of both supply and demand forces and measure both input and output.

Some Empirical Findings

When we examine empirical data on outputs and inputs of marketing firms and establishments, using the best measures for these that we can contrive, what do our findings show concerning differences between firms of different types or between the same firms over a period of time? Barger's study of the period 1869-1949 indicates that output per manhour in retail and wholesale trade—the volume of finished goods weighted by distributive margins and divided by manhours employed—rose 1.0 percent per year,

---

[7] George, op. cit., pp. 28-34.

while that in agriculture rose 1.9 percent, in mining 2.6 percent, and in manufacturing 2.3 percent.[8]

Studies of similar firms or establishments at one point in time, such as the detailed analysis by Hall, Knapp, and Winsten of food and clothing stores in Great Britain, Canada, and the United States; by George of 35 firms in Great Britain in both 1961 and 1966; and by David Schwartzman of productivity in retail trade in various types of retail stores for the census years between 1929 and 1963, have been more helpful than aggregative studies in revealing the sources of changes in productivity. Both George and Schwartzman were able to estimate the effects of certain factors related to changing productivity ratios.

In his analysis of changes in sales in constant dollars of 35 retail firms, George divided the change in total real output into three segments—that related to the change in labor, that related to the change in the amount of capital, and that related to technical and organizational change. Real sales rose 5.37 percent per annum between 1961 and 1966. (This figure ranged from 0.14 percent for cooperatives to 7.64 percent for grocers.) The labor input (wage bill = number of workers times unit wage in constant pounds) increased 2.25 percent per annum during this period, the capital used (total assets = fixed capital + capitalized value of rental property + inventories) increased 1.86 percent per annum, and the increased output due to applied technical and organizational knowledge (total increase in output minus 2.25 percent due to labor and 1.86 percent due to capital) was imputed at 1.26 percent per annum.[9]

Analysis by type of retail operation (cooperative, department store, grocery, etc.) revealed a positive relationship between the change in the amount of capital employed and the change in output related to technical and organizational knowledge. Changes in capital investment were further analyzed in terms of conversions to self-service, refittings, and extensions of old shops and, of course, new shops. It was found that output was higher for conversions than for extensions and refittings and that new shops showed slightly higher rates of productivity than older shops of the same type.

Using *Census of Business* data for the United States for the years 1929-1963 and measuring growth in output in sales per manhour in constant dollars, Schwartzman related changes in output to changes in transaction size and service per transaction, with the results indicated in Table 23.2. His analysis shows clearly the positive effect that increase in the size of transactions has on sales per manhour and the importance of decreased service per transaction on productivity in retailing as a whole, and particularly in apparel, general merchandise, furniture, and automotive stores. He found that the increasing size of transactions was related to rising incomes, and the decreasing service per transaction to the net interaction of rising incomes (which would induce consumers to buy more service) and the rising price of services (which would iduce them to buy less service). The decline in services was due to the rising price of retail services, which was not fully offset by the increasing demand associated with rising incomes.[10]

---

[8] Harold Barger, *Distribution's Place in the American Economy Since 1869*, National Bureau of Economic Research, General Series, no. 58 (Princeton, N.J.: Princeton University Press, 1955), pp. 37-52. Beckman analyzed census data for the years 1935, 1939, 1948, 1954, and 1958 and concluded that productivity per manhour in retailing increased 91 percent between 1935 and 1958, compared with 34 percent in wholesaling, and 63 percent in all manufacturing. Theodore N. Beckman, op. cit.

[9] George, op. cit., pp. 21-51.

[10] Schwartzman, op. cit., pp. 153-190.

Table 23.2 Contribution of Output per Manhour, Transaction Size, and Service per Transaction to the Average Annual Rate of Growth of Sales per Manhour in Retail Trade in the United States, 1929-1963[a]

Kind of Business	Output per Manhour (1)	Transaction Size (2)	Service per Transaction (3)	Sum of Components (1 + 2 + 3) (4)	Rate of Growth of Sales per Manhour (5)	Residual (5 – 4) (6)
Retail Trade	– .2	2.0	.4[b]	2.2	1.8	– .4
General merchandise stores	– .2	.2	2.2	2.2	1.9	– .2
Food stores	1.3	4.0	– 1.6	3.7	2.6	– 1.1
Automotive dealers	– .2	1.1	1.2	2.1	2.0	– .2
Gasoline stations	–	2.4	–	2.4	3.1	.7
Apparel stores	– 1.2	– .5	2.4	.7	.9	.3
Furniture stores	– .7	1.6	1.9	2.7	2.3	– .4
Drug stores	– .1	2.4	– .2	2.1	2.0	– .1

[a]See original for an explanation of methods of measurement or estimation.

[b]Includes the effect of shifts in sales between store types on service per dollar of sales and sales per manhour.

Source: David Schwartzman, *The Decline of Service in Retail Trade,* Washington State University, College of Economics and Business, Bureau of Economic and Business Research, Study no. 48 (Pullman: Washington State University, 1971), p. 14.

Factors Related to Technical Efficiency in Marketing

We have cited only a few of the empirical studies of marketing productivity. Studies of retail productivity are more numerous than those of wholesaling. In general, it has been found that over time output per manhour in marketing has increased less than in nonmarketing industries,[11] and probably less in retailing than in wholesaling. We shall explore possible reasons for these trends in terms of productivity potentials inherent in the capital, labor, and managerial resources employed in marketing firms.

CAPITAL

One of the most significant factors accounting for increased productivity in manufacturing is the use of capital and the substitution of capital for labor. Utilization of capital in marketing is constrained because of the nature of the output, which remains essentially a personal service. To the extent that customers demand information that can be dispensed only on a personal basis and to the extent that negotiation remains personal, varying from transaction to transaction, there are limitations to the substitution of capital for labor. If advertising is regarded as a form of capital investment and can serve as a substitute for personal selling, it may be substituted for labor. However, advertising that buyers do not want does not contribute to productivity but serves only to increase inputs without commensurate increase in buyer utilities. The substitution of mass displays for

---

[11] An exception to this generalization is in Beckman's study of productivity in retailing, wholesaling, and manufacturing. See footnote 8.

personal selling in self-service retailing is another case in which capital has been substituted for purchased labor, but this does not take into account the unpaid customer labor that is utilized.

Capital investment in fixed plant and equipment has increased in both retailing and wholesaling, but its use is not commensurate with that in manufacturing. Most of the physical capital employed in marketing is for the storage, display, and movement of goods. Some has been employed in accounting (cash registers, bookkeeping machines) and control (computer, marking machines). The computer is the one capital good that probably holds the greatest promise of making a substantial contribution to marketing productivity. Its effectiveness, of course, depends upon the development of appropriate systems of control that are compatible with valid decision models. If the computer's digestion system can be made to equal its voracious appetite, it holds much promise for dealing with the problems of the multiproduct, multiservice firms that characterize so much of marketing.

Another form of capital in marketing is inventories. However, George found that only about 20 percent of total capital employed during the early 1960s by retail firms was merchandise stocks.[12] These, of course, can be used more intensively in large establishments and firms, and the tendency toward increasing size of stores and of retail firms over the years has probably increased productivity related to this form of capital.

LABOR

Labor is the most important single productive factor in marketing, a labor-intensive industry. Failure of output per manhour in marketing to rise as much as that in other industries is tied to the limitations on the use of capital in marketing and the competitive position of marketing employees, and particularly retailing employees, in the total labor market.

Average weekly earnings in wholesaling were $154 in 1972, compared with $155 in manufacturing, $186 in mining, $224 in construction, and $187 in transportation and public utilities. The lowest earnings were in retail trade, where they averaged $91, compared with $108 in services and $128 in finance, insurance, and real estate.[13]

Labor in retailing has traditionally been low-wage labor, related to the low productivity potential of the work situation and, conversely, to the low quality of labor utilized. Part-time employment is not uncommon, and its use is encouraged by the inability of retailing management to control the flow of output through the workweek and the consequent necessity of having additional employees on hand to take care of customer-determined peak loads that occur seasonally, within a week, and within a working day. While many positions in retailing are quite well paid, the average employee in retailing has lower earnings than in other industries because of low productivity. This, in turn, has made it more difficult to attract high-quality labor. Some of the tasks of retailing are performed by marginal workers when viewed as part of the total labor force spectrum.

But an important change has occured in the labor market from which marketing firms draw their employees. Over the years rising productivity in certain industries, particularly

[12] George, op. cit., p. 24.

[13] U.S., Bureau of the Census, *Statistical Abstract of the United States: 1973*, 94th ed. (Washington, D.C.: GPO, 1973), p. 241.

manufacturing, has resulted in higher wage rates. If employees are able to perform the tasks of *either* manufacturing or marketing, the wages of the two types of occupation will be related. Rising wage rates in general, resulting partly from increased use of capital in manufacturing processes, have caused wages of marketing employees to rise. In addition to rising wage rates per hour, the workweek in both retailing and wholesaling declined more than in manufacturing during the 60 years surrounding the turn of the century.

Higher hourly wage rates in combination with shorter workweeks forced management to seek means of increasing labor's productivity. This came about through increased use of capital where possible, increased efficiency through work organization (such as the introduction of self-service), and decreased services (by letting customers do their own product collection and transportation, for example, or, in the case of wholesaling, by shifting services forward to retailers or backward to manufacturers, thereby encouraging circumvention of the wholesaler). The other way in which efficiency has been increased has been through changes in the scale of operation, and hence in work organization, which permits more intensive use of one or more productive factors with resulting economies of scale. Larger firms and establishments are one evidence of this.

Still another method of achieving increased productivity in the face of rising labor costs is to divert marketing resources into product development and promotion in order to alter the nature of the output and, it is hoped, consumers' valuation of output. If, for example, the seller increases the quality and variety of products he offers, and along with that his promotional efforts, he seeks a more favorable consumer response. Such an increase in consumer satisfaction would be interpreted in productivity analysis as an increase in output. It seems reasonable to believe that the market power associated with large volume, access to large quantities of resources, control over private brands, and the ability to use advertising and promotional methods effectively and efficiently have been significant factors in accounting for the increasing size of marketing firms and establishments and the tendency for increased vertical integration.

The extent to which changes in product quality, increased variety and differentiation, and increased promotional effort have increased consumer welfare is not clear, however. If consumers demonstrated their preference for these compenents of the marketing mix by greater patronage of firms whose outputs included these elements than of firms whose outputs did not include them, this would be evidence of a genuine differential in output as measured by revealed preference. But for consumers to demonstrate this preference, outputs *with* and *without* these compenents must be equally accessible to them. We cannot be certain that competition has operated in such a way as to ensure the availability and consumer awareness of these clearly defined alternatives.

MANAGEMENT

As a result of managerial decisions, it is probable that there has been some increased productivity in marketing. Increased use of decision models in determining the location and movement of merchandise stocks and marketing outlets, utilization of policies and techniques to control the flow of output through time in outlets where the customer's discretion in the timing of purchases is considerable, expansion of firm and enterprise size in order to achieve economies of scale, and organization of work flows within the marketing institution are among the ways that management has been able to achieve greater output with a given quantity of labor and capital input.

It seems unlikely, however, that the rate at which increased productivity has occurred in these areas of decision making and control has kept pace with the increased range of alternatives that have been generated through product innovation and the stimulus of the imperfectly competitive environment within which managerial decisions are made in marketing. On the contrary, it would appear that the complexity of decisions has been increased more rapidly than the means for making decisions and effecting control. Such a statement is, of course, necessarily based on a judgment in which the range and complexity of problems confronting management are arrayed against the scope of problem-solving methods. Although we recognize that some problem-solving methods in use today are far superior to some in use yesterday, such as in the control of physical stocks and merchandise flows, rising levels of consumption and greater diversity and discretion in consumer choices have probably widened the need for solutions more than the means of arriving at solutions.

One more complication involved in the assessment of managerial competence in marketing is the fact that increased competence in one respect sometimes leads to increased consumer disutility in another. For example, widening of market areas leads to economies of scale, but this comes at the cost of congestion in the trading center and increased travel time. Standardization of operating procedures may lead to lower average costs but result in neglect of minority demands. Changes in managerial techniques are not improvements in a social sense unless they result in increased total utility. If managerial methods are improved in some areas more readily than in others, there may sometimes be backwash effects on those "other" areas, with attendant social costs not taken into account in the calculus of the market place. Social costs must therefore be considered in any complete evaluation of managerial productivity.

SOCIAL EFFICIENCY AND THE MARKETING SYSTEM

The problem of appraising the effectiveness of the marketing system as a whole is far more complex than that of evaluating the efficiency of individual markets or firms that are a part of that system. Systems of social organization are created to meet the goals of individuals—goals that are themselves the product of the culture within which the individual lives, grows, and expires. The total social system is comprised of several subsidiary systems, of which the economic system is one of the most important. The marketing system is, in turn, a subsystem within the economic system. As such, it must be judged on the basis of its efficacy as an integral part of the economy and of the total society. We shall consider some of the problems inherent in making such an assessment.

Evaluation of an Economic System

PARETO OPTIMALITY

The economic system is the social organization through which society's scarce resources are employed for human welfare. Those whom it serves are both individual and social entities. According to the Paretian criterion, maximum welfare is achieved when no changes can be made that would result in benefits to anyone without losses to another.[14] But economic change—whether in the physical, technical, functional, or institutional

---

[14] Discussions of the conditions of Pareto optimality may be found in E. J. Mishan, "A Survey of Welfare Economics, 1939-1959," *The Economic Journal 70*, no. 278 (June 1960): 197-256, reprinted in his *Welfare Economics—Five Introductory Essays* (New York: Random House, 1964), pp. 3-97; I. M. D. Little, *A Critique of Welfare Economics*, 2d ed. (Oxford: Oxford University Press, 1957), esp. pp. 84-116; Kenneth J. Arrow, *Social Choice and Individual Values* (New York: Wiley, 1951).

processes of producing, distributing, or consuming the goods and services that society produces—seldom results in benefits to one segment of society without also possibilities of costs to another segment. To deal with this possibility the notion of Pareto optimality may be extended to that of potential Pareto optimality. A movement toward potential Pareto optimality could occur if a change would yield benefits to one group and costs to another in amounts sufficient to permit the group that benefits to compensate the group that loses by an amount large enough to offset their loss and, at the same time, leave the benefited group with some net advantage over its former position. The inclusion of this compensation possibility in the specification of conditions of optimality extends the Pareto principle to embrace a wider range of production and distribution possibilities.

Changes in economic processes or market behavior seldom occur without resulting in changes in the distribution of total output, and redistribution frequently means that someone is better off and someone else is worse off. Although the compensation principle in the extended Pareto optimality criterion can be employed as a basis for altering the net effects of this redistribution to society, we know that compensation, even if possible, is frequently not paid, and that there may be indirect effects from changes for which compensation is not calculable. In many of these cases, society has employed an ethical principle in lieu of the utility principle that underlies the Pareto optimum. Wherever a change occurs that increases someone's utility and decreases another's utility, society must make a judgment as to whether the resulting redistribution is preferable to the prior distribution. This is done either by authority or by consensus. Examples are numerous: use of revenue from the income tax to pay welfare benefits, exemption of food from sales taxes in some states, subsidies to agricultural producers, free school lunches, excise taxes on liquor and cigarettes, tuition fees at public educational institutions that are less than educational costs.

Policies governing the redistribution of society's income can also be implemented by legislation that regulates rather than taxes. For example, laws creating protective tariffs that yield no revenue, prohibiting price discrimination, making possible resale price maintenance, prohibiting the sale of adulterated products, prohibiting false and misleading advertising, establishing standards for products, and setting ceilings on rents, interest, or other prices are legal means of effecting income redistribution by regulation.

INDIRECT BENEFITS AND COSTS

The problem, however, is even broader than we have indicated. Individuals and social groups are becoming increasingly aware of the indirect or social costs and benefits—that is, the external or spillover effects—that are not, and cannot be, measured by market prices but are a significant element in the total social benefit or cost of certain economic decisions. External effects occur when the impact of a specific action is felt not only by those directly involved but also indirectly by others.

External effects can be positive or negative. Most of the concern for external effects has focused on the indirect costs of certain private actions on society as a whole. We do not include as an external cost the results of ineffective use of funds, since these are questions of technical efficiency. Rather, we include those effects that are not priced by the market mechanism. In these cases, it is not possible for an individual who is hurt by the external effects of a business policy to use the pricing mechanism to receive compensation from the business firm. Nor is it possible for the business firm to charge the recipient of positive external benefits for the value of those benefits to him. For example, if advertising offends some television viewers, it is difficult to use the price mechanism as a means of compensating those individuals for the displeasure they have experienced. Or if a consumer is stimulated to work harder and thereby raise his level of consumption as a result of the stimulus of advertising (as advertisers are wont to claim), it would be difficult to charge that particular consumer for the "benefits" he receives from the advertising.

Pollution is one of the external effects of many production decisions. Marketing activity can generate both physical and sociopsychological pollution. Advertising, though pleasing to some, is offensive to many. Product variations permit producers to meet diverse needs of some customers but may merely add to the confusion of others and to the price of goods of those who do not benefit from the broadened range of choice. Appealing packaging may please many buyers but result in waste disposal problems for society as a whole. Sales promotion that creates dissatisfaction among owners of "old" goods who have been persuaded to prefer "new" items has to be evaluated against the benefits of promotion to the firm and to those individuals who receive enhanced utility from their positive response to it.

In the absence of a market mechanism for dealing with indirect effects of economic actions, it is necessary that social action be taken. Lacking market prices, society is forced to develop a procedure for social evaluation of benefits and costs, and such a procedure is likely to be judgmental, based on social values arrived at by consensus rather than on market values arrived at by the interaction of forces of demand and supply. We cannot ignore these aspects of marketing and shall include them in our subsequent consideration of the effectiveness of the marketing system.

WELFARE CRITERIA AND TIME

Individual and social welfare, which are the ultimate objectives of marketing activity, have to be defined within a time dimension. A number of important issues center on the balance between current and future welfare. Shall we be concerned with today or tomorrow, with this year or next, with our well-being or that of our grandchildren? Some of these comparative values can be established in the market place through, for example, the discounting of future welfare to arrive at a present value, or through the compounding of benefits forward to arrive at an expected terminal value. The rate of discount or interest is clearly a function of social values, for it must represent in part the consensus of members of society as to their relative preference for goods now or later.

But there is another facet of time that is of unusual importance in evaluating the marketing system, and this concerns both its adaptability in the short run and its viability in the long run. Specifically, does the marketing system clear the market in the short run, and as the forces of demand and supply and the institutional structure within which they operate change, does the market show the degree of flexibility necessary to sweep the market clean so that supply and demand are in fact brought into equilibrium? The question of viability in the longer run is equally important: Does the marketing system result in sufficient stability to perform its fundamental role of resource and output allocation with a minimum of cyclical imperfection? In the still longer run, can the marketing system survive or respond optimally to alternative systems of economic control by expanding, contracting, or adapting? We shall consider some questions of viability, stability, and perpetuity in the following discussion.

Evaluation of the Marketing System

The purpose of the marketing system is to provide the institutional structure and processes by which decisions of independent buyers and sellers are brought into unity. It is concerned with the transmission of information, the coordination of complementary decisions, the reconciliation of competing decisions, and the unification of complementary and competing decisions into a system. Specifically, its functions are to provide a merchandise mix of amounts and varieties appropriate to production potentials and buyer demands, to have such goods located so that they are optimally accessible to potential buyers, to make available information necessary for buyers and sellers to make economic decisions, and to enable buyers and sellers to arrive at prices and terms of sale that will effect an optimal level and mix of output and an optimal distribution of that output among potential users in the economy. Given these functions, how can the market be judged in terms of its efficiency?

GENERAL CRITERIA

Several individuals have wrestled with the problem of establishing criteria by which an industry's market might be evaluated, or the marketing system as a whole might be judged in terms of social efficiency.[15] We propose two broad criteria, one pertaining to short-run market efficiency and the other to long-run efficiency. In the short run, we propose that the returns to resources utilized in marketing be compared with the returns such resources might earn in nonmarketing industries. In the evaluation of the market's long-run functioning, we propose that the transactions actually effected be evaluated against potential transactions. Such criteria are conceptually far simpler than their transformation into operational criteria that are amenable to empirical measurement. We shall now consider the approaches to such a transformation.

APPROACHES TO EMPIRICAL MARKET EVALUATION

Two basic approaches have been employed in judging marketing efficiency empirically. One is to specify the conditions under which optimum decisions would be expected to be arrived at and to determine the extent to which such conditions actually exist in the market or market system under investigation. The other approach is to determine what constitutes evidence of optimum decisions and to evaluate observed behavior, or results of behavior, against that standard. The first approach is concerned with structure and conditions; the second is concerned with conduct and performance. In both cases, and particularly the second case, we often use proxies to indicate what we are attempting to measure. For example, price-cost relationships are neither structural nor behavioral but

---

[15] Criteria for evaluating the marketing system as a whole have been developed in Barger, op. cit., Reavis Cox et al., *Distribution in a High-Level Economy* (Englewood Cliffs, N.J.: Prentice-Hall, 1965); Raymond G. Bressler, Jr., and Richard A. King, *Markets, Prices, and Interregional Trade* (New York: Wiley, 1970). Studies of specific markets may be found in Hall, Knapp, and Winsten, op. cit.; George, op. cit.; George and Hills, op. cit.; James B. Jefferys, Simon Hausberger, and Göran Lindbold, *Productivity in the Distributive Trades in Europe* (Paris: Organization for European Economic Cooperation, 1954); Schwartzman, op. cit. Among more recent studies dealing with some of the broader questions of marketing efficiency are Lee E. Preston and Norman R. Collins, "The Analysis of Market Efficiency," *Journal of Marketing Research* 3 (May 1966): 154-162; Stephen H. Sosnick, "Operational Criteria for Evaluating Market Performance," in Paul L. Farris, ed., *Market Structure Research* (Ames: Iowa State University Press, 1964), pp. 81-125, with discussions by Stanley K. Seaver and Willard F. Mueller, pp. 125-137; George J. Stigler, "Public Regulation of the Securities Markets," *Journal of Business* 37 (April 1964); 117-142; Harold Demsetz, "The Cost of Transacting," *Quarterly Journal of Economics* 82 (February 1968): 33-53.

are an evidence of behavior. We shall describe briefly some specific conditions and performance criteria that might be used in the assessment of market efficiency.

1. *RESOURCE MOBILITY*. One condition conducive to optimal short-run returns to resources employed in marketing is a mobility of resources that will permit existing market participants to increase or decrease the amount of resources they are devoting to marketing activities. This would be manifest through the ease of varying the product and product mix, the amount and quality of market information available, and the ability to alter the size, location, and movement of stocks of merchandise.

Long-run resource mobility is associated with ease of entry and exit in the industry, which is closely tied to liquidity of the long-term capital market in periods of both expansion and contraction. Long-term entry and exit may involve the creation of new firms and establishments or the abolition of existing ones. It may also come through the "side-way" entry of existing institutions into the purchase or sale of new lines of merchandise not related to its old lines, or the "side-way" exit of firms from particular lines of merchandising.

2. *RATE OF INNOVATION*. One evidence of efficiency is rate of innovation in products, in techniques of processing, in marketing, and in consumption. Particularly important in long-run market efficiency is the quality of the climate for innovation. On the assumption that it is socially desirable for new products and new methods of production to be introduced when technically possible, we would say that that marketing system is preferred which in the long run contributes to such a climate. It is particularly important that the climate be conducive to an *optimum* rate of innovation—one that has the greatest long-run benefits for total consumption without gross disruptions to production and consumption processes. An excessive rate of innovation can be quite wasteful.

3. *PRICES AND PRICE RESPONSIVENESS*. Prices should in the short run effect proper resource reallocation, or secure optimum resource allocation once it is achieved. Price flexibility is desirable in the short run if it reflects adaptation to changing demand and supply conditions; but price flexibility may reflect disequilibrium conditions that are not a desirable market attribute. A comparison of price variance with average prices may be suggestive of price responsiveness of a given market, or of the marketing system as a whole in both the short and long run. Long-run price-cost relationships may be indicative of the competitive structure of the market, a condition influencing market performance. Price stability has some advantages in encouraging orderly marketing and in facilitating long-run planning, but it is not desirable if it reflects control or inflexibility. Viability and stability of the market, as evidenced by price variability and price responsiveness to changes in demand and supply conditions, are important market attributes that reflect efficiency. These criteria are probably more useful in comparing one market with another than in evaluating the marketing system as a whole. The latter is possible if actual measures of viability and stability can be placed against some standard of optimum performance.

4. *PROFITS*. One evidence of long-run market efficiency lies in profit rates. These are often compared with those of nonmarketing industries. Long-run returns to other productive factors might also be compared between marketing and nonmarketing industries. Unfortunately profits are an incomplete measure of marketing efficiency, since

they fail to indicate consumer (or buyer) utility. Were they viewed along with some measure of aggregate buyer satisfaction, they would be far more useful than when viewed in isolation, for large profits that result from monopoly control are not indicative of efficiency. Long-run negative profits, however, are more likely to indicate overcapacity or some other imperfection.

CONCLUDING COMMENTS ON STRUCTURAL AND PERFORMANCE CRITERIA

This brief review of efficiency criteria for judging a market or the marketing system has not yielded very satisfactory results. We have observed that it is easier to evaluate one market against another, in which we conclude that one is more efficient than another with respect to the criteria employed. But the marketing system cannot be judged against the nonmarketing system except, perhaps, with respect to the comparative returns to comparable resources in both the short and long run. Where resources are not comparable such a comparison is not meaningful. Nor can profits be used to compare the efficiency of one marketing system with another without also comparing consumer utilities in the two systems.

Evaluation of several conditions or evidences of behavior may be necessary in order that different facets of the picture may be placed in focus. This suggests the importance of avoiding simplistic yardsticks unless simple measures can be justified.

In all cases, however, judgment is important in appraising a particular set of data. Such judgment may involve assumed standards, or standards only partially based on objectively derived criteria. It may involve the searching for market strengths and weaknesses in light of possibilities that can be conceptualized. For example, we know theoretically that excess capacity will result in unusually low profits, or even negative profits. On the basis of profit data and observation of operations at less than full capacity, we could say that gasoline retailing in the United States, at least before 1974, was less efficient than it could have been. Was it consumer convenience that demanded this extra capacity? To some extent it was, but many consumers demonstrated a willingness to wait in line for gasoline service if the price differential were sufficient. This does not prove that there was overcapacity, but it lends support to the judgment that there was. It is this type of analysis, based on facts, deduction, and judgment, that is probably what the analyst of the marketing system will have to employ until our theory and our facts provide us with a firmer basis for evaluation. We shall attempt to utilize such an approach in the chapter that follows.

24

The Market System and Social Welfare

The Universe is not operating on a basis in which
the Star Sun opines ignorantly that it can no
longer afford to let Earth have the energy to keep
life going because it hasn't paid its last bill:
"We Stars have got to make a profit!"

—R. Buckminster Fuller

We now turn to some of the broader issues concerning markets as means of economic control. We shall consider the nature of alternatives to the market system of economic control and the limitations of the marketing system that have led to modifications of its role in many economies, and in some cases to the substitution of alternative systems for arriving at decisions with respect to resource allocation.

MARKET VERSUS NONMARKET SYSTEMS OF RESOURCE ALLOCATION

Nature of the Market System

A market system is the structure of exchange relationships that are established between buyers and sellers who, through their offers, reflect their ability and willingness to exchange ownership of resources and, through their transactions, determine the allocation of resources to the production of goods and services and the distribution of goods and services among market participants. The extent and character of competition in a market indicates the degree of freedom that individuals, groups, and institutions have to participate in market activities and the degree of control that particular participants have over the participation of others and, hence, over the transactions that are actually effected.

The beauty of the market system of control lies in the impersonal framework that it provides for production units to realize the benefits of specialization and for nonspecialized consumption units to acquire access to and ownership of the output of producers through the pricing mechanism, which, if effective, directs production, distribution, and consumption in a network through which individual preferences and society's production potential are unified. A "good" marketing system brings the actions of its decision-making components into balance with optimum rapidity and accuracy, distributing society's income in a way that achieves maximum social welfare.

Throughout this volume, we have described and analyzed the structure and functioning of the marketing system. We have noted not only how the marketing system does certain things very well but also how it fails at times to function efficiently. There are, however, additional questions that we need to ask about the effectiveness of the market as a means of economic control.

Alternatives to the Market System

If we examine the market system as it exists in different economies at various levels of economic and social development, its characteristics reflect the impact of physical and social technology on that society's economic organization. Also reflected are the individual and social values of that society and the role that these play in the making of economic decisions.

LEVELS OF COLLECTIVE ACTION

The marketing system, however, is not the only mechanism by which economic control can be achieved. An individual may decide not to use the market place as a means of reaching his economic goals. He may plant his own garden, paint his own house, and play his own guitar. Even though he is probably not able to avoid use of the market when he sells his labor or buys his vegetable seeds, his paint and paintbrush, and his guitar, nevertheless he still has some options open. Groups of individuals can avoid some aspects of market participation by pooling their resources and buying jointly or establishing a cooperative. Larger clusters, such as the firm, may internalize market transactions by integration. Chain stores, for example, perform "wholesaling" and "manufacturing" functions as well as "retailing" functions, thereby performing within the firm certain coordinating functions that in the absence of integration are achieved through market interactions.

On a still more aggregative level, society as a whole may choose to provide public goods in lieu of private goods, because (1) such goods cannot be provided at all through a market system, (2) such goods cannot be provided as efficiently through a market system as they can by public action, or (3) society wishes to distribute such goods in ways other than those that would result from use of the market system of allocation. Thus public schools, the army, police and fire protection, public highways, and parks enter the spectrum of services available to consumers outside the marketplace or through a combination of market and public provision. The public's role in marketing may follow a still different route through regulation of marketing institutions and marketing behavior to establish constraints or opportunities that would otherwise not exist for market participants.

THE MARKET-AUTHORITARIAN CONTINUUM

It is helpful to view these alternatives along a continuum. At one extreme, we have goods and services produced by individuals, groups, or institutions who participate externally in markets in which they buy and sell. The social system by which distribution, coordination, and control are achieved among these private decision makers is the market. At the other end of the continuum, we have goods and services produced and distributed by the government on the basis of public decisions made by governmental units—legislative and/or executive. In a democracy, governmental units will be accountable to the public; in an autocracy, such accountability will not exist except to the extent that the autocracy finds it expedient (to minimize the probability of revolt, for example) or chooses to do so (as a beneficient dictator, for example).

Between these two extremes are many possible degrees of variation and overlap. Public control over the production and distribution of goods and services need not rest on complete substitution of governmental authority for marketing control. The government may choose not to undertake the physical transformation of goods and services through government-owned enterprises but instead enter the market as a buyer and redistribute its purchases among members of the society according to principles established by legislative or administrative directive. The military, for example, buys aircraft, ships, food, and clothing from private firms. Thus the government is a market participant, and the control of resource allocation is effected partly by the operation of the market but primarily by governmental authority. The market is the instrument through which governmental control is achieved. Public control of marketing activities may also be achieved by regulation of market structure, market behavior, or internal nonmarket behavior of private units.

There is still another control alternative on the continuum between private decision-making units controlled by market forces and public decision-making units controlled by government. Sometimes private decision-making units, such as firms, assume a quasi-public status by virtue of their market power and/or integration of functions. In this case, markets continue to play an important role, for they are the medium through which the large, integrated firm acquires some of the resources it uses and through which it sells its final output, but internalization of many of the controls that would otherwise have come through market operations means that some of the functions of markets have been absorbed into the firm's internal operations. Such units are "private" in a legal sense because of their private ownership of resources, but the internalization of economic control and the broad impact of their decisions on society give them some of the character of a public institution. The various operating units of General Motors could, for example, be disaggregated and coordinated through market relationships. Instead, they are coordinated largely by administrative control. Because of a large market share and internalized controls, such a firm is a quasi-private/quasi-public institution.

The basic question to which we now turn is why alternative means have been developed for distributing goods and services and for coordinating and controlling the allocation of resources. Specifically, what are the limitations and weaknesses of the marketing system that account for public intervention through regulation of markets and marketing practices, governmental participation in marketing, or publicly owned enterprises?

LIMITATIONS OF MARKETS AS CONTROL MECHANISMS

In considering the limitations of markets and marketing, we must deal with many factors that do not lend themselves to quantification. We would prefer to offer definitive answers to the questions we shall raise, but the observations on which such answers would have to rest are often not amenable to precise valuation. Where this is true we shall not pretend to precision but shall offer instead a judgment rather than a definitive solution. We share the view of Peter Steiner, who, in discussing public expenditure policy, said:

> I would rather measure only what I have confidence in measuring with some accuracy and leave "incommensurables" to be decided by explicit choice. . . . As has been said in another connection, it may be better to be vaguely right than precisely wrong.[1]

---

[1] Peter O. Steiner, "The Public Sector and the Public Interest," in *The Analysis and Evaluation of Public Expenditures: The PPB System,* A Compendium of Papers Submitted to U.S., Congress, Joint Economic Committee, 91st Cong., 1st sess. (Washington, D.C.: GPO, 1969), I, 42.

The factors that contribute to the ineffectiveness or failure of the market mechanism can be grouped into three categories: (1) transaction costs, (2) market imperfections, and (3) market externalities.[2] These are described as follows:

1. Transaction costs
   a. Costs of information and analysis. Sometimes called costs of search, these are actually broader in scope than that. They include the cost of acquiring, interpreting, and analyzing data. They are affected by the amount of information needed, the amount available, its accessibility, its reliability and validity, the ease and accuracy of its transmission, the complexity of the requisite model, and the delays in action that occur while the optimum allocation is being calculated.
   b. Costs of negotiation. These are costs of communication and haggling between buyer and seller and are affected by the quantity and quality of information obtained in the search procedure, by the quality of the communication medium and the noise in transmission between buyer and seller, and by the bargaining skill of market participants.
   c. Costs of exclusion. These are incurred in order to prohibit those who do not meet the terms specified (usually by the seller) from receiving benefits from market activity.
2. Market imperfections or failure
   a. Functioning markets may result in more or less than optimal allocation owing to
      (i) incompleteness or imperfection of information, analysis, negotiation, or exclusion, causing inefficient organizational structure or performance, or
      (ii) structural constraints resulting from the private use of market power for ends inconsistent with those that would result in optimum social welfare.
   b. Markets may fail to exist at all owing to
      (i) inordinate risks resulting from inadequate information, or
      (ii) inability to exclude or exclusion possible only at excessive cost.
3. Externalities of marketing. Marketing externalities are costs (negative) and benefits (positive) that do not enter into the price of marketing but are created by functioning of the marketing system and are borne by, or accrue to, society as a whole, or a segment of society, outside the market relationship.

Most of our discussion throughout this volume has been concerned with the structural characteristics of markets and the behavior of market participants as these relate to transaction costs and the efficiency of markets, that is, their ability to move toward social

---

[2] The classification and listing that we use are modifications of several ideas suggested by Steiner, op. cit., pp. 21-22, and Kenneth J. Arrow, "The Organization of Economic Activity: Issues Pertinent to the Choice of Market versus Nonmarket Allocation," in *The Analysis and Evaluation of Public Expenditures: The PPB System,* U.S., Congress, Joint Economic Committee, Subcommittee on Economy in Government, 91st Cong., 1st sess. (Washington, D.C.: GPO, 1969), I, 47-64.

It will be noted in this discussion that costs of transportation and storage, which we have included throughout this volume as a part of marketing costs, are given scant attention. This is justifiable in this context since the optimal movement of goods through space and time should be the same under any system of economic control. The question with which we are dealing here is whether the market system of control is better or worse than an authoritarian system of control through government. To the extent that transportation and storage costs are affected by, or affect, the information, negotiation, exclusion, imperfection, and externality costs which we note, they would enter into consideration in choosing the preferred system of resource allocation.

optima. We have not treated externalities in any detail. In the following sections we shall review some of the important characteristics of transaction costs, comment on the nature of market imperfections, and then consider in some detail the externalities of marketing.

Transaction Costs

Transaction costs are direct marketing costs that enter into the price of marketing. These are the costs of doing the tasks of marketing, and such tasks must be undertaken whether a market system of control or an alternative system is employed. The determination of what to produce, what production techniques and resources to utilize, and how to distribute the output to members of society requires information, analysis, and decision regardless of the form of economic organization a society may have. The market place provides the informational and regulatory mechanisms that the authoritarian society has to create by other means.

TRANSACTIONS IN THE NONMARKET ECONOMY

There are, however, some differences in the nature and size of these "marketing tasks" as they appear in market economies compared with nonmarket economies. Negotiation costs, for example, are to some extent internalized under a system of public ownership. However, that which negotiation accomplishes in the market must be achieved by other means if haggling and bargaining do not take place. Bargaining, for example, generates information essential for economic decision making. In the absence of private bargaining between buyers and sellers, with resulting prices and transactions, other sources of the information thereby lost must be found.

Most socialistic economies have in fact found it desirable to maintain markets for consumer goods in order that consumer preferences could be matched with the goods produced. To some extent such markets can also be utilized as a source of information to guide production decisions to the extent that public authorities choose to let individual preferences serve as a guide. Consumer markets in socialistic societies perform a significant role in the making of production and allocation decisions. Such markets are in fact often more efficient than the minds of bureaucrats, even when the latter are aided by beautiful bureaucratic models and computers.

Costs of exclusion also are not peculiar to the market system of control so long as human desires exceed resources, for some system of rationing has to be instituted to make allocation decisions. Sometimes, however, it is easier to exclude under public control than under a market system where the power of individual participants is more restricted.

Sales promotion and advertising would probably be significantly different in an authoritarian economy from what they are in a market economy. Yet even in a socialistic economy errors of analysis might lead to the need for promotional efforts in order to complete the distribution of surplus goods.

Market research is another activity required in both market and nonmarket economies. The search for information and knowledge necessary to make intelligent production and distribution decisions is both more difficult and easier in the authoritarian economy: more difficult because the free play of demand and supply are obscured by controls; easier because the requisite information can be obtained by command rather than by voluntary cooperation or inference, as it often must be in the market economy.

TRANSACTION COSTS AS A DEDUCTION FROM TOTAL OUTPUT

Transaction costs should be viewed as a deduction from the total social output of the economy. Their significance in evaluating a market economy relative to other systems of economic control has been described by Arrow as follows:

> In a price system, transaction costs drive a wedge between buyer's and seller's prices and thereby give rise to welfare losses as in the usual analysis. Removal of these welfare losses by changing to another system (for example, governmental allocation on benefit-cost criteria) must be weighed against any possible increase in transaction costs (for example, the need for elaborate and perhaps impossible studies to determine demand functions without the benefit of observing a market).[3]

The higher transaction costs are, the wider the wedge driven between users and producers and the lower the level of output of the goods and services that are not associated with making transactions possible.

If the decisions arrived at by the transaction process can be arrived at by nontransactional means at a total cost lower than total transaction costs, such an alternative would be preferable to a system of markets. There are two questions involved. One question, to which we have confined ourselves, is whether efficiently executed market transactions are the most economical means of making allocation decisions in the economy. The second question is whether market transactions are in fact performed efficiently. If not, what are the sources of inefficiency? It is to this second question that we now turn.

Marketing inefficiency results in marketing costs higher than necessary to perform the tasks of marketing. The transactional costs involved are those of information collection and analysis, negotiation, and exclusion. It is possible for inefficiencies to arise in each of these, resulting in costs higher than necessary, thereby encouraging governmental intervention in the form of regulation or control. In certain extreme cases market failure may result.[4]

MARKET INFORMATION

The importance of market information to decision making increases as the volume and variety of goods and services increases and as the degree of risk and uncertainty in

---

[3] Arrow, op. cit., p. 60.

[4] We have reserved the term *market failure* to refer to those extreme cases where markets fail to exist at all owing to the extremely high risks that inhere in market participation or to the excessively high costs of excluding nonparticipants. In one sense this is a market inefficiency of such serious proportions that it results in the collapse of a market. An example would be a futures market that fails to materialize because buyers and sellers are both surrounded with much uncertainty as to what future demand and supply will be. In this case, probabilities cannot be assigned to future prices, costs, or transaction volumes, and buyers and sellers are unwilling to become market participants. Better information, or perhaps the pooling of risks if the problem is one of variability in the incidence of predictable risk, would make such a market viable. In this sense, the problem is one of efficiency in information collection and distribution or in scale of operation. Excessive costs of exclusion refers to those cases where exclusion is impossible or, if possible, is not practical.

Since the imperfections of functioning markets and the problems that give rise to complete market failure are so closely related, we think it is better to discuss these together rather than separately. We

markets increases. The longer the time span between market commitments and the consummation of market transactions, the greater the risk is likely to be. Also, the more dynamic the market is, the greater the degree of risk. Information can reduce uncertainty to risk, or reduce the degree of risk, thereby lessening the costs of marketing. Imperfections in the acquisition and distribution of information will reduce market efficiency. The major issues in market information concern the amount of information available, its accuracy, its distribution among potential participants, the rapidity with which it is made available to buyers and sellers, and its analysis. Defects associated with each of these as a result of private market operation may encourage governmental intervention.

1. *AMOUNT AND ACCURACY.* There are economies of scale in obtaining and distributing information. All buyers may benefit from the same information, and all sellers may want the same information. Also, much information is valuable to both buyers and sellers. If buyers and sellers are too small to provide information economically, centralized provision may be desirable, either through private collection agencies or through government. The need for accuracy injects another variable. A great deal of market information is provided in private markets by sellers *for* buyers—through advertising, salesmen, and labeling—and questions of accuracy can easily arise. In these cases, governmental intervention in the form of either independently produced information or regulation of the quality of private information may be desirable.

2. *DISTRIBUTION.* The distribution of market information is unequal. Firms are more likely to be able to provide information for themselves economically than consumers. Public provision of unbiased information to consumers may reduce the degree of inequality in the distribution of information among market participants, and may do so with some possibility for efficiency in its production and control of its veracity. Large firms are more likely to be able to acquire information economically than small firms. Again, public participation in information collection and dissemination may be a desirable alternative for the small production unit.

Farmers and businessmen have both been served by information made available through the U.S. Department of Agriculture, the Cooperative Extension Service, the U.S. Department of Labor, and the U.S. Department of Commerce. Consumers have been served by labeling requirements for foods, drugs, hazardous substances, textiles, and automobiles and by some fairly nonrigorous controls over advertising. Only recently, however, has there been concerted concern for the coordination and expansion of consumer information services of the federal government. Private organizations, such as Consumers Union, have done far more than the federal government in making available to consumers accurate information on product quality and market alternatives needed for making intelligent market choices.

3. *"FAST" INFORMATION.* The utility of "fast" or "timely" information, as well as its cost, may also make centralized production and distribution economical. The cost of getting information rapidly relates to the cost of fast collection and dissemination, while

---

shall make clear in our consideration of costs of exclusion those conditions under which such costs lead to less than perfect markets and those under which they lead to a complete collapse of the market.

its utility is largely that of preventing costly delays in action while information is being obtained, or errors of action prior to the acquisition of information.

4. *ANALYSIS.* One of the aspects of "information" that we included in our consideration of transaction costs was the analysis of information. This involves evaluation of the information's reliability and validity, but especially the incorporation of information into decision models. Although the usefulness of decision models depends in part on the quality of the information that goes into them, the quality of the models themselves can vary from buyer to buyer and from seller to seller. The quality of models is largely a function of the knowledge, analytical skill, and experience of the model builder.

In addition to their personal differences, either the seller or the buyer may be at an advantage over the other as a result of their relative scales of operation. Yet this is an area where public participation has been limited except through the public's role in education. If a relatively free market is to be relied upon for economic control, subject to public action that specifies and monitors the rules of operation, decision making would almost have to be decentralized. It would appear judicious for the government to focus on the quantity and quality of information and its distribution rather than on the decision making itself. Government intervention in the latter can easily become tantamount to the substitution of government decisions for private decisions. If, therefore, private decision making is valued as a social policy, public intervention might be directed more effectively toward the provision of an environment that is conducive to efficiency in private decision making, which will, in turn, make possible the realization of social optima.

NEGOTIATION

The actual bargaining and haggling that characterizes market transactions is more obvious in some markets than in others. Consumer goods markets in relatively mature economies are not those in which ostensible haggling takes place, but such haggling is conspicuous in consumer goods markets in many economies. Where the bargaining is not apparent, it occurs through the actions of price-sensitive consumers who search until they find acceptable terms of trade. Their ultimate action bears, therefore, on all potential sellers whose offerings were searched, and on all buyers, whether they are bargain hunters or not.

Haggling is likely to be more common in industrial goods markets, and particularly where risk and uncertainty are high. The imperfections of bargaining may drive firms to internalization of these processes. This would occur if information flows within a firm are found to be more efficient than between firms because the employees of a firm have common objectives, are subject to common controls, and have common incentives. Where risk and uncertainty are high, the range of possibilities is enhanced, and sellers or buyers may find it is more efficient to internalize the operation, thereby avoiding the market transaction and effecting greater control over the matching of costs and benefits.

Still another aspect of risk in negotiations in capital goods markets is the need to monitor the transaction, particularly if it involves a span of time and possibilities of variability in the price, contingent on future developments. Under these circumstances, either sellers or buyers may find it more efficient to internalize the operation and conduct the monitoring within the firm rather than through the market place. Markets do not work efficiently where there is an absence of trust between buyers and sellers. In the absence of trust, policing is necessary. Policing by fiat may therefore be found to be more efficient than by the enforcement of legal rights associated with the market transaction.[5]

If the conditions that we have described are important in particular situations, firms may choose to internalize the negotiation process, achieving the same end by administrative control rather than through the market place. This constitutes a rejection of the market as the preferred means of control. But this can give rise to another source of inefficiency—that resulting from the substitution of firm control for market control. We shall consider this facet of inefficiency in our discussion of monopolistic or semimonopolistic market power.

EXCLUSION

One of the problems of private buyers and sellers is that of preventing freeloaders from benefiting from the market transaction. Freeloaders do not meet the terms of the transaction. If, for example, the manager of an outdoor movie theater cannot prevent people from viewing his movie from the highway, he has a problem of exclusion, for many may view the movie who do not pay the admission fee. Retailers exclude nonbuyers by having store buildings, checkout counters, and guards who catch shoplifters. Yet they cannot exclude the shopper who uses the store's stock as a source of information and who, after carefully inspecting the inventory and noting price and quality, returns home and uses this information as a basis for placing a mail order with a discount store. Hallmark can exclude nonbuyers from the use of Hallmark cards (though not from receiving them!), but it cannot exclude nonbuyers from viewing its television programs, whose cost is borne by the purchasers of Hallmark cards. Where exclusion is possible and not too costly, the market participant can be segregated from the nonparticipant, and only the one who pays the price gets the utility from the service rendered.[6]

This notion of exclusion opens up a vast area of services that are nonmarketable or for which nonmarket means of allocation and control are deemed preferable to market control.[7] Nonmarket means of production and distribution may be preferred because market exclusion is impossible, impractical, costly, or not desired.[8]

1. *IMPOSSIBLE EXCLUSION.* Clean air is desired by everyone and benefits everyone. If air is dirty to begin with and resources are used to make it clean, it would be almost impossible to distribute this clean air by the market system, at least if it is to be marketed outdoors, for how would nonbuyers be excluded? If it is marketed indoors, however,

---

[5] Possibilities for greater efficiency in the flow of information and for more efficient control over information veracity within the firm than between firms are discussed in considerable detail by Oliver E. Williamson, "The Vertical Integration of Production: Market Failure Considerations," *American Economic Review* (May 1971): 112-123.

[6] It should be noted that costs incurred to achieve exclusion are costs incurred to prevent positive externalities. A market externality is an effect from a market transaction that does not enter into the price of the good or service marketed. A positive externality exists when that effect is beneficial to the recipient, and a negative externality when the effect is costly to the outside recipient. In the case of market exclusion, sellers (or buyers) want to prevent nonpaying users from being users, hoping thereby to increase the seller's (buyer's) return by channeling all market participants through the transactional route.

[7] We use the term *services* to refer to the utilities from both "goods" and "personal services."

[8] See Steiner, op. cit., pp. 18-20.

only buyers could be admitted and the market system would work. This is how cooled air is often sold.

Still another example of a service that is not marketable is national defense. One can hardly conceive of any kind of market mechanism that, without public intervention, would result in the maintenance of military forces and matériel sufficient to provide the level of national defense that a country like Russia, the United States, or Great Britain would deem desirable. Even a mercenary army would have to be financed by public funds. While all individuals would presumably benefit to some degree from the presence of defense forces, it is unlikely that a market system would alone evoke the amount of funds necessary to maintain a potentially effective military force in peacetime. Even in wartime, when the utility of such defense would be more clearly calculable for each citizen and group in the society, it is unlikely that private purchases in the market place would suffice to secure a sufficient defense force in light of the joint output and joint consumption that characterizes its production and consumption.

2. *IMPRACTICAL EXCLUSION.* This brings us, then, to problems that arise out of the impracticality of relying on market exclusion to achieve the desired level of output and distribution. Sometimes the information essential for individuals to make intelligent market choices may be lacking, or sometimes the benefits of a decision are partly individual and partly joint. For example, if fire protection is sold on the market, a resident can calculate the probability of his house's burning down provided that all his neighbors also buy an agreement with the fire company to put out any fire when it occurs. But if one neighbor does not buy such protection, his burning house could endanger all others in the neighborhood while he, at the same time, benefits from the protection that each of the others has on his house. In this case, it is possible but not practical for fire protection to be provided on a market basis. A more desirable level of protection, at lower unit cost, would be achieved by public provision of such a service.

Weisbrod has suggested another example.[9] This is the option demand in which a group of people may be willing to pay for the option of having a market alternative, particularly at some time in the future. For example, I would be willing to pay something to have the local cinema stay in business in case I ever want to go to the movies. I seldom go, but it is worth something to me to have this option open. I am willing to pay something to have the middle Snake River without dams. I do not go there often, but I like to have it there when I want to go. These are all cases in which an occasional user *could* be assessed for the value to him of this option so long as all users are occasional users; that is, all potential users could be charged a price high enough to cover the costs of preserving the service for those infrequent occasions when it is demanded. But if some users are regular users and some are infrequent users, the latter with option demands, it is difficult to separate these two groups and to assess the two at different prices through a market mechanism. Under such circumstances the government may choose to subsidize the service for which there is an option demand owing to the rigidity that makes its marketability impractical.[10]

---

[9] Burton A. Weisbrod, "Collective-Consumption Services of Individual-Consumption Goods," *Quarterly Journal of Economics* 78 (August 1964): 471-477.

[10] Would it not seem that the existence of Israel may have served Zionists throughout the world in this particular way?

3. *COSTLY EXCLUSION.* This brings us to the third reason for the use of nonmarket means of controlling the production of certain services. In many cases the production and distribution decisions could be made by market participants, but the cost is extremely high. If so, it may be better for control to be effected by means of decisions arrived at through authoritarian methods. If there is only one buyer and one seller, a market system of control may be extremely costly. If there is uncertainty with respect to sales, prices, technology, competition, or product quality, buyers and sellers may be prohibited from market participation because of the cost. If a monopoly is the most economical means of production, it may be better for the monopoly to be permitted and protected and for governmental control to be substituted for the chaos that might result from excessive entry and duplication. Public utilities are of this type. Or perhaps the risks of production are so high that private sellers cannot enter the market except at prices that exceed those that buyers will accept. Someday private firms may engage in traffic in outer space, but until then public intervention may be necessary to provide the resources necessary for its exploration, since the uncertainties and risks are so great.

4. *UNDESIRED EXCLUSION.* Finally, we come to that very broad area in which a society decides that it does not desire to have production and distribution decisions made through the market process because the result is inconsistent with the social goals of the group. In one sense we have come full circle, for we could say that society's preference for nonmarket decision control is a reflection of the fact that some of the variables that the society wishes to take into account in making a resource allocation decision cannot be reflected in market values. To this extent, we are back to our first point—that one of the reasons for the use of nonmarket means of allocation is the *impossibility* of achieving the desired allocation through market operation. If there is a social concern with the quality of output, the society may opt for socially produced goods and services rather than privately produced output. Thus control of quality can be ensured if it is technically feasible. Other types of services that society prefers to distribute without sole reliance on the marketing system are education, parks, health care, beaches, museums, school lunches, libraries, and some types of housing. In these cases, social intervention is often partial rather than complete; for example, there are both private and public schools. But the social goal is to make education available to all—or nearly all—within certain socially defined constraints related to ability and conduct.[11] Health care is provided partly by private market activity, but an increasing portion comes through public support. Housing is still essentially a market-controlled good, with substantial intervention by the federal government in the availability and terms of housing credit and in many cases the quality of housing.

Substitution of public for private action is even more dramatic when we consider

---

[11] This is an especially interesting public good, for the hidden costs to the individual who gets the education are considerable. For small children work opportunities are so limited that most of the direct cost of education is reflected in the school budget. Yet even here the cost to individuals of books and supplies and school-related needs may not be inconsequential to many students. As we approach higher education the opportunity cost of college attendance is largely the earnings forgone during those years, and this greatly exceeds the direct cost that the student incurs. It represents a substantial part of the total cost of education met by both the individual recipient and society. See Theodore W. Schultz, *The Economic Value of Education* (New York: Columbia University Press, 1963).

welfare programs, social security, and other attempts to effect a redistribution of the real income of the economy. These can be viewed as consumption choices made manifest through social action in the sense that members of society recognize that the utility that one individual receives is a function of another's consumption. If most citizens get satisfaction from redistributing income from the wealthy to the poor, such a redistribution will be sought. This is a case where collective action is required to meet individual demands, since the market mechanism is not adequate to achieve the goal sought.

There are some interesting issues at stake in this type of production and distribution decision. One concerns the way in which this kind of allocation is to be viewed. When we look at the market, it is clear that there is an aggregating of individual demands to make up a total demand, and of individual supplies to comprise a total supply. Thus by an additive process the total output and total consumption are determined, and individual demands and supplies determine the distribution of output among components of these aggregates. But a social demand, and the resulting social supply, is not necessarily the summation of individual demands. It seems better to view the demand for and supply of social welfare as a function of social values that are a product of human interaction and the melding, reinforcement, and extension of individual values into a system of social values. The latter system is different from the individual values from which it is derived, and to which the individual is willing to commit himself. The difference arises because the individual comes to value the society itself within which social values are generated. The individual must effect a harmony between his own and society's values if he is to live at relative peace with the two as a part of his total value system, and this he does by incorporating into his personal scheme of values some that are social in origin and nature.[12]

Social values may or may not be realized via market mechanisms. To the extent that they emphasize more goods and services, greater differentiation, and survival by market success and expiration by market failure, the market can be relied upon to achieve them. To the extent that they emphasize individual welfare of all, concern for minority demands, and human compassion, the market is likely to be found wanting, and positive social intervention in the production and distribution of goods and services is likely to result.

If we view the drift of "capitalistic" countries throughout history toward more and more social intervention in economic processes, we cannot ignore the significant role that the evolution of social values has played. This is not, of course, the only reason for the

---

[12] There is controversy over whether this distinction is necessary and/or desirable. It can be argued that if an individual extends the horizon of his values to embrace those generated and perpetuated by society as a whole, such socially determined values have in fact become a part of the individual's package of values. In this sense, social welfare becomes an objective of individual action and need not be separated from the goals of the individual that are more "personal."

Although society, in both the broad and narrow senses, can be said to be the origin of all values, except those few that are the product of instinct, we take the position that it is *useful* to think of social values as something more than a mere summation of individual values. We accept the view of Jerome Rothenberg and Peter Steiner that society can be perceived as an independent entity with its own value orderings, and that this approach makes it possible to understand some social decisions and actions that are not easily analyzed within the neater but conceptually more difficult notion of a summation of individual values, part of which are "personal" in origin and effect and part of which are "social." See Jerome Rothenberg, *The Measurement of Social Welfare* (Englewood Cliffs, N.J.: Prentice-Hall, 1961), and Peter O. Steiner, op. cit., pp. 24-30.

drift. Rising levels of income have made it possible for people to turn their attention away from the question of how to make two blades of grass grow where one grew before to the questions of what *can be done* with the second blade and also what *ought to be done* with it. Affluence makes it possible for members of a society to have social concerns, since it costs them less in terms of sacrifice when such concerns can be attended to out of a full market basket.[13]

Market Imperfections and Failures

MARKET POWER

One of the costs of market disequilibrium of great social concern is that associated with short- or long-term monopoly positions that make it possible for the monopolizer to make decisions different from those that would lead to a social optimum. Imperfect competition, rather than outright monopoly, is more often characteristic of the marketing system in highly developed economies. The forms that this takes have been treated throughout this volume—product differentiation through quality differences, branding, labeling, packaging, variations in the clustering of product attributes, and services and servicing, as well as sales stimulation through promotion and advertising. Some of these are designed to adapt products to differences in demand; some are designed to stimulate sales by persuasion. All are designed to increase the net returns to sellers of goods.

Forms of imperfect competition are not without merit, for some of them provide one means by which innovations can be encouraged as an integral part of the marketing process. These are necessary for continual increases in the quantity and variety of goods and services made available. But innovation gives the innovator opportunities for exclusion, and it is the use of this power that may work against the social welfare. Equally important is whether the marketing system provides the means for establishing the optimum *direction* of innovation. If the demand for differentiation is single peaked at the middle, monopolistic competition may easily result in excessive bunching of output around that point with too little attention to minority demands. If demand is double or triple peaked, or distributed evenly over a spectrum (of quality, for example), there is a greater probability that all demands will be met under a system of monopolistic competition in which there are large numbers of producers. If demand is dispersed within a multidimensional attribute space, it is still more likely that product differentiation will result in output closer to the social optimum.

The possibility of restricted output or price rigidities associated with monopolistic or semimonopolistic power is a more serious problem. Such power may arise out of economies of scale associated with capital requirements or out of ownership of limited productive resources. Even in areas such as retailing and wholesaling, where monopoly is far less common than imperfect competition, privately imposed market controls, resulting

---

[13] It would be nice to think that there is another reason why such an attitude develops under conditions of affluence. This would be that one of the ingredients of affluence is the *ability* to be concerned about another. This notion implies that affluence is not merely a market basket full of goods but a market basket full of goods plus increased human sensitivity. Unfortunately the history of humankind yields scant evidence that this is so.

from site monopolies or differentials in bargaining power, can lead to resource misallocation. Where monopoly power is a result of economies of scale, public ownership or control is desirable. Where it is a result of abuses of the marketing system, the establishment and enforcement of rules of conduct by the public is clearly called for. Where it is a result of errors that the market system is unable to correct completely or quickly, public regulation of the structure of markets and of marketing practices may be necessary as a substitute for the self-regulating forces that the market fails to generate.

Imperfect competition, monopoly, and gradations of monopoly (and monopsony) have been the focus of work in industrial organization for a long time, and the impact on consumer welfare of policies developed in these markets has been the basis for a long history of market regulation in the United States and of public enterprise in a number of western economies. The principal objective of such intervention has been to create mechanisms for correcting market defects or for substituting socially oriented decision-making processes for private decision making that is found not to be effectively monitored within the market structure.

MARKET FAILURE

We shall consider two types of market failure, one in which buyers have negative wants and one in which they have positive wants. In each case the market mechanism is totally or partially nonresponsive.

Marketing is concerned with the transfer of title to goods and services that have value. But some things may have a negative value; that is, consumers would be willing to pay to get rid of them. Buyers may wish to avoid illness, death, or bodily harm, or perhaps to silence the jukebox. Some of these can be provided through the market mechanism. For example, the services of physicians are demanded and paid for by consumers, not because they "enjoy" those services, but because failure to buy them will entail discomfort or even death. But even in this case, markets fail to provide all of the health services that members of society want for all people. Therefore private markets are increasingly supplemented by public action. In order to prevent murder one could hire a bodyguard. But prevention of murder is more likely to be accomplished by government fiat and action than by a market relationship. Protection against "bads," in contrast to the acquisition of "goods," often is not a marketable service.

There are also some "goods" that may not be produced by the market system. Consider, for example what is sometimes referred to as "the market for ideas." This may include the market in which the activities covered by the First Amendment are bought and sold,[14] and it would also include all of the arts, education, research, and communcation media. Is the market mechanism adequate to generate the quantity and quality of output that society demands in these areas of human activity? Probably not. We can buy and sell books, magazines, operas, education, and works of art, but the market mechanism falls short of stimulating the level of productivity that most societies seek from actual and potential participants in these areas of endeavor. Nor are all ideas marketable. In many cases, for example, exclusion may be impossible. Sometimes a work of art will have no market value in the short run but a very high market value in the long run. To the extent that markets for ideas do exist, the role of government in establishing and enforcing the rules governing their operation is quite different from its role in

---

[14] R. H. Coase, "The Market for Goods and the Market for Ideas," *American Economic Review* 54 (May 1974): 384-391.

commodity markets. Should the government have the same power to regulate the market for ideas as it does for commodities? John Milton believed it should not.

> Truth and understanding are not such wares as to be monopoliz'd and traded in by tickets and statutes and standards. We must not think to make a staple commodity of all the knowledge in the Land, to mark and licence it like our broad cloath and our wooll packs.[15]

On the other hand, Ronald Coase questions whether we can logically support such strongly opposing policies in these two types of markets. Our concern in this discussion, however, is with the failure of markets to exist for many kinds of ideas and creations that have long-run value to society.

Externalities of Marketing

Externalities of marketing are the effects of marketing that are felt by parties not included in the marketing transaction. They are spillover effects that do not enter into the price of marketing. Yet they may yield benefits, costs, or some combination of benefits and costs to society. We shall refer to those that yield net benefits as *positive externalities* and those that result in net social costs as *negative externalities*.

We shall exclude from consideration in this section one set of market effects that in a strict sense could be "externalities" but that we believe are more appropriately considered as a separate set. These are the effects of imperfections or market failure that cause a demand not to be met. For example, we shall not classify as an externality market failure arising out of the fact that a particular good or service is not marketable or can be provided more efficiently by means other than the market system. Nor shall we consider imperfections that result in unmet demands as "externalities."

In one sense, of course, market imperfections and failure could be considered as externalities, for they are opportunity costs of marketing that society incurs because of defects or inadequacies of the marketing system. We believe, however, that it is better to restrict the term *externalities* to effects that are actually felt and not to include consequences that are desired but fail to occur. For example, one of the spillover effects that we *shall* regard as an external effect is that of advertising on the quality of entertainment provided by television broadcasters. This impact is known to be large and the social significance not inconsequential. It is something that happens—not something that fails to happen.

In order to complete our assessment of the market system as a means of economic control, it is essential that the external effects of marketing be taken into account. We shall attempt to do this in the sections that follow. Once again we shall be confronted with the problem of identifying areas of impact in which the degree of impact does not generally lend itself readily to quantification.

MARKETS AND THE QUALITY OF CONSUMPTION

If markets work efficiently and completely, the quality of consumption that is made possible is a function of consumer preferences and resource potentials. If they function

---

[15] John Milton, *Areopagitica: For the Liberty of Unlicend'd Printing* (1644), ed. John W. Hales (Oxford: Clarendon Press, 1886), p. 33.

inefficiently or incompletely, they will, as noted earlier, result in less than the total level of consumption possible, and a distribution of consumption among goods and services in a way that distorts the realization of optimum allocation. Are there, in addition, external effects of marketing on the quality of consumption?

Not only do we consume the goods and services that move to us through the market place, but also the environmental effects of their production and distribution. If their production results in pollution of the air we breathe, the airwaves through which we hear, and the landscape we view, these social costs must be taken into account as a part of the cost of the economic output that the marketing system transmits. Total private consumption is reduced by the cost of public pollution. To what extent this pollution can be said to be a part of the marketing system's output is not easy to say. Certainly marketing has accelerated product differentiation with the resulting proliferation of items, brands, and product types and a much more rapid rate of obsolescence and economic depreciation than would otherwise occur. While marketing has accelerated the search for something better, with positive benefits, it has also accelerated the search for something different, with sometimes positive benefits and sometimes social costs.

Still another example is packaging, an important tool in the marketing of certain kinds of goods. Paper, cartons, and bags of various types protect products and promote them, but they also add to a disposal problem of no small proportions.

Another example is transportation. Trucking contributes enormously to the flexibility and versatility of the transport system, but it has negative effects for the traveler with whom it shares the roadways. Trucks are noisy, and they make some drivers nervous and nearly all drivers weary. They have contributed to the cost of constructing and maintaining highways, and they have no doubt contributed to loss of life. Not all the cost of getting one's furniture delivered to him 15 days late is borne by him; part of it is also borne by the harried travelers around whom his furniture was swished or who were forced to tarry behind it.

Nor should we ignore the effects of marketing on the landscape. In addition to billboards, the retailing system is responsible for the blatant ugliness of most of our urban shopping centers. Some are not ugly; some, in fact, are attractive. But it does not seem unreasonable to say that in general the exterior of our retail and wholesale trading centers subtracts more than it adds to the physical environment within which mankind lives. In a market economy people have to have stores, and stores have to have exteriors. But exteriors can range all the way from ugly to beautiful, and so they do, and as with most of the frequency distributions in the social sciences, generally with a positive skew.

Some of these externalities could be priced, with prices used as a means of encouraging positive externalities and discouraging negative ones. Some can be regulated by public action, as with billboard regulations, zoning and building codes, product quality requirements, and highway license fees and travel regulations. Marketing may not be society's biggest polluter, but it is not without its share of responsibility for some of the social costs thereby incurred. These have to be set against the benefits derived from such things as lower transportation costs for passengers due to disproportionately high social transport costs for freight if such differentials are found to exist.

CONSUMER PERCEPTION

How consumers perceive goods and services is a function of the cultural environment within which their perception is activated and their patterns of perception are shaped. One of the ingredients of that environment is advertising. We do not take the position that advertising determines demand but, rather, that it influences demand. To the extent that this is done, it can have benefits by increasing awareness of market alternatives and possibly even serving as a stimulus to increased productive efforts of both buyer and seller. But the negative social effects cannot be ignored, for it can also lead to dissatisfaction with existing goods and thereby create obsolescence. Not wanting something is not necessarily virtuous, but converting a nonwant into a want when the want cannot be met because of existing constraints also is not virtuous. Such frustrations can properly be regarded as social costs.

There is yet another way in which advertising and promotion may affect consumer perception. Suppose that through advertising and promotion consumers come to believe that goods are better than they are. Is this a positive or negative externality? If consumers are happier, thinking they have a superior product, perhaps it is a positive benefit. If they find out later that they have been hoodwinked, it would then clearly be a social cost. If the consumer values truth more than illusion, even though the illusion is pleasant, it would be a social cost. Overall, we would probably have to judge deception, misleading information, or persuasion on the basis of false pretenses as socially costly in the sense that they make people behave in ways different from the ways they would behave were their information complete and accurate. In fact perhaps the biggest social cost of advertising results from the lack of objectivity in the information projected and the impact of this on consumer choice. An equal amount of resources devoted to the generation and distribution of complete and accurate information would yield far greater social utility. The social disutility to which we refer is the result of inaccurate and incomplete information and, therefore, of choices that are less than optimal.

There is, however, another angle that we should not ignore. Some people like to be fooled. Some are solaced by reading advertising after the fact of purchase to reinforce their decision.[16] Awareness of a discrepancy between what one wishes to believe and what one knows is fact can generate a need that may be met by advertising. In these cases, one would have to say that the advertising has benefits for the individual unless we move fearlessly into the assessment of the worthiness of felt needs. In general, we would probably say that truth is better than nontruth, but this may not always be so. Sometimes illusions are mighty fine things to have.

MARKETING AND COMMUNICATION MEDIA

One area in which marketing has had the most dramatic effect on consumption has been through the impact of advertising on communications. Newspapers, periodicals, radio, and television are dependent on advertising revenue for a substantial portion of their income. The nonadvertising content of newspapers and magazines appears to have been less affected by advertising than radio and television programs, where program content is to a larger degree controlled by the advertiser. The advertiser will have an incentive to direct program content toward the largest possible audience that is likely to buy his product, and it is this mass appeal that governs the quality of many of the programs that appear on the airwaves. That such an important means of social communication is left to the control of private advertisers is one of the socially unfortunate attributes of the American scene. This marriage of marketing and communication has produced some very

---

[16] See Leon Festinger, *A Theory of Cognitive Dissonance* (Stanford, Calif.: Stanford University Press, 1957), pp. 1-31.

mediocre offspring and some downright deplorable ones. As in most monogamous societies, there are even some bastards.

Not all the effects of advertising on programing are negative, however; some of the superior programs of television have been financed by private funds and made available "free" to all. But this is little justification for the system. If newspapers and magazines, radio and television programs are desired at low or zero cost per user, with the costs to be borne by society as a whole, surely there are superior ways of achieving that end than waiting for the self-seeking advertiser to put in his appearance. Whether or not advertisers exercise much control over the nonadvertising content of newspapers and magazines has often been debated. There are cases in which great editorial independence has been demonstrated, and other cases where such independence is not found at all. From a social point of view, it is very difficult to equate the social costs of advertiser control of much of the output of certain communications media with the benefits that may result from the "free" availability of that output. In fact it would be better that it not be "free" in order that the price mechanism might be more effectively utilized in determining the quantity and quality of programs.

Another possibility for external effects looms on the horizon in the form of closed-circuit television. The following statement is based on information from Lawrence G. Chait, president of the Association of Direct Marketing Agencies (ADMA), concerning closed-circuit TV:

> American Intertel, owned by Holiday Inns, hopes to tie hotel and motel rooms together for an audience of traveling businessmen. Sitting on top of the TV set in the hotel room would be an order form for the product. The form could be filled in and dropped off at the registration desk. American Intertel expects eventually to tie together about 250,000 rooms or more using as a starting base the 155,000 in the Holiday Inns.

> Thus, if we want to reach an audience of traveling businessmen, we would use this network during the hours of the day when the men would be in their rooms. Maids are told to turn the sets to the closed-circuit channel. Before most men would realize they're a captive audience, they've already gotten the message.

> When they make their first group of hotels available for this in January, we expect to start experimenting with it and see what the cost-effectiveness relationship is. Once again this is a kind of targeted marketing—a direct approach to a known audience, at a known place, at a known time.[17]

The social costs and benefits of such an experiment cannot, of course, be quantified, but such costs and benefits (if any) would have to be known for a full social evaluation to be made of such a marketing practice.

MARKETS AND THE QUALITY OF LIFE

There are several important spillover effects from marketing that affect not merely the consumption of goods and services, in the narrow sense of consumption, but also what we might call the quality of life—the nature of the total environment of living, of which goods and services constitute a part, but that also includes interpersonal relationships and the intellectual and ethical dimensions of human experience.

---

[17]Reprinted from Thomas E. Caruso, "Direct Marketing Agencies Form Association, Study New Media," *The Marketing News* 5 (mid-September 1971): 4-5 published by the American Marketing Association.

1. *INTERPERSONAL RELATIONS.* One of the fascinating features of the history of mankind is the role of markets in human relationships. Although all markets have revolved around transactions in which the ownership of rights to goods and services are established, it would be wrong to ignore the importance of human interaction through market participation. We shall leave to historians, anthropologists, and sociologists the task of developing the noneconomic reasons for the evolution of markets. But an economist cannot ignore the role of trade in providing a medium for human experience as exciting and challenging as almost any.

Physical production may appeal to some because of the opportunities it affords for creative experience with natural and man-made "things." Social interaction in small primary groups, in large institutional settings, and in various gradations of human clusters between these extremes is a significant element in human development and experience. These experiences, whether formal or informal, systematic or irregular, structured or unstructured, form the basis for the creation of the socialized human being.

Markets, in which everyone participates at some time or another, are one of the structures through which social interchange takes place, and to this extent are a part of the social environment within which humans work and live. Some people hate to be market participants; others enjoy it. Whatever its character, it does provide one medium for human interaction. We can hardly judge its usefulness in this respect without a more careful analysis of its effects on human personality, attitudes, and development. We can, however, observe an extremely important attribute of markets as media for human interaction. This is the dichotomous character of the human relationships therein engendered—partly competitive and partly cooperative. Let us examine this facet of markets further.

2. *COMPETITION AND COOPERATION.* Marketing is characterized by a strange mixture of cooperative and competitive relationships. Buyers compete with buyers for the offerings of sellers. Sellers compete with sellers for the custom of buyers. Buyers and sellers bargain with one another for terms favorable to each. Finally, however, a transaction results and both buyer and seller are benefited. Thus competition is replaced by a final cooperative act. Is marketing basically cooperative or competitive? There is no categorical answer, of course, but it would seem offhand that the struggle supercedes the delightful moment of transformation in the scope of its effects. Witness, for example, the following quotation from a talk by Harry C. McCreary, president of the McCreary Tire and Rubber Company, before the Akron, Ohio, Chapter of the American Marketing Association, March 3, 1971:

> I wish . . . the professional economists and bureaucrats in this country would take just one lousy year out of their lives and . . . get the heck out of their ivory towers and retreats and try to SELL something to somebody. . . . Frankly, what I see being written by some of these economists and what I see in some of the bureaucrats' attempts to regulate business . . . scares me! I think I see a very basic, underlying, gut-feeling type of assumption . . . that happens to be *completely false:* "About all business has to do is sit around, dreaming up new products for the marketplace; and once relatively perfected, business then has only to very efficiently (and profitably) cram these products down the throats of the defenseless consumers."
>
> The economists and bureaucrats seem to have (this false) gut-feeling that selling the product really represents very little problem. If you stop and think about that, you'll see some very serious implications for private-enterprise business . . . because if they . . . convince a majority of the VOTERS their assumption is correct, then we're going to see regulation of business like you ain't never seen the likes of before!

. . . if they (had ever had to sell anything to anybody), they just might understand what a bitter competitive struggle it is. They might have friends fired because a sales quota wasn't met. They might know of vice presidents fired because of the loss of a fraction of a percent in a market position. And they might have heard the word "NO" enough times themselves to realize that selling anything is damned hard work.[18]

If this describes what does in fact go on in the market place, we can legitimately ask if the results justify the individual and social cost indicated. Granted that competition may be essential in certain situations to bring to the surface some of the sterling qualities of humankind and make possible survival of superior social units, there is no assurance that the kind of competition that Mr. McCreary describes will achieve these ends.

There are surely optima to the amount and kind of competition that a social system engenders. Competition is not without great merit in terms of its effects on both individual development and social welfare. Just as competitive sports may be a stimulus to physical development and performance, competition between individuals and social groups can encourage innovation, growth, and achievement. The question, however, is one of balance between cooperative and competitive effort. There is something almost paradoxical about an economic system whose productivity is so clearly a product of cooperative effort among specialized consumption and production units but is, at the same time, dependent upon direction and control by competition between those units. What happens to an individual at the interface of these two forms of interpersonal relations? It is possible to reconcile these seemingly conflicting routes to our goals, or are we perched precariously on the interstice of two inconsonant pigeonholes?

3. *MARKET VALUES AND SOCIAL VALUES.* In the long route we have followed in our discussion of marketing institutions, policies, and practices, and in our search for the principles that govern market operation, we have tried to show the role of marketing in meeting individual and social needs. We have not been critical of what those needs are, nor of their manifestation in the market place, for we have accepted as our responsibility that of trying to describe and, where possible, explain the structure and behavior of the marketing system and evaluate the effectiveness with which it meets individual and social needs as given. It is not inappropriate, however, to conclude our discussion by raising what we believe is one of the important questions facing the society that has created, and benefits from, the market system of economic control.

The question we raise concerns the relationship of human values and market values. Human values reflect the utility assigned by individuals or by society to various human experiences, the ordering of those experiences, and their placement within life's space. Consumption of goods and services is one of the means by which human experience is achieved, and many of the goods and services that are consumed move to users through the market place. The market place becomes, therefore, the aperture through which many human preferences are made manifest and through which production potentials are brought into some kind of balance with those preferences.

In our discussion of the effectiveness of the market as a mechanism for the allocation of resources, we have raised such questions as whether it transmits information fully and accurately, whether it provides an efficient means of screening and bringing into balance the demands of buyers and the supplies of sellers, and whether there are circumstances

---

[18] Reprinted from "Marketing Remarks," *The Marketing News* 4 (first-of-September 1971): 8, published by the American Marketing Association.

under which it simply fails to function at all. In all these cases we have been asking: If individuals make their preferences known in the market place, does the market do an adequate—preferably good—job of reconciling those preferences with the economy's production potential? We have observed that there are some cases where market information, negotiation, and exclusion are imperfect; where inefficiency exists; or where monopoly or risk prevent the realization of market potential. We have, however, gone further than this and asked an additional question: Where social values are more than a mere summation of individual values, is the market mechanism adequate for such significations to direct choices in the economic system? If, for example, a society's values reflect concern for distribution of personal income (and hence, personal consumption expenditures), does the market provide adequately for the expression of this preference and its realization? In this case, we concluded that the answer was no, and that social action beyond the market mechanism was necessary to achieve the end sought. In other cases, however, we found the market to be an effective mediator. Our answer, then, to the question of market adequacy is necessarily a mixed one in which we will have to say, "It depends."

We turn now to a still different facet of the question of congruency of market and human values. This time we ask the question: Through its role as an integral part of the economic system, does the marketing system stimulate or generate human values that are different from what they would be without the market, or does it alter or suppress human values that would otherwise govern human behavior?

We have already said a good deal about the role of advertising and sales promotion in marketing and the objective of these in terms of shaping the pattern of human preferences. We have pointed out that if successful, advertising and promotion do alter specific demands, although it is by no means clear that they can significantly alter the underlying cultural bases of general demands.

At this point, we would like to broaden the range of our inquiry and view the question of the impact of marketing on human values, not in the narrow terms of advertising and promotion alone, but rather in terms of the total marketing system and its possible impact on human values. Has the marketing system that was created to be responsive to human values become sufficiently powerful that it has, in turn, helped shape those values? Obviously we cannot answer this question categorically. Even if we could answer it, we would still have the more controversial normative question of whether the marketing system should or should not be allowed to influence human values. But we can make some observations and judgments relevant to the questions we have raised.

The central focus of marketing in western society is without doubt that of selling more and more. Our whole economy—not just the marketing system—bears that focus. Increasing gross national product, expanding investment, increasing disposable personal income, and rising personal consumption expenditures are generally regarded as "good." The marketing system, with its emphasis on promotion, on product and service innovations, on more intensive and extensive distribution, and on an increasing volume of sales, has shared mightily in this total social objective. True, concern with per capita income and sales has often been the emphasis, rather than just total income and sales, but even in this case, growth objectives underlie most of the policies fostered by both public and private institutions.

It is not correct to say that the marketing system alone has caused this emphasis, but it is correct to say that the marketing system, which has evolved as an instrument to achieve economic ends, has developed into far more than a mere instrument in this process. Marketing has been a significant contributor to, and to some degree creator of, the drive for economic growth and the premium that society places on growth. In one sense it is the success of the marketing system in achieving this that has created the dilemma, for it is "market success" that has made the system's output such a dominant factor in our total level of living.

We ask if this materialistic focus is indeed what Western society really wants. Certainly we do not wish to condone poverty. But is our desire for more and more insatiable? The more goods we have, the more effort we must put into their management and use. Moreover, human effort directed toward the production of more and more goods inevitably subtracts from the human effort available for other kinds of activities.[19] Maximum output is not necessarily the same as optimum output. It is our judgment that growth that leads to an increasing range and depth of human experience can be desirable. We question, however, whether the goods society, which our marketing system has helped generate and perpetuate, does in fact lead to the range and depth of human experience that would be possible were it tempered by the selective use of alternative means to individual and social goals.

Quite apart from the normative question of whether a continually rising level of consumption is desirable is the pragmatic question of the compatability of a marketing-oriented society to a world with resource limitations. The seriousness of the discrepancy between growth objectives and resource constraints has surfaced so rapidly and so dramatically that a very careful reassessment of the appropriate social role of marketing is called for.

There is yet another aspect of the marketing system that we should consider, and this concerns its role in determining the quality of consumption. The problem arises not because of weaknesses inherent in the market system but because of the abuse of market potentials through the garnering of market power. There is good reason to question whether the objectives and behavior of the large firm that is able to achieve a handsome measure of market power are compatible with the desires and demands of consumers. Is such a market sufficiently sensitive to the spectrum of demands of any one individual, or to those of all the diverse segments of society? We can observe examples of excessive and trivial differentiation, defective products, and false and misleading advertising. Nor is it sufficient to say that because consumers buy a good they obviously like it. Consumers often buy products not because they prefer them to possible alternatives but because they have no other choice. When its potentials are abused through the exercise of power that inhibits entry and a free range of communication and choice, the market system is not allowed to do what it is capable of doing.

It is our conviction that the market system, even with its defects, is an enormously important—indeed magnificent—subsystem within the total social system. At this point in the evolution of our understanding of market processes, the movement of the marketing system closer to realization of its potential contribution to human welfare must come through an intelligent social delineation of its role and structure, and through continuous public and private monitoring of its performance. Only if our perceptions and analyses of the market economy are undertaken within the frameworks established by our best intellectual efforts will it be understood, its potentialities known, and its possibilities realized. We hope increased understanding of the marketing system will, in turn, contribute to the eventual development of a unified theory of social systems.[20]

---

[19] A lucid exposition of this viewpoint is that of Staffan B. Linder, *The Harried Leisure Class* (New York: Columbia University Press, 1970).

[20] A significant movement toward this threshhold is Alfred Kuhn, *The Logic of Social Systems* (San Francisco: Jossey-Bass, 1974).

APPENDIX

THE RELEVANCE OF MARKETING TO OTHER SOCIAL SYSTEMS

We have focused upon marketing as a part of the economic system, but we should note that the structure and some of the techniques of marketing are often employed where interpersonal and social relationships entail different, and sometimes more subtle, forms of exchange or transfer than those that we have considered in this volume.

In public welfare programs certain marketing techniques have been utilized with varying consequences. Voucher schemes—for food, rent, other "necessities," or all consumer goods and services—have been employed, and a body of analysis concerning the effects and efficiency of their use has been developed.[1] Part of the debate over the negative income tax pivots around the comparative merits of transfers in money and transfers in kind, each resulting in different degrees of market participation by the public and by welfare recipients.[2] Welfare programs in general represent a total or partial substitution of public allocation for market allocation, and among the questions most often asked are those that concern the degree of freedom the individual recipient should be given in deciding the composition of the transfer made to him and the effect of such transfers on productive incentives.

Marketing techniques have also been employed in military logistics, although this is a case where the military may have contributed as much to marketing as the other way around.

Promotional techniques are most highly developed where their potential yield is greatest, and this is as likely to be in politics, religion, and college football recruiting as in the markets in which goods and services are bought and sold. Politicians make extensive use of advertising and person-to-person contacts to peddle themselves to their potential constituency. Evangelists and other men of the cloth, no less than academicians, the Metropolitan Opera, the Community Chest, the Marines, and the American Medical Association's lobby use marketing's promotional methods to try to persuade if not to convince. The Chamber of Commerce, the AFL-CIO, and the President of the United States are as market conscious as the corporation. Nor do the selling tactics of the junior executive, working his way up to the executive washroom, or of the local Kiwanis president, leading his constituents to his own persuasion by indirection, differ markedly from the tactics of your friendly Avon representative.

These are but a few of the many areas in which marketing methods and techniques, and sometimes marketing institutions, are used to achieve, alter, or affect human relationships. In these nonmarket cases, the interpersonal and social relationships involved must be studied within the framework of those disciplines most appropriate to the social system within which such relations exist. Some of these exchanges are closest to those we observe in markets for services. Sometimes, however, the unique character of interpersonal and social relationships in these other kinds of situations alters the nature and effect of the exchange. In some cases there in only a one-way transfer. Charity and politics and friendships and Social Security are not governed by the same distribution

---

[1] See, for example, Edgar O. Olsen, "Some Theorems in the Theory of Efficient Transfers," *Journal of Political Economy* 79 (January-February 1969): 166-176.

[2] Lester C. Thurow, "Cash Versus In-Kind Transfers," *American Economic Review* 64 (May 1974): 190-195.

processes or decision rules as are market commodities, even though all of these often share certain common attributes.

If the relationships entail (1) an explicit *quid pro quo* exchange, and (2) explicit or covert choice-making by the participants in each exchange, they can be understood within the economic framework we have employed in this volume. Economics, the science of decision making, can be a powerful tool in the analysis of some of the choices entailed in these exchange relationships. But usually more than a single disciplinary approach is needed to understand the character and procedural modes of nonmarket relationships. As we study both market and nonmarket interactions, we hope areas of commonality will appear as we gain new insights through a multidisciplinary approach to interpersonal and intergroup relations, contributing eventually to a viable and useful theory of social systems.

Name Index

Subject Index

75 76 77 9 8 7 6 5 4 3 2 1

DATE DUE

PRINTED IN U.S.A.